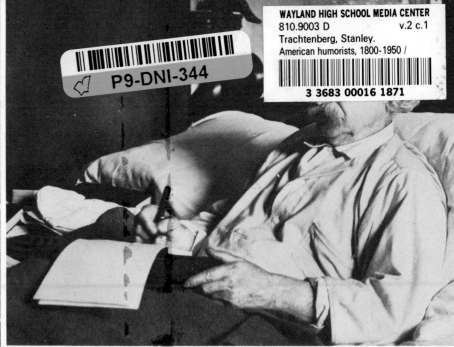

Dictionary of Literary Biography • Volume Eleven

American Humorists, 1800-1950

Part 2: M-Z

Dictionary of Literary Biography

1: *The American Renaissance in New England*,
   edited by Joel Myerson (1978)

2: *American Novelists Since World War II*,
   edited by Jeffrey Helterman and Richard Layman (1978)

3: *Antebellum Writers in New York and the South*,
   edited by Joel Myerson (1979)

4: *American Writers in Paris, 1920-1939*,
   edited by Karen Lane Rood (1980)

5: *American Poets Since World War II*, 2 volumes,
   edited by Donald J. Greiner (1980)

6: *American Novelists Since World War II*, Second Series,
   edited by James E. Kibler, Jr. (1980)

7: *Twentieth-Century American Dramatists*, 2 volumes,
   edited by John MacNicholas (1981)

8: *Twentieth-Century American Science-Fiction Writers*, 2 volumes,
   edited by David Cowart and Thomas L. Wymer (1981)

9: *American Novelists, 1910-1945*, 3 volumes,
   edited by James J. Martine (1981)

   Yearbook: 1980,
   edited by Karen L. Rood, Jean W. Ross, and Richard Ziegfeld (1981)

10: *Modern British Dramatists, 1900-1945*, 2 volumes,
    edited by Stanley Weintraub (1982)

11: *American Humorists, 1800-1950*, 2 volumes,
    edited by Stanley Trachtenberg (1982)

   Yearbook: 1981,
   edited by Karen L. Rood, Jean W. Ross, and Richard Ziegfeld (1982)

American Humorists, 1800-1950

Part 2: M-Z

Edited by Stanley Trachtenberg
Texas Christian University

A Bruccoli Clark Book
Gale Research Company • Book Tower • Detroit, Michigan 48226
1982

Advisory Board for
DICTIONARY OF LITERARY BIOGRAPHY

Manufactured by Braun-Brumfield, Inc.
Ann Arbor, Michigan
Printed in the United States of America

Copyright © 1982
GALE RESEARCH COMPANY

Library of Congress Cataloging in Publication Data

Main entry under title:

American humorists, 1800-1950.

(Dictionary of literary biography; v. 11)
"A Bruccoli Clark book."
Contents: pt. 1. A-L—pt. 2. M-Z.
1. Humorists, American—Biography. I. Trachtenberg,
Stanley. II. Series.
PS430.A44   817'.009[B]   81-20238
ISBN 0-8108-1147-X (set) AACR2

Contents

Part 1

Foreword...xi

Preface...xii

Permissions and Acknowledgments..................xiii

George Ade (1866-1944).........................3
   William W. Hoffa

Max Adeler
   (see Charles Heber Clark)

Josiah Allen's Wife
   (see Marietta Holley)

Bill Arp
   (See Charles Henry Smith)

Joseph Glover Baldwin (1815-1864)..................12
   L. Moody Simms, Jr.

John Kendrick Bangs (1862-1922).......................17
   William W. Hoffa

Robert Benchley (1889-1945)..............................22
   Eric Solomon

Ambrose Bierce (1842-1914?).............................38
   Matthew O'Brien

Hosea Biglow
   (see James Russell Lowell)

Josh Billings
   (see Henry Wheeler Shaw)

Hugh Henry Brackenridge (1748-1816)............49
   Lucille M. Schultz

John Brougham (1810-1880)..............................56
   Shelley Armitage

Charles Farrar Browne (1834-1867)..................60
   Robert E. Abrams

Gelett Burgess (1866-1951)..................................68
   John Wenke

Charles Heber Clark (1841-1915).......................77
   John Lang

Samuel Langhorne Clemens
   (see Mark Twain)

Irvin S. Cobb (1876-1944).................................82
   Sandra Lieb

Geoffrey Crayon
   (see Washington Irving)

Davy Crockett (1786-1836).................................89
   William Bedford Clark

Will Cuppy (1884-1949)......................................94
   Sandra Lieb

T. A. Daly (1871-1948)......................................100
   Patricia Owens Williams

Charles A. Davis (1795-1867)............................103
   Craig Turner

Clarence Day (1874-1935).................................108
   Richard Alan Schwartz

George Horatio Derby (1823-1861).................114
   John Lang

Diogenes, Jr.
   (see John Brougham)

Q. K. Philander Doesticks, P. B.
   (see Mortimer Thomson)

J. Downing, Major
   (see Charles A. Davis)

Major Jack Downing
   (see Seba Smith)

Finley Peter Dunne (1867-1936)......................123
   James DeMuth

William Faulkner (1897-1962)...........................134
   M. Thomas Inge

Corey Ford (1902-1969)....................................147
   Patrick Day

Montague Glass (1877-1934).............................151
   Gregory S. Sojka

Asa Greene (1789-1838).....................................156
   Mark A. Keller

27482

Contents

Milt Gross (1895-1953)......................................160
  Bill Blackbeard

Arthur Guiterman (1871-1943) 165
  Philip G. Terrie

Thomas Chandler Haliburton (1796-1865)......169
  Edward E. Waldron

Marion Hargrove (1919-   ) 176
  Robert Secor

George Washington Harris (1814-1869) 180
  Milton Rickels

Joel Chandler Harris (1848-1908) 189
  R. Bruce Bickley, Jr.

Samuel Hoffenstein (1890-1947) 202
  Paul C. Wermuth

Marietta Holley (1836-1926) 206
  Jane A. Curry

Johnson Jones Hooper (1815-1862) 211
  Mark A. Keller

Kin Hubbard (1868-1930)..................................219
  James C. McNutt

Washington Irving (1783-1859)........................224
  William Bedford Clark

Major Joseph Jones
  (see William Tappan Thompson)

Orpheus C. Kerr
  (see Robert Henry Newell)

Diedrick Knickerbocker
  (see Washington Irving)

Arthur Kober (1900-1975)................................237
  Sanford Pinsker

Ring Lardner (1885-1933) 242
  Elizabeth Evans

Charles G. Leland (1824-1903)........................256
  David E. E. Sloane

Charles B. Lewis (1842-1924) 267
  Shelley Armitage

David Ross Locke (1833-1888)..........................270
  Dennis E. Minor

Augustus Baldwin Longstreet (1790-1870)......276
  Paul R. Lilly, Jr.

Anita Loos (1893-1981)....................................283
  Thomas Grant

Sut Lovingood
  (see George Washington Harris)

James Russell Lowell (1819-1891)....................291
  Thomas Wortham

Contributors..305

Part 2

Permissions and Acknowledgments....................ix

Don Marquis (1878-1937) 309
  Dan Jaffe

Abe Martin
  (see Kin Hubbard)

Phyllis McGinley (1905-1978)...........................317
  Nancy Walker

H. L. Mencken (1880-1956) 323
  Elton Miles

Petroleum Vesuvius Nasby
  (see David Ross Locke)

Ogden Nash (1902-1971) 331
  St. George Tucker Arnold, Jr.

Joseph C. Neal (1807-1847) 344
  David E. E. Sloane

Robert Henry Newell (1836-1901)....................350
  Michael Butler

C. F. M. Noland (1810?-1858) 360
  Lorne Fienberg

Bill Nye (1850-1896)..364
  David B. Kesterson

Dorothy Parker (1893-1967) 369
  Thomas Grant

S. J. Perelman (1904-1979) 382
  Steven H. Gale

John Phoenix
  (see George Horatio Derby)

M. Quad
  (see Charles B. Lewis)

John Riddell
  (see Corey Ford)

Will Rogers (1879-1935)....................................404
  Terry L. Heller

Leonard Q. Ross
  (see Leo Rosten)

Leo Rosten (1908-   ).............................410
  Ellen Golub

Damon Runyon (1880-1946)...........................419
  Thomas Grant

Henry Wheeler Shaw (1818-1885)....................429
  David B. Kesterton

B. P. Shillaber (1814-1890) 434
  Clyde G. Wade

Max Shulman (1919-   ) 439
  Francis Hodgins

Sam Slick
  (see Thomas Chandler Haliburton)

Charles Henry Smith (1826-1903)...................447
  William E. Lenz

H. Allen Smith (1907-1976)...........................452
  L. Moody Simms, Jr.

Seba Smith (1792-1868)...................................459
  Edward E. Waldron

Donald Ogden Stewart (1894-1980) 466
  James C. McNutt

Edward Streeter (1891-1976)...........................474
  Roy Arthur Swanson

Squibob
  (see George Horatio Derby)

Simon Suggs
  (see Johnson Jones Hooper)

Frank Sullivan (1892-1976) 478
  Betsy Erkkila

William Tappan Thompson (1812-1882).........485
  Paul R. Lilly, Jr.

Mortimer Thomson (1831-1875) 491
  David E. E. Sloane

Thomas Bangs Thorpe (1815-1878).................497
  Mark A. Keller

James Thurber (1894-1961)............................505
  Peter A. Scholl

Mark Twain (1835-1910)..................................526
  Pascal Covici, Jr.

Artemus Ward
  (see Charles Farrar Browne)

Carolyn Wells (1862-1942)...............................556
  Zita Zatkin Dresner

Colonel Pete Whetstone
  (see C. F. M. Noland)

Frances Miriam Whitcher (1814-1852).............560
  Clyde G. Wade

E. B. White (1899-   ) 568
  Edward C. Sampson

Appendix I: American Humor: A Historical
  Survey 585

East and Northeast 587
  Stanley Trachtenberg

South and Southwest.......................................597
  Sandy Cohen

Midwest 603
  Nancy Pogel

West...619
  David B. Kesterson

Appendix II: Humorous Book Illustration......623
  Bill Blackbeard

Appendix III: Newspaper Syndication of American
  Humor 641
  Bill Blackbeard

Appendix IV: Selected Humorous Maga-
  zines (1802-1950)......................................653
  Richard Marschall and Carol J. Wilson

Appendix V: Supplementary Reading List......679

Contributors...683

Cumulative Index..691

Permissions

The following people and institutions generously permitted the reproduction of photographs and other illustrative materials: Culver Pictures, pp. 310, 316, 324, 333, 346, 357, 370, 420, 435, 457, 468, 472, 479, 507, 520, 528, 533, 538, 559, 622; The Granger Collection, pp. 318, 326, 406, 423, 430, 454, 609; The Bettmann Archive, Inc., pp. 329, 339, 364, 378, 384, 405, 433, 460, 553, 590, 591, 592, 595, 596, 614, 621; Matthew J. Bruccoli, pp. 340, 341; Wide World Photos, pp. 407, 408; Arthur Rothstein, p. 411; Eileen Darby, p. 428; Martha Holmes, p. 440; Harvard University Archives, p. 475; Harper & Row, pp. 569, 575; Cornell University Library, p. 578; H. Mitgang, p. 581; University of Virginia Library, p. 603.

Acknowledgments

This book was produced by BC Research.

Karen L. Rood is the senior editor for the *Dictionary of Literary Biography* series.

The production staff included Mary L. Betts, Joseph Caldwell, Betty Davidson, Angela Dixon, Joyce Fowler, Karen Geney, Robert H. Griffin, Patricia S. Hicks, Sharon K. Kirkland, Cynthia D. Lybrand, Shirley A. Ross, Walter W. Ross, Robin A. Sumner, Cheryl A. Swartzentruber, Carol J. Wilson, and Lynne C. Zeigler. Anne Dixon did the library research with the assistance of the following librarians at the Thomas Cooper Library of the University of South Carolina: Michael Freeman, Dwight Gardner, Michael Havener, David Lincove, Donna Nance, Harriet Oglesbee, Paula Swope, Jane Thesing, Ellen Tillett, Gary Treadway, and Beth Woodard. Special thanks are due to Jamie Boozer and Jean Rhyne of Thomas Cooper Library, Keith Walters, the staff of the Humanities Research Center at the University of Texas, Philip Eppard of Harvard University Libraries, and Bill Blackbeard of the San Francisco Academy of Comic Art. Photographic copy work for this volume was done by Pat Crawford of Imagery, Columbia, South Carolina.

Dictionary of Literary Biography • Volume Eleven

American Humorists, 1800-1950

Part 2: M-Z

Dictionary of Literary Biography

Don Marquis

(29 July 1878-29 December 1937)

Dan Jaffe

University of Missouri, Kansas City

BOOKS: *Danny's Own Story* (Garden City: Double-day, Page, 1912);

Dreams & Dust (New York & London: Harper, 1915);

The Cruise of the Jasper B. (New York & London: Appleton, 1916);

Hermione and Her Little Group of Serious Thinkers (New York & London: Appleton, 1916);

Prefaces (New York & London: Appleton, 1919);

Carter, and Other People (New York & London: Appleton, 1921);

Noah An' Jonah An' Cap'n John Smith, A Book of Humorous Verse (New York & London: Appleton, 1921);

The Old Soak, and Hail and Farewell (Garden City & Toronto: Doubleday, Page, 1921);

Poems and Portraits (Garden City & Toronto: Doubleday, Page, 1922);

The Revolt of the Oyster (Garden City: Doubleday, Page, 1922);

Sonnets to a Red-Haired Lady (by a Gentleman with a Blue Beard) and Famous Love Affairs (Garden City: Doubleday, Page, 1922);

The Old Soak's History of the World (Garden City: Doubleday, Page, 1924; London: Heinemann, 1924);

The Dark Hours, Five Scenes from History (Garden City: Doubleday, Page, 1924; London: Heinemann, 1924);

Pandora Lifts the Lid, by Marquis and Christopher Morley (New York: Doran, 1924; London: Cape, 1924);

Words and Thoughts, A Play in One Act (New York & London: Appleton, 1924);

The Awakening and Other Poems (London: Heinemann, 1924; Garden City: Doubleday, Page, 1925);

The Old Soak: A Comedy in Three Acts (New York & London: French, 1926);

The Almost Perfect State (Garden City: Doubleday, Page, 1927; London: Heinemann, 1927);

Out of the Sea, A Play in Four Acts (Garden City: Doubleday, Page, 1927; London: Heinemann, 1927);

Archy and Mehitabel (Garden City: Doubleday, Page, 1927; London: Benn, 1931);

Love Sonnets of a Cave Man and Other Verses (Garden City: Doubleday, Doran, 1928);

When the Turtles Sing, and Other Unusual Tales (Garden City: Doubleday, Doran, 1928);

A Variety of People (Garden City: Doubleday, Doran, 1929);

Off the Arm (Garden City: Doubleday, Doran, 1930);

Archys Life of Mehitabel (Garden City: Doubleday, Doran, 1933; London: Faber & Faber, 1934);

Chapters for the Orthodox (Garden City: Doubleday, Doran, 1934);

Master of the Revels, A Comedy in Four Acts (Garden City: Doubleday, Doran, 1934);

Archy Does His Part (Garden City: Doubleday, Doran, 1935; London: Faber & Faber, 1936);

Sun Dial Time (Garden City: Doubleday, Doran, 1936);

Sons of the Puritans (New York: Doubleday, Doran, 1939);

the lives and times of archy and mehitabel (New York: Doubleday, Doran, 1940).

Born of indeterminate parents but probably of *Periplaneta americana* or *Periplaneta fuliginosa* stock (American or Smoky Brown), Archy the cockroach discovered a patron and admirer in the offices of the *New York Evening Sun*. It was 1916 when Archy came to the attention of Don Marquis, columnist, short-story writer, playwright, poet, and epigrammatic philosopher. Archy claimed to have been transmigrated, that in one of his earlier lives he had been a free-verse bard. Beginning on 29 March 1916, Marquis "transmitted" Archy's messages, typed on Marquis's typewriter and addressed "dear boss," to the wider public via his column, "The Sun Dial." Because Archy could not press the shift key and a letter key at the same time, none of his messages contained capital letters. When Marquis first collected his Archy columns in *Archy and Mehitabel* (1927), *Archys Life of Mehitabel* (1933), and *Archy Does His Part* (1935), the books were printed with capital letters, but later editions of these still popular books were published without them to conform to Archy's typography. In 1940 the three books were collected under the title *the lives and times of archy and mehitabel*. In his often-quoted introduction to *archys life of mehitabel* Marquis attributed to Archy and Mehitabel the cat "a kind of vitality" that seemed to exist beyond his control: "I tried to kill them off at least half a dozen times. But they would not stay dead. Every time I killed them, I got hundreds of letters from their devoted readers demanding an immediate resuscitation. It was easy enough to manage these resurrections; every time I stepped on Archy and slew him, his soul could transmigrate into another cockroach without missing a strophe. I finally began to understand that for some reason or other (or possibly for no reason at all) there was a certain public which wanted them."

Donald Robert Perry Marquis was born on 29 July 1878 to James Stewart and Virginia Whitmore Marquis in Walnut, Illinois, at 3 P.M. during an eclipse of the sun. In his uncompleted "Egobiography" Marquis commented, "to be born with an eclipse over you is to be born with a kind of cosmic caul covering you." The name Marquis is Scottish in origin; and Marquis's ancestors came to Winchester, Virginia, via Northern Ireland. They were, according to Don Marquis, "Calvinists who believed in Infant Damnation, Calomel, and Scotch Whiskey." As a boy, Marquis learned from his grandfather, William or Captain Billy Marquis, how his great-grandfather had been a soldier in the Revolutionary War and how he had trekked west to Ohio in 1798. Captain Billy Marquis had fought in the War of 1812, and Marquis's father was a doctor. Although Marquis was born in Illinois, he was to become in the minds of many as firmly associated with New York as Damon Runyon.

Marquis got to New York via Washington, D.C., and Atlanta. He had been early attracted to newspapers, enthusiastically reading Eugene Field in a Chicago paper as a boy. After getting experience on weekly newspapers in and around Walnut, he moved to Washington in 1900, first working for the census bureau and then going to work for the *Washington Times*. He then worked briefly for a newspaper in Philadelphia before going on to Atlanta where he was employed first by the *Atlanta News* and later by the *Atlanta Journal*. He began to write poetry seriously during this period; but most of his poems, he claimed, were thrown out by the janitor. Five years after he had moved to Atlanta, Marquis became associate editor of *Uncle Remus's Home Magazine*, started in 1907 by Joel Chandler Harris. The magazine had a national circulation and Marquis, whose writing had been limited primarily to editorials, now began to write book

Don Marquis

reviews and parodies as well. In one of his parodies he suggested that Upton Sinclair research a novel about upper-class life in Newport by disguising himself as a servant or even a cockroach. After Harris's death in July 1908, Marquis became dissatisfied with his work on the magazine. In late 1909, after marrying Reina Melcher on 8 June 1909, he left Atlanta. The Marquises were to have two children, Robert (born in 1915) and Barbara (born in 1918).

The Atlanta days proved to be extremely significant. In addition to his friendship with Harris he was during those years a companion and associate of Grantland Rice, who would become one of the best-known and most influential sportswriters in America, and Frank Stanton, the famous Southern newspaper columnist. Stanton encouraged Marquis to keep trying the columnist's trade. Marquis stopped briefly in Cleveland, then rushed on to New York. He wanted to make a name for himself as a New York columnist. He had left his wife behind in Atlanta for a short time while he looked for work. He arrived in New York, he said later, with a dozen books of poetry and a pair of old socks. Until 1912 the Marquises supported themselves mainly by free-lance writing, and Marquis worked briefly, on various occasions, for several New York newspapers.

During the summer of 1911, Marquis's wife encouraged him to complete a novel he had begun writing in Atlanta. *Danny's Own Story* (1912) was published by the first publisher Marquis sent it to, Doubleday, Page. *Danny's Own Story* reflects Marquis's devotion to Mark Twain and in many ways echoes *Huckleberry Finn*. At eighteen Danny runs away from the parents who found him on their doorstep as an infant, and goes with Dr. Kirby, who is operating an Indian medicine show. Like Huck, Danny's travels involve him in a series of disillusioning experiences. In Kentucky he observes night riders; in Georgia he finds out about lynching. In the course of his escapades Danny discovers Doc Kirby is his real father, how and why he was left on the doorstep, and what happened to his mother. The novel was praised for its style, its "savor and charm." But even admirers of Marquis, such as Christopher Morley and Lynn Lee, have objected to its derivative quality.

In 1912 Marquis's ambition to be a newspaper columnist was fulfilled when he was hired to write "The Sun Dial" column for the *New York Evening Sun*. By the time he left the *Sun* in 1922 to write "The Lantern" column for the *New York Tribune*, he and the characters he created for his columns had become famous, and his first play had had a successful run on Broadway.

Marquis's second book, *Dreams & Dust* (1915), a collection of poetry he later regretted having had published, was followed by a second novel, *The Cruise of the Jasper B.* (1916). Like *Danny's Own Story* it is melodramatic and mock-romantic, a purposeful burlesque of the popular swashbuckling novels written by Richard Harding Davis. *The Cruise of the Jasper B.* has a complicated and contrived plot. Clement J. Cleggett, a copyreader on a New York newspaper, inherits $500,000. He buys a ship and sets out for adventure, during which, among other things, he marries a young woman who has been carting around a large box of ice (which turns out to contain a corpse) and fights a duel with a villain who wears a scarf pin in the likeness of a skull. After winning out over evil, Clement has four sons, names them D'Artagnan, Athos, Porthos, and Aramis, and refuses a title from the King of England because he values his American citizenship more. The novel is entertaining because Clement's daring deeds are so ridiculous.

During the next fourteen years, Marquis had twenty books published, many of them collections of his columns and pieces that appeared widely and regularly in other newspapers and magazines. In his columns Marquis included poems, parodies, vignettes, commentaries, and epigrams, and he introduced a number of comic characters who reappeared in later columns, with friends, and gained audiences of followers.

One of the first of these characters to show up in "The Sun Dial" was a wealthy dilettante named Hermione, whose monologues were included in *Hermione and Her Little Group of Serious Thinkers* (1916). Without commenting on what they say, Marquis permits Hermione and her friends to reveal their own silliness, and the result is an ironic attack on those who talk but do not produce, the newest literary or sociological fads, and the self servers who contribute to their own and others' delusions. Most memorable of the members of Hermione's group is Fothergil Finch, a vers libre poet who combines shallowness with posturing, pretentiousness with banality. In these and other columns, Marquis attacks pseudo-intellectuality, superficiality, and the whole tendency to self-congratulate or to exaggerate. He works at putting things into perspective, a perspective most likely to disturb those who know absolutely, the fanatics, the too-easily enthusiastic, and those in charge.

Marquis's next book, *Prefaces* (1919), includes Marquis's introductions to thirty-two imaginary books. These books include a calendar, a memorandum book, a hangman's diary, a cookbook, a book of safety pins, and a book of fishhooks. Each sketch uses the proposed subject being introduced in order to satirize people and literature. The best story in Marquis's next book, the collection of short stories *Carter, and Other People* (1921), is probably the title story, originally published in *Harper's* as "The Mulatto." Based on the Atlanta race riot of 22 September 1906, it reveals Marquis's hatred of racism. In another of his 1921 books, Marquis topped *Hermione and Her Little Group of Serious Thinkers* with a collection of twenty-two columns about another character he had created, one of the "most memorable characters in modern American humor," the likable drinking man Clem Hawley. In *The Old Soak* Clem first lives in Flatbush and then moves to rural Baycliff, Long Island. Clem comments on how the world should be run and complains about Prohibition. Because the bars are closed he cannot keep up with politics or sports. He says that Prohibition keeps a man at home so much that he fights with his wife. He is suspicious of those who too strongly profess religious morality. He suggests that a dry country is hardhearted and hardly harmonious. The popularity of *The Old Soak* resulted in a second collection, *The Old Soak's History of the World* (1924). Marquis's first play, *The Old Soak*, opened on Broadway in August 1922 and ran for 325 performances. A second Old Soak play, *Everything's Jake*, ran for seventy-six performances in 1930.

Like much of Marquis's other work, the Old Soak columns undercut human weaknesses. Clem sees even biblical figures as flawed and rejects cultural superiority of all sorts, especially the tendency to be overawed by the ancient and the European. He has colloquial common sense and sees most people as imperfect but worth having around. In his time Clem became a kind of folk hero with whom all sorts of people identified, in part because of the general antagonism toward Prohibition and the excesses associated with it. In his *New York Times* review of the play *The Old Soak* Alexander Woollcott called Clem "a cheerful likeable old drunkard." Woollcott noted that the plot was too predictable—the erring son has led the family into financial difficulty; the drunk father is wrongfully suspected; the mother weeps bitter tears—but he admired the "humor, charm and whimsicality" of the author. Even if the plot was thin, the audiences responded to the play's humor and sympathy. The *Times* reviewer of *Everything's Jake* responded similarly, commenting that as one would expect everything turned out well and everyone earned a fortune. It was not profundity that made the play worthwhile, he said, but Marquis's scintillating use of American English.

Marquis's professional successes in the early 1920s were marred by tragedy. In February 1921 his five-year-old son died, and in December 1923 Reina Marquis died suddenly. Despite continuing financial problems, in 1925 Marquis decided to give up his column so that he could work at home and be close to his young daughter who had been traumatized by her mother's death.

On 2 February 1926 Marquis married actress Marjorie Potts Vonnegut, a friend of Reina Marquis's with whom she had shared an interest in Christian Science. Marjorie Marquis admired her husband's humor writing, but according to Edward Anthony she was "fundamentally a serious-minded woman," who was more impressed with his serious writing, particularly his biblical play, *The Dark Hours, Five Scenes from History*, which had been published by Doubleday, Page in 1924. When she staged the play in 1932, it was far less successful than Marquis's humorous plays, running for only eight performances. Yet Brooks Atkinson in the *New York Times* said that Marquis should be "properly respected as the author of a modern play of the passion," and he thought that the script, which depicted five scenes from Christian history, was superior to the production.

Marquis's other attempt at serious drama had been similarly unsuccessful. *Out of the Sea* ran for only sixteen performances in 1927. A modern version of the Tristram legend, set on the coast of Cornwall, the play chronicles the doomed love of a minor American poet, John Harding, who loves a young married woman, Isobel Tregesal, who is dominated by her tyrannical husband. John and Isobel plan to escape together, but after her husband confronts her, Isobel kills him and drowns herself. Atkinson in the *New York Times* said satirically that Archy "would have little patience with such star-struck drama."

As with Hermione and the Old Soak, a wide audience of readers was already familiar with Archy the cockroach and Mehitabel the cat by the time the first book about them was published in 1927. For many readers it was not necessary to explain that sometime in March 1916 Marquis had discovered a gigantic cockroach jumping up and down on the keys of his typewriter, "head downward, and his weight and the impact of the blow were just sufficient to operate the machine, one slow letter after another." It was fairly common knowledge that Archy could not operate the shift lever to type capital letters and that his labor was so excruciating that he did not bother to punctuate. Marquis explained that he left paper in the typewriter, and each night Archy typed a message.

archy and mehitabel consists of forty-eight columns mostly in the form of free-verse poems, and introduces a host of characters, including Freddy the rat, a jealous literary type; Marty Bliggens the toad; a South American tarantula; a gentleman with a long brown beard who seems to have eaten his own eye; Shakespeare; Ben Jonson; and the mummy of the Egyptian pharaoh in the Metropolitan Museum.

Despite the wide range of characters there are a number of central concerns that Archy returns to repeatedly. Archy believes in transmigration and ghosts. He was once a free-verse poet; Mehitabel the cat was once Cleopatra; one of Mehitabel's lovers was once François Villon. Archy wonders about what happens between states.

Although this is a comic work it repeatedly confronts death. Mehitabel cavorts among the bones of the Paris catacombs. Freddy the rat dies, probably from poisoned cheese but perhaps in a battle with a tarantula. A spider and a fly have a discussion about cosmic purposes in which the spider justifies his killing the fly by pointing out that he, as a web maker, is a creator of beauty while the fly represents the merely utilitarian. Yet, says Archy, the talk makes no difference in the outcome. Archy is aware that all things come to naught, and he is not surprised that a free-verse poet is trapped in the body of a cockroach, that the queen of the Nile has become an alley cat.

Archy emphasizes the resilience of the poor. Hurt can be disguised by exaggeration. His messages leave no doubt about his social consciousness. He is aware of the haves and the have-nots, the bloodthirstiness of the powerful, how rationalization is used to hide anti-social activity, how widespread is intolerance. He rails against individual self-delusion and the arrogance, foolishness, and lack of compassion inherent in judging hastily and superficially.

While *archy and mehitabel* has the greatest range of characters and places, many of the themes in the first book about Archy are picked up and amplified later. There is here, as in the later books, an overwhelming sense of isolation. Archy feels alone and stranded. He tries to communicate, but he feels threatened especially by human beings. Despite his bravado and his faith in the beauty of art, he is afraid that the act of writing may be futile. Maybe

Archy typing a message to Marquis as Mehitabel looks on, illustration by George Herriman

writers, even free-verse poets, are no better than anyone else. Even Shakespeare, Archy has it on good testimony, felt he had sold out by writing for the theater. Still, throughout *archy and mehitabel*, there is a sense of rejuvenating energy that enables Mehitabel to be a free spirit in spite of all, to always be a "lady," "toujours gai." Energy and compassion inform the book as Archy calls for "less justice and more charity."

By the time *archys life of mehitabel* was published six years later (1933), Mehitabel had developed considerably. She almost takes over the book—so much so that Archy revolts and refuses to finish telling her story. Before their falling out, a number of things about Mehitabel's background become clear: she has been taught to drink at an early age by a kitchen maid; her mother and her dissolute father were "high born"; and she was born in a stable in Greenwich Village. While her brothers and sisters were sent early to a watery grave, she was a pampered kitten until she fought with a foolish dog named Snookums and scratched her mistress. After Mehitabel was tossed into an ashcan, she wandered off into a barroom where she caused a pair of drunks to think they were having delusions as she sipped beer from a glass on their table. Soon she was the barroom cat, until she sneaked into a man's fur pocket and went home with him. Archy has been dutifully reporting all in his messages to Marquis, but at this point Mehitabel gets a swelled head from so much publicity and demands that her picture be published; an annoyed Archy reasserts himself and calls for a revolt by the insects of the world, emphasizing the importance of the small:

> i can show you love and hate
> and the future
> dreaming side by side
> in a cell
> in the little cells where
> matter is so fine it merges
> into spirit

Thus, he illustrates that this comic work is never far from the cosmic.

In much of *archys life of mehitabel* Archy's concerns are literary. After eating a lot of Kipling's poetry in a secondhand bookstore, he launches into a parody of Kipling's literary ballads. He emphasizes the strenuousness of his labors as a writer, his consequential poverty, the resistance of the machine he must operate, and the importance of the self. And he fiddles with style, typing half a poem in capital letters when he finds the shift keys locked and, in another, spelling out all the names of punctuation marks. Perhaps it is Archy's self-consciousness that makes him underline repeatedly the inferiority of man. Having made this point, he lets Mehitabel back into the book. Once again he reports her tales of her suffering, her fall from the good life, and how she got revenge with her claws. Seeking to become movie stars, Archy and Mehitabel go to Hollywood, but after Mehitabel is "forcibly rejected at least twice from every moving-picture studio," they begin to hitchhike back. In New Mexico Mehitabel has an affair with a coyote she calls "cowboy bill." Back in New York she scrapes a living out of fish heads from the cans of Shinbone Alley and has a batch of kittens that act like dogs. Near the end of the book, Archy visits her and hears her singing,

> i have had my ups i have had my downs
> i never was nobodys pet
> i got a limp in my left hind leg
> but theres life in the old dame yet

Archy concludes that the artist always pays, that the world is incomprehensible. But he signs his last letter to the boss, "yours for rum / crime and riot." C. G. Poore, writing in the *New York Times*, said "Archy has written one of the outstanding biographies of the year. It was not easy for him; as half the world knows, each word that this sapient cockroach types is accomplished only through gruelling labor. . . ."

The third book of the Archy epic, *archy does his*

part, is the longest of the three and has considerably more social criticism. Reflecting the mood of the Depression, Archy criticizes the New Deal and government and politicians in general. In this book antagonisms harden. There are conflicts between Archy and Pete, a Boston bull terrier, between Archy and Marquis, between Marquis and some of his readers. A good portion of the book concerns itself with Archy's strike against the column, complete with scabs, picketing, and negotiations. Archy asks for "economic justice and a living wage," for a Paris vacation, and for a few crumbs. He also visits Washington and comments prophetically about events to come in Europe. As he surveys the circumstances of the planet he becomes more and more disillusioned with the ways in which humans mishandle their affairs. The book ends with his account of the ecological disaster man has visited on the planet:

> america was once a paradise
> of timberland and stream
> but it is dying because of the greed
> and money lust of a thousand little kings
> who slashed the timber all to hell
> and would not be controlled
> and changed the climate
> and stole the rainfall from posterity.

He predicts that

> one day the mississippi itself
> will be a bed of sand
> ants and scorpions and centipedes
> shall inherit the earth.

But he is hardly satisfied, and he signs off,

> dear boss
> i relay this information
> without any fear that humanity
> will take warning and reform
>   archy

Marquis had a distinguished career aside from his writings about Archy and his friends, but more than fifty years after its inception, Archy's epic continues to generate an enthusiastic audience, and this kind of popularity has not followed Marquis's other work.

the lives and times of archy and mehitabel explores the American language. It is written in colloquial idiom, getting a particular zest from its nonpoetic elements. Archy speaks with inimitable run-on

Archy beginning his biography of Mehitabel, illustration by George Herriman

rhythms, memorable refrains, and a peculiar way of exaggerating and then flattening the emphasis, and he particularly enjoys quoting others, most often Mehitabel, who in turn may quote others. Archy is a marvelous instrument of absorption. His is "underside" speech, but it is full of borrowings that reflect all the levels of America's complex culture. Archy knows how everyone sounds and can echo the street-wise, parody the elitist. He likes to juxtapose the lingo of the bar with the biblical or the Shakespearean. As Bernard DeVoto wrote of *the lives and times of archy and mehitabel*, "There has never been anything like Archy or Mehitabel and there never will be. Don Marquis got all his rich and strange talent into a cockroach who had the literary urge . . . and a cat . . . who was always a lady in spite of hell. Only fantasy was wide or versatile enough to contain him. . . ."

Despite the popularity of Archy and Mehitabel, Marquis often needed money during the late 1920s and early 1930s. In 1928-1929 he went to

work as a screenwriter in Hollywood, where he hoped the climate would be beneficial to his daughter's poor health. In 1931 he worked in Hollywood for nineteen weeks, during which his daughter died. Although he worked in Hollywood off and on until 1936, he was not a successful screenwriter, and the novel based on his Hollywood experiences, *Off the Arm* (1930), is generally unsuccessful. Full of familiar caricatures of Hollywood types, the book, however, does have a sharp portrait of Charlie Chaplin in Douglas Fairbanks's swimming pool. One of its main characters, Gerald Wadleigh, an overweight, middle-aged popular novelist, is probably a self-caricature of Marquis.

Marquis's iconoclasm reveals itself in two other books written and published during the same time the stories of Archy and Mehitabel were appearing in book form. In *The Almost Perfect State* (1927) he maintained that "The Almost Perfect State will not be governed by businessmen, but by artists." This notebook for a utopia is "half serious, half whimsical," containing serious ideas and comic relief. On the one hand Marquis insists that the almost perfect state would be possible only if people were capable of self-government, that in such a state a man would not cut down a tree unless he planted at least two. On the other hand he comments, "You may clothe part of the people all of the time or all of the people part of the time, but you cannot force all of the people to wear all their clothes all the time." Bernard DeVoto found this generally unsalable book admirable but "exasperating." The twelve chapters in *Chapters for the Orthodox* (1934) nearly all deal with Jehovah, the Christ, and the Devil in New York City. In one of them Christ is arrested at an Italian restaurant for changing water to wine and is charged with being a bootlegger. These chapters do treat serious ideas such as free will, evil, and the relationship of God and man. God is seen as irrational; man rejects his love and kindness. In "Miss Higginbottom Declines" Jehovah decides to send "another Begotten son" and chooses Miss Higginbottom for the role originally played by Mary, but she refuses on the grounds that bearing a child out of wedlock is abhorrent and a threat to her virtue.

The last years of Marquis's life were difficult. He had had a heart attack in Hollywood in January 1929, and shortly before the opening of his play *The Dark Hours* in November 1932, he was struck by uremic poisoning or some sort of "vascular disturbance." On 25 October 1936 Marjorie Marquis died. Marquis, who had had a series of strokes that year and lost the power of speech, lingered. When he died on 29 December 1937 he was heavily in debt, although widely acclaimed. He had always handled money generously and ineptly. His death resulted in editorials and eulogies throughout the country. In New York, the *Times*, the *Herald Tribune*, and the *World-Telegram* said prominent goodbyes. Said the *Times*, "Don Marquis was an Elizabethan

Don Marquis

born out of his time. . . . all that he wrote or imagined was racy of the central prairies. But he could have been at home in the Mermaid Tavern raising a tankard to Ben Jonson, even rubbing elbows with Will Shakespeare, and quoting the profound Biblical misquotations of the Old Soak in praise of good liquor."

When he died Marquis left an uncompleted novel that might have become his best. *Sons of the Puritans* (1939) was published in its unfinished form

with a preface by Christopher Morley and Marquis's notes on how he might finish it. Set in Hazleton (really Walnut, Illinois), the novel develops the conflict between fundamentalism and agnosticism as Jack Stephens, orphaned son of a fire-and-brimstone preacher, rebels against the repressive atmosphere of his college. Marquis planned to have him leave for New York and become involved in the literary and artistic movements there just prior to World War I.

Edward Anthony, in *O Rare Don Marquis*, cites numerous reviewers who praised Marquis's "serious" poetry, and encourages the view that the comic Don Marquis, although clever, entertaining, and inventive is less significant than the playwright and poet who wrote the poems in *Dreams and Dust* and the New Testament drama *The Dark Hours*. In fact Anthony calls *The Dark Hours* "the supreme effort of Marquis's years as a writer." Marquis himself was likely to misjudge his work, giving priority to the "serious." In 1927 when *archy and mehitabel* was published he was working most seriously on his play, *Out of the Sea*, which now seems dated and inflated, and he sometimes expressed disappointment about the responses to his "most ambitious work." Louis Untermeyer in *A Treasury of Laughter* quotes Marquis as saying, "It would be one on me if I should be remembered longest for creating a cockroach character."

Marquis charmed people with his wit and congeniality, in person as well as through his column. His friends included many humorists and literary men such as Christopher Morley, Will Rogers, Homer Croy, and John Dewey, who was a tenant of Marquis's in New York. Marquis and Dewey had long chats but Marquis complained he could not get the famous utilitarian philosopher to reveal any of the "Great Mysteries." Marquis's fans included Theodore Roosevelt and Edwin Arlington Robinson.

Perhaps Marquis's significance is best expressed in the privately printed pamphlet presented to the Cleveland Public Library by his friend and sometimes contributor to his column, Benjamin Casseres, the year after Marquis's death. The pamphlet entitled *Don Marquis* is a biblical parody in which Marquis appears before "the Great Impresario" as a modern Job, blind and poverty-stricken. He has lost his family. He has been beset by Satan. But before his interview is over Satan has been banished. "Angels of Laughter" fill the heavens. Don Marquis has been lifted to "the Kingdom of Cosmic Mirth."

Plays:

The Old Soak, New York, Plymouth Theatre, 22 August 1922;

Out of the Sea, New York, Eltinge Theatre, 5 December 1927;

Everything's Jake, New York, Assembly Theatre, 16 January 1930;

The Dark Hours, New York, New Amsterdam Theatre, 14 November 1932.

Biography:

Edward Anthony, *O Rare Don Marquis, A Biography* (Garden City: Doubleday, 1962).

References:

Benjamin Casseres, *Don Marquis* (N.p.: Privately printed, 1938);

Bernard DeVoto, "Almost Toujour Gai," in his *The Easy Chair* (Boston: Houghton Mifflin, 1955);

Dan Jaffe, "Archy Jumps Over the Moon," in *The Twenties: Fiction, Poetry, Drama*, edited by War-

ren French (De Land, Fla.: Everett/Edwards, 1975), pp. 427-437;

Lynn Lee, *Don Marquis* (Boston: Twayne, 1981);

George Middleton, *These Things Are Mine* (New York: Macmillan, 1947);

Christopher Morley, *Letters of Askance* (Philadelphia & New York: Lippincott, 1939);

Morley, *Shandygaff* (Garden City: Doubleday, Page, 1919);

Morley, "A Successor to Mark Twain," *Michigan Alumnus Quarterly Review* (Summer 1937);

Stuart P. Sherman, "Don Marquis—What Is He?," *New York Herald Tribune Book Review*, 8 February 1925;

Simeon Strunsky, "Goodbye, Don," *New York Times*, 30 December 1937, pp. 18-19;

Norris Yates, "The Many Masks of Don Marquis," in his *The American Humorist: Conscience of the Twentieth Century* (Ames: Iowa State University Press, 1964), pp. 195-216.

Phyllis McGinley

(21 March 1905-22 February 1978)

Nancy Walker
Stephens College

BOOKS: *On the Contrary* (Garden City: Doubleday, Doran, 1934);

One More Manhattan (New York: Harcourt, Brace, 1937);

A Pocketful of Wry (New York: Duell, Sloan & Pearce, 1940);

Husbands Are Difficult; or, The Book of Oliver Ames (New York: Duell, Sloan & Pearce, 1941);

The Horse Who Lived Upstairs (Philadelphia: Lippincott, 1944);

The Plain Princess (Philadelphia: Lippincott, 1945);

Stones from a Glass House: New Poems (New York: Viking, 1946);

A Name for Kitty (New York: Simon & Schuster, 1948; London: Muller, 1950);

All Around the Town (Philadelphia: Lippincott, 1948);

The Most Wonderful Doll in the World (Philadelphia: Lippincott, 1950);

Blunderbus (Philadelphia: Lippincott, 1951);

The Horse Who Had His Picture in the Paper (Philadelphia: Lippincott, 1951);

A Short Walk from the Station (New York: Viking, 1951);

The Make-Believe Twins (Philadelphia: Lippincott, 1953);

Love Letters (New York: Viking, 1954; London: Dent, 1955);

The Year Without a Santa Claus (Philadelphia: Lippincott, 1957; Leicester, U.K.: Brockhampton Press, 1960);

Merry Christmas, Happy New Year (New York: Viking, 1958; London: Secker & Warburg, 1959);

Lucy McLockett (Philadelphia: Lippincott, 1959; Leicester, U.K.: Brockhampton Press, 1961);

The Province of the Heart (New York: Viking, 1959; London: Catholic Book Club, 1963);

Times Three: Selected Verse from Three Decades, with Seventy New Poems (New York: Viking, 1960; London: Secker & Warburg, 1961);

Sugar and Spice: The ABC of Being a Girl (New York: Watts, 1960);

Mince Pie and Mistletoe (Philadelphia: Lippincott, 1961);

Boys Are Awful (New York: Watts, 1962);

The B Book (New York: Crowell-Collier, 1962; London: Collier-Macmillan, 1968);

A Girl and Her Room (New York: Watts, 1963);

How Mrs. Santa Claus Saved Christmas (Philadelphia: Lippincott, 1963; Kingswood, Surrey, U.K.: World's Work, 1964);

Sixpence in Her Shoe (New York: Macmillan, 1964);

Wonderful Time (Philadelphia: Lippincott, 1966);

A Wreath of Christmas Legends (New York: Macmillan, 1967);

Wonders and Surprises: A Collection of Poems (Philadelphia: Lippincott, 1968);

Saint-Watching (New York: Viking, 1969; London: Collins, 1970);

Christmas con and pro (Berkeley: Hart Press, 1971);

Confessions of a Reluctant Optimist, edited by Barbara Wells Price (Kansas City, Mo.: Hallmark Editions, 1973).

One of the best-known and most prolific writers of light verse in twentieth-century America, Phyllis McGinley enjoyed a long career which was highlighted in 1961 by her receiving the Pulitzer Prize for *Times Three: Selected Verse from Three Decades, with Seventy New Poems*, the first time that award had been given for a volume of light verse. Her verse has been widely praised for its technical virtuosity. W. H. Auden, in the foreword to *Times Three*, places her in the tradition of Hood, Belloc, and Chesterton, and she is often compared to Dorothy Parker, though more on the basis of her sex and her long association with the *New Yorker* than for similarities of style and subject matter. A consistently staunch defender of woman's role as homemaker and mother, McGinley celebrated that role in her poetry and in humorous essays published in a wide variety of magazines, and in addition, wrote nineteen books for children.

McGinley was born to Catholic parents of German and Irish descent—Daniel and Julia Kiesel McGinley—in Ontario, Oregon, but the family soon moved to a ranch in Iliff, Colorado, where McGinley and her brother attended a small country school. The isolation of ranch life fostered her enthusiasm for reading; she said in a *Time* interview in 1965, "I am probably the only person left living who has read the entire works of Bulwer-Lytton—when I was ten years old." She began writing verse at the age of six,

Phyllis McGinley

though her talent for humor did not emerge until she was an adult.

When her father died in 1917, McGinley moved to her mother's family's home in Ogden, Utah, where she attended Sacred Heart Academy and Ogden High School. After beginning college at the University of Southern California, she transferred to the University of Utah, from which she graduated in 1927. While at Utah, she consistently won prizes for poetry, short stories, and essays that she entered pseudonymously in university competitions. Determined to be a poet, she began to submit work to New York magazines while teaching school in Ogden, and in 1929, after having poems accepted by several publications, she moved to New Rochelle, New York, where she taught English in a junior high school while continuing to write what she has called "serious, sad, Swinburne-ish" poetry.

McGinley's conversion to the humorous poetry for which she became famous was motivated by a note from *New Yorker* fiction editor Katherine White, which said, "we are buying your poem, but why do you sing the same sad songs all lady poets sing?" Encouraged by the *New Yorker*'s enthusiasm for the light verse she began to write, McGinley resigned her teaching post in the early 1930s and moved to New York City, where she worked briefly as an advertising copywriter and as poetry editor for *Town and Country* while attempting to establish a career as a free-lance writer.

The subjects of McGinley's poetry range from the topical and even trivial to issues of worldwide significance, and the tone accordingly varies from lighthearted mirth to incisive wit. Often the distinction between light verse and serious poetry blurs, as in "Ballade of Lost Objects," in which McGinley uses the devices of light verse to convey a wistful, nostalgic message. And some of her poems, such as the sonnet "Midcentury Love Letter," are wholly serious. The distinction between light verse and poetry, McGinley said in a 1965 article in the *American Scholar*, is "impact.... Serious poetry engages the emotions. Light verse aims at the intellect which it wishes to amuse and divert." As a writer of the latter, she identified her themes as the "topical or the domestic. The views from my own terrace are the ones I describe, small, personal and suburban."

McGinley's first three books of light verse, however, have urban themes. Her first collection, *On the Contrary* (1934), includes a number of light-hearted satires on fashions, department stores, and newspaper items. The tone of most of the poems is playful, as she reflects on the fads and minutiae of city life: the "socially prominent" couple in "The Odious People," the raising of prices at Woolworth's in "Death in 40th Street," and the inconveniences of having to commute to the suburbs in "Song from New Rochelle":

> But just when the height is at its fun
>   And the yodeler's growing vocal,
> I am the one who needs must run
>   To catch the Stamford local.

The volume also includes several poems about "Oliver Ames," McGinley's fictional embodiment of male habits and foibles, and several, such as "Atavism," which deal more generally with the uneasy relationship between the sexes. The poems display McGinley's early mastery of many of the devices of light verse—polished form, rhyme, conversational tone, and wordplay—but the topicality of their subjects was no doubt one factor in McGinley's decision to include only seven of them in *Times Three*. As she said in a 1960 *Newsweek* interview, "At first, . . . I was writing real light verse. I mean *really* light verse."

In *One More Manhattan*, published in 1937, McGinley employs many of the same themes. Still a city dweller, as the title suggests, she comments wryly on women in from the suburbs for a day of shopping ("A Day in the City"), the rigors of weekends in the country ("Song to Be Sung After Labor Day"), and, in "Midsummer Meditations," the inadvisability of sidewalk cafes in Manhattan, where "airs of August, gusty, / Waft cinders toward the soup." Two thematic emphases differentiate this volume from the earlier one. Attesting to her status as a colleague of other prominent humorists of the era are several poems which allude to their works. "Ballade for a Bard" is an appreciative review of Franklin P. Adams's *The Melancholy Lute* (1936), and in "Evolution of a Benedick" she reviews Ogden Nash's *The Bad Parent's Garden of Verse* (1936), employing Nash's characteristic devices of forced rhymes (e.g., "nursery" and "versery") and irregular line lengths. The Depression and threats of war in Europe provide the basis for several poems in the ironic mode. In "Trinity Place," fat pompous pigeons are contrasted with jobless men on park benches: "It is only the men who are hungry. The pigeons are fed." And in "Carol with Variations," the peaceful lyrics of Christmas carols are transmuted into horrified commentary on a warlike world: "Sing the candle, sing the lamp, / Sing the Concentration Camp." Many of the poems in *One More Manhattan* appeared first in the *New Yorker*, which continued to publish her light verse throughout the 1930s.

On 25 June 1937 McGinley married Charles L. Hayden, a telephone company employee and part-time jazz musician. By the time their first daughter, Julie (Julia Elizabeth), was born in 1939, the Haydens had moved from Manhattan to suburban Larchmont. Eventually, domesticity and suburbia would alter the tone and themes of McGinley's work, but her 1940 collection, *A Pocketful of Wry*, has much in common with *One More Manhattan*. Many of the poems in each collection had been first published in the *New Yorker*, the *Saturday Review of Literature*, the *Saturday Evening Post*, and *Red Book Magazine*. The first two sections of *A Pocketful of Wry* consist of poems on light, topical subjects: newspaper items, radio programs and films, fashions, and the urban scene. The third section, "Private and Personal," contains the often-reprinted "Apology for Husbands" and "Why, Some of my Best Friends are Women," while in the fourth, "A Troubled Pool," she turns to the world situation, especially the bombing of London, in ironic parodies. A nursery rhyme provides the framework for "Old Rhyme" ("You make a fine target / Say the bells of St. Marg'et"), and in "Mr. Browning Revises—1940," she uses the structure of Browning's "Home-thoughts, from Abroad" to describe bomb shelters and gas masks.

Most of McGinley's early poems on the war between the sexes are collected in the 1941 *Husbands Are Difficult; or, The Book of Oliver Ames*. Dedicated to "C.L.H." (Charles L. Hayden), the volume includes the Oliver Ames poems from earlier volumes and other poems on the foibles of men which had originally been published in the *New Yorker*, the *Saturday Evening Post*, and *Good Housekeeping*. The poems are consistently light in tone, and play upon stereotypical descriptions of men as well-intentioned and necessary creatures who are nevertheless messy, impractical, and often annoyingly ill-tempered or vain. In contrast, the woman whose voice is heard in the verses is blessed with common sense and patience enough to keep the relationship on an even keel. McGinley's contentment with her suburban domestic lot is apparent throughout the volume, and is summarized in the final poem, "View from a Suburban Window," a parody of Milton's "On His Blindness," which ends with the line "I might have done much worse. I might, at that."

After the birth of her second daughter, Patsy (Phyllis Louise), McGinley turned her talents for humor to writing children's books, beginning with *The Horse Who Lived Upstairs* in 1944, and for the rest of her career she wrote for both children and adults with equal success. In *Sixpence in Her Shoe* (1964), she calls children "the finest audience in the world . . . enormous in numbers, avid for fulfillment, and immensely loyal." The dimeter and trimeter lines of her "lightest" light verse adapted well to the jog-trot rhythms of children's verse.

In *Stones from a Glass House: New Poems* (1946), a collection of light verse published originally in the *New Yorker* and other magazines from 1940 to 1946, such short lines are rarely used. The poems rely more on wit than on playful devices, though the subjects are sometimes ephemeral (the dieting of the Dionne quintuplets, the magazines in beauty parlors). The more enduring poems in this as in other collections use the devices of light verse, especially parody and consistency of meter and rhyme scheme, to convey themes of widespread appeal. Half of these poems were selected by McGinley for inclusion in *Times Three*, notably "Occupation: Housewife," "The Velvet Hand," "Confessions of a Reluctant Optimist," "The 5:32," "Dido of Tunisia," and "V-Day."

The prosuburban sentiments in "Confessions of a Reluctant Optimist" and "The 5:32" recur with force in *A Short Walk from the Station* (1951); most of the "Sonnets from Westchester" in this volume are reprinted from *Stones from a Glass House*. *A Short Walk from the Station* was intended as a defense of suburban life, and is prefaced by McGinley's essay "Suburbia, of Thee I sing," which had appeared in *Harper's* in December 1946. Condemning the suburbs has become, McGinley says, "a literary cliché," and "Spruce Manor" (Larchmont) "has become a symbol of all that is middle class in the worst sense." But she contends that such charges are uninformed and unfair, and maintains that the suburban way of life will, "in a world of terrible extremes, . . . stand out as the safe, important medium." The poems in *A Short Walk from the Station* present the scenes and people of the suburbs with gentle humor and little satire. The *Time* reviewer noted a "new McGinley, . . . a suburban Frost who shows all the signs of trying to slip unobtrusively from light verse into homely poetry." The subjects are child raising ("The Velvet Hand"), the school system ("P.T.A. Tea Party"), social life ("Hostess"), husbands ("Volunteer Fireman"), and other aspects of life in suburban Westchester County, where McGinley and her family lived for twenty-six years before moving to Weston, Connecticut, in 1964.

Love Letters, published in 1954, brought McGinley the Edna St. Vincent Millay Memorial Award, the first in a series of honors which included election to the National Institute of Arts and Letters the following year. *Love Letters*, her last collection of verse before the publication of *Times Three* in 1960, sold unusually well for a volume of poetry: 40,000 copies in the six years before the appearance of *Times Three*. The *New Yorker* had, as usual, been the place of initial publication for the majority of these poems, but McGinley was also placing poems more and more frequently in women's magazines such as *Good Housekeeping* and *Mademoiselle*. The mellow tone of *Love Letters* is heralded by the opening poem, "Apologia," in which she admits that age has altered her approach to life. The poem begins:

> When I and the world
> Were greener and fitter,
> Many a bitter
> Stone I hurled.

But, she adds,

> Now, like a miser
> All that I own
> I celebrate.

Most of the poems do celebrate rather than satirize. The key poem in the volume is "In Praise of Diversity," which was written for commencement at Columbia University in 1953 and which she also read at the White House Festival of the Arts in 1965. Arguing against strict dichotomies, McGinley urges the reader to "bless the delightful fact" that there are "Twelve months, nine muses, and two sexes." She reverts to the satiric mode in the series of brief sketches "A Gallery of Elders," which includes "The Old Feminist" and "The Old Radical," and takes several swipes at television in the series titled "The Jaundiced Viewer"; but the humor of most of the poems is the gentle amusement of "Eros in the Kitchen" and "A Kind of Love Letter to New York." Also in this volume is a series of poems about various saints of the Catholic church, a long-standing interest which McGinley would later explore in *Saint-Watching* (1969), a collection of essays about the lives of the saints.

All but a few of the poems in *Love Letters* are included in the Pulitzer Prize-winning *Times Three*. The volume contains almost 300 poems, including seventy not previously collected in book form, arranged in reverse chronology by decade. Less than half of McGinley's published poetry is included; omitted are the most topical and ephemeral verses, but the volume nonetheless provides a retrospective of McGinley's themes and techniques. The 1930s are represented by a number of poems about the New York scene, a handful of the Oliver Ames poems, and the best of the more ironic poems about war and depression. The largest category in this section is "Personal Remarks," which includes "Lament for a Wavering Viewpoint" and "Why, Some of My Best Friends Are Women." The poems from the 1940s demonstrate a mastery of technique and a wide range of tone and subject matter. Irony is a common mode, not only in the section "The War Before the Last," but also in poems about various kinds of intolerance, such as "The Town That Tries Men's Souls" and "Moody Reflections." Two sections, "I Know a Village" and "Domestic Affairs," are devoted to community and children; here are the popular "Ballroom Dancing Class" and "Anniversary." "Sonnets from the Suburbs" is a series of ten sonnets which shows McGinley's facility with the form. The poems of the 1940s are less conversational, more reflective than those of the 1930s, and the reader is invited to smile more often than to laugh.

The McGinley poems of the 1950s reveal a woman with strong opinions and a variety of styles with which to express them. The techniques of her lighter verse range from the playful invention of "The Importance of Being Western" ("Wyatt Earp / Rides tall in the stearp") to literary parody ("I wandered lonely as a fareless cabby"). Many of the poems mingle the humorous with the serious, such as "The Doll House" and "A Garland of Precepts," and the section includes the wholly serious sonnet "Midcentury Love Letter." Short lines and singsong rhythms characterize the satiric portraits in "Reformers, Saints, and Preachers," whereas the poems about teenaged children in "A Certain Age" have more complex structures and a tone of mock despair. David McCord, reviewing *Times Three* for the *Saturday Review*, praised McGinley's "compassion, her intuition, her ability to pare the world's wormy apple with a razor blade."

After *Times Three*, McGinley's major publications for adults were collections of essays. In 1959, the year before *Times Three* appeared, she had published *The Province of the Heart*. In her "Note to the Reader" she explains why, "after twenty-five years of being a moderately respectable writer of verse, I should suddenly commit a collection of prose." The volume is a rebuttal to those, like John P. Mar-

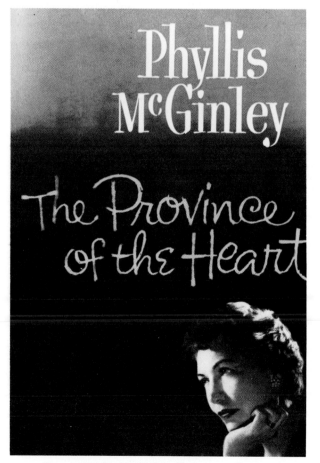

Dust jacket for McGinley's first essay collection

quand, who pictured suburbia as a "dreary strong-hold of mediocrity." As she had done in verse, especially in such poems as "Confessions of a Reluctant Optimist," McGinley here defends the role of the housewife and mother against those who find it limiting or demeaning. As one reviewer noted, "only a wit as blithe as Miss McGinley's could make [this defense] palatable." Her tone ranges from the gentle chiding of "The Honor of Being a Woman" to the hilarity of a neighbor's malapropisms in "I Knew Mrs. Tuttle." "Suburbia, of Thee I Sing" is reprinted in this volume, and the majority of the other selections were originally published in various women's magazines.

Being known as the chief spokesman for traditional womanhood occasionally made McGinley uncomfortable, however. In an interview in *Newsweek* in 1960, she said, "I'm so sick of this 'Phyllis McGinley, suburban housewife and mother of two.' . . . That's only an eighth or a tenth of my work. The rest is different. There's a hell of a lot of straight social criticism." But between 1960 and 1964 McGinley wrote a series of semi-autobiographical articles for the *Ladies' Home Journal* on woman's "oldest profession," and these were published as *Sixpence in Her Shoe*. Intended by her publisher as a rebuttal to Betty Friedan's *The Feminine Mystique* (1963), *Sixpence in Her Shoe* sold slowly at first, but eventually spent many weeks on the best-seller list in 1964 and 1965. Some of the essays, such as "Are Children People?," seem intended purely for amusement; others, like "A Jewel in the Pocket" and "The Pleasures of Thrift," convey serious messages with the aid of wit. The tone of the essays, like that of her poetry, ranges from sarcastic to nostalgic as she alternately rails against forced competition for children ("Keeping Up with the Joneses, Jr.") and remembers homemade ice cream ("The Myth of Grandmother's Cooking").

Following her husband's death in 1972, McGinley moved from the suburban setting with which she had so long been identified to a New York apartment. On her seventy-first birthday she composed the quatrain:

> Seventy is wormwood
> Seventy is gall
> But it's better to be 70
> Than not alive at all.

When she died in 1978, the *New York Times* noted that "her cheerful approach to life and love distinguished her from the mordant breed of poet."

Phyllis McGinley's reputation as one of the foremost writers of light verse in the twentieth century seems secure. Her technical skill is undeniable, and the thematic development of her poetry mirrors the changes in American humor and in woman's role in American society. The urbane iconoclasm of the early *New Yorker* period gave way to an affirmation of traditional values at mid-century, and McGinley increasingly found an audience among middle-class women who found comic perspective on their own lives in both her verse and her prose. Though feminist critics may find her views uncongenial, McGinley's virtuosity should outlive political debate, especially as the personal, conversational tone of much contemporary poetry continues to blur the distinction between light verse and serious poetry.

Cover, Time Magazine, *16 June 1965*

Play:
Small Wonder, lyrics by McGinley, New York, Coronet Theatre, 15 September 1948.

Screenplay:
The Emperor's Nightingale, English narration by

McGinley, Jiri Trnka (Czechoslovakia), 1951.

Other:

Wonders and Surprises: A Collection of Poems, edited by McGinley (Philadelphia: Lippincott, 1968).

Periodical Publication:

"The Light Side of the Moon," *American Scholar*, 34 (Autumn 1965): 555-568.

Interviews:

"The Lady in Larchmont," *Newsweek*, 56 (26 September 1960): 120-122;

"The Telltale Hearth," *Time*, 85 (18 June 1965): 74-78.

References:

L. F. Doyle, "Poems of Phyllis McGinley," *America*, 92 (18 December 1954): 320-322;

David McCord, "She Speaks a Language of Delight," *Saturday Review*, 43 (10 December 1960): 32;

K. Sullivan, "Phyllis McGinley," *Catholic World*, 185 (September 1957): 420-425;

Linda Welshimer Wagner, *Phyllis McGinley* (New York: Twayne, 1971).

H. L. Mencken

(12 September 1880-29 January 1956)

Elton Miles
Sul Ross State University

BOOKS: *Ventures into Verse* (Baltimore: Marshall, Beck & Gordon, 1903);

George Bernard Shaw: His Plays (Boston: Luce, 1905);

The Philosophy of Friedrich Nietzsche (Boston: Luce, 1908; London: Unwin, 1908);

A Book of Burlesques (New York: John Lane, 1916; revised edition, New York: Knopf, 1920; London: Cape, 1923);

A Little Book in C Major (New York: John Lane, 1916);

A Book of Prefaces (New York: Knopf, 1917; London: Cape, 1922);

Damn! A Book of Calumny (New York: Philip Goodwin, 1918); republished as *A Book of Calumny* (New York: Knopf, 1918);

In Defense of Women (New York: Philip Goodwin, 1918);

The American Language: A Preliminary Inquiry into the Development of English in the United States (New York: Knopf, 1919; revised and enlarged, 1921; London: Cape, 1922; revised and enlarged again, 1923; corrected, enlarged, and rewritten, New York: Knopf, 1936; London: Paul, Trench & Trubner, 1936; *Supplement I* (New York: Knopf, 1945); *Supplement II* (New York: Knopf, 1948);

Prejudices: First Series (New York: Knopf, 1919; London: Cape, 1920);

Prejudices: Second Series (New York: Knopf, 1920; London: Cape, 1921);

Prejudices: Third Series (New York: Knopf, 1922; London: Cape, 1923);

Prejudices: Fourth Series (New York: Knopf, 1924; London: Cape, 1925);

Selected Prejudices (New York: Knopf, 1926);

Notes on Democracy (New York: Knopf, 1926; London: Cape, 1927);

Prejudices: Fifth Series (New York: Knopf, 1926; London: Cape, 1927);

Prejudices: Sixth Series (New York: Knopf, 1927; London: Cape, 1928);

Treatise on the Gods (New York & London: Knopf, 1930);

Making a President (New York: Knopf, 1932);

Treatise on Right and Wrong (New York: Knopf, 1934; London: Paul, Trench & Trubner, 1934);

Happy Days, 1880-1892 (New York: Knopf, 1940; London: Paul, Trench & Trubner, 1940);

Newspaper Days, 1899-1906 (New York: Knopf, 1941; London: Paul, Trench & Trubner, 1942);

Heathen Days, 1890-1936 (New York: Knopf, 1943);

Christmas Story (New York: Knopf, 1946);

A Mencken Chrestomathy (New York: Knopf, 1949);

A Carnival of Buncombe, edited by Malcolm Moos

(Baltimore: Johns Hopkins Press/London: Oxford University Press, 1956);
Minority Report: H. L. Mencken's Notebooks (New York: Knopf, 1956);
A Bathtub Hoax, and Other Blasts & Bravos from the Chicago Tribune, edited by Robert McHugh (New York: Knopf, 1958);
H. L. Mencken on Music, edited by Louis Cheslock (New York: Knopf, 1961).

Of German-American descent, Henry Louis Mencken was born on 12 September 1880, in Baltimore, Maryland, where he lived all his life, most of it in the same house. His prosperous, conservative family was in the tobacco trade, and he took just pride in his ancestral line of European professors and lawyers. When he was nine he was playing the piano and had discovered *Huckleberry Finn*, a book he never ceased to celebrate and to claim as a personal influence. During his ten years of formal schooling, he became a voracious, systematic reader in all subjects. In 1899 he began his journalistic career as a reporter at the *Baltimore Herald* as morning editor. By 1903, at the age of twenty-three, he was city editor of that paper. In 1906 Mencken left the *Herald* to become editor of the *Baltimore Sun*; he retained a lifelong connection with the *Sunpapers* as writer and member of the board of directors.

After 1908 Mencken made a stir in American letters as literary critic of the *Smart Set* magazine, of which he became coeditor with George Jean Nathan from 1914 to 1923. With biting humor he defended naturalists such as Theodore Dreiser and satirists such as Sinclair Lewis, while sarcastically opposing the genteel tradition in such authors as William Dean Howells and Henry James. He also baited reformers and their banning of "immoral" literature from the mail and from libraries. Thus, he won a following of students, artists, and journalists eager for a fruition of the fin de siecle revolt against Victorian standards in art, thought, and morality. In 1924 he continued to lead the intellectual rebellion as coeditor with Nathan of the *American Mercury*, though his interest in literature declined as it grew in ideas and institutions. (Nathan's relationship with the magazine ended in August 1925, and Mencken continued as editor until December 1933.) In 1926 Mencken added to his national notoriety by openly getting himself arrested in Boston for publicly selling the so-called "Hatrack" number of the *American Mercury* (April 1926). It had been outlawed there because it included Herbert Asbury's story "Hatrack," about a small-town prostitute. During twenty-five magazine years, Mencken's fame as a

H. L. Mencken

newspaperman also grew. He reported the circus atmosphere at national political conventions from 1920 to 1948 (excepting 1944) for *Sunpapers*, and his coverage of the Scopes "Monkey Trial" in Dayton, Tennessee, during the summer of 1925 was nationally syndicated.

During World War I Mencken saw fit to abstain from newspaper work, because of his anti-British and seemingly pro-German sentiment. He devoted much time to *The American Language* (1919), and later, during World War II, he would concentrate on its supplements partly for the same reason. His reputation, somewhat tarnished, suffered during the 1930s because of his scorn for Franklin Delano Roosevelt and the New Deal, which he called "a milch cow with 125,000 teats." His conservative views at odds with those of the public and circulation dropping as a result, Mencken left the *Mercury* at the end of 1933 to continue newspaper work and book writing. By 1934 he had authored more than a score of books.

In 1930 he married author and English professor Sara Haardt; she was frequently ill throughout their marriage and died in 1935. Afterward, he lived quietly with his brother August in their Baltimore home place. In 1948 he suffered a stroke that left him unable to read or write. He died in his sleep on 29 January 1956.

Mencken's style, the mainstay of his humor, appears to be a refinement of that used by many a fiery frontier journalist, especially in the South and West, who flourished at the end of the nineteenth century. He admired Mark Twain and Ambrose Bierce and less notable writers such as W. C. Brann, who was shot and killed in Waco, Texas, in 1898, because of his pejorative writing. Mencken "distinctly" remembered (as he said) placing an article in *Brann's Iconoclast* and recalled it as a ribald treatment of one of his everlasting targets, the Methodists. In his literary criticism he acknowledged Edgar Allan Poe as the American forerunner in levelheaded, acid-penned judgments, and he praised the work of James Huneker for its identical qualities.

Mencken's inscription to F. Scott Fitzgerald in Prejudices: Second Series

It is appropriate to compare Mencken with Voltaire, Swift, and Samuel Johnson, as commentators have done. Like Johnson he uttered conservative thought with sharp wit and he produced an important philological work. Like Swift he yanked the garment of delusion off mankind to expose naked pretension, quackery, and stupidity. Like Voltaire he wrote entertainingly on a multitude of subjects, enlivening them with the magic of laughter. Unlike Swift and Voltaire, however, he left behind no creative masterpiece like *Gulliver's Travels* or *Candide* to warrant himself a standing among literary greats.

After his first book, *Ventures into Verse* (1903), a juvenile volume of poems of which he grew to be ashamed, Mencken wrote *George Bernard Shaw: His Plays* (1905), a sympathetic treatment of the merits of Shaw's work. Later he was to write scornfully of Shaw as "The Ulster Polonius." Of greater importance in understanding Mencken himself and his writing is his next book, *The Philosophy of Friedrich Nietzsche* (1908), the first American book to popularize the German philosopher. Though the gentlemanly Mencken always denied any pretense to superiority, many sense in his writing a posture aspiring to that of a Nietzschean superior person. He was a skeptic in all matters, scornfully amused at any opinion contrary to his own, ready to demolish the opposition with raillery and invective, and prepared to exert his literary power against the intellectually weak and therefore undeserving world of lesser human beings, the bourgeois "boobery." In 1937 when Mencken saw Edward Stone's dissertation about him, he told the scholar, "I was under the impression that my debt to Nietzsche was very slight," but "your argument rather shakes me." He admitted, "Nietzscheanisms . . . undoubtedly got into my own stuff."

In his adamant conservatism, Mencken liked to say that his attitudes did not change after his fifth year. Some of his more generally disturbing opinions may be found in his "Jazz Webster" in *A Book of Burlesques* (1916), reminiscent of Bierce's *Devil's Dictionary*:

BALLOT BOX. The altar of democracy. The cult served upon it is the worship of jackals by jackasses.

CIVILIZATION. A concerted effort to remedy the blunders and check the practical joking of God.

EVIL. What one believes of others.

IMMORALITY. The morality of those who are having a good time.

LOVE. The delusion that one woman differs from another.

PATRIOTISM. A variety of hallucination.

PROGRESS. The process whereby the human race has got rid of whiskers, the vermiform appendix, and God.

Book of Calumny (1918), slashing at conventions in American life, literature, and music.

In *A Book of Prefaces* Mencken produced a landmark in American literary criticism. He stirs up literary controversy and sets a new standard for realistic literary taste and criticism. His style is to

Mencken and George Jean Nathan

In Mencken's rural America of the "hog and Christian endeavor belts" one finds "farmers plowing sterile fields behind sad, meditative horses, both suffering from the bites of insects." In the cities are "ticket-choppers in subways, breathing sweat in its gaseous form." Everywhere are "women confined for the ninth . . . time, wondering hopelessly what it is all about."

The next three important volumes illustrate the range and trend of Mencken's subject choices in his works before 1930. Starting mainly with literary matters, they deal increasingly with social and political topics at large, most of the articles drawn from their author's newspaper and magazine pieces. In addition, Mencken's self-acquired scholarly mastery of language studies asserted itself. They are *A Book of Prefaces* (1917), *In Defense of Women* (1918), and *The American Language*. Less significant is a culling of journalistic pieces, *Damn! A*

verbally smite his prejudiced and moralistic opponents and to praise his favorite writers to the exclusion of others; he defends authors beset by censorship, and attributes to them his own belief in freedom of expression, amorality, and determinism.

Concluding *A Book of Prefaces* is one of the most important documents in American letters, "Puritanism as a Literary Force." Here Mencken attributes the deplorable state of American letters of his time to a Calvinistic doctrine that made God "a superior sort of devil." That doctrine survives, says Mencken, among Methodists and Baptists who now, through a growing belief in divine grace, cower only before a God that "is scarcely worse than the average jail warden." Sprouting from this tawdry creed, a "moral obsession has given a strong color to American literature" to the point that "a novel or a play is judged among us, not by its artistic honesty, its perfection of workmanship, but almost entirely

by its orthodoxy of doctrine, its platitudinousness, its usefulness as a moral tract." He argues that the effort of so great a writer as Mark Twain was intimidated and diluted by critical threats emanating even from his friend Howells, for Howells and Henry James both "showed that timorousness and reticence which are the distinguishing marks of the Puritan." In the American critic was a puritanical "prejudice against beauty as a form of debauchery and corruption—the distrust of all ideas that do not readily fit into certain accepted axioms—the belief in the eternal validity of all moral concepts—in brief, the whole mental sluggishness of the lower orders of men." After tracing the history of American organized and governmental opposition to what is good in the arts, Mencken expounds in documented detail on the censorious force of the Comstock Postal Act to ban from the mail "obscene" materials, including Thomas Hardy's *Jude the Obscure* and Harold Frederic's *The Damnation of Theron Ware*. Nevertheless, observes Mencken, there is hope: "We have yet no delivery, but we have at least the beginning of a revolt, or, at all events, a protest." In his own book, of course, Mencken is protesting. "We are sweating through . . . our spiritual measles," he concludes, prophesying that America may soon get her Hardy, Conrad, and Synge. (But when Faulkner, Hemingway, O'Neill, and Fitzgerald emerged, their artistry and their importance were lost upon Mencken.)

Perhaps the most successful of Mencken's early books, in terms of sales, was *In Defense of Women*, which by 1928 was in its eleventh American printing; there had also been a British publication and translations into French, German, and Hungarian. Though it now seems dated in some ways, the subject choice may be Mencken's most universal and perennially significant. His thesis is that women are more intelligent than men. Though they are entering more professions than previously, he says, they will never wholly enter into men's tasks, because if women "get on all-fours with men in such stupid occupations," they would "commit spiritual suicide."

The American Language met with popular success of a magnitude neither Mencken nor his publisher, Alfred Knopf, anticipated. The first edition was only 1,500 copies, which were sold almost overnight. For years Mencken had sometimes studied and written about the growth of an American English and had made himself a highly informed amateur authority on the subject. Yet he was amazed that *The American Language* was received with genuine seriousness as well as delight. He re-

turned to *The American Language* throughout his career, revising and enlarging it in 1922, 1923, and 1936. He wrote supplements to the work, which were published in 1945 and 1948. *The American Language* earned Mencken new respect as a philologist, distinct from his reputation as the whip-tongued "Blond Beast of Baltimore."

In the 1920s Mencken continued to lash out with stinging but comical invective, attacking whatever and whomever annoyed him. In his *American Mercury* he carried on and amplified the *Smart Set* attack on convention in the arts, liberalism in ideas and institutions, and conservatism in religion. He wrote less on literature and more on ideas, politics, institutions, and manners. As editor, Mencken encouraged a vigorous regional realism in all branches of American letters. Though he discovered no great writers, he consistently published works of writers who became important in their own regions; thus, he helped break the stranglehold of New York and New England on American culture. Like Poe, Mencken proved to be not only an important critic but an effective magazine editor as well, and the *American Mercury* briefly rivaled *Harper's* and the *Atlantic Monthly* in stature.

Mencken's most significant work during the 1920s was *Prejudices*, six volumes published between 1919 and 1928. His topics in *Prejudices* deal progressively less with literature and the arts. In *Prejudices: First Series* (1919) 80 percent of the numbered sections deal with literary or artistic subjects. Thirteen pieces concern writers, including Emerson, Poe, Howells, Hamlin Garland, Jack London, and Bernard Shaw. In the last, *Prejudices: Sixth Series* (1927), literature and the arts claim only 18 percent of the main headings (one of which is "Ambrose Bierce"). Of the more memorable of Mencken's *Prejudices*, that on "Professor Veblen" occurs in the 1919 volume, after Mencken had reread the economist's "singularly laborious and muggy . . . incomparably tangled and unintelligible works." He illustrates America's "lack of an intellectual aristocracy—sound in its information, skeptical in its habit of mind." Because America's ruling plutocracy is "ignorant, hostile to inquiry, tyrannical in its power, suspicious of ideas of whatever sort," a "stray rebel" like Veblen goes over to the mob in America, where the populace is "more capable of putting idiotic ideas into execution, than anywhere else."

Another striking Mencken essay, "The Sahara of the Bozart," appears in *Prejudices: Second Series* (1920). In the South, he says, "The arts, save in the lower reaches of the gospel hymns, the phonograph and the Chautauqua harangue, are held in suspicion." Perhaps his most vicious attack is that in "The Husbandman," *Prejudices: Fourth Series* (1924), against the American farmer. "It is hard," he says, "to tell which end of him is made in the image of God and which is mere hoof." He asks, "Has anyone ever heard of a farmer practising or advocating any political idea that was not absolutely self-seeking . . . to loot the rest of us for his gain?" In *Prejudices: Fifth Series* (1926) are found Mencken's account of the "Monkey Trial" and his critical obituary of William Jennings Bryan. "He couldn't be president," Mencken points out, "but he could at least help magnificently in the solemn business of shutting off the Presidency from every intelligent and self-respecting man."

In 1926 Mencken assembled *Selected Prejudices*, collecting those articles he thought important from the first four series of *Prejudices*. His main headings are *Arts*, *Ideas*, *Institutions*, and *Persons*. In "Education" he believes that schoolteachers should ardently love the subjects they teach. "But this would mean exposing children to contact with monomaniacs, half-wits, defectives? Well, what of it? The vast majority of them are already exposed to contact with half-wits in their own homes; they are taught the word of God by half-wits on Sundays; they will grow up into complacent half-wits in the days to come." But, he says, "the system combats their natural enthusiasm diligently and mercilessly. . . . It orders them to teach . . . by formulae as baffling to the pupil as they are paralysing to the teacher." In "Das Kapital" he supports laissez-faire in the business world and charges that the "barbaric manners and morals" in commerce occur because "capitalism, under democracy, is constantly under hostile pressure" from government and politics.

Notes on Democracy (1926), *Treatise on the Gods* (1930), and *Treatise on Right and Wrong* (1934) are commonly referred to as Mencken's trilogy. Of these, only the first is in the familiar ripsnorting style. Democracy is unsound, says Mencken, because "The whole life of the inferior man, including his so-called thinking, is purely a biochemical process, and exactly comparable to what goes on in a barrel of cider." *Treatise on the Gods* demonstrates that all religions are doubtless man-made, and that while a civilized man cannot prove that religion is not true, "he has at least proved that it is not necessary." Notable especially for its treatment of free will, *Treatise on Right and Wrong* avoids definition of right, wrong, sin, and virtue as useless. If there is a thesis of the book, it is that a scientific approach to ethics is possible. To Mencken's disappointment, his trilogy did not succeed with the public and it met with coolness from the critics.

In 1937, however, he won the greatest acclaim of his career with the fourth edition of *The American Language*, corrected, much enlarged, and rewritten. In it Mencken alters the thesis of the 1919 first edition, having observed that "American has become so powerful that it has begun to drag English with it," though "the two languages are still distinct in more ways than one." He omits his hilarious common American version of the Declaration of Independence (published in the third edition) to dispel the error of some British commentators that it represents what he thought English should be. He follows the plan of his original studies, mainly along historical lines. First, he depicts "The Two Streams of English" and the attitudes of the learned and others toward American aberrations. Then he traces "The Beginnings of American" from the first Indian loan-words through "The Period of Growth" of the American vocabulary and alteration of conventional forms, to "The Language Today" and a comparison of "American and English." The remainder of the study is devoted to American pronunciation, spelling, proper names, slang, and—in "The Common Speech"—American grammar. Throughout, he illustrates the movement of the nonstandard spoken language into acceptability as standard American. In "The Future of the Language" he concludes: "As English spreads over the world, will it be able to maintain its present form? Probably not, but why should it?" Mencken believed that there is no such thing as a permanent standard English. Included in this edition are the appended "Non-English Dialects in American," an indexed "List of Words and Phrases," and a general index. The whole is liberally footnoted. *Supplement I* (1945) enlarged upon the first six chapters of the fourth edition; *Supplement II* (1948) the remainder.

The occasional subtle humor befits the subject and is not as strident as in earlier works. In his discourse on differences between American and English, Mencken notes that, "The hospital itself, if it takes pay for entertaining the sick, is not a hospital at all, but a *nursing-home*, and its *trained* or *registered* nurses (as we would say) are just plain *nurses*. . . . And the white-clad young gentlemen who make love to them are not *studying medicine* but *walking the hospitals*." In "The Common Speech" he describes the vigor of American, pointing out that "the indefatigable schoolmarm has been trying to put down the American vulgate, but with very little success. . . . the moment [her pupils] get beyond the reach of her constabulary ear they revert to the looser and more natural speech-habits of home and work-place." Mencken's attacks against language conservatives are gentle but pointed. Some scholars, he says, believe that "the natural growth of language is wild and wicked." He tells how the National Council of Teachers of English, "following that hopeful custom which gave the nation Mother's Day and . . . Eat More Cheese Week" virtually failed "to make the first seven days of November Better-Speech Week." Though "The higher variety of gogues are somewhat less naive . . . they show a considerable reluctance to deal with American as a living language of a numerous and puissant people, making its own rules as it goes along and well worthy of scientific study." In his *American Language* series, Mencken has more space than did Johnson for whimsical definition and etymology; as in *Supplement I*: "One of the most mysterious American verbs is *to goose*. Its meaning is known to every schoolboy, but the dictionaries do not list it. . . . The preponderance of medical opinion, I find, inclines to the theory that the verb was suggested by the fact that geese, which are pugnacious birds, sometimes attack human beings, especially children, by biting at their fundaments. . . . The question remains why

one person is *goosey* and another is not. Some resent *goosing* no more than they resent a touch on the arm, whereas others leap into the air, emit loud cries, and are thrown into a panic," etc.

In the early 1940s Mencken completed the autobiographical trilogy that occupied his temporary retirement from newspaper work during World War II. Composed with wit, charm, and pleasant humor, they record his past in the afterglow of time lapsed: *Happy Days, 1880-1892* (1940), *Newspaper Days, 1899-1906* (1941), and *Heathen Days, 1890-1936* (1943). In *Heathen Days*, for example, Mencken relates how he began at the piano "playing trios and quartettes with an outfit that devoted four hours of every week to the job— that is two hours to actual playing and the other two to the twin and inseparable art of beer-drinking." In 1922 the group played Beethoven's first eight symphonies in one session, beginning at 4 P.M. Sometimes flagging, "we decided," Mencken says, "to knock off for an hour and find out what the malt had to offer in the way of encouragement." Nobody remembered for sure how they finished, about 5 A.M., but one musician said that "we were chased out by our host, assisted by hunting dogs."

In 1948 Mencken covered the Democratic and

Mencken covering the Republican National Convention in 1948, his last year as a newspaperman

Republican national conventions for the *Evening Sun*, fuming as always about the ineptness of politicians. In his last column, on desegregation, he was indignant "to find so much of the spirit of the Georgia Cracker surviving in the Maryland Free State." Attacking one of his favorite targets, he insisted that "relics of Ku Kluxery should be wiped out." It was Mencken's last rant. A week after he filed his last report on the Republican convention, he had a stroke that left him largely incapacitated for the last eight years of his life.

At the end of his productive career, Mencken had made two books of imaginative humor, *A Book of Burlesques*, near the beginning, and *Christmas Story* (1946), near the end. In "Death: A Philosophical Discussion," the first of the fifteen sketches in *Burlesques*, a set of pallbearers exchanges platitudes: "It don't do no good to kick. When a man's time comes he's got to go." Perhaps the most original, "From the Programme of a Concert," is a travesty on fictitious music for a poem by Nietzsche. The musical notations contain melodies with sour notes, unplayable themes, and a seven-bar rest that ranges from *mf* to *pppp*. There are satires on concert artists, weddings, the sexes, and Americans traveling abroad. In a powerful sketch, "From the Memoirs of the Devil," Satan appears as a sort of Reverend Davidson from *Rain* trying to convince an innocent but condemned girl of her sinfulness. Throughout, Satan buttresses his discourse with accurate and appropriate biblical references.

To the extent that H. L. Mencken was a comic writer, the humor resides in his caustic style and his irreverent, opinionated tone. However sincere and whatever his subject, he wrote to entertain. He described his own comic propensity as "a capacity to discover hidden and surprising relations between apparently disparate things, and to invent novel and arresting turns of speech." An editorializer on an encyclopedic range of subjects, his solid contributions to American culture were amplified by his tart, often shocking humor. Summing up his own achievement near the end of his career, Mencken wrote, "Those who explore [my] pages will find them marked with a certain ribaldry, even when they discuss topics commonly regarded as grave. I do not apologize for this, for life in the Republic has always seemed to me far more comic than serious. We live in a land of absolute quackeries, and if we do not learn how to laugh we succumb to the melancholy disease which afflicts the race with viewers-with-alarm. I have had too good a time

of it in this world to go down that chute."

Letters:

Letters of H. L. Mencken, edited by Guy J. Forgue (New York: Knopf, 1961).

Bibliography:

Betty Adler and Jane Wilhelm, *H. L. M.: The Mencken Bibliography* (Baltimore: Johns Hopkins University Press, 1961).

Biographies:

Isaac Goldberg, *The Man Mencken: A Biographical and Critical Survey* (New York: Simon & Schuster, 1925);

Edgar Kemler, *The Irreverent Mr. Mencken* (Boston: Little, Brown, 1950);

William Manchester, *Disturber of the Peace: The Life of H. L. Mencken* (New York: Harper, 1950);

Charles Angoff, *H. L. Mencken: A Portrait from Memory* (New York: Thomas Yoseloff, 1956);

Sara Mayfield, *The Constant Circle: H. L. Mencken and His Friends* (New York: Delacorte, 1968);

Carl Bode, *Mencken* (Carbondale: Southern Illinois University Press, 1969);

Douglas C. Stenerson, *H. L. Mencken: Iconoclast from Baltimore* (Chicago: University of Chicago Press, 1971);

H. Allen Smith, "A Friend in Baltimore," in *The Best of H. Allen Smith* (New York: Trident Press, 1972);

Charles A. Fecher, *Mencken: A Study of His Thought* (New York: Knopf, 1978).

References:

C. M. Babcock, "Mark Twain, Mencken, and the Higher Goofyism," *American Quarterly*, 16 (Winter 1964): 587-594;

Malcolm Cowley, "Mencken and Mark Twain," *New Republic*, 108 (8 March 1943): 321;

Joseph Epstein, "Show-Biz Mencken," *New Republic*, 159 (14 September 1968): 31-33;

James Grossman, "Mencken: Buffoon of Truth," *Nation*, 170 (13 May 1950): 451;

Irving Howe, "Comedian Playing Hamlet," *New Republic*, 134 (21 May 1958): 17-18;

Gerald W. Johnson, "Reconsideration," *New Republic*, 173 (27 December 1975): 32-33;

Elton Miles, "Mencken's *Mercury* and the West," *Southwestern American Literature*, 3 (1973): 39-48;

R. Olivar-Bertrand, "Mencken's This World Satire," *Contemporary Review*, 23 (October 1973): 202-206;

William Saroyan, "The American Clowns of Criticism," *Overland*, new series, 87 (March 1929): 77-78;

V. E. Simrell, "H. L. Mencken, the Rhetorician," *Quarterly Journal of Speech Education*, 13

(November 1927): 399-411;

Carl Van Doren, "Smartness and Light," *Century*, 105 (March 1923): 791-796.

Papers:
The largest Mencken manuscript collection is in the Enoch Pratt Free Library, Baltimore, Maryland.

Ogden Nash

St. George Tucker Arnold, Jr.
Florida International University

BIRTH: Rye, New York, 19 August 1902, to Edmund Strudwick and Mattie Chenault Nash.

EDUCATION: Harvard University, 1920-1921.

MARRIAGE: 6 June 1931 to Frances Rider Leonard; children: Linell Chenault, Isabel Jackson.

AWARDS: Member of the American Academy of Arts and Sciences and the National Institute of Arts and Letters.

DEATH: Baltimore, Maryland, 19 May 1971.

SELECTED BOOKS: *The Cricket of Carador*, by Nash and Joseph Alger (Garden City: Doubleday, Page, 1925);

Born in a Beer Garden or, She Troupes to Conquer, by Nash, Christopher Morley, Cleon Throckmorton, and others (New York: Foundry Press/R.C. Rimington, 1930);

Hard Lines (New York: Simon & Schuster, 1931); enlarged as *Hard Lines, and Others* (London: Duckworth, 1932)—adds selections from *Free Wheeling*;

Free Wheeling (New York: Simon & Schuster, 1931);

Happy Days (New York: Simon & Schuster, 1933);

Four Prominent So and So's, lyrics by Nash, music by Robert Armbruster (New York: Simon & Schuster, 1934);

The Primrose Path (New York: Simon & Schuster, 1935);

The Bad Parents' Garden of Verse (New York: Simon & Schuster, 1936);

I'm a Stranger Here Myself (Boston: Little, Brown, 1938; London: Gollancz, 1938);

The Face is Familiar: the Selected Verse of Ogden Nash (Boston: Little, Brown, 1940; London: Dent, 1942; revised edition, London: Dent, 1954);

Good Intentions (Boston: Little, Brown, 1942; enlarged edition, London: Dent, 1942; revised edition, London: Dent, 1956);

One Touch of Venus, by Nash and S. J. Perelman (Boston: Little, Brown, 1944);

Many Long Years Ago (Boston: Little, Brown, 1945; London: Dent, 1945);

Ogden Nash's Musical Zoo, music by Vernon Duke (Boston: Little, Brown, 1947);

Versus (Boston: Little, Brown, 1949; London: Dent, 1949);

Family Reunion (Boston: Little, Brown, 1950; London: Dent, 1951);

Parents Keep Out: Elderly Poems for Youngerly Readers (Boston: Little, Brown, 1951; enlarged edition, London: Dent, 1962);

The Private Dining Room, and Other New Verses (Boston: Little, Brown, 1953; London: Dent, 1953);

The Christmas That Almost Wasn't (Boston & Toronto: Little, Brown, 1957; London: Dent, 1958);

You Can't Get There from Here (Boston & Toronto: Little, Brown, 1957; London: Dent, 1957);

Custard the Dragon (Boston: Little, Brown, 1959; London: Dent, 1960);

Verse from 1929 On (Boston: Little, Brown, 1959); republished as *Collected Verse from 1929 On* (London: Dent, 1961);

A Boy Is a Boy: The Fun of Being a Boy (New York:

Watts, 1960; London: Dent, 1961);

Scrooge Rides Again (Berkeley, Cal.: Hart, 1960);

Custard the Dragon and the Wicked Knight (Boston & Toronto: Little, Brown, 1961);

Everyone But Thee and Me (Boston & Toronto: Little, Brown, 1962; London: Dent, 1963);

Girls Are Silly (New York: Watts, 1962; London: Dent, 1964);

The New Nutcracker Suite and Other Innocent Verses (Boston & Toronto: Little, Brown, 1962);

The Adventures of Isabel (Boston & Toronto: Little, Brown, 1963);

A Boy and His Room (New York: Watts, 1963);

A Boy and His Room and The Adventures of Isabel (London: Dent, 1964);

Marriage Lines: Notes of a Student Husband (Boston & Toronto: Little, Brown, 1964; London: Dent, 1964);

The Untold Adventures of Santa Claus (Boston & Toronto: Little, Brown, 1964; London: Dent, 1965);

The Animal Garden (New York: Evans, 1965; London: Deutsch, 1972);

The Mysterious Ouphe (New York: Spadea Press, 1965);

The Cruise of the Aardvark (New York: Evans, 1967; London: Deutsch, 1972);

Santa Go Home: A Case History for Parents (Boston & Toronto: Little, Brown, 1967; London: Dent, 1968);

There's Always Another Windmill (Boston & Toronto: Little, Brown, 1968; London: Deutsch, 1969);

Bed Riddance: A Posy for the Indisposed (Boston & Toronto: Little, Brown, 1970; London: Deutsch, 1971);

The Old Dog Barks Backwards (Boston & Toronto: Little, Brown, 1972; London: Deutsch, 1973);

I Wouldn't Have Missed It: Selected Poems of Ogden Nash, selected by Linnel Smith and Isabel Eberstadt (Boston & Toronto: Little, Brown, 1972).

During his lifetime, Ogden Nash was the most widely known, appreciated, and imitated American creator of light verse. The many Nash admirers, both scholars and the general public, would maintain, with considerable justification, that the poet's reputation has grown still further in the years since his death. The continuing sales of his books lend substantial support to their views. Certainly few writers of light or serious verse can claim the same extensive dissemination of their poems that Nash's works enjoy, both with and without citation of the author. Certain Nash lines, such as "If called by a

panther, / Don't anther," and "In the vanities / No one wears panities," and "Candy / Is dandy, / But liquor / Is quicker" have become bits of popular American folklore. As Nash remarked in a late verse, the turbulent modern world has much need for the relief his whimsy offers: "In chaos sublunary / What remains constant but buffoonery?" Nash's peculiar variety of poetic buffoonery combines wit and imagination with eminently memorable rhymes.

Frederick Ogden Nash was born in Rye, New York, to Edmund Strudwick and Mattie Chenault Nash, both of Southern stock. Nash's great-great-grandfather was governor of North Carolina during the Revolution, and that ancestor's brother was General Francis Nash, for whom Nashville, Tennessee, was named. This pedigree did not in the least restrain the poet-inheritor of the Nash name from gently but thoroughly deflating genealogical pretensions, along with other pomposities, in his verses. He was raised in Savannah, Georgia, and several other East Coast cities, as his father's import-export business necessitated that the Nashes make frequent moves. Nash described his unique accent as "Clam chowder of the East Coast—New England with a little Savannah at odd moments" and attributed it to the influence of his family's peripatetic existence during his formative years. Following his secondary education from 1917 to 1920 at St. George's School in Newport, Rhode Island, Nash attended Harvard for the 1920-1921 academic year, and then, as he put it, he "had to drop out to earn a living." He first tried teaching at his alma mater, but after a year he fled from St. George's, "because I lost my entire nervous system carving lamb for a table of fourteen-year-olds." Throughout his life Nash was a bit of a hypochondriac—one who, a friend recalled, "seemed to enjoy poor health."

After St. George's Nash tried working as a bond salesman on Wall Street. The results left something to be desired; he sold one bond—"to my godmother"—but had the chance to "see lots of good movies." Following his failure at high finance, Nash took a job writing streetcar advertising for Barron Collier. He moved on in 1925 to the advertising department at the Doubleday, Page publishing house, which was to become Doubleday, Doran in 1927. Nash had considerable aptitude for advertising, according to George Stevens, a colleague at Doubleday, Doran, who felt that Nash could have made quite a success at the business. Stevens later recalled Nash's ad copy for Booth Tarkington's *The Plutocrat* (1927), one of the house's titles which was

Ogden Nash

then high on the best-seller lists. Nash's slogan, "First in New York, First in Chicago, and First in the Hearts of his Countrymen," was effective and catchy but, much to Stevens's delight, Nash's paraphrase of the epithet commonly applied to George Washington scandalized an elderly vice-president at the company. (In the 1940s Nash was to suggest a new slogan to Western Union: "Don't write, telegraph. We'll mail it for you.")

Nash's humorous advertising sallies were by no means his sole writings during this period. In off hours, he tried to write serious poetry. "I wrote sonnets about beauty and truth, eternity, poignant pain," he remembered. "That was what the people I read wrote about, too—Keats, Shelley, Byron, the classical English poets." Yet Nash's final judgment on his serious literary efforts was that he had better "laugh at myself before anyone laughed at me," and he restricted himself increasingly to writing the whimsical verse that was to make him famous. Nash began to refine his focus upon what he called "my field—the minor idiocies of humanity."

Early in his stay at Doubleday, Page, Nash made his first attempt at writing a children's book, collaborating with his friend Joseph Alger on *The Cricket of Carador* (1925). This slight but imaginative fantasy forecast his lifelong fascination with animals. Yet the majority of Nash's spare time was not devoted to literary production. As George Stevens reminisced on his and Nash's life during Prohibition, "It was the era of the ignoble experiment, and we ignored the law in each other's society more than once. We used to go to Yankee Stadium to see Babe Ruth in his greatest year and the Yankees in theirs. In May we drove to Mineola and saw *The Spirit of St. Louis* a few days before her pilot took off for Paris. During the presidential campaign of 1928 both of us were enthusiastically for Al Smith, and, as I recall it, we were as much surprised as disappointed when Hoover swamped him."

While working at Doubleday, Doran, Nash collaborated with Christopher Morley and another colleague to create his first published piece of comic writing, an effusion of youthful good spirits that parodies various forms of serious literature: *Born in a Beer Garden or, She Troupes to Conquer: Sundry Ejaculations by Christopher Morley, Cleon Throckmorton, and Ogden Nash, and Certain of the Hoboken Ads, with a Commentary by Earnest Elmo Calkins* (1930). It was at Doubleday, Doran, as he faced Stevens across their desks, that Nash began scrawling brief verses on pieces of yellow paper and pitching them over to his friend. Some of these bits of poetry appeared in Nash's first book of humorous verse, *Hard Lines* (1931), and Stevens later wondered why he had been unable to recognize the poetic squibs and one-liners for more than trifles. Nash's first published humorous poem occurred to him one summer afternoon in 1930 as he gazed out his office window at an urban prominence, a mound covered by high-rise buildings, but still euphemistically called a "hill." Nash, casting about for thoughts to keep his mind off the business of writing advertising copy, idly jotted down some lines of verse, which he soon threw into a trash bin. Later he retrieved the paper, titled the verse "Spring Comes to Murray Hill," and mailed the poem to the *New Yorker*, which accepted it. The poem shows the characteristic mental process of the Nash poetic voice, or, more precisely, the Nash character's voice: a moment's boredom spiraling into an absurd festival of fractured rhyme and novel syllabication, as these lines suggest:

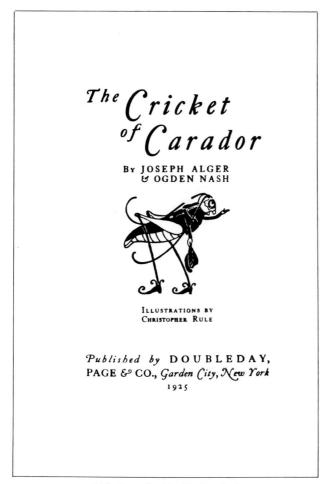

Title page for Nash's first book

> I sit in an office at 244 Madison Avenue
> And say to myself you have a responsible job,
> havenue?
> Why then do you fritter away your time on
> this doggerel?
> If you have a sore throat you can cure it by
> using a good goggerel
> If you have a sore foot you can get it fixed by a
> chiropodist
> And you can get your original sin removed by
> St. John the Bopodist.

The poem epitomizes Nash's whimsical style and projects the essence of the comic vision that was to amuse Nash's readers from that time to the present. Here, too, is Nash's cheerful maiming of conventional syllabication and pronunciation, his novel reorganization of stresses, his near rhymes, and the extended, straggling line, which he so frequently employed and likened to "a horse running up to a hurdle but you don't know when it'll jump." In the introduction to *I Wouldn't Have Missed It* (1972) Archibald MacLeish, considering that afternoon in 1930 on which Nash's poetic career began, com-

OF COURSE I'M A TURTLE,
BUT AM I REAL OR MOCK?
I LEAVE IT TO
HILAIRE BELLOC.

Drawing by Ogden Nash

mented, "as one approaches thirty, things have a way of happening." And on that afternoon, said MacLeish, "He found himself—or, if not precisely himself, then a form of language he could speak." MacLeish noted that if one does not see Murray Hill beyond the copywriter's head as he leans from the window, "one can at least smell it: that penetrating pharmaceutical scent of face powder and sex which pervades the metropolises of our cosmetic civilization." There is something empty about the young man's hope, MacLeish stressed, "Even the defeated artist's pain. The drugstore on the corner can take care of everything, and that longing for the long-unwritten poem is no worse—or better—than a brief sore throat." The poem suggests that Nash had found his major theme—the countless banalities of the contemporary city, and the futility of the quest for meaning there—all expressed in the language of the whimsical.

Nash soon had a second poem taken by the *New Yorker*, quickly gained additional acceptances from other periodicals, and in 1931 saw his first collection of verses, *Hard Lines*, with Otto Soglow's illustrations, published by Simon and Schuster. The

book's success was immediate and substantial as seven printings of *Hard Lines* were sold out in 1931 alone. In a very short time Nash noticed that he was making more money from selling poetry—about forty dollars a week—than he was receiving from his advertising job. Quitting the advertising business, he took a position on the staff of the *New Yorker* in 1932 but kept the job only three months and thereafter wrote on a free-lance basis.

Pretending to acknowledge a profound debt to the major sources of his inspiration, Nash dedicated *Hard Lines* to Dorothy Parker, Samuel Hoffenstein, Peter Mark Roget, and "The Sweet Singer of Michigan, without a complete and handy set of whose works this book could not have been written so quickly." This invocation honors the would-be poetic warblings of Julia Moore, the 1870 farm-woman-versifier whose stabs at poetry, heavy with stock moralizing, overdone sentimentality, extensive cliches, awkward inversions, grotesquely tortured rhythms, and dreadful rhymes, offer an index to the sins of which the talentless poet may be guilty. While Nash claimed cheerfully that he was culpable of the full range of poetic wrongs with which the Sweet Singer might be charged, he avoided the rustic and the sentimental. Close scrutiny of his verse, moreover, points up how Nash transformed the pattern of other Julia Moore gaffes into something rich and rare. In Nash's verse the unusual usages are wild; the standard cliches, literary borrowings, and moralistic saws of banal poetry become altered and refocused with hilarious effects and considerable loss of the expected conventional moral relevance in such lines as "A good way to forget today's sorrows / is by thinking hard about tomorrow's," or "When I consider how my life is spent / I hardly ever repent." The reader's expectations are constantly overturned: "A man is very dishonorable to sell himself / for anything other than quite a lot of pelf." *Hard Lines* also shows the variety of ways in which Nash first demonstrated his cheerful sabotage of conventional spelling which was to be his trademark. Orthography yields to phonology in such lines as "Philo Vance / needs a kick in the pance"; "Many an infant that screams like a calliope / could be soothed by a little attention to its diope"; and "Like an art lover looking at the Mona Lisa in the Louvre / is the New York *Herald Tribune* looking at Mr. Herbert Houvre."

In other more earnest poems in *Hard Lines*, Nash's comments on his society set the tone that was to mark his later satiric verse. His targets were rarely too deeply offended by his barbs, thanks to the whimsical tone in which they were expressed. He voices his negative feelings for clerics who devote themselves to criticizing what Nash sees as unobjectionable amusements enjoyed by their congregations in these lines from "The Pulpiteers Have Hairy Ears":

> I wonder why it is that so many clerics
> Must be perpetually in hysterics.
> It's odd, but at any hint of gaiety
> On the part of the laity
> Their furies and rages
> Fill pages and pages.

Hurt that certain of the clergy have condemned the beautiful Ziegfeld girls, the "amorous, clamorous dryads" created by T. H. White, and Lewis Carroll's "charming undraped nimpse," Nash wishes that these critics would desist, for "I am sure none of those lovely girls has done anyone any harm / for who is any the worse for the view of a shapely artistic feminine leg or arm?" He goes on to wonder at ministers' disapproval of all modes of combat except one: "Neither do clerics like prize fighting, cock fighting, bull fighting, or any other kind of fighting / unless it is a war, in which case they urge people to / go out and do a lot of smiting." Never genuinely hostile, the poet stresses that he is speaking of only a fraction of the clergy, the 25 percent who "seem to be / as unhappy as ex-kings."

Nash's satire sometimes strikes politicians as well. "Invocation" makes light of Mormon Senator Reed Smoot's crusade against pornography. "Senator Smoot (Republican, Ut.) / Is planning a ban on smut. / Oh rooti-ti-toot for Smoot of Ut. / Smite, Smoot, Smite for Ut., / Grit your molars and do your dut." As the reader has an increasingly hard time taking the crusading senator seriously, Smoot's quest suffers corresponding loss of dignity:

> Senator Smoot is an institute
> Not to be bribed with pelf;
> He guards our homes from erotic tomes
> By reading them all himself.
> Smite, Smoot, smite for Ut.,
> They're smuggling smut from Balt. to Butte.

The poems of *Hard Lines* introduce other Nash themes and affinities. These famous lines from "Autres Betes, Autres Moeurs" suggest how the animal world inspired Nash:

> The Turtle lives 'twixt plated decks
> Which practically conceal its sex.
> I think it clever of the turtle
> In such a fix to be so fertile.

But Nash, for all his delight in them as comic capital, does not long to join the creatures in their habitats; when he shifts his focus from the natural to the human world, he celebrates not man in the fields, but man in the city. "I Want New York" stresses, in one of his reversed cliches, how content Nash is with his urban environment. "That's why I really think New York is exquisite. / It isn't all right just for a visit / . . . I'd live in it and like it even better if you gave me the place." His feeling for the city is echoed in another *Hard Lines* poem, "Hymn to the Sun and Myself," in which Nash expresses his delight in himself and his world. Celebrating that "At 11:07 a.m. I'll be 27 ¾ years old," Nash delights in who he is, where he is, what he is doing. "Oh, what fun to be young and healthy and alive / and privileged to do some of the work of the world from nine to five!" he cries. Nash exults in minor triumphs like not having been hit by a streetcar, or not having had the price of a ticket on the Titanic, and ends, "Oh, let every day for a long time not be my last!"

This celebratory tone, however, is countered in another verse in *Hard Lines*, the strikingly somber "Old Men," with which the volume ends. This is the first of the rare but poignant meditations on aging and death which contrast the more cheery or satiric majority of Nash's verses. "People expect old men to die," he begins, and then he notes that the world at large is perfectly complacent to the death of old men. "They do not really mourn old men." Yet Nash takes the little considered point of view of the other aged men, as they witness the death of one of their number: "But the old men know when an old man dies."

Presenting the essence of his comic vision, *Hard Lines* introduced Nash's comedy and the occasional more serious directions in his thought with great success, as the book's sales emphasized. Nash followed it up in the same year with *Free Wheeling*, in 1933 with *Happy Days*, and in 1935 with *The Primrose Path*. These volumes reflected approximately the same focus and emphasis as *Hard Lines*, and all enjoyed good sales and repeated printings as Nash began to attract greater and greater public attention.

The next significant addition to the themes in his verse occurred, naturally enough, as Nash and his wife—he married Frances Rider Leonard on 6 June 1931—began their family. *The Bad Parents' Garden of Verse*, which appeared in 1936, expresses a variety of new concerns. His wife had borne him two baby girls by this time, and Nash, in his role as protective father, had developed new views on boys. In "Song to be Sung by the Father of Six-months-old-Female Children," the father of girls expresses a special anxiety about the unknown little boy baby who may someday marry his daughter: "I never see an infant (male), / a-sleeping in the sun, / Without I turn a trifle pale / and think, is *he* the one?" Nash the father fantasizes about tormenting the wooer-to-be of his daughter: "Sand for his spinach I'll gladly bring, / and tabasco sauce for his teething ring. . . ," until the potential courter decides that "perhaps he'll struggle through fire and water / to marry somebody else's daughter."

The parent in Nash's "Children's Party" projects a less-than-delighted image of his role as host to a horde of little ones. "Of similarity there's lots" he muses, "'twixt tiny tots and Hottentots." As he watches her joyous complicity in the mayhem about her, the battered father muses "Oh, progeny playing by itself / Is a lonely fascinating elf, / But progeny in roistering batches / Would drive St. Francis from here to Natchez." When the tykes turn hoses on each other and on him, and flip ice cream "with spoons for catapults," the father yields the field. He begs the dog for the key to the doghouse. Nash regularly discusses the infant's strategy for manipulating the parent, taking the child's point of view, as in "A Child's Guide to Parents." "The wise child handles father and mother / by playing one against the other. / Don't! cries this parent to the tot / The opposite parents asks, Why not?"

As he settled, supposedly with much comic catastrophe, into parenthood, Nash continued to feature his thoughts on children along with his original themes in *I'm a Stranger Here Myself* (1938), *The Face is Familiar* (1940), *Good Intentions* (1942), and *Many Long Years Ago* (1945).

Nash did not often discuss his comic patterns, but did once explain his formula for the telling use of cliches: "The trick is that it must be somebody else's cliche and not the author's own." Typical is the treatment that Nash gives to the overworked advice, "Hate the sin but love the sinner," in "Nevertheless," from *Many Long Years Ago*. Nash celebrates a number of sins while detesting the wretches who commit them. He says of a glutton:

> Bibesco Poolidge is a man of jowl
> I've never seen a dewlap, but on him;
> He shines with the grease of many a basted
>   fowl;
> Ten thousand sauces round his innards swim.
> The ghosts of hosts of kine about him prowl,
> Lamb, pig, and game blood trickles from his
>   chin;
> I cannot look on him without a scowl;
> I hate the sinner. But what a luscious sin!

The verses in *Many Long Years Ago* give evidence of Nash's hypochondria; poems on the topic of his health appear with increasing frequency in the later collections. In "When the Devil Was Sick Could He Prove It?" from *Many Long Years Ago*, Nash's comic speaker thinks about how embarrassing it is when you feel "unspecifically off-color," but "still you can't produce a red throat or a white tongue . . . or any kind of symptom / and it is very embarrassing that whoever was supposed to be passing out the symptoms skymptom." Thermometer gazing and pulse taking are featured in a number of Nash's poems from this time and later, poems usually ending in a mild self-criticism: "I can get a very smug Monday, Tuesday, Wednesday, Thursday / or Friday in bed out of a tenth of a degree. / It is to this trait I am debtor / for the happy fact that on week ends I generally feel better." This theme grew so compelling to Nash that in 1970, he compiled his lifetime dialogue with his body's real or imagined ills into a poetic compendium of medical complaints, *Bed Riddance*.

Whatever the nature of his ailments, however, they did not keep Nash from traveling or living happily away from the East Coast. From 1936 to 1942 he had a well-remunerated but frustrating sojourn in Hollywood. He wrote three screenplays for MGM: *The Firefly* (1937), his adaptation of Otto A. Harbach's play; *The Shining Hair* (1938), coauthored with Jane Murfin; and *The Feminine Touch* (1941), written with George Oppenheimer and Edmund L. Hartman. None of these met with success.

During this screenwriting interlude, however, Nash met S. J. Perelman, who was in Hollywood on similar business. The two quickly became friends and decided to collaborate on a musical, for which Kurt Weill was recruited to provide the score. The resulting effort, book by Perelman, lyrics by Nash, and music by Weill, was *One Touch of Venus*, a smash hit of the 1943 Broadway season that ran for 567 performances. A song from the musical, "Speak Low," has continued to be popular. Although Nash was to try two more musicals, he did not repeat the success he achieved with his first attempt.

Nash had more consistent if less spectacular luck with radio and television than he did with the stage. In the 1940s he was heard on radio's "Information, Please!" and on the Bing Crosby and Rudy Vallee shows. He was a regular panelist on the guess-the-celebrity show "Masquerade Party" in the 1950s, and was in frequent demand as a panelist for other such shows. He also wrote lyrics for the television show *Art Carney Meets Peter and the Wolf*, based on Sergei Prokofiev's *Peter and the Wolf*, and for two other television specials for children based on Camille Saint-Saëns's *Carnival of Animals* and Paul Dukas's *The Sorcerer's Apprentice*.

In the 1950s and 1960s Nash gave increasing attention to writing children's poems, while he continued his steady output of adult-oriented whimsy. Works such as *Parents Keep Out: Elderly Poems for Youngerly Readers* (1951), *The Christmas That Almost Wasn't* (1957), *Custard the Dragon* (1959), *Custard the Dragon and the Wicked Knight* (1961), and *Girls are Silly* (1962) give a sense of Nash's increasing emphasis on poetry for children, and poetry addressed to adults that focuses on children. Numerous poems in these collections suggest the affection Nash felt for his daughters: "Roses red and violets blue, / I know a girl who is really two. / Yesterday she was only one; / today, I think, will be twice the fun." He returned often to his so-called advice for parents, in such works as *Santa Go Home: A Case History for Parents* (1967). He continued also to address his younger readers in fantasies that demonstrated his imaginative communion with them, such as *The Mysterious Ouphe* (1965). Nash's thoughts on the grandparently role are expressed in poems such as "The Ring in Grandfather's Nose," and "Preface to the Past," from *You Can't Get There from Here* (1957). The first points up the strains of baby-sitting the next generation: "My pretty new watch goes tickety-ticket, / Whenever I wind it / it chips like a cricket. / The second hand / hippety hippety hippety hops / Till shaken by baby; / then pretty watch stops." The grandpa baby-sitter laments about what else he might be doing, and what his friends are doing—sleeping, playing poker, watching chorus girls—while he baby-sits. "Preface to the Past" gives a much softer view, as Nash reviews the amazing speed with which his two daughters have gone from phase to phase: "I tried to be as wise as Diogenes / in the rearing of my two little progenies, / but just as I hit upon wisdom's essence / they changed from infants to adolescents." He sees the cycle's end: "Now I'm counting, the cycle being complete, / the toes on my children's children feet. / Here lies my past, good-by I have kissed it; / Thank you, kids, I wouldn't have missed it."

In Nash's adult-oriented later works, considerable emphasis is given to mild complaints about aging and sickness, yet the comedy that always introduces and accompanies the complaint, the implied criticism that introduces the complainer, gives a very limited sense of morbidity. Nash always saw his role as that of cheerful light entertainer, and maintained it to the last in his writing.

Not only did Nash use the fractured cliche to destroy the cliche, he also demonstrated, with hilarious results, the way that a zany idea can become its own motivation in his imagination. The comic confusion can destroy all the boundaries of conventional perception. Typical of this pattern, Walter Blair notes, is "The Strange Case of Mr. Ballantine's Valentines," from *I'm a Stranger Here Myself*. A lawyer named Ballantine is unhappy about his lifelong failure to receive any valentines. He relates his misery to his law partner, Mr. Bogardus, who gets plenty of valentines and finds them boring. Ballantine laments the identical fate he has to face each Valentine's Day, when all that greets him on his desk is a pile of affadavits. "Affadavit," Mr. Bogardus consoles, "is better than no bread." The word affadavit now begins to dominate the consciousnesses of both lawyers. Ballantine recites "affadavit, affadavit, onward, into the valley of death rode the six hundred." Bogardus criticizes anyone who would rhyme "onward" with "six hundred," and finally mentions that he did not know "who was the king before David, but Solomon was the king affadavit."

This sort of mental-verbal confusion, and the triumph of the strange word, or combination of words, over common sense appears often in the comic quandaries of such modern writers as James Thurber and Robert Benchley, writers of what Blair terms the "dementia praecox" school of humor. These writers' "little man" characters are often victimized by words and phrases that turn on them in this nonsensical way. Nash's poem concludes on a deranged note with more verbal confusion. Ballantine seems to have solved the problem of his solitude when he hits it off with Herculena, the strongest woman in the world, who, it turns out, is also troubled by never having received any valentines. Yet Ballantine dooms his love affair when he mishears his love, who asks him, in a coquettish moment, to pinch her muscle. "He thought she said bustle," says the speaker, and Ballantine recovers consciousness "just in time to observe the vernal equinox."

In this context, Nash is connected not only with Thurber, but with a wide range of modern humorists who display that, on occasion, their comic personae have their perceptions shaped by minds not altogether under control. Nash's speaker often finds himself pursued by his own curious associations and perceptions, and at points they seem to replace volition in his mind. When a cabbie turns out to be both adamant and an eavesdropper, Nash's comic personae seems compelled to make a pun, calling him "an Adam-ant-Eves-dropper." Similarities of sound often entrap Nash's speakers, who seem unable to extricate their thoughts from the associated sounds and the imagistic momentum they develop. This tendency is seen in such titles as "Everything's Haggis in Hoboken, or, Scots Wha Hae Hae," "To Bargain Toboggan, To-Whoo!," "Roulette Us Be Gay," and "Curl Up and Diet." The sounds of words also lead Nash into conscious spelling errors in order to maintain the phonic accuracy of his rhyme. Such spelling appears in the limerick "Arthur," from *Many Long Years Ago*:

> There was an old man of Calcutta,
> Who coated his tonsils with butta,
> Thus converting his snore
> From a thunderous roar
> To a soft, oleaginous mutta.

The comic speaker's memory is also a frequent saboteur of his thoughts in the present; ancient ditties, ads, nursery rhymes both accurate and altered, grammar drills from grade school, pieces of verse and song, all flood his mind at inappropriate times, and make a hash of his current reflections. Wordsworth's "Ode: Intimations Of Immortality" runs through the speaker's head as he lowers his eyes to a plate of intricate hors d'oeuvres, which he despises. Hence, "My heart leaps down when I behold gadgets with cocktails."

Nash's speaker, in a certain group of poems written throughout his career, shares with Benchley and Thurber a conviction that he is being pursued by inanimate things. In one of his verses, he receives a splinter in his foot as he steps from bed. In another

Nash and S. J. Perelman, playwrights

Ogden Nash
30 OLMSTED GREEN · BALTIMORE, MARYLAND 21210
January 4 1971

I was living in New York at the time of Hemingway's crash, and his words on his return from the jungle caught my ear. I wrote the words, beginning "A bunch of bananas and a bottle of gin Lets the hunger out and the happiness in." Took them to Mack Goldman, then vice-president of Harms Inc, Madison Ave and 52nd St, who liked them, gave them to a composer, I think Dick Manning, who set them to a gay Calypso tune. Took the song to Mitch Miller, then head of pop recordings for Columbia. He liked, but insisted on revisions, which I made but didn't like. It was recorded by Rosemary Clooney and José Ferrer, at that time felicitously married. I heard it on the air twice, after which it was barred by the networks; I was told because its extolling of gin was taboo. It then vanished into oblivion. I have neither a copy of the song nor the record. I never heard anything from Hemingway, but have been told that it amused him.

Yours sincerely,

Ogden Nash

Nash's comments on "A Bunch of Bananas"

Ogden Nash's 1954 song inspired by Ernest Hemingway's plane crash

he cannot keep his seemingly animated bedcovers on as he tries to stay warm in the night; they ingeniously defy his best efforts to keep himself covered. Nash has much in common with Thurber and Benchley when he strives to make peace with mechanical antagonists. Nash's nemesis resides in such demons as malfunctioning children's toys and the faulty plumbing in a vacation cottage: "if there is one thing that makes me terrified and panical / It is anything mechanical and nowadays everything is mechanical." Nash also pictures himself as foiled by paperwork—income-tax returns, bills to be kept straight. In "Prayer at the End of A Rope," from *I'm A Stranger Here Myself*, Nash appeals for divine assistance in avoiding gaffes financial and social, beseeching the aid with the humblest sort of supplication:

> I ask no miracles nor stunts,
> No heavenly radiogram;
> I only beg for once, just once,
> To not be in a jam.

In a couplet Nash gives the sense of himself as a fall guy to fate, thanks to his own perverseness: "The things I want to do, I won't / and only do the things I don't."

Yet, in his several laments for himself in the role of victimized little man, however effectively self-deprecatory those verses may be in themselves, Nash does not reverse the reader's abiding sense that, when he voices his insecurity, Nash is not speaking in his truly characteristic tone. Despite his occasional similarities to such comic writers as Thurber and Benchley, Nash finally appears as one who, for all his momentary self-doubts, does indeed have a firm sense of identity and security. In the majority of his works, he seems united with less neurotic humorists of earlier periods. His more compact bits of witty social criticism, his most telling observations of human folly, are more in the tradition of Benjamin Franklin. Many of Nash's pithier aphorisms contain such concise and witty punch that they might have been penned by Franklin, or—with worse spellings—by Josh Billings: "It is easier for one parent to support seven children than for seven children to support one parent" (*The Private Dining Room*, 1953); "One way to be very happy is to be very rich" (*Hard Lines*); "The reason for much matrimony is patrimony" (*Many Long Years Ago*); "Why did the Lord give us so much quickness of movement / unless it was to avoid responsibility?" (*Private Dining Room*).

The speaker of these aphorisms is troubled little by insecurity. These one-liners all have their basis in Nash's close observation of the way things are in a world of compromises. The reality principle and the American respect for pragmatism that Blair identifies as "horse sense" underpin the great majority of Nash's verses. Nash's moral relativism is characterized with precision in "Golly, How Truth Will Out," from *Many Long Years Ago*, when Nash cheerfully contemplates how vital it is to become skilled at the fine social art of smooth and convincing prevarication.

> How does a person get to be a capable liar?
> That is something that I respectfully inquiar,
> . . . .
> Oh to be Machiavellian, Oh to be unscrupu-
> lous,
> Oh to be glib!
> Oh to be ever prepared with a plausible fib!
> Because then a dinner engagement or a con-
> tract or a treaty is no longer a fetter,
> Because liars can just logically lie their way
> out of it if they don't like it or if one comes
> along that they like better;

William Soskin refers to Nash's verses as "a compendium of bitter insanity, wry foolishness and considerably inspired lunacy."

Yet Nash's darker side appears infrequently. In most of the poems that brought him fame, the whimsical tone and the classic innocent's pose predominate. Most project, moreover, an abiding easy-going feeling that the poet is fairly content with his quite comfortable middle-class life, even while he is poking gentle fun at it. In his most characteristic pose, Nash is a good-natured observer of the passing scene, hopeful that it is going to yield him adequate curiosities to turn into comic capital. One critic has called Nash "a philosopher, albeit a laughing one," who writes most typically of the "vicissitudes and eccentricitudes of domestic life as they affected an apparently gentle, somewhat bewildered man."

The sorts of things that bewilder or mildly irritate Nash point up his general contentment with things as they are. The good life, as he pictured it, is essentially urban and essentially well-heeled. The kind of conflicts that are featured in Nash's verse, too, make it clear that things in town are not too bad at all, from where the poet sits. A characteristic long-term abuse that Nash, as the subject of his verse, has suffered in society is expressed in "Coffee With the Meal" from *I'm a Stranger Here Myself*; his problem is the difficulty he has in making it clear to waiters that he does *not* want his coffee after dinner, he wants coffee to accompany the repast:

> I don't want coffee in a glass,
> And I don't want a miserable demi-tasse,
> But what I'll have, come woe come weal,
> Is coffee with, coffee with, coffee *with* the
> meal.

His strenuous plaints and threats to the headwaiter avail the wretched diner not a whit, of course, and, "One hour later Monsieur, alas! / Got his coffee in a demi-tasse."

Nash often suggests some of the drawbacks of living in the metropolis. In "City Greenery," from *Many Long Years Ago*, he comments,

> If you should happen after dark
> To find yourself in Central Park,
> Ignore the paths that beckon you
> And hurry, hurry to the zoo,
> And creep into the tiger's lair.
> Frankly, you'll be safer there.

Probably the events Nash most often satirizes, however, are the social gatherings in upper-middle-class suburban homes and country clubs. In "Out is Out," from *I'm a Stranger Here Myself*, Nash scowls poetically upon suburban hosts and hostesses who find it novel to eat dinner outside.

> Oh, it's drizzling a little; I think perhaps
> The girls had better keep on their wraps;
> Just strike a match and enjoy the way
> The raindrops splash in the consomme.
> You probably won't get botts or pellagra
> From whatever lit on your pate de foie gras.

Nash was also intrigued with frictions between his friends and neighbors during their recreation at the country club. In one verse his speaker plays a somewhat Machiavellian role when he introduces two fellow country clubbers, who, considering their personal temperamental peculiarities, ought to destroy each other once they get tennis rackets in their hands:

> This is Mr. Woolley, Mrs. Dixon;
> This is Mrs. Dixon, Mr. Woolley;
> Mr. Woolley, Mrs. Dixon is a vixen;
> Mrs. Dixon, Mr. Woolley is a bully.
> . . . .
> And let the welkin shout that it's I who
> brought about
> The meeting of the vixen and the bully.

Watching the two decimate one another with violent outbreaks of temper, Nash's speaker is satisfied at the outcome of his harsh experiment in human relations: "To both of you more power, and may your meeting flower / In the slaughter of a vixen and a bully."

Nash's other themes range widely, but always keep to the comic treatment of the everyday—dining, buses and taxis, cocktails, the common cold, fashion, love, language, the theater, travel, conscience, money, birthdays, card games, the weather, football, matrimony, child rearing, family arguments, and even death. In "The Buses Headed for Scranton" (*You Can't Get There from Here*), he created a funny but somewhat eerie folktale of sorts when he considered a wayward bus that disappeared mysteriously. For all the other buses' sturdiness, for all their drivers' daring, for all their passengers' spunk, the buses are haunted by the memory of the fate of one of their number which essayed the perilous passage to Scranton alone, and was later found "near a gasoline pump—moss grown, / Deserted, abandoned, like the *Mary Celeste*." The verse goes on to detail the appearance of the abandoned vehicle, the inexplicable traces of her missing passengers:

> Valises snuggled trimly upon the racks
> Lunches in tidy packets.
> Twelve *Daily Newses* in neat, pathetic stacks,
> Thermoses, Chiclets, and books with paper
> jackets.

The possible causes of their disappearance are considered, but without satisfaction to the tale-teller:

> Some say the travelers saw the Wendigo
> Or were eaten by bears.
> I know not the horrid answer, I only know
> That the buses headed for Scranton travel in
> pairs.

Nash's much less comic consideration of death in "Old Men" suggests his awareness of death and the ominous possibility of one's passing meaning very little to others, but Nash's own death was not unmourned. Throughout his life he enjoyed not only the popularity accorded him by his sizable readership but also the much rarer tribute of respect from his competitors in the creation of light verse. At the time of his death, in 1971, his admirers, both amateur and professional, accorded Nash the sincerest form of flattery as, with varying degrees of success, they attempted to couch their farewell tributes in Nash-like mangled meter. For example, poet Morris Bishop wrote:

> Free from flashiness, free from trashiness,
> Is the essence of ogdenashiness.
> Rich, original, rash and rational
> Stands the monument ogdenational.

Any attempt to place Nash's work in the context of other American humorous writing, or the humor of any other country, for that matter, tends initially to highlight his singularity. George Stevens notes this particularity. "Nash was not the only writer who could make frivolity immortal. But he was unique—not at all like Gilbert or Lear or Lewis Carroll, still less like his immediate predecessors in America: Dorothy Parker, Margaret Fishback, Franklin P. Adams. By the same token, he was and remains inimitable—easy to imitate badly, impossible to imitate well."

Play:
One Touch of Venus, by Nash and S. J. Perelman,
music by Kurt Weil, New York, Imperial Theatre, 7 October 1943.

Screenplays:
The Firefly, MGM, 1937;
The Shining Hair, by Nash and Jane Murfin, MGM, 1938;
The Feminine Touch, by Nash, George Oppenheimer, and Edmund L. Hartman, MGM, 1941.

Other:
P. G. Wodehouse, *Nothing But Wodehouse*, edited by Nash (Garden City: Doubleday, Doran, 1932);
The Moon is Shining Bright as Day: An Anthology of Good-Humored Verse, selected, with an introduction, by Nash (Philadelphia: Lippincott, 1953).

References:
Lavonne B. Axford, *An Index to the Poems of Ogden Nash* (Metuchen, N. J.: Scarecrow Press, 1972);
Louis Hasley, "The Golden Treasury of Ogden Nashery," *Arizona Quarterly*, 27 (Spring 1971): 241-250.

Joseph C. Neal
(3 February 1807-17 July 1847)

David E. E. Sloane
University of New Haven

BOOKS: *Charcoal Sketches; or, Scenes in a Metropolis* (Philadelphia: Carey & Hart, 1838); republished as volume 2 of *The Pic Nic Papers. By Various Hands*, 3 volumes, edited by Charles Dickens (London: Colburn, 1841);
In Town and About (Philadelphia: Godey & McMichael, 1843);
Peter Ploddy, and Other Oddities (Philadelphia: Carey & Hart, 1844);
Charcoal Sketches, Second Series, edited by Alice B. Neal (New York: Burgess, Stringer, 1848); republished as *"Boots:" Or, the Misfortunes of Peter Faber, and Other Sketches* (Philadelphia: Getz, 1855); republished as *The Misfortunes of Peter Faber, and Other Sketches* (Philadelphia: Peterson, 1856);
Neal's Charcoal Sketches, Three Books Complete in One (Philadelphia: Peterson, 1865).

Popular in his own era, Joseph C. Neal was quickly forgotten after his death. Given Neal's limited canon and the unobtrusiveness of his brief life in Philadelphia as newspaper editor and urban comedian, it is understandable how later anthologists could so easily confuse his work with that of John Neal, the Yankee humorist. As well as Neal expressed his bemusement at the petty vanities of city life, the world has passed him by.

Joseph Clay Neal was born to the Reverend James A. Neal and Christiana Palmer Neal on 3 February 1807 in Greenland, New Hampshire. James Neal had moved with his pregnant wife from Philadelphia to Greenland because of his failing health, leaving his position as principal of "one of the first female academies of celebrity" in the United States in order to become minister of a Congregational church. When her husband died two years later, Christiana Neal returned to Philadelphia with Joseph, her only living child. Neal was raised in the city and lived the greater part of his life there. Christiana Neal appears to have been an affectionate and devoted mother; according to Morton M'Michael, Neal's friend, she was a woman of cultivated taste, wide-ranging knowledge, and active and genuine courtesy. Mrs. Neal's fond interest in her child may account for a persistent interest in the training of children expressed in Neal's sketches.

Little is known of Neal's childhood, but it is clear from M'Michael's 1844 biographical essay that he was neither particularly well off financially nor socially well connected. Although they lived in genteel poverty, Mrs. Neal did not neglect her son's education. According to Joseph Jackson, Mrs. Neal ran a bookstore from the time of her return to Philadelphia through 1832, and she is identified in Philadelphia city directories as conducting the Union Circulating Library through 1841. Thus, Neal was surrounded by books, and his family history would account for his scrupulous and moral education.

About 1829 Neal journeyed to the Pennsylvania coalfields hoping to make his fortune. He spent two years in Pottstown, Pennsylvania, gaining newspaper experience but not making much money. According to M'Michael, this "frontier" experience offered Neal "the wide field of observation thrown open to his view, when Schuylkill County was an El Dorado, forming a centre of attraction to all sorts of people, who rushed thither to secure fortunes at a grasp, and to become nabobs in an hour." In 1831 Neal returned to Philadelphia, taking up residence with his mother and entering into a career as editor of the *Philadelphia Pennsylvanian*.

The *Pennsylvanian* was a four-page, seven-column newspaper with a wide circulation among Democrats. In 1831 it was a weekly newspaper, but by 1832 it was published daily. Two columns on the newspaper's front page were devoted to literature. News and editorial comments, including Neal's serious reports of the regular meetings of Philadelphia's "Democratic Hickory Club," appeared on page two. Commercial news and advertisements filled the last two pages. The literary columns appear to be Neal's writing, and he seems to have written some of the notes on the second page, which reflect his voice and his taste in the material chosen from the newspaper exchanges which formed a national news network in the pre-Civil War era. Numerous items on the editorial page are clearly by Neal, including a note in the 11 April 1833 number

that other papers were cribbing many of the *Pennsylvanian*'s comic items and cutting their "heads and tails" off. Neal's conclusion is in character: "Well this is a wicked thieving world and we must put up with it." The *Pennsylvanian* reprinted much humor from other papers, generally with acknowledgment, including comic, lower-class dialogue such as police-court sketches from a "London paper." Neal wrote serious editorials and also his "Charcoal Sketches" for the paper. Neal also sought new and "Western" sources such as Solitaire (John S. Robb) for contributors. The urban misfits of Neal's sketches seem natural in this company.

As editor of the *Pennsylvanian*, Neal was, according to every commentator, the "beau ideal" of an editor. Although he defended Democratic party positions, he did not engage in personal vituperation. Upon leaving the *Pennsylvanian* in 1844 because of ill health, he commented that after thirteen years as editor he had earned an honorable discharge from politics, "especially when during all this fierce campaigning, I never asked a favor from the hand of patronage, and never received one." A list of political events which Neal wrote about suggests the intensity of this era: the veto, Biddle and the Bank, the panic, the war of 1836, and the political campaigns of 1840 and 1844. National events and local happenings made a tempestuous mix. "It was something, at one time, to be politically virtuous in Philadelphia," Neal commented. Neal did, in fact, petition Sen. James Buchanan in 1838 for an office for a friend, but the fate of the request is unknown. Neal's favorable attitude toward immigrants and the poor may well have put him at odds with Buchanan's conservative and legalistic viewpoints. Buchanan complained in 1840 that the *Pennsylvanian*, which did not become a Buchanan organ until 1845, after Neal had retired, had never done him common justice.

While editing the *Pennsylvanian*, Neal was also involved in other ventures which led to his fame as a humorist. In July 1835 he became assistant editor to Charles Alexander on the *Gentlemen's Vade Mecum: or the Sporting and Dramatic Companion*, then in its first year of publication. The paper provided a mix of sporting and financial news, accompanied by comic items, fiction, and advice on manners. Neal was active as both editor and contributor, compiling material from the exchanges, composing editorial paragraphs, and contributing his earliest series of "City Worthies," describing Philadelphia vagrants and urban misfits, which were subsequently reprinted in the *Pennsylvanian*, where they had their widest circulation.

Joseph C. Neal

Neal's "Peter Brush, the Great Used Up," the most famous and widely reprinted of his sketches, was part of the series that appeared in the *Gentlemen's Vade Mecum*. Peter Brush is a disappointed seeker of political office and spoils, bewailing his fortunes in the city gutters. As Neal later pointed out, he took pains not to show Peter as a partisan of any particular party. Brush is a "cowboy," like the thieves depicted in Cooper's *The Spy* (1821), unprincipled and self-interested, seeking patronage from any politician, regardless of his party. With a briefer philosophical introduction than most of Neal's sketches, "Peter Brush" is one of Neal's most compact, and the target was a new political type of city spoils seeker and loafer who represented a corrupted component of the democratic process in a country that was becoming increasingly urban.

The structure of "Peter Brush" is generally representative of all Neal's sketches. There is little dramatic action, and a treatise on the melancholy November weather of Philadelphia ends by introducing the central figure. Peter Brush is sitting on a curb, "out at elbows, out at knees, out of pocket, out of office . . . as *outré* a mortal as ever the eye of man

did rest upon." Peter addresses a soliloquy to the street, in which he quotes his ma's advice, "Peter, my son, put not your trust in princes." From a hodgepodge of parental guidance and popular philosophy, Peter fabricates his complaint in such a way that his ineffectual cynicism is revealed in his own vulgar idiom: "I don't care which side they're on, for I've tried both, and I know. Put not your trust in politicians, or you'll get a hyst." Failing to promote a "circular recommend" in a drunken approach to a homeowner, Brush then saunters off into the city night, cynical and truculent to the end.

The publication history of "Peter Brush" illustrates how widely Neal's works were published, often without recognition for Neal himself. The sketch first appeared in the *Gentlemen's Vade Mecum* in the early fall of 1835 and was widely reprinted, frequently without attribution, through the newspaper exchanges. On 13 August 1836 a revised version was reprinted in the *Philadelphia Saturday News* (the *Gentlemen's Vade Mecum*'s successor) as number six in a series titled "City Worthies." In this version, Peter argues with a "Charley" (slang for "officer") who accuses him of being a gentleman's son, and Brush declares, "I love my country, and I want an office!" The *Pennsylvanian* reprinted the sketch on 15 August and it again circulated in the exchanges. William Trotter Porter's New York humor magazine, *Spirit of the Times*, was among others that reprinted it without credit to Neal; Porter's attribution was to the *Cincinnati Farmer*. Neal collected it in *Charcoal Sketches* in 1838. It was reprinted almost in full in an article on American humor in the *Knickerbocker* magazine in August 1857, but the *Knickerbocker* noted only that Neal was the author of a "peculiar species of newspaper humor extremely amusing in its inception."

Charles Alexander was involved in five or six other publishing ventures at the same time as the *Gentleman's Vade Mecum*, and in 1836 he withdrew from work on the magazine. Louis Godey became the magazine's publisher, and Neal and M'Michael its editors. On 2 July 1836 it appeared under a new title as the *Philadelphia Saturday News and Literary Gazette*. In numerous advertisements the new venture was touted as a "Mammoth Sheet," and "A Real Monster!" The newspaper was double-size, supposedly the largest ever printed in the United States, and advertised as "dog cheap," capable of being read by a large family circle all at one time. *Gentlemen's Vade Mecum* subscribers were told that they would have their subscriptions finished off with the *Saturday News*, for which the "City Worthies" would be prepared "expressly and exclusively." The first of the *Saturday News* "City Worthies" series was a scene from the life of "Neddy Slowe," never reprinted by Neal but quickly circulated through the exchanges, frequently without credit. By 21 January 1837 the "City Worthies" series had reached sixteen, holding its own beside Dickens's *The Pickwick Papers* and other English works that were appearing in family newspapers at about the same time. "City Worthies" sketches from the *Saturday News* regularly appeared in the *Pennsylvanian* two or three days later. The *Saturday News* continued for two years, ceasing publication on 5 January 1839.

The popularity of Neal's sketches invited a book publication, and the result was *Charcoal Sketches*, copyrighted in 1837 and published early in 1838. The volume included eighteen sketches of city characters such as Duberly Doubtington, the man who couldn't make up his mind; Fydget

Title page for Neal's first book, etching by D. C. Johnston

Fyxington; "Orson Dabbs, the Hittite," who believes that hitting people solves arguments, until he is "macerated" by the night watch; and Peter Brush, the original brushed-off street politician. The sketches usually follow a similar format, beginning with a description of the city and either the character's comic personal history or his burlesque philosophy expressed in his own words. The character of the "hero" is then described with or without vulgar comic dialect, and the better sketches include some bits of comic action. Finally, the character exposes his own weaknesses through a soliloquy and is sent away by the night watch. Neal's introduction to *Charcoal Sketches* modestly recommended the illustrations by David C. Johnston as worthy of attention if the stories were not.

Despite their prior publication in the *Gentlemen's Vade Mecum*, the *Saturday News*, the *Pennsylvanian*, and the exchange columns of other newspapers, the sketches provoked wide interest. A second edition appeared in 1838 with a third and fourth in 1839; by 1841 the book was in its sixth edition. The *Knickerbocker* for April 1838 commented in a long, favorable review, "Our author has gone out into the by-ways and thoroughfares of the metropolis, and from among the greasy multitude selected rare specimens of that numerous class of wights who hang loose, like rags, upon the back of society, and has made them 'heroes in history.'" Neal's wit, philosophy, and Hogarthian touches were praised. Edgar Allan Poe, however, satirized Neal's style and format in "Peter Pendulum, the Business Man," which appeared in the February 1840 issue of *Burton's Gentleman's Magazine* and captured Neal's use of soliloquy and interest in childhood character formation. Perhaps the sincerest "flattery" was the outright piracy of Neal's work by the London publisher Henry Colburn in 1841. *The Pic Nic Papers*, "Edited by Boz," played on the popularity of Dickens's *The Pickwick Papers*, offering short stories by several English contributors. The second volume, according to Dickens made up without his knowledge, contained the entire contents of *Charcoal Sketches*, listed merely as "appended from an American source" without further acknowledgment. Neal's works appeared widely, but, true to the economics of newspaper publishing in his era and because of the absence of the international copyright, the actual return was small.

Neal continued to write in much the same vein for the rest of his brief career, although ill health seems to have caused some variations in his life. He continued to live with his mother at 16 South Seventh Street in Philadelphia, but in 1841-1842 he left Philadelphia and his work on the *Pennsylvanian* to tour Europe and Africa in an attempt to restore his health, eroded by the effect of daily newspaper editing on his delicate constitution. By 1843 Neal was back in Philadelphia and again editing the *Pennsylvanian*. He was also contributing sketches to the *United States Magazine and Democratic Review*, which also published work by such writers as Nathaniel Hawthorne. Neal's "The Boys that Run with the Engine," "The Newsboy," and "Street Corner Loungers" appeared in this magazine with illustrations by F. O. C. Darley, and late in 1843 the three sketches were republished in a thin volume titled *In Town and About*. A fourth Darley-Neal offering, "The Black Maria," describing the Philadelphia prison van, appeared in *Godey's* in November 1843.

In 1844 *Godey's* and *Graham's* both included sketches by Neal, and in October 1844 Carey and Hart published *Peter Ploddy, and Other Oddities*. The four sketches he had written to accompany Darley's drawings were included, along with Neal's most Hawthornesque short story, "Jack Spratte's Revenge," in which the wickedness of a revengeful suitor first ruins and then reforms his victims. A second edition of *Peter Ploddy* was not called for until 1853. Some of Neal's most interesting statements on the transition to the modern era appear in this volume, symbolized best in "The Newsboy," where a peasant at Waterloo boils potatoes in a knight's helmet.

In 1844 Neal retired from the *Pennsylvanian* permanently, both for reasons of health and in hope of more rewarding work on a venture of his own, *Neal's Saturday Gazette and Ladies Literary Museum*, which first appeared on Saturday, 12 October 1844. *Neal's Saturday Gazette* was a literary newspaper offering romances by Meta Duncan, Robert Morris, Lydia Peirson, and others. Other periodicals were reviewed in "Literary Intelligence," and "Editorial Chit-chat," a popular feature; a further series of "Charcoal Sketches" was also offered. Along with material by English writers, Neal was genuinely eager to publish American humorists, and by the second year, Neal claimed Solitaire, Ned Buntline, and others as regulars in what one critic described as the most "thoughtful" of the weeklies published in Philadelphia. By October 1845 all of Neal's weakening energy was devoted to the weekly.

Two women figure prominently in Neal's life during his years as editor of the *Saturday Gazette*, Emily Bradley and Miriam Berry. Emily Bradley's work began appearing in *Neal's Saturday Gazette* in the spring of 1845 under the pen names Cousin

Alice or Alice C. Lee. Her stories, which Allibone's dictionary describes as improving the heart while gratifying the imagination, fitted well into a journal which circulated "in New England and other precise places" and among the ladies. Neal developed a personal relationship with the young author which led to their marriage on 13 December 1846; the bride was eighteen when she returned with Neal to take up residence in the house on Seventh Street. After their marriage Neal encouraged his wife to keep the name Alice (due to a second marriage in 1853, biographical reference books often list her as Alice B. Haven). Francis Miriam Berry [Whitcher] ("The Widow Bedott") became known to Neal in 1846 through submissions to his *Saturday Gazette*. Neal prevailed on the doubtful author to offer her material not only to *Neal's Saturday Gazette*, where it had drawn favorable attention, but also to Louis Godey. Alice Neal continued to encourage "The Widow Bedott" after Neal's death and wrote an introduction to the *Widow Bedott Papers* in 1855.

Neal's Saturday Gazette continued to prosper throughout early 1847. Neal, however, knew himself to be seriously ill and requested his unbelieving bride to collect and edit his last volume of sketches. His actual collapse on Saturday morning, 17 July, however, came as a surprise to the publishing community of Philadelphia, who praised his wit and mourned the passing of a congenial friend. The cause of death was given as "congestion of the brain." Consoled by Neal's widowed mother, Alice Neal continued to conduct *Neal's Saturday Gazette* well into the 1850s, writing the literary departments herself and expanding readership among the ladies and children.

Neal's last volume, *Charcoal Sketches, Second Series*, was published by Burgess, Stringer in New York in 1848. It was republished in 1850 and in 1855 appeared as *"Boots:" Or, the Misfortunes of Peter Faber, and Other Sketches*. Peterson's included it in a series of comic works in 1856 as *The Misfortunes of Peter Faber, and Other Sketches*. The *Literary World* mourned that the country could ill afford to lose such an opponent of cant, and reprinted in its review Alice Neal's foreword in which she described Neal's charge to her and pointed out his intention to use humor to instruct, an intention which Alice Neal's editing emphasized through the selection of several pieces which had no dramatic action or dialect whatsoever to alleviate their didactic generalizations. "Peter Faber" and "Quintus Quozzles' Catastrophe" are well dramatized, however, along with "Timothy Tantrum," featuring a hero to whom "creation is a porcupinity."

After Neal's death attention to his work fell

away rapidly. Poe had attacked Neal's sketches in "A Chapter on Autography," calling them tediously repetitious and uninventive, employing the same character and plot over and over without any new departure. Poe admitted that taken singly Neal's sketches are excellent police reports with a streak of burlesque. Rufus W. Griswold, in *The Prose Writers of America* (1847), took a corresponding position in castigating Neal's choice of burlesque names and lack of genial sympathy, but praised Neal as the "moral historian" of a new class of characters. Since that time Neal has received only passing mention. His early portraits of the urban vulgarian have not secured for him recognition as an innovator in American humor. Peterson published *Neal's Charcoal Sketches, Three Books Complete in One* in 1865, the last separate edition of Neal's works.

An assessment of Neal's importance in American humor is complicated by the slimness of his canon and his personal reticence—no personal journals and not more than ten letters are known to exist. Few of his writings were signed in the *Pennsylvanian* or elsewhere, with the exception of the "Charcoal Sketches" themselves. His sketches, which won for him the name "The American Boz," showed the urban down-and-outer in a variety of guises, and showed a new type of American character in dialect and burlesque action, but, as Poe observed, the sketches seem largely similar when taken as a whole. "The Black Maria," "The Newsboy," "Orson Dabbs," and "Peter Brush" do indeed have the Hogarthian realism for which critics praised them, but without more exposure for his type of Northern urban comedy, Neal is likely to continue a modest and unrecognized figure in the development of American humor.

References:

"American Humor," *Eclectic Magazine*, 33 (September 1854): 137-144;

Will M. Clemens, "Joseph C. Neal," *Famous Funny Fellows* (Cleveland: William W. Williams, 1882), pp. 123-129;

Rufus W. Griswold, *The Prose Writers of America* (Philadelphia: Carey & Hart, 1847), pp. 518-522;

Joseph Jackson, *Literary Landmarks of Philadelphia* (Philadelphia: McKay, 1939), pp. 234-237;

Morton M'Michael, "Joseph C. Neal," *Graham's Magazine*, 25 (February 1844): 49-52;

Frank Luther Mott, *A History of American Magazines, 1741-1850* (New York: Appleton, 1930);

Alice B. Neal, Introduction to *Widow Bedott Papers* by Frances Miriam Whitcher (New York: J. C. Derby, 1856), pp. ix-xix;

Ellis P. Oberholtzer, *The Literary History of Philadelphia* (Philadelphia: Jacobs, 1906);

Edgar Allan Poe, "A Chapter on Autography," *The Works of Edgar Allan Poe* (Chicago: Stone & Kimball, 1895) IX: 206-207;

Review of *Charcoal Sketches, Second Series*, *Literary World*, 2 (1 January 1848): 532-533;

Henry Simpson, *The Lives of Eminent Philadelphians* (Philadelphia: Brotherhead, 1859), pp. 741-742;

Bertha M. Stearns, "Philadelphia Magazines for Ladies: 1830-1860," *Pennsylvania Magazine*, 69 (July 1945): 207-219.

Papers:

Though the New York Public Library, Yale, Haverford College, and Harvard each hold one or two letters, the Pennsylvania Historical Society's collection provides the most valuable resources. It contains six letters—including an autobiographical statement covering the 1832-1844 period—and files of Philadelphia newspapers edited by Neal, which contain the only texts of numerous sketches which were never reprinted in his three collections of stories.

Robert Henry Newell
(Orpheus C. Kerr)
(13 December 1836-July 1901)

Michael Butler
University of Kansas

SELECTED BOOKS: *The Orpheus C. Kerr Papers* (New York: Blakeman & Mason, 1862; London: Hotten, 1866);

The Orpheus C. Kerr Papers. Second Series (New York: Carleton, 1863; London: Hotten, 1866);

The Palace Beautiful, and Other Poems (New York: Carleton, 1865);

The Orpheus C. Kerr Papers. Third Series (New York: Carleton, 1865; London: Hotten, 1866);

Avery Glibun; or, Between Two Fires (New York: Carleton; London: Low, 1867);

Smoked Glass (New York: Carleton; London: Low, 1868);

The Cloven Foot: Being an Adaptation of the English Novel "The Mystery of Edwin Drood" (By Charles Dickens) To American Scenes, Characters, Customs, and Nomenclature (New York: Carleton; London: Low, 1870; republished as *The Mystery of Mr. E. Drood* (London: Hotten, 1871);

Versatilities (Boston: Lee & Shepard; New York: Lee, Shepard & Dillingham, 1871);

The Walking Doll; or The Asters and Disasters of Society (New York: Felt, 1872);

Studies in Stanzas (New York: Useful Knowledge Publishing, 1882);

There Was Once a Man (New York: Fords, Howard & Hulbert, 1884).

During the Civil War, Robert Henry Newell was one of the North's most popular humorists. His satirical *The Orpheus C. Kerr Papers* were particular favorites of Abraham Lincoln who, according to Carl Sandburg, once declared "Any one who has not read them is a heathen."

Newell was the child of a prosperous New York City couple, Robert and Amy Lawrence Newell. His father was a successful inventor who had been awarded gold medals at international expositions in London and Vienna. He perfected a bank lock the combination of which could be changed daily and a sewing machine that anticipated Elias Howe's invention by several years. Young Newell was educated in private schools and was preparing for college when financial problems following his father's death in 1854 forced him to give up plans for further schooling. Newell turned to journalism for a living and apparently succeeded very quickly. In 1858, only three months after selling his first free-lance pieces, he was made literary editor of the *Sunday Mercury*, one of New York's largest papers. According to biographers of his future wife, actress Adah Isaacs Menken, the position immediately made him a powerful figure in the city's literary circles. For the next few years, Newell produced "a variety of verse and current comment all of which," according to Stephen Leacock, "has proved as ephemeral as it was successful."

With the inauguration of Lincoln in 1861, Newell turned his attention to Washington and began the series of newspaper letters which made him a national figure—*The Orpheus C. Kerr Papers*. Originally done for the *Sunday Mercury* and then continued in other publications, the Kerr letters provided the nation with a running commentary on American civilian and military affairs during the Civil War and first years of Reconstruction. At first, *The Orpheus C. Kerr Papers* were ostensibly letters written home by a Yankee from "north of the Connecticut River," one of the horde of aspirants after political preferment who descended upon the capital in the early days of Lincoln's administration. The name Orpheus C. Kerr is a play upon "office-seeker." It would be a mistake, however, to see only a pun, which in fact soon became irrelevant, and overlook other implications of Newell's choice of a name for his mouthpiece. From the beginning, either Orpheus Kerr was intended to be more than a run-of-the-mill political hack or Newell was unable to keep much distance between himself and his creation—he did retain the pen name for most of his career. Kerr very much resembles the narrative personae of eighteenth-century English periodicals like the *Tatler*, the *Spectator*, or the *World*. He is intelligent and well educated, both literate and literary. Unlike such roughly contemporary characters as George Washington Harris's Sut Lovingood, Charles Farrar Browne's Artemus Ward, or David Ross Locke's Petroleum V. Nasby, he writes a correct, if at times inflated, prose. He does not write in dialect; his spelling, grammar, and syntax are correct, and, if for that alone, *The Orpheus C. Kerr Papers* are among the easiest of nineteenth-century American comic works to read.

Kerr's rhetoric reflects an awareness of the best and worst in literature. He indulges in literary and social criticism; he rambles philosophically. He enjoys the mental play of parody and punning—the most frequently used comic device in the letters. Orpheus Kerr is an intellectual—albeit of the small town variety—and, perhaps more important, an ironist—about both others and himself. The second paragraph of his first letter states: "Though you find me in Washington now, I was born of respectable parents, and gave every indication, in my satchel and apron days, of coming to something better than this,—much better, my boy." Much of the comedy in the letters lies in mock heroic or slapstick accounts of military doings, but more comes from the narrator's commentaries on those doings—or anything else he happens to think of.

Aside from their narrator, the very first Kerr letters offer little to distinguish them from the run of contemporary American comic writing. They might even be less interesting than most. The fall of Fort Sumter, announced in letter 4, suddenly focused Newell's writing, however, and gave it a new energy and intensity. With the outbreak of war, Orpheus Kerr ceases to be a job seeker; acquires a horse, the steed Pegasus; and attaches himself to the Northern army. From then on, *The Orpheus C. Kerr Papers* are tied together by the usually farcical adventures of the Conic Section, Mackerel Brigade of the Army of Accomac—a military unit characterized by its "remarkable retrograde advances."

For seven years, from 1861 to 1868, Newell reduced the events of the Civil War and Reconstruction to the size of his comic world with its growing cast of characters. The Northern military is represented in *The Orpheus C. Kerr Papers* by officers less willing to sit at the head of armed men in motion than to retire from the field and take "the Oath"—three or four times, hot or cold, from bottle or glass, preferably with a little sugar. They include Captain Villiam Brown, who appears most frequently; Captain Bob Shorty; Colonel Wobert Wobble; Colonel Wobert Wobinson; Rear Admiral Head, who spends most of the war on Duck Pond fishing from the back seat of the Union navy; and the general of the Mackerel Brigade, who for two series of *The Orpheus C. Kerr Papers* Newell used to lampoon George McClellan, general in chief of the Union army. Like McClellan, the Mackerel com-

mander makes Napoleonic orations to his troops, pursues the same strategy of procrastination, and shares the same political ambitions. The general in fact spends less time prosecuting the war than he does vehemently denying his candidacy for the presidency in 1865. When he is finally removed from command, the troops express fear for their lives.

The South is represented by a collection of dim-witted crackers, hysterical maidens, and arrogant cavaliers, chief among them Captain Muchausen and his brother Loyola. Newell's Southerners are vicious, violent, and bigoted deadbeats who preach honor but do not honor their debts. His treatment of them suggests a dislike growing into hatred as the war endured, an impression supported by statements he made in later works. Three Northern politicians play prominent roles in the letters. One, the venerable Gammon, is an antique politician friendly to the South who sprinkles references to his "old friend George Washington" throughout pronouncements like: " 'My friends, this war is like a great struggle between two hostile armies; it will continue until it has ceased, and it will cease when it is no longer continued. Peace,' says the Venerable Gammon—waving indulgent permission for the sun to go on shining,—'peace is the end of the War, as war is the end of peace; therefore, if we had no war, peace would be without end, and if we had no peace, war would be endless.' " The Gammon's fellow conservative, the Kentuckian, is a Unionist only by virtue of the armed occupation of his state. He possesses all the characteristics of Southerners but a ragged gray uniform. Like them and all their friends in the Kerr papers, he is an egomaniac; he once confuses his shadow on the wall for a map of the United States. His aim is to ensure that the struggle between the states remains a "White Man's war" and to ensure that it "be carried on without detriment to the material interests of the South." "Kentucky," he says, "will stand no nonsense whatsomever."

Entering the Kerr letters near the end of the first series of *The Orpheus C. Kerr Papers*, the Kentuckian signals Newell's growing exasperation with the North's prosecution of the war. Abraham Lincoln reflects similar changes in Newell's attitudes. Newell started out treating Lincoln—whom Kerr once describes as bowing "like a graceful door-hinge"—like just another comic character. Early appearances of the president emphasize his ugliness, his ungainliness, and his seemingly obsessive bent for telling very long anecdotes about the folks back home. Over the course of *The Orpheus C. Kerr*

Papers, however, Lincoln's stories become more pointed. Apparently as Newell's pessimism grew, so did his respect for the president. By the end of the war Newell had come to see Lincoln as a rock among men of wax, the only man in Washington still pursuing "the obvious Right." With the assassination his admiration was transformed into veneration. "All that is beautiful and good in the world," he wrote in response, "must mourn his irreparable loss."

A chaplain is the last major character to enter the Kerr papers. He is the least comic of all the Mackerel Brigade and consequently seems another sign of Newell's growing awareness of the realities of his subject and, perhaps, growing uneasiness with his comic approach to it. In the midst of continuous bickerings by politicians and political soldiers about property rights, the status of contraband blacks, and "the White Man's war," the chaplain remains a committed abolitionist. He is also one character who consistently reduces the rhetoric of glorious battles to the facts of war. The following passage from the third series of *The Orpheus C. Kerr Papers* is representative: "Just as the spectacled veterans gained this side of Duck Lake again, my boy, the Mackerel Chaplain was accosted by a Republican chap from Boston, and says he: 'This really looks like action at last my friend. Our troops are evidently all enthusiasm to be led once more against the foe.'

"The Chaplin shaded his eyes with his hand, to look at the speaker, and says he:

" 'They are indeed enthusiastic, my friend. So enthusiastic, in fact, that at least half of them would not come back to this side at all.'

" 'Ah!' says the Chaplain, as softly as though he were speaking in a sick-room; 'they remain there sleeping upon their arms. And, oh, my friend, they will never come back again.' "

As should be expected of a group of newspaper articles written over seven years under various journalistic pressures, *The Orpheus C. Kerr Papers* are loosely organized. The books into which they were collected—and single letters—jump from subject to unrelated subject, approach and wander away from major and minor points, swing through contrasting emotions. History gives them some order. Such battles and events as Bull Run, Fredericksburg, Antietam, Chancellorsville, the Emancipation Proclamation, and the Alabama affair are mentioned in, or with changed names, comically described in their pages and provide a sense of the time along which the letters are strung. Essentially the papers are not ordered by external events, however, but by the mind of their narrator and by the

topics, ideas, and attitudes he returns to again and again. Some of these are directly related to the war and its conduct—to the stupidity, incompetence, lack of resolve, dishonesty, wastefulness of civilian and military leaders: to the arrogant intransigence and inhumanity of the South and its allies. Some are not.

In the latter category lie many digressions on literature scattered throughout the books. Perhaps as a practicing critic Newell could not stray from the subject for long; perhaps it offered him and his readers an escape from the war. Whatever the case, Newell's comments on literature and literary taste in America range from thrown away lines like his quick mention of a Boston man's nightly prayer to Dickens, or the same character's reverence for Ticknor and Fields's new bookshop as one of the nation's most sacred institutions, through longer parodies, burlesques, and imitations. Among the last are sentimental poems and, in the second series of *The Orpheus C. Kerr Papers*, the tales of the Cosmopolitan Club, a number of exotic and sensational stories of Spanish romance, Turkish revenge, French homicide, and Transylvanian metamorphosis of the kind popular before the war. These stories are so true to their models a reader might take them for parody. Yet the serious manner in which they are related as well as some characteristics of Newell's postwar writings suggests they are not.

Most of Newell's parodies and burlesques are poems, many of which were later collected in *Versatilities* (1871). He produced grotesque versions of popular songs and poems ludicrous in their ingenuity. One twenty-six-line work runs through the alphabet in order with all the words in each line starting with a certain letter. According to Carl Sandburg, Lincoln was particularly fond of a poem which mocked McClellan's constant call for more troops in the fable of a monkey who, while fighting a serpent, keeps crying out to Jupiter for more tail. The parodies include a series of supposed reactions to the Civil War by English poets and some very amusing submissions to the contest for choosing a new national anthem written by H. W. L----- of Cambridge, the Hon. Edward E----- of Boston, John Greenleaf W-----, Dr. Oliver Wendell H-----, William Cullen B-----, and others. Ralph Waldo E-----'s contribution reads:

Source immaterial of material naught,
   Focus of light infinitesimal,
Sum of all things by sleepless Nature
           wrought,
   of which abnormal man is decimal.

Robert Henry Newell

Refract, in prism immortal, from thy stars
    To the stars blent incipient on our flag,
The beam translucent, neutrifying death;
    And raise to immortality the rag.

Thomas Bailey A----- submitted:

The little brown squirrel hops in the corn,
    the cricket quaintly sings;
The emerald pigeon nods his head,
    And the shad in the river springs,
The dainty sunflower hangs its head
    On the shore of the summer sea;
And better far that I were dead
    If Maud did not love me.

I love the squirrel that hops in the corn,
    And the cricket that quaintly sings;
And the emerald pigeon that nods his head,
    And the shad that gayly springs.
I love the dainty sunflower, too.
    And Maud with her snowy breast;
I love them all;—but I love—I love—
    I love my country best.

Another nonmilitary subject often discussed

in the letters is the women of America whose artificiality, silliness, and egocentricity are frequently displayed in their inane gifts to the men of the Mackerel Brigade. Their first offerings to the men at arms are handmade havelocks—light cloth cap covers of the kind worn by French legionnaires—which the troops mistake for very large shirts. Later a "girl of about seventy" ships the brigade 10,000 pious tracts. Another sends large feather fans. A wife sends her husband, who is starving on short rations, a copy of the temperance pledge, a pair of skates, two bottles of toothache drops, and six sheets of patent flypaper. Another writes to berate her mate as "a unnatural and wicious creetur" for not sending her a new dress and some hair pins; the husband notes that American women sometimes die "when there's new and expensive tombstones in fashion."

For Newell such female absurdity came to be extremely serious for he decided it revealed not only an innate silliness but a complete lack of understanding of the Civil War, which, in his opinion, soon deepened into a petulant desire not to be bothered by it. The second series of *The Orpheus C. Kerr Papers* contains this letter to the author: "My ma requests me to tell you that you ought to be ashamed of yourself, you hateful thing, for encouraging the vulgar people to be in favor of this nasty war, that is causing their superiors so much trouble, and has given away the opera and made enemies of those nice Southerners, with their beautiful big eyes and elegant swearing.

". . . why don't you advocate a compromise . . . and get Mr. Lincoln to stop the Constitution and order the war to be ended before there's any more assassinations and things?"

This comic passage, more serious than jokes about outsized cap cloths and feather fans, is one of many expressions of the theme which seems if not to dominate then to focus the later papers. That is the failure of the civilian population, and to a certain extent the military, to commit itself to the war and its ideals. Newell's home front seems made up of silly women, slackers, grafters, profiteers, and Copperheads. Early letters treat the fools behind the lines as relatively harmless absurdities. Later Newell and his subjects get meaner, and his humor grows increasingly bitter. One letter describes a family of Northern profiteers at home; another is centered on the New York draft riots. In one letter, a representative of the Great North-West arrives in Washington to complain that the war is interfering with real estate speculation in his part of the country and to insist that The Great North-West has "no quarrel with" and wants no part in "this here Black Republican New England war upon the sunny South." In another, Orpheus Kerr encounters a former slave owner who has come into occupied territory to establish an African school and water cure establishment. Years before he had realized the evil of slavery. "I could not bear the sting of conscience," he says, "and I resolved to make a sacrifice for the sake of principle—to cease to be a slaveholder! I called my slaves together. . . . I bade them be good boys and girls, and then I—SOLD EVERY ONE OF THEM!" When, immediately after telling his story, this character's student body is scattered by cavalry, he demands that the slaves be returned to the South—for this is a white man's war. "Otherwise," he states, "future reconciliation and reconstruction will be impossible."

That last emphasizes the idea emerging from Kerr's letters that not only do the women, the profiteers, and the conservative politicians like the Venerable Gammon, the Kentuckian, Horace Greeley, and General McClellan fail to commit themselves to the war, they fail to understand it. For Newell, the Civil War was a struggle aimed both at freeing the black from slavery and making him a citizen of the United States. In *Avery Glibun*, a novel published in 1867, he referred to the Civil War as "the second creation of Man." He was frustrated by all reluctance to face the issue of emancipation. He scorned alternatives offered by Northern politicians. The first general of the Mackerel Brigade pushes colonization as a solution to the slave question and is miffed by the "selfishness" of blacks who quietly reject his offer to move to the barren island of Nova Zembla and live by hunting bears. Newell also derided the reluctance to let blacks serve in the army, the resistance to granting them citizenship, the fear of their moving North and taking up jobs of "honest working-men." In a letter written in 1863, the Kentuckian proclaims his disgust at seeing "how the Black Man is continually being raised above the White man." In response, Orpheus Kerr discusses the superiority of white skin to black: "So highly, indeed, do many possessors of this complexion admire its prevailing whiteness, that they perform their ablutions with an artistic design to leave here and there certain picturesque streaks of delicate shading, thereby causing the whiteness of the intervening spots to appear all the more dazzling." Upon black skin, he continues: "the beautiful virtue of Modesty cannot paint itself in a blush when the owner is detected in the act of taking a bribe; nor is it susceptible of that beautiful sunset-tint which the genial merit of being able to punish four bottles at a sitting delights to leave upon a face of Caucasian extraction." He concludes: "we cannot blame the White Man for entertaining a wholesome contempt and loathing for the Black Man; and the truly hearty manner in which many of our more pallid fellow-countrymen breathe ingenious execrations whenever the latter is mentioned, may be accepted as a beautiful and touching proof that they appreciate God's benignity in giving them a superiority of skin; even though He may have seen best, in His infinite wisdom, to leave them occasionally without brains."

Impatience with the military, anger at the home front, despair over the fate of his ideals turned Newell's humor darker as the war endured. The cheerfulness which once allowed Orpheus Kerr to reduce great campaigns to slapstick battles for henhouses deserted Newell. A letter appearing in *The Orpheus C. Kerr Papers. Third Series* suggests his ultimate evaluation of his subject: "To the youthful soul," he wrote, "This war is a vast phantasmagoria of almighty giants struggling together in the clouds. There was a time when I, too, was able to see it to that extent; but time, and some experience in Virginia, have reduced my giants in the clouds to brigadiers in the mud; and from seeing our national banner in the character of a rainbow dipped stars, I have come to regard it as an ambitious attempt to represent sunrise in muslin, the unexpected scantiness of the material compelling the ingenious artist to use a section of midnight to fill up."

The pessimism toward public events which haunts the later letters may have been reinforced by some unhappy turns taken by Newell's private life in 1862 and 1863. In September 1862, he married the actress Adah Isaacs Menken. Theirs was a marriage which has always befuddled her biographers. By all accounts, Adah Menken was a person of remarkable physical and intellectual attractions. One of the most notorious women of her time, she was known throughout America as "the Naked Lady" because at the climax of her most famous vehicle, the play *Mazeppa*, she appeared wearing only pink tights and strapped to the back of a horse which pranced down the aisle of the theater and up a ramp onto the stage. Newell was her third husband; his immediate predecessor was James Heenan, a famous boxer, who had deserted Menken when he sailed off to England for a championship fight. He later increased the scandal associated with the pair by claiming they had never actually been legally married. Adah Menken's literary talents brought her into contact with Newell, who had published her poetry in his paper. He thought her the most intelli-

Adah Isaacs Menken

gent woman he had ever met; he also believed that with his help she could be reformed into the most remarkable literary woman of their age. He dreamed of her leaving the stage, deserting her bohemian friends—Walt Whitman among them—and retreating to a two-libraried house in New Jersey where they could hide away, devoting themselves wholly to art and each other. In later years, Newell judged his dream "an immature fanaticism for some supremely unselfish achievement." "I falsified nature," he wrote, "and assumed the most critical of social relations as though it had been merely a nominal one, that I might with the greater facility essay a full grown human soul's regeneration. It was a cruelty no less than an egotism when I dreamed that it was a salvation and a self-sacrifice. God and man were justified in punishing my sacrilegious presumption."

The language of this confession suggests how badly the two were matched. Newell was shy and retiring—in the words of her biographers, "sour" and "sullen." He was conservative in his behavior, social values, and his ideas about women whom he

believed in the main weak, silly, erratic, and always in need of man's strong hand. Adah Menken was neither silly nor weak. Outgoing, unconventional, and ambitious, she loved, perhaps craved, publicity. She espoused advanced feminist ideas; she smoked cigarettes in public. Why she accepted Newell's suit is possibly even more a mystery than why he pursued her. Only one of her biographers, Paul Lewis, believes she could actually have been attracted by the man or his genius. Most believe that she married on the rebound either to forget Heenan or to find refuge from the scandal surrounding their separation.

Whatever the case, the marriage of Robert Newell and Adah Menken was a short one. One of her biographers claims that in reality it lasted only two weeks. Then, after she had rejected Newell's demands that she leave the stage, and he had reacted by imprisoning her in the house in New Jersey, she climbed out a window and escaped to New York. Another insists the marriage went smoothly for several months until an eccentric Baltimore admirer sent her a diamond and emerald bracelet worth $1,500 which, in defiance of Newell, she refused to return. In July of 1863, the couple attempted a reconcilation and traveled together to California. By their return to New York about nine months later, the marriage was definitely finished. Menken sailed alone to Europe and friendships with celebrities like Charles Dickens and Charles Reade, and more intimate relationships with Alexandre Dumas the elder and Algernon Swinburne. In 1865, she sued Newell for divorce charging desertion. He did not contest the action. Newell never remarried and, when he died in 1901, friends of his later years were surprised to learn that he had not always been a bachelor.

After the breakup of his marriage, Newell returned to New York journalism. He held literary editorships with various papers, served as a war correspondent for the *New York Herald*, and continued writing Kerr letters, the last volume of which was published in 1868 under the title *Smoked Glass*. About half of that book is devoted to what Newell called the great American theatrical, "Impeachment, or The Man Without a Friend." A partial listing of the drama's cast suggests Newell's opinion of the proceedings: Man Without a Friend—A. Johnson; Macbeth—B. Wade; Mephistopheles—Thaddeus Stevens; Corps de Bully—Butler, Bingham & Co. (Wade, Stevens, Butler, and Bingham were among the Radical Republicans in the House of Representatives who managed the impeachment proceedings against Johnson.) Although he believed impeachment unjust, Newell was no fan of Andrew Johnson; in fact he seems by this time to have become disgusted with everyone in American government whether Northerner, Southerner, Democrat, or Republican.

The second half of *Smoked Glass* chronicles the adventures of Orpheus Kerr and Villiam Brown with an army of occupation at Chipmunk Courthouse, Virginia. The tone of these letters is lighter than those written near the end of the war but in other ways they seem nastier, more forced. Running under their surface appears to be a mixture of exasperation and despair that the war accomplished so little. The Munchausens are back in control and they are as chivalrous as ever—as arrogant, as violent, as highly mortgaged. The Ku Klux Klan has begun its night rides. Nevertheless the last of the Orpheus C. Kerr letters reminded Newell's readers and perhaps Newell himself that something of real, if compromised, value had been gained by the years of conflict. As Kerr and Brown retreat from the South, their attention is drawn to "a miserably dilapidated roadside house, through the windows of which a feeble light and the voices of men singing came out upon the thickening darkness of the night. Moving softly to the half-open door, we looked in, and beheld many member of the free-negro race kneeling in the wretched room, around the figure of a one-armed sable soldier of the Union, who, holding a lighted tallow candle in his only hand, beat time with it to the supplication all were singing. Here and there in the kneeling congregation appeared the blue uniform which, in every other attitude than that, had stood out a score of times in the red flash of battle; and, as the voices of homely praise and prayer went up to Him who no less gave blackness to the raven than whiteness to the goose, I thought it was fitting that the light, in its intoning rise and fall, should alternately call from the shadows of a far corner and restore to them again the bust of ABRAHAM LINCOLN. / Yours, reverently, / Orpheus C. Kerr."

While writing the last of the Kerr letters, Newell worked on his first novel, *Avery Glibun; or, Between Two Fires*, which was published before *Smoked Glass* in 1867. A dedication to nobody—"in grateful recognition of the individual sympathy, encouragement, and generous praise extended to the author at a time when he really needed such disinterested help"—labels the book an "experimental combination of the old and new schools of fiction." Parts of *Avery Glibun* seem drawn from the warehouses of sensational fiction; parts are obviously drawn from Newell's physical and psychological experiences. The novel contains many plots; it is in fact several novels—a gothic romance involving a magnetic villain called the King of Diamonds, strange women of many identities, and babies switched in their cradles; a political satire revolving around attempts to buy the New York state senatorial election; a social comedy of manners among the new rich; and the chronicle of the title character's rise to manhood. Its most interesting technical characteristic is the use of two narrative points of view. Chapters related in the third person by an omniscient narrator alternate with those told in first person by an innocent less aware than the reader of what is going on around him. The novel swings back and forth between sensational and fairly realistic fiction. Avery Glibun's adventures take him, for example, from a wealthy home dominated by a cruelly sinister father who seeks his death, to a Dickensian boarding school, to a gypsy camp, to a secret hideout in the New York underworld, to the offices of a literary journal, to the accounting department of a large dry goods store. The book also offers extended and detailed pictures of conditions among the criminal classes of New York, its literary bohemians, and its retail clerks.

Avery Glibun is not primarily a comic novel but it does contain many humorous observations and episodes. In it Newell jibes at the theory and practice of education in America; describing his excitement at going off to school, for example, Avery Glibun says: "Motherless and insignificant as I was, no one thought it worthwhile to encourage my imagination with that finely nervous ideal of the coming school-master which causes very little boys to regard learning as the expiation of crime." He told his usual jokes about the Irish and about silly women—although in one scene a woman writer who seems fairly sensible says: "I don't believe it would be possible for a man to be funny without some slur upon women." He satirized literary fashions, publishing practices, and the business "realities" which force American artists to Europeanize their art. He attacked Tammany politics and legislative corruption. He passed from irony into sarcasm when discussing the treatment of the poor, or lack of it, by greedy doctors who demand cash in advance, or the exploitation of underpaid employees by sanctimonious merchants. Much of *Avery Glibun* seems to be about money: about the power, corruption, suffering, hypocrisy often tied to it. At one point a clerk shouts out, "We are just salaries, we are not men." At another, a description of the worst New York slums begins: "Money is the root of all evil, and so is bread." Much of the wit of Orpheus C. Kerr can be found in *Avery Glibun*, less of the humor.

In 1869, Newell joined the staff of the *New York World*, where until 1874 he edited a social studies column. During this period, he published his last comic novels—*The Cloven Foot* in 1870 and *The Walking Doll* in 1872. For an American reader, *The Cloven Foot* is one of the more interesting of the many attempts to complete Dickens's unfinished *Mystery of Edwin Drood*. In his preface to the book, Newell stated that he intended it to make a point in a long-running literary debate. He quotes a review in which he had repeated Hawthorne's argument that the American writer is hampered by the lack of a permanent romantic background for his fiction and had then gone on to claim it a mistake if not an injustice to compare American and European fiction. He also quotes several contemporaries who based rebuttals of his assertions on the argument that, because men and women are the same no matter what their country, background is essentially an irrelevant element in fiction. In response to that, Newell reports he "conceived the idea of serio-comically demonstrating the assumed accuracy of his views by deliberately reducing the current work of some great foreign novelist to American equivalents."

The Cloven Foot is essentially a translation of *The Mystery of Edwin Drood* from English into American—a translation of language, character, and place. Dickens's John Jasper, the English opium eater become John Bumstead, American clove eater—referring to the nineteenth-century drinker's use of clove as a "breath freshener." Dickens's city of Cloisterham with its venerable cathedral and nuns' house becomes suburban Bumsteadville with its ritualistic church and alms house. A professional philanthropist is transformed into an insurance agent, and a chapter entitled "Philanthropy in Minor Canon Corner" into "Insurance in Gospeller's Gulch." The English heroine, Rosa Bud, becomes the American, Flora Potts. Throughout *The Cloven Foot* Newell followed Dickens's original very closely—practically paragraph by paragraph. A representative sample of the result is the opening to the second chapter. Dickens began a description of a church emptying out after service: "Whosoever has observed that sedate and clerical bird, the rook, may perhaps have noticed that when he wings his way homeward towards nightfall, in a sedate and clerical company, two rooks will suddenly detach themselves from the rest, will retrace their flight for some distance, and will there poise and linger; conveying to mere men the fancy that it is of some

occult importance to the body politic that this artful couple should pretend to have renounced connection with it." Newell's American version reads: "Whosoever has noticed a party of those sedate and Germanesquely philosophical animals, the pigs, scrambling precipitately under the gate from out a cabbage-patch toward nightfall, may, perhaps have observed, that, immediately upon emerging from the sacred vegetable preserve, a couple of the more elderly and designing of them assumed a sudden air of abstracted musing, and reduced their progress to a most dignified and leisurely walk, as though to convince the human beholder that their recent proximity to the cabbages had been but the trivial accident of a meditative stroll." Whether it proves Newell's point or not, *The Cloven Foot* is an amusingly double-edged literary parody.

Robert Henry Newell

Judged by conventional literary standards, *The Walking Doll; or The Asters and Disasters of Society* is perhaps Newell's most successful novel—even if not the most interesting. It is more cohesive than *Avery Glibun*; it does not contain the schizophrenic shifts from comic to serious that characterize his earlier work. There are serious passages but they are less frequent and more muted here. The novel is naturally more self-contained than *The Cloven Foot*—although Newell still had literary models in mind when he wrote this last comic work. His preface reads: "The 'Great American Novel' has been long expected by the Critics who / 'in their foolishness, / Passion and mulishness,' / have dictated that it shall possess and rival all the worst beauties / of Dickens, Reade, Wilkie Collins, Thackeray, and Miss Braddon. / Well—here it is!"

The Walking Doll brings together a number of plots, none of which seems particularly important to the progress of the book. In one, Geoffrey Dapple, a toymaker, struggles to reinvent a walking doll mechanism hidden years before by a wife he thinks he murdered. In another, Adelaide Aster, a powerful and scheming woman, works to get two stepsons disinherited in favor of her own child. In the most prominent, a bizarre young man behaves in ways no one can understand. That young man, Jack Aster, is the successful embodiment of a literary criticism Newell made in *The Orpheus C. Kerr Papers* and then repeated in each of his later works. In the first series of *The Orpheus C. Kerr Papers*, Newell wrote that woman's genius "as displayed in gushing fiction, is a power of creating an unnatural and unmitigated ruffian for a hero, my boy, at whose shrine all created crinoline and immense delegations of inferior broadcloth are impelled to bow." In illustration, he made the first of many references in his work to Charlotte Brontë's Rochester, a character "done-over scores of times" and "still 'much used in respectable families.' " In *Avery Glibun*, Newell created Plato Wynne, the hero's false father, a gambler, counterfeiter, political fixer, and "the incarnation of all that cows, commands, and universally infatuates women. He was an embodied jeer, insult, and stealthy lash, to his wife; yet that once proud, imperious, and tigerish woman loved him with all the invincible fidelity of a spaniel." Jack Aster is a burlesque of the type. Forced from his father's house by a scheming stepmother, Jack becomes a romantic outcast, the driver of a horse cab. Arrogant, self-centered, and rude, he is "proudly sensitive . . . so morbidly alive to any human notice not devoted exclusively to himself." He walks with a rolling Byronic gait. He lives with "a skeleton newsboy" whom, he tells an acquaintance, "I found starving in the streets one night and have adopted as my valet." When in full costume, wearing his mighty sombrero far down over his nose, flourishing a long old-fashioned Spanish cloak, or wrapper, from his broad shoulders, and pulling his moustache impatiently with his left hand, he might have been taken for a desperate Academy of Design artist come to paint a portrait by violence." Aster seems to court both heroines of the novel, Lucy Lardner, the daughter of a respectable merchant, and Dolly Dapple, the child of the toymaker. When accused of that seeming infidelity or any other ungentlemanly behavior, he always shouts "Hay?" and runs from the room—often getting caught up in his Spanish cloak and tumbling down stairs.

Like *Avery Glibun*, *The Walking Doll* spins a gothic web. Characters, few of whom are what they seem or who they pretend to be, all turn out to be connected to one another in complicated ways. Dr. Canary, a poetical dentist's assistant, is, for example, found to be a ruined aristocrat and the first husband of the wicked stepmother. Mrs. Dedley, a nurse, is discovered to be the long-thought-dead wife of the toymaker. And the mystery of Jack Aster's strange behavior is cleared up with the revelation that Jack is both John Phillip Aster and John Francis Aster, identical twins who unknown to each other have adopted the same sombrero, Spanish cape, tortoiseshell goggles, and bravo behavior. As Orpheus C. Kerr declares at the end of the novel, "Man is a strange being, and it is curious that no author ever remarked it before."

In *The Walking Doll*, Newell returned to his favorite subjects and themes. Women are worked over once again. By accident and design they are at the center of most of the troubles experienced by characters of the novel. The two Jacks are almost done out of their inheritance by the scheming stepmother who had already ruined one husband. The toymaker's wife, a nag, drove him insane by hiding the mechanism for his walking doll. Lucy and Dolly are Newell's usual simpletons; the worse the Jack Asters behave, the more they love them. One, Jack's landlady, is an advocate of woman's rights who responds to his complaints about the monotony of the board by shouting: "The tyranny of your sex has put it upon woman to set the table, and if your sex don't like hash, it can lump it." The South is here in Dimwiddie Pamunkey, an accomplice of the stepmother, and in a tale of a Southern wedding at which all participants kill each other off. There are also digressions on rude salesclerks, the Irish, corrupt Tammany politicians, and American art, particularly the tyranny of Europe and Boston over American writers, painters, and public.

Although *The Walking Doll* is lighter entertainment than *Avery Glibun*, the novel still contains very serious passages—most notably some discussing the plight of the children of the drinking poor and the lack of social concern among the New York rich. Another interesting aspect of the book is Newell's continuation of the indictment of doctors begun in *Avery Glibun*. Here the accusation is one we might not expect in a novel of the time; Newell attacked the doctors of large hospitals for their sexual harassment of nurses.

In 1874 Newell joined the *Daily Graphic* and shortly after became editor of the illustrated weekly paper *Hearth and Home*. In 1876, a nervous affliction forced his retirement from active journalism. He began working on "Didaschelle," an autobiographical novel, but severe writer's cramp and letter blindness forced him to quit the book after completing only half of it. In 1884 his last novel, *There Was Once a Man*, appeared. Not a comic work, the book's argument nevertheless relies on one of Newell's favorite comic targets from the past and bases an attack on the theory of evolution upon what in earlier works would no doubt have been presented as an anti-Irish joke typical of the times. *There Was Once a Man* is set in Borneo and deals in part with the civilizing efforts of the English governor, Sir James Brooke, and in part with the efforts of a materialistic Scottish doctor to prove his orangutanlike creature, Oshonsee, a missing link in the evolution of ape into man. In the end, the semiintelligent beast is found to be the descendant of a degenerate Borneo woman and a retarded Irishman named O'Shawnessy, and consequently a strong argument for the counterview of devolution. In some ways, the front matter for *There Was Once a Man* is more interesting and more thought-provoking than the novel. On the dedication page, blank space allows the buyer—The One, Tried and Proved, UNSELFISH FRIEND of My Maturer Years—to write in his own name. A poem in an odd form of Greek which attacks the publisher for not letting Newell properly proofread the typescript is signed "Orpheus in Hades."

Newell died in early July 1901 at his home in Brooklyn. Because his sister and servants had gone on vacation, his body lay undiscovered for days. A two inch obituary notice in the *New York Tribune*, which mixed up the dates of his life and misspelled the title of a book, summed him up as follows: "Mr. Newell was fond of animals and took an active interest in the work of the Society for the Prevention of Cruelty to Animals. He liked to see the streets kept clean, and if he saw a piece of paper on the sidewalk he would invariably throw it into the gutter."

The obscurity shrouding Newell's work when that paragraph was written has lasted to the present. In 1901, a "Retrospect of American Humor" published in *Century Magazine* gave only brief attention to his writings but included Newell among the five political humorists of importance between 1830 and 1870. A recent major study of American humor mentioned him only in a footnote listing the pseudonyms of nineteenth-century writers. Possibly Newell's reputation has suffered not only because of the brevity of his career but also because of a modern tendency to judge nineteenth-century comic writers by how much their work anticipates *The Adventures of Huckleberry Finn*. Newell's writings contain few of the more obvious foreshadowings found in the work of more vernacular contemporaries. Nevertheless, whatever their current status, *The Orpheus C. Kerr Papers* are undeniably important in the history of American literature. If nothing else their immense popularity at the beginning of one of American humor's most fertile periods must have made them an influence on some of our best comic writers.

Yet in truth there seems to be nothing in the literary quality of Newell's work which could demand our renewed attention. His short career could not be said to have shown any interesting development. The favorite subjects of his early books are the favored topics of his later ones; the treatment is essentially the same. In a sense, his jokes never changed; only the words in them did. Newell was not a literary master. He never put together a cohesive, well-organized work of art. His plots seldom make sense; he created no unforgettable or strikingly original characters. Although his work done after the Kerr papers contains some graphic depictions of the criminals, bohemian artists, merchants, and retail clerks of New York—characters not commonly encountered in the fiction of his time—he did not produce any sustained realistic portraits of American life. At the same time, ironically enough, his work is too topical. Many of its references are so specific they are lost on modern readers—although it is interesting to see how many "temporary concerns" of Newell's day like woman's rights, bureaucratic waste, political corruption, even the Great American Novel have endured to become the "temporary concerns" of our own times. Newell's work is often very funny. It is witty; it contains many amusing turns of phrase, many good lines. It is usually genuinely amusing in ways other nineteenth-century American humor often is not. That is simply not enough, however, to rescue it from obscurity.

But *The Orpheus C. Kerr Papers* should be rescued from neglect, for they are important for their cultural observations as well as their literary merit. Certainly no other work in any more entertaining fashion offers insights into the Civil War era in our nation's history or challenges the myths that have grown up about it. For the general reader, the chief value of *The Orpheus C. Kerr Papers* may now be historical but that is nonetheless a very real value.

C. F. M. Noland
(Colonel Pete Whetstone)
(23 August 1810?-23 June 1858)

Lorne Fienberg
Iowa State University

BOOKS: *Pete Whetstone of Devil's Fork: Letters to the Spirit of the Times*, edited by T. R. Worley and E. A. Nolte (Van Buren, Ark.: Argus Press, 1957);

Cavorting on the Devil's Fork: The Pete Whetstone Letters of C. F. M. Noland, edited by Leonard Williams (Memphis: Memphis State University Press, 1979).

The literary career of Charles Fenton Mercer Noland poses unusual problems for both the biographer and the critic. It is difficult to evaluate the artistic achievement of a writer whose entire body of work consists of a series of 250 brief sporting epistles and humorous sketches which appeared under three pseudonyms in William T. Porter's New York *Spirit of the Times* between 1836 and 1856. It is even more difficult to argue for the literary influence of a figure who saw himself primarily as a newspaper editor, lawyer, politician, breeder of thoroughbreds, and gentleman, and only incidentally as a frontier humorist who never attached his own name to his pieces, and whose works never appeared in book form until almost 100 years after his death. And yet Col. C. F. M. Noland was not only the first contributor of original humorous sketches to the *Spirit of the Times*; he was for several decades the most prolific and most flatteringly imitated correspondent to that journal, which would pioneer in the publication of humorous tales from all regions of the United States. As the creator of Colonel Pete Whetstone and the brawling revelers Dan Looney and Jim Cole, Noland's experiments in depicting the comic characters, incidents, and dialects of the frontier Southwest provided suggestive models for Thomas Bangs Thorpe, Johnson Jones Hooper, and George Washington Harris, his better-known colleagues in the "Big Bear School of Humor."

Noland was born in Loudoun County, Virginia, most probably on 23 August 1810 (although here his biographers, his military records, and even the family Bible provide conflicting evidence). His father, William, apparently envisioning a glorious

military career for his son, enrolled Fenton in the United States Military Academy at West Point some months before his thirteenth birthday. The younger Noland disappointed his father's hopes by flunking out of the academy in less than two years.

C. F. M. Noland

In 1826 the family emigrated to Batesville, Arkansas, perhaps in shame, perhaps as a punishment to Fenton for his academic shortcomings. At any rate, Arkansas proved more paradise than purgatory to the young Noland. He began reading for the legal profession and wrote political broadsides in the Batesville newspapers under the pseudonym "Devereux." One such article in January 1831 provoked a duel of honor in which he killed William Fontaine Pope, a nephew of the governor. Once more finding himself in embarrassing circumstances, Noland retreated to Fort Gibson in the Indian territory where he joined the U.S. Army. His peregrinations with the Mounted Rangers lasted until 1834 when he resigned from active duty, apparently in high dudgeon over his failure to achieve suitable promotions. In 1836 Noland was admitted to the bar and the following year he entered into a law partnership in Batesville with William F. Denton. It was during his first years as a lawyer in Batesville that Noland made the acquaintance of Lucretia Ringgold who became his wife in 1840.

Noland's entry into Arkansas politics was an inauspicious one. On 29 January 1837, after participating in the convention which drafted a constitution and petition for statehood, Noland was elected courier to bear the official copy of the petition to Washington. While journeying by steamboat to Mobile and by horseback overland to Richmond and Washington, he was repeatedly delayed by blizzards. When he arrived in Washington on 8 March, he discovered that a copy of the petition sent by United States mail had arrived and been submitted to Congress a week earlier. Something of the same futility dogged his political career. Despite his election to the Arkansas legislature as a Whig representative from Independence County, and subsequent reelection in 1838, 1840, and 1846, he was constantly at odds with the Democratic majority.

After careers as a soldier, political commentator, attorney, and state legislator, Noland became editor in February 1855 of the *Arkansas State Gazette and Democrat*. He added to these occupations an enduring passion for all kinds of outdoor sports and pastimes, in particular the breeding of thoroughbred horses. Although he was not by birth a member of the planter aristocracy, he was a plantation owner and he counted among his friends the elite of Southern society.

In addition to his multitude of vocations, Noland's personality was of fabled complexity. In a work entitled *The Lives and Adventures of the Desperadoes of the South-West* (1848), Alfred W. Arrington describes his extraordinary friend "Fent Noland": "Such is the versatility of his genius that he seems equally adapted to every species of effort, intellectual or physical. . . . In genteel society, a more polished gentleman never moved on the earth. To see him . . . in the salon with the ladies, we would swear that he had studied nothing all his life but the science of refined courtesy, and the art of saying the most beautiful things. But this view presents only one half of the man. Observe him in a circle of Desperadoes—listen to the roars aroused by his wild anecdotes—hear him sing his favorite, 'Such a gittin up stairs,' or 'The Hudson was a Bully Boat'; . . . or see him practising at ten paces, driving out the centre every shot, or bringing down the sparrow on the wing;—and you would reverse your former judgment of the man."

Noland was, then, both the refined gentleman, adept in all the genteel social graces, and the "desperado," glorying in a world of prodigious physical exploits in the frontier backwoods. His contributions to the *Spirit of the Times* celebrate this versatility in the character of the ideal Southern gentleman (himself), but the striking duality of the gentleman's roles offers us a clue to the diversity of literary personae which Noland created in his letters and sketches.

In writing his first sporting epistle to William T. Porter's journal, it is doubtful that Noland had any particular literary aspirations; yet he would surely have been attracted by the editorial mission of the *Spirit of the Times*. In an issue of 1837, editor Porter could boldly assert that his publication "is designed to promote the views and interests of but an infinitesimal division of those classes of society composing the great mass. . . . we are addressing ourselves to gentlemen of standing, wealth and intelligence—the very corinthian columns of the community." Indeed, it was with all the solidity of a "corinthian column" that Noland submitted his first offering to the *Spirit of the Times* entitled "A Glance at the Southern Racing Stables etc." under the pseudonym "N. of Arkansas." In this account of the state of the breeder's art in Alabama, and in the more than 200 sporting epistles which followed, N. of Arkansas endeared himself to readers of the *Spirit of the Times* primarily for the polish and formality of his prose, and for the keen accuracy and insight with which he analyzed the sporting life. Such accounts provided few hints that their author would help to pioneer in the writing of a distinctive brand of humorous fiction from the frontier Southwest.

But Noland's single weakness as a sporting correspondent—his incorrigible fondness for digression upon the more rustic and uncouth incidents of frontier life—became his most engaging quality as a writer of humorous sketches. Irresistibly, N.'s correspondence would drift off into bits of gossip about wilderness hunts; the presentation of sketches of frontier types, replete with vernacular dialect; and the recounting of celebrated tall tales, such as the one about the greenhorn soldier who mistakenly fears he has been bitten by a rattler, when he has in fact only been squatting on his own spurs. His account of the drunken revels during a Fourth of July celebration in the backwoods abounds in riotous details of boisterous songs and pranks, a rigged poker game, and the repeated emptying and refilling of a jug of moonshine. But whatever his enjoyment of the festivities, N. is always in these accounts the detached satirist commenting in a cultivated way upon the rude behavior of his social inferiors. Such condescension would have been appropriate to the social pretensions of the *Spirit of the Times* and its readers. Critics of Southwestern American humor have frequently observed that much of the humor of these frontier sketches depends upon the teller's achieving a satiric distance from the events and characters he is describing. However, Noland's creation of a second literary persona, Colonel Pete Whetstone, enabled him to depict the antics of backwoods characters from the perspective of an involved narrator.

Norris W. Yates has observed that in the forty-five Pete Whetstone letters Noland was "the first southwestern author to eliminate his own cultivated personality from the story as far as direct presentation of character and atmosphere was concerned." Accordingly, cultivated readers derive amusement from Pete's unconscious abuse of the rules of spelling and grammar, and from his uninhibited use of the flamboyant diction and metaphors of the backwoods vernacular. But Pete Whetstone's character, his opinions, and his accounts of frontier incidents remain closely linked to the more gentlemanly letters of N. of Arkansas. In his first letter, Pete significantly asserts that N. of Arkansas is his best friend. They witness the same thoroughbred races; they travel together to New York, Virginia, and New Orleans, and they even share an audience with President Van Buren. Repeatedly, Pete's and N.'s accounts of similar events appear on the same pages of issues of the *Spirit of the Times*. Noland's achievements as a writer of humorous sketches stem not from the removal of the cultivated voice of the gentlemanly narrative, but from the sophisticated juxtaposition of two voices, one genteel and proper, the other rustic and liberated from formality and polite convention. N.'s letters operate as a framing device which enables the reader to determine the parodic intent of Pete Whetstone's style and beliefs. A recent edition of the Pete Whetstone letters by Leonard Williams, entitled *Cavorting on the Devil's Fork: The Pete Whetstone Letters of C. F. M. Noland* (1979), offers readers of American humor, the first accurate sampling in book form of Noland's work. But, because the edition omits all but passing reference to the correspondence of N. of Arkansas, it fails to convey this parodic relationship or the full extent of Noland's

sophistication as a literary stylist and technical innovator.

Pete's first letter to the *Spirit of the Times* on 14 February 1837 defiantly challenges the decorum customarily observed by sporting correspondents such as N. of Arkansas. There is a brief apology in which Pete begs editor Porter to "excuse my familiarity, for you must know us chaps on the Devil's Fort [sic] don't stand on ceremony." Then throwing ceremony to the winds, Pete introduces the members of his family and a host of backwoods characters, including the brawling Dan Looney and Jim Cole. He boasts of his trusty rifle, his skilled hunting dogs, and his horse Bussing Coon. The narrative itself consists of several mildly offensive political squibs, the account of a challenge match between Bussing Coon and Warping Bars, and the nose biting and eye gouging which occur during the celebration of Bussing Coon's victory. Next morning, Pete sets out on a bear hunt, despite his cuts and bruises, and he concludes his "sporting epistle" by promising to send Porter "the particulars" at a later date.

This initial letter established the dialect, the tone, and the substance for the forty-four other letters which appeared, at first in quick succession (twenty-nine appeared between 1837 and 1839), and then at sporadic intervals until 1856. Pete does occasionally emerge as the keenly sensitive and knowledgeable observer of the frontier sporting life. More often, he is the reporter of sporting travesties such as the "Race Between 'Worm Eater' and 'Apple Sas,'" of his stupefaction upon hearing the first "pe-anny" in Arkansas, or of witnessing the wiles of the "ventrilokist" who "can talk way out of doors and stand in the house." Best of all, Pete loves a fight, and Jim Cole and Dan Looney figure prominently in the inhuman brutalities which occasionally occur in the sporting life of the backwoods. Repeatedly, Pete challenges the reader to object to his spirited improprieties: "Look here, mister, if you don't like the smell of fresh bread, you had better quit the bakery"; or, "Mister, if you don't like the smell of the apples, you had best quit the cider press." But there is always immense pleasure to be derived from such aromas.

Nevertheless, Noland's ambiguous response to Pete's uncouth ways and to his social pretensions emerges in a series of letters Pete writes from Little Rock between 1837 and 1839 after he has been elected to the Arkansas state legislature. If we remember that Noland was himself a successful Whig politician struggling against the popular tide of Jacksonian Democracy, we can appreciate his satire of Colonel Pete Whetstone, the upstart Democratic politician. Noland could remain gentle in his criticisms of Pete's social and political antics as long as he himself remained in legislative office. But in December 1844 N. of Arkansas brings to the pages of the *Spirit of the Times* the news of his defeat (presumably Noland's own) as a Whig political candidate. Here begins the process of Noland's disillusionment with the shape of Southern society and the series of personal reversals which were to culminate in his death from consumption on 23 June 1858.

Noland's political defeat precipitated a return to his law office in 1850. There, despite continuing activity as a land agent, sometime editor of the *Arkansas Gazette*, and even a brief return to the political arena in an appointment to the unexalted position of Swamp Land Commissioner, his persistent cough and loss of weight signaled his declining health. But throughout his later years, Noland's literary efforts reveal not only his personal decline, but a process of social disillusionment as well. N. of Arkansas's letters to the *Spirit of the Times*, once a celebration of the qualities of the Southern gentleman, become in the 1840s and 1850s increasingly elegiac in their account of the deaths of great thoroughbreds like Blue Dick, of personal friends among the Southern gentry, and by extension, of a faltering social ideal.

The extent to which Noland viewed with distaste the decline of Southern gentility and the corresponding rise of the uncouth frontiersman is revealed in his introduction of a third set of letters, written to the *Spirit of the Times* by the drunken Jim Cole. Jim, in his ignorance, vulgarity, and virtual illiteracy is a thoroughly debased version of Pete Whetstone, stripped of Pete's imaginative wit, physical vigor, and keen eye for the sporting life. His obsession with fighting dogs and drunken riots is not so critical as the news that his friend Dan Looney is a Democratic candidate for the "Legislater." Southern gentlemen have been thrust from their positions of political power and responsibility, only to be replaced by the scum of Southern society.

It is fruitless to speculate whether Noland's declining health cut short his efforts to see any of his literary work published in book form. Certainly, by 1858, Noland's fellow contributors to the *Spirit of the Times*—Thorpe, Hooper, and Harris—had achieved this distinction. But even in their uncollected periodical form, Noland's letter sequences proved to be influential models of the characterizations, subjects, and literary techniques of the humor of the Old Southwest. Noland pioneered in the realistic depiction of local color, in the accurate transcription of frontier vernacular, and in the use of the framing device to establish his distinctive perspective on frontier life. Just as significant, perhaps, Noland's letter sequences helped to establish the peculiar social vision of much Southwestern humor, with its simultaneous attraction to the vitality of exploits in the backwoods and exposure of the boorishness and brutality of the people who lived there.

Other:

"Old Sense of Arkansas," in *The Big Bear of Arkansas, and Other Sketches, Illustrative of Characters and Incidents in the South and Southwest*, edited by William T. Porter (Philadelphia: Carey & Hart, 1845), pp. 143-145.

References:

Lorne Fienberg, "Colonel Noland of the *Spirit*: The Voices of a Gentleman in Southwest Humor," *American Literature*, 53 (May 1981): 232-245;

James R. Masterson, *Tall Tales of Arkansaw* (Boston: Chapman & Grimes, 1942);

Norris W. Yates, *William T. Porter and the Spirit of the Times* (Baton Rouge: Louisiana State University Press, 1957), pp. 26-29, 62-75, 179-180, 193-194.

Bill Nye

(25 August 1850-22 February 1896)

David B. Kesterson
North Texas State University

SELECTED BOOKS: *Bill Nye and Boomerang; or, The Tale of a Meek-Eyed Mule, and Some Other Literary Gems* (Chicago: Belford, Clarke, 1881);

Forty Liars, and Other Lies (Chicago: Belford, Clarke, 1882);

Boomerang Shots (London & New York: Ward, Lock, 1884);

Hits and Skits (London & New York: Ward, Lock, 1884);

Baled Hay. A Drier Book Than Walt Whitman's "Leaves o' Grass" (Chicago & New York: Belford, Clarke, 1884);

Bill Nye's Cordwood (Chicago: Rhodes & McClure, 1887);

Remarks (Chicago: A. E. Davis, 1887);

Nye and Riley's Railway Guide, by Nye and James Whitcomb Riley (Chicago: Dearborn, 1888); republished as *Nye and Riley's Wit and Humor* (New York: Neely, 1896); published again as *On the "Shoe-String" Limited* (Chicago: Thompson & Thomas, 1905);

Bill Nye's Chestnuts Old and New. Latest Gathering (Chicago & New York: Belford, Clarke, 1888);

Bill Nye's Thinks (Chicago: Dearborn, 1888);

An Almanac for 1891 (New York: Privately printed, 1890);

Bill Nye's Red Book (Chicago: Thompson & Thomas, 1891);

Sparks from the Pen of Bill Nye (Chicago & New York: Neely, 1891);

Bill Nye's History of the United States (Philadelphia: Lippincott, 1894; London: Chatto & Windus, 1894);

Bill Nye's History of England From the Druids to the Reign of Henry VIII (Philadelphia: Lippincott, 1896);

A Guest at the Ludlow and Other Stories (Indianapolis & Kansas City: Bowen-Merrill, 1897);

Bill Nye, His Book (Chicago: Smith, 1900);

Bill Nye's Grim Jokes (Chicago: Conkey, n.d.).

Edgar Wilson Nye was one of the late nineteenth century's most prominent humorists. His reputation so rivaled Mark Twain's that Twain was jealous of the younger man's talents. Except for one attempted novel, Nye mainly wrote short comic essays, sketches, and fictional vignettes, though he also produced two books of burlesque history, an almanac, and two Broadway plays. Moreover, he was a famous newspaper columnist, editor, and comic lecturer. He even tried his hand at poetry.

Though Nye was born in Shirley, Maine, he remained a Yankee for only a short time. At about two years of age, as he humorously tells it, he took his "parents by the hand and gently led them away" to Hudson, Wisconsin. It was in the Midwest that Nye was raised. While there he received brief formal education in a Hudson academy and a nearby military school, but his main learning derived from his various experiences as farmer, miller, teacher, and student of law. It was also during the Wisconsin years, 1852-1876, that Nye became interested in writing and tried his hand at journalism for local

Bill Nye

newspapers, such as the *Hudson Star* and *Chippewa Falls Weekly Herald*.

Nye liked Wisconsin, but he was struck with wanderlust. Having failed to secure positions on major Midwestern newspapers, he left the area at age twenty-six and headed west, stopping in the territory of Wyoming when his funds ran low. It was in Wyoming, over a seven-year period, that Nye found success and early fame. After a stint on the *Laramie City Sentinel*, he cofounded and became the first editor of the *Laramie Boomerang* (named for his pet mule), a daily and weekly newspaper for which he wrote a humor column. Nye was also busy in public life in Laramie, serving as justice of the peace, notary public, United States land commissioner, and postmaster. He even ran for the territorial legislature, though unsuccessfully. Admired for his ready wit and congenial nature, he was chosen to chair the "Forty Liars Club" that met for witty conversation and the exchange of tall tales. Also while in Laramie, in 1877, Nye married Clara Frances Smith from Illinois, his beloved "Fanny" or "Catalpa," and their first two children were born there.

Nye's lively columns for the *Boomerang*, consisting of comic sketches, short narratives, essays, and occasional burlesque poems, were so popular locally that their fame spread. Soon he was contributing to Cheyenne, Denver, even Detroit newspapers, as well as such renowned periodicals as *Peck's Sun*, *Puck*, and *Texas Siftings*. He was eager for his works to appear in book form, however, and while living in Laramie *Bill Nye and Boomerang* (1881) and *Forty Liars, and Other Lies* (1882) were published. *Baled Hay* (1884) was begun there. These books are largely collections of Nye's Wyoming newspaper sketches and essays. The brief selections are characterized by informal structure and relaxed tone. Though they lack the sharp control and fine chiseling of a Josh Billings aphoristic essay, they still evince artful design. Nye was a careful writer, even under pressures of journalistic deadlines.

Most of the selections in these three books relate to the American West in some way, treating such topics as Indians, Mormons, Chinese labor, mining and miners, the landscape and weather, and regional customs. If Nye is often critical of Indians and Mormons—he unfortunately had blatant prejudices—he is still genuinely fond of the West and even defends its ways against criticisms from the "effete" East. He praises Western women and lauds Wyoming's granting women's suffrage in 1890. In short, these books reveal a Nye much at home in the West and proud of being there despite

what he discerns as the area's climatic and cultural shortcomings. The sketches are also characteristic of Nye's brand of humor: the droll, inane observations and bizarre situations, use of understatement and anticlimax, occasional violent or "sick" humor, and an abundance of lively satire and irony.

Caricature of Nye by Eugene Zimmerman

Nye's residence in the West cannot be given enough emphasis, for much of the writing he did throughout the remainder of his career reflects the influence of the West. Certainly his humor was shaped by the harsh, rugged, often dangerous modes of living he witnessed there. Even his pen name came from the West. When he began writing for Wyoming newspapers, Western audiences' familiarity with Bret Harte's character Bill Nye in the popular poem "Plain Language from Truthful James" in a sense forced the name "Bill" on Nye, and the name stuck.

Nye was forced to leave the West in 1883 when he was stricken with cerebrospinal meningitis and had to retreat to lower altitudes. After penning a famous letter of resignation, "A Resign," from the Laramie post office facetiously addressed to the president of the United States, Nye and his family moved to Greeley, Colorado, where he convalesced, and then back to Wisconsin.

The Wisconsin interlude, 1883-1886, brought Nye's first attempts at playwriting—*Gas Fixtures* (1886) and *The Village Postmaster* (1886), the latter rewritten in 1891 as *The Cadi*—and his debut as comic platform lecturer. His lecturing flourished when he moved to New York in 1887 as humor columnist for the *New York World*. The *World* column increased his visibility and public demand, and Nye suddenly found himself one of the stars of the lecture circuit sponsored by Maj. James B. Pond's Lyceum Bureau. In his peak years he earned as much as $30,000. From 1888 through 1890 he joined company with Hoosier friend and poet James Whitcomb Riley; billed as the "Twins of Genius," they trooped over the country, delighting lyceum audiences with Riley's dialect poems and Nye's zany anecdotes and comic sketches.

Title page for Nye's first book

Nye's success as a stage comic was enhanced by his personal appearance and mannerisms: tall and angular with a shiny bald head, he assumed an utterly blank facial expression; a quaint, droll manner of speaking was accompanied by exaggerated gestures. After 1890, when Riley left the stage, Nye continued to lecture both alone and with other partners. He found lecturing stimulating but terri-

bly exhausting. In fact the rigorous demands of the circuit undoubtedly aggravated his already frail physical condition and led to his death.

While lecturing and writing weekly "letters," as he called his columns, for the *New York World*, Nye was producing more books. *Remarks* (1887) is another volume of essays and sketches on the order of his first three, but the writing is much fuller and more polished and mature, the pieces generally longer and more diverse in subject matter. The Western influence is still discernable, but so is Nye's experience as a stage artist who had learned a great deal about developing an oral sketch or essay in order to hold an audience's attention. One of Nye's best short burlesque narratives, "Twombley's Tale," a farce about the narrator's falling down a mine shaft, appears in *Remarks*.

The popular *Nye and Riley's Railway Guide* (1888) capitalized on the twosome's platform fame by offering representative material in printed form designed for the entertainment of railroad passengers. The same bonanza year saw the publication of *Bill Nye's Chestnuts Old and New* and *Bill Nye's Thinks*, volumes that contain selected newspaper columns and reprints from earlier books. The former is distinguished by many "Smaller Chestnuts," brief aphoristic pieces more on the order of a Josh Billings utterance than Nye's usual fare. They comment on such topics as the transiency of life, fame, gun control, firmness of resolve, the English joke, true marriage, and contemporary fiction. *Bill Nye's Thinks* is another book shaped for railway entertainment; its twenty-eight selections cover such topics as Nye's Washington, D.C., experiences, the sights of New York, the status of Indian affairs, the establishment of journalism schools, and farmers' problems with high tariffs. A variety of lively topics makes *Bill Nye's Thinks* one of the most enjoyable of Nye's books today. One nineteenth-century reviewer accurately observed that it "contains some of the popular humorist's happiest hits."

As part of his work for the *New York World* and, after 1891, the American Press Humorists Association, Nye was sent on attractive correspondent assignments here and abroad. In 1889 it was to Paris to cover the international exposition. A second trip abroad materialized in 1893; in London Nye was a guest at a celebration dinner for Emile Zola. He reported on the Chicago World's Fair in the summer of 1893, spent the winter of 1894 observing the workings of government in Washington, D.C., and early in 1895 steamed for the Bahamas, though the voyage proved nearly disastrous because of a shipwreck near Nassau. All these excursions, plus lec-

"Still Dropping in Occasionally from the Back Districts," drawing by F. Opper

ture experiences and other activities of Nye's constitute the material in the newspaper columns in the *World* and some eighty syndicated newspapers from 1887 to 1896. It is a rich record that serves as an index to the mature Nye's interests and literary methods while at the same time serving as a fascinating guide to the interests of the age. These writings of roughly his last ten years are his most varied and sophisticated.

Nye bid farewell to New York City early in 1891, moving his family to the North Carolina hills. He had grown tired of the bustle of urban life and the cold Northern climate. Before moving, however, he arranged with *World* owners Joseph Pulitzer and John Cockerill for the continued publication of his columns. Later in the year his Sunday "letter" was bought for syndication when a managerial change in the *World* office caused Nye to become disenchanted with the paper and dissolve his contract.

For the remaining five years of his life, Nye's headquarters and dateline were first Skyland, then Arden, North Carolina, two small hamlets near Asheville. At Arden Nye built his commodious rural retreat, Buck Shoals, on 100 wooded acres of land adjoining the vast Biltmore manor of George W. Vanderbilt II, a proximity that prompted several satirical columns by Nye. He became such an advocate of western North Carolina that some of his columns read like chamber of commerce propaganda; he boasts about the climate, wildlife, natural growth, people, and customs of the area.

The North Carolina years were Nye's most productive literarily in both quantity and variety of output. He wrote two popular books of burlesque history, a major (and final) volume of essays and sketches, a novel (though the manuscript was lost in the Nassau shipwreck), one Broadway play and the libretto for another, all the while continuing to write his weekly columns, lecture, and travel as a correspondent.

Nye's dramatic success followed close on the heels of his move south. *The Cadi*, the rewritten 1886 *Village Postmaster*, ran for 125 performances on Broadway late in 1891. Though the text does not survive, reviews show that the play was a three-act comedy featuring a Nye-like persona, played by actor Thomas Q. Seabrooke. It appears to have been a largely autobiographical treatment of Nye's life as a public servant. Nye was less fortunate with *The Stag Party*, a musical travesty coauthored with dramatist Paul M. Potter. The play ran for twelve shaky performances in December 1895 before folding. Critically it was panned; no copy survives, but the play apparently failed because of a ridiculous plot, a poor combination of humor and music, and the lack of a Nye persona to attract public interest.

The most distinguished literary accomplishments late in his career were the two books of burlesque history, *Bill Nye's History of the United States* (1894) and *Bill Nye's History of England From the Druids to the Reign of Henry VIII* (1896). These books were a logical culmination of his lifelong use of satire and interest in historical events and famous people. The United States volume, spanning American history from Columbus's discovery to Grover Cleveland's administration, contains some of Nye's best writing. With a lively, polished style, Nye is at his peak in description, narration, and analysis. The whole book exudes his enthusiasm for history—so much so that he sometimes forgets to be funny, as in the long section on the Civil War. Despite its burlesque of pedantry and historical legend, the book contains serious themes, especially that of the superiority of democracy over monarchy or any type of tyranny.

The United States history was so successful that Nye's publisher, J. B. Lippincott, asked for a companion volume. Thus in 1895 Nye began writing *Bill Nye's History of England*, a book that begins with pre-Roman England and stops in the middle of the reign of Henry VIII. The narrative would have progressed to the late nineteenth century had Nye not fallen ill and died before its completion. The book presents a rather harsh view of early England, emphasizing social, religious, and political turmoil and monarchial license. Absent are many of the burlesque devices of the United States volume. What humor there is lies mostly in Nye's witty expression and exaggeration of historical events. Both of the history books are fully and cleverly illustrated.

When Nye died in February 1896 at age forty-five, his final book of essays and sketches, *A Guest at the Ludlow* (1897), was in press. This book enjoyed critical and public acclaim. Most of the twenty-eight selections are reprinted from Nye's *New York World* columns. The range of subjects is broad—from a sketch of New York's Ludlow Street jail to essays on change and growth in American society—and reflects Nye's broad interests and experiences. The variety and high quality of the material make the book enjoyable reading today.

Nye's writings were so popular that during his lifetime there were pirated editions of his works, and after his death publishers continued to capitalize on his fame by bringing out both new and reprinted collections of his essays under such titles as *Nye and Riley's Wit and Humor* (1901) and *The Funny Fellow's Grab-Bag* (1903), the latter a collection of essays by Nye and other humorists.

Nye was generally regarded by his contemporaries as a genial humorist who looked on humanity and its problems with sympathy and keen insight. He had the rare ability to see the lighter side of his own misfortunes and discomforts. In Laramie City, for example, when the *Boomerang* had the

dubious distinction of being housed above a livery stable, Nye erected a sign that directed visitors either to climb the stairs at the rear of the stable or "twist the tail of the iron-gray mule and take the elevator." And during bouts of serious illness, he continued to compose some of his funniest Sunday "letters."

"Nye as the Duke of Sandy Bottom," drawing by F. Opper

There is a darker side to Nye's humor, however, that has often gone undetected. His view of life could be grim, even cynical, at times. He sometimes speaks of life as a "pathway to the grave" and ponders the transiency of life and the vanity of human wishes. He is also occasionally harsh and cutting in his humor, attacking individuals or groups and indulging in invective. Even cruel or sick humor is sometimes evident, especially in his Western writings. Thus Nye emerges as a complex individual who employs humor both as a means of entertainment and as a way of approaching life's harshest realities.

In the twentieth century, Nye's reputation has declined along with the fortunes of the other literary comedians. It is hard to believe now that he was once so popular that critic Will M. Clemens in 1882 raved over Nye's having "written a larger quantity and a better quality of first-class, genuine humor, than any other funny man in America." As tastes changed, Nye's popularity declined. With recent renewed appreciation of the literary comedians, however, there is an increased interest in him. Moreover, the *Laramie Boomerang* has begun reprinting his old columns, and several books have appeared which deal with Nye's life and works. It is unlikely that Bill Nye will ever again be a household name, but much of his writing still provides lively entertainment and pertinent views on a wide range of subjects.

Plays:

The Cadi, New York, Union Square Theatre, 21 September 1891;

The Stag Party, by Nye and Paul M. Potter, New York, Garden Theatre, 17 December 1895.

Other:

His Fleeting Ideal: A Romance of Baffled Hypnotism, a composite novel with chapter 12 by Nye (New York: J. S. Ogilvie, 1890).

Periodical Publications:

"The Autobiography of a Justice of the Peace," *Century*, 43 (November 1891): 60-67;

"Autobiography of an Editor," *Century*, 45 (November 1892): 156-159;

" 'Bill Nye' on the Art of Lecturing," *Century*, 80 (June 1910): 316-319.

References:

Walter Blair, "The Background of Bill Nye in American Humor," Ph.D. dissertation, University of Chicago, 1931;

Louis Hasley, ed., *The Best of Bill Nye's Humor* (New Haven: College & University Press, 1972);

David B. Kesterson, *Bill Nye (Edgar Wilson Nye)* (Boston: Twayne, 1981);

Kesterson, *Bill Nye: The Western Writings* (Boise: Boise State University, 1976);

T. A. Larson, ed., *Bill Nye's Western Humor* (Lincoln: University of Nebraska Press, 1968).

Dorothy Parker

(22 August 1893-7 June 1967)

Thomas Grant
University of Hartford

SELECTED BOOKS: *Men I'm Not Married To*, by Parker, and *Women I'm Not Married To*, by Franklin P. Adams (Garden City: Doubleday, Page, 1922);

Enough Rope (New York: Boni & Liveright, 1926);

Sunset Gun (New York: Boni & Liveright, 1928);

Close Harmony, or The Lady Next Door, by Parker and Elmer Rice (New York & London: French, 1929);

Laments for the Living (New York: Viking, 1930; London: Longmans, Green, 1930);

Death and Taxes (New York: Viking, 1931);

After Such Pleasures (New York: Viking, 1933; London: Longmans, Green, 1934);

Collected Poems: Not So Deep As A Well (New York: Viking, 1936; London: Hamilton, 1937); republished as *The Collected Poetry of Dorothy Parker* (New York: Modern Library, 1944);

Here Lies (New York: Viking, 1939; London: Longmans, Green, 1939); republished as *The Collected Stories of Dorothy Parker* (New York: Modern Library, 1942);

The Viking Portable Library Dorothy Parker (New York: Viking, 1944); republished as *The Indispensable Dorothy Parker* (New York: The Book Society, 1944); published again as *Selected Short Stories* (New York: Editions for the Armed Services, 1944); revised and enlarged as *The Portable Dorothy Parker* (New York: Viking, 1973); republished as *The Collected Dorothy Parker* (London: Duckworth, 1973);

The Ladies of the Corridor, by Parker and Arnaud d'Usseau (New York: Viking, 1954);

Constant Reader (New York: Viking, 1970); republished as *A Month of Saturdays* (London & Basingstoke: Macmillan, 1971).

There was a time when it seemed that all things bright, clever, or malicious spoken in New York were ascribed to Dorothy Parker. That time was the 1920s, when wit was as plentiful as bathtub gin and, when dispensed by her, just as lethal. "You know," she was remembered as saying among friends about an accomplished contemporary with amorous proclivities, "that woman speaks 18 languages? And she can't say 'No' in any of them." When conversation turned to an actress who had fallen and broken a leg in London, Dorothy Parker became distraught: "Oh, how terrible! She must have done it sliding down a barrister." She could mock herself as well. "One more drink," goes her famous party line, "and I'd be under the host." Even in later years she could be heard delivering memorably witty lines with undiminished spontaneity. "I had an office so tiny," she recalled in an interview about the office she shared with Robert Benchley, "that an inch smaller and it would have been adultery." When Tuesday Weld and her mother moved onto her Hollywood street, she told visitors: "Have you met Tuesday Weld's mother, Wednesday, yet?" "Don't worry about Alan," she said after her divorce from second husband, Alan Campbell, "Alan will always land on somebody's feet." In *An Unfinished Woman*, Lillian Hellman said that she enjoyed Dorothy Parker more than any other woman: "for me, the wit was never as attractive as the comment, often startling, always sudden, as if a curtain had opened and you had a brief and brilliant glance into what you would never have found for yourself."

This exceptionally bright woman was born Dorothy Rothschild in West End, New Jersey, in 1893 to a Scottish Presbyterian mother who, she felt, deserted her by dying in her infancy and a wealthy Jewish father who regularly, among other cruelties she remembered, hammered her wrists at table for the slightest infraction. According to John Keats's biography, *You Might As Well Live: The Life and Times of Dorothy Parker*, she was a late, unexpected arrival in a loveless family, from which a stepmother, another Scottish Presbyterian, sent her to a Catholic convent school in order to save her soul from the curse of being a Jew's daughter. "Mongrel" was the title she selected for the autobiography she never got around to writing. About adolescence spent among the nuns, she remembered only her departure: "I was fired from there, finally, for a lot of things, among them my insistence that the Immaculate Conception was spontaneous combustion." Actually, she probably bit her tongue more often than she admitted, since she was accepted at the prestigious and progressive Miss Dana's School in Morristown, New Jersey, where she thrived under the rigorous curriculum that stressed the classics, creative writing, elocution, and discussion

of current events. According to Keats, she was remembered as a diminutive, demure, but exceptionally brilliant member of the class of 1911.

Dorothy Parker

Little is known about the next five years except that Dorothy Rothschild lived in a Manhattan boardinghouse where she supported herself by playing the piano at night in a dancing school. She began writing poetry in convent school and during this time she was collecting magazine rejection slips, until 1915 when one of her verses was finally accepted by *Vogue* editor Frank Crowninshield, who gave her a job on the magazine writing captions for fashion illustrations. Successful captions required the inventor to design a verbal line as succinct, yet as striking and high-toned, as the visual line of the fashion apparel they were meant to help sell. Several of hers remain memorable: "Brevity is the Soul of Lingerie, as the Petticoat said to the Chemise"; "This little pink dress will win you a beau"; "Right Dress! For milady's motor jaunt."

Crowninshield was so delighted by his new discovery that in 1917 he invited her to join *Vanity Fair*, a more sophisticated, primarily literary, magazine and, at the time, the nation's arbiter of taste. He elevated her to drama critic. That year she met and married Edwin Pond Parker II of an old

Hartford, Connecticut, family and thus completed the transformation of Dorothy Rothschild into Dorothy Parker—"I married him to change my name," she confessed not long after—and escaped from the "mongrel" past she later said she despised. As a rising young journalist with a name she considered acceptable, "Mrs. Parker," as she preferred to be called, became the first, and for a time the only woman among the regulars of the so-called Algonquin Round Table who met for lunch at the Algonquin Hotel. Original members included Franklin P. Adams, Alexander Woollcott, Heywood Broun, and George S. Kaufman, and later members included Robert Benchley, Robert Sherwood, Edna Ferber, and Harold Ross, who in 1925 founded the *New Yorker*. Acceptance into the group required of tyros such as Parker a talent for the devasting phrase dryly delivered; the reward would be the honor of being quoted in an influential daily column, such as Adams's "The Conning Tower." Significantly, Parker was quoted most frequently. Word games became a special luncheon challenge and in these, too, she was the Round Table's King Arthur rather than its Guinevere. When neither Benchley nor Sherwood could, for example, hatch a witty sentence with the word "horticulture," she volunteered: "You can lead a horticulture, but you can't make her think." Her sly, scornful barbs, all the more devastating for being delivered by so small and outwardly gentle a lady, quickly made her enemies among the powerful. When Parker wrote a negative review of a performance by Billie Burke in 1920, Burke's husband, influential impresario Florenz Ziegfeld prevailed upon Frank Crowninshield to fire Parker. Fellow *Vanity Fair* columnists Robert Sherwood and Robert Benchley quit in sympathy.

Unemployment for the three was, however, short lived. Parker was hired by *Ainslee's* to write a monthly theater column, which allowed her time to free-lance. She contributed poetry and character sketches in prose to *Ladies' Home Journal, Saturday Evening Post* and, over a three-year span, ninety-one pieces to *Life*, a satirical magazine imitative of *Punch*, whose contributors included Benchley, Sherwood, Donald Ogden Stewart, Don Marquis, and Christopher Morley. In 1924, she coauthored with Elmer Rice a domestic comedy, *Close Harmony* (1929), about two frustrated people whose fumbling attempts at an adulterous affair frighten them back to their mates. Parker wrote a sprawling first draft that includes some sprightly dialogue, and Elmer Rice shaped it into a play; but it closed on Broadway after four weeks. Later in the decade, she wrote a

monthly column for *McCall's*, she reviewed books for the *New Yorker* between 1927 and 1931 under the by-line "Constant Reader," and in 1931 she substituted for Robert Benchley as the *New Yorker's* drama critic. In her book reviews she championed rare talents such as Ring Lardner, Dashiell Hammett, Elinor Wylie, and Ernest Hemingway, and deflated merely popular ones, such as William Lyon Phelps and Elinor Glyn. Of a book by popular lady wit Margot Asquith, Parker declared: "The affair between Margot Asquith and Margot Asquith will live as one of the prettiest love stories in all literature."

Caricature of Parker by Hirschfeld

Parker's scathing wit was likely sharpened by the two years she spent under pressure at *Vogue* forced to dream up witty lines to decorate the years' changing fashions. But the epigrammatic clarity and precision of her style was forged, as Arthur Kinney has shown, from her study and imitation of classical Latin poets begun at Miss Dana's School and perfected by her reading of classical imitators among her contemporaries. Roman wit suffuses her own, abundantly demonstrated in her poetry. From Catullus, by way of Housman, she learned to express the disappointments of love in deceptively simple, conversational, yet elegantly polished and succinct songs that at their best strike the reader as both unabashedly confessional and ironically distanced in tone. Hence, "Summary":

> Every love's the love before
> In a duller dress.
> That's the measure of my lore—
> Here's my bitterness:
> Would I knew a little more,
> Or very much less!

From Horace, by way of the Horatian imitations of Eugene Field and F. P. Adams, she learned to contrive cocky but concise mock odes that build upon initial hyperboles and end with an ironic flourish, such as in "Godspeed":

> Oh, seek, my love, your newer way;
> I'll not be left in sorrow.
> So long as I have yesterday,
> Go take your damned tomorrow!

From Martial, by way of the English epigram tradition, she learned the severely compressed economy of hyperrestricted form, as shown in "The Flaw in Paganism":

> Drink and dance and laugh and lie,
> Love, the reeling midnight through,
> For tomorrow we shall die!
> (But, alas, we never do.)

From them all, she learned wry Roman resignation, a deeply pagan sense of man's, and woman's, limitations. And from other female poets, Edna St. Vincent Millay and Elinor Wylie, both steeped in the Roman poets, she acquired fluency in longer forms, such as the sonnet, and, through their work, found her own personal voice. Hence, "On Being a Woman":

> Why is it, when I am in Rome,
> I'd give an eye to be at home,
> But when on native earth I be,
> My soul is sick for Italy?
>
> And why with you, my love, my lord,
> Am I spectacularly bored,
> Yet do you up and leave me—then
> I scream to have you back again?

These classical and modern influences per-vade Parker's collections of poetry, beginning with *Enough Rope* (1926). This slim volume was a sensational best-seller, especially for a book of poems. Throughout, she shows herself to be technically accomplished in several poetic modes: the lyric, the Horatian ode, ballade, ballad stanza, sonnet, epigram, and even epitaph. A classicist, she seems to relish the challenge to adhere to the requisites of traditional form. Her prevailing subject is love's labor's lost (or threatened loss) usually examined at the moment when initial disappointments have for the woman passed into rueful, self-deprecating humor, as in "One Perfect Rose":

> A single flow'r he sent me, since we met.
>   All tenderly his messenger he chose;
> Deep-hearted, pure, with scented dew still
>   wet—
>   One perfect rose.
>
> I knew the language of the floweret;
>   "My fragile leaves," it said, "his heart
>   enclose."
> Love long has taken for his amulet
>   One perfect rose.
>
> Why is it no one ever sent me yet
>   One perfect limousine, do you sup-
>   pose?
> Ah no, it's always just my luck to get
>   One perfect rose.

Although a man of limited sensitivity is politely but justly abused, as well as the speaker herself for foolishly awaiting his overtures—that curtailed refrain damns with faint praise—Parker is really attacking the sentimental proprieties which hold the speaker, as well as all women, in her proper place. Hence, she knowingly mimics the cloying cliches that embalm true affections: "deep-hearted, pure, with scented dew," "My fragile leaves . . ."—the trite "language of the floweret" which decorates florist shop missives and greeting cards. The speaker's wish for a more functional gift ("one perfect limousine") nicely betrays the transparencies of her suitor's polite evasions, just as the poem itself burlesques trite romantic lyrics. The subtle enemy of love is hollow conventions hypocritically preserved in insincere expressions. In "Unfortunate Coincidence," the enemy is the seductive vocabulary of vows:

> By the time you swear you're his,
>   Shivering and sighing,

And he vows his passion is
    Infinite, undying—
Lady, make a note of this:
    One of you is lying.

In "Comment," it is the luring promises of songs:

Oh, life is a glorious cycle of song.
    A medley of extemporanea;
And love is a thing that can never go wrong;
    And I am Marie of Roumania.

Sometimes, Parker succumbs herself to romantic cliches, as in "A Well-Worn Story," which seems only to be itself well-worn—the posture affected, the cadences mechanical, the images sentimental:

Together we trod the secret lane
And walked the muttering town.
I wore my heart like a wet, red stain
On the breast of a velvet gown.

When she dwells lugubriously upon the plight of the spurned woman, rather than wrench from sorrow some momentary triumph in mordant wit, Parker falls back upon the polite jargon of Housman and Millay at their worst.

Parker's second slim volume, *Sunset Gun* (1928), was nearly as popular as her first. She continued to experiment in traditional forms, including a daring cycle of epigrams, "A Pig's-Eye View of Literature," a sort of barnyard glance up at the classics. Lesser luminaries naturally inspire the truer lampoon:

Upon the work of Walter Landor
I am unfit to write with candor.
If you can read it, well and good;
But as for me, I never could.

She continues, too, her well-informed assault upon empty vows and false promises peddled in popular songs and whispered in attentive ears. In "Theory," a weary woman knocks her head for the dumbness of her heart:

Into love and out again,
    Thus I went, and thus I go.
Spare your voice, and hold your pen—
    Well and bitterly I know
All the songs were ever sung,
    All the words were ever said;
Could it be, when I was young,
    Some one dropped me on my head?

In "For a Lady Who Must Write Verse," Parker attacks vacuous but facile poets:

Let your rhymes be tinsel treasures,
    Strung and seen and thrown aside.
Drill your apt and docile measures
    Sternly as you drill your pride.

Parker can be deeply reflective too; when she writes about the dichotomy between the claims of the heart and those of the head her wit becomes startlingly metaphysical. The exquisitely wrought "Interior" echoes Emily Dickinson, save for the final line:

Her mind lives in a quiet room,
    A narrow room, and tall,
With pretty lamps to quench the gloom
    And mottoes on the wall.

There all the things are waxen neat
    And set in decorous lines;
And there are posies, round and sweet,
    And little, straightened vines.

Her mind lives tidily, apart
    From cold and noise and pain,
And bolts the door against her heart,
    Out wailing in the rain.

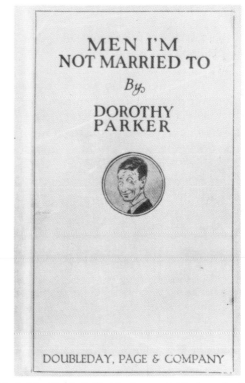

MEN I'M
NOT MARRIED TO
By
DOROTHY
PARKER

DOUBLEDAY, PAGE & COMPANY

Dust jacket for Parker's first book, an upside-down book bound with Women I'm Not Married To

The wailings of *Enough Rope* diminish in *Sunset Gun*, but so too does the cockiness, the disarming whimsy, the wry skepticism. By the time *Death and Taxes* (1931), her third slim volume, was published, Parker's sadness had given way to bitter cynicism, that of a mind which had settled for the only certainties, the two of her title. In "Cherry White," the humor, such as it is, is macabre:

> I never see that prettiest thing—
> A cherry bough gone white with Spring—
> But what I think, "How gay 'twould be
> To hang me from a flowering tree."

She continued, however, to experiment with traditional forms, including another cycle of epigrams, all shadowed by a funereal title, "Tombstones in the Starlight." The best retain a glimmer of saving wit, as in "Sanctuary":

> My land is bare of chattering folk;
> The clouds are low along the ridges,
> And sweet's the air with curly smoke
> From all my burning bridges.

The wit fades in "The Lady's Reward" as the cocky smirk resolves into a despairing grimace:

> Never serious be, nor true,
> And your wish will come to you—
> And if that makes you happy, kid,
> You'll be the first it ever did.

Parker continued to linger over grief, despair, and death, too close to her own experience, as her stories better revealed. When she published her three collections of poetry in one volume in 1936, with some deletions and five additions, she entitled it with the aptly funereal phrase, *Not So Deep As A Well*—from dying Mercutio's sardonic quip (*Romeo and Juliet*, act 3).

In an article written in 1937, Parker disagreed with the belief "that ridicule is the most effective weapon"; as she put it, "there are things that never have been funny, and never will be. And I know that ridicule may be a shield, but it is not a weapon." Ridicule, so exquisitely phrased in her best poetry, was her sharpest weapon against proper manners and hypocritical observances; but the acerbic personae who speak her mind also know they are not superior to the dumbest of either sex. In that knowledge, wit becomes a defense, first against pain and then despair. The contradictions inherent in

being a bright woman vexed by a heart yearning for what the mind must mock gives uncommon subtlety to her verse and distinguishes her poetry from the glut of flapper verse of the 1920s. Her technical skill in translating classical forms into a modern idiom and the complexity of her wit prompted Arthur Kinney to call Parker "the best epigrammatic poet in our country, in this century."

Parker's evolving mastery as a social satirist is given fuller rein in her prose, particularly her stories published between 1922 and 1957, beginning with "Just a Pretty Little Picture" in the December 1922 issue of Mencken and Nathan's *Smart Set*. When the *New Yorker* was launched in 1925, she contributed stories, actually "character" sketches, beginning with "Oh, He's Charming!" in the first issue (16 February 1925); her last story, "The Banquet of Crow," was also published in the *New Yorker* (14 December 1957). Brendan Gill has recently insisted that Parker was one who "helped to invent what the world came to call the 'New Yorker' short story." She was certainly first to map the territory. To the woman with upper-class pretensions in "A Certain Lady" (*New Yorker*, 28 February 1925), geography is all: "Although she lives as far from Park Avenue as it is possible to do and still keep out of Jersey, Mrs. Legion is cozily conversant of all the comings and goings, or what have you, of Avenue dwellers." She populated the narrow neighborhood with memorable Manhattanites, including the obligatory psychiatrist, and enjoyed deflating their pretensions in devastating phrases: "It was a big factor in Dr. Langham's success that she had the ability to make wet straws seem like sturdy logs to the nearly submerged" ("The Banquet of Crow"). In addition to her attentive ear for modulating inflections developed over the years, Parker has an exceptionally alert eye for detecting personality draped by well-cut clothes. Her men are walking fashion ads, *New Yorker* mannequins surely, and about as complex: "From the young man's coat, more surely than from his palm, might be read the ingredients of his character. Whimsy peeped around the lapels of that coat; balance showed in the double march of its buttons; and the color of its material, the dreamy blue of a spring midnight, confessed a deep strain of sentiment. The face above the jacket was neat and spare, and wore, at the moment, a look of pleading" ("The Young Woman in Green Lace"). Her women seldom just weep; they literally come apart: "The color left her cheeks and collected damply in her nose, and rims of vivid pink grew around her pale eyelashes. Even her hair became affected; it came away from the pins, and stray ends of it wandered limply over her neck" ("Mr. Durant").

The familiar features of the *New Yorker* story—the striving characters, the distilled, acerbic style, the acute metropolitan sense of place—are stamped in these lines. Parker's talents for prose portraiture minutely rendered evolved naturally from her mastery of epigrammatic style and method. She concentrated upon a few characters whose self-absorption hampers or prevents true communication, leading to misunderstanding, estrangement or, worse, loneliness. She seldom strayed from the closed interiors of high-rise apartments and dwelt upon those casual, brief encounters in which apparent harmonies suddenly unravel into discord. She captured the strained gestures and banal conversations that lay bare inner anxieties, and thereby she opened up desperate lives to our sympathy as well as our scorn.

Parker's first collection of stories was *Laments for the Living* (1930), which, as the title suggests, is similar thematically to her poetry. As in "New York to Detroit," a sketch in dialogue about a bad phone connection used by a couple to excuse a faltering affair, these stories tend to be concerned with bad connections, missed or unfulfilled opportunities. In "The Sexes," a suitor is demoralized by his date's unfounded jealousy; when he tries to be reconciled, she turns his candor to her advantage: " 'Well, the minute you came in the room,' she said, 'you started making such a fuss over Florence Leaming. . . . You two seemed to be having such a wonderful time together, goodness knows I wouldn't have butted in for anything.'

" 'My God,' he said, 'this what's-her-name girl came up and began talking to me before I even saw anybody else, and what could I do? I couldn't sock her in the nose, could I?'

" 'I certainly didn't see you try,' she said." Parker's subject is never the sexes embattled, but most often couples, as in "The Sexes," maneuvering for advantage, each driven to preserve self-esteem by pride, whether the virtue or the vice. Frequently, their success will require the sacrifice of what they seek—love, of course, but also honor. In "The Last Tea," a couple linger over their breakup, both absorbed in saving self-respect by talking vacuously about the attention each is being given by new, more accommodating mates. In the well-known soliloquy, "A Telephone Call," the same searching girl awaits a mate, and appears willing to strike a Faustian wager with God: "I think he must still like me a little. He

couldn't have called me 'darling' twice today, if he didn't still like me a little . . . You see, God, if You would just let him telephone me, I wouldn't have to ask You anything more. I would be sweet to him, I would be gay. I would be just the way I used to be, and then he would love me again." Contemporary readers may find such fawning too appallingly slavish, except that the girl knows all too well how men, if only unwittingly, often require it of her: "I don't think he even knows how he makes me feel. I wish he could know, without my telling him. They don't like you to tell them they've made you cry. They don't like you to tell them you're unhappy because of them. If you do, they think you're possessive and exacting. And then they hate you. They hate you whenever you say anything you really think. You always have to keep playing little games." This fluttering flapper shows herself to be more astute than she can let on, least of all to the man whose call she foolishly awaits. As in the poetry, established proprieties are Parker's enemies. The very form of the girl's confession, the soliloquy, dramatizes her powerlessness and reinforces her sense of a woman's dilemma as she is torn between the truths she knows and, should the phone ring, the lies she is ready to tell.

The rueful consequences of not abiding by the rules of the "little games" are worked out in the dramatic monologue, "Just A Little One," in which an apparently self-assured flapper visits a speakeasy with Fred, and, at first, comes on as flip and flashy: "Oh, I like this place better and better, now that my eyes are getting accustomed to it. You mustn't let them tell you this lighting system is original with them, Fred; they got the idea from the Mammoth Cave. This is you sitting next to me, isn't it? Oh, you can't fool me. I'd know that knee anywhere." Gradually, and after a few drinks, the girl's brash confidence declines as Fred's preoccupation with another girl rises, thus making her depend on her wit more desperately, which in turn becomes increasingly more acerbic, until she begins to sound like Parker over lunch at the Algonquin: "Was Edith here with you, Thursday night? This place must be very becoming to her. Next to being in a coal mine, I can't think of anywhere she could go that the light would be more flattering to that pan of hers. . . . Now to me, Edith looks like something that would eat her young. Dresses well? *Edith* dresses well? Are you trying to kid me, Fred, at my age. . . ? You mean those clothes of hers are *intentional*? My heavens, I always thought she was on her way out of a burning building." Her barbs, dipped in jealousy, hardly faze Fred, whose silence throughout denotes his power, his superiority. Again, dramatic form enfeebles a woman, isolating her in her very words. They poison her hopes too, thus proving that men "hate you whenever you say anything you really think." Knowing she has botched the rules, she collapses into self-pity, ending up a whimpering drunk pleading absurdly with Fred to buy her a horse, "just a little one."

Parker's omnisciently told stories from *Laments for the Living* tend to be more savage. Not just follies but hypocrisies abound, which require her unmediated scorn. In "Arrangement in Black and White," an obnoxious socialite eager to meet the latest black celebrity betrays her prejudices by her insistence that she has none. Her many gaucheries are forecast in the first lines: "The woman with the pink velvet poppies twined round the assisted gold of her hair traversed the crowded room at an interesting gait combining a skip with a sidle . . ." "Mr. Durant" concerns a married man's cruelty to his secretary whose affair with him ends in an abortion he has demanded but will not totally pay for. "Elimination of bother," says the narrator, "was the main thing." His heartlessness is shrewdly prefigured by his "whimsy": "Mr. Durant had the odd desire to catch his thumb-nail in the present end of the run [of the secretary's stocking], and to draw it on down until the slim line of the dropped stitches reached to the top of her low shoe." Later, at home, when a stray dog is taken in as a family pet, the righteous Mr. Durant recoils in disgust, oblivious of both his hypocrisy and his callousness: "You have a female around, and you know what happens. All the males in the neighborhood will be running after her. First thing you know, she'd be having puppies—and the way they look after they've had them, and all! That would be nice for the children to see, wouldn't it? I should think you'd think of the children, Fan." In "Big Blonde," the focus shifts to the girl, a model who settles for apparent security with a man whose own insecurity leads them both to drink; both slide separately into alcoholism and she ends up a much used, self-loathing party girl. This is a grim tale about a "good sport" who turns into "a rotten sport," spoiling men's games and ruining her own life. Although this story won the O. Henry Short Story Award of 1929 and has been much anthologized since, the fall of Hazel Morse is rendered so unrelentingly brutal—by an outraged, overbearing narrator—that her slide into despair seems preordained, predictable, and finally only pathetic. When Parker's narratives venture beyond the accounts of brief encounters, her stories turn into melodramas.

Parker's second volume of stories, *After Such Pleasures* (1933), shows her less reliant upon editorial omniscience and more willing to allow dramatic scenes to unfold through the play of voices written for her characters. The title comes from John Donne's "Farewell to Love": "Ah cannot wee, / As well as cocks and lyons jocund be, / After such pleasure?" Most of these stories answer no, but the focus as well as the art, as in the first collection of stories, is in the games people play, the tyranny of rules and the futile attempts to break free of them. Some stories are lightly amusing, others sardonic, a few corrosive. In the dramatic monologue "The Waltz," social convention dictates that the girl not only accept an invitation to dance, but say so with the approved deference: *"Shall we? Oh, yes, it's a waltz. Mind? Why, I'm simply thrilled."* To herself, however, she fumes: "I most certainly will *not* dance with you, I'll see you in hell first. Why, thank you, I'd like to awfully, but I'm having labor pains. Oh, yes, *do* let's dance together—it's so nice to meet a man who isn't a scaredy-cat about catching my beri-beri." Imaginary rejoinders make up her arsenal of weapons, but social courtesy prevents their deployment. A worse fate than a waltz awaits her should she have to return to an emptied table and actually *talk* to this "triple threat." "A girl's best friend," quipped Parker, "is her mutter"; but talk is her worst. When the girl friend in "Dusk Before Fireworks" risks her mate's displeasure by disclosing her jealousy, he turns the reassuring words of love she really seeks against her, as if to shame her precisely for her honesty: "Kit, you ought to know, without my saying it. You know. It's this feeling you *have* to say things—that's what spoils everything."

The penalty for honesty in a woman is long hours spent alone being brilliantly witty. In "The Little Hours," a soliloquy which itself confirms a woman's isolation, an unidentified woman is afflicted by insomnia worsened by a plague of bad rhymes: "Yes, and you want to know what got me into this mess? Going to bed at ten o'clock, that's what. That spells ruin. Early to bed, and you'll wish you were dead. Bed before eleven, nuts before seven." Notably, Parker burdens her alter ego with her own splendid talent for witticisms: ". . . let them keep their La Rochefoucauld, and see if I care. I'll stick to La Fontaine. Only I'd be better company if I could quit thinking that La Fontaine married Alfred Lunt. . . . And I'll stay off Verlaine too; he was always chasing Rimbauds." The residue of humor turned sour is the vinegar of sentiment, revealed in a companion soliloquy called "Sentiment." A woman of the same personality, homeward bound in a taxi, ruminates during the trip over an affair just ended, and her desperate wit dissolves into forced epigrams sprung from lines by favorite romantics: "It's sentimental to know that you cannot bear to see the places where once all was well with you, that you cannot bear reminders of a dead loveliness. Sorrow is tranquility remembered in emotion. It—oh, I think that's quite good. 'Remembered in emotion'—that's a really nice reversal. I wish I could say it to him."

read the papers, but nothing in them except that Mona Wheatley is in Reno charging *intolerable cruelty*. Called up Jim Wheatley to see if he had anything to do tonight, but he was tied up. Finally got Ollie Martin. *Can't* decide whether to wear the white satin or the black chiffon or the yellow pebble crepe. Simply *wrecked* to the *core* about my finger nail. Can't *bear* it." In "Lady with a Lamp," a woman just recovering from the trauma of an abortion in the hospital is visited by a friend whose sympathy quickly gives way to chastisements that reduce the weary patient to hysterical tears: "Well, Mona! Well, you poor sick thing, you! Ah, you look so little and

Marc Connelly, Dorothy Parker, Harpo Marx, and Robert Sherwood, from Life's *"News-Stand" parody issue*

In other interior monologues from this second collection, the self-centered social climbers of earlier stories return, but to condemn themselves. Parker burlesques their mindless blather, exaggerating their inflections to reveal women truly driven by the need to secure social and emotional advantage. The haughty socialite of "From the Diary of a New York Lady" makes a crisis of a cracked fingernail and the insufferable archness of her tone is perfectly inappropriate to her actual condition. She is desperate for a date: "Started to

white and *little*, you do, lying there in that great big bed. That's what you do—go and look so childlike and pitiful nobody'd have the heart to scold you. And I ought to scold you." The cloying voice deadens all feeling as it drones endlessly. Mona's "friend" blunders on, scolding self-righteously, oblivious of her harming effects, or cruelly eager to foment them: "Oh, I wish you'd get over that Garry McVicker. If you could just meet some nice, sweet, considerate man, and get married to him, and have your own lovely place—and with your *taste*, Mona!

—and maybe have a couple of children . . . why, Mona Morrison, are you crying? Oh, you've got a cold? You've got a cold, too?"

The need to alienate affections and destroy true compassion is also powerfully evoked in "Glory in the Daytime," an omnisciently told tale of much greater subtlety than "Big Blonde." Parker juxtaposes three kinds of womanly affection: Mrs. Murdock's girlish adoration of Lily Wynton, a famous actress, Hallie Noyes's lesbian attachment to the actress; and the actress's utter devotion to herself. When Mrs. Murdock is invited to tea by Miss Noyes to meet Lily Wynton, she discovers a desperate hag, decayed in body, twisted in mind and full of haughty disdain: " 'What a clever little face,' said Lily Wynton. 'Clever, clever little face. What does she do, sweet Hallie? I'm sure she writes, doesn't she? Yes, I can feel it. She writes beautiful, beautiful words. Don't you, child?' " Her hostess and lover picks up her cue: " 'Tiny one doesn't write, Lily,' Miss Noyes said. She threw herself back upon the divan. 'She's a museum piece. She's a devoted wife.' " Mrs. Murdock is nonplussed but holds to her adoration of the actress until Mr. Murdock later calls Hallie "Hank," thus forcing the truth about the lesbian lovers that compassion prevented Mrs. Murdock from acknowledging. Among these hardened realists, only "the devoted wife," however naive, remained devoted to "the glamour and beauty and romance of living."

When Parker was reviewing books as "Constant Reader" in the *New Yorker*, she said in a review of *Men Without Women*: "Hemingway has an unerring sense of selection. He discards details with a magnificent lavishness; he keeps his words to their short path." Parker too has this unerring sense of correct brevity, understatement, and conciseness. She also found these qualities in Ring Lardner, another important influence on her prose. In a review of his 1929 short-story collection, *Round Up*, she singled out Lardner's "unparalleled ear and eye, his strange bitter pity, his utter sureness of characterization, his unceasing investigation, his beautiful economy." She possessed what she praised in others, especially that "strange bitter pity" for kindred sufferers that frequently tempered her scorn.

The petite, demure lady whose scathing wit won her the respect and admiration of powerful men also lost her the lasting affections of men she chose to love, most notably Hemingway and Charles MacArthur, if we are to believe the accounts of sympathetic friends. Hence, she did not bear her sorrow quite as stoically as her characters; in fact, by

Dorothy Parker

all accounts, the pain of rejection was considerably worsened by the shattering indignities of abortion and several suicide attempts, one in 1923, another in 1925—some have said there were more.

She was Mr. Durant's secretary and the woman in the hospital following the abortion—"so little and white and *little*"—as well as "Little Mrs. Murdock," the carefree (and careless) flappers, and also "Big Blonde," the "good sport" who slides into alcoholism, promiscuity, and lonely despair. Her most repugnant characters, and the most vividly drawn, are women, many of whom seem cursed with Parker's own intellectual talents as well as her emotional liabilities. "Boy, did I think I was smart," she confessed in an interview in her last years; "I was just a little Jewish girl trying to be cute." Her passage from society's scourge to self-scourger owes something to the social pressure on an exceptionally bright, ambitious girl in an allegedly emancipated era to be fashionably clever, even brassy, one of the boys. "It was the great fiction of the 1920's," observed John Keats, "that women could and should be the great pals of men." Women thus wore their hair bobbed, donned mannish clothes, bandaged their breasts flat and behaved outrageously. Parker obliged the times too well and "pals" of lesser talent and fewer regrets patronized her as "Our Mrs. Parker" and "Our Little Dottie." "Dammit, it *was* the twenties," she rationalized in later years, "and we *had* to be smarty. I wanted to be cute. That's the terrible thing. I should have had more sense."

After her divorce from Edwin Parker in 1928, a distant, shadowy figure in her life by then, she had several unhappy affairs; in 1933 she married Alan Campbell, an actor eleven years her junior, and half-Jewish like herself. She endured an unsatisfying though lucrative screenwriting career with him in Hollywood. Because of her reputation as a mistress of repartee, she was hired by MGM to add dialogue to several films while both worked as a rewrite team. In 1936, they received screen credit for three films: *The Moon's Our Home*, starring Margaret Sullavan (additional dialogue); *Suzy*, starring Jean Harlow and Cary Grant (screenplay); and *Lady, Be Careful*, starring Lew Ayres (screen adaptation of a play). In 1937, their screenplay for *A Star is Born*, with Fredric March and Janet Gaynor was nominated for an Academy Award. They also added dialogue to *Woman Chases Man* with Miriam Hopkins and Joel McCrea. In 1938, they wrote the screenplay for *Sweethearts*, starring Nelson Eddy and Jeannette MacDonald and in 1939 the screenplay for *Trade Winds*, starring Fredric March and Joan Bennett. Between 1933 and 1939, the Campbells received screen credit for sixteen films. In 1941, they received screen credit for additional dialogue and scenes to Lillian Hellman's *The Little Foxes*, starring Bette Davis, and in 1942 collaborated on the original screenplay for Hitchcock's *Saboteur*. Campbell took to writing scripts with ease and proved competent at it; Dorothy hated the hackwork of adding lustre to false pearls and filled up her days by evading the work, drinking, and spending their high salary.

She jeopardized her health during this period, becoming pregnant in 1935 at age forty-two, risking the miscarriage that occurred after three months. She put all her hopes in the new child and even took up knitting infant clothes, to the dismay of cynical friends; afterwards, she was devastated. She even jeopardized their career by her ardent, though naive, devotion to Communist causes, supporting the needy at home and the politically oppressed abroad. In 1933, she became an organizer, with Lillian Hellman, of the Screen Writers Guild; in 1936, she helped to found the Anti-Nazi League; and in 1937, she reported the Loyalist cause from Spain for *New Masses*. Her avowed Marxism, questioned by friends like F. Scott Fitzgerald as romantic, caused her to be blacklisted and subpoened to testify before the House Un-American Activities Committee.

Moreover, she jeopardized her marriage, according to friends, by being the suspicious, sullen, and bickering wife—the very kind of unpleasant, emotionally dependent woman savaged in her earlier stories. The Campbells were divorced in 1947, remarried in 1950, and separated two years later; they settled down to a marriage of sorts in 1956 and remained together primarily in Hollywood while she worked as an occasional book reviewer for *Esquire* until his death in 1963.

During these long twilight years Parker found story writing more difficult and she wrote less than before. Her standards remained high, but her sardonic wit was shadowed, not only by her own unhappiness, but also by the reality of bleaker economic times. Victims of the Depression walk New York streets in "The Custard Heart" and one, a young man selling pencils, receives from rich, idle Mrs. Lanier her momentary sympathy, but no help: "In gentlest delicacy she would slip away, leaving him with mean wares intact, not a worker for his livelihood like a million others, but signal and set apart, rare in the fragrance of charity." While she awaits her younger man, Mrs. Lanier wistfully hopes—"If only I had a little baby, . . . I think I could be almost happy." A mother's sympathy for the oppressed suffuses "Clothe the Naked," about a black woman's devotion to her blind grandson; a motherlike sympathy for blind youth suffuses "Soldiers of the Republic," about the chivalry of a few Loyalists on leave. These three stories were included in a new collection of twenty-four stories, drawn from the two previously published collections and given another funereal title, *Here Lies*, published in 1939 and dedicated to Lillian Hellman. Although reviews were mixed, William Plomer's laudatory notice in *The Spectator* captured perfectly the compatibility between vision and style that make Parker's stories seem so faithful to the complexities of actual experience: "The urbanity of these stories is that of a worldly, witty person with a place in a complex and highly-developed society, their ruthlessness that of an expert critical intelligence, about which there is something clinical, something of the probing of a dentist: the fine-pointed instrument unerringly discovers the carious cavity behind the smile. . . . Mrs. Parker may appear amused, but it is plain that she is really horrified. Her bantering revelations are inspired by a respect for decency, and her pity and sympathy are ready when needed."

That "expert critical intelligence," softened by a sympathetic heart, inspired a few new stories, five of which were added to those collected in *Here Lies*, including "Cousin Larry," published in the early 1930s, to compose *The Viking Portable Library Dorothy Parker* (1944), selected poetry and fiction arranged by the author, introduced by Somerset Maugham and dedicated to Lieutenant Alan Campbell. This collection was revised and expanded in 1973 to include three stories written during the 1950s, book reviews, including the entire "Constant Reader" reviews in the *New Yorker* (separately published in 1970), and some uncollected articles, with a new introduction by Brendan Gill. Of the first ten Viking Portables (of which there are now over seventy-five), "seven have been dropped or replaced by new editions," says the publisher's note; "only *Shakespeare, The World Bible,* and *Dorothy Parker* have remained continuously in print and selling steadily through time and change." The best of the new stories are the familiar ones, revelations in dialogue, in which pride or vanity prevent sympathy or compassion and thus lead to estrangement. In "The Lovely Leave," based on Parker's own separation from Campbell during World War II, a couple's reunion is spoiled when the wife is told that her husband's leave has been unexpectedly cut to only a few hours. Now her courage will be tested, but she knows that "the little games" women must play include the waiting game: "There had been rules to be learned . . . and the first of them was the hardest: never say to him what you want him to say to you. Never tell him how sadly you miss him." Instead: "Set down for him the gay happenings about you, bright little anecdotes, not invented, necessarily, but attractively embellished." But when he prefers to spend his shortened leave by soaking in a hot tub, she abrogates the rules to speak the truth she knows should be at this time kept suppressed: "You have a whole new life—I have half an old one." Efforts by each to reach the other lead to misunderstanding, more difficult for her because she must, in the end, sacrifice their love to his apparently nobler sacrifice in the war effort. When she tells a friend her reunion of less than an hour was "lovely," she is ironically forced to use the cheerful talk she had prepared for him. In the 1944 Portable edition, Parker placed this story first, where it appears in the 1973 revision and in subsequent reprintings.

Other stories are loosely autobiographical, including the three from the 1950s, written during a period of strain preceding the Campbells' first divorce. "I Live on Your Visits," "Lolita," and "The Bolt Behind the Blue" all dwell mordantly upon older embittered women whose abandonment long ago by husbands is worsened in their eyes by grown children enjoying happy lives without them. These grim tales were partially offset by her last published story, "The Banquet of Crow," written shortly after the Campbells were reconciled (though the story is not included in the revised Portable). Characteristically, Parker begins by setting the social scene in her usually terse and sardonic way: "It was a year when wives whose position was only an inch or two below that of the saints—arbiters of etiquette, venerated hostesses, architects of memorable menus—suddenly caught up a travelling bag and a jewel case and flew off to Mexico with ambiguous young men allied with the arts." Then the chronicler focuses upon the familiar Parker Manhattanite with "a list of proven talents as wife, chum, and lover" who finds herself left by her husband after eleven years. She responds first by worming condolences from friends until they no longer can stand her, then by searching out his old acquaintances, and finally by visiting a female psychiatrist, who tells her that her husband is going through a mid-life crisis. The husband's sudden return for a suitcase provides the wife's opportunity to implement her psychiatrist's plan for a reconciliation by making the husband "eat crow." It becomes clear that her self-delusion, not her husband's menopause, ruined their marriage: " 'No. It wasn't abrupt,' he said, 'I'd been saying it to you for six of those eleven years.'

" 'I never heard you,' she said.

" 'Yes, you did, my dear,' he said, 'You interpreted it as a cry of "Wolf," but you heard me.' " Yet the wife still fails to understand her husband, and cowers behind her doctor's diagnosis: "You know what's the matter with you? You're middle-aged. That's why you've got these ideas." Significantly, the psychiatrist is a woman blinded by her own eagerness to savor another woman's revenge. In the story's devastating final line—"She went to the telephone and called Dr. Langham"—we know who the banquet of crow has been set for.

The final story of abandonment and remorse—of a woman faulted and sentenced to life alone—is the one Parker endured herself in her last years. She prophesied and even rehearsed her final agonies more than a decade before her death in *The Ladies of the Corridor* (1954), a play written with Arnaud D'Usseau in 1953. Earlier with coauthor Ross Evans, she had tried her hand at writing tragedy in her second play, *The Coast of Illyria* (1949), a searing portrayal of the tortured lives of Charles and Mary Lamb. In *The Ladies of the Corridor*, which she said was among the works she was most proud of, she brought tragedy home in a searing portrayal of the tortured lives of embittered old women who endure their final days alone in a seedy mid-Manhattan hotel. Their laments are familiar: "We weren't part of [our husbands'] lives; and as we got older we weren't part of anybody's lives, and yet we never learned how to be alone." Moments of humor, such as they are, are desperate attempts to stave off fear and terror. Mrs. Tyson, a broken alcoholic of forgotten talents, seems most reminiscent of the wisecracking, self-deprecating wit her inventor once was: "Let's see. What are my talents? Think I could teach French? I used to speak very nice French, all in the present tense. Maybe I could give music lessons to backward children. There must be lots of backward children around. I took music lessons for years. I finally got so I could play the 'Minute Waltz' in a minute and a half." After a life of lies, self-delusion and endless disappointments, Mrs. Tyson at the end leaps out a window on a bellhop's dare: "Why don't you take a running jump for yourself?"—the only false note in an otherwise moving play. Parker herself, having peered more than once into the abyss (on less than a dare), drew back this last time. After the death of Campbell ten years later, in 1963, she became a lady of the corridor, first in a Hollywood apartment and then in an eastside Manhattan hotel, where she was found dead of a heart attack in her shabby room in 1967. She was seventy-three.

Dorothy Parker aspired to be a serious, disciplined writer like the few she admired, and only in her last years did she put it so: "I want to be taken seriously as a short story writer." In those later reviews for *Esquire* which she found so difficult to write, she showed that she kept even more vigorously than before to her high standards, singling out for praise those writers who have since become regarded as major prose stylists: Nabokov, Barth, Capote, and Updike. But Dorothy Rothschild's apparent need to be "Mrs. Parker" and thus win approval from established male contemporaries transformed her instead into the funny lady at the head table. Although part of her needed to believe that she bargained away her talents acting "smarty" in order to appear "cute," another, better part of her was quietly wrenching triumph from failure by translating the bitter contradictions in her own experience into exquisitely crafted poetry and prose rich in original insights into women's lives in the modern city.

Humor was essential to the success of her art. "I am unable to feel that a writer can be complete without humor," she declared in 1931. More than being an intelligent woman's weapon to annihilate lesser mortals, more than being an emotionally dependent woman's shield against the pain of rejection, certainly more than "the appreciation of things comic," as she once defined it, humor was, paradoxically for Parker, a necessary corrective to excess, whether of style or sensibility: "the possession of a sense of humor entails the sense of selection, the civilized fear of going too far," she observed. Humor, as Parker realized, depends upon a standard of decency and compassion: "Humor, imagination, and manners are pretty fairly interchangeably interwoven." To single out the humorist in Dorothy Parker is to identify the magnitude of her high seriousness as a disciplined writer, the estimation she wanted and now deserves.

Plays:
Round the Town (revue), New York, Century Roof Theater, 21 May 1924;
Close Harmony, or The Lady Next Door, by Parker and Elmer Rice, New York, Gaiety Theater, 1 December 1924;
Shoot the Works (revue), New York, George M. Cohan Theater, 21 July 1931;
The Coast of Illyria, by Parker and Ross Evans, Dallas, Margo Jones Theater, April 1949;
The Ladies of the Corridor, by Parker and Arnaud D'Usseau, New York, Longacre Theater, 21 October 1953.

Screenplays:
Here is My Heart, Paramount, 1934;
One Hour Late, Paramount, 1935;
Big Broadcast of 1936, Paramount, 1935;
Mary Burns, Fugitive, Paramount, 1935;
Hands Across the Table, Paramount, 1935;
Paris in Spring, Paramount, 1935;
Three Married Men, Paramount, 1936;
Lady, Be Careful, Paramount, 1936;
The Moon's Our Home, Paramount, 1936;
Suzy, MGM, 1936;
A Star Is Born, United Artists, 1937;
Sweethearts, MGM, 1938;
Crime Takes a Holiday, Columbia, 1938;
Trade Winds, United Artists, 1938;
Flight into Nowhere, Columbia, 1938;
Five Little Peppers and How They Grew, Columbia, 1939;
Weekend for Three, RKO, 1941;
Saboteur, Universal, 1942;

A Gentle Gangster, Republic, 1943;
Mr. Skeffington, Warner Brothers, 1944;
Smash Up: The Story of a Woman, Universal, 1947;
The Fan, Twentieth Century-Fox, 1949.

Television Scripts:
The Lovely Leave, *A Telephone Call*, and *Dusk Before Fireworks*, adapted for the Festival of Performing Arts, WNEW-TV, 8 May 1962.

Other:
The Portable F. Scott Fitzgerald, edited by Parker (New York: Viking, 1945);
Dorothy Parker: Poems and a Story, recording by Parker, Spoken Arts 726, 1962;
The World of Dorothy Parker, recording by Parker, Verve V-15029, 1962;
Short Story: A Thematic Anthology, edited by Parker and F. B. Shroyer (New York: Scribners, 1965).

References:
Marion Capron, "Dorothy Parker," in *Writers at Work*, edited by Malcolm Cowley (New York: Viking, 1957);
Wyatt Cooper, "Whatever You Think Dorothy Parker Was Like, She Wasn't," *Esquire* (July 1968): 56-57, 61, 110-114;
Frank Crowninshield, "Crowninshield in the cubs' den," *Vogue* (15 September 1944): 162-163, 197-201;

Corey Ford, *The Time of Laughter* (Boston: Little, Brown, 1967);
James R. Gaines, *Wit's End: Days and Nights of the Algonquin Round Table* (New York: Harcourt, Brace, Jovanovich, 1977);
Brendan Gill, *Here at The New Yorker* (New York: Random House, 1975);
Gill, Introduction to *The Portable Dorothy Parker*;
Lillian Hellman, *An Unfinished Woman* (Boston: Little, Brown, 1969);
John Keats, *You Might As Well Live: The Life and Times of Dorothy Parker* (New York: Simon & Schuster, 1970);
Arthur F. Kinney, *Dorothy Parker* (Boston: Twayne, 1978);
W. Somerset Maugham, "Variations on a Theme," introduction to *The Viking Portable Dorothy Parker*;
Alexander Woollcott, "Our Mrs. Parker," in *While Rome Burns* (New York: Viking, 1934).

Papers:
Dorothy Parker's papers are the property of The National Association for the Advancement of Colored People, to whom they were willed by the author, administered by Parker's legal executrix, Lillian Hellman. Letters and memorabilia are owned by several American university libraries, with the Houghton Library at Harvard University possessing the largest recorded holdings outside private ownership (twenty-two letters).

S. J. Perelman

Steven H. Gale
Missouri Southern State College

BIRTH: Brooklyn, New York, 1 February 1904, to Joseph and Sophia Charra Perelman.

EDUCATION: Brown University, 1921-1925.

MARRIAGE: 4 July 1929 to Laura West; children: Adam, Abby Laura.

AWARDS: New York Film Critics Award for *Around the World in Eighty Days*, 1956; Academy of Motion Pictures Arts and Sciences Oscar for best

screenplay, *Around the World in Eighty Days*, 1956; special National Book Award for his contribution to American letters, 1978.

DEATH: New York, New York, 17 October 1979.

BOOKS: *Dawn Ginsbergh's Revenge* (New York: Liveright, 1929);
Parlor, Bedlam and Bath, by Perelman and Quentin J. Reynolds (New York: Liveright, 1930);

Strictly from Hunger (New York: Random House, 1937);

Look Who's Talking! (New York: Random House, 1940);

The Night Before Christmas, by Perelman and Laura Perelman (New York: French, 1942);

The Dream Department (New York: Random House, 1943);

One Touch of Venus, by Perelman and Ogden Nash (Boston: Little, Brown, 1944);

The Best of S. J. Perelman (New York: Random House, 1944; London: Heinemann, 1945); republished as *Crazy Like a Fox* (New York: Modern Library, 1947);

Keep It Crisp (New York: Random House, 1946; London: Heinemann, 1947);

Acres and Pains (New York: Reynal & Hitchcock, 1947; London: Heinemann, 1948);

Westward Ha! or Around the World in Eighty Clichés (New York: Simon & Schuster, 1948; London: Reinhardt & Evans, 1949);

Listen to the Mocking Bird (New York: Simon & Schuster, 1949; London: Reinhardt & Evans, 1951);

The Swiss Family Perelman (New York: Simon & Schuster, 1950; London: Reinhardt & Evans, 1951);

The Ill-Tempered Clavichord (New York: Simon & Schuster, 1952; London: Max Reinhardt, 1953);

Hold that Christmas Tiger! (Berkeley: Hart, 1954);

Perelman's Home Companion: A Collector's Item (the Collector Being S. J. Perelman) of 36 Otherwise Unavailable Pieces by Himself (New York: Simon & Schuster, 1955);

The Road to Miltown; or, Under the Spreading Atrophy (New York: Simon & Schuster, 1957); republished as *Bite on the Bullet; or, Under the Spreading Atrophy* (London: Heinemann, 1957);

The Most of S. J. Perelman (New York: Simon & Schuster, 1958; London: Heinemann, 1959);

The Rising Gorge (New York: Simon & Schuster, 1961; London: Heinemann, 1962);

The Beauty Part, by Perelman and Ogden Nash (New York: Simon & Schuster, 1963);

Chicken Inspector No. 23 (New York: Simon & Schuster, 1966; London: Hodder & Stoughton, 1967);

Baby, It's Cold Inside (New York: Simon & Schuster, 1970; London: Weidenfeld & Nicolson, 1970);

Vinegar Puss (New York: Simon & Schuster, 1975; London: Weidenfeld & Nicolson, 1976);

Eastward Ha! (New York: Simon & Schuster, 1977; London: Eyre Methuen, 1978);

The Last Laugh (New York: Simon & Schuster, 1981).

COLLECTION: *A Child's Garden of Curses* (London: Heinemann, 1951)—includes *Crazy Like a Fox*, *Keep It Crisp*, and *Acres and Pains*.

S. J. (Sidney Joseph) Perelman was born in Brooklyn, New York, on 1 February 1904 to a father who had immigrated to the United States twelve years earlier. He grew up in Providence, Rhode Island, where, as he told *New York Times Magazine* interviewer William Zinnser in 1969, his father was a machinist, ran a dry goods store, and tried unsuccessfully to raise poultry: "It was the American dream that if you had a few acres and a chicken farm there was no limit to your possible wealth. I grew up with and have since retained the keenest hatred of chickens." Perelman was a voracious reader, perhaps stimulated by the success stories of Horatio Alger and others. He was soon reading the variety of books that captured the attention of the youngsters of that time: the Toby Tyler books, *Graustark*, *Girl of the Lumberlost*, *Trail of the Lonesome Pine*, *The Mystery of Fu Manchu*, *The Winning of Barbara Worth*, *Scaramouche*, *Pollyanna*, and the novels of Charles Dickens. In many ways the style and subject matter of these books supply the foundation for Perelman's humor.

As a young man, Perelman had no interest in writing. He told Zinnser that his "chief interest always was to be a cartoonist," and he spoke of drawing "cartoons in my father's store on the long cardboard strips around which the bolts of Amoskeag cotton and ginghams were stored." In fact, while at Brown University as a premedical student, he joined the staff of the *Brown Jug*, the campus humor magazine, as a cartoonist. John Held, Jr., the recorder of the flapper era, was the prime influence on his drawing and, even though Perelman later became the magazine's editor and thus began to write for publication, his humor always contained the deceptive simplicity and somewhat stylized feeling of a cartoon. Perelman's editorials (advocating, among other things, "the dismissal of the dean and all the other pompous old fools on the faculty") reflect the first literary influence that he recalls: "H. L. Mencken was the Catherine wheel, the ultimate firework.... He loosened up journalism. With his use of the colloquial and the dynamic, the foreign reference, and the bizarre

S. J. Perelman

word like *Sitzfleisch* he brought adrenalin into the gray and pulpy style of the day." When he left Brown in 1925, Norman Anthony, the editor of *Judge*, a popular weekly humor magazine, offered him a contract "to provide two cartoons and one humor piece every week." The cartoons were not great—in one a pasha is seen saying to his grand vizier, "Who's been eating my Kurds and why?" Perelman remained with *Judge* until 1929.

In 1930 Perelman moved to *College Humor*, and it was there that a style of his own began to emerge. "I was beginning to develop a sense of parody," he told Zinsser, "and of lapidary prose." His style shows the influence of many writers, but as most great artists, Perelman had the ability to make what he borrowed his own, and to go beyond his source, even though, as he admits in a 1963 *Paris Review* interview, he "stole from the very best sources." The first author to influence him as a humorist was George Ade. "He had a social sense of history," Perelman told Zinsser. "Ade's humor was rooted in a perception of people and places. He had a cutting edge and an acerbic wit that no earlier American humorist had." Other writers mentioned by Perelman as having influenced his writing were

Stephen Leacock, Max Beerbohm, Ring Lardner ("at his best . . . the nonpareil"), Robert Benchley, Donald Ogden Stewart, Frank Sullivan, and Flann O'Brien. In addition, he told Myra MacPherson of the *Washington Post* in 1970, he "developed a fondness for whatever Dickens" he read, which may be related to his admission that "My names and titles spring out of my lifetime devotion to puns." Raymond Chandler (who "took the private eye legend . . . and refined it and added an element that was not very obvious, and that was humor"), E. M. Forster ("His story, 'Afternoon at Pretoria,' is one of the finest pieces of comic writing I know"), Henry David Thoreau, George Jean Nathan, and James Joyce ("I've come over the years to realize that *Ulysses* is the greatest work of the comic imagination that exists for me") are among those more serious writers whom Perelman recognizes as having had an influence on his writing.

Much of Perelman's work that originally appeared in magazines has been reprinted in book form. While many of the pieces appear in two or more of his twenty volumes of prose, his output is astounding. Four hundred forty-one of his essays were collected. Most of these were written for the *New Yorker*, with a number of pieces being published in *Holiday* and later in *Travel and Leisure*, but his work also appeared in such magazines as *Broun's Nutmeg*, *Brown Jug*, *College Humor*, *Contact*, *Diplomat*, *Escapade*, *Funny Bone*, *Judge*, *Life*, *McCall's*, *Redbook*, *Stage Magazine*, the *Country Book*, the *New Masses*, the *Saturday Evening Post*, *This Week Magazine*, *TV Guide*, *Venture*, and *What's New*.

In 1929 Horace Liveright published Perelman's first book, though through an oversight the author's name was not printed on the title page. The collection, entitled *Dawn Ginsbergh's Revenge*, bore the legend "this book does not stop in Yonkers," and this bewildering non sequitur epitomizes the forty-nine stories contained in the volume. Most of the selections in this first volume originally appeared in *Judge*, and some of the characteristic elements of Perelman's comic style are already evident. These early pieces are short, and they are not the work of a mature writer, but there are moments of Perelman at his best in the collection. "Puppets of Passion," for instance, is a satirical look at a young woman, Dawn Ginsbergh, who is courted by three suitors, "any one of them an ideal catch": "Nicky Nussbaum, tall, dashing, soldierly . . . DuBois Moskovicz of the Foreign Legation, and Hastings Berman, the great portrait painter." A parody of women's magazine romances of the early twentieth century, the tale (subtitled "A Throbbing Story of Youth's Hot Re-

Title page from which Perelman's name was omitted

volt Against the Conventions") shows Perelman's predilection for having fun with the names of his characters, for punning, for incongruity, and for reversal. Dawn's room is described as "large enough for the whole Sixty-ninth Regiment. To tell the truth, the Sixty-ninth Regiment *was* in the room, in undress uniform." From the beginning of a Perelman story there is seldom any question that the author's approach is humorous: "Dawn Ginsbergh lay in her enormous sixteenth-century four-poster bed and played tag with her blood pressure.

"Oh, it was so good to be alive on this glorious May morning instead of being dead or something. Dawn, you must know was very fond of being alive. In fact, as she used to remark . . . 'I would rather be alive than be Alderman.' "

Perelman joyfully made fun of purple prose, as when he describes Dawn: the "impetuous dashing Dawn of the flame-taunted hair and scarlet lips bee-stung like violet pools and so on at ten cents a word for a page and a half." And he made elaborate puns: "A knock on the door aroused Dawn from her lethargy. She hastily slipped it off and donned an abstraction. This was Dawn, flitting lightly from lethargy to abstraction and back to precipice again. Or from Beethoven to Bach and Bach to Bach again." Dawn's mother is a "slim nervous woman, nervous like a manatee or a Firpo," a description that combines Perelman's appreciation for incongruity with his constant allusions. The manatee is a

Dust jacket for Perelman's first book

huge, docile mammal, in no way nervous; Firpo was Luis Firpo, an Argentinian boxer who fought for the heavyweight championship in 1923. "Puppets of Passion" concludes with Dawn proposing marriage to the iceman, whom she has never seen before, and romantically proclaiming that she will work with him on his route.

The remaining selections in *Dawn Ginsbergh's Revenge* demonstrate similar elements. " 'Bell's Folly,' or the First Telephone" begins, "The other day, the whilst I was glancing through my encyclopedia for a corkscrew which had gone astray. . . ." "Sea-Serpent Menace Again Rears Ugly Head" contains a picture (of an old-fashioned bathtub) with the caption "The sea-serpent following the steamer" and takes place on the tramp steamer "Max Beerbohm," crewed by "one Jim Hawkins, a powder monkey" who "had got thirsty for an apple and had crawled in a barrel"; Israel Hands; and Long John Silverman (names taken in part from Robert Louis Stevenson's *Treasure Island*). "Why I Should Like to be a White Slave" has nothing to do with white slavery, though there is a character named Bjack Bjohnson. (Jack Johnson, a black man who was heavyweight champion from 1908 to 1915, got into legal trouble for traveling with a white woman.) It is a nonsense sketch that moves from Bjohnson to a horse who substitutes as a college dean (and subsequently is court-martialed and shot), to Germany's declaration of war on Latvia for the third time, to the narrator's wife's renewing a dog's license, to his conclusion: "The next afternoon we motored out . . . and were divorced by Vincent Lopez [the leader of a popular big band]. I now have a good job in the Water Department and no longer need fear the hydrant-headed monster of Jealousy. And to think that a fuzzy little wire-haired wombat first drew us together!"

The year after his first book appeared, *Parlor, Bedlam and Bath*, written in collaboration with Quentin Reynolds, was published by Liveright; but it was not until seven years later, in 1937, that Perelman's next collection of stories, *Strictly From Hunger*, was published. In the meantime, Perelman was "seduced" by the Marx Brothers to Hollywood where he worked on eight movies in ten years for Paramount and MGM, he wrote for Broadway, and he started writing for the *New Yorker* in 1934.

Strictly From Hunger was Perelman's first collection to be published by Random House. It includes several of what are generally considered his earliest masterpieces: "Waiting for Santy" (a take-off on Clifford Odets), "Scenario" (one of his first parodies of Hollywood motion pictures, in which he

runs together hundreds of B-movie cliches), "The Love Decoy" ("A Story of Youth in College Today"), and "A Farewell to Omsk" (subtitled "The terrifying result of reading an entire gift set of Dostoevsky in one afternoon").

In the eight years since *Dawn Ginsbergh's Revenge* appeared, Perelman had matured both as a humorist and as a stylist. When he moved from *Judge*, he began to write longer pieces in which he was able to develop his points more fully. In addition, his use of language became much sharper and lost the sophomoric tinge of his earlier writing, though he still maintained an exuberant tone. "The Idol's Eye" is in many ways the best and most representative piece in *Strictly From Hunger*. The tale begins with the narrator, Clay Modeling, explaining how he and three others spent a weekend at the villa of a mutual friend, Gabriel Snubbers. Snubbers, who speaks with an affected accent, has come into an inheritance and refuses to leave home so Gossip Gabrilowitsch, the Polish pianist, Downey Couch, the Irish tenor, Frank Falcovsky, the Jewish prowler, and the narrator cycled down from London. In "The Idol's Eye," Perelman relies on four of the humorous devices that characterize his style: outlandish names, puns, understatement, and nonsense. Perelman's first pun is delivered in the description of the guests' arrival when Snubbers leads them up a "great avenue of two stately alms." Understatement comes into play when the party discovers that the entire left wing of the house, incidentally containing Snubbers's aunt, has just burned down, an event casually dismissed by Snubbers. Literalism is another source of humor, as when the host offers his guests "a spot of whiskey and soda," which turns out to be a spot of whiskey on a piece of paper that his "sleekly Oriental" servant, Littlejohn, shows them, and baking soda. The thread of conscious literalism that leads to nonsense runs through the rest of the selection as a counterpoint to the tale that Snubbers tells: " 'I was going through some of my great-grandfather's things the other day . . .'

" 'What things?' demanded Falcovsky.

" 'His bones, if you must know,' Snubbers said coldly. 'You know, Great-grandfather died under strange circumstances. He opened a vein in his bath.'

" 'I never knew baths had veins,' protested Gabrilowitsch.

" 'I never knew his great-grandfather had a ba—' began Falcovsky derisively. With a shout Snubbers threw himself on Falcovsky. It was the signal for Pandemonium, the upstairs girl, to enter and throw herself with a shout on Couch. The outcome of the neckingbee was as follows: Canadians 12, Visitors 9, Krebs and Vronsky played footie, subbing for Gerber and Weinwald, who were disabled by flying antipasto." The story that continues is Snubbers's account, in detail, of how his great-grandfather managed to steal the huge flawless ruby that served as the eye of a temple idol. It is a plot straight out of the B-movies and serials of the 1930s and 1940s, even to the particular of the dark face appearing at his window. The twist comes when Snubbers reveals the upshot of the case: "the movers took away his piano. You see . . . Great-grandfather had missed the last four installments." "And—and the ruby?" inquires one of the listeners. " 'Oh, *that*,' shrugged Snubbers. 'I just threw that in to make it interesting.'

"We bashed in his conk and left him to the vultures."

Soon after the period in his life that Perelman regarded as "without question my formative education"—at around eleven, when he began reading the numerous books mentioned above—he was exposed to a second major influence in his artistic development, the movies. These two sources were later remembered fondly in Perelman's "Cloudland Revisited" series.

The overall effect of "The Idol Eye," as with most of Perelman's humor, is to keep the reader logically off balance, and the random, fast delivery of lines and thoughts are the elements in Perelman's work that first attracted the attention of the Marx Brothers. In the early 1930s Perelman's career was permanently affected by what he then considered a lucky break. Groucho Marx had written a dust jacket blurb for *Dawn Ginsbergh's Revenge*. Although Perelman was not well known, the Marx Brothers, who "were feverish to get into radio," Perelman recalls, "detailed me and Will B. Johnstone, another comic artist, to contrive a program. We had a conception of them as four stowaways immersed in the hold of a trans-Atlantic liner, and there our invention stopped. They said, 'This isn't our radio show, it's our next movie.' They took us up to Jesse Lasky in the Paramount Building, and three weeks later we were barreling westward on the Chief to write 'Monkey Business.' "

So began an association with Hollywood that Perelman detested. He readily admits that the sole motivation for his connection with Hollywood was money—"and the characters who ran the celluloid factories were willing to lay it on the line"—but he remembers the experience as tawdry at best: "After all, it was no worse than playing the piano in a whorehouse." In his 1963 *Paris Review* interview, Perelman expressed his impression of the city and the industry: "a dreary industrial town controlled by hoodlums of enormous wealth, the ethical sense of a pack of jackals, and taste so degraded that it befouled everything it touched. I don't mean to sound like a boy Savonarola, but there were times, when I drove along the Sunset Strip and looked at those buildings, or when I watched the fashionable film colony arriving at some premiere at Grauman's Egyptian, that I fully expected God in his wrath to obliterate the whole shebang. It was—if you'll allow me to use a hopelessly inexpressive word—*dégoutant*." Interestingly, it was after this period of the 1930s, of living in such a "hideous and untenable place . . . populated with few exceptions by Yahoos," that Perelman's writing began to reflect a slightly bitter cynicism.

Perelman viewed his relationship with the Marx Brothers ambiguously. On the one hand, Perelman has been quoted as saying "I'm sure that knowing Groucho Marx has meant a great deal," in a context in which he was expressing admiration for Robert Benchley and Dorothy Parker and admitting how important and helpful they were in his career. The first five Marx Brothers films are generally considered their best, and Perelman scripted the third (*Monkey Business*, 1931) and the fourth (*Horse Feathers*, 1932). On the other hand, Perelman has expressed his distaste for the brothers: "As far as temperaments and their personalities were concerned, they were capricious, tricky beyond endurance, and altogether unreliable. They were also megalomaniac to a degree which is impossible to describe. . . . I did two films with them, which in its way is perhaps my greatest distinction in life, because anybody who ever worked on any picture for the Marx Brothers said he would rather be chained to a galley oar and lashed at ten-minute intervals than work for these sons of bitches again." While Perelman and Johnstone worked on the screenplay for *Monkey Business*, the Marx Brothers played the London Palladium. According to Perelman, "when they got back [to Hollywood] they summoned us for a reading of our script. They came with their lawyers and accountants and masseurs and dentists—23 people, plus Zeppo's Afghans and Chico's schnauzer—and I read for 85 minutes in absolute silence. At the end Chico said, 'Whaddya think, Groucho?' Groucho took the cigar out of his mouth and said 'Stinks!,' and they all got up and walked out. So we started again, and in 1932 the picture was done and was a hit."

Horse Feathers was released the year after *Mon-*

S. J. and Laura Perelman in Hollywood

key Business. Directed by Norman McLeod and starring the four Marx Brothers along with Thelma Todd, David Landau, and Nat Pendleton, this film is in much the same vein as its predecessor, but it is cinematically much better. Bert Kalmar and Harry Ruby were signed to work on the filmscript with Perelman.

Meanwhile, Perelman was also trying his hand at writing for the stage. In 1932 *Walk a Little Faster*, a series of sketches that Perelman wrote with Robert MacGunigle, opened at the Music Box in New York. Beatrice Lillie played in the starring role, but apparently her talents did not suit Perelman's material, at least in the opinion of the *New York Times* theater critic Brooks Atkinson. The following year Perelman and his wife wrote *All Good Americans*, a comedy about Americans living in Paris. Atkinson enjoyed the play's jokes, but he still felt that "Mr. and Mrs. Perelman have written a second-rate Barry comedy with a trying scene of whimsical pantomime toward the end." Eight years later, in 1941, Atkinson again was disappointed in the lack of plot in a Perelman play. *The Night Before Christmas*, also written in collaboration with his wife Laura, contained hilarious segments but the play as a whole was unsuccessful.

Of the eight plays and parts of plays that Perelman wrote either by himself or in collaboration with others, *One Touch of Venus* proved to be the most popular. Cowritten with Ogden Nash, with music by Kurt Weill, the play opened at the Imperial Theatre in New York on 7 October 1943, starring Kenny Baker as Rodney Hatch and Mary Martin, whom Perelman called "the most agreeable and disciplined performer I've ever known," in the role of Venus. In 1948 a movie version based on Perelman's screenplay was released; directed by William A. Selter, it starred Ava Gardner, Robert Walker, Dick Haymes, and Eve Arden.

The two-act play is divided into twelve scenes and set in New York City, primarily at the Whitelaw Savory Foundation of Modern Art. The play opens with a chorus singing a comic song which is used to set the tone. Savory (John Boles) has purchased a three-thousand-year-old statue of Anatolia in Istanbul and today it is delivered.

The plot is simple. Rodney Hatch (Baker, who "exuded boyish charm") is a barber who happens to be in the studio when the statue is delivered. He puts his girl friend's engagement ring on the statue's finger and it suddenly comes to life—the goddess of love in search of love, especially sensual love. After some complications and coincidences including the "murder" of Rodney's girl friend and the appearance of an Anatolian religious fanatic trying to recover his goddess, Rodney falls in love with Venus, who has been pursuing him avidly. His perception of married life is too prosaic for her, though, and in spite of her protestations of undying love, Venus cannot stand the punctuality and humdrum promised as part of her life in the suburbs of Ozone Heights so she returns to an inanimate state. While Rodney stands in the museum gallery looking at the resurrected statue and mourning the loss of his love, a simple girl from Ozone Heights who looks amazingly like Venus wanders in and the two go off to live happily ever after. The comedy is Perelman's best-known stage play, but it is sophomoric. Altogether there are fourteen songs, the most famous of which is "Speak Low," and two ballets in the play, and it has its share of funny lines, as when one character reports to another, "Tony's in bed with Sciatica." "Why tell me? Tell Mr. Sciatica," the second answers. *One Touch of Venus* is theatrical, yet it does not exploit the medium in ways that make it any more effective than Perelman's essays. It is typical popular Broadway fare, providing an entertaining evening but lacking enduring significance.

Perelman's fourth collection of essays, *Look Who's Talking!*, was published in 1940. The twenty-four selections first appeared in the *New Yorker*, the *New Masses*, and *Broun's Nutmeg*. *Look Who's Talking!* contains several selections that are regarded as classics. "Down With the Restoration," for example, starts out by establishing the author's expertise: "I haven't made a prediction since the opening night of *The Women* some years ago, when I rose at the end of the third act and announced to my escort, a Miss Chicken-Licken, 'The public will never take this to its bosom.' Since the public has practically worn its bosom to a nubbin niggling up to *The Women*, I feel that my predictions may be a straw to show the direction the wind is blowing away from." He then goes on to make an astonishing prophecy: "One of these days two young people are going to stumble across a ruined farmhouse and leave it alone." The story that follows is a parody of those articles that filled the pages of magazines such as the *American Home-Owner*: Mibs and Evan completely remodel a farmhouse for $51.18 with the help of one of a long line of handymen named Lafe.

Parody is one of Perelman's primary devices and in "Somewhere a Roscoe . . ." he provides an example of the sort of writing that leads him to parody and its effect on him. Two years ago, he

begins, he was "almost a character in a Russian novel," lying in bed for days and drinking tea out of a glass. Then he picked up *Spicy Detective*, a pulp magazine, and his life changed dramatically. The essay continues with excerpts from a number of episodes in the Dan Turner saga. Turner, "the apotheosis of all private detectives," is forever finding himself in situations, described in the same terms in story after story—though there are minor differences, as in the sound of gunfire. Guns always cough or belch "Kachow," "Chow-chow," "Kachow," or simply "Chow," and the victim is always a woman, usually well-endowed and dressed suggestively, often one who has an Oriental servant. A similar look at science fiction is the basis for "Captain Future, Block that Kick!," and books about medical practice written by doctors come under fire in "Boy Meets Girl Meets Foot."

In 1943 *The Dream Department*, containing twenty-five selections reprinted from the *New Yorker* and the *Funny Bone*, followed *Look Who's Talking!* It was dedicated to Perelman's close friend and brother-in-law, novelist Nathanael West. The first selection, "Counter-Revolution," returns to one of Perelman's favorite topic clusters—advertising, shoddy workmanship and merchandise, and the cavalier treatment of customers by sales clerks who insinuate that they would rather not sell anything to this particular schlemiel of a customer anyway. From the very beginning of his career Perelman was preoccupied with the absurdities contained in advertising. "Counter-Revolution" begins with an explanation of how the narrator came to purchase a bottle of Major's Cement and his incredulity upon reading the extended disclaimer that came with the bottle. Typically, Perelman takes a notion to the extreme in order to demonstrate the full implications of what might normally be accepted as an unimportant inconvenience. It is exactly these minor irritations and what they reflect about the people who perpetrate them and about the people who allow them to continue without a whimper that occupies Perelman's interest. He not only relates his own experiences, reactions, and frustrations, but he simultaneously accomplishes the primary function of comedy in his satires—he points out society's foibles.

Advertisements for the film version of Somerset Maugham's life of painter Paul Gauguin, *The Moon and Sixpence*, stimulate Perelman's mockery in "Beat Me, Post-Impressionist Daddy." The narrator claims to have unearthed some letters between the artist and his own father's barber (who lived in the family's bureau, which is where the letters were discovered). Following the lines of the advertisements, which distort Maugham's work by overemphasizing Gauguin's passion for women, at least, Perelman notes, as it is displayed in the painter's journal (*Avant et Après*) and correspondence, these spurious letters are filled with provocative lines. Women will not leave him alone, he declares, pleading with him to abuse them: " 'I'm a strange little beast!' she cried. 'Beat me 'til your arm aches!' . . . what could I do? I bounced her around a bit, knocked out several of her teeth," but still he is "surrounded by hordes of beauties begging me to maltreat them."

"To Sleep, Perchance to Steam" is a short piece about insomnia, enlightened by Perelman's own special brand of inanity: "I shuddered for approximately half an hour to relax my nerves, plugged a pair of Flents into my ears, and tied on a sleep mask. I probably should have waited until I got into bed before doing so, as I took a rather nasty fall over a wastebasket." Perelman never lets us forget that we cannot make any assumptions or take anything for granted. "I read several chapters of Durfee's *Monasteries of the Rhône*," he informs us, "with no success whatever until I discovered I had forgotten to remove my mask." "Woodman, Don't Spare that Tree!" is a scenario that returns to the author's dismay at the projects of decorators, and "A Pox on You, Mine Goodly Host" presents Jiggs and Maggie types (the narrator's pseudopersona metaphorically implied) trying to establish their credentials so that they can be served at Schrafft's.

By 1946, when *Keep It Crisp* was published, Perelman's reputation had been established and most of his work was appearing only in major magazines. *Keep It Crisp*, for example, was compiled of twenty-five reprints from the *New Yorker* and the *Saturday Evening Post*. The best known of these pieces is "Farewell, My Lovely Appetizer," a parody of Raymond Chandler's thrillers, especially those about hard-boiled private detective Philip Marlowe, the detective in Chandler's *Farewell, My Lovely*. In the *Paris Review* interview Perelman admits his pleasure that Chandler praised the piece in a collection of his letters, *Raymond Chandler Speaking*: "I ran across a very flattering reference he made to a parody of his work I had done."

Perelman does indeed capture the feeling of the genre. Mike Noonan, at the Atlas Agency—Noonan and Driscoll ("but Snapper Driscoll had retired two years before with a .38 slug between his shoulders, donated by a snowbird in Tacoma"), enters the "crummy anteroom we kept to impress clients," growls at his secretary, Birdie Clafflin, and is informed that a "looker," a Swede named Sigrid Bjornesterne, is looking for him. When Sigrid returns they take turns concealing information from one another ("playing it safe until I knew where she stood") until she finally hires him to find out how the herring that she serves her husband is given its pinkish tones. After an adventurous afternoon, avoiding possible tails while ferreting out information, Noonan returns to his office where Sigrid is awaiting him, pistol in hand. Noonan, having determined that Sigrid intends to poison her husband with the herring, disarms her, refuses to be seduced, and calls the police.

A successful parody depends on more than just a plot outline, however, and Perelman's stylistic imitation is masterful. The passage in which Noonan greets Birdie is a good example: " 'Well, you certainly look like something the cat dragged in,' she said. She had a quick tongue. She also had eyes like dusty lapis lazuli, taffy hair, and a figure that did things to me. I kicked open the bottom drawer of her desk, let two inches of rye trickle down my craw, kissed Birdie square on her lush, red mouth, and set fire to a cigarette."

Parody and motion pictures blend in "How Sharper Than a Serpent's Tooth" when a viewing of *Mildred Pierce* induces Perelman to write a scenario in which parents undergoing a divorce are forced to reveal the embarrassing source of their livelihood to their son. "Hell in Gabardines," "Garnish Your Face with Parsley and Serve," and "Physician Steel Thyself" also parody the movies.

Dedicated to Robert C. Benchley, *The Best of S. J. Perelman* was published by Random House in 1944 and later republished under the title *Crazy Like a Fox* in their Modern Library series in 1947. Most of the selections already had been collected in *Look Who's Talking!*, *Strictly from Hunger*, *The Dream Department*, and *Keep It Crisp*. There is an amusing introduction to the book purportedly by one Sidney Namlerep of 1626 Broadway, New York City—Namlerep is Perelman spelled backwards and the Broadway address was the location of Perelman's office.

Acres and Pains, also published in 1947, was the first of what might be called Perelman's few thematic collections. Instead of following the usual pattern of his books, which are merely anthologies of the best but unrelated essays written over several years, *Acres and Pains* is a collection of stories that, Perelman claims, are "the by-product of a dozen years of country living." Twenty of the twenty-one segments originally appeared in the *Saturday Evening Post*; the other was published in the *Country Book*.

All are set on Perelman's farm, Rising Gorge, near Tinicum Township in Bucks County, Pennsylvania. Each segment deals with a specific aspect of country living, with topics ranging from neighbors to architects and remodeling, from swimming pools to maids, from milk cows to country doctors, from hoboes to dogs. Among the best chapters is that on vegetable gardening, in which the trials and tribu-

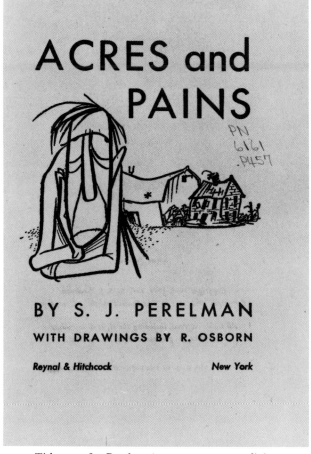

Title page for Perelman's essays on country living

lations experienced by everyone who has tried to raise vegetables are recaptured—searching through seed catalogues, fighting to bring the plants to the point that they are "poking their heads through the lava and broken glass, just in time to be eaten by cutworms, scorched by drought and smothered by weeds." Chapter 13 examines the country dweller's experience with solitude. In Perelman's world, though, solitude is in no way akin to that lauded by Thoreau at Walden Pond. Instead of reveling in marvelous thoughts, the inhabitant of Perelman's farmhouse cringes under the bed covers, joined by the family dogs, terrified by the un-

identified creakings and whispers of noise that surround him at night.

These two chapters sum up the concept underlying *Acres and Pains*: rural life is not for civilized man. Nowhere in Perelman's trek back to nature does he discover the noble savage among the locals who continually take advantage of his pocketbook, gullibility, naivete, and inexperience in things rural. Rather than a georgic the author has produced a near diatribe. His idealized vision of life in the manor house is soon replaced by the reality of chiggers, dry wells, cracked walls, dying trees, termites, and mosquitoes. And after nature is through with him he must face his neighbors who either laugh at his follies or take advantage of him or, most frequently, both.

Written in the first person, the apocryphal anecdotes about commonplace adventures usually end with Perelman as the butt of his own joke. He portrays himself as a softheaded sucker who has only the vaguest romantic conception of the life that he has adopted and this conception frequently comes back to haunt him when he misunderstands or grasps just a particle of the truth: "I started wearing patched blue jeans," he informs us, and "mopped my forehead with a red banana." It was some time later that he realized he should have been using a red bandanna. In chapter 6 his mechanical misadventures might be attributed to his confusing stopcocks with bushings and storage tanks with flanges. There is an echo of Benchley when he admits to "a slight headache caused by exposure to poisoned bourbon." And there is the ever-present play on words, as when he describes the outcome of trying to build a swimming pool, which ultimately has to be dynamited because it leaks, floods his neighbor's yard, and becomes a haven for poisonous snakes, among other things: "When the dust finally settled, I had enough firewood for the next fifty years, most of it right inside the house where I could get at it. And when *I* finally settled, the man next door had a new front porch and a glass eye you couldn't tell from the other one."

Perelman's definition of a farm is "an irregular patch of nettles bounded by short-term notes, containing a fool and his wife who didn't know enough to stay in the city." *Acres and Pains* illustrates the aches and pains that life in such an environment can produce. There are humorous passages throughout as the proverbial little man confronts forces that he can neither control nor overcome. The volume, which has a more fictive ring to it than do some of Perelman's later collections, is filled with amusing concepts (all hired hands are named Lafe) and funny lines ("My wife and I were still knee-deep in a puddle outside our front door, exchanging shrill taunts and questioning each other's legitimacy, when our first visitor drove up"). Still, the book seems to suffer from the artistic problem encountered by any writer of serial comedy—humor as a single topic is difficult to sustain throughout a book.

Westward Ha! or Around the World in Eighty Clichés, published in 1948, was the first of Perelman's volumes to be published by Simon and Schuster, the publishing house that would publish his last thirteen books. All twelve of the selections in this collection were initially printed in *Holiday* and are considerably longer than the average Perelman essay. The subtitle gives a clear indication of the kind of fare to be expected. Perelman had published travel pieces before, but this was his first collection devoted entirely to his travel experiences. The journey in this case was an around-the-world trip he undertook with Al Hirschfeld, the theatrical caricaturist from the *New York Times* who became Perelman's illustrator and to whom the author dedicated this book.

Not only is *Westward Ha!* Perelman's first travel volume, it is also his best. The content is well balanced between providing insights to the writer (and exploring the human condition through the metaphor of travel) and commenting on the locales he visits. Perelman's normal attitude toward himself combines obvious posturing with self-deprecation, the first making him fair game for the second. In "Please Don't Give Me Nothing to Remember You By" the narrator describes himself thus: "A simple, unpretentious man of a grave but kindly mien. . . . His loosely woven tweeds were worn with all the easy authority of a man accustomed to go into a pawnshop, lay down his watch, and take his four dollars home with him." To this he adds bits of biographical data dropped here and there at random, but in a constant flow (he was, for example, a premed student for two years). He continually makes himself the butt of his jokes: in "Boy Meets Gull" he claims to have been "a deep-water sailor since boyhood," but subsequently refers to "the man whose duty it was to drive the ship—the chauffeur or the motorman or whatever you call him." He proclaims that he relishes a joke "even at my own expense," yet, when knocked down by the Prince Regent's Belgian shepherd in "The Road to Mandalay," he finds nothing funny in the situation: "what there was in my plight to provoke screams of laughter, I do not know. Possibly they had never seen a man on a dog before."

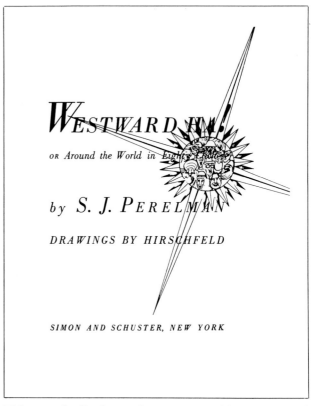

Title page for Perelman's first collection of humorous travel pieces

Hirschfeld illustration for Westward Ha!

Stylistically, too, *Westward Ha!* is superior to most of the travel pieces that follow it. It is rich and compact, much in the manner of the dialogue in *Horse Feathers*. Instead of a few brilliant gems scattered through each piece, in the tales of *Westward Ha!* every line is either funny or building to a funny line.

The beginning of Perelman's third decade of publishing was marked by the publication of *Listen to the Mocking Bird* in 1949. This volume is especially notable because it features the author's "nostalgia kick," the "Cloudland Revisited" series. The importance of this *New Yorker* series of affectionate reminiscenses about books and movies from Perelman's youth is underlined by the fact that the writer used this format twenty-two times in the short period from 30 October 1948 ("Into Your Tent I'll Creep," which is included in this collection) through 10 October 1953 ("Shades of Young Girls Among the Flummery").

"Into Your Tent I'll Creep" establishes the pattern for the series. Perelman introduces his subject, E. M. Hull's novel *The Sheik*, by explaining the circumstances under which he read it—as a Brown University sophomore, standing behind the counter of a cigar store where he was the night clerk. The occasion for writing this essay is Perelman's rereading of the novel twenty-five years later. He summarizes the plot and supplies quotes as specimens of the novelist's stylistic accomplishment. Other pieces in this volume bear some of Perelman's classic titles: "The Sweeter the Tooth, the Nearer the Couch" (a confrontation between Perelman, who is trying to protect a store of candy in a hotel room in Panang, British Malaya, and the horde of tiny red ants that manages to wrest it away from him), "Don't Bring Me Oscars (When It's Shoesies that I Need)" (a calamitous home movie filming session—the announcement of which is met by his wife's usual enthusiasm: " 'A really crackpot notion,' she admitted, confusing the word with 'crackerjack' "), "Danger in the Drain" (a mock nineteenth-century detective story), "Methinks He Doth Protein Too Much" (food imagery as applied to a female love object, literally), and "Stringing Up Father" (business competition between father and son).

The Swiss Family Perelman, like *Acres and Pains*, is a collection of articles all written on the same subject. Published in 1950, *The Swiss Family Perelman*'s twelve chapters chronicle a trip taken by the author, his wife, Laura, their twelve-year-old son,

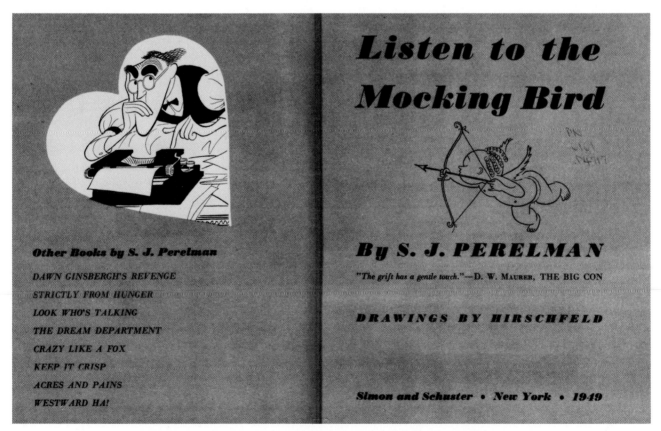

Other Books by S. J. Perelman

DAWN GINSBERGH'S REVENGE
STRICTLY FROM HUNGER
LOOK WHO'S TALKING
THE DREAM DEPARTMENT
CRAZY LIKE A FOX
KEEP IT CRISP
ACRES AND PAINS
WESTWARD HA!

Listen to the Mocking Bird

By S. J. PERELMAN

"The grift has a gentle touch."—D. W. MAURER, THE BIG CON

DRAWINGS BY HIRSCHFELD

Simon and Schuster • New York • 1949

Card page and title page for collection featuring Perelman's nostalgia series

Hirschfeld illustration for Listen to the Mocking Bird

Adam, and ten-year-old daughter, Abby, across the United States by train and then, after a short stopover in Hollywood, on to Honolulu, Manila, Hong Kong, New Guinea, Bali, Bangkok, India, Istanbul, Rome, Nice, Paris, London, Dublin, Denmark, Germany, and back to New York. The stories, first published in *Holiday* and illustrated by Hirschfeld, begin in medias res with "Rancors Aweigh" as the family is aboard the S. S. *President Cleveland* out of San Francisco and bound for Hong Kong. There is a flashback in "Low Bridge—Everybody Down" to explain how they arrived in San Francisco, and then in "The Wild Blue Yonder" they are back on shipboard. Starting much like a normal narrative with straightforward description and exposition, the account soon becomes typically Perelmanesque. It fits into that category of personal adventures that the author occasionally writes about (often detailing his travels), embellished by his unique style and personality—frequently exposing himself as the source and object of his humor. Along the way Perelman manages to acquire a talking mynah bird in Siam, suffer through several bouts with fellow travelers who are decidely anti-American, undergo a number of unpleasant (though usually funny) incidents, and meet a

"chemically blonde" French chanteuse. When he finally returns home in "The Roaring Traffic's Boom" ready to settle in for an extended stay, he is informed by the superintendent that his apartment building is scheduled for demolition at the end of the month.

The Swiss Family Perelman does not sustain the level of humor and style found in much of Perelman's other works, but as in everything he does there are moments, lines, and images that carry us happily along. Like Woody Allen's work, which was greatly influenced by Perelman, some of his writing is rather bland until one of these moments appears. There are elements in common with his other writing, of course, and one of these is the wondrous mixture of references and allusions to all areas of life, some familiar and some esoteric, often juxtaposed with one another.

In 1952 *The Ill-Tempered Clavichord* was published. With the exception of "Young as You Feel," reprinted from *Redbook*, the twenty-three selections first appeared in the *New Yorker*. Five of the pieces are part of the "Cloudland Revisited" series. Among the other "sportive" essays in the collection is a digression on bravery, "Up the Close and Down the Stair," in which the narrator proves his sensibility in staying out of scrapes ("when the Princess Pats stood at Passchendaele in '17, I was damned careful to be twelve years old and three thousand miles to the rear"), only to be caught in an embarrassing situation when he mistakes a neighbor dumping trash for a burglar. "A Girl and a Boy Anthropoid Were Dancing" deals with one of the writer's most beloved subjects, striptease dancers. "The Hand that Cradles the Rock" is based on a biographical portrait of Fleur Fenton Cowles, directress of *Look*, *Quick*, and *Flair*. It deals with the editor's (Hyacinth Beddoes Laffoon's) handling of the yes-men who surround her.

"Nesselrode to Jeopardy" begins with a supposed excerpt from a *Times* news story. This is one of Perelman's most frequently used techniques, and some critics have complained that it is a little heavy-handed and that he employs this stratagem too often, but it is effective. Beginning a piece in this manner introduces the subject matter, elicits a sense of authority, sets the scene, implies the author's attitude toward his topic, and generally saves time by letting him avoid the otherwise necessary background explanations. In this piece the narrator becomes involved in an international attempt to track down the source of contaminated hollandaise sauce, told somewhat in the mode of Eric Ambler. "Chewies the Goat but Flicks Need Hypo" is a movie treatment designed to appeal to the "gustatory as well as the visual instinct." The intent is to make fun of theater owners' efforts to prod audiences over to the concession stand for popcorn and other goodies, and Perelman sees film as a perfect medium for this endeavor and for his mockery as well. During a feast scene, he suggests, why not insert dialogue on the order of "Thanks, Baroness. . . . And, speaking of matters edible, the fans watching this need not fall prey to the green-eyed monster, for adjacent to their chairs they will lamp a pleasing selection of mint drops, chocolate creams, and candied apples to beguile themselves stomach-wise." Again Perelman has extrapolated a trend to the point of its logical absurdity.

In "Personne Ici Except Us Chickens" Perelman uses a magazine advertisement to get his narrator and a gullible neighbor to Europe on a wild-goose chase. Imagined Russian agents become involved, and the author leaps about illogically, in the manner of some of his early works. He winds things up with a sort of reversed deus ex machina—the husband suddenly appears: " 'Name of a name!' exploded Grimalkin. 'Why have I never heard of this husband before?' / 'Ze exposition was too extensive to plant 'is existence,' she hissed."

Perelman's Home Companion was published in 1955. Subtitled *A Collector's Item (the Collector Being S. J. Perelman) of 36 Otherwise Unavailable Pieces by Himself*, most of the selections in this volume were, in fact, reprinted from *Look Who's Talking!* and *Keep It Crisp*. *The Road to Miltown; or, Under the Spreading Atrophy* was published in New York in 1957. It was published simultaneously in London under the title *Bite on the Bullet* since English readers would not be likely to recognize the reference to an American tranquilizer. Of the thirty-four pieces, thirty-one were reprints from the *New Yorker*, two were from *Holiday*, and one was new. "Who Stole My Golden Metaphor" is the new piece included in the anthology. In it, Vernon Equinox (a name Perelman resurrects for his 1962 play *The Beauty Part*) is cast as an artist upset because Truman Capote had plagiarized a metaphorical concept that he had used in describing himself. "I said I was about as tall as an Osage bow and just as relentless," Equinox asserts. Capote said of himself, "I'm about as tall as a shotgun—and just as noisy." "I guess his eyes *are* really heated, though," Equinox muses. "The only time I ever saw him, in the balcony of Lowe's Valencia, they glowed in the dark like a carnation."

"De Gustibus Ain't What Dey Used to Be," which Perelman also drew upon for *The Beauty Part*, is set in April Monkhood's apartment where Cyprian Voles, not Lance Weatherwax, as in the play, is her would-be lover. Instead of talking on the telephone with her former husband, Sensualdo, as in the play, this version has her husband passionately sweep her out of the apartment as she admits, "To kiss anyone else is like a mustache without salt." Cyprian, meanwhile, stands rigid, disguised as a hitching post. *Harper's Bazaar*, one of Perelman's favorite targets, comes under fire in "The Saucier's Apprentice." Delivered in the style of a B-movie Interpol detective story (hearkening back to the "Nesselrode to Jeopardy" hollandaise sauce caper in *The Ill-Tempered Clavichord* and earlier pieces), the essay follows the determined efforts of the narrator and Inspector Marcel Riboflavin to track down the person who polluted a sauce bearnaise served at Maxim's in Paris. The mystery is solved by the revelation that the perpetrator, who turns out to be the inspector's wife, was gathering material for a magazine article. "The holley had a trot-box! . . . I mean, the trolley had a hot box" are the first words spoken in "I'll Always Call You Schnorrer, My African Explorer," an essay that recounts the narrator's first exposure, in 1916, to the Marx Brothers, then a vaudeville team performing in Providence, Rhode Island. From this introduction the narrative jumps to the early 1950s when the storyteller is invited by Groucho to visit the RKO lot in Hollywood where he is filming *A Girl In Every Port* with William Bendix and Marie Wilson. The dialogue could easily come from a Marx Brothers movie: " 'Gravy, gravy!' shouted Groucho. 'Everybody wants gravy! Did those six poor slobs on the *Kon-Tiki* have any gravy? Did Scipio's legions, deep in the African waste, have gravy? Did Fanny Hill?'

" 'Did Fanny Hill what?' I asked.

" 'Never mind, you cad,' he threw at me. 'I'm sick to death of innuendo, brittle small talk, the sly, silken rustle of feminine underthings. I want to sit in a ballpark with the wind in my hair and breathe cold, clean popcorn into my lungs. . . .' "

Between the scripting of *Horse Feathers* in 1932 and 1959, Perelman wrote nine credited screenplays as original screen stories. The first was *Paris Interlude* (1934). Then came *Florida Special* (cowritten with his wife, Laura, and released in 1936). Directed by Ralph Murphy, the movie featured Jack Oakie and Sally Eilers in a romantic murder mystery that takes place aboard a southbound train. *Florida Special* was followed by *Sweethearts* (1938), directed by W. S. Van Dyke and starring Jeanette MacDonald and Nelson Eddy, along with Frank Morgan, Ray Bolger, and Mischa Auer. With its Victor Herbert songs this color film about two operetta stars who constantly fight when offstage is considered one of MacDonald and Eddy's best. Perelman in *Westward Ha!* called *Sweethearts* "a pestilence" and described MacDonald as "The Iron Butterfly" and Eddy as "The Singing Capon." Next came three films cowritten by the Perelmans, *Ambush* (1939), for which, Perelman quipped, "Laura and I were supposed to introduce the humorous element," *Boy Trouble* (1939), and *The Golden Fleecing* (1940). In 1942 Perelman wrote the original story for *Larceny, Inc.* Directed by Lloyd Bacon, the picture included an impressive cast: Edward G. Robinson, Jane Wyman, Broderick Crawford, Jack Carson, Anthony Quinn, and Edward Brophy, and Jackie Gleason in a bit part. A highly regarded comedy, *Larceny, Inc.* concerns three ex-cons (Robinson, Crawford, and Brophy) who use a luggage store as a front for their shady activities. The plot is complicated when another gangster (Quinn) tries to move in on them. MGM's Irving Thalberg hired the Perelmans "to work on a loathsome little thing called 'Greenwich Village' because we had once lived on Washington Square." The movie, released in 1944, was an uninspired musical directed by Walter Lang and starring Carmen Miranda, Don Ameche, William Bendix, Vivian

Blaine, Felix Bressart, Tony and Sally DeMarco, and the Step Brothers. In 1948 *One Touch of Venus* was adapted to the screen, though Perelman was not credited with the screenplay. Interestingly, in this version the hero falls in love with a store-window statue of Venus that comes to life. Perelman was also assigned the task of translating Dale Carnegie's *How to Win Friends and Influence People* into a screenplay as a vehicle for Joan Crawford and Fanny Brice, but the project was "mercifully never completed." Ironically, Perelman wrote some of the same kinds of movies that he often parodied in his prose.

In 1956 Perelman, along with James Poe and John Farrow, received the New York Film Critics Award and an Oscar for the year's best screenplay with *Around the World in Eighty Days*, adapted from the novel by Jules Verne. Perelman's experience with the giant-screen extravaganza produced by Michael Todd and directed by Michael Anderson was not fondly remembered. In "Disquiet, Please, We're Turning!" from the "Around the Bend in Eighty Days" series, Perelman calls Todd "a cheap chiseler reluctant to disgorge royalties, a carnival grifter with the ethics of a stoat." Nevertheless, the movie, filmed in gorgeous color on location around the world and featuring forty-four international stars in cameo roles, was the winner of the Academy Award for best picture.

In 1958 *The Most of S. J. Perelman*, dedicated to Perelman's wife, Laura, was published. The majority of the 120 pieces contained in this collection originally appeared in the *New Yorker*, with other works from *Holiday*, the *Saturday Evening Post*, the *Country Book*, *College Humor*, *Contact*, and *Life*. In addition, there is an introduction by Dorothy Parker based on a piece she had written for the *New York Times Book Review*. Several of the selections first were published in earlier volumes (*Crazy Like a Fox* and *The Road to Miltown*), but with the exception of one piece which had not been published previously, all of the selections in this volume (including the whole of *Acres and Pains* and *Westward Ha!*) had already appeared in book form. The sampling represents twelve of the writer's fourteen books published to that time. (Omitted are *Dawn Ginsbergh's Revenge* and *Parlor, Bedlam and Bath*.) Only five collections of Perelman's work were published later, so *The Most of S. J. Perelman* serves as an excellent introduction to Perelman's prose.

Published in 1961, *The Rising Gorge* was dedicated to Al Hirschfeld, Perelman's illustrator. Most of the thirty-four selections, previously uncollected, originally appeared in the *New Yorker*, with a sprinkling collected from *Holiday*, *Redbook*, *This*

Week Magazine, and *What's New*. By 1961 Perelman's prose could be called well-wrought, but it had lost much of its frothiness. The light, fey style of his earlier works had given way to verbal density; the sprightliness of Perelman's youth was replaced by a sense of self-assuredness.

Still, he continued to exercise his skills in a variety of ways. "Eine Kleine Mothmusik" is constructed as a series of letters exchanged between Perelman and his dry cleaner. In "Dial 'H' for Heartburn" the author adopts the persona of a young woman (recalling *Dawn Ginsbergh's Revenge*). "Is You Is or Is You Ain't, Goober Man?" is an "expose" of Mr. Planters Peanut, written as a playlet. "Dr. Perelman, I Presume, or Small-Bore in Africa" is a collection of seven articles about the writer's precarious East African travels. Perelman's deft use of language in this collection produces a slightly different kind of humor from his earlier work. More aware of his craft as a writer, less concerned with being funny, he was clearly a writer in control of his medium.

On 26 December 1962 Perelman's second stage collaboration with Ogden Nash, *The Beauty Part*, was mounted at the Music Box Theatre on Broadway. With Bert Lahr playing five characters, the comedy lampooned the "cultural explosion" that seemed to make it "incumbent on everyone to express themselves in words or paint" or "to leap around in homemade jerseys," as Perelman explained in interviews. The reception of the play was promising with laudatory reviews by critics such as Howard Taubman of the *New York Times*, but a New York City newspaper strike robbed the play of important reviews and publicity, and as a result it closed after two and a half months. In addition to Lahr in multiple roles as Milo Leotard Allardyce Duplessis Weatherwax, Hyacinth Beddoes Laffoon, Harry Hubris, Nelson Smedley, and Judge Herman J. Rinderbrust, several other players appeared in multiple parts: Alice Ghostley (Octavia Weatherwax, Kitty Entrail, and Grace Fingerhead), David Doyle (Mike Malroy, Bunce, Maurice Blount, Curtis Fingerhead, Wagnerian, and Hanratty), Gil Gardner (Van Lennep, Fish-Market Boy, Elmo, and Policeman), Bernie West (Sam Fussfeld, Seymour Krumgold, Wormser, and Poteat), William Le Massena (Hagedorn, Boris Pickwick, Emmett Stagg, Hennepin, and Bailiff), Arnold Soboloff (Vishnu, Vernon Equinox, Rukeyser, and Joe Gourielli), Charlotte Ray (Gloria Krumgold, Mrs. Younghusband, Rowena Inchcape, and Mrs. Lafcadio Mifflin), and Fiddle Viracola (Chenille Schreiber and Sherry Quicklime). Also in the comedy were Larry Hagman and Patricia Englund. The play was directed by Noel Willman.

The two-act (eleven scenes) play is set in New York and California. It opens in the luxurious Weatherwax triplex on Park Avenue where multimillionaire Weatherwax, his wife, and their Yalie son Lance are introduced. Upon learning that the family fortune (which is so great that "There's loose rubies all over the foyer") is based on the Weatherwax All-Weather Garbage Disposal Plan, the embarrassed Lance declares that he is separating from the family to pursue his love, April Monkhood, and a life as a creative artist. The rest of the play concerns Lance's efforts to realize these goals, with many interrelated characters and themes woven into the plot.

Money is a major concern. April abandons Lance when he reveals that he has renounced his family ties to the Weatherwax fortune, and various other characters (notably Harry Hubris) become interested in Lance only after they become aware of his financial connections. Hyacinth Beddoes Laffoon's interest in Lance as a member of her editorial staff is formed on this basis, and their relationship cools when she learns that the Weatherwax Trust and Loan Company will not give her a loan. Unable to get help from either April or Mrs. Laffoon to become a writer, Lance turns to the renowned painter Goddard Quagmeyer to serve as an apprentice but is disillusioned when Quagmeyer sells out his artistic sensibilities and principles for the money offered by Hollywood producer Hubris. Act 1 ends with Hubris proclaiming that Lance will become a movie director: "To show my faith in you, I'm going to let your folks put up the money for an independent production!"

In Act 2, Lance and Hubris, disguised as a Chinese houseboy and his father, are in Santa Barbara trying to steal the manuscript of a Civil War novel that they intend to adapt to the screen. ("Nobody before ever looked at the Confederacy through the eyes of a Creole callgirl.") Everything becomes farcically confused when the author's jealous husband tries to substitute his wife's work for his own so that he can sell his novel to a pornographic-book publisher. Next, Lance becomes involved in an outrageous television project in Pasadena. The "Communist Plot" and problems with unions and blue collar workers are included in a series of adventures that conclude with April ("an attractive girl in her early twenties given to self-dramatization and endowed with magnificent secondary sexual characteristics and practically no sense of humor") being hauled into court by the vice squad for popping out of a fake pie "clad in the world's scantiest bikini." The court is presided over by Judge Herman J. Rinderbrust, who uses the televised proceedings to advertise business concerns, such as a cemetery, in which he has stock. Justice is tempered by the judge's economic interests, and April's case is dismissed when Lance produces some "relevant and germane" evidence, a check in the judge's name in the amount of $500,000. The play ends with the traditional fertility ceremony celebration of comedy—April and Lance are married—and Milo Weatherwax showers everyone, including the audience, with "a little bundle of happiness. . . . everybody's joy"—greenbacks.

It is often difficult to assess individual contributions to a collaborative effort. In the case of *The Beauty Part*, though, the identification of specific lines, indeed, whole scenes, many of them among the best in the play, is simplified by the fact that a great deal of the material is taken from Perelman's prose pieces from as much as fifteen years earlier (see "Farewell, My Lovely Appetizer," "How Sharper Than a Serpent's Tooth," "De Gustibus Ain't What Dey Used to Be," and "The Hand That Cradles the Rock"). Perelman's points are evident. Money controls everything, even creativity. False culture takes its lumps, too. "Every housewife in the country's got a novel under her apron," laments Quagmeyer before his defection to the service of Mamon, "And the dentists are even worse. Do you realize that there are twice as many dentists painting in their spare time as there are painters practicing dentistry?" When Mrs. Krumgold is asked what the subject should be of a painting that she has commissioned, she replies, "Oh, who cares? So long as it doesn't clash with the drapes. They're silver blue." The superficiality is summed up in an exchange between Lance and Hubris about the actor hired to play the title role in a picture about the life of John Singer Sargent:

> HUBRIS: Mentality's one problem you won't have with Rob Roy Fruitwell. Strictly a matzo ball.
> LANCE: But John Singer Sargent was a genius.
> HUBRIS: (*Triumphantly*): That's the beauty part. This cluck is a sensitized sponge that he'll soak up the info you give him and project it . . .

Dialogue is an excellent mode through which Perelman's love of words can be expressed and it is probable that his recognition of the format's pos-

sibilities for extending the manipulation of language in a natural seeming way lay behind his frequent use of the scenario form in his essays.

Chicken Inspector No. 23 was published in 1966. Eight of the thirty-three selections contained in the collection come from *Holiday*, the *Saturday Evening Post*, *TV Guide*, *Diplomat*, and *Venture*, but following the normal pattern, the majority of the pieces included first appeared in the *New Yorker*. "Are You Decent, Memsahib?" is an "autobiographical" account of how a young beauty from Scranton, Pennsylvania (stage name, Sherry Muscatel), performs such a tasteful act of striptease that she turns the head of Lam Chowdri, an Indian maharaja from the state of Cawnpone who is currently attending Harvard. They are soon married and, in order to be near his wife all the time, Chowdri renounces his title. A Parsee lawyer named Mr. Nuroddin is sent to fetch Chowdri home, but the heroine's charms quickly turn his head too and he becomes an ardent courter. In short order Uncle Nooj, the regent, arrives to extricate his nephew and lawyer from the narrator's wiles, only to fall for her himself. The story ends with Sherry treating them all as servants.

"Nobody Here 'cep' Us Riffraff" is prefaced by an excerpt from the *Observer* (London) that takes notice of Americans in London who pursue literary celebrities. In the format of a diary written by a female English literature major three years out of Wellesley, the piece traces the young woman's midadventures as she seeks the famous and uncovers the phonies, who seek only sex and money from her. "Walk the Plank, Pussycat—You're on Camera" is derived from television actor Nick Adams's announcement to his wife on national television that he was divorcing her. Perelman presents a television script contrived to take advantage of the exploitive nature of certain types of programming and of the audience's voyeurism. In "A Soft Answer Turneth Away Royalties," Perelman once more turns to an exchange of letters to make his point. This time he lampoons both publishers and authors. He also demonstrates the strength of his convictions in typical Perelmanesque fashion: "For a moment, I thought of vindicating my profession dramatically with a right cross to the man's jaw, but it occurred to me that he might vindicate his with a right cross to mine, and I forbore."

Perelman's next collection is even further removed than *Chicken Inspector No. 23* from the type of merriment seen in his early writings. The author's first book since 1966, *Baby, It's Cold Inside* was published in 1970. Of this collection, all but six of the thirty-two pieces originally appeared in the *New Yorker* from 1961 through 1969, the others coming from *Holiday*, *TV Guide*, and *Venture*. It may be significant that Perelman dedicated this book, his eighteenth, to J. D. Salinger, for in some ways the selections it contains reflect a kind of loss of innocence, a continuation of the maturing, perhaps, that was beginning to become apparent in *Chicken Inspector No. 23*. The 1960s were a time of national unrest—Viet Nam, college sit-ins, political assassinations—and this collection reflects the decade. Perelman's point of view has changed; he is no longer the madcap, freewheeling blythe spirit of the 1930s and 1940s, or even the mature observer of the 1950s, looking back on fondly remembered books and films from his youth to point out that they were often ridiculous and frequently not as good as they should have been. Instead, in *Baby, It's Cold Inside*, Perelman's perspective is more tempered. Playing with the popular song title, "Baby, It's Cold Outside," he becomes introspective in his tone. There is still satire, reflecting his amusement and amazement at human failings, but the outrageously absurd connections of "The Idols' Eye" and the language of *Westward Ha!* are gone. The pieces are humorous, but there is an undertone of seriousness. Perelman seems to look upon his material with a somewhat sadder and wiser detachment than had been apparent previously.

Representative of this period in Perelman's development as a writer is "And, in the Center Ring, That Stupendous, Death-Defying Daredevil...," in which the narrator recalls being enthralled by the acrobatic expertise displayed by trapeze artists in the movie *Variety*. The typical Perelman trademarks are present. Remembrance, particularly of movies, literary references, unsupported Mittyesque imaginings, outrageous names, and the quick turn based on juxtaposing elevated language with cliches or slang. As the story progresses, the protagonist is introduced to a female aerialist whose act he has been admiring. He is disillusioned, for not only is she broad shouldered, but her account of the performance has nothing to do with art or discipline. Her focus while on the high trapeze, she reveals, is money—the cost of the rope used to swing her back and forth. As the narrator leaves this meeting with the friend who arranged the introduction, they discuss the breaking of illusion, as when the friend went through "fire and water" to meet Picasso only to find the artist preoccupied with the expense of camel's hair brushes. When a limousine carrying Sophia Loren passes them, though, the despondent friend is suddenly ready to gallop after her—"I'd go

through fire and water to meet her.... A person like this could change your whole life, give you a new perspective...." His adolescent illusions live on.

In the summer of 1970 Laura Perelman died. A few weeks later Perelman sold their farm and in October he moved to London. The move, as he had told a *New York Times* reporter in September, was an attempt to escape from "insanity and violence," "twice breathed air," the current political climate from "the co-author of the Mundt-Nixon bill . . . to every hard hat and red-neck in the country," and incivility, but "The fact that I think it's volcano time in this country is not responsible for the move, though I'm just as appalled as everyone about the conditions." More important, he said, "I've reached the point where I regard my existence as an artichoke, and I'm stripping away the outer layers." "I've had all the rural splendor I can use," he reported, "and each time I get to New York it seems more pestilential than before." On the other hand, he found life in London more "rational": "The obvious good manners and consideration of people there toward each other may be only selfish, but it's good enough for me." Within two years Perelman was back in New York, stating that he had been sated by British couth: "I found myself surrounded in Kensington by stiff-backed Anglo-Indian women living in genteel penury, stalking out three or four times a day to buy one egg or one lemon—a condition that can only be described as tight-assed."

Early in his English sojourn Perelman set out on an eight-day world tour. The idea was for the *New Yorker* to publish his Phileas Fogg-like travel journal in serial form and then for Simon and Schuster to reprint the account as a book. *Vinegar Puss* (1975) included thirty-one selections from the *New Yorker*, *Travel and Leisure* ("Nostasia in Asia"), *Holiday*, *McCall's*, and *Escapade*. Among these were the six pieces grouped under the subtitle, "Around the Bend in Eighty Days." The first anthology that Perelman published after his return from his two years in London, *Vinegar Puss* was well received by reviewers, as usual, but it is not up to Perelman's standard level. There are still funny lines but it lacks the liveliness of the author's early writing. Perelman is clever as always, yet his writing in this collection is more stolid than most of his previous work, and there is nothing new thematically or stylistically. For instance, in "Hail, Hail, the Ganglia's All Here," the eleven-year-old hero is named S. G. Pefelman, an obvious play on the author's name, but the story of how young Pefelman solves a problem that has been baffling police simply is not very funny. In "Missing: Two Lollopaloozas—No Reward," Perelman returns to a device and a theme used before, but with less verve. The story is prefaced by a blurb, ascribed to *Variety*, about an actress in India who is being sued for having walked out in the middle of thirteen pictures. The Perelman character, with pertinent references to Noel Coward, Laurence Harvey, Barton MacLane, and others, meets the actress, Shasta Allahjee, in Bombay, a woman with the face of a nineteen-year-old Ava Gardner mixed with a dash of "an Oriental Catherine Deneuve" and a body that makes Elke Sommer look like "a dried-up old prune" in comparison. The combination of current and past references is effective, and the narrator's blatant attempts to impress Miss Allahjee are amusing and in the same vein as many of Perelman's earlier pieces with the everyman underdog scurrying to overcome the obstacles between him and his idealized and unreachable object of desire. As to be expected, in the end, although he has managed to save her from the evil clutches of the pursuing producers and at the same time established her as a worldwide star of the first magnitude, all through a single stroke of genius, she rejects him.

"Around the Bend in Eighty Days" is a series of six tales about how Perelman and his companion, Sally-Lou Claypool (a 6' 1" beauty from Memphis), came to try to retrace Phileas Fogg's route—fifteen years after the movie was shot—as described in the Jules Verne novel. "Disquiet, Please, We're Turning!" has a few high spots: Candide Yam, Todd's beautiful Chinese secretary; the exemplification of Todd's miserliness; the description of the events during the six-week location shooting in Spain and later an incident in Paris. "New Girdle, With Lots of Support" explains how Perelman's discovery of factual errors in Verne's story stimulated his interest in the trip (and points out that there was no hot air balloon in the original tale; Todd borrowed the balloon episode from another Verne story, *Five Weeks in a Balloon*). It also describes the writer's selection of his traveling companion. "The Turkey Trot: One Step Forward, Two Steps Back" details the first leg of the trip (Rome) and provides insight into Sally-Lou, who, when Perelman discourses on the "vanished glory of the Ottomans," admits that cushioned footstools turn her on, too. Generally, the series is a straightforward account, embellished by Perelman's perspective and unique reactions.

Eastward Ha! (1977) was the last book published in Perelman's lifetime. Another collection of travel pieces, the major part of the text originally

Dust jacket for Perelman's last collection of travel pieces

appeared in *Travel and Leisure*. Basically a catalogue of impressionistic views as opposed to a descriptive travelogue, the nine chapters that compose the book relate Perelman's experiences on his last trip around the world.

Scotland, the setting for his first adventure and "Looking for Pussy," contains a number of Perelman's trademarks. For example, the expected puns are present, there are cinematic allusions and references to other literati (recalling certain exploits of Thurber and Beerbohm), and the narrator adopts the stance of a man whose constant admiration for the ladies is unreturned and whose desires remain unrealized: "I felt I could lean on her shoulder should I ever need support. But that, of course, was academic since I never got her number. Perhaps it was because the moment she'd seen me, she instinctively got mine." "Paris on Five Dolors a Day!" traces his meanderings through the City of Light—meeting an old friend, having his fortune told, being on board a sinking sightseeing boat. "The Millenium, and What They Can Do With It" takes place in Russia (Moscow, Kiev, Leningrad), and contains a typical Perelmanesque exchange: " 'I am what Puritans scornfully call a womanizer. It's sort of a lay preacher.'

" 'You revere women?' she asked puzzled.

" 'I worship the ground they walk on,' I admitted. 'Not the women, you understand, just the ground they walk on.' " "The Nearer the East, the Shorter the Shrift" details the writer's trip to Istanbul and then on board the *Ankora* on a voyage to a Greek isle in search of a tailor to deepen the pants pockets of a suit that he had bought there while passing through the previous year. A five-hour conversation with one of his favorite authors, Isaac Bashevis Singer, highlights Perelman's visit to Israel as described in "Unshorn Locks and Bogus Bagels" (about a barber and a gentleman who wears a ceramic bagel on a chain around his neck). Perelman's attitude toward Singer contrasts interestingly with the throwaway lines that repeatedly pepper his writing, reflecting his love for Conan Doyle and his dislike for "hacks" like Irving Wallace and Harold Robbins who are frequently mentioned in passing. In "Rosy and Sleazy, or Dream and Reality in Asia," the traveler relates the changes he sees that have taken place in Bangkok since his visit to Thailand in 1947 (and fondly reported in *Westward Ha!*) and then skips lightly through Malacca and Hong Kong—where he felt the freedom not to do the things customarily incumbent on tourists. Perelman also writes about Malaysia in this section, with Penang being singled out as one of the few places in all of his travels that he finds attractive and unchanged and that consequently receives sympathetic affectionate treatment. There is a quick swing "To One cup of Java, Add One Snootful of Tahiti" and the book concludes with "Back Home in Tinseltown," an account of his stay in Los Angeles.

The style of *Eastward Ha!* is much more relaxed than *Vinegar Puss*, published two years earlier. It may be that the greater distance in time from his wife's death had a calming effect. Whatever the cause, his style is better suited to the themes and topics of his later writing here. At the same time, though, his sexual allusions and double entendres are more harshly worded in his later writing. As with most of his travel writing, the pieces are designed not to map out the history of the local sights but rather to catch the national flavor in what might be called a montage. A series of similar episodes, largely romantic imaginings a la Walter Mitty, revolving around airline stewardesses on flights between countries, serves as a unifying character line for Perelman's narrator persona. On the serious side, his essays include occasional social commentary and he incidentally describes some points of interest in connection with plot developments (almost always located in major cities), but Perelman's prime concern is Perelman. He is his own best subject, and it is often difficult to distinguish between reporting and fiction in the tales of his peregrinations. The accounts are built around fact, but they also contain exaggeration that supplies the essential reality instead of a superficial, photographic reality. Accidents, mishaps, scraps, emotional reactions, relationships with his fellow travelers, how he sees himself in relation to the world around him—these are Perelman's subjects.

It is appropriate that Perelman's final book was admiringly reviewed on the cover of the *New York Times Book Review*, by Tom Wolfe. The posthumous work, published in 1981, bears the title *The Last Laugh*. It consists of fourteen *New Yorker* stories, four chapters from the author's unfinished autobiography, "The Hindsight Saga" (a project Perelman alluded to some years earlier and whose title mock's John Galsworthy's *The Forsyte Saga*), and an introduction by Paul Theroux. Wolfe expresses disappointment that the autobiography must remain incomplete and the writer's abilities in the subgenre untested, but a large percentage of Perelman's

S. J. Perelman

writing was in effect based on autobiographical events.

S. J. Perelman is one of the most popular writers of humor in the history of American literature, and the disparate writers who claim to be "quite an admirer" of Perelman, in contemporary British dramatist Harold Pinter's words, include Pinter himself, Dorothy Parker, Robert Benchley, Somerset Maugham, Ogden Nash, T. S. Eliot, E. B. White, and Eudora Welty. Benchley once noted that "It was just a matter of time before Perelman took over the dementia praecox field and drove us all to writing articles on economics" and White stated that "Sid's stuff influenced me in the early days. . . . he has, from the beginning, bowed to no one." John Hollander, in a commemorative article that appeared in the BBC's the *Listener* magazine, states that Perelman "and Henry Miller were both tremendously important influences on all kinds of novelists, not only karmic ones but, of course on comic ones as well." In the same article Woody Allen recalls, "I discovered [Perelman] when I was in high school. I came across certain pieces that he had written and I immediately was stunned by them. I thought they were just the best and the funniest things that I had ever read, and not at all heavy-handed, which most humour writers are. . . . Perelman . . . is just as light as a souffle. What happens to you when you read Perelman and you're a young writer is fatal because his style seeps into you. He's got such a pronounced, overwhelming comic style that it's very hard not to be influenced by him." Peter Sellers and Spike Milligan, from British television's "The Goon Show," claimed Perelman as their mentor.

In spite of his popularity (hundreds of individual pieces, over twenty books, eleven films, work in television and for the stage, done over a period of fifty years) and in spite of his acknowledged influence on other twentieth-century authors, there has been almost no scholarly attention paid to Perelman's writing. A doctoral dissertation in progress in France, a couple of interviews, and three or four articles in scholarly journals compose the critical commentary on his canon. As might be expected with a writer of comedy, Perelman was not studied by scholars during his lifetime, nor is he remembered now for any special or significant thematic content, as Louis Hasley points out in "The Kangaroo Mind of S. J. Perelman," though he does occasionally imply dissatisfaction with certain governments and agencies. Instead, it is his mastery of the English language and his manipulation of prose for comic effect that draw praise, and his ability was such that he could apply his style to any topic to produce humor. E. B. White, a contemporary, admirer, and friend of Perelman's, tells a story that sums up both the man and his work: "Sid commands a vocabulary that is the despair (and joy) of every writing man. He is like a Roxy organ that has three decks, 50 stops, and a pride of pedals under the bench. When he wants a word it's there. He and Laura showed up at our house in Sarasota a couple of winters ago. They had been in an automobile accident—a bad one, the car a complete wreck. Laura came out of it with some bruises, Sid with a new word. The car, he learned, had been 'totaled.' I could see that the addition of this word to his already enormous store meant a lot to him. His ears are as busy as an ant's feelers. No word ever gets by him."

The attention concentrated on Perelman's use of language is in no way meant to belittle humorous writing or the social functions of humor. His work is read for enjoyment and to commiserate with a kindred spirit in a vindictive world—but it is not read for its philosophy or great thoughts. Columnist Hal Boyle described him as "a man who looks with skepticism on everything in life except the messages he finds in Chinese cookies." "These," Perelman tells Boyle, "I accept literally," and he goes on to deny being a cynic, though he admits the possibility that he is an idealist. At the base of his writing is a sense of perspective, an ability to see ridiculous or amusing aspects in quotidian experiences through his wire-rimmed glasses. This is coupled with the talent for communicating his discoveries to his audience so that they can share in the laughter. Catastrophe is avoided—it is catastrophe enough to be trapped in a restaurant by a former flame who has been caught in compromising situations by a progression of husbands in spite of being "a giantess in an emerald-green frock, trimmed with salmon beads, a veritable grenadier of a woman. . . . Askew on her head . . . a fawn-colored duvetyn turban whose aigrette was secured by the Hope diamond or its rhinestone equivalent . . . [with] the odor of malt pervading her embrace," as he relates in "Call and I Follow, I Follow!"

As an author Perelman was a society writer rather than a writer on social concerns. His topics were not politics, but everyday subjects—films, books, travel, appliances, advertisements—topical but timeless only in the strictest sense of the word in that they represent annoyances that will always plague mankind, not the larger questions about the nature of existence. "Humor is purely a point of view, and only the pedants try to classify it," he told William Zinnser. "For me its chief merit is the use of the unexpected, the glancing allusion, the deflation of pomposity, and the constant repetition of one's helplessness in a majority of situations. One doesn't consciously start out wanting to be a social satirist. You find something absurd enough to make you want to push a couple of antipersonnel bombs under it. If it seems to have another element of meaning, that's lagniappe. But the main obligation is to amuse yourself."

Perelman has also said, "I regard myself as a species of journalist." The length of his essays, then, is imposed on his writing to some extent by their place of publication. Because of this there are some affinities with other journalist-humorists such as Mark Twain and Finley Peter Dunne. In fact, some of his protagonists display traits similar to those exhibited by various Twain personae or Mr. Dooley. Thus two elements of Perelman's style converge. His writing contains the exuberance and the straight-faced exaggeration that are common elements in traditional American humor; it has an American tone to it. There is simultaneously a bite in what he writes. "Generally speaking," he claims, "I don't believe in kindly humor." At the same time, journals are his element and Edgar Allan Poe's strictures about the short story are applicable (especially since the short stories referred to appeared in journals). This means that the quick effect is sought. "His pieces usually had a lead sentence, or lead paragraph, that was as hair-raising as the first big dip on a roller coaster," reflects E. B. White. The need to be concise led to a use of language that has a British feel to it. Puns and other forms of word play, non sequiturs, cliches (both phrases and situations—which are sometimes taken literally when they are meant figuratively), and literary allusions all have been noted above, and Perelman used his tools with the sure hand of a superb craftsman. Indeed, it is his knowledge of these tools that makes him such a capable parodist.

Perhaps Perelman's insistence on labeling himself a journalist and writer of short humorous pieces carries its own challenge. As he remarks, "No other kind of writer risks his work so visibly or so often on the high wire of public approval. It is the thinnest wire in all literature, and the writer lives with the certain knowledge that he will frequently fall off."

The final story in the last collection published in Perelman's lifetime, in which he supposedly winds up marrying Gabrielle de Casabas, the paragon of womanhood who wants only him, fittingly ends with a line that summarizes his life and his writing: "Oh, well, kid, I decided, drink up—you win a little, you lose a little. Isn't that what it's all about?" Indeed, Perelman may have found life a little naughty at times, but he always enjoyed being involved in its celebration and he happily shared this with all of us.

Plays:
The Third Little Show, sketches by Perelman, New York, Music Box Theatre, 1 June 1931;

Walk a Little Faster, sketches by Perelman and Robert MacGunigle, New York, St. James Theatre, 7 December 1932;

All Good Americans, by Perelman and Laura Perelman, New York, Henry Miller's Theatre, 5 December 1933;

Two Weeks with Pay, sketches by Perelman, tour, 1940;

The Night Before Christmas, by Perelman and Laura Perelman, New York, Morosco Theatre, 10 April 1941;

One Touch of Venus, by Perelman and Ogden Nash, music by Kurt Weill, adapted from F. Anstey's *The Tinted Venus*, New York, Imperial Theatre, 7 October 1943;

Sweet Bye and Bye, by Perelman and Al Hirschfeld, music by Vernon Duke, lyrics by Nash, New Haven, Conn., Shubert Theatre, 10 October 1946;

The Beauty Part, by Perelman and Nash, New York, Music Box Theatre, 26 December 1962.

Screenplays:
Monkey Business, by Perelman and Will B. Johnstone, Paramount, 1931;

Horse Feathers, by Perelman, Bert Kalmar, and Harry Ruby, Paramount, 1932;

Paris Interlude, MGM, 1934;

Florida Special, by Perelman, Laura Perelman, David Boehm, and Marguerite Roberts, Paramount, 1936;

Sweethearts, MGM, 1938;

Ambush, by Perelman and Laura Perelman, Paramount, 1939;

Boy Trouble, by Perelman and Laura Perelman, Paramount, 1939;

The Golden Fleecing, by Perelman, Laura Perelman, and Marion Parsonnet, MGM, 1940;

Larceny, Inc., Warner Brothers, 1942;

Greenwich Village, MGM, 1944;

Around the World in Eighty Days, by Perelman, James Poe, and John Farrow, United Artists, 1956.

Television Scripts:
Omnibus, contributed scripts, including "Malice in

Wonderland," 18 January 1959, NBC, 1957-
1959;
"The Changing Ways of Love," *Seven Lively Arts*,
CBS, 3 November 1957;
Elizabeth Taylor's London, CBS, 6 October 1963.

Interviews:
William Cole and George Plimpton, "S. J. Perel-
man," *Paris Review*, 30 (Fall 1963): 147;
William Zinsser, "Perelman of Great Price," *New
York Times Magazine*, 26 January 1969, pp. 26,
72, 74, 76.

Bibliography:
Steven H. Gale, "Sidney Joseph Perelman: Twenty
Years of American Humor," *Bulletin of Bib-
liography*, 29 (January-March 1972): 10-12.

References:
Woody Allen, Caskie Stinnett, and John Hollander,

"Perelman's Revenge or the Gifts of Provi-
dence, Rhode Island," *Listener*, 102 (15
November 1979): 667-669;
Walter Blair and Hamlin Hill, *America's Humor:
From Poor Richard to Doonesbury* (New York:
Oxford University Press, 1980);
Russell Davies, "S. J. Perelman: 1904-1979," *New
Statesman*, 98 (26 October 1979): 646-647;
Douglas Fowler, *S. J. Perelman* (New York: Twayne,
forthcoming, 1982);
Louis Hasley, "The Kangaroo Mind of S. J. Perel-
man," *South Atlantic Quarterly*, 72 (Winter
1973): 115-121;
Terry Heller, "Sidney Joseph Perelman," *Critical
Survey of Short Fiction* (Los Angeles: Salem,
1981), pp. 2079-2084;
J. A. Ward, "The Hollywood Metaphor: The Marx
Brothers, S. J. Perelman, Nathanael West,"
Southern Review, 12 (July 1976): 659-672.

Will Rogers
(4 November 1879-15 August 1935)

Terry L. Heller
Coe College

SELECTED BOOKS: *The Cowboy Philosopher on the
Peace Conference* (New York: Harper, 1919);
The Cowboy Philosopher on Prohibition (New York:
Harper, 1919);
The Illiterate Digest (New York: A. & C. Boni, 1924);
Letters of a Self-Made Diplomat to His President (New
York: A. & C. Boni, 1926);
There's Not a Bathing Suit in Russia (New York:
A. & C. Boni, 1927);
Ether and Me (New York & London: Putnam's,
1929);
*Twelve Radio Talks Delivered by Will Rogers During the
Spring of 1930* (New York: E. R. Squibb &
Sons, 1930);
The Autobiography of Will Rogers, edited by Donald
Day (Boston: Houghton Mifflin, 1949);
Sanity is Where You Find It, edited by Donald Day
(Boston: Houghton Mifflin, 1955);
The Writings of Will Rogers, edited by Joseph A.
Stout, Jr., and James M. Smallwood (Stillwa-
ter: Oklahoma State University Press,
1973-)—volumes published through 1980 in-
clude: *Ether and Me* (1973), *There's Not a Bath-*

ing Suit in Russia & Other Bare Facts (1973), *The
Illiterate Digest* (1974), *The Cowboy Philosopher on
the Peace Conference* (1975), *The Cowboy
Philosopher on Prohibition* (1975), *Convention
Articles of Will Rogers* (1976), *Letters of a Self-
Made Diplomat to His President* (1977), *Will
Rogers' Daily Telegrams*, 4 volumes (1978), *Will
Rogers' Weekly Articles*, 1 of 6 volumes (1980).

William Penn Adair Rogers, according to his
biographers, was the last of the cracker-barrel
philosophers, that tradition of American humor
which includes Benjamin Franklin, Abraham Lincoln, Mark Twain, Marietta Holley, and Finley
Peter Dunne and which evokes the image of rural
types gathered about the cracker barrel of a general
store, transfixed by a witty talker who keeps them
chuckling while he sums up their thoughts in
amusing tales and pungent aphorisms. "All I know
is what I read in the papers"; variations on this
sentence were often included in Rogers's
monologues and articles. He made his reputation as
an ordinary man who read the papers carefully and

pointed out the ridiculous as well as the grimly humorous in the activities of the body politic. Calling himself the cowboy philosopher, he reached a huge audience through his lectures, films, stage plays, newspaper and magazine articles, books, and radio broadcasts. At his death, many commentators thought him one of the most influential private citizens in the United States.

Rogers proudly proclaimed throughout his life that he was an Oklahoma cowboy and one-quarter Cherokee Indian. These connections with the blood and soil of America branded him, in his own mind, as an authentic American. The last of eight children of the well-to-do Clement Vann Rogers and Mary American Schrimsher, he was born on his parents' ranch near Claremore, Oklahoma, on 4 November 1879. Though he achieved the rough equivalent of a high-school education, he never graduated; he was apparently more interested in cowboy-show arts, especially riding and roping tricks. After running away from the military school which his father had vainly hoped would settle him, the eighteen-year-old Rogers worked and traveled. Tiring of managing and working on his father's ranch, he sailed to South America, then worked his way to South Africa where he started in show business with Texas Jack's Wild West Show as a trick rider. He then toured with a circus in New Zealand and Australia. After returning home in 1904, he joined another wild west show which eventually took him to New York City. There he began working vaudeville shows as a trick roping performer.

Rogers's career began to develop when he discovered he had a talent for humor and started telling jokes as part of his rope act. During his apprentice years, 1905-1916, he worked regularly without becoming a headliner. In 1908 he married Betty Blake and they soon had three children, Will, Jr., born in 1911, Amelia, born in 1913, and James Blake, born in 1915. In 1916 Rogers began an eleven-year run as a regular performer in the Ziegfeld Follies and rose quickly to stardom. His discovery, at his wife's suggestion, of newspaper stories as a source for humorous topical commentary made it possible for him to produce enough new material for three daily performances. His wad of gum, his Oklahoma drawl, and his casual stage presence became trademarks of his humor as he mastered techniques for making jokes about contemporary events and personalities. By 1919 his jokes were so successful that he was able to collect them in his first two books: *The Cowboy Philosopher on the Peace Conference* (about the Paris Peace Conference following World War I) and *The Cowboy Philosopher on Prohibition*. Both books sold well because they expressed ideas with which most of his readers would agree and because they captured the flavor of his oral delivery.

Rogers's career took another direction when he appeared in a movie, *Laughing Bill Hyde* (1918). He signed a two-year film contract with Sam Goldwyn and moved his family to California soon after the birth of his fourth child, Freddie; the baby died there of diphtheria. Rogers was a reasonably successful actor, but he lost his contract when the Goldwyn operation was sold. His subsequent attempt to produce his own films failed financially, forcing him to return to the Follies. However, he kept his home in Beverly Hills for ten years before moving to a ranch at Santa Monica. In New York financial necessity moved him to yet another stage in his career; he became an after-dinner speaker. His success on the circuit attracted the attention of the McNaught Newspaper Syndicate, and in 1922 he began writing for them the syndicated weekly column which ran until his death. In this column Rogers developed his abilities as a writer.

In 1924 he collected his favorites among the first two years of his columns for publication in *The*

Will Rogers in costume for his vaudeville act

William Jennings Bryan and Will Rogers

with accounts of meetings with famous people such as Lady Astor and George Bernard Shaw. While in Europe he proposed to send the *New York Times* a daily telegram. Published as "Will Rogers Says," the telegrams became a syndicated daily wire which ran until his death. The Russian portion of his tour appeared in his next book, *There's Not a Bathing Suit in Russia* (1927). These two travel books are more unified than his earlier efforts; they show Rogers sustaining humorous narrative and presenting a cohesive view of the world. Nineteen twenty-six was also the year of Rogers's first radio broadcast which led eventually to a popular series of weekly broadcasts beginning in 1930. In his columns, books, and broadcasts, the format remained the same: a short witty commentary on a contemporary topic with illustrative stories worked in. An example is his June 1930 radio broadcast in which he argues that Prohibition is not important enough to absorb so much of the nation's energy. During his monologue he invokes biblical authority: "Right in the first book of Genesis, you don't read but just a few pages until Noah was lit up like a pygmy golf course. Here is just

Illiterate Digest. This book was well received, prompting reviewers to recognize him as a spokesman for the ordinary American. The targets of his irony and humor included Congress, government in general, American business, and world disarmament. In a typical column, he ridiculed a philanthropist's offer of a reward for a workable plan to end wars: "Can you imagine the bunch of Multi-Millionaires made by the last war agreeing to stop all chances of a future war for 100 thousand dollars? I am only an ignorant Cowpuncher but there ain't nobody on earth . . . ever going to make me believe they will ever stop wars." In a more bitter, less typical column he wrote, "You wire the State or the Federal Government that your Cow or Hog is sick and they will send out experts from Washington and appropriate money. . . . You wire them that your Baby has the Diphtheria . . . and see what they do."

In 1926 Rogers traveled to Europe for the *Saturday Evening Post* and produced a series of articles which became *Letters of a Self-Made Diplomat to His President* (1926). Rogers's reputation opened doors for him, and he was able to enrich his columns

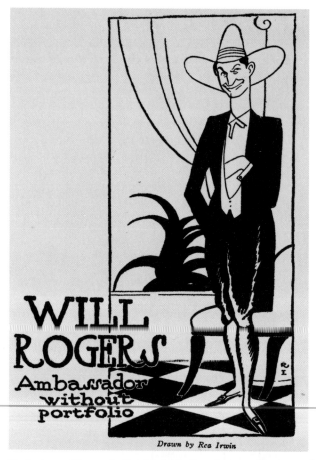

Caricature of Rogers by Rea Irwin for frontispiece of Letters of a Self-Made Diplomat to His President

how it started. . . . Right in the start of Genesis . . . it says, 'And Noah became a husbandman and planted a vineyard.' The minute he became a husband he started in raising the ingredients that goes with married life. So you can trace all drink to marriage, see. What we got to prohibit is marriage.

"In the very next verse . . . it says, 'And he drank of the wine and was drunk.' Now that was Noah himself, our forefather. Practically all of us can trace our ancestry back to him. . . .

"Now you see Noah drank and he didn't drink water and he was a man that knew more about water than practically any man of his time. . . . Old Noah was an expert on water, but the Lord is very farseeing, and everything He does is for the best. Through Noah partaking of too much wine and going on this little spree, that is just why the Lord picked on him to pick out these animals to take in to the Ark. He was the only man that had even seen all of them. So if Noah hadn't drunk, today we would be without circuses and menageries."

Rogers's popularity increased rapidly in the late 1920s with his wide exposure on the radio, in his columns, and with his humanitarian activities, which were given generous coverage in the press. In 1927 he toured the Mississippi flood areas, gave benefit performances for the victims, and testified in favor of flood relief before Congress. By 1928 he was a recognized commentator on national political conventions. In addition to earning good reviews for his performance in the 1928 Broadway show, *Three Cheers*, he was nominated by *Life* as the Anti-Bunk party's presidential candidate. He ran a campaign in his columns which kept his readers laughing at all the candidates. As he became a national figure, the movies again sought him and he began a new career in sound films with *They Had to See Paris* (1929). He soon was appearing on several "most popular actor" lists. His popularity resulted at least in part from his policy of appearing only in films which he felt were suitable for family viewing. His best known films include *A Connecticut Yankee in King Arthur's Court* (1931) and *Steamboat 'Round the Bend* (1935).

Rogers's 1929 gallstone operation provided the material for *Ether and Me* (1929), perhaps his only book that has not become dated. The book reveals the personal side of Rogers, showing his family life and his ability to laugh at himself; it also touches on the more serious theme of his own mortality, foreshadowing in some ways Rogers's more serious approach to his material in the 1930s.

Rogers's broadcasts and columns of the De-

Will and Betty Rogers

pression era reveal him at his most mature and accomplished. He moderated some of his more extreme opinions. In the 1920s he had admired Mussolini, supported American isolationism, and often expressed the view that the American government should be run like one of Henry Ford's factories. In the 1930s he changed his mind about Mussolini and became ambivalent about Ford. His frequent and extensive travels which carried him around the world three times and often took him to troubled areas may have increased his sympathies for the unfortunate everywhere, but his opinions about American involvement in the squabbles of foreign governments did not change. During the Depression he spoke out, sometimes bitterly, against those who blamed victims for their misfortunes. He called repeatedly for relief and welcomed Franklin Roosevelt and the New Deal. He gave benefit performances for American drought and flood victims. He toured the areas devastated by a Central American earthquake and gave benefits for the homeless.

Throughout his career, Rogers's opinions reflected the paradoxes of public opinion in America. He always thought the American government inefficient, yet he supported every president in office, came to think that only the government could remedy the ills of the Depression, and frequently repeated that the American government was the best in the world. He spoke strongly in favor of individual self-determination for persons and nations, yet he found dictatorship attractive at times. He usually seemed optimistic about the long range future and pessimistic about the short range. He ridiculed those traits of human nature which lead to paternalism, intolerance, and war, but he praised the "normal majority," supported American participation in the arms race of his day, and admitted admiration for several individual congressmen.

In 1931 Will Durant requested from Rogers a statement of his philosophy of life. He replied: "There aint nothing to life but satisfaction. . . . Indians and primitive races were the highest civilized, because they were more satisfied, and they depended less on each other, and took less from each other. We couldent live a day without depending on everybody. So our civilization has given us no Liberty or Independence."

"Suppose the other Guy quits feeding us. The whole thing is a 'Racket,' so get a few laughs, do the best you can, take nothing serious, for nothing is certainly depending on this generation. Each one lives in spite of the previous one and not because of it. And dont start 'seeking knowledge' for the more you seek the nearer the 'Booby Hatch' you get.

"And dont have an ideal to work for. Thats like riding towards a Mirage of a lake. When you get there it aint there. Believe in something for another World, but dont be too set on what it is, and then you wont start out that life with a disappointment. Live your life so that whenever you lose, you are ahead."

Though often quoted as a definitive statement of his general views, these remarks are more pessimistic and cynical than Rogers's articles normally were. The realism and humility of the statement are characteristic of his attitudes throughout his career, but his pessimism about American civilization is indicative of his frustration with Hoover's Depression policies. Perhaps the general trend of his thinking is better revealed in his description of a member of the "big honest majority," who goes along "believing in

Will Rogers and Wiley Post in Fairbanks, Alaska, on 18 August 1935, the day of their fatal plane crash

right, doing right, tending to his own business, letting the other fellows alone. He don't seem simple enough minded to believe that EVERYTHING is right and he don't appear to be Cuckoo enough to think that EVERYTHING is wrong." Rogers combines a strong skepticism about social progress with a faith in the abiding values of community: loyalty to family, friends, honest dealings, an easy toleration of the views of others, and a love for his native soil. To these he adds an appreciation of personal liberty and an accompanying sense of personal responsibility for others.

Rogers died in the middle of the Depression. He was killed in a plane crash with Wiley Post near Point Barrow, Alaska, on 15 August 1935. His death in an airplane is ironic because Rogers was an enthusiastic supporter of flying and air safety all his adult life, and the purpose of Post's flight was to survey safer mail and passenger routes to Russia. After Rogers's death the nation mourned as never before the passing of a mass-media personality.

Rogers's chosen epitaph, "I never met a man I didn't like," indicates one of the reasons for his popularity despite his role as a public critic. Though his humor was often pointed, he did not enjoy hurting people. When his victims protested, his typical response was to remind them that humorists should not be taken too seriously. More important to his popularity and his success was his skillful use of irony. Rogers was a master at appearing just ignorant enough to show his listeners that, like them, he saw through the sham and hypocrisy of those who try to take advantage of ordinary people. This combination of gentleness and subtle toughness together with his comic talents and his homely presence endeared Rogers to the American people. His sense of public decency also appealed to average Americans. Rogers took his obligation to satisfy public mores so seriously that shortly before his death, he gave up his part in a California stage production of Eugene O'Neill's *Ah, Wilderness!* (1932) when a Pasadena clergyman protested that he had been embarrassed when he took his fourteen-year-old daughter to a performance. The American public so liked and admired Rogers that when *Life* announced in 1928 that he had been elected "unofficial" president of the United States, the title stuck.

When the Will Rogers memorial was dedicated at Claremore, Oklahoma, on 4 November 1938, President Roosevelt described Will Rogers's achievement: "I doubt if there is among us a more useful citizen than the one who holds the secret of banishing gloom, of making tears give way to laughter, of supplanting desolation and despair with hope and courage. . . . His appeal went straight to the heart of the nation."

References:

Paul E. Alworth, *Will Rogers* (New York: Twayne, 1974);

Walter Blair and Hamlin Hill, *America's Humor: From Poor Richard to Doonesbury* (New York: Oxford University Press, 1978), pp. 520-529;

William R. Brown, "Will Rogers: Ironist as Persuader," *Speech Monographs*, 39 (1972): 183-192;

Homer Croy, *Our Will Rogers* (New York: Duell, Sloan, & Pearce, 1953);

Donald Day, *Will Rogers* (New York: David McKay, 1962);

Norris Yates, *The American Humorist* (Ames: Iowa State University Press, 1964), pp. 113-127.

Leo Rosten
(Leonard Q. Ross)
(11 April 1908-   )

Ellen Golub
University of Pennsylvania

BOOKS: *The Education of H*Y*M*A*N K*A*P*L*A*N*, as Leonard Q. Ross (New York: Harcourt, Brace, 1937; London: Constable, 1937);

The Washington Correspondents (New York: Harcourt, Brace, 1937);

Dateline: Europe, as Leonard Ross (New York: Harcourt, Brace, 1939); republished as *Balkan Express* (London: William Heinemann, 1939);

The Strangest Places, as Leonard Q. Ross (New York: Harcourt, Brace, 1939; London: Constable, 1939);

Adventure in Washington, as Leonard Ross (New York: Harcourt, Brace, 1940);

Hollywood: The Movie Colony, The Movie Makers (New York: Harcourt, Brace, 1941);

112 Gripes About The French (Washington, D.C., United States War Department, 1944);

The Dark Corner, as Leonard Q. Ross (New York: Century, 1945; London: Walter Edwards, 1946);

Sleep, My Love, as Leonard Ross (New York: Triangle, 1946); republished as *Dors, Mon Amour*, translated by Elisabeth Granet (Paris: Hachette, 1949);

The Return of H*Y*M*A*N K*A*P*L*A*N (New York: Harper, 1959; London: Gollancz, 1959);

Captain Newman, M.D. (New York: Harper, 1961; London: Gollancz, 1961);

The Story Behind The Painting (New York: Doubleday-Cowles, 1962);

The Many Worlds of L*E*O R*O*S*T*E*N (New York: Harper & Row, 1964); republished as *The Leo Rosten Bedside Book* (London: Gollancz, 1965);

A Most Private Intrigue (New York: Atheneum, 1967; London: Gollancz, 1967);

The Joys of Yiddish (New York: McGraw-Hill, 1968; London: W. H. Allen, 1970);

People I Have Loved, Known, or Admired (New York: McGraw-Hill, 1970; London: W. H. Allen, 1973);

A Trumpet for Reason (Garden City: Doubleday, 1970; London: W. H. Allen, 1971);

Leo Rosten's Treasury of Jewish Quotations, edited by Rosten (New York: McGraw-Hill, 1972; London: W. H. Allen, 1973);

Rome Wasn't Burned in a Day: The Mischief of Language (Garden City: Doubleday, 1972; London: W. H. Allen, 1973);

Dear "Herm"–With a Cast of Dozens (New York: McGraw-Hill, 1974; London: W. H. Allen, 1975);

O K*A*P*L*A*N! My K*A*P*L*A*N!, as Leonard Q. Ross (New York: Harper & Row, 1976);

The 3:10 to Anywhere (New York: McGraw-Hill, 1976);

The Power of Positive Nonsense (New York: McGraw-Hill, 1977);

Passions & Prejudices: or, Some of My Best Friends Are People (New York: McGraw-Hill, 1978);

Infinite Riches: Gems From a Lifetime of Reading (New York: McGraw-Hill, 1979);

Silky! A Detective Story (New York: Harper & Row, 1979);

King Silky! (New York: Harper & Row, 1980).

Although known as a social scientist of some reputation, Leo Calvin Rosten is best recognized as a humorist who often writes under the pseudonyms Leonard Ross and Leonard Q. Ross. His extraordinarily popular first book, *The Education of H*Y*M*A*N K*A*P*L*A*N*, earned comparisons to the comic works of Dickens and Shakespeare. That book is also the keynote of a prolific career which includes ethnic humor, melodramas, screenplays, and writings on economics, social science, and lexicography. No matter what the literary form, Rosten's persistent subject is what his malaprop-cursed, mispronouncing, unwitting character, Hyman Kaplan, calls "good English." Rosten's interest and comic talents are consistently engaged in presenting the mysteries, misuses, and vagaries of language as spoken and written by fallible beings.

Rosten was born in Lodz, Poland, to Samuel C. and Ida Freundlich Rosten and was brought at the age of three to the United States when his parents immigrated. The Rostens settled in a poor neighborhood in Chicago, the city in which Leo received much of his education. As Rosten writes, "Chicago must bear the responsibility for my misguided childhood; it was there I spent my grammar school days reading Frank Merriwell and Rabelais. My high school years, of a higher order, were devoted to banging my hands with hammers (woodshop), cutting my fingers off neatly at the joint (tin shop), and pouring hot lead over my toes once a week (foundry). I was also exposed to mechanical drawing, which left me drawn and unmechanical." By his teenage years, Rosten had read Chekhov, Maupassant, and many of the masters whose collected works were being peddled by book salesmen and consumed by the knowledge-hungry immigrants and their children among whom he lived. Samuel Rosten attended a night school for immigrants, and to his son fell the unusual task of helping him with his homework. Both parents became U.S. citizens and, as a result, Leo Rosten became a naturalized American citizen.

At the University of Chicago, which virtually subsidized four years of his college education, Rosten pursued multiple interests, studying everything "from anthropology to zoology." He studied in Europe for six months in 1928, returned to spend a year in law school, and received his Ph.B. degree from Chicago, Phi Beta Kappa, in 1930. Graduating at the beginning of the Depression, Rosten searched for employment for two years, during which time he worked as a bus boy, a salesman, a camp counselor, a lecturer, a real-estate salesman's assistant, and a maker of fake antique coins. His most notable job was as a part-time teacher of English to adults in a Chicago night school much like the one his father had attended. It was from this experience that *The Education of H*Y*M*A*N   K*A*P*L*A*N* derived.

"In 1932," Rosten writes, "I came to the realization that I was a remarkably ignorant young man." Accordingly, Rosten spent the next decade pursuing serious research. He enrolled in the graduate school of Political Science and International Relations at the University of Chicago (1932), where he later became Harold Lasswell's research assistant in political science (1934) and a lecturer in international politics (1934-1935). He studied briefly at the London School of Economics and Political Science in 1934 and during that year sold his first piece of written work, a study of British Fascist leader Oswald Mosley and English fascism, to *Harper's* magazine.

Rosten's serious work continued as he left Chicago for Washington to receive a grant from the Social Science Research Council. There he con-

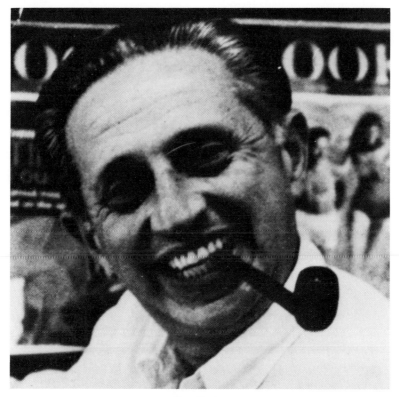

Leo Rosten

ducted sixteen months of research on the Washington press corps, its function, techniques, composition, and effects on public opinion, for his Ph.D. thesis. He also began writing articles on the psychology of politics, while serving as a research staffer on President Roosevelt's Committee on Administrative Management. Concurrent with this work, Rosten began writing fiction for fun and profit. He wrote under the pseudonym Leonard Q. Ross (lest his professors and the research council should think him neglectful of his scholarly duties) and sold humorous sketches for three years to the *New Yorker*.

The publication of these stories coincided with the illness of Rosten's wife, Priscilla Ann Mead, and helped to pay debts incurred by her appendicitis and pneumonia. (She died after bearing Rosten three children: Philip, Madeline, and Peggy. In 1960 Rosten married Gertrude Zimmerman.) Their publication also branded Rosten as a humorist, earned him an award from the National Conference of Christians and Jews, and immortalized the character of Hyman Kaplan.

In 1937 Rosten published two diverse books, one serious and the other humorous. He received his Ph.D. from the University of Chicago for the result of his Washington research and published *The Washington Correspondents*, a 436-page reference volume in the field of public opinion research and analysis. The book was heralded by critics as well written, socially important, and of lasting value; it identified the typical Washington correspondent as a thirty-seven-year-old family man who became a journalist by choice, lived in a small city, had a liberal arts background, and received $5,987 per year to write what his publisher wanted to hear. In identifying the typical correspondent, Rosten approached as a social scientist an issue which he confronts in his humorous work as well: the transmission of information and how it becomes distorted by the comic devices, whether accidental or intentional, of a speaker's or listener's communication.

Rosten explains that the kind of writer he is prefers "to work simultaneously on quite different subjects." Accordingly, as Leonard Q. Ross, he published in 1937 his collected stories which had for three years been appearing in the *New Yorker*. This book received even more attention than did *The Washington Correspondents*; it is *The Education of H*Y*M*A*N K*A*P*L*A*N* and it earned Leo Rosten his lasting reputation as a humorist. His university sponsors and other academics were delighted with the revelation of Rosten's other identity; the *New Yorker* was relieved that he was not one

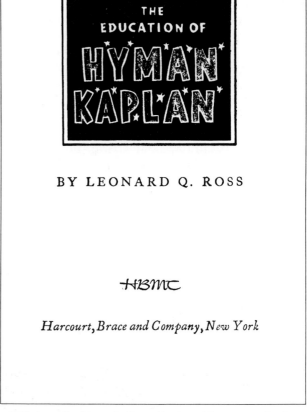

Title page for Rosten's first collection of humorous sketches

of their own staff writing under an assumed name in order to supplement his income. Many critics mourned the publication of the collection fearing that its appearance signaled the end of the Kaplan saga. Joseph Wood Krutch wrote, "It would be a pity to see Mr. Kaplan decline like the Falstaff of the *Merry Wives* . . . it is also hard to imagine a world without him. I at least shall feel, not that he has ceased to exist, but that through some calamity I have ceased to hear of the stupendous yet justifiable blunders which he is somewhere still making in obedience to the laws of his being." Sir Isaiah Berlin of Oxford called the book "one of the great comic creations of the 20th century."

Rosten's concern, in *The Education of H*Y*M*A*N K*A*P*L*A*N*, was for getting Kaplan's dialect exactly and, secondary to that, getting the right rhythm of speech. Scholar and creative artist were merged in the careful construction of sentences and the product is a hilarious jabberwocky of the English language. Hyman Kaplan is an ardent pupil, the ironic star in the American Night Preparatory School For Adults. He is a charming, red-faced, cherubic man, always smiling, disarmingly naive. Singlehandedly, he dismantles the English language with his misguided passions for it, his malapropisms and monstrous diction, his well-intentioned but specious logical deductions.

Enamored of American history and literature, he writes essays on Abraham Lincohen, Valt Viterman, Mocktwain, and Jack Laundon. Inimitably, he grammaticizes the plural of "sandwich" into "delicatessen," "blouse" into "blice," and "cat" into "katz." Superlatives for Kaplan move from "good" to "batter" to "high-cless"; verbs conjugate into "fail, failed, bankropt"; the opposite of "new" is "second-hand." In pronunciation "Salome" descends into "salami" and "memory" into "mamory." As Mr. Kaplan unveils his humorous character in composition, he never fails to hyperbolize his own name in red and blue crayon, each letter followed by a green star.

The personable Mr. Kaplan is the very spirit of a class peopled by other funny characters, each with his own peculiar flair. There is Miss Rochelle Goldberg, constant consumer of jellybeans and caramels; Mr. Norman Bloom, Kaplan's grammatical nemesis; the blushing Miss Mitnick, and the shy Mrs. Moskowitz. Kaplan's "dip thinking" and inept locutions ("If your eye falls on a bargain, pick it op.") are ministered to by Mr. Parkhill (Mr. Pockheel to Kaplan), a scion of native English speakers whose nerves Kaplan pushes to the point of breaking. But for all Parkhill's pleas for rational syntax and proper pronunciation, Kaplan always gets the last word, a cheerful "Hau Kay!"

Following his success with *The Education of H*Y*M*A*N K*A*P*L*A*N*, Rosten (as Leonard Q. Ross) published two books in 1939 and undertook the researching of a more serious volume. The first book, a novel called *Dateline: Europe*, is described as an adventure story "in the Graustarkian manner," and it details the exploits of an ace European correspondent, Peter Strake, his two girl friends (a society girl and a reporter), and the assassination of the king of Belgovena somewhere in the Balkans. Critics found it "admirably giddy" and "pure Hollywood in conception, plot, characters, and incident, it should make a good movie."

The Strangest Places, also a product of 1939, is a collection of sketches about New York, Chicago, San Francisco, and New Orleans and the people who lived there. Many of these sketches had appeared previously in *The New Yorker* in what Rosten

has termed "less lusty form." All fourteen pieces were judged by critics as "dizzily humorous reading, for Mr. Ross has a keen eye for spotting the incongruous, the pretentious, the phony and the funny." The craziest of the sketches, uncannily contemporary, is about a Los Angeles religious cult, "The Mighty I Am." This cult abhors and disdains red and black, liquor and tobacco, meat and onions, garlic and sex. Notable among the eight New York sketches is one about an East Fifty-seventh Street family court. The doorman, when asked what he thought of the institution, replied (in reminiscent Kaplanese), "Don't ask me, Mister. It's big—complicated . . . I'm just a clog in the wheel."

Adventure in Washington (1940) was Rosten's second novel, this one about a domestic correspondent. Jeffrey Brett, Rosten's superhero, works for a Midwestern newspaper, becomes involved with a villainous Washington lobbyist, and is aided by a beautiful girl. Rosten was complimented by critics for his knowledge of Washington news coverage, but his book was dubbed uninteresting and his characters cardboard.

Rosten claims that his two novels, *Dateline: Europe* and *Adventure in Washington*, "were both intended as money-making potboilers. . . . The first was written in seventeen days, the second in nineteen." Both were written for the purpose of relaxation and were originally sold to magazines. Indeed, Rosten continued to be a diligent political and social scientist and wrote fiction, at least initially, for fun and profit.

In 1939, having begun to work as a screenwriter and having sold original stories to moviemakers, Rosten found himself more interested in the sociology of the motion picture industry than in the writing of screenplays. He received a grant from the Carnegie Corporation of New York, and a grant one year later from the Rockefeller Foundation, and set to work with a "corps of statisticians and questionnaire analysts" to gather and analyze information on the movies and their makers. The result, published and reviewed the week of Pearl Harbor in 1941 (and therefore overshadowed by the war) was *Hollywood: The Movie Colony, The Movie Makers*, a 436-page study of "the life, practices, and values of Hollywood; it explores the manners and mores of the movie colony, the pattern and spirit of Hollywood which permeates its incomes, spending, homes, parties, romances, politics, prestige, and so on. The Movie Makers is concerned with the four major groups in Hollywood: movie producers, actors, directors, writers." The book is a storehouse of information and was acknowledged as a significant contribution to sociology. It was seen as an "attempt to make an extraordinary community comprehensible." The negative criticism, curiously, focused on Rosten's language, calling it "infected with the higher Goldwynism."

Rosten's coining of nouns like "publicization," and adjectives like "intricated," his seeming misuse of language, indicates the uniqueness of his playful style, and his ever-present concern for words and rhythms of language as hypersensitive vehicles of communication. Even in his nonfictional sociological research, we find the spirit of Hyman Kaplan, the crafty and personable *litterateur* giving voice to unique and exotic creations. Such linguistic playfulness marks the meeting ground of all Rosten's work, both factual and fictional. At any rate, the book was hardly an immediate commercial success, reviewed as it was on the front page of the book section of the Sunday *New York Times* on 7 December 1941.

The war drew Rosten back to Washington where he became a consultant for the National Defense Advisory Committee and the Office for Energy Management. In 1942 he became chief of the Motion Picture Division of the Office of Facts and Figures, and from 1942 to 1944 he served as director of the Office of War Information. His wartime tasks, based upon his peacetime training, were in planning the War Department's program of training, information, and orientation films. He was particularly involved in work dealing with the psychology of propaganda and the means by which Nazi propaganda could be counteracted in the United States. In 1945 Rosten was given the rank of colonel and sent overseas by the Office of the Secretary of War to advise on the morale problems of and information programs for American occupational forces in France and Germany; there he was attached to the Information and Education Branch of Supreme Headquarters, American Expeditionary Forces.

After extensive travel in Europe, Rosten returned to the United States and worked as a social science consultant to the Rand Corporation (1947-1949) in Santa Monica, California. He lived for two years "in the golden sun and the lovely pagan outdoors of California" while some of his screenplays were made into films. But finally Rosten, claiming to be a city boy raised on city streets, returned to New York. He became an editorial advisor specializing in popular culture for *Look* magazine and divided his remaining time between writing and traveling.

Rosten spent as much time as he could in Europe; he indulged his "museumphilia" at the Louvre, the Uffizi, and the cadre of great galleries in London, Paris, Madrid, Rome, Venice, Munich, and Vienna. When *Look* asked him to write a piece about Holbein's portrait of Anne of Cleves, he put his interest and decades of reading art criticism together and produced *The Story Behind the Painting* (1962), a beautifully illustrated volume about painters and their art which skirts the "pose" and "purple suffocations . . . with which aestheticians insist on trying to convert English into Choctaw."

Another successful project, a book called *A Guide to the Religions of America*, was edited by Rosten and grew out of his association with *Look*. During the years 1952-1955, that magazine ran a popular series on the major religious groups in the United States. Typical of Rosten's work as a social scientist, it is a lucid compendium—question and answer style—in which important religious leaders elucidate the tenets of their faiths. Immensely popular, the book has been reprinted frequently.

In a 1964 interview, Rosten articulated the attractions that various forms of fiction have for him. As he says, "I have always enjoyed writing melodramas because it takes nothing out of me, emotionally—it's one form of writing that, for me at least, is sheer diversion, problem-setting and problem-solving; it doesn't spring from my own life. I don't have to hammer out basic truths about the human experience. Melodramas are play, the structuring of surprise, the plotting of the unexpected and its delights." Humor has always been more difficult than the easily created melodrama for Rosten. As he says, "I'd rather turn out ten melodramas than one piece that's funny." Perhaps that is why twenty years after *The Education of H*Y*M*A*N K*A*P*L*A*N*, Rosten (sans pseudonym) published the long-awaited sequel, *The Return of H*Y*M*A*N K*A*P*L*A*N* (1959), which was welcomed by critics from Evelyn Waugh to Rebecca West and dubbed "the most momentous literary return since Sherlock Holmes rematerialized." In the preface to this volume, Rosten appends a tongue-in-cheek explanation of the writing of dialogue and dialect humor; he says that dialect is not transcription but actually a new creation by the artist which strives for inventiveness as much as for accuracy.

Indeed, the Kaplanese dialect is rendered with both inventiveness and accuracy as the irrepressible immigrant makes his timeless reappearance amid a collection of old friends and new acquaintances ready, once again, to learn "Inklish" in the beginner's class of the American Night Preparatory

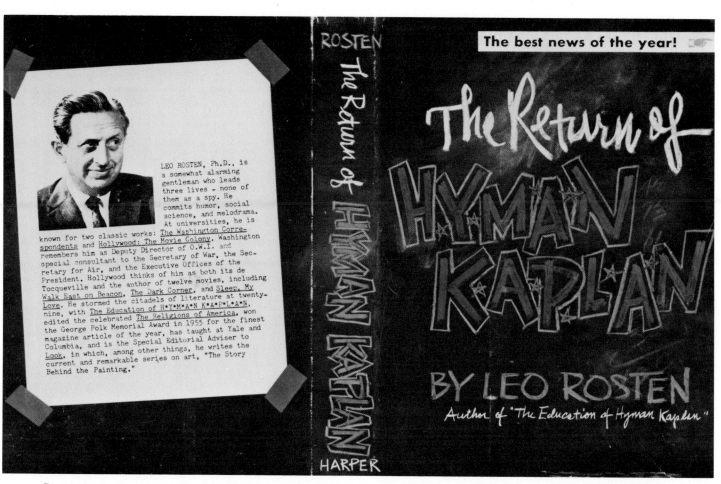

Dust jacket for Rosten's sequel to The Education of H*Y*M*A*N K*A*P*L*A*N, *published twenty-two years after the original*

School for Adults. Many of the episodes include new faces and accents: Olga Tarnova, "a sort of faded Cleopatra, floating down a Slavic Nile, lost in dreams of the days when men (were) maddened by her beauty"; Stanislaus Wilkomirski, who answers Parkhill's roll "I am"; Lola Lopez; Gus Matsoukas; and Nathan P. Nathan who reveals in one hilarious episode that he was born in a train over Niagara Falls and, depending on the train's location at his birth, may be the class's only native American student.

With the exception of a touching focus on the private habits of Mr. Parkhill, the teacher of somewhat patrician background who brings grammar to the alien (Rosten compares this to bringing God to the heathen), Kaplan reigns supreme. A diameter, he reasons, is a machine for counting dimes. The first president is Judge Vashington; other American patriots include Tom S. Jefferson, L. X. Hamilton, Tom Spain, John Edems, and James Medicine; the Chinese leader is Sanghai Jack,

and—with his cavalier comprehension of history and reality—Kaplan paraphrases Patrick Henry, "Julius Scissor had his Brutus, Cholly de Foist had his Cornvall, an' if Kink Judge got a bren in his had he vil make a profit from soch a semple." Despite Hymie Kaplan's humorous ethnic vernacular, the critics were less amused than previously and thought Rosten more distant from his earlier experience.

In 1960 Rosten received a one-year appointment as Visiting Professor of Political Science at the University of California, Berkeley, and was appointed a consultant to the Commission on National Goals. Also, after Hyman Kaplan's return to print, Rosten became interested in reworking some of his wartime experiences into fiction. Having contemplated them for fifteen years, Rosten feels he dared himself to bring off a story which he felt very deeply, a story of people and events. As he says, "I wondered whether I could bring off a story that shifted emotional gears, as it were, from chapter to chapter. That is, I hoped that in one chapter I could make people roar with laughter, then make them weep; I wanted to move from comedy to tragedy to fantasy to farce, moving from mood to mood without keying the story to one central story line."

The result was *Captain Newman, M.D.* (1961), the story of a creative and compassionate psychiatrist loyal to and tenaciously supportive of the war bedeviled inmates of his Air Force mental ward. The book vaguely resembles Joseph Heller's *Catch-22* (published the same year) as it casts a sympathetic eye upon the irony of sending healthy men into combat, resurrecting their traumatized egos, and returning them to combat to be killed or wounded. Typical of Rosten is the book's heavy dependence on dialogue (and dialect) as a means of characterization, a device which lends an air of authenticity and truth as well as comic ethnicity and regionalism. Initially the book was praised for these qualities. *Times Literary Supplement* called it "gentle, constantly entertaining and deeply compassionate." Others praised it for "wild humor" and "pathos." *Captain Newman, M.D.* was excerpted in American literature anthologies, taught to psychiatry students in medical schools, and—perhaps the ultimate praise—made into a successful Hollywood film. Still, in retrospect, the book appears dated and simplistic as it stereotypes the shrewd Jew, the simpleminded Negro, and the all-American boy traumatized by war. As one critic later observed, "The author skillfully alternates chapters of situation comedy with melodrama to suggest emotional range, but all sequences are as neatly rounded out as in a television series."

The epilogue to *Captain Newman, M.D.*, its last nine pages, were republished that same year (1961) by Harper & Row as *Hope and Honor and High Resolve*. They are a contemplative and philosophical nine pages, told by the narrator, about loneliness, faith, and suffering as he learned about them from the wise Dr. Josiah Newman, whose virtue is "the capacity to confront intolerable ideas with equanimity." Rosten cites the contents of this booklet as the essence of his philosophy.

The Many Worlds of L*E*O R*O*S*T*E*N (1964) derives mostly from Rosten's previously published articles and books and is an amusing collection described on the title page as "stories, humor, social commentary, travelogues, satire, memoirs, profiles, and sundry entertainments never before published; with a special introduction, background notes, revelations and confessions, all hand-written and themselves worth the price of admission." While Rosten was absent as a persona

from many of his most successful humorous pieces, a personal voice figures in this collection. He is observer and analyst, exploring human experience through an encyclopedic range of topics from Greek morality to Grouch Marx. The ever-prolific Rosten published *A Most Private Intrigue* in 1967 to high critical praise. A spy thriller of "counter-counter espionage," it is another of the melodramas he writes for pleasure.

While a faculty associate of Columbia University and while still living in New York, Rosten compiled a lexicon of Yiddish (or, as he prefers to call it, "Lexicon of Yiddish in English"). When *The Joys of Yiddish* (1968) was published, it became a smash success. Ever interested in the nuances and complexities of language, Rosten explores the interrelationship between Yiddish and English (becoming "Yinglish" and "Ameridish"). In a voice which alternates between serious explication and hilarious monologue, he frequently employs examples from Yiddish humor and folk sayings. The book both informs and delights as it defines the many Yiddish words which have entered the English language, such as the familiar bagel, yenta, bubeleh, and shtup; and the more esoteric yeshiva bucher, yachne, tzaddik, and shtuss. "Shmaltz," he explains, is cooking fat but understood also as good luck, as in "He fell into a tub of *shmaltz*"; "Nu" is the most frequently used Yiddish word and, in tandem with other words or phrases, can mean everything from "How are things with you?" to "What's the hurry?" to "I hate to mention it, but . . ."; "yiches" means pedigree or family status. *The Joys of Yiddish* joins *The Education of H*Y*M*A*N K*A*P*L*A*N* as the two works most responsible for Rosten's reputation as a humorist. Over the next ten years (1970-1980), while he was greatly prolific, he did not produce any work which equaled the popularity of these two volumes.

In 1970 Rosten published *People I Have Loved, Known, or Admired*, which contains thirty-seven character sketches of people from Freud to Groucho Marx to Rosten's friend Wilbur. Some characters sketched are imaginary and many benefit from Rosten's wit in his attempts to make them human, "which is to say childish, mature, vain, humble, flabbergasting, charming, giftless, shallow, brilliant, cheerful, somber, lyrical, flat, sublime, outrageous, ordinary, and astonishing."

During the sixties, still on the staff of *Look*, Rosten published columns under the heading, "The World of Leo Rosten." Three such pieces were combined and expanded into *A Trumpet for Reason* (1970), a shrill and slender volume of ideas in response to student protest movements and the civil disobedience of the Viet Nam era. The typically lighthearted Rosten turns here to sarcasm, anger, and pedantry as he rails against youth culture.

In 1972 Rosten pursued his interest in Jewish lexicography and the insatiability of his audience by assembling *Leo Rosten's Treasury of Jewish Quotations*. That same year, he produced *Rome Wasn't Burned In a Day: The Mischief of Language* (with illustrations by Robert Day), "a medley of English sentences each of which, through the delicious imprecision of a word or the innocent refurbishing of a phrase, becomes a sudden transformation of an intense expectation into *something*—something startling or funny and illuminating and instructive." Rosten continues in his introduction to this book to discourse on the history of malapropisms and puns, misnomers and slips of the tongue—262 of which he collects in the book. Also, in 1973 Rosten began writing a column called "Diversions" in *Saturday Review World*, and through 1974 published six short stories there.

In *Dear "Herm"–With a Cast of Dozens* (1974) Rosten returns to the same type of humorous fictional exploits which brought him fame with Hyman Kaplan. To Leo Rosten, author and persona, arrives a series of letters from an old high-school acquaintance, Herman Klitcher. Herm, anxious to renew acquaintance with the famous author, writes a series of letters to Rosten in which he portrays himself, his family, and friends as foolish, doggedly persistent, lamentably unselfconscious, and in dire need of Rosten's advice on subjects from psychoanalysis to theology to the solution of brain twisters. Most outstanding in Herm's letters is his inscrutably comic misuse of language and logic which Rosten pointedly displays by responding with supercilious and knowing rejoinders. The book is quite funny in its puns and malapropisms, but the superior stance of the author's persona to his subject is a disturbing device which counteracts much of its potency. As Rosten explained in *O K*A*P*L*A*N! My K*A*P*L*A*N!* (1976), ". . . if a reader recognizes a comic intention or spots a seed planted to sprout into jest, he is impelled to resist the writer's purpose."

Rosten's purpose is less obvious in his third Kaplan book, *O K*A*P*L*A*N! My K*A*P*L*A*N!*, and the book is better for it. The book is a compendium of the two previous Kaplan collections, rewritten and complemented by new characters and situations: twins Milas and Tomas Wodjik, identical in every way; the nearsighted and farsighted Reuben Olshansky; the mutterer Olaf Umea; the nitpicking principal, Loulla Schnepfe, and the familiar Nathan P. Nathan. In this last Kaplan volume, the cavalier immigrant continues outrageously to re-

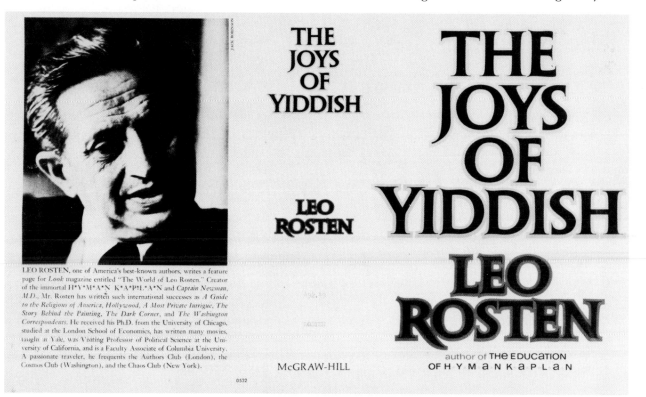

Dust jacket for Rosten's "relaxed lexicon . . . with serendipitous excursions into Jewish humor, habits, holidays. . . ."

construct life and language "to suit his heart's desire."

Since 1976 Rosten has published a variety of books which illustrate both his versatility as a writer and his interest in that craft. *The 3:10 to Anywhere* (1976) is a treasury of stories and incidents recalled from Rosten's many travels; typically, it is peppered with sentimental or funny anecdotes about human experience and its varied international character. *The Power of Positive Nonsense* (1977) is equally anecdotal, but its purpose is more pointed: the debunking of conventional wisdom in the face of sometimes incredible facts or logical truths. Also typical of Rosten is the dependency of the book's success upon the punch of single lines wittily delivered and the ludicrousness of human nature, illustrated by a careful and crafty use of language.

Passions and Prejudices (1978) is another of Rosten's volumes debunking conventional or unfounded pieties. In a first-person wandering discourse on human nature, he discusses happiness, politics, famous personalities, the press, and art, always with due attention to history and psychology and with a style which favors characterization through dialogue. Springing from Rosten's ear for the absurd and the well-spoken word, *Infinite Riches: Gems from a Lifetime of Reading* (1979) is a collection of his favorite aphorisms, insights, acerbities, stories, and discourses garnered from thousands of other writers in a lifetime of wide reading.

Rosten's most recent project is the Silky series, two novels which represent a curious recapitulation of his writing to date. In *Silky! A Detective Story* (1979) and *King Silky!* (1980), Sidney "Silky" Pincus is private eye, former cop, and comic hero who rescues and loves rich and beautiful ladies from the perils of swashbuckling New York. Pincus, the self-proclaimed "Cowboy from Kishinev," speaks the tough-guy language of 1930s gangster movies peppered with Yiddish acerbities. Here in Silky's dialogue Rosten weds his love of potboiling melodrama with his devotion to language. Both *Silky!* and *King Silky!* contain Yiddish glossaries which refer to *The Joys of Yiddish* and help to clarify the humor of Silky's comment to a cabdriver that he's from "Gay in dred, Idaho," or that he must slip a fin to a "schnorrer." Pincus is an American-born Hyman Kaplan, a bold Jewish detective as ludicrous and tenacious as his immigrant student forebear. He becomes a hipster in the Big Apple, a melting putz of Yiddishisms and Americanisms—a speaker of what Rosten delights in labeling "Yinglish."

Starting as a social scientist interested in the problems of precise communication in an imprecise world, Leo Rosten was led to humor as a natural means of expression. He has explored many literary forms and devices, but has been most successful with the representation of dialect which he says "reveals what it conceals . . . creates plausible deceptions, persuasive flows of expectation which must be outwitted by surprising and amusing payoffs." Rosten defines humor as "the affectionate communication of insight. Humor depends on characters. It unfolds from a fondness for those it portrays. Humor is not hostile. It is not superior to its plays. Unlike wit, it is not corrosive; unlike satire, it is not antiseptic; unlike slapstick, it is not ludicrous; unlike buffoonery, it is not banal. Humor is a compassionate account of human beings caught in the carnival and tragedy of living." In some of his later works, Rosten loses the power of "plausible deceptions," with an intrusive authorial voice seeking to instruct or moralize from the point of view of superior insight. Perhaps this is why he will be best remembered for *The Joys of Yiddish* and the Hyman Kaplan series, where the mysteries of language and human behavior remain, for the most part, untouched by narrative vanity, producing in Rosten's own words the "greatest pleasure in the unexpected appearance of the felicitous."

Screenplays:

All Through the Night, screen story by Rosten, Warner Brothers, 1942;

The Conspirators, by Rosten and Vladimir Pozner, Warner Brothers, 1944;

Lured, United Artists, 1947;

Sleep, My Love, screenplay by Rosten and St. Clair McKelway, United Artists, 1947;

The Velvet Touch, screen story by Rosten, RKO, 1948;

Where Danger Lives, screen story by Rosten, RKO, 1950;

The Whistle at Eaton Falls, additional dialogue by Rosten, Columbia, 1951;

Double Dynamite, screen story by Rosten, RKO, 1952;

Walk East on Beacon, screen story and screenplay by Rosten, Columbia, 1952.

Other:

A Guide to the Religions of America, edited by Rosten (New York: Simon & Schuster, 1955); republished as *Religions of America* (London: Heinemann, 1957); revised as *Religions in America* (New York: Simon & Schuster, 1963); revised again as *Religions of America* (New York: Simon & Schuster, 1975).

Papers:

A Rosten manuscript collection is at Brandeis University, Waltham, Massachusetts.

Damon Runyon

(4 October 1880-10 December 1946)

Thomas Grant
University of Hartford

BOOKS: *The Tents of Trouble. Ballads of the Wander-bund and Other Verse* (New York: Fitzgerald, 1911);

Rhymes of the Firing Line (New York: Fitzgerald, 1912);

Guys and Dolls (New York: Stokes, 1931; London: Jarrolds, 1932);

Blue Plate Special (New York: Stokes, 1934);

Money From Home (New York: Stokes, 1935);

More Than Somewhat, selected by E. C. Bentley (London: Constable, 1937);

Take It Easy (New York: Stokes, 1938; London: Constable, 1938);

Furthermore, selected by E. C. Bentley (London: Constable, 1938);

The Best of Damon Runyon, edited by E. C. Bentley (New York: Stokes, 1938);

My Old Man (New York: Stackpole Sons, 1939; London: Constable, 1940);

My Wife Ethel (Philadelphia: McKay, 1939; London: Constable, 1939); republished as *The Turps* (London: Constable, 1951);

A Slight Case of Murder (New York: Dramatists Play Service, 1940);

Runyon à la Carte (Philadelphia: Lippincott, 1944; London: Constable, 1946);

The Three Wise Guys and Other Stories (New York: Avon, 1946);

In Our Town (New York: Creative Age Press, 1946);

Short Takes, Reader's Choice of the Best Columns of America's Favorite Newspaperman (New York & London: Whittlesey House/McGraw-Hill, 1946; London: Constable, 1948);

Poems for Men (New York: Duell, Sloan & Pearce, 1947);

Trials and Other Tribulations (Philadelphia: Lippincott, 1948);

Runyon First and Last (Philadelphia: Lippincott, 1949); republished as *All This and That* (London: Constable, 1950);

Runyon From First to Last (London: Constable, 1954).

Damon Runyon was one of the most popular journalists and writers during the first half of this century. After he died in 1946, Jo Swerling and Abe Burrows adapted Runyon stories and characters into the Broadway musical hit, *Guys and Dolls*, which opened in 1950 and ran for 1,200 performances; five years later, the musical was made into a movie starring Marlon Brando and Frank Sinatra. Since then, Runyon's star has dimmed considerably. During his lifetime, however, Runyon was widely regarded as an accomplished and eccentric humorist. Like Mark Twain, Ring Lardner, and James Thurber, Runyon came to comic writing from journalism and from many years spent listening attentively to "the real language of men," to recall Wordsworth. He took Twain's advice that successful storytelling in America required a writer's artful telling. He began writing in time to work the rich vein of the frontier fable, and he brought the tall tale to the modern city.

Alfred Damon Runyan was born in Manhattan—a prairie town in Kansas—in 1880, the son of an itinerant printer and publisher of small-town newspapers named Alfred Lee Runyan—a corruption of his French ancestral name, Renoyan—and Elizabeth Damon, a descendant of one of the original settlers of the Massachusetts Bay Colony. In 1887, Alfred Runyan moved his family to Pueblo, Colorado, where he took a job as a printer on the *Pueblo Chieftain*. When Elizabeth Runyan died of tuberculosis shortly afterward, seven-year-old Alfred was let loose onto the dirt streets of Pueblo, a wide-open mining boom town, where he worked as a messenger boy in the thriving red-light district and roamed the neighborhoods with a gang of other poor toughs. He was taking after his father, an incurable vagabond and carouser who spent his free time in Pueblo saloons panhandling drinks by telling stories about Western heroes such as Buffalo Bill Cody and Bat Masterson, who at the time were being spirited into legend, and embellishing his own military exploits with General Custer. In a very early story, "My Father" (*Everybody's*, 1911), young Alfred used his father as a model for frontier roarer Bill Kivingson of whom it was said, "They's been a-many a-ring-tailed, red-eyed son o' trouble turned loose in these here parts. . . . I seen 'em come and I seen 'em go, but they's never been no white man could claw within a foot o' the neck o' ole Bill. . . ."

The real-life hellraiser managed to get his wayward son off Pueblo streets in his early teens by securing a job for him on the *Pueblo Evening Press*, where he worked for Col. W. B. McKinney, who promptly sent him back onto the streets as roving reporter. Al was a full-time reporter by the age of fifteen and by seventeen had received his first by-line with the *Evening Post*, another McKinney-owned paper in Pueblo. When a printer's error caused his name to come out "Runyon," he decided to keep the new spelling. The following year, 1898, the sinking of the battleship *Maine* inspired him to enlist; though rejected by the Colorado Volunteers because he was underage and undersized, he managed to bluff his way into the Thirteenth Minnesota Volunteers and went to the Philippines in 1898. Runyon wrote a variety of material for *The Manila Freedom*, the soldiers' newspaper, and for *Soldier's Letter*, an illustrated magazine published in Manila.

After his discharge from service in 1899, he spent all his money during a drinking binge in San Francisco, so he was forced to "ride the rods" back to Pueblo, where he worked for a while as a reporter for the *Chieftain*. He soon took to the rods again, bumming around the Rocky Mountain region, working for short periods on small-town dailies, living in hotels and, when he was broke, in hobo jungles. In 1905, he landed a job as a sports reporter for the *Denver Post*, a maverick paper trying to dethrone the reigning *Rocky Mountain News*. To beat the competition, *Denver Post* reporters were encouraged to take liberties with the facts and color the news with human interest angles. Runyon proved too obliging and was fired in the spring of 1906, but the rival *Rocky Mountain News* took him on and widened his beat to cover city politics and party conventions, including the Democratic National Convention held in Denver in 1908. As a rising metropolitan reporter, he met Ellen Egan, a social news writer for the *Rocky Mountain News*, but their courtship was stymied by her disapproval of his heavy drinking bouts in the company of sporting cronies and his wanderings in the red-light district of Denver—the pattern of life he had come to prefer since his early days in Pueblo.

During this more prosperous decade for Runyon in the new century, perhaps crowned in March 1908 when he was named a director of the Denver Press Club, he began to publish verses and stories in national magazines, such as *Collier's* and *McClure's*. Although the Spanish-American War failed to make a hero of him, he perfected his inherited talent for improvising barroom ballads (in print at least) and spinning yarns, taking as his subject Philippine camp life among the bragging victors. His ballads were strictly newspaper filler, mostly

Damon Runyon

humorous doggerel in rough imitation of Kipling. "A Song of 'Pants'" begins,

> I'm a-comin' up from stables in me ragged
> pantaloons
> An' me shirt tail's flyin' freely out be-
> hind;
> An' me ridin' seat has patchin's grinnin' like a
> pair o' moons—
> 'Tis a job I did me ownself, d'ye mind.

His stories smell of enlisted men's barracks. Typical is "Fat Fallon" (*Lippincott's*, 1907) in which Private Hanks, Runyon's persona in several early wartime stories, reminisces about "Flash Fat" Fallon, coach and star of the barracks baseball team, who blunders through army maneuvers, leading his troop, adrift on a barge, into a storm on a large Philippine lake. Their distress is cause, not of alarm, but merriment, even some Tom Sawyer-like adventure inspired by "yellow-back" novels: "The storm kept up 'most all day, and nary a sign of our tow did we see. Fat decided that we'd be pirates and prey upon the vessels that come across our path." They proceed to mock the authorities that have so ill served them by parodying army hierarchy: "We had an election of officers, and Fat was made captain and me first mate. Fat called himself Bloody Biscuit, the Loose Character of the Laguna, and I was Jiggering Jasper, the Pie-eyed Pirate of the Peskyhanna. We had Renegade Rube and Three-fingered Jack and Desperate Dave and Gory John; we had Stephen Stubbs, the Squint-eyed Scout, and all the other names you ever read in the yellow-backs. Fat had a christening of the boat. Someone had a bottle of pickles in his haversack, so we busted that over the bow—inside the boat, so the pickles wouldn't escape—and Fat says: " 'I christen thee the Bum Steer!' "

In these early wartime tales, Runyon established his permanent fictional world—that of men who are outcasts, undesirables or merely misfits, like Fallon's doughboys; they are bound together by a common fate that directs their lives. Their duties may in time change from war making to bet making, from base running to gin running, but Runyon's men thrive upon a camaraderie born of a community of the elect, sustained by gentlemanly codes of honor and deference. The outward expression of camaraderie is the argot of the group and changes with each group. Even the nicknames help cement fellowship, by conferring status upon members and often signifying their roles in a hierarchy. From his fertile frontier imagination, working upon memory and desire, Runyon, himself an outsider and something of a self-styled outcast, created a world elsewhere, one that in time would seem to mock the "straight" world, even as it imitated many traditional customs and upheld many traditional values.

In 1910, Runyon lost money when the Colorado State Baseball League he invested in collapsed; he subsequently courted ruin by excessive drinking and carousing. When Charles E. Van Loan, formerly a *Denver Post* sports reporter, traveled through Denver on his way to San Francisco to cover the Jack Johnson-James J. Jeffries heavyweight title fight for the Hearst newspapers, he left with Runyon, who went with him to San Francisco and later joined him in New York. He offered Runyon a room in his New York apartment in exchange for short story plots. Runyon arrived in New York early in 1911, obliged his benefactor, and occasionally wrote his own stories, managing to place his work in such popular magazines as *Everybody's* and *Harper's*. To get by, he persuaded publisher Desmond Fitzgerald to print *The Tents of Trouble* in 1911, a thin volume of ballads about wanderers, beachcombers, and hoboes that out west earned him the title, "The Kipling of Colorado."

But he soon needed a steady job and through Van Loan's connections, landed one in the sports department of the morning *New York American*, one of the most spirited dailies in the growing Hearst chain. Sports editor Harry Cashman thought his new reporter's name—Alfred Damon Runyon—too pompous and struck "Alfred" from his by-line.

When he learned about Runyon's freewheeling way with the news from Denver press clippings, Cashman sent him to San Antonio in early 1911 to cover spring training of the New York Giants. Runyon enjoyed hobnobbing with another special fraternity, the baseball players, many of them heroes of his youth; and he befriended a few of these, especially Arthur "Bugs" Raymond, an eccentric former pitching star whose antics he recounted in dispatches sent back to New York. Readers soon preferred these stories to conventional summaries of game strategy and recitations of statistics concluding with box scores. Hence, he was encouraged to write about the players, and by the time he returned to New York following the exhibition season, he was a recognized baseball writer and a key reporter for a successful Hearst New York daily. He could now persuade Ellen Egan to marry him since he had finally met her requirements—a steady job and permanent abstinence from liquor.

Since Runyon had already learned in Denver how to increase his readership by turning "hard" news into "human interest" stories, he succeeded easily in the new field of sports journalism, which required his talent for mixing fact and fantasy. He worked at flamboyance, often by assaulting the reader with verbal barrage—the kind of hype that nowadays is left to electronic scoreboards. "As for you, Roger Bresnahan," he wrote on 22 July 1911 about the manager of the St. Louis Cardinals, "with your oily voice and city ways—take that! Zam! Bumpety Bump-Bump! (Noise of villain falling off the front stoop, bleeding from the nose.)" He would enliven any baseball account, especially when the Giants lost. About a loss to the Cincinnati Reds, managed by Clark Griffith, Runyon bellowed: "Viva la Mique Donlin, anyway! Mique pecked a home run into the right field bleachers at the Polo Grounds yesterday afternoon after Griffith's Cuban Stouts had built up the foundation and super structure of an 8 to 2 score, the said home run keeping it from being 8 to 1." The remainder of Runyon's account wanders from the game to comparisons of the nationalities of the players, and only at the end does he return to the game and an inning-by-inning account. "I always made covering a standard story," he later said, "like a big race or a ball game more or less of a stunt."

Because of his "stunts," the *New York American* sought in 1913 to increase circulation by promoting him as the paper's official humorist. As biographer Edwin P. Hoyt notes, "the promotion department, in heralding his coverage of National League baseball, informed readers: 'Mr. Runyon has entertained for several seasons narrating the game in his inimitable humorous style and at the same time furnishing enough detailed description to satisfy the most rabid fan.' " He applied his "inimitable humorous style" to other sports, covering horse shows at Madison Square Garden and Ivy League football games, and converted many a boring contest into an interesting, readable story. His growing fame allowed him to prevail upon the publisher of his first collection of ballads to publish another, *Rhymes of the Firing Line*, in 1912. In 1914 Runyon took on an additional daily column for the *New York American* called "The Mornin's Mornin'," in which he was permitted to write strong editorials about whatever he wished. He continued to follow the Giants in Texas spring training, but he also noted Pancho Villa's movements in Mexico, the 1916 Republican Convention, then Allied troops in the Argonne during World War I. In mid-1919 he wrote "A Tale of Two Fists," a series of articles in the *American* promoting boxing's new world heavyweight challenger, his acquaintance and fellow Coloradan, Jack Dempsey.

As the 1920s began, Runyon settled into a regular habit of spending afternoons at his office typing his column and long nights in conversation at Broadway bars that catered to the New York sporting and journalist crowd, most notably Lindy's, a brassy all-night delicatessen-restaurant—Mindy's in Runyon's later fiction. He roamed a narrow territory, Broadway between Times Square and Columbus Circle, and named it "Jacob's Beach," after a tout of that name, because the sidewalks were the Jones Beach of the boxing and racing crowd. Since Prohibition was in effect, his collection of cronies had swelled to include gangsters and gin runners, and again, Runyon relished their company, even courting classier rogues, such as gambler Arnold Rothstein, a teetotaler like himself, and mobster Al Capone, who would later become a winter neighbor in Miami. Runyon's unceasing search through endless Prohibition nights for colorful material to feed into his popular daily column led in time to the total neglect of his wife and family. Ellen Runyon turned to alcohol and died early. Her death contributed to Runyon's long estrangement from his two children, the painful consequences of which are recounted by his son, Damon Runyon, Jr., in his memoir, *Father's Footsteps* (1954).

To support his carousing and gambling, Runyon augmented his column with weekly sketches for the Sunday magazine of the *American*. From "Mornin's Mornin'," he borrowed a narrative voice he had used on occasion, "A. Mugg," and fleshed him out as "Amos Mugg," a kind of saloon philosopher, but straight out of the cracker barrel. The ambling, colloquial style of the later Broadway stories is apparent in these sketches, as in "The Homecoming of Hero McBride," which appeared in the 10 August 1919 issue. "The other night I run into Chelsea McBride, who is just back from France, where he puts in nearly two years in the war business. In the old days before the Kaiser gets to be such a stinker, this Chelsea McBride is one of the lads around Broadway, and is well known to one and all, though what Chelsea's racket is nobody knows, except that he does thus and so, and one thing and another. He is just a good man, which is a way of saying he does the best he can, and he does all right, at that." Although Runyon had occasionally slid into the historic present in his columns, these Sunday sketches marked his first sustained use of this stylistic oddity. Other McBride stories followed—successors to the Private Hanks stories of the preceding decade—spun from Runyon's World War I memories.

In 1922, these evolved into the "Grandpap Mugg" stories in the Sunday *American* that became the "My Old Home Town" series in 1923 and 1924. These are nostalgic sketches about ordinary life in a remote Western town (clearly Pueblo) in an earlier, simpler period, narrated either by "Grandpap," who recalls Runyon's yarn-spinner father, or by "a young squirt," his worshipful son. As Runyon harks back to olden days out west, reminiscence swells into tall tale. Typical is "The Old Man of the Mountain," which begins: "Many a strange thing happens back in my old home town out West, but nothing stranger ever happens than the time old Zeb Griscom suddenly hauls off and drops out of sight, leaving his wife, Mrs. Griscom, mourning for him more than somewhat." Old Zeb's friends set off to find him, only to get lost, thus requiring more search parties, until his wife is forced to go looking, and discovers in a cave "as jolly a party as anybody will wish to find with Mr. Hathaway, the banker, doing some cooking over a big fire, and my Grandpap dealing out drinks, and everybody laying around looking very happy indeed, until they see my Grandmaw." This humorous sketch, a Rocky Mountain version of Rip Van Winkle, in which men harassed by wives and

Runyon in his apartment

responsibilities seek and find a haven of rest and camaraderie, harks back to Runyon's earlier barracks tales—and farther back, to the nostalgia laden mining camp tales of Bret Harte. As Runyon's roaring camp past became more remote, his need to recapture it in fantasies of male escape seemed to increase.

These Western tales began to appear in the editorial section of the *American* in 1924 under the heading "Greatest American Humorists," along with contributions by Bugs Baer, Gene Fowler, and Ring Lardner. Most of Runyon's tales, called "My Home Town," bear too obviously the stamp of Harte, but occasionally Runyon broke free to follow Twain's comic practice of allowing the teller to ramble solemnly while describing a string of ludicrous events. In "A Slight Hitch in *Uncle Tom's Cabin*," a Twain-like title, the grandson tells about the time Lem Beaman's hungry greyhounds had to play the bloodhounds in the stage performance of Harriet Beecher Stowe's play, destroying it and driving the heroine from the theater. The teller remains un-

fazed, however, as Twain insisted an American storyteller must, and concludes drily, "But everybody admits this *Uncle Tom's Cabin* is as good as ever they see, figuring in the chase, and all."

Still, Runyon was working in an antique mode, and fortunately abandoned the "My Home Town" material in 1926. He kept up his column, "The Mornin's Mornin'," but his enormous popularity began to level off in the mid-twenties. He took on other assignments, most notably sensational trials, beginning in 1926 with the lengthy Hall-Mills murder case in New Jersey, which he called a theatrical extravaganza, "worthy of Belasco." Again, he wrote his dispatches as human interest stories, embellishing the facts with capsule portraits. Runyon changed the name of his column in the summer of 1928 to "I Think So," which allowed him a broader scope, but the next year he returned to sports journalism, this time specializing in boxing and horse racing. His column was renamed "Between You and Me."

Runyon's long, if not always distinguished,

practice as spinner of Western tales, as sports journalist, as crime reporter, as omnipresent Broadway columnist, and bon vivant prepared him well for another round of fiction writing, this time his most significant and longest sustained series, comprising the so-called "Broadway stories" written mostly for *Collier's* between 1929 and 1940. Most of these are heavily, sometimes mechanically, plotted urban tales after the manner of O. Henry, in which Runyon dwells affectionately upon a recurring assortment of underworld types based loosely on real-life cronies and acquaintances. Too often he shows that he was still working in the outmoded frontier vein of Harte, playing the tough-guy world for laughs and dissolving artificial crises with surprise endings.

His first Broadway story, about a rivalry between a gangster and a reporter over the former's girl friend, practically announces by its title, "Romance in the Roaring Forties" (*Cosmopolitan*, 1929), Runyon's debt to O. Henry and Harte, even to the point of implying that "Jacob's Beach," not implausibly, is a new roaring frontier. Runyon's familiar, first-person narrator has reappeared, but now his world and its lingo are truly contemporary and also quite appealing. Runyon delights in coining words by adding intensives or humorous suffixes to standard words (as in "stinkeroo" for pipe or "phonus balonus" for counterfeit); he uses colloquialisms and freely sprinkles his stories with the argot of his tribe (calling racehorses "giddyaps": waitresses "biscuit shooters": and mafiosi "mustache Petes"). He is also inclined to humorous euphemisms that indicate his flip acceptance of rude events. The pending electrocution of a killer moves him not to sympathy but to eloquence: ". . . on the morrow [Gentleman George] is to be placed in Mister Edison's rocking chair in the room adjoining his cell, and given a very severe shock in the seat of his breeches." Runyon's humor thus lies in the inventiveness of language and in the incongruity between highly serious events and the vernacular.

Alliterative names for his characters abound: Harry the Horse, Joe the Joker, Hot Horse Herbie, Overcoat Obie, and Frankie Ferocious. As in his early sketches, nicknames indicate camaraderie and rank for Runyon, this time in the rather strict hierarchy of the underworld, in which a lowly gambler like Feet Samuel treads at the bottom, a middling gangster, Dave the Dude, struts in the middle; and The Brain, a recurring figure and master gambler (modeled on Runyon's friend, Arnold Rothstein), sits on top.

By contrast, women in Runyon's gangster world, when they are not shrews as in "The Old Men of the Mountain," are "dolls," "judys," "broads," "pancakes," or "cupcakes"; the affectionate, but condescending, labels reveal their subordinate role as obedient, bejeweled playthings of their "guys." All these features served Runyon's purpose of glorifying the new outlaw class in the glamorous city.

In his first *Collier's* story, "Lillian" (1930), a drunken vaudevillian and an alcoholic cat, Lillian, save a boy from a tenement fire; the vaudevillian reforms and marries the boy's wealthy mother, while the cat continues to drink, led on by a bootlegger who urges her to harass dogs. In this bracing tale, one of Broadway's lowly habitues is lifted from the gutter through his courage, which is amply, and justly, rewarded. Eleven years later in "Johnny One Eye" (*Collier's*, 1941), Runyon worked this plot with a waif and a one-eyed cat to illustrate the inherent goodness of a toughened gangster. Waifs, human and animal, appear frequently in Runyon's stories since they permit him to display the tenderness his characters normally keep well hidden. In "Little Miss Marker" (*Collier's*, 1932), an infant, "a little doll" (later played by Shirley Temple in a movie based on the story) is left with Sorrowful, an old burned-out bookie as a "marker" for a two-dollar bet. The child grows up on Broadway, diverting the crowds at Mindy's by her dancing, but catches pneumonia one evening after a performance and, while at death's door, is suddenly reclaimed by her father who finally pays his debt—after he learns that his daughter is soon to become an heiress. In this tale about Broadway's lower orders, Runyon tugs mercilessly at the reader's heartstrings, but his chief purpose is to celebrate the self-sacrifice of his imagined outlaw class. Sorrowful and his friends are poor, but they unselfishly care for the child; as she grows up, they deny her nothing, while her real father cares only for the wealth soon to come under his control. After her good fortune is disclosed, Sorrowful keeps his self-respect by demanding from her father only the price of the bet: "You owe me a two-dollar marker for the bet you blow on Cold Cuts, and I will trouble you to send it to me at once, so I can wipe you off my books."

Occasionally, Runyon examines the allure of the underworld. In "Social Error" (*Collier's*, 1930), Miss Harriet MacKyle from Park Avenue, one of "many legitimate people [who] are much interested in the doings of tough guys, and consider them very romantic," believes ". . . all the junk the newspapers print making heroes out of tough guys," and she goes slumming among Broadway "jernts." At the

Hearts and Flowers Club, she becomes infatuated with "a little guy who wears horn cheaters and writes articles for the magazines," introduced to her by the playful narrator as "Bad Basil Valentine, who will kill you quicker than you can say scat, and maybe quicker." Basil and Harriet fall for each other—for he, too, comes from the straight world and shares her fascination with street toughs—but he is forced to act out the role the narrator has created for him. After the usual turns of the plot, including a shooting, "Bad Basil" ironically proves his toughness to Harriet, and they get married, still clinging to their fantasy.

Runyon's stories of the underworld proved enormously popular, if not compellingly realistic; in less than two years after he began the Broadway stories, he published his first collection of them, entitled *Guys and Dolls* (1931). Though the volume was a best-seller, reviewers stressed the popular appeal of the stories and were not impressed with their literary qualities. The *New York Times* reviewer, for example, praised the humorist in Runyon, but missed the fairy tale quality of his work, "The stories were written to get laughs, and they often do. The

characters are too thin for any long life. Mr. Runyon knows what interests most people, arouses their curiosity and makes them laugh."

At a time when moviegoers had a seemingly insatiable taste for gangster films, Runyon capitalized on his popularity, and increased his income, by selling movie rights to his stories. From 1934, when he worked on the screenplay for "Little Miss Marker," until the mid-1940s, Runyon was frequently on Hollywood studio payrolls, making $2000 a week and sometimes more.

In 1934, Runyon's second collection of stories was published. He had wanted to call it "More Guys and Dolls," but his editors insisted upon *Blue Plate Special*—perhaps to advertise Runyon's unrefined, yet palatable, fare. Whether he is writing about Broadway, uptown Manhattan, Saratoga, or Miami, a horse race, a football game, or some bizarre wager, Runyon sticks to the formula that made *Guys and Dolls* so popular: he wrote vernacular stories about tough yet sentimental gangsters. The Depression casts a shadow over some of these new stories. In "The Snatching of Bookie Bob" (*Collier's*, 1931), Broadway's "citizens," as Runyon called them, are

Dust jacket and title page for Runyon's first collection of Broadway stories

so broke that they are reduced to wearing last year's clothes and "snatching" competitors. However, the proprieties continue to be upheld, honor is practiced—as it is not in straight society, Runyon implies—and Bookie Bob endures his fate "like a gentleman." Other stories collected in *Blue Plate Special* exploit Depression fantasies about sudden wealth descending "miraculously" upon the resourceful and the virtuous—fairy tale romances easily convertible into sentimental movie fantasies by the Frank Capras of Hollywood, as many were. In "The Lemon Drop Kid" (*Collier's*, 1934), a tout by that name earns a cash reward for apparently curing a millionaire's arthritis (with a placebo of lemon drops), but only after he has shown his altruism by helping a poor family, into which he marries. In "Three Wise Guys" (*Collier's*, 1933), a trio of gangsters reenacts the Christmas story playing the three kings, while in "Dancing Dan's Christmas" (*Collier's*, 1932), a jewel thief plays Santa Claus to a poor young girl and her destitute grandmother, then vanishes after a good deed deftly done.

One story from *Blue Plate Special* is notably atypical, "The Old Doll's House" (*Collier's*, 1933), a remarkably underplayed version of a familiar romance motif. It begins more self-consciously than most in a fairy tale vein: "Now it seems that one cold winter night, a party of residents of Brooklyn comes across the Manhattan Bridge in an automobile wishing to pay a call on a guy by the name of Lance McGowan, who is well-known to one and all along Broadway as a coming guy in the business field." Lance's callers are rival "importers" and they are coming to execute him. He escapes by sneaking into a Manhattan mansion in which an old spinster, Miss Abigail Ardsley, lives alone, except for a few ancient servants. She sits dressed in white before the fireplace waiting for her young suitor, who died forty years ago just outside the house after her repressive father expelled him. When Lance wanders in through the door once bolted against her lover, she in her senility thinks her lost lover has finally returned and, to save his skin, Lance is forced to play into her fantasy. His criminal argot contrasts effectively with the language of the sophisticated Miss Ardsley, whom he must strain to imitate: "Why I am greatly surprised to hear your statement about the doors around here being so little used. Why, Sweetheart, if I know there is a doll as good-looking as you in the neighborhood, and a door unlocked, I will be busting in myself every night. . . . Listen, Sweetheart, do you happen to have a drink in the joint?" Later, after Lance's competitors are murdered at midnight and he is arrested for the crime,

the old lady testifies in court that the defendant was in her company at the time, then turns to him and whispers: "I will be expecting you again some night, young man." The final revelation preserves the fairy tale's fragile enchantment, "But of course it is just as well for Lance that Miss Abigail Ardsley does not explain to the court that when she recovers from the shock of the finding of her ever-loving young guy frozen to death, she stops all the clocks in her house at the hour she sees him last, so for forty-five years it is always twelve o'clock in her house."

In 1935, Runyon collaborated with Howard Lindsay on a Broadway play, *A Slight Case of Murder*, a familiar Runyonesque farce about an ex-bootlegger who sends his staff of crooks to dispose of the bodies of some robbers they found on the top floor of his new house, but instead, after they find there is a $30,000 reward for the robbers, they bring the bodies back to the ex-bootlegger's house. The play was dismissed as trivial by critics and closed after seventy performances. Runyon also published a third collection of stories in 1935, *Money From Home*, a fourth, *Take It Easy*, in 1938, and in that same year, *The Best of Damon Runyon*, which collected stories in previous volumes along with new material. His popularity spread abroad as separate collections under new titles were published in London. Plots and characters proliferate astonishingly, but they obey the same sentimental formula. Time, history, social change hardly matter. The best story from these new collections is clearly "A Piece of Pie" (*Collier's*, 1937; in *Take It Easy*), which, like "The Old Doll's House," is happily free of Runyon's special pleading for the moral superiority of the outlaw class. It revolves around a gangland epic eating contest that is unabashedly absurd, a tall tale fit for the "roaring forties." The reputations of New York and Boston, the cities of the combatants, are at stake, and Runyon's narrator builds up the match as if it were a Dempsey-Tunney championship fight. But promoters discover that New York's best eater, Nicely-Nicely, is on a diet to please his fiancee, and Miss Violette Shumberger, who "has a face the size of a town clock and enough chins for a fire escape," is chosen to represent the city. During the actual contest, suspense balloons along with the contestants. Then, suddenly, Boston's Joel Duffle quits on the desserts while ahead, demoralized by Violette's apparent request for more food, when in fact she is secretly admitting that she can't even eat what's before her. Her unexpected triumph takes on epic proportions when she admits, "I forget about the contest and eat my regular dinner of pig's knuckles and sauerkraut an hour before the contest starts."

She even wins Nicely-Nicely too, as he sheds his diet along with his fiancee and moves to Florida with Violette, where they are "running a barbeque stand and, the chances are, eating like seven mules."

By the early 1940s, when the harsh realities of contemporary history revealed just how dated Runyon's stories had become, his Broadway legend making was finally exhausted. By the late 1930s, after he had returned to writing a column for the tabloid *New York Daily Mirror* when the *New York American* suspended publication in 1937, he developed a new, more contemporary mode, a series of folksy letters addressed to an imaginary editor by Joe Turp, a patriotic working-class husband from Brooklyn. These were collected and published in 1939 as *My Wife Ethel* (republished in 1951 as *The Turps*). Turp's letters are undistinguished, but they are typically Runyonesque in their sentimentalized portrayal of good-hearted urbanites from the lower social orders.

In 1938, Runyon developed throat cancer and began to forsake the gambling and high living that had attracted him so strongly. He was embittered by his exclusion from yet another war he was now too old to fight in or even report on, and his second marriage, to a chorus girl much younger than he, was beginning to turn sour. He was divorced in 1946 after fourteen years of marriage. He even lashed out against humor, though without identifying any specific target: "Most American humour is in bad taste and growing worse under the present vogue for the suggestive and the downright obscene in the spoken and written word."

After a throat operation in 1944, when malignancy was discovered, Runyon could not speak. He sought refuge from his anguish among newspaper cronies in New York, where he still enjoyed an impressive following. He tried to cling to his Broadway past, writing a few new Broadway tales, but the best of these meager efforts, "Blonde Mink" (*Collier's*, 1945), seems unusually sinister and disturbingly portentous, closer to Poe than to O. Henry and Harte. It concerns a "doll's" violation of a deceased gangster's request to use his money to buy him an impressive gravestone. When she buys an expensive blonde mink instead, a crony of the dead gangster kills her so the gangster's ghost will be quieted. This tale of retribution perhaps reflects the author's bitterness toward his young wife who he felt abandoned him in his painful old age.

Toward the end of his life, Runyon wrote sketches to save his sanity, one a dialogue called "Death pays a Social Call." Death finally did call on 10 December 1946. A week later, World War I

Runyon, Walter Winchell, and Sherman Billingsley at the Stork Club

Vivian Blaine as Miss Adelaide and Sam Levene as Nathan Detroit in Guys and the Dolls, *the Broadway play based on Runyon's characters*

flying ace Eddie Rickenbacker flew over Broadway and scattered Runyon's ashes.

"Damon was the self-installed President of the Hard Boiled Egg Club," said Scoop Gleason, a fellow journalist, after Runyon's death. "He liked to pretend he was as hard as he was tough. He worked at creating that image, but behind the façade was a sentimental and tender side." The pretense may owe much to Runyon's early poverty, to the early death of his mother, and to the powerful spell cast by his hard-boiled, ring-tailed roarer father, while his phenomenal commercial success betrayed his true character as a fanatical subscriber to the gospel of hard work, an attribute that poverty often fosters. His measure of success was therefore never quality, only money; if he can be believed: "I have no interest in artistic triumphs that are financial losers. I would like to have an artistic success that also made money, of course, but if I had to make a choice between the two I would take the dough." This obsessive gambler in life played it utterly safe in art, always picking a sure winner. Had Runyon been a risk taker like the colorful gamblers he admired and created, he might have used his mastery of plot and his idiosyncratic style to create a substantial corpus of urban comic lore to rival that of his gifted contemporary, Ring Lardner. Still, he

should be read as one of the original stylists of a time rich in imaginative styles—"the last local colorist," as a recent critic has dubbed him. Certainly as a humorist, he has left a few rare "stunts" that will assure him a notable place in the American comic tradition.

Play:

A Slight Case of Murder, by Runyon and Howard Lindsay, New York, 48th Street Theatre, 11 September 1935, 70 [performances].

References:

Calvin S. Brown, "The Luck of Miss Marker," *Western Humanities Review*, 11 (1957): 341-345;

Tom Clark, *The World of Damon Runyon* (New York: Harper & Row, 1978);

LeRocque DuBose, "Damon Runyon's Underworld Lingo," *University of Texas Studies in English*, 32 (1953): 123-132;

Gene Fowler, *Skyline: A Reporter's Reminiscence of the 1920s* (New York: Viking, 1961);

Edwin P. Hoyt, *A Gentleman of Broadway: The Story of Damon Runyon* (Boston: Little, Brown, 1964);

John O. Rees, "The Last Local Colorist: Damon Runyon," *Kansas Magazine*, 7 (1968): 73-81;

Damon Runyon, Jr., *Father's Footsteps* (New York: Random House, 1954);

Jean Wagner, *Runyonese: The Mind and Craft of Damon Runyon* (Paris: Steckert-Hafner, 1965);

Edward H. Weiner, *The Damon Runyon Story* (New York: Longmans, Green, 1948).

Papers:

Significant holdings of letters are owned by the University of California, Berkeley, and Temple University. The only notable collection of manuscripts not in private hands is housed in the New York Public Library.

Henry Wheeler Shaw
(Josh Billings)
(21 April 1818-14 October 1885)

David B. Kesterson
North Texas State University

SELECTED BOOKS: *Josh Billings, Hiz Sayings* (New York: Carleton, 1865);

Josh Billings on Ice, and Other Things (New York: Carleton, 1868);

Josh Billings' Farmer's Allminax, published annually (New York: Carleton, 1870-1879); collected as *Old Probability; Perhaps Rain—Perhaps Not* (New York: Carleton, 1879); recollected as *Josh Billings' Old Farmer's Allminax, 1870-1879* (New York: Dillingham, 1902);

Twelve Ancestrals Sighns in the Billings' Zodiac Gallery, reprinted from 1874 *Allminax* (New York, 1873);

Everybody's Friend, or Josh Billings' Encyclopedia and Proverbial Philosophy of Wit and Humor (Hartford, Conn.: American Publishing Company, 1874);

Josh Billings' Wit and Humor (London: Routledge, 1874);

The Complete Comical Writings of Josh Billings (New York: Carleton, 1876);

Josh Billings' Trump Kards: Blue Grass Philosophy (New York: Carleton, 1877);

Josh Billings' Cook Book and Picktorial Proverbs (New York: Carleton, 1880);

Josh Billings Struggling with Things (New York: Carleton, 1881);

The Complete Works of Josh Billings (New York: Dillingham, 1888).

By the middle 1860s, when Mark Twain was still relatively unknown, Henry Wheeler Shaw (Josh Billings) had achieved national fame as one of the foremost literary comedians in America. He made his reputation as a coiner of clever aphorisms, a writer of familiar essays, sketches, and burlesque almanacs, and as a comic lecturer. He was a humorist, a homespun philospher, and a conscious literary artist. One of his chief strengths was originality; in such a graphic epigram as "when a feller gits a goin down hil, it dus seem as tho evry thing had bin greased for the okashun," even the deliberate misspellings fade into the background behind the compelling image.

Shaw was born on 21 April 1818, in Lanesboro, Massachusetts, located in the heart of the Berkshire Hills. Young Henry was brought up in an enlightened, active family—both his paternal grandfather and father being involved in national and state politics. His formal education consisted of district schooling, college preparatory study at a private academy, and a little over a year's work at Hamilton College in 1833-1834. Shaw was a restless and questing young man, inclined to be venturesome and prankish rather than scholarly. Thus it is not surprising that he was expelled from Hamilton for climbing a lightning rod and removing the clapper from the chapel tower bell. Though Shaw left school forever, he had learned enough about life during these early years to pique his keen curiosity about a wide variety of subjects.

Yielding to wanderlust, Shaw spent ten years (1835-1845) traveling and working in the Middle West and West. He even signed up for two geographical explorations in those regions. Then at age twenty-seven he returned to Lanesboro and married his childhood sweetheart, Zilpha Bradford (a descendant of William Bradford). For nine years the Shaws moved about, Shaw trying his hand at farming and supervising the mining of coal before settling in Poughkeepsie, New York, where he and Zilpha decided to raise their two daughters. In Poughkeepsie Shaw worked as auctioneer and real-estate agent and was elected to the city council in 1858. It appeared that, as he now approached middle age, he had found his niche as businessman and solid citizen.

In the late 1850s, however, Shaw began writing humorous sketches for area newspapers to while away his leisure time. Using such pseudonyms as Efrem Billings, Si Sledlength, and finally Josh Billings, he found his first major success in 1864 with the quaintly written "Essa on the Muel, bi Josh Billings," a piece that employed misspellings and faulty grammar in the mode of Artemus Ward's writings. It was snapped up by a Boston newspaper and reprinted in three comic journals within a month. The way was now paved for Shaw to collect his witticisms and sketches in a book; with the help of Charles Farrar Browne (the creator of Artemus Ward), *Josh Billings, Hiz Sayings* was published in 1865. The book was highly successful, and "Josh Billings" was launched.

Josh Billings, Hiz Sayings and Shaw's next book, *Josh Billings on Ice, and Other Things* (1868), both contain the aphorisms, short essays, and sketches so characteristic of Shaw's writings. The aphorisms are pithy, incisive statements conveying general truths. Written in characteristic cacography and distorted grammar, they cover every subject from beauty to boredom. They are filled with comic devices of understatement ("[I] found the ice in a slippery condition"), anticlimax ("Buty is power; but the most treacherous one i kno ov"), and antiproverbialism (" 'Give me liberty, or giv me deth'—but ov the 2 I prefer the liberty"). Occasional puns and malapropisms are also present. Shaw's "afferisms" convey a sense of ease and spontaneity that belies the actual effort and time that went into their composition. He once said he worked three hours on one particular saying, just "to get it right." The imagery is sharp and original, and the sayings excel in succinctness. Walter Blair has observed that regardless of the subject, "Josh Billings showed a great gift for squeezing much lore into few words." Shaw himself averred that "ginowine proverbs ar like good kambrick needles—short, sharp, and shiny." The sayings were widely appealing to the reading populace of his time, a people nurtured in the traditions of honesty, frugality, and moral righteousness. Shaw as cracker-barrel philosopher was much in demand.

The essays and sketches in *Josh Billings, Hiz*

Henry Wheeler Shaw

Sayings and *Josh Billings on Ice* cover a multitude of subjects; they are short (rarely more than 500 words) and seemingly artless and informal in structure. In actuality, they are usually constructed around carefully chiseled individual sentences. On the surface the essays might seem little more than series of epigrams; but a closer look reveals their true artistry, especially in unity and stylistic charm. Shaw was a well-read man, and literary models for his essays can be found in Addison, Steele, and Goldsmith: the clarity, ease, and charm with which these classic eighteenth-century authors wrote are apparent in Shaw's work. So adept is Shaw in the genre of the short essay that Walter Blair calls him "primarily an essayist." His subjects range from topics of the day, such as women's suffrage and trends in language and literature, to timeless views of types and characteristics of people and animals. Indeed, Shaw's numerous essays on animals are among his most memorable (witness "Essa on the Muel"). His method in both the human and animal essays is to single out the traits of each type, discuss them humorously, and occasionally draw a fitting moral from his observations. In the animal essays his method differs from Aesop's in that he dwells more on natural history than on moralistic fables involving animal characters and actions.

Following the success of *Josh Billings, Hiz Sayings*, Shaw moved to New York City where in 1867 he launched his long-lived career as humor columnist on the *New York Weekly*. His column, variously called "The Josh Billings Papers," "Josh Billings' Spice Box," and "Josh Billings' Philosophy," consisted of a variety of material: aphorisms, essays and sketches, narratives and travel accounts, letters to correspondents, and even occasional poems and mock dramatic interludes. The material published in these columns, for which Shaw was paid $100 per installment, makes up most of the contents of his printed books, though much of it was revised before republication. Shaw's *Weekly* column became so popular that it continued for the remaining eighteen years of his life and was even rerun for several years posthumously. (The publishers simply did not announce Shaw's death in 1885.) Moreover, the columns were frequently pirated by other newspapers.

While employed as an "Exclusive" by the *Weekly*, Shaw was free to continue to write books and to lecture. In 1869 he released the first installment of the soon famous *Josh Billings' Farmer's Allminax*, published annually until 1879. The *Farmer's Allminax* was his most successful literary venture, during its first year selling over 90,000 copies, the second year over 127,000, the third and fourth years over 100,000, and never less than 50,000 during the next six years. That Shaw's endeavor won such acclaim is not surprising, for he astutely capitalized on two highly popular types of almanacs at the time—the comic and the farmer's. Shaw's satiric *Allminax* combines the jokes, humorous tales, poems, and crude illustrations of the former with the mixture of informative and entertaining material in the latter, the result being an almanac that is both a burlesque of the typical almanac format and

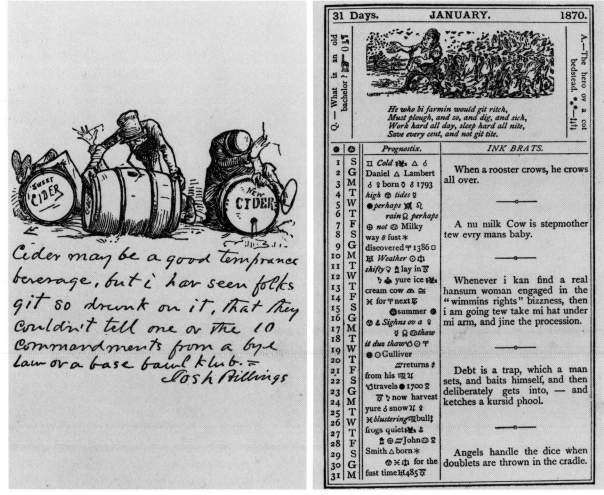

January 1870 entry from Josh Billings' Old Farmer's Allminax

contents and, simultaneously, a lively jest book of Shaw's usual humorous aphorisms, essays, and miscellaneous pieces. Its burlesque touches on all the popular elements of the typical farmer's almanac: the Man of the Signs, monthly horoscopes, the farmer's calendar, weather predictions, and other odds and ends of interest to rural readers. The *Allminax* offers pleasant browsing even today. The burlesque of astrology is delightful, the monthly entries witty, and the humorous aphorisms among Shaw's most catching. When Shaw's original ten-year contract for the *Allminax* terminated in 1879, he gathered the ten issues together in the book that was his favorite: *Old Probability: Perhaps Rain–Perhaps Not*, the volume he referred to fondly as "My little Waif."

Beginning in 1873, with *Twelve Ancestrals Sighns in the Billings' Zodiac Gallery*, reprinted from the *Allminax* for 1874, Shaw published a series of jest books—brief, inexpensive paperback volumes containing assorted humorous material from jokes and conundrums to comic drawings. This type of book was highly popular during Shaw's day, a trend encouraged by the proliferation of comic periodicals and humorous newspaper and magazine columns during the last half of the nineteenth century. The lengthiest and most diverse of his jest books are the several different volumes published as *Josh Billings' Spice Box* (1874 and following). Actually, much of the material in these entertaining volumes was only collected and edited by Shaw rather than written by him. *Josh Billings' Trump Kards: Blue Grass Philosophy* (1877) offers sixteen essays and sketches and nearly twenty pages of witty aphorisms and illustrations. A more obscure work is *Josh Billings' Cook Book and Picktorial Proverbs* (1880), a slender volume containing thirteen humorous recipes along with comic illustrations, aphorisms, and miscellaneous tidbits. In his preface Josh informs the public that the recipes "are the suggestions ov a man who never haz been able to cook hiz own goose just exactly right"; the reader who finds the dishes disappointing should take comfort in the thought that "they aint enny wuss than they are, and yu hav gained sumthing bi the experiment." In literary terms, *Josh Billings Struggling With Things* (1881) is the least interesting of the jest books, the small number of illustrated aphorisms seeming to exist primarily for the sake of the copious advertising that clutters its pages.

By the time Shaw made the move to New York to write for the *Weekly*, he had begun to make his name as a platform funny man. Though his early attempts at lecturing were abortive, he eventually became so successful that he was sponsored by famed lecture circuit entrepreneur James Clark Redpath, who signed Shaw up as a "$100-a-night" man. For seventeen consecutive seasons Shaw was to read his lectures for as many as 100 nights a year in, as he said, "every town in Texas and California and in all the Canada towns and then down South from Baltimore across to Memphis and New Orleans." As one of Redpath's star performers, he became friends with other renowned lecturers such as Mark Twain and David Ross Locke (Petroleum V. Nasby).

Shaw's lectures were usually on one of three topics—"Buty and the Beasts," "What i Kno About Hotels," and the frequently given "Milk." These were open-ended topics that allowed Shaw, in the persona of Josh Billings, much latitude. Each lecture was delivered in short, often aphoristic paragraphs. Transitions between subjects were purposely illogical and strained, a stylistic device that delighted the audience. The comic tone of a lecture was enhanced by Shaw's personal appearance, mannerisms, and carefully studied stage techniques. Tall and stoop-shouldered, Shaw had a large head and face, accentuated by long, shaggy hair and an unkempt beard. He wore solemn black suits and boots, shirts with oversized collars, and no necktie. His whole demeanor was half-serious, half-humorous, an appearance that created laughter in itself. Shaw sat to lecture, often next to a table with an untouched and unexplained pitcher of milk sitting on it. His halting delivery and superb comic timing capped off each successful performance.

While Shaw was well under way with his lecturing, he published *Everybody's Friend, or Josh Billings' Encyclopedia and Proverbial Philosophy of Wit and Humor* (1874), a collection of most of his writings to date except the *Allminax*. Two years later his *The Complete Comical Writings of Josh Billings* appeared. Then in 1884 he began contributing aphorisms to the *Century Illustrated Monthly Magazine* under the pseudonym Uncle Esek. So popular was "Uncle Esek's Wisdom" that the *Century* carried the column three years after Shaw's death. The Uncle Esek sayings differed from Shaw's usual aphorisms in that they were written in standard spelling and grammar.

Shaw remained active and prosperous in his old age, until the summer of 1884 when his health began to fail. A year later he journeyed to the Pacific coast where his physicians thought the climate might prove resuscitative. But the sojourn there

Josh Billings lecturing on the probabilities of life

ticular topics apropos of his times, such as women's rights and current fashions, are treated in his essays and aphorisms, his best pieces are usually those that deal with timeless, universal subjects and truths. The humor Shaw created, as Walter Blair has pointed out, is one of "phraseology rather than of character." His writings are so fresh and startling in use of imagery that Max Eastman viewed Shaw as a "poetic humorist" and went so far as to pronounce him the "father of imagism." Most of his language is in the cacography so faddish in his school and times. Early in his career Shaw resisted adoption of misspellings and substandard grammar until he realized these techniques would bring him popularity. He also sensed that moral apothegms phrased in unorthodox language would be more palatable than if presented unadorned and with high seriousness. The misspellings do cause some problems in reading and appreciating Shaw today; however, they also lend to the richness and quaintness of his style and combine forces with his wit to create humor.

Though there were some detractors among Shaw's contemporaries, critics of his age generally praised his brand of humor and clever use of language. He was labeled "a Jacques and a Touchstone in one and the same person" and an "Aesop and Ben Franklin, condensed and abridged." At present, little is written critically about Shaw, the later twentieth century having largely relegated him to his historical place among the literary comedians. There are a few important exceptions, however; Shaw and the literary comedians have undergone recent critical reevaluation and drawn appreciative commentary in such books as Jesse Bier's *The Rise and Fall of American Humor* (1968); *The Comic Imagination in American Literature* (1973), edited by Louis D. Rubin; David B. Kesterson's *Josh Billings* (1973); and Walter Blair and Hamlin Hill's *America's Humor: From Poor Richard to Doonesbury* (1978). These critics and others have mainly concentrated on Shaw's brand of humor, his contributions to literary realism, and his striking use of the language. Jesse Bier rightly feels that Shaw was one of America's first comic theoreticians. Joseph Jones's enlightened view is that Shaw is far more than a cracker-barrel philosopher: he is "a rather severely self-disciplined artist."

lasted only a few months; he died unexpectedly from apoplexy on 14 October 1885 in Monterey, California.

Shaw had a broad, classical concept of humor that matched his general philosophy of life. He interpreted his comic talent as the ability to cause a "smile continually on the face of every human being on God's footstool, and this smile should ever and anon widen into a broad grin." Humor should both entertain and inform. Chaucerian in his world view, Shaw found amusement in and even pardoned the foibles of mankind. Though deep enough a thinker to ponder the failures of civilization and sometimes judge the progress of mankind with skepticism, he usually managed to override gloom with lighthearted witticisms that convinced an audience that life was worth living after all.

In content, Shaw's writings are less political than those of many of his fellow literary comedians; nor did he write much fiction. Even though par-

Shaw was influenced by writers such as Shakespeare, Dickens, Burns, Goldsmith, Pope, Homer, Vergil, and Franklin. In turn he left his stamp on the likes of Mark Twain, Bill Nye, Kin Hubbard, Will Rogers, and the whole school of rural, cracker-barrel humorists. He contributed to the rise of realism in American letters with his probing critical barbs that lie beneath the surface of his humor. In all, he was a gifted man and writer who earned his place as a key figure in the development of American humor.

Other:

Josh Billings Spice Box, a periodical collection of humor edited by Shaw published in New York by various publishers—including Carleton, Street & Smith, and Ogilvie—in 1874 and afterward.

B. P. Shillaber

(12 July 1814-25 November 1890)

Clyde G. Wade
University of Missouri, Rolla

SELECTED BOOKS: *Life and Sayings of Mrs. Partington and Others of the Family* (New York: J. C. Derby, 1854);

Knitting Work: A Web of Many Textures Wrought by Ruth Partington (Boston: Brown, Taggard & Chase, 1859);

Partingtonian Patchwork (Boston: Lee & Shepard, 1873).

B. P. Shillaber made his way into literature over the same indirect route taken by a Bostonian of an earlier day, Benjamin Franklin. In 1847 he slipped a sketch of his into the *Boston Post*, where he worked as a compositor, and gained instant notice. Other sketches followed, and Shillaber was suddenly famous as the creator of Mrs. Partington. (A Yankee to the marrow, Mrs. Partington nevertheless owes her name to the English author Sydney Smith. Smith's Mrs. Partington was a Devonshire woman who once tried to sweep the ocean out of her kitchen. This comic episode was on Shillaber's mind when by chance he overhead the remark that inspired the first humorous saying he was to attribute to his Mrs. Partington: it "made no difference to her whether flour was dear or cheap, as she always had to pay just so much for a half-dollar's worth.") Along with Frances Whitcher's Widow Bedott, Mrs. Partington made a genuine impact upon American humor, introducing herself as comic rival to such comic male figures as Jack Downing and Sam Slick and quickening the evolution of American humor to an emphasis upon more authentic comic portraiture.

It was an emphasis that affected the writing of humor. There was, for example, less reliance upon political and other external events to create laughter. Writing techniques also changed in response to the interest in character. While Jack Downing's vehicle had been letters to the folks back home, Mrs. Partington relied upon the monologue. Shillaber's command of Yankee vernacular in large measure accounts for the enormously popular success of Mrs. Partington. That success, in turn, added its influence to the evolution of authentic vernacular speech as the natural vehicle for much of the best American humor to emerge in succeeding decades.

Shillaber's work as journalist and editor further adds to his historical importance. First as a printer and then as a young newspaperman for the *Post*, he became acquainted with the humorists of the 1840s. Thus when he founded and edited a short-lived but important journal of humor, the *Carpet-Bag* (1851-1853), he was able to publish some of the best humorists of the day—including early work of two youthful unknowns, Artemus Ward and Mark Twain.

Benjamin Penhallow Shillaber began his indirect route to success in Portsmouth, New Hampshire, where he was born, one of six children of William and Sarah Shillaber. He attended Portsmouth district schools until he began to learn the printer's trade. From 1829 until the spring of 1833 he served as a printer's devil. In 1833 he became a book compositor with the Boston firm of Tuttle and Weeks. He acquired the rating of journeyman printer in 1835 at the age of twenty-one, but in October of that year he experienced such violent nasal hemorrhages that he left for the tropics. For about two years he was a compositor on the *Royal Gazette of British Guiana*. Returning to Boston in July 1838, he married Ann Tappan de Rochemont the following August 15. Shortly there-

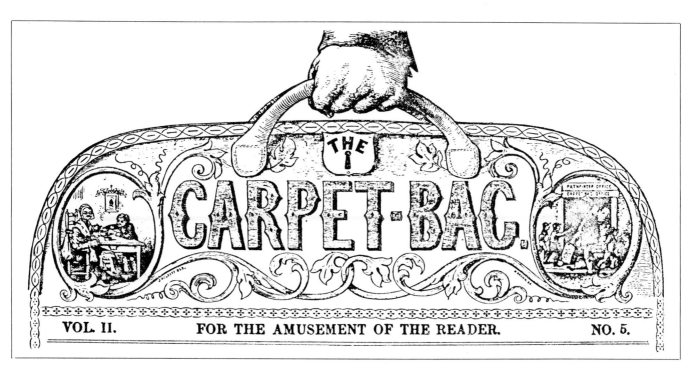

The flag for Shillaber's humorous weekly magazine

after he joined the *Boston Post* as a printer, apparently with no further ambitions, until he slipped the first Mrs. Partington sketch into the newspaper's pages nine years later.

In 1854, after the *Carpet-Bag* was discontinued, Shillaber was back with the *Post* when J. C. Derby, a New York publisher, pointed out that a compilation of Mrs. Partington sketches "would make a pretty good selling book" and asked Shillaber to supply enough copy for about 300 pages. Orders for 20,000 copies of the book had been placed before publication, and it sold well thereafter—at least another 10,000 copies. Although other volumes of Mrs. Partington sketches followed, selling well and emphasizing Shillaber's popularity as a humorist, the *Life and Sayings of Mrs. Partington and Others of the Family* (1854) includes Shillaber's best sketches and presents his principal characters, Mrs. Partington and her nephew Ike, more effectively than the later volumes.

In the 1860s and 1870s Shillaber adjusted to the changing tastes of his audience but at the expense of his stature as a humorist. He wrote more leisurely narratives, developing in them such humorous characters as Dr. Spooner and Blifkins "the martyr." The twenty-one brief chapters that constitute the "Blifkins Papers" in *Partingtonian Patchwork* (1873) provide more than 100 pages of pleasantly amusing, genteel narratives but little else.

B. P. Shillaber

Portents of a loss of strength and vigor come with the first Blifkins episode, "Blifkins's Summer Retreat." In that story Shillaber reverses the history of Mrs. Partington who comes to Boston from a rural Down East village. Blifkins is a man of the city who, on vacation, is hopelessly and sometimes humorously out of place in a rural setting. Like other Down East humorists from Seba Smith to his principal rival, Frances Whitcher, Shillaber becomes just another genteel writer when he gets away from the manners and vernacular speech of his region. Hence *Life and Sayings of Mrs. Partington* remains his best work.

Two qualities of *Life and Sayings of Mrs. Partington* reflect importantly upon Shillaber's humor. First, except for the thirty-three page "biography" of Ruth Partington which served as an introduction, the book consists mostly of materials shaped for the columns of the *Boston Post* or the *Carpet-Bag*. Some entries are nothing more than random anecdotes and one-liners, obvious newspaper filler. Shillaber never entirely escaped the limitations of the newspaper column, not even after *Life and Sayings of Mrs. Partington* demonstrated an audience for humorous books featuring his characters. Second, Shillaber was devoted almost exclusively to the amiable humor that dominated his first book, good-naturedly uniting laughter and sensibility.

As he told Derby, Shillaber initiated the Mrs. Partington sketches with the intention of "creating a smile" and seeking "pleasantry for the moment." Subsequent volumes reveal that he was generally satisfied with the good will and laughter of a popular audience who asked little more than to be touched and amused by predictable characters, clever plays on words, and uncomplicated jests and anecdotes. The "Lubricatory" to *Partington Patchwork* echoes the prefatory comments of his first volume and confirms that Shillaber's attitude toward humor remained unchanged over the years: "but he [the author] deems that if it [*Partingtonian Patchwork*] succeed in making the reader for a moment forget his worldly cares and pains, and awakens a smile at eccentricities of thought and speech, it will have done as much good as though it made more pretension." The consequence of his continuing satisfaction with amiable prose sketches and stories that studiously avoid the less pleasant realities of his day is that Shillaber's career as a humorist reflects no especially remarkable intellectual or artistic growth.

Nevertheless, Shillaber was successful in the characterization of Mrs. Partington. The emphasis upon sensibility which he shared too readily with his era undoubtedly helped to shape her character. A widowed, grandmotherly woman of rural New England lately come to Boston, she regards the world with a mixture of naivete and folk wisdom; and she exudes, in Shillaber's words, such benevolence of "act, intention and sentiment" as to win through the years the affectionate approbation of a large following, including such notable folk as Oliver Wendell Holmes and Henry Ward Beecher. Many a sketch declines into sentimentality insufficiently checked by humor. But on occasion the sentiment clashes with the genial humor and exacerbates a problem for Shillaber of reconciling the genial outlook of the sketches with complexities of actual experience which, obviously, often troubled him.

The most interesting and meaningful humorous sketches attempt to reconcile that genial humor with reality. Shillaber tries to solve the problem with cruelty in "The Cat and Kittens." Mrs. Partington discovers a litter of kittens in her work basket, lying upon the black gloves and handkerchief she habitually wore in memory of her departed husband. She cries in anger, "I'll drownd 'em, every one of 'em!" Ike is ordered to dispatch the kittens in the big tub. Swift to obey, he is not prompt enough to escape a novel impulse to charity: "'Stop, Isaac, a minute,' she cried, 'and I'll take the chill off the water; it would be cruel to put 'em into it stone-cold.'" Shillaber's purpose in compromising Mrs. Partington's charity is made baldly explicit: "Perfection belongeth not to man or woman, and we would throw this good pen of ours into the street . . . could we pretend that Mrs. Partington was an exception to this universal rule." Although he finds the cruelty of the drowned kittens "rather gratuitous," Jesse Bier perceives in the uses of cruelty an urge in Shillaber and other American humorists to be wholly truthful. "Against a nauseatingly prettified ideal of American life," he writes, "humorists set their cruelty as a particular redressment of reality."

In this respect Mrs. Partington's "roguish" nephew Ike is the principal counterforce to superficial amiableness. Ike not only drowns the kittens, he subsequently hangs the cat when he deliberately misconstrues a command of his aunt. Later he foists off on her a preposterous tale of cat suicide. His most imaginative act of violence against cats comes in "Ike in the Country" when he ties smooth clamshells to each foot of a local cat and then places the animal on the frozen river so that the wind carries it to almost certain destruction in the cold waters of the bay. Yet the sketches which feature Ike reveal that he is prompted more by boredom than viciousness. Moreover, at the age of eleven he is "just upon the dividing line between accountability and indulgence." Thus he is potentially better suited than his aunt for revealing the whole truth about experience within the confines of an amiable humor. The Ike "juveniles" which Shillaber continued to write for many years demonstrate the importance of Ike and also Shillaber's determination to create a more substantial youth than the traditional good little boy of literature. This response to the falsification of youth is remarkably like that of his younger contemporary, Mark Twain.

For all of Ike's potential as a character, however, it is not he who brought Shillaber to fame but Mrs. Partington. She, more than any of the characters who surround her, defines Shillaber's humor. The most famous malapropist of her day, Mrs. Partington reveals through her verbal blunders the worst and best of Shillaber's humor. The worst is mere verbal cuteness as in the sketch "Fancy Diseases" where such malapropisms as "two buckles" for tuberculosis and the more obvious "hermitage of the lungs" and "jocular vein" can but faintly amuse. In other sketches such confusions as "pasture" for pastor and "Santa Cruz" for Santa Claus suggest a humorist laboring to be funny.

At their best, Mrs. Partington's "inaccuracies of speech," as Shillaber described them, are truly expressive of her character, reflecting a believable mind and a personality smacking of life. The words then pour out of a consciousness that has a hopelessly faulty, inherently comic grasp of language. *Omnibus* becomes *ominous*, chateau is confused with *chapeau*, oratorio with *Ontario*, and *trough* with *troth*. There are also the burning lather of Mount Vociferous, the King James Aversion, and Johnson's Decency (dictionary).

When Shillaber exploits the naivete of her rural background, the humor derives even more satisfactorily from her character and achieves greater success. She got the amused attention of the nation during the Pierce administration with her response to comments about relations between the United States and Mexico: "The Mexicans had better not trouble any of our relations, I can tell 'em!" Accepting with entire literalness the news that there will be a "canvassing [of] the state," she launches into an attack upon the "extravagance and costiveness of government." In "A Home Truth" Mrs. Partington's sympathy with slaves leads to an observation that has the bite of reality and is indeed closer to home: "But some of our folks don't do much better. I know a poor old colored man here in Boston that they treat jest like a nigger." Similar successes occur in "A Substitute" when Mrs. Partington,

short of cash, responds to a call for alms with two sausages and when in "Mild Weather" she counters a wealthy man's chuckle that mild days in winter are "good weather for poor people" with a shrewder observation that allows no complacency about poverty. "Cold weather is the best for the poor, for then the rich feel the cold . . . and feel more exposed to give 'em consolation and coal." The malapropism fully justifies itself, adding force as well as humor to Mrs. Partington's insight.

Life and Sayings of Mrs. Partington was followed by other volumes devoted to Mrs. Partington, notably *Knitting Work* (1859) and *Partingtonian Patchwork*. Though Ike continued to occupy Shillaber's attention, the possibilities of Mrs. Partington and Ike were not fully realized by Shillaber, in good part because, too closely wedded to the newspaper sketch, he never cultivated the richer, more spacious literary forms such as the novel that encourage character development and complex humor. But Shillaber had a good reputation as a popular humorist in his day, and history provides an instance of the strongest proof that he was both avidly read and remarkably influential.

The potential of Mrs. Partington and Ike was in fact realized by Mark Twain in the characters of Aunt Polly and Tom Sawyer. The points of similarity between the women and the boys are too great for any other conclusion. There is even a remarkable visual proof of their kinship in the illustration entitled "Contentment" in *The Adventures of Tom Sawyer* (1876). A representation of Aunt Polly, it first appeared above the caption "Ruth Partington" in *Life and Sayings of Mrs. Partington* twenty-two years earlier. So close was Twain's unconscious identification with Mrs. Partington that he attributed the drowning of the kittens to his mother upon whom he consciously based the character of Aunt Polly. Critics have thoroughly examined the relationships, and Walter Blair's summary in *Native American Humor* is readily accessible, succinct, and convincing—particularly in the juxtaposition of remarkably similar passages from *Knitting Work* and chapter 3 of *Tom Sawyer*.

The juxtaposition of Twain and Shillaber emphasizes that whatever Shillaber's place in the history of American humor, it is less than that of a major writer. Though minor, his place is nevertheless respectable. His sympathetic identification with other writers of humor, his efforts as editor, particularly of the *Carpet-Bag*, and his own writing substantially support a claim to an influential role in the development of American humor. All the activities taken together seem to confirm Franklin J. Meine's

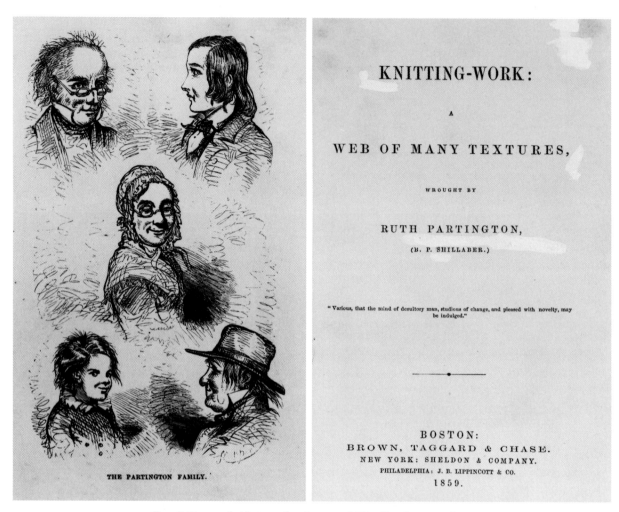

KNITTING-WORK:

A

WEB OF MANY TEXTURES,

WROUGHT BY

RUTH PARTINGTON,

(B. P. SHILLABER.)

"Various, that the mind of desultory man, studious of change, and pleased with novelty, may be indulged."

BOSTON:
BROWN, TAGGARD & CHASE.
NEW YORK: SHELDON & COMPANY.
PHILADELPHIA: J. B. LIPPINCOTT & CO.
1859.

THE PARTINGTON FAMILY.

Frontispiece and title page for the second Mrs. Partington volume

perception of him as a "connecting link" between the generation of humorists who flourished before the Civil War and the generation who flourished after it. Recent histories of American humor such as Jesse Bier's *The Rise and Fall of American Humor* (1968) and especially Walter Blair and Hamlin Hill's more inclusive *America's Humor: From Poor Richard to Doonesbury* (1978) give good evidence that Shillaber's place is sufficiently established. Bier, who finds little importance in the humor itself nevertheless begins his study with B. P. Shillaber. Blair and Hill include him among the "reputable" (as opposed to "subversive") humorists, one in whose work "tradition, decorum, justice, and sanity played significant parts."

Other:
Carpet-Bag, edited by Shillaber, 1851-1853.

Periodical Publications:
"Experiences During Many Years," *New England Magazine* (June 1893-May 1894).

References:
Jesse Bier, *The Rise and Fall of American Humor* (New York: Holt, Rinehart & Winston, 1968);

Walter Blair, *Native American Humor* (New York: American Book Company, 1937);

Blair and Hamlin Hill, *America's Humor: From Poor Richard to Doonesbury* (New York: Oxford University Press, 1978), pp. 155-156, 186, 280;

George W. Bungay, *Off-Hand Takings; or Crayon Sketches of the Noticeable Men of Our Age*, third edition (New York: Robert M. De Witt, 1854), pp. 372-376;

J. C. Derby, *Fifty Years Among Authors, Books and Publishers* (New York: Carleton, 1884), pp. 407-413.

Max Shulman

(14 March 1919-   )

Francis Hodgins
University of Illinois

SELECTED BOOKS: *Barefoot Boy With Cheek* (Garden City: Doubleday, Doran, 1943);

The Feather Merchants (Garden City: Doubleday, Doran, 1944);

The Zebra Derby (Garden City: Doubleday, 1946);

Sleep Till Noon (Garden City: Doubleday, 1950);

The Tender Trap, by Shulman and Robert Paul Smith (New York: Random House, 1955);

Rally Round the Flag, Boys! (Garden City: Doubleday, 1957);

Anyone Got a Match? (New York, Evanston & London: Harper & Row, 1964);

Potatoes Are Cheaper (Garden City: Doubleday, 1971; London: Joseph, 1973).

COLLECTIONS: *The Many Loves of Dobie Gillis* (Garden City: Doubleday, 1951);

I Was a Teen-Age Dwarf (New York: Random House, 1959; London: Heinemann, 1959).

Looking back on his work in mid-career, Max Shulman saw that humor had from the first been his defense against the harshness of social reality. "I know now," he wrote in 1961, "why I turned early to humor as my branch of writing. The reason is simply that life was bitter and I was not. All around me was poverty and sordidness but I refused to see it that way. By turning it into jokes, I made it bearable." However ingenuous this deflection may appear as a protective device, it accurately indicates the limits of Shulman's humor, which typically transforms potentially disturbing social material into escapist entertainment. His satires either stop comfortably short of serious criticism or bypass social reality altogether for the still greater safety of farce. Unpleasant social conditions are acknowledged only to be dismissed: an indistinct slum in *Sleep Till Noon* (1950), for example, is merely the background for a farce about life among the rich; the depiction of ghetto poverty in *Potatoes Are Cheaper* (1971) not only escapes bitterness through jokes but makes life an exhilarating game in which nothing is at risk but money; and even such undeniably sordid social facts as racism and anti-Semitism lose their menace as they become the material for

bright one-liners. Indeed, the intention of Shulman's humor is to present a world without either risk or menace, a reassuring context that allows his stories to take up current social issues without having to take them seriously. It is humor that rarely reaches beyond the immediate laugh, that is neither an instrument of criticism nor the means to an irreverent or socially radical comic perspective. But within these limits Shulman's humor has proved a durable source of light entertainment in many literary forms—novels and short stories, plays and screenplays, television scripts, and a syndicated column in college newspapers. From the publication of his popular first book, *Barefoot Boy With Cheek*, in 1943, Shulman has had a recognized place among American humorists.

His early awareness of "poverty and sordidness" came from growing up during the Depression years in St. Paul, Minnesota, where he was born and lived until he was graduated from college. Sometime during those early years his interest in writing—along with his recourse to humor—was established. He attended the University of Minnesota as a journalism major and wrote regularly for campus publications, most notably for *Ski-U-Mah*, the humor magazine. Shortly before his graduation in 1942 his humor columns came to the attention of an editor for Doubleday who thereupon invited him to write a book. "I was too green to panic," Shulman reports, "so I wrote *Barefoot Boy With Cheek*. Doubleday published the book in 1943 with trepidation, but somehow the college kids turned it into a runaway." Shulman's bare-bones account of his first book publication does little to convey the drama of an event that has the quality of a Hollywood legend of the discovery of a star. Seemingly without effort, and certainly without a struggling young writer's painful apprenticeship to his craft, he had passed from anonymous college boy to literary celebrity—and as a result of a book that was little different from his college columns. Craft, as it happened, would have to come later.

By the time his book appeared, Shulman had enlisted in the Army Air Force, where he served until 1946. It could scarcely be said, however, that the war interrupted his new literary career, which went forward with impressive speed on the line laid down by *Barefoot Boy With Cheek*. Intent upon following up that first success, he devoted every spare moment to his writing: "During the war (at night, on Sundays, on furloughs), I turned out two novels—*The Feather Merchants* and *The Zebra Derby*—and a couple of dozen short stories." When the war ended, Shulman was therefore well established as a productive humorist whose primary appeal was still to college undergraduates (including those about to return to college from the armed services), and his own return to civilian life did not signal any apparent change in his work. In fact, one of his first postwar projects (again by invitation) was the adaptation of *Barefoot Boy With Cheek* as a musical comedy—an approach to a new form but through the familiar materials of an established success. Having married while he was still in college, he now had a growing family to support and was, as he said, paying his bills "with a raft of short stories" in the magazines and with a fourth novel, *Sleep Till Noon*, a dreary repetition of the devices of his first books that had none of their energy or invention. In the early 1950s he published a collection of still more college stories, *The Many Loves of Dobie Gillis* (1951), from which he would later create a popular television comedy series that ran from 1959 to 1963. With Robert Paul Smith he also wrote a play, *The Tender Trap*, that was produced on Broadway in 1954 and made into a movie the next year. But despite the apparent variety of these literary activities, Shulman had not moved far from his first formulas for writing humor, and it seems significant that in 1954 he returned to the field of his earliest recognition by writing a syndicated weekly humor column for college newspapers.

The next year, as if to survey his market and to assess his amateur competition, he compiled an anthology, *Max Shulman's Guided Tour of Campus Humor*, in which he collected examples from college humor publications across the country and from several periods. But, as he explained in the introduction, the collection was less historical than he had intended because he found the humor of World War I and the 1920s to be "hopelessly dated" and so had included little of it. Shulman's own early books now seem just as severely dated. The form of these books is farce, not as an element in other kinds of comedy, but as the nearly exclusive basis for humor. This use of farce meant relying for comic effects upon exaggeration, caricature, broad verbal play, gags, and ludicrous situations; but above all it meant that extemporaneous invention—digression

Max Shulman

following digression—was the essential element of structure, far outweighing plot or character or story line. Farce used as a structure in this way made a book essentially a series of skits (not unlike Shulman's college humor columns) about subjects that are unrelated to each other or to any narrative development; in this context the occasional admission "But I digress" is not an apology for straying but part of the joke, for there is nothing but digression, nothing to digress from. The test of such writing is its capacity to entertain through inventiveness alone. Each zany incident, beginning and ending nowhere and having no point beyond its incongruities, must be a separate infusion of energy to carry the book forward. When this energy flags, there is neither plot nor character nor story to sustain interest.

Barefoot Boy With Cheek is nominally "about" Asa Hearthrug's freshman year at the University of Minnesota, but of course it is equally about any number of other things, from the first digression (the pointless history of a female relative who "Latinized her name to Yanqui Imperialismo" to fight bulls in Bolivia) to the last (an equally pointless legend of how the campus once belonged to a nation where everyone was named Chalmers, only first cousins were permitted to marry, and the people worshiped a statue of Franklin Pierce). The humor is relentlessly juvenile, and its sole premise is that incongruities are funny. Occasionally the jokes flirt with vulgarity, as in naming a symphony "Filligree on Derriere's Variation of a Theme of Merde." More often they depend upon the kind of under-graduate knowingness that finds it humorous to refer to El Greco's influence on Kate Douglas Wiggin or to have William Jennings Bryan ask, at the end of the Cross of Gold speech, "What will it be, gentlemen, rum, romanism, or rebellion?"

Somewhere within these digressions Asa is given his college physical by health service doctors too busy reading *Film Fun* to notice his presence; is abducted by means of a mantrap into Alpha Cholera Fraternity (Roger Hailfellow, president; Shylock Fiscal, treasurer; and a rush committee wearing side arms); and is assigned a program of courses (including three in the language, literature, and government of Lett) that will make him "a well-rounded-out personality." He divides his romantic interests between Noblesse Oblige, a sorority girl whose vocabulary consists mostly of "I mean," and Yetta Samovar, a "finely mustached" Communist in "close-knit burlap" who takes him to meetings of the Subversive Elements' League to sing songs like "Let the Bosses Take the Losses." During the year Asa also eludes the clutches of a libidinous housemother ("I'm home all the time"); submits a story to *Poignancy*, the literary magazine (unintelligible poetry, proletarian fiction); and, as Alpha Cholera's only freshman, runs for student council as a horse so dark that he is kept locked in his room throughout the campaign.

Barefoot Boy With Cheek does not develop these matters beyond the immediate joke. The best possibilities of satire are lost in simple caricature, as, of course, are all possibilities of characterization and story development. The intentionally pointless digressions too often collapse in mid-flight for lack of narrative energy and inventiveness: as the pattern becomes predictable, it becomes boring. Twelve years later, in the introduction to his *Guided Tour of Campus Humor*, Shulman listed three characteristics common to college humor: "a) an irreverence toward authority; b) a love of the outlandish; c) a preoccupation with sex." Of these, his own first book is almost exclusively given over to his love of the outlandish and to the self-indulgence that went with it. His work needed something—theme, plot, or structure—to give shape to his talent for slapstick.

But in his next three books Shulman seemed to be stuck with the formulas of the first one. Part of the enormous success of *Barefoot Boy With Cheek* was due to its timeliness, to catching the accent, in exaggerated form, of a period of college life. In *The*

Feather Merchants (1944), Shulman tried to do the same thing for civilian life in wartime, from the perspective of a serviceman home on leave. In *The Zebra Derby* (1946), Asa Hearthrug has "come home from the wars to live and prosper in a new world of peace, opportunity, and universal plumbing facilities." The last of these early books, *Sleep Till Noon*, is not timely in this way, since it is vaguely placed in the Depression years, but this transition book in Shulman's career clings to the old formulas even as it shows their exhaustion.

The Feather Merchants (in defining the term, *Dictionary of American Slang* cites Shulman as its primary source) is easily the most readable of these books now. One reason is that farce is less dominant here. Much of the humor again depends upon exaggeration, caricature, crude verbal play, and elaborate gags. Digressions are again prominent and present the same temptations to self-indulgence. But this time there is a firmer story line, the characters are more developed, and the mild satire focuses on the self-deceptions, patriotic belligerence, and sheer foolishness of an unendangered and thoroughly prosperous civilian society in wartime. If the jokes about price-gouging and hoarding are predictable ("She had so much flour and sugar hidden in her house that when she had a fire last winter, after they put it out there was a two-story cake standing there"), there is genuine comic pathos in the yearning of ordinary people to feel that their lives have been touched by the heroic significance of a world war. Shulman deals with this only in the broadest way, but his parodies of war-time movies, songs, newspaper and newscast rhetoric—and the speech of citizens as they relate themselves to "total war"—are humor in the service of social history. The most important advance over his first book, however, occurs in the development of character. In Daniel Miller, the soldier home on leave, *The Feather Merchants* has a significantly more flexible and realistic narrator; and in Miller's friend Sam Wye, a trickster with a fertile imagination, Shulman creates a character who is the self-conscious agent of comic inventions rather than the butt of them. In *The Feather Merchants* the characters, even the type characters, have, beyond their absurdities, traits and idiosyncrasies that connect them to the world and give them interest.

Shulman's next two books repeat the formulas of *Barefoot Boy With Cheek* in a mechanical fashion that suggests little of that first book's exuberance. *The Zebra Derby* revives several of the earlier characters (in addition to having, as a protest against the false modesty of authors, twenty-four characters named Max) as Asa Hearthrug seeks his "destiny" in a world where peace promises imminent social perfection. But the book is less an exploration of comic possibilities in "the new, fulfilled America" than a frenzied search for laughs as it takes Asa through an unimaginative round of supposedly funny activities, from selling cookie cutters to joining Yetta Samovar (still wearing burlap) in a workers' paradise defined as free love and ideological drama. There is a return briefly to the University of Minnesota for some tepid jokes about veterans in college. But every scene in this book is both a quick take and a meaningless excursion, and Shulman seems bored by his rehearsal of old tricks. The book ends, appropriately, with Asa back home in Whistlestop and assuring himself that, despite "atomic energy and radar and the federating of nations," his own world is "unchanged," even "static."

Sleep Till Noon, which concerns the rise of an Asa-like character from poverty to inadvertent business success, is a still more feeble book. The lackluster digressions seem merely obligatory padding, and that in turn makes the absence of structure all the more awkward. Such books might, as Shulman said, pay the bills, but he was clearly tired of them.

In these books Shulman's love of incongruity is sometimes condensed in one-line jokes, including, in *Barefoot Boy With Cheek*, a repetition of Ring Lardner's classic line: " 'Shut up,' he explained." Occasionally there is evidence of a perspective which might, had Shulman's aims been different, have made him an effective satirist, as in this brief burlesque (complete with reference to that famous turtle) of the agrarian Oklahoma that Steinbeck had sentimentalized in *The Grapes of Wrath*: "In the shade of CCC-planted trees loose-hung farmers squatted in a position no city-bred man can even approximate and drew pictures of biological manifestations in the dirt with blunt sticks. Calico-clad farm wives, their supper sidemeat cooking in immemorial pots, sat sluggishly fanning themselves with parity checks. A turtle crossed the road to get on the other side." Although it is never more than intermittent in his work, this astringent side of Shulman's wit shows the potential for a far more complex comic perspective on social issues, as in this exchange from *Anyone Got a Match?* (1964): " 'I like you, Mr. Shapian. Fact is, I like practically all you Jew fellers.'

" 'Not that it makes any difference,' said Ira, 'but I'm an Armenian.'

" 'You're right,' said Jefferson. 'It don't make any difference.' "

By the middle 1950s Shulman was fully established in the life he would thereafter follow as a professional writer who turned his hand to many forms of literary entertainment. But his career as a writer and humorist was about to take a new direction. The change came in 1956, when, Shulman later reported, "I finally buckled down to write *Rally Round the Flag, Boys!* Whatever its faults—and it has plenty—it is the only book I ever wrote that came out exactly as I planned it." His plan for the book, although he did not say so, meant turning away from the kind of fiction he had thus far written. His new fiction would have a firm plot and a clear story line, and its humor would be based in character and situation. As his fiction became conventional in structure, his humor became social in a new way, taking its material from contemporary social concerns and even introducing, as the observations of a "journeyman sociologist," some minor social analysis. This is not to say that Shulman's humor would ever become critical or penetrating, let alone iconoclastic; but his social notations would have a certain shrewdness.

Rally Round the Flag, Boys! (1957) concerns the establishment of a Nike missile base in a Connecticut village not unlike Westport, where Shulman then lived. But the Nike installation is only the occasion for a lighthearted survey of the social classes and types of the village and, more especially, of the ways of modern love, from the courting rituals of teenagers to the equally obligatory adulteries of the middle-aged. Gone are the gags and puns of the earlier books, and farce of the former sort appears only in a final scene, when a Nike is fired by accident and becomes the grand climax of the village's Fourth of July fireworks display. Discarding his reliance upon the merely outlandish, Shulman shows an unexpected talent for pertinent exaggeration and deft caricature, as in summarizing an Oklahoma farm boy's career in country music: at the age of six he was taken to hear Ernest Tubb sing "from the heart" and was inspired to become a "big star" himself; at ten, using his father's half-filled silo as an echo chamber, he composed "You Lied to Me Oncet Too Often," despite his limited experience of betrayal in love; at sixteen, when he was ready for Oklahoma City as a stepping-stone toward Nashville, he was the author of "upwards of three thousand songs," including such titles as "Red Eye Whiskey Is My Buckler, but the Bible Is My Shield" and "Dear God, I'm Glad You Took My Ethel, She

Was Much Too Good for Me." Here the exaggeration points up the pious sentimentality of country music, and the titles are almost plausible.

Although the love stories are the narrative core of the novel, the humor more often comes from Shulman's observations, at times amounting to small sociological essays, on social relations in the village. Putnam's Landing, we find, has "three distinct social categories, vertically divided": old Yankee families, descendants of Italians who first came to build the New Haven railroad, and New York commuters. What is also quickly apparent is that this vertical social division conveniently eliminates the usual class structure with its inevitable underclass; Putnam's Landing is a benign vision of a social system without losers. The Yankees still hold political power but have no more oppressive intent than to keep the village out of "the murky valley of deficit financing" and welcome the fiscally conservative Italians as allies. There are "no prejudices of a religious or social nature" in the village, no social conflicts deeper than the parliamentary wrangles at town meetings when the commuters' zeal for civic improvements meets the Yankees' resistance to change. In Putnam's Landing, we are told, even the juvenile delinquent is a rebel only in dress, language, and the frequency with which he spits; typically he comes from a "ranch house on two well-kept acres, and the sight of a switchblade would have put him in shock."

This carefully circumscribed version of reality is the necessary frame for Shulman's new kind of humor, which has become social and superficially "relevant" while still assuring us that nothing of consequence is at stake. *Rally Round the Flag, Boys!* provides a comforting view of the world. The love stories sort themselves out with all the participants appropriately matched. Adultery does not permanently damage the hero's marriage. Love not only conquers all, it sweeps everything else out of sight. Even the chief New Delinquent is allowed a small triumph as matters are rounded off: sent to a military school for discipline, he has singlehandedly changed the fashion of the academy in favor of long sideburns. Social issues are equally disposable. A dustless, noiseless, nonpolluting Nike missile base is finally no more threatening an intrusion into village life than the equally noiseless and odorless new garbage disposal plant to which, in fact, it is thematically related. In this sanitized context the humor comes from minor social notations: the editorial in the local paper giving a grudging welcome to the Nike base—and to the air force and navy too, if they

A WONDERFULLY FUNNY NOVEL ABOUT LOVE AND MISSILES

Dust jacket for Shulman's 1957 novel about love and missiles in a middle-class suburb

want to come—because it is at least preferable to more commuters; the "Yankee Clippers" who prey happily upon the commuters by selling them everything from wet building lots (by means of the imaginative nomenclature that transforms a salt meadow into Flintlock Ridge) to wall sealers for damp basements and power tools to rust in them; a twinkly Norman Rockwell version of a village doctor whose refreshing candor about his lack of knowledge (so unlike the arrogance of New York doctors, Shulman observes) is always praised by his patients, "those who lived"; and of course the "tweedy and fervent" commuters with their passion for civic virtue and amateur theatricals, their "special emergency protest meetings" of the PTA to deal with a hole in the school playground, and their overextended life-styles that keep them "skewered . . . on the two horns of fixedness and cashlessness. . . ."

Although Shulman's books generally received only cursory reviews, his next novel, *Anyone Got a Match?*, provoked a review by R. V. Cassill which touched a substantial issue for all of Shulman's later books. "This novel means nothing," Cassill wrote, "but in its own terms it is exquisitely skillful. . . . The pacing is beautiful. The selection and manipulation of characters is a triumph. All that's wrong is that the intention in every detail and every larger dimension is to perpetuate a fraud, to feint a serious satirical intent and then to cancel it totally." What Cassill objects to is Shulman's refusal to make his humor an instrument of social criticism even when his subject is itself socially significant. *Anyone Got a Match?* has such a subject—in fact it has several, including the cigarette industry, commercial television, the southern California life-style, race relations, and even the role of adultery in contemporary marriage. But the most prominent subject is food additives and the effect they may be having on the health of Americans.

The basic story seems promising for satire. Tobacco magnate Jefferson Tatum is looking for a "black hat" to divert public attention from "that so-called Surgeon General," whose report has raised the threat of lung cancer and depressed cigarette sales. Tatum finds his black hat in the food industry. Since, "like any other tobacco tycoon," he owns a college, he will order research into the chemicals that enter the American diet from pesticides and additives, put the results on national television, and drive a worried public back to smoking. To make the research credible, he must reluctantly permit Acanthus College, a denominational diploma mill with the nation's lowest admission standards and heaviest undergraduates (both essential to the football program) and a faculty who are all "elders of the Don't-Fiddle-With-The-Gospel Brotherhood," to be made over into a bona fide college, which means not just racial integration and nonathletic students "with straight 'A' averages and glasses" but professors who are free even to investigate the methods Tatum uses to run this Southern town as a private fiefdom.

Cassill is of course right in claiming that Shulman's satire avoids the seriousness of social issues. If there is a conclusion to be drawn about food additives and pesticides, it is that "it is the business of chemistry to take intelligent risks" and that pure-food zealots probably overstate those risks. The book's somewhat less prominent concern with race relations is treated with equal blandness. Here the conclusion is that "patience, courage, and steady, intelligent pressure" on the part of blacks (as op-posed to "these ridiculous, random, disorganized marches and demonstrations") will combine with the economic interests of whites to bring about a fully integrated society; Jefferson Tatum, a genial racist, does more than any revolutionist to reduce discrimination, just through selfish interest in having a tractable labor force and a peaceful town, and even, as he puts it, "got a plaque for racial tolerance from them Hebes at B'nai B'rith." Nor does any serious issue derive from the tobacco industry's enormous economic power, despite an offhandedly cynical appraisal of its relations with Congress and with the American Medical Association. As always, it is Shulman's purpose to turn aside serious questions with a joke.

Three years earlier, as if anticipating criticism of the kind Cassill advances, Shulman published a somber article in *Yale Review* setting forth his views on humor. "American Humor: Its Cause and Cure" is by far his fullest word on the subject, and it is an uncharacteristically systematic and "serious" denigration of humor as a form of literature. At bottom, Shulman argues, humor has a "dreary" effect because it "holds up a distorting mirror" to life, and this is finally depressing. Because of this distortion, "no humorist has ever cast light into the dark corners of the human soul"—a position which immediately forces him to exclude all major writers from the ranks of humorists. Shakespeare and Shaw, for example, despite their occasional concern with humor, are to be understood on quite different grounds, and Mark Twain will be valued not for his humor but for "his astute and angry social commentary."

This is the strategy of the essay, to deprive humor of stature and significance by narrowing its associations and lowering its functions. Lacking an essential element of dignity, humor "cannot be art. Humor is to art . . . as a satyr to Hyperion." Nor is humor, as is often claimed, an effective instrument of social criticism. "It is, of course, true that humorists have taken political and social injustice as their themes. But once they render it into comedic terms, they necessarily distort it to the point where the impact is lost." This inevitable distortion, Shulman argues, makes humor and social criticism incompatible. "When a humorist is sufficiently exercised by the state of the world, he gives up humor." Like Mark Twain, Ring Lardner is for Shulman a case in point: "Lardner fortunately had the talent to write seriously. Most humorists do not." As proof that humor has no real social impact, Shulman offers a long list of modern humorists, including Robert Benchley, S. J. Perelman, Dorothy Parker,

Don Marquis, Clarence Day, and E. B. White. "All," he observes, "have entertained with skill and taste. . . . All have failed to leave a ripple in the main current of American thought."

But Shulman's criticism of humor is not only for its lack of artistic stature or social importance. To entertain might seem function enough for humor—until we examine the means it employs. If by distorting reality humor makes us "feel comfortable," it also makes us "feel superior" by "pandering" to an apparently ineradicable need for "cruelty" that is only "silted over by the forces of civilization. . . ." For whatever reason, cruelty had become the inescapable element of bad conscience in all humor for Shulman. It links the way we "look down" on Charlie Chaplin to the overt violence of the cartoon mouse "whacking" the cartoon cat, since the one is "as much an appeal to cruelty" as the other. Our transactions with humorists no doubt serve our needs, but they do not, in the way of art, elevate our nature: "By all means let wealth accrue to humorists, but not honors. Let humorists be respected as any honest merchant is respected, but let us not confuse them with benefactors of mankind, with movers and shakers, with historical forces, with artists." Unlike the "cause" of humor, the "cure" for it is never specified, but it would obviously require a radical perfecting of human nature, reminding us of Mark Twain's remark that there is no humor in heaven.

Even as Shulman dismisses humor as "a very minor form of literary craft," his indictment seems overdrawn, disclaiming too much and concealing an emotional repudiation of the humorist's role. In part his argument is self-serving, since by implication it would justify his own career. He could have become a social critic only by ceasing to be a humorist, and like "most humorists" he lacked the talent for serious writing. If his work distorts reality, that is what the humorist does in making us "feel comfortable." If reviewers complain that his books are more slapstick than satire, that has been his way of avoiding greater cruelties, of whacking the cartoon cat instead of Charlie Chaplin. Most of all, his argument places his work beyond significant literary judgment by making humor unimportant and the humorist safely inconsequential, neither an artist nor a social force but merely a merchant who serves our less creditable needs. In effect, Shulman defends his trade by making it too trivial to count.

Whatever this bleak assessment may have meant to Shulman personally, its greatest import for his work was in the acknowledgment of the place of cruelty in humor, a point which recalls the old saying that only equals laugh together. This is the key to an important shift of tone in Shulman's latest books, where his humor has a new edge, a new aggressiveness. This is only intermittently evident in *Anyone Got a Match?* There the aggressive humor is directed to such safe subjects as the competitive practices of commercial television, the "soft, shiftless life of the California rich" that produces children who are "bronzed, vacuous, untroubled, muscular, and semi-aquatic," and the more familiar corruptions of college football. (The building that a visitor would mistake for the Acanthus chapel is actually the residence of the football coach, and the stained-glass windows reflect contemporary religious experience by depicting "the wing-T formation, pass interference, and the red dog.") But in a book where Shulman's most socially "important" subjects—food additives and race relations—are nearly exempt from satire, his newly aggressive humor could have only limited range.

There are no sacred subjects in *Potatoes Are Cheaper*, Shulman's most recent novel. Once again his work has changed directions, this time away from any concern with social issues or relevance. The setting is the St. Paul of Shulman's late adolescence in 1936 and 1937, years so deep in the Depression that a steady job was something remembered from "olden times." But the Depression is not a political or social issue in the novel; it is simply a condition which makes getting money the primary object of life. It might be, as Eddie Cantor sang, that "potatoes were cheaper. . . , but who the hell had money to buy any except maybe Eddie Cantor?" Yet poverty is not an issue either. Shulman does not mean to emphasize the hardships of the Depression or to air old injustices. Nobody starves. Nobody even suffers except for comic effect. Poverty is not a degradation; it is only a lack of money, and that is only a challenge to "making it."

But Shulman is turning back to the Depression from the perspectives of the 1960s, and *Potatoes Are Cheaper* is more contemporary than his novels about contemporary social issues. For one thing, as if to take his modest place in a major literary movement, he has discovered in this book the literary value of his Jewish heritage—or at least the comic possibilities of a Jewish group identity. For another, after many years of something close to literary prudishness, he for the first time adopts current standards and, with a couple of notable exceptions, makes liberal use of the four- and five-letter words that were formerly taboo. Above all, the narrative voice of the novel takes its tone from the 1960s, both from the liberalized—and often coarse—sexual attitudes of that period and from its ready cynicism about any cultural heritage.

Potatoes Are Cheaper is relentlessly "Jewish" on every page. Since, from the perspective of Selby Avenue in St. Paul, nearly all the known world seems to be Jewish, anti-Semitism is no more a social issue than ghetto poverty. Informed that one of her favorite radio performers is an anti-Semite, the prototypical Jewish mother replies: "So who's not?" This is a key to Shulman's own ambivalence in this book, which sets his basic affection for a Jewish cultural heritage against his awareness of its parochialism and other unattractive qualities and so makes him in that sense "anti-Semitic." If "myths" about Jews are to be funny, they must imply an "outside" perspective and audience: "It's not a myth, incidentally, this myth about how Jews love fruit. They will kill for fruit. But here is a curious fact you may not know: they have no interest at all in green vegetables." Informed through the school nurse that her son needs green vegetables, the Jewish mother sees to it that he gets one "every single day: a dill pickle." All the usual components of "Jewish" fiction are exaggerated here. Counting the hero's aunts, there are five Jewish mothers, every one a terror of the neighborhood "even though they were little teensy women, none of them much bigger than a ferret." The five Jewish fathers are predictably faceless and impotent and huddle in corners "trying to look invisible" whenever the "hollering" starts. Jewish mothers not only threaten on every occasion to die for your sins, but it is said

that "even if they go they leave a curse."

But Shulman's real subject in *Potatoes Are Cheaper* is neither the myths nor the facts of Jewish life but the vulgarity of the period. To explore this he returns for the first time since his early farces to a first-person narrator, Morris Katz, a suitably vulgar hero who is far removed from the world of Asa Hearthrug. Katz's only talent is for sexual seduction, and his only hope of "making it" is to marry someone with money. The story turns upon the question of whether to aim for a millionaire's daughter or to follow the advice of an older con man who says ". . . guys like you and me only got one way to win: steal small." From this comes Shulman's caustically comic survey of the culture—family life, religious practices, weddings, movies, college poetry, socialist poetry (by Itzik Fishel, "The Sweet Singer of the Sweat Shops"), and what Morris Katz would call "love." Although Shulman's survey does not explore these matters in depth, this is nevertheless his best book. In his memories of the Depression he found a way of life which was at once close to him and yet available to humor, including the cruelty of humor. *Potatoes Are Cheaper*, for all its lightheartedness, reminds us that we laugh from a sense of superiority. The evidence of Shulman's career is that he did not come easily to this view, but in *Potatoes Are Cheaper* it is a firm perspective and it gives a new edge to his humor. However his work may ultimately be measured, this most recent of his novels must mark a substantial development in his craft.

Frank Faylen as Mr. Gillis, Dwayne Hickman as Dobie Gillis, and Bob Denver as Maynard G. Krebs in The Many Loves of Dobie Gillis, *the television show based on Shulman's characters*

Plays:

Barefoot Boy With Cheek, adapted from Shulman's novel by Shulman and George Abbott, New York, Martin Beck Theatre, 3 April 1947;

The Tender Trap, by Shulman and Robert Paul Smith, New York, Longacre Theatre, 13 October 1954;

How Now, Dow Jones, New York, Lunt-Fontanne Theatre, 7 December 1967.

Screenplays:

Confidentially Connie, by Shulman and Herman Wouk, MGM, 1953;

The Affairs of Dobie Gillis, MGM, 1953;

Half a Hero, MGM, 1953;

House Calls, by Shulman, Alan Mandel, Charles Shyer, and Julius J. Epstein, Universal, 1978.

Television Scripts:

The Many Loves of Dobie Gillis, created by Shulman, CBS, 1959-1963;

House Calls, created by Shulman and Epstein, CBS, 1979-

Other:

Max Shulman's Guided Tour of Campus Humor, edited by Shulman (New York: Hanover House, 1955).

Periodical Publications:

"Ten Tips for Writers," *Writer*, 74 (August 1961): 10-11;

"American Humor: Its Cause and Cure," *Yale Review*, 51 (October 1961): 119-124.

Charles Henry Smith
(Bill Arp)
(15 June 1826-24 August 1903)

William E. Lenz
Chatham College

SELECTED BOOKS: *Bill Arp, So Called* (New York: Metropolitan Record Office, 1866);

Bill Arp's Peace Papers (New York: Carleton, 1873);

Bill Arp's Scrap Book; Humor and Philosophy (Atlanta: J. P. Harrison, 1884);

The Farm and the Fireside: Sketches of Domestic Life in War and in Peace (Atlanta: Constitution Publishing, 1891);

A School History of Georgia: Georgia as a Colony and a State, 1733-1893 (Boston: Ginn, 1893);

Bill Arp: From the Uncivil War to Date, 1861-1903 (Atlanta: Byrd Printing, 1903).

Charles Henry Smith wrote more than 2,000 humorous letters under the pseudonym "Bill Arp" between 1861 and 1903, most of which were published in Southern newspapers such as the *Atlanta Constitution*. "Bill Arp" joined Charles Farrar Browne's "Artemus Ward," David Ross Locke's "Petroleum V. Nasby," and Henry Wheeler Shaw's "Josh Billings" as one of a new breed of humorists produced by the Civil War period, literary comedians whose timely epistles and lectures made capital of the comic misspellings, misquotations, caricatures, and twisted literary dialect of an illiterate persona. Carrying on the humorous tradition of a cracker-barrel philosopher writing a letter to the editor of a local newspaper—a tradition including Benjamin Franklin's "Silence Dogood" and James Russell Lowell's "Hosea Biglow"—Smith's Bill Arp expressed what he himself called "the silent echoes of our people's thoughts" during the turbulent era of the Civil War, Reconstruction, and into the twentieth century. Bill Arp's inspiration and audience were not Northerners or Union sympathizers, as were those of Artemus Ward, for example, but stalwart Confederates, "Rebels, *so called*." His importance resides in his immediate record of the times that "try men's soles," in the intelligence with which he gave voice to the sentiments of the average Southerner, and in his insistence on the humanity and vigor of Southern men and women. Smith's knowledge of his people's thoughts came from his occupations as a storekeeper, lawyer, soldier, supply commissioner, judge, and political figure; and when the letters of Bill Arp began appearing, Arp was heralded as a Southern Artemus Ward, a spokesman for the Confederacy around whom the entire region could rally.

Charles Henry Smith was born in Lawrenceville, Georgia, in 1826, to Asahel Reid Smith, a native of Vermont who became a storekeeper and schoolteacher in Liberty County, Georgia, around 1817, and Caroline Ann Maguire Smith, one of his students whose father had fled Ireland for the new world. Charles Henry Smith was raised in a financially secure middle-class home of ten children, attended the Gwinnett County Manual Labor Institute (which his father had helped found), and in 1844 entered Franklin College (later to become the University of Georgia), which he had to leave a few months shy of graduation because his father's declining health required him to manage the family store. In 1849 he married Mary Octavia Hutchins, daughter of the wealthy Judge Nathan L. Hutchins of Lawrenceville, a man reported to own more than 100 slaves. Following a brief period of study, Smith was admitted to the Georgia bar and began to ride the local court circuit under the wing of his father-in-law. Smith's apprenticeship was typical of many Southern lawyers and humorists; Augustus B. Longstreet, author of *Georgia Scenes* (1835), Johnson J. Hooper, author of *Simon Suggs' Adventures* (1845), and James G. Baldwin, author of *Flush Times of Alabama and Mississippi* (1853), all learned both law and storytelling on the legal circuit, and managed to juggle several professions throughout their lives. In 1850 the first of Smith's thirteen children was born, and the next year the Smith family moved to Rome, Georgia, where Charles Henry Smith formed a new law partnership with John W. H. Underwood. As Bill Arp wrote later, these years of experience taught him human nature as well as law, ingraining in him an intelligent skepticism that informed his letters: "We are engaged in manufakturin [the law] by holesale, and atter while it will be retaled out by the lawyers to any body that wants it. It's an esy bisiness to make law, but the greatest diffikulty is in onderstandin it atter it is made. Among the lawyers this difficulty don't seam to lie so much in the hed as in the poket. For five dollars a lawyer can luminise sum, and more akkordin to pay." Like his predecessors Longstreet, Hooper, and Baldwin, Smith was a respected member of his community, becoming clerk of the city council in 1852 and city alderman in 1861. At the beginning of the Civil War in that year, Smith enlisted as a Confederate private in the Rome Light Guards, then became a member of the Cherokee Artillery, Phillips' Brigade, and joined the Eighth

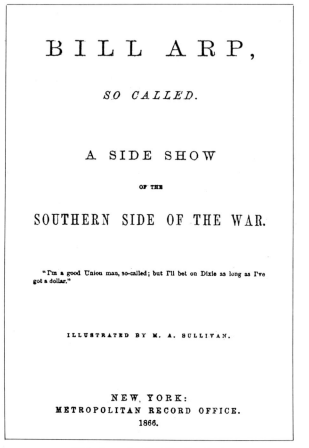

BILL ARP,

SO CALLED.

A SIDE SHOW

OF THE

SOUTHERN SIDE OF THE WAR.

"I'm a good Union man, so-called; but I'll bet on Dixie as long as I've got a dollar."

ILLUSTRATED BY M. A. SULLIVAN.

NEW YORK:
METROPOLITAN RECORD OFFICE.
1866.

Title page for Smith's first book

Georgia Regiment in July 1861, where he was ranked as a major and served as a supply commissioner on the staffs of Generals Francis S. Bartow and George Thomas Anderson. In April 1861, Smith sent the first letter signed "Bill Arp" to a local newspaper, the *Southern Confederacy*. In 1862 Smith was reelected city alderman; in 1863 he was made first lieutenant in the Forrest Light Artillery Company; in 1864 he again became city alderman and was appointed a Confederate judge advocate in Macon; and in 1865 he resumed residence in Rome where he set up as a storekeeper and was promptly elected to the new Georgia senate. *Bill Arp, So Called*, the first collection of Smith's letters, was published in 1866 by the Metropolitan Record Office of New York. It was an immediate success, as was *Bill Arp's Peace Papers* in 1873; each new volume contained reprints of early letters with some newer material. But between 1867 and 1878 Smith spent less time on literature than in serving the cause of regional politics as a lawyer, the mayor of Rome (1867), and city alderman (four terms). In 1878, the emphasis of his career shifted, as he gave the first of several hundred public lectures and began contributing a weekly letter to the *Atlanta Constitution*, which he continued until 1903. *Bill Arp's Scrap Book; Humor and Philosophy* appeared in 1884, *The Farm and the Fireside: Sketches of Domestic Life in War and in Peace* in 1891, *A School History of Georgia: Georgia as a Colony and a State, 1733-1893* in 1893, and *Bill Arp: From the Uncivil War to Date, 1861-1903*—the most complete edition of his letters—was published in 1903. He died on 24 August 1903 at Cartersville, Georgia.

The first and perhaps most famous letter to be written by "Bill Arp" was addressed to "Mr. Linkhorn—Sur," dated "Rome, Ga., Aprile 1861," and sent to a Georgia newspaper in response to President Lincoln's order for Southern military and militia units to disband. This first "spontanyous combustion" set the tone for all Smith's wartime letters. "We received your proklamation, and as you have put us on very short notis, a few of us boys have conkluded to write you, and ax for a little more time. . . . I tried my darndest yisterday to disperse and retire, but it was no go. . . . If you can possibly xtend that order to thirty days, do so. We have sent

you a CHECK at Harper's Ferry [scene of an early Confederate victory over Union troops] but if you positively won't xtend, we'll send you a chek drawn by Jeff Davis [president of the Confederacy], Borygard endorser [that is, a threat backed by the military forces of General P. Q. T. Beauregard], payable on sight anywhere." Bill Arp's satiric humor struck a responsive chord in 1861, and Southern newspapers reprinted the letter, catapulting its author into instant celebrity. With each new letter Bill Arp's fame, popularity, and confidence increased, so that he soon became what James C. Austin called "a Southern institution, a kind of national jester for the Confederacy."

Although the tortured misspellings and low cracker dialect may strike the modern reader as forced and artificial, in 1861 they were part of a comic tradition practiced in the period 1830 to 1860 by Southwestern humorists Augustus B. Longstreet, William T. Thompson, Johnson J. Hooper, T. B. Thorpe, James G. Baldwin, and George W. Harris. Misspellings and mispronunciations were funny to a mass audience which had recently become literate on a large scale, and they allowed readers to feel superior to the uneducated and unsophisticated comic persona. Browne's Artemus Ward, to whom Bill Arp even addressed one of his letters in an explicit admission of his progenitor, achieved success by mispronouncing, misusing, and mistaking words, confusing their meanings and implications and typically deflating his own pretensions to knowledge, his own mouthing of cliches, and his own hypocrisies. The illiterate persona as used by Browne and Smith also allowed the literary comedian to assume the role of the humble cracker-barrel philosopher, the common man who though powerless to effect change has clear insights into the simple truth of complex issues. In the guise of Bill Arp, Smith expressed the joy and the pain, the anger, fear, and frustration of the average Southerner toward the North, ridiculing its efforts to dictate its laws to the Confederacy, its military disasters at Harper's Ferry and Bull Run, and its generally inefficient—not to say ignorant or corrupt—administration. In his second letter to "Mr. Abe Linkhorn, Senterville, Ginnerwerry 12, 1862," reprinted in *Bill Arp's Peace Papers*, he notes that "we hav not been able to disperse as yet. Me and the boys started last May to see you pussonally, and ax fer an xtension of your brief furlo, but we got on a bust in old Virginny, about the 21st of Jewly, and like to hav got run over by a passel of fellers runnin from Bull Run to your city." Bill Arp buoyed the spirits of the Confederates during a long and

Charles Henry Smith

bloody war, reminded them of their triumphs and made them laugh during their defeats, gave voice to Smith's middle-class Southerners, and served as a rallying point for common men and women throughout his long career.

Unlike George Washington Harris's Sut Lovingood, whose Tennessee dialect letters attacked Lincoln and the Yankees in vicious and almost rabid fashion, Smith's Bill Arp maintains for the majority of his letters a tone of skeptical but reasonable inquiry, satirizing such topics as draft dodgers, high taxes, and corrupt officials. In *Bill Arp, So Called* he satirizes all three beginning with draft dodgers: "Such is the rapid progress of human events in these fighting times, that a man who was only forty last year, can be forty-six this. . . . Before this developing war, it was not thought possible for so much rheumatics and chronics, so many sore legs and weak backs, to exist. . . . We will have a race of people after a while that ain't worth a curse. The good ones are getting killed up, but these *skulkers* and *shirkers* and *dodgers* don't die. There ain't one died since the war broke out." Bill Arp on taxes: "There's the city tax, and the county tax, and State tax, and Confederate tax, and general tax, and special tax, and church tax, and charity tax, and tax in kind, and tax unkind, and shoe tax, and salt tax, and speculator's tax in general; and they scourge a man hard and they scourge him frequent, and poor human nature caves in." And on corruption: "Pollytix is a fateegin subject. . . . Before the war it had its ups and downs, and ockasionally, was varygated and pekulyer. Now-a-days it's settled down into two principuls which is to plunder the goverment and umble the South. We've sorter got used to the first, for it's dun with a knife that cuts both ways, but the other makes a new sore evry time, and nocks the skab off the old one before it gits well." Despite the wit and intelligence revealed by his observations, Bill Arp never admitted the equality of blacks, and his belief in their natural inferiority should be remembered; as late as 1893 Smith published in the magazine *Forum* an essay entitled "Have American Negroes Too Much Liberty?" Writing without benefit of his nom de plume, Smith argued that blacks could never achieve equality with whites, and that in time they would disappear from America in accordance with Darwinian laws.

When analyzing the reasons for the Civil War, however, Bill Arp did not ultimately place blame on politics, economics, or abolition; in *Bill Arp's Peace Papers* he writes that the war "wur kaused xklusively by Gen. States Rights goin to sleep one day, and old Kolonel Federlist cum along and tride to kut his

ham-string." Arp's repeated references to issues of fundamental Southern importance—like states' rights, which had been a point of contention for thirty years in states such as Georgia and North Carolina—locate him at the center of Confederate experience, enabling his letters to be read as a record of the Southern mind and heart. In his third

Bill Arp, by M. A. Sullivan

letter to President Lincoln, dated 2 December 1862, Arp sends his greetings to "Madam Harriet Beechers toe," revealing in his wordplay the Rebels' confidence that complete victory is almost within reach: "But alas for human folly—alas for all subloonery things—our peepul will not believe, these crazy Rebels will not konsider! . . . The *Lee* side of any shore are onhelthy to your populashun! Keep away from them Virginy waters kourses. Go round em or under em, but for the sake of ekonomy don't try to kross em. It is too hard on your burryal squads and ambylance hosses." Bill Arp's bluster gave continual boosts to Confederate morale both on the battlefield and on the home front; he could refer to a Southern victory as a successful bluff in a game of poker, while he could with accurate humor describe himself fleeing the city of Rome before the terrible advance of General Sherman as a "Roman runagee." In the preface to *Bill Arp, So Called* Smith writes that "These letters may be worthy of preservation as illustrative of a part of the war. . . . At the time they appeared in the press of the South, these sentiments were the silent echoes of our people's thoughts, and this accounts in the main for the popularity with which they were received. Of course they contain exaggerations, and prophecies which were never fulfilled; but both sections were playing 'brag' as well as 'battle.'. . . ." The Confederacy, despite this bravado, collapsed before the Union forces, and Bill Arp found himself recording the destruction of his beloved South: "Could you stand upon the hills of this desolate city and see its wasted and withered beauties . . . I know you would feel that there was no fitness in a union with that people. The wanton destruction . . . has murdered our Christian charity and stabbed our forgiveness to the quick."

After the end of the fighting, Bill Arp turned his attention to the inequalities and injustices of Reconstruction: "it aint the war that our peepul is mad about no how. Its this confounded, everlastin, abominabal peace—this tail to the comet—this rubbin the skab off before the sore gets well." In 1865 he appealed to Artemus Ward and "our four fathers" for merciful justice for the Confederacy, affirming ironically that "I'm tryin to harmonize": "*I'm* a good Union man, *so-called. I* ain't agwine to fight no more. *I* shan't vote for the next war. *I* ain't no gurilla. I've done tuk the oath, and I'm gwine to keep it, but as for my being subjugated, and humilyated, and amalgamated, and enervated . . . it ain't so—nary time. I ain't ashamed of nuthin neither—ain't repentin—ain't axin for no one-horse, short-winded pardon. Nobody needn't be playin priest around me. I ain't got no twenty thousand dollars. Wish I had; I'd give it to these poor widders and orfins." Although he admitted in a fine parody of a popular elementary school primer that perhaps "In Dixie's fall, / We sinned all," Reconstruction politics angered him, appearing to be nothing more than a convenient device for milking the South of its last drops of pride. Yankee greed, corrupt officials, harsh military rule, the inefficient Freedman's Bureau, and self-righteous Northern senators provoked his pen again and again. Yet as his letters were collected in books—five

in all— Smith desired his own tone and style to undergo reconstruction and correction; although originally "spontanyous combustions," the inflammatory tone of his early letters became extinguished as he revised for posterity. The more reconciled Bill Arp divided people into two types without regard for regionalism; there are "those who have seen better days, and those who haven't." The antebellum plantation system he now judged an "economy of waste," and he seemed resigned that the days of the Old South were over. In its place he saw the rise of a new system based not upon blood or race but upon ambition, hard work, and luck; this new union of spirit, muscle, and energy he admitted was "the best all-around team the South has ever had." As Bill Arp was transformed into a Georgia institution, writing his weekly column for the *Atlanta Constitution* beginning in 1878, his satire softened into sentiment. The last collection of his letters, *Bill Arp: From the Uncivil War to Date*, begins with an autobiographical reminiscence entitled "A Pretty Story." The cynicism and skepticism of the earlier pieces is almost entirely absent from these later writings; in their place is a nostalgic sentiment clearly indicated by a random glance at this volume's contents: "The Voice of Spring," "The Ups and Downs of Farming," "The Family Preparing to Receive City Cousins," "Old Things are Passing Away, And All things Have Become New," "The Old School Days," "A Mother is a Mother Still, the Holiest Thing Alive," and "Children a Heritage from the Lord." Although Smith once again includes "The Roman runagee" in this 1903 collection, he corrects Bill Arp's spelling and grammar. The shift in orthographics reflects a shift in the taste of Smith's more national audience, one that has become more sophisticated and securely literate, and a shift in Smith's own interests and intentions; what concerns him after 1878 are the pleasures and comforts of hearth and home, as is evident in his 1891 publication of *The Farm and the Fireside* and his 1893 *A School History of Georgia*. The unity of family, state, and nation is now more important than keeping fresh memories of regionalism and secession. A comfortable nostalgia has replaced Bill Arp's insistent skepticism; "Arp's Reminiscences of Fifty Years" ends with the mature reflection that "the clock will not be set back, and so we must all be content with things as they are and make them better if we can." The Civil War itself recedes before this impulse: "The civil war was a play, a thrilling tragedy, in which great armies were the players and the world the witnesses." When it forces itself to consciousness, the war is not romanticized by flag-waving and patriotic cliches, but is seen in all its grim reality: "neither victories nor defeats are to be compared to the horrors of battle, the things that are behind the scenes and are never published. During the seven days' fight across the Chickahominy, hundreds of the dead were hastily buried head to foot a foot or so under the surface, and the earth heaped over them; for you must know, my friends, that on a battlefield there are neither shrouds nor graves, nor coffins nor mourners." The graphic detail of this description (which continues for several paragraphs) is clearly nonpartisan. It is as if Bill Arp has stepped aside and Charles Henry Smith has taken his place; the comic persona has merged with its creator, and Bill Arp has become a conservative middle-class family man from northern Georgia.

Smith's Bill Arp compares favorably with Browne's Artemus Ward and other literary comedians of the postwar era. Smith's wit, intelligence, and insight made Bill Arp a more reasonable and tolerant spokesman for the Southern cause than George W. Harris's Sut Lovingood, while Smith's epistolary accounts of the Civil War are invaluable records of the average Confederate's point of view; his fine sense of humor and common sense almost always redeem the letters from charges of artificiality or bigotry. As he notes in *Bill Arp's Scrap Book*, "I joined the army and succeeded in killing about as many of them as they of me." Today he is remembered primarily for his early Bill Arp letters with their firsthand testimony of the ordinary Georgia man's—and woman's—understanding of events local and national. Unlike Joel Chandler Harris and Kittrell J. Warren, who wrote fiction with a Southern slant, Smith wrote "spontanyous combustions," "illustrative of a part of the war—as a side-show to the Southern side of it—an index to our feelings and sentiments. . . ." The *Savannah Press* once said of him, "In the dark days he kept southern hearts from breaking," and after his death in 1903 many newspapers on both sides of the Mason-Dixon line paid tribute to "the best loved man in all the Southland." Smith's Bill Arp left a unique record of the common Southerner's impressions of the Civil War, Reconstruction, and the Gilded Age; he might have been summing up his own contribution when he wrote in his last essay, "It is well for the children to know these things for they are worth knowing."

Periodical Publication:
"Have American Negroes Too Much Liberty?," *Forum*, 16 (October 1893): 176-183.

References:
James C. Austin, *Bill Arp* (New York: Twayne, 1969);
Jesse Bier, *The Rise and Fall of American Humor* (New York, Chicago & San Francisco: Holt, Rinehart & Winston, 1968), pp. 78ff.;
Walter Blair and Hamlin Hill, *America's Humor From Poor Richard to Doonesbury* (New York: Oxford University Press, 1978), pp. 88ff.

H. Allen Smith
(19 December 1907-24 February 1976)

L. Moody Simms, Jr.
Illinois State University

BOOKS: *Robert Gair: A Study* (New York: Dial, 1939);
Mr. Klein's Kampf (New York: Stackpole Sons, 1940);
Low Man on a Totem Pole (Garden City: Doubleday, Doran, 1941);
Life in a Putty Knife Factory (Garden City: Doubleday, Doran, 1943);
Lost in the Horse Latitudes (Garden City: Doubleday, Doran, 1944);
Rhubarb (Garden City: Doubleday, 1946);
Lo, the Former Egyptian! (Garden City: Doubleday, 1947);
Larks in the Popcorn (Garden City: Doubleday, 1948);
We Went Thataway (Garden City: Doubleday, 1949);
Low and Inside: A Book of Baseball Anecdotes, Oddities and Curiosities, by Smith and Ira Lepouce Smith (Garden City: Doubleday, 1949);
People Named Smith (Garden City: Doubleday, 1950);
Three Men on Third: A Second Book of Baseball Anecdotes, Oddities and Curiosities, by Smith and Ira

Lepouce Smith (Garden City: Doubleday, 1951);

Mister Zip (Garden City: Doubleday, 1952);

Smith's London Journal; Now First Published From the Original Manuscript (Garden City: Doubleday, 1952);

The Compleat Practical Joker (Garden City: Doubleday, 1953);

The Rebel Yell (Garden City: Doubleday, 1954);

The Age of the Tail (Boston: Little, Brown, 1955);

Write Me A Poem, Baby (Boston: Little, Brown, 1956);

The Pig in the Barber Shop (Boston: Little, Brown, 1958);

Don't Get Perconel With a Chicken (Boston: Little, Brown, 1959);

Let the Crabgrass Grow: H. Allen Smith's Suburban Almanac (New York: Geis, 1960);

Waikiki Beachnik (Boston: Little, Brown, 1960);

How to Write Without Knowing Nothing (Boston: Little, Brown, 1961);

To Hell in a Handbasket (Garden City: Doubleday, 1962);

A Short History of Fingers and Other State Papers (Boston: Little, Brown, 1963);

Two-thirds of a Coconut Tree (Boston: Little, Brown, 1963);

Son of Rhubarb (New York: Trident, 1967);

Buskin' With H. Allen Smith (New York: Trident, 1968);

The Great Chili Confrontation (New York: Trident, 1969);

The View From Chivo (New York: Trident, 1971);

Low Man Rides Again (Garden City: Doubleday, 1973);

Return of the Virginian (Garden City: Doubleday, 1974);

The Life and Death of Gene Fowler (New York: Morrow, 1977).

Called "the screwball's Boswell" by Fred Allen, H. Allen Smith achieved overnight success as a humorist with the publication of *Low Man on a Totem Pole* in 1941. Turning out sequels at the rate of nearly one a year, he was rarely off the best-seller lists during the 1940s. Between 1941 and 1946, his works reportedly sold 1.4 million copies. Though his output, sales, and reputation declined during his later years, his numerous books, essays, and articles were more than enough to establish him in the front rank of the American humorists of his day. Smith also built a reputation as a real-life character, who purportedly took the first legal drink after Prohibition, "kidnapped" Albert Einstein from a banquet in his honor, and once greeted the austere J. P.

Morgan with a jaunty "Hiya, toots!"

One of nine children, Harry Allen Smith was born on 19 December 1907, in McLeansboro, Illinois, to Catholic parents, Harry Arthur and Addie Allen Smith. He later jokingly referred to his southern Illinois birthplace as "the sorriest piece of real estate in the U. S., nurturing a miserable tribe of human beings whose equal for depravity and ignorance has not been seen in the whole history of the world." The Smith family moved to Decatur, Illinois, then to Defiance, Ohio, before settling in Huntington, Indiana, in 1919. Smith attended St. Mary's parochial school in Huntington and, as an altar boy, regularly helped serve Mass. Once asked if he believed in baptism, he is said to have replied: "God yes, I've seen it done." He later related that he and fellow altar boys prayed for prominent members of the parish to die because of the "cash gratuities attendant on funerals."

Smith abandoned his formal education after the eighth grade and went to work in a barbershop as a shoe-shine boy and general handy man. In 1922, a sister's suitor helped him get a job as proofreader on the *Huntington Press* at three dollars a week. Devoting his spare time to reading, he soon became a reporter. The itch to write led him to compose an imaginative piece entitled "Stranded on a Davenport" (1924), which was circulated through the community by some girls in a typewriting class of the local high school. It discussed in detail how a young man had his way with a young woman on the piece of furniture mentioned in the title. The local justice of the peace judged it to be "lewd, licentious, obscene and lascivious." Fined $22.50 and ostracized by his neighbors, Smith fled Huntington at the age of seventeen.

For the next few years, Smith was a wandering reporter, a career that trained a number of American humorists. After a brief stint as a reporter in Jeffersonville, Indiana, where he passed himself off as ten years older than he was, he then worked on the *Evening Post* and the *Times* in Louisville, Kentucky. At the age of nineteen, Smith became editor of a lively daily, the *Sebring* (Florida) *American*. When the *American* folded in 1926, he caulked boats and then tried promoting small-town directories in Texas, a project which was a dismal failure. Pawning his portable typewriter, he reached Tulsa, Oklahoma, early in 1927, where he worked on the *Tribune* for a short time. On 14 April 1927 Smith married Nelle Mae Simpson, a graduate of the University of Missouri School of Journalism who had been the society editor of the *Sebring American*.

Smith went to Denver in the summer of 1927.

Taking a job on the *Denver Post*, he joined a staff of well-educated, well-read young men. At their suggestion, Smith read the works of Dickens, Anatole France, and H. L. Mencken, authors who became lifelong influences. While he was at the *Post*, Smith's family grew. In 1928, a son, Allen Wyatt, was born. The following year, after the birth of daughter Nancy Jean, Smith quit the *Post*, sent his family to his wife's home in Missouri (they would join him later), and went to New York.

He arrived in New York City on Labor Day 1929 with ten dollars and no position. Two days later, he took a job as a feature writer for United Press, where he worked until 1934. After brief jobs with several radio and film companies, he joined the *New York World-Telegram* in 1936 as a rewrite man. He soon became established on the *World-Telegram* as a feature interviewer, one of the best in the country. He also penned humorous articles for the newspaper on "major and minor celebrities, human oddities, and ordinary mortals." A natural enemy of pomposity and pretense, Smith took special delight in skewering stuffed shirts and those whose reputations he believed to be greater than their achievements.

Smith's first book, *Robert Gair*, appeared in 1939. Its subject was a Brooklyn manufacturer of paper bags who pioneered in the development of the pasteboard carton. Favorably reviewed, the book is a collection of anecdotes illustrating Gair's masterful will, Scotch thrift, and vigorous self-assertion. Smith's next book, a novel entitled *Mr. Klein's Kampf* (1940), received little notice. Written in thirteen days, it is the story of one Orson Klein, an actor who could make himself up to look like Hitler.

Smith burst upon the literary scene as a humorist of best-selling proportions with *Low Man on a Totem Pole*, a collection of interviews, autobiographical articles, and trivia, with an introduction by Fred Allen. After recounting his early life, Smith introduced the reader to people he had interviewed as a newspaperman, ranging from chorus girls ("barefoot up to their chins"), stripteasers, and the man who perpetually bounced eggs on a bar, to the storekeeper who habitually rang "No Sale" on his cash register and spit in the penny compartment and the newspaperman who suffered the delusion that Herbert Hoover had bladders on his feet. Well received by the critics, the book is light, lively, and funny. Its contents—like those of many of the works which followed—reveal that Smith had not forgotten the origins of his success. Years later, he observed: "I am generally classified as a humorist, but I don't particularly care for that designation. I pre-

Smith as low man on a totem pole

fer to think of myself as a reporter, a reporter with a humorous slant. I am funny in the sense that the world is funny."

The success of *Low Man on a Totem Pole* brought Smith an offer from the United Feature Syndicate to write a daily column called "The Totem Pole." He accepted and left the *World-Telegram* in 1941. In February of 1942, he agreed to act as a master of ceremonies on a weekly radio network program called "Swop Nite." After ten weeks, he quit the show in an argument over money.

Though his syndicated column was successful, Smith canceled his contract in April 1942, believing that the war would cause newspapers to tighten up and discard newer features. With numerous magazine assignments and a contract to write another book, he left newspaper work and for the rest of his life devoted himself full-time to professional writing.

Published in 1943, *Life in a Putty Knife Factory* is a collection of interviews and pen portraits. A number of them deal with Hollywood and the world of radio, two subjects Smith knew well, the former through his celebrity interviews and other show-business contacts, the latter through his work as a radio show host. Reacting to some of this experience negatively—he disliked pomposity wherever he found it—he uses his putty knife as a scalpel, taking special pleasure in heckling the "high-class morons of Hollywood." Though the *Time* reviewer found *Life in a Putty Knife Factory* filled with the "sort of talk that might be had . . . from any boozy, bawdy, abundant newspaper man," others found it every bit as amusing as *Low Man on a Totem Pole*.

Smith's commentary on Hollywood earned him an invitation to visit the film capital of the world. His next work, *Lost in the Horse Latitudes* (1944), is a book of humorous essays dealing, for the most part, with the author's experiences in Hollywood. He described these experiences in "the land of the false eyelash and the flying custard pie" with impish frankness and the calculated touch of irreverence which had become his hallmark. For example, a movie studio reminded him of a newspaper office "on a large scale, crowded with eccentric, capricious, temperamental screwballs." Geniuses were everywhere and came in three sizes: "those who are geniuses and know they are geniuses and speak about it frequently; those who are actually not geniuses but somebody told them they were so they do everything but wear badges proclaiming it; and genuine geniuses who keep their mouths shut about their affliction and do their work." From today's vantage point, *Lost in the Horse Latitudes* can

be seen as one of the most discerning books yet published on the zaniness of Hollywood.

By the mid-1940s, Smith was widely known as a somewhat bawdy humorist with a fast-paced style. He was making a very comfortable living solely from his writing. Smith's early books, though they contain some of his best writing, have a reduced appeal today because so many of the people he discussed—Maxie Rosenbloom, Joe E. Brown, Constance Bennett—have faded from interest.

Toward the end of World War II, Smith moved his family into a large white house on a hill in Mount Kisco, New York, situated in Westchester County, about forty miles from Manhattan. Following the publication of *Rhubarb* (1946), a novel about a cat who inherits a million dollars and a baseball team, and *Lo, the Former Egyptian!* (1947), a collection of autobiographical musings occasioned by a visit to his southern Illinois birthplace, Smith presented some observations on his new life in Westchester County in *Larks in the Popcorn* (1948). An exile from New York City, he decided to raise three crops—watermelons, strawberries, and popcorn; instead, he found out quite a bit about poison ivy and wasps in his new home. The book is notable for some fine pages on the author playing at country squire and on Smith's country neighbors—a collection of salty, down-to-earth theater personalities, literary people, and Wall Street brokers. Having escaped commuting, at least temporarily, Smith enjoyed his special position until a neighbor commiserated with him because he had to stay home all the time with his wife.

During the late 1940s and early 1950s, Smith produced a volume a year, most of which sold moderately well and typically received respectful notices. Works of this period include *Low and Inside* (1949) and *Three Men on Third* (1951), both with Ira Lepouce Smith, and both collections of anecdotes and jokes about baseball; a compilation of information and stories about *People Named Smith* (1950); *Smith's London Journal* (1952); and *The Compleat Practical Joker* (1953), a survey of practical jokes in different centuries and countries.

At the same time, Smith focused a great deal of attention on the American West of fact and fancy. In *We Went Thataway*, published in 1949, he recounted a trip through parts of the West, purportedly to investigate the "Western Menace" for the members of the Mount Kisco Philosophical Society. The book takes the reader cross-country, surveying a land of motels and filling stations, of souvenirs and neon lights, of indigestion, roadside zoos, and dude ranches.

Recalling his journey across the Great Plains, Smith writes: "The prairie impresses us only because we have been conditioned to regard it with emotion; it has been romanticized down through the years, peopled with skulking redskins, with outlaw bands made up of men who wear black hats and black shirts and have black mustaches and black horses and black hearts, and, most important of all, with the Great American Hero—fresh out of the barber chair, his guns slung low, his white hat bigger than any road agent's black hat, his horse whiter than his hat and endowed with a genius for untying knots, and his heart nine tenths of one per cent purer than Ivory Soap. It does no good to say that no such person ever raced across these prairies. It does no good to say that the heroes of this immense flatland looked more like Gabby Hayes than Roy Rogers—with matted whiskers and few if any teeth and with a body odor that would send coyotes screeching in the direction of Saskatchewan."

Smith's *Mister Zip* appeared in 1952. It deals with the cowboy hero and the delusion of an ideal West. Also a satire on Western movies, its hero is Mr. Zip, a hard-riding idol of Hollywood, who was born plain Clifford Humphrey in a small Midwestern town. Zip LeBaron has definite ideas about the cowboy's attire: "when he became a cowboy actor he insisted on a hat with a limp brim. . . . The production people agreed that it looked good, looked even thrilling when the wind was beating the brim back against the crown; but all too often the wind flapped it downward, covering Zip's eyes as he rode in pursuit of the outlaws. It was ridiculous . . . for a cowboy hero to come riding hell-for-leather across the plains with the brim of his black hat plastered down against his face, covering not only his eyes but his nose." With its many sharp insights into our national character, the novel is a revealing document as well as a humorous one. Elton Miles, in his introduction to *The Best of H. Allen Smith* (1972), has called *Mister Zip* and Smith's *The Age of the Tail* (1955) "American masterpieces of satire."

Two of Smith's best works appeared in the mid-1950s. Published in 1954 to generally favorable reviews, Smith's *The Rebel Yell* was viewed by its author as "a carpetbagger's attempt to establish the

DRAWINGS BY LEO HERSHFIELD

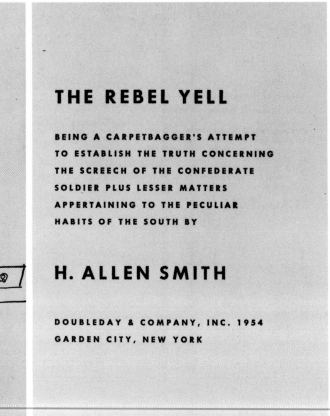

THE REBEL YELL

BEING A CARPETBAGGER'S ATTEMPT
TO ESTABLISH THE TRUTH CONCERNING
THE SCREECH OF THE CONFEDERATE
SOLDIER PLUS LESSER MATTERS
APPERTAINING TO THE PECULIAR
HABITS OF THE SOUTH BY

H. ALLEN SMITH

DOUBLEDAY & COMPANY, INC. 1954
GARDEN CITY, NEW YORK

Frontispiece and title page for Smith's account of the South as seen by a "carpetbagger"

H. Allen Smith

truth concerning the screech of the Confederate soldier plus lesser matters pertaining to the peculiar habits of the South." In reality the book is a satire on chauvinistic fondness for the past. In a hilarious section on racial and sectional prejudice, "Revolt of a Damyankee," Smith calls for a friendlier feeling between the North and South. However, such a relationship would not develop if Southerners "continue their intolerant sniping at us. . . . Just because they are so powerful in Washington, just because they have all that cotton and all that tobacco and all that pellagra and all that grits and all that rubbery talk—that doesn't give them the right to look down their patrician noses" at Northerners.

In Smith's *The Age of the Tail*, published in 1955, all babies born after 22 September 1957 have tails. The book is ostensibly a social historian's report, written in 1997-1998, about this development

and how it affects the human race. It is in fact an ironic commentary on greed, vanity, the lust for power, and what Smith saw as the delusion of human dignity. At book's end, Smith's social historian can only "hope that mankind will not discover methods for using his tail as a weapon, as the monitor lizard and the sting ray use it."

During the late 1950s and early 1960s, Smith continued to publish prolifically. *Write Me a Poem, Baby* (1956) and *Don't Get Perconel with a Chicken* (1959) are collections of children's prose and verse with commentary by Smith. *Let the Crabgrass Grow* (1960) is an evocation of life in the wealthy suburbs of New York. A visit to the Hawaiian Islands resulted in *Waikiki Beachnik* in 1960. Smith's *How to Write Without Knowing Nothing* (1961) deals with the use and misuse of language, while *A Short History of Fingers and Other State Papers* (1963) is a collection of miscellaneous pieces. *Two-thirds of a Coconut Tree* (1963) is an impressionistic journal Smith kept during a short stay in Tahiti.

Two of Smith's books from this period stand out among the others. Published in 1958, *The Pig in the Barber Shop* is a perfectly balanced travel book based on a three-month tour of Mexico. Though Smith's zany brand of humor is uppermost, exemplified in his account of an annual Cussing Fiesta at Alvarado, there is an undercurrent of seriousness and evidence of a genuine fondness for Mexico and its people.

To Hell in a Handbasket (1962) is the irreverent autobiography of a newspaperman. Smith depicts his youth in Illinois, Ohio, and Indiana, his struggles as an itinerant newspaperman and as an editor, and his years in New York as a feature writer and interviewer. Throughout the book, Smith exhibits his knack for vitriolic comment and his strange, almost avuncular pride in the ridiculous things his fellow human beings insist on doing. Yet he also notes that it is "increasingly painful to laugh at the human race and the incredible situation it has got itself into in the Glorious Year of Advanced Civilization, 1962."

By 1967, Smith had been looking for several years for a place to live far away from Mount Kisco. As a result of New York's urban sprawl, Mount Kisco's streets were constantly crowded and its stores filled with people he did not know. To his mind, Arizona, California, and Florida, where he spent a good deal of time looking, were spoiled. Settling on Texas, he eventually made his home in Alpine, a small town he had visited in 1947 while collecting material for *We Went Thataway*.

The books Smith wrote during the final decade of his life were not as widely reviewed as his earlier ones. The time of his great popularity had passed years before. Tastes in humor had changed, and many of those readers who had placed him consistently on the best-seller lists of the 1940s remembered him vaguely or not at all.

Two novels about cats date from this last period—*Son of Rhubarb* (1967) and *The View From Chivo* (1971). Appearing in 1968, *Buskin' with H. Allen Smith* is a compilation of favorite jokes. *The Great Chili Confrontation* (1969) recounts Smith's experiences at a weekend chili cook-off held in a Texas ghost town called Terlingua. Published in 1973, *Low Man Rides Again* is a collection of magazine and newspaper articles, while *Return of the Virginian*

(1974) is a free-form burlesque on the manners and morals of Caliche, Texas. Smith's last book, *The Life and Legend of Gene Fowler*, an anecdotal, high-spirited biography, appeared posthumously in 1977.

Smith died in San Francisco on 24 February 1976. His last book was published nearly forty years after his first. In his *The World, the Flesh, and H. Allen Smith* (1954), Bergen Evans places Smith squarely in a long tradition of American humorists, ranging from Davy Crockett through Mark Twain, Finley Peter Dunne, and George Ade. Writing in 1976, Gregory Curtis maintained that Smith's "preferences—for the bawdy, for cussing, for dialect, for yarns—place Smith personally and as an author in a literary tradition known as the Humor of the Old Southwest."

Smith once defined a humorist as "a fellow who realizes, first, that he is no better than anybody else, and second, that nobody else is either." He was contemptuous of anyone in authority and those who disagreed with him. As a folk humorist and a man of self-professed peasant tastes, he found Culture with a capital C to be fair game. Though he sometimes tried to conceal it, he sympathized with the defeated, the frustrated, and the hopeless. Consequently, his work had great appeal for a broad range of common readers. As an observer of the passing scene, Smith had few equals. The strength of his humor, which is detached, skeptical, hearty, boisterous, and ribald, lies in his observation of the misfortunes and follies of individuals.

Other:

Desert Island Decameron, edited by Smith (Garden City: Doubleday, Doran, 1945).

References:

Gregory Curtis, "The Dream House of H. Allen Smith," *Texas Monthly* (February 1976);

Bergen Evans, ed., *The World, the Flesh, and H. Allen Smith* (Garden City: Hanover House, 1954), pp. ix-xvi;

Elton Miles, ed., *The Best of H. Allen Smith* (New York: Trident, 1972), pp. 1-3;

Joe Nawrozki, "Humor Was Serious Stuff for Smith," *Baltimore News-American*, 29 February 1976;

Robert van Gelder, "An Interview with Mr. H. Allen Smith," *New York Times Book Review*, 24 August 1941, pp. 2, 22.

Seba Smith
(Major Jack Downing)
(14 September 1792-28 July 1868)

Edward E. Waldron
Yankton College

SELECTED BOOKS: *The Life and Writings of Major Jack Downing of Downingville, Away Down East in the State of Maine, Written by Himself* (Boston: Lilly, Wait, Colman & Holden, 1833);

Powhatan, A Metrical Romance in 7 Cantos (New York: Harper, 1841);

May-Day in New York (New York: Burgess, Stringer, 1845); also published as *Jack Downing's Letters by Major Jack Downing* (Philadelphia: Peterson, 1845);

Dew-drops of the Nineteenth Century (New York: J. K. Wellman, 1846);

New Elements of Geometry (London: Bentley, 1850);

Way Down East or Portraitures of Yankee Life (New York: Derby, 1854);

My Thirty Years Out of the Senate (New York: Oaksmith, 1859).

With the creation of Jack Downing (later, Captain, then Major Jack Downing), Seba Smith introduced a new character into the annals of American literature: a comic Yankee who was realistically portrayed. Although this character type had appeared on the stage in various forms for years before Smith brought Jack into the world, Smith created in Jack Downing a different breed of Yankee, one whose dialect was relatively unexaggerated and whose humor depended not so much on his long-winded anecdotes as on his naive view of American politics and politicians. As Jeanette Tandy observed in *Crackerbox Philosophers in American Humor and Satire* (1925), "The first attempt at presentation of the unlettered philosopher and critic in American literature . . . resulted in a notably realistic and unaffected characterization." Seba Smith's Jack Downing, drawings of whom eventually led to the standard caricature of Uncle Sam, set the stage for a host of comic figures to follow, including Sam Slick, Hosea Biglow, and Mr. Dooley.

Seba Smith was born in a log cabin in Buckfield, Maine, the son of Seba and Aphia Stevens Smith. In 1799 his father moved the family to Bridgton, about thirty-five miles north of Portland; the elder Smith served for a time as post-rider from Portland to Waterford. Young Seba worked at odd jobs through his youth. Although he had relatively little formal schooling in those years, he learned enough to be able to teach school at Bridgton when he was eighteen. In 1815, at the age of twenty-three, he entered Bowdoin College (then only fourteen years old itself) as a sophomore; he graduated with honors in 1818.

After teaching for a year in Portland, Smith journeyed to the Carolinas and, later, across the Atlantic to Liverpool, probably working his passage as he went. When he returned to Maine, he became the assistant editor of the *Eastern Argus*, a Democratic newspaper in Portland, and thus started his journalistic career. In 1823, after he had been made editor of the *Argus*, he married Elizabeth Oakes Smith of Portland, a young woman who was to have her own measure of fame as a writer and lecturer on the lyceum circuit.

In the fall of 1829, Seba Smith began the *Portland Courier*, his own newspaper, with no political ties; it was the first daily paper to be issued in Maine. The *Courier* was the vehicle Smith used to launch his Downing letters, beginning in January 1830. The widely reprinted letters ran for several years in the *Courier* and, later, in other papers. They became so popular, in fact, that a host of imitators sprang up, using Jack's name but rarely capturing Smith's gentle satiric touch.

The origin of Jack Downing is touched on briefly by Smith in his preface to *My Thirty Years Out of the Senate* (1859). In January 1830 the Maine Legislature, meeting in Portland, was almost evenly split, so that nothing could be accomplished for all the intricate maneuverings to gain a balance of power for one of the parties. That month Smith, "wishing to show the ridiculous position of the legislature in its true light, and also, by something out of the common track of newspaper writing, to give increased interest and popularity to his own little daily paper," created a plan—and a character—to achieve his goal: "the plan [was] to bring a green, unsophisticated lad from the country into town with a load of axe-handles, hoop poles, and other notions, for sale, and while waiting the movements of a dull market, let him blunder into the halls of the legislature, and after witnessing for some days their strange doings, sit down and write an account of them to his friends at home in his own plain language. The plan was successful almost beyond parallel."

Selecting the name for his character was simply an arbitrary decision, according to Smith. He said the name was "original to the author, who had never heard or seen the name before." The nature of his character, while not so completely original as his name, still carries an air of originality. Jack Downing is, at first, the "green, unsophisticated lad" his creator invented. He can't understand, for example, why the legislature would debate whether a gentleman should have a seat when there are obviously many chairs available in the chamber. In later years, after he has been the confidant of presidents, Jack assumes a little more worldliness, but he never loses that "plain" touch which was the source of the charm in his original letters.

In an introductory essay included in both *The Life and Writings of Major Jack Downing of Downingville* (1833) and *My Thirty Years Out of the Senate*, Jack presents a "Sketch of My Early Life." In the sketch the reader is introduced to the characters who fill out the cast of the Downing literature: Grandfather Zebedee Downing, who never tires of telling the story of the "fatigue of Burgwine" and who is an inspiration to Jack when the latter is called upon by President Jackson to rescue the prisoners at Madawaska and to put down the Nullifiers in South Carolina; Uncle Joshua Downing, who is, as Jack tells Jackson, "the most thorough-going Republikan in Downingville" and Jack's constant advisor on political matters; Cousin Obediah Downing, who helped Jack read his way through school; and Jack's father, who dreamed he saw a curious plant grow out of his son's head and interpreted it, as did Jack, as a sign that "Downingville wouldn't be big enough to hold" Jack Downing. Other letter writers and receivers over the years include Jack's Cousin Ephraim, who receives the first letter from Jack, and Cousin Nabby, who keeps Jack informed of social matters in Downingville, including the preparations for a presidential visit that never happens.

The letters Smith printed in the *Portland Courier* drew national attention. Over the years, Major Jack Downing was praised as a brilliant creation and his writings were received with warm approval. In the publisher's preface to *My Thirty Years Out of the Senate*, Appleton Oaksmith, Seba Smith's eldest son and publisher of the volume, quotes the *New York Courier and Enquirer*, 3 July 1839: "There is no doubt that the author is the *best painter of Yankee peculiarities that ever wrote*. He is true to nature and never caricatures, but without caricaturing is most amusing." On 27 February 1844 the same paper said, in reference to the Downing letters: "Those letters were written in the true and genuine spirit of Yankeedom, and were clothed in the real vernacular of the land. Some of them deserve a higher and more lasting reputation than seems to have awaited them. . . . They ought to be considered standard exhibitions of New England peculiarities of style, feeling and sentiment at the time, and be cherished as authentic mementoes of the pilgrim opinions and pilgrim dialects of the generation in which they appeared." On 16 July 1845 the *Courier and Enquirer* further noted about Seba Smith: "He is, in point of fact, the only writer who has ever been entirely successful in the genuine dialect of Yankee land." Clearly, Smith was regarded by his contemporaries as an important contributor to the building of what became a truly national character.

One of the problems that accompanied Seba Smith's success with Jack Downing was the rush of imitators who assumed his character's name and epistolary mode and unashamedly published many "Jack Downing" letters of their own. Of all the Smith imitators, the best known is Charles A. Davis, a New York iron and steel merchant who published "Downing letters" in the *New York Daily Advertiser* beginning in 1833. In 1834 he published *Letters of J. Downing, Major, of Downingville Militia, Second Brigade, to his old friend, Mr. Dwight of the New York*

Seba Smith

Jack Downing, by L. A. Howard

Daily Advertiser. Living in New York, Davis had the chance to get his letters on various national events presented to the metropolitan reading public days before Smith's letters on similar events would arrive from Maine.

To add to the confusion, several pirated editions of *both* men's writing were issued, including one still listed frequently as a Smith publication: *Letters Written during the President's Tour Down East; by Myself, Major Jack Downing of Downingville* (Cincinnati: J. J. James, 1833). This publication contains six Smith letters and six Davis letters, along with nine imitations. One clear way to distinguish the Smith and the Davis letters is by the signatures: Smith always signed his letters "Captain [or Major] Jack Downing," while Davis signed his letters "J. Downing, Major." Even after decades there is still confusion concerning the authorship of some "Jack Downing" literature.

The appearance of all the imitation Downing letters and the very real threat that someone else might get credit for his creation prompted Smith to bring out the first collected edition of Downing letters, *The Life and Writings of Major Jack Downing of Downingville*, in 1833. Included in the collection were letters in which Jack attacked the "rascally" counterfeiters who were using his name. He writes to his "old friend," the editor of the *Portland Courier*: "there is the most rascally set of fellers skulking about somewhere in this part of the country that I have heard of, and I wish you'd blow 'em up. They are worse than the pickpockets. I mean them are fellers that's got to writing letters and putting my name to 'em, and sending of 'em to the printers. And I heard there was one sassy feller . . . that got on to a horse, and rid about town calling himself Major Jack Downing. . . . Isn't it Mr. Shakespeare that says something about 'he that steals my munny-pus steals trash, but he that steals my name ought to have his head broke?' I wish you would find that story and print it."

In an editorial note in *My Thirty Years Out of the Senate*, Smith is even more direct in his accusation. (The specific incident alluded to is a minor problem encountered during a presidential visit to New York.) Smith says: "one individual . . . made a bold and systematic rush at the Major, and attempted to strip his well-earned laurels from his brow, and entwine them around his own head. This was a respectable merchant, a heavy iron dealer in New York. Violently seized with a literary mania, he sat down and wrote a Downing letter, giving an account of the arrival of the Presidential party in New York, signed it with the Major's name, and published it in the old Daily Advertiser." The references to "a heavy iron dealer in New York" and to the *Daily Advertiser* make clear that Davis is the target for the satiric attack from Smith which follows the above account. Earlier in the note Smith observes: "The popular man is like the child who holds a nice stick of candy in his hand; all the children around are on tiptoe to get a nibble. It is not strange, therefore, that many in different parts of the country, endeavored to get a taste of Major Downing's popularity by attempting to imitate his writings."

The reason for Jack Downing's popularity becomes evident after reading only a little of Smith's writing. Jack is charmingly naive and has a simplicity of style that is welcome in the ordinarily cumbersome prose of the mid-nineteenth century. Consider, for example, his preface to *The Life and Writings of Major Jack Downing of Downingville*, in which he discusses his surprise at learning he would have to write a preface at all: "Arter I got my book all done, and had looked it over every day as the printer went along with it, till I got clear to the last page, so as to see it was done right, the printer comes to me, and says he, we want a Preface now. A preface! says I, what in nater is that? Why, says he, it is something to fill up the two first pages with. But, says I, aint the two first pages filled up yet? I thought we had jest got through the last page; I hope our cake aint all turning to dough again. O, it's all right, says he, we always print the first pages last; all we want now is the preface, to fill up them are two first pages. Well, says I, but this is a pretty curious piece of business, this duin work backwards."

Jack also answers the printer's question concerning why Jack wrote the book (something all prefaces should have): "In the first place . . . I wrote the book because I couldn't help it; if I hadn't made it, I dont believe but what I should have split. And in the next place, I made it so as to get my letters all together, out of the way of the rascally counterfeits, so that folks might know the good eggs from the rotten ones." In concluding his remarks, Jack makes clear his political ambitions, kindled by the popularity he has gained in the nation: "as to what [the book] is good for, it will tell folks more about politics, and how to get offices, than ever they knew before in their lives; and what is the best ont, it will be pretty likely to get me in to be President."

While Jack's adventures never led him to the office he sought, they did take him from his native Downingville to far-off places; and, while he never served as president, he was a friend to men who did. Jack begins his career after going to Portland to sell assorted goods and to strike out on his own. Business being bad, he wanders into the state legislature to observe the goings-on. He is puzzled by the dissatisfaction with a speaker who seems to be doing just fine and the refusal to give a Mr. Roberts from Waterborough a seat: "Some said he should n't have a seat because he adjourned the town meeting and wasn't fairly elected. Others said it was no such thing, and that he was elected as fairly as any of

'em. . . . when they came to vote, they got three or four majority that he shouldn't have a seat. And I thought it a needless piece of cruelty, for they wan't crowded, and there was a number of seats empty. But they would have it so, and the poor man had to go and stand up in the lobby." These and other comments Jack sent to Cousin Ephraim Downing; later letters also went to Uncle Joshua Downing and were sometimes sent to the *Portland Courier* to be forwarded to him.

Adding to the scope of Smith's concept is the idea of having Jack's relatives write to him as well. There are almost as many letters from Uncle Joshua, Cousin Ephraim, and Cousin Nabby to Jack as there are letters from him to them. After Jack enters President Jackson's confidence, Uncle Joshua even writes to "the Gineral" himself. In a letter dated 6 November 1831 and addressed to "General Jackson," Joshua Downing describes the raising of the militia in Downingville to help his newly commissioned "neffu," Jack, in his campaign to free the prisoners of Madawaska. (The "prisoners" later disappoint Jack by walking away from their British "captors," so there is no war for Captain Jack Downing to wage.) When the Downingville militia marches into Washington City a few years later to help Jack fight against the Nullifiers in South Carolina, another battle that never happens, Jackson mistakes them for the Nullifiers and almost calls out the federal troops against them.

After his initial observation of the legislature, Jack decides to hang around Portland for a time. During the course of events Jack is nominated in Downingville for governor of Maine and receives all 117 votes cast in his hometown. Unfortunately, in spite of his following the tradition of giving voters rides to the polls, he receives no votes in Portland, or anywhere else. Not one to sit around in defeat for long, Jack decides to head for Washington City after President Jackson's cabinet "blows up" with an eye to securing for himself a position in the new cabinet.

That idea falls flat, but Jack does gain entry into Jackson's White House and soon finds himself in the thick of federal doings, including the "campaign" in Madawaska and the never realized, but fully prepared-for excursion against the Nullifiers in South Carolina mentioned above. The latter incident gained him his rank of major. In fact, Jack was later offered a promotion to colonel, but he refused: "that are . . . story, that the President gave me a curnel's commission jest before we started Down East isn't exactly true. The President did offer me one, but I thanked him, and told him if he would excuse me, I should rather not take it, for I

L. A. Howard's cartoon of South Carolina nullification

had always noticed that majors were more apt to rise in the world than curnels." Part of Smith's satire was aimed at the spoils system operating under Andrew Jackson, a system which rankled the fairly conservative newspaperman. His satire is never so vicious as others at the time, but he does use his easy-going character to point out the weaknesses of the system in a most effective manner.

Another point of interest in Smith's approach (and one echoed by his imitators) is that he used real situations and inserted Jack into the thick of them, in order to provide his unique perspective on events. True to the gossip of the times, Jack's view of the "cabinet explosion" centered on what was rumored to be in-fighting among the cabinet officers—and their wives—over the reputation of the wife of Secretary of War Eaton. What was historically a matter of positioning to see who would succeed Jackson to the presidency becomes, in Jack's view of things, a matter of fisticuffs between Eaton and Secretary of the Treasury Ingham. It is at the latter's doorstep, in fact, that Jack steps in to offer his services. When Eaton and his party learn that their opponent is "*Jack Downing*, of the State of Maine," they drop their heads and leave immediately. As Jack says, "They were afraid I should

have 'em all before the President today, and have 'em turned out of office; for it's got whispered around the city that the President sets a good deal by me, and that I have a good deal of influence with him."

The attitude of Jack Downing, and his naivete, are part of the humor of Seba Smith's writing, perhaps the larger part. While Smith does use some of the humorous devices in vogue at the time— misspellings and malapropisms, mainly—he does not overexaggerate Jack's spelling or word use, at least not nearly as much as his contemporaries and later writers did in their writing. "General" becomes "gineral" and "there" becomes "are," but none of Jack's spelling or usage is unrecognizable. Charles Davis followed Smith's example for the most part, but he and the other Smith imitators did create some terribly burdensome prose in attempting to effect a dialect for Jack. Here is one example from Davis: "There was a swod of fine folks, and dreadful handsome galls; and the house was nigh upon church full." Compare that to a similar passage from Smith: "But what made the Gineral hold his head up . . . was when we marched along the street by them are five thousand galls all dressed up, and looking as pretty as a million of butterflies." In the opinion of the editor of the *Morning Courier and New York Enquirer*, "the attempts to touch off the oddities of an uneducated New Englander, by the imitators of the real Major, are as far removed from real Yankeeism as they are from the language of a Somersetshire peasant."

Clearly, in the eyes of many of his contemporaries, and certainly in the eyes of modern critics, Seba Smith was the original, the creative force behind the comic literary Yankee character. There may have been confusion during various parts of his lifetime concerning who was the originator of Jack Downing, but today we can acknowledge Smith's efforts without a doubt. Jack Downing's career, and Seba Smith's writing, continued beyond the publication of *The Life and Writings of Major Jack Downing of Downingville*. Smith published the *Downing Gazette* in Portland, Maine, for a few years in the mid-1830s. Then, in 1836 the original Major Jack Downing, exhausted by his duties as editor and by the competition, became seriously ill and died. He had a splendid funeral, dutifully reported in the *Portland Courier and Family Reader* on 1 April 1836 by Cousin Nabby and Uncle Joshua. Someone published "J. Downing, Major" letters in the *New York Daily Express* between 1837 and 1839, and one must assume Davis was the author.

Meanwhile, Seba Smith's personal life had undergone several changes. After losing most of his money in land speculation in Maine, he tried to regain his losses by selling a cotton-cleaning device to growers in South Carolina. Failing there as well, he moved to New York with Elizabeth and their four sons. For a few years both of the Smiths wrote articles for the *Southern Literary Messenger* and other periodicals. By 1843 Smith had resumed his editorial role, first with the *Rover*, a weekly magazine, from 1843 to 1845, and then intermittently with Emerson's *United States Magazine* from 1854 to 1859. In 1859 he established the short-lived *Great Republic*, an enterprise that lasted only one year.

During this period, Smith also published several books: *Powhatan* (1841), a metrical romance; *New Elements of Geometry* (1850), an original and highly inaccurate dissertation on geometry; and *Way Down East* (1854), a collection of tales on Yankee customs and characters. He also began a new series of Downing letters at this time and published a small collection of the old letters.

May-Day in New York or *Jack Downing's Letters by Major Jack Downing* (it was published under both titles) was brought out in 1845. Although the book has been credited to Davis, Mary Wyman (*Two American Pioneers*) argues that the book "bears the stamp of Smith from the cover to the postscript." Smith evidently wrote the preface himself, and it

"Major Downing Getting Over a Gap in History," by L. A. Howard

includes a review of the Downing letters and the first letter of the original Major, dated 18 January 1830. Later, reference is made to Jack's "ducking" at Castle Garden, when "a new set of Downing letters commenced, and C. A. D——, a Broad Street merchant, was most delighted at his success." Wyman concludes: ". . . the preface is ostensibly written to explain to the mystified public who the original Major was and to show the injustice of Davis' claims." The book even contains stories signed "Seba Smith," stories that were later included in *Way Down East*. As Wyman claims, the book was compiled under the direction of Smith, at the very least.

Smith began the second series of Downing letters in 1847, publishing them in the *Daily Intelligencer* in New York. In 1859 he collected some of the later letters and, along with the best of the earlier letters and assorted "docyments," brought them out in book form under the title *My Thirty Years Out of the Senate*, a parody of Thomas Hart Benton's book of a similar title. In the publisher's preface to Smith's book, Appleton Oaksmith, echoing his father's style, presents Jack's reasons for the book—and the title: "The veteran politician, Colonel Thomas H. Benton, has given to his countrymen a comprehensive and very valuable work entitled: 'THIRTY YEARS IN THE UNITED STATES SENATE; Or, A History of the Working of the American Government for Thirty Years,' &c.

"Now, that other veteran politician, Major Jack Downing, who declares positively that there is an outside as well as an inside to everything, has prepared to lay before his countrymen *his* comprehensive and valuable work entitled: 'THIRTY YEARS "OUT" OF THE UNITED STATES SENATE; Or, A History of the Working of American Politicians for Thirty Years,' &c."

In this last book, Jack has gained the confidence of two more presidents, Polk and Pierce, and serves them in various capacities. He goes to the war zone as Polk's confidential emissary during the Mexican War and relates in his dispatches his special observations. Santa Anna, for example, is "as slippery as an eel, and has as many lives as a cat." Smith, like most of the nation, opposed Polk's attempts at the annexation of Mexico, and the Downing material reflects that criticism. In one letter Jack reports a dream in which the country, having annexed all of North and South America, has turned into a huge ship of war and set sail for Europe, Asia, and Africa looking for new conquests. Polk, the captain, sings out: "Don't stop for birds'-egging round the West India Islands; we can

pick them up as we come back along." (At this time, James Russell Lowell began *The Biglow Papers*, and with Hosea Biglow, his character, he uses a much sharper satiric thrust than that of Smith in attacking Polk's war.)

Jack also visits the Democratic Presidential Convention of 1852 when Pierce was nominated. He looks at the process of trying to select a candidate as an attempt to haul a wagon up a hill; the "Old Fogy" teams of Cass and Buchanan were pulling against the Douglas team, "made up mostly of young steers." Finally, the Franklin Pierce team is the only one with enough power to pull all the factions to the top. When Jack writes Uncle Joshua to tell him who the candidate is to be, Uncle Joshua writes back with a question: "Major, who is General Pierce? It ain't a fictious name, is it?"

In his last appearance in print, Jack Downing also concerned himself with international affairs. One letter draws a comic picture of relations between Russia and Turkey, in which the "foolish Sultan . . . told Mr. Bear to clear out of his cornfield in fifteen days, or he'd set the dogs arter him." And in the early fifties, when the annexation of Cuba was a popular issue, Jack sets off in his ship, *The Two Pollies*, to join the filibusters heading toward Cuba. He ends his career much as he started it, by commenting on a legislative body—this time the House of Representatives in Washington. To quiet Pierce's concerns over a delay caused by the House's inability to choose a Speaker, Jack offers to bring the guns of *The Two Pollies* to bear upon the capitol. In spite of a postscript in which Jack indicates that his activities will continue, this collection is the last known appearance of new material by Smith's Jack Downing.

In 1860 Seba Smith retired from active life and spent his last years in Patchogue, Long Island. His health failed during the fall of 1867; and, after a lingering illness, he died on 28 July 1868. Unfortunately, he had lived to see the once popular Major Jack Downing almost forgotten. Hardly any reference to Jack was made in accounts of Smith's death.

Seba Smith was, by nature, a shy and retiring man. He was essentially conservative and was concerned about the dangers he saw to the solidarity of the Union. But, while readers remember Jack Downing for his use as a political foil, Seba Smith considered the characterization of the New England Yankee the most important part of his work. Referring to the Downing letters in 1858, he said: "Genuine Yankee delineations do not consist in mere out of the way modes of expression, but in a subtle quaintness of thought, which under the simplest language conveys a homey truth or a statesman-like idea. So far is the genuine Yankee from being an awkward talking boor, he is on the contrary singularly wise, penetrating, and observant, reproducing in our day, from traditional use the language of Shakespeare and Milton."

The contributions of Seba Smith to American humor are twofold. First, he gave us a record and life of a "genuine" Yankee from Down East, in a subtle and gentle form; second, he set a new pattern for American humor in his political satire issuing from the pen of a simple country philosopher. Those who followed him—from Thomas Chandler Haliburton and James Russell Lowell to Finley Peter Dunne and Will Rogers—might often have surpassed him in literary style or wit, but they—and we—owe a great debt to the man who started it all.

Doubtful Attributions:
Letters Written During the President's Tour "Down East" (Cincinnati: J. J. James, 1833);
The Life of Andrew Jackson (Philadelphia: T. K. Greenbank, 1834);
Jack Downing's Song Book (Providence: Wheeden and Cory, 1835);
John Smith's Letters (New York: Colman, 1839).

Reference:
Mary Alice Wyman, *Two American Pioneers* (New York: Columbia University Press, 1927).

Donald Ogden Stewart
(30 November 1894-2 August 1980)

James C. McNutt
University of Texas at Austin

BOOKS: *A Parody Outline of History* (New York: Doran, 1921);
Perfect Behavior (New York: Doran, 1922);
Aunt Polly's Story of Mankind (New York: Doran, 1923; London: Brentano, 1927);
Mr. and Mrs. Haddock Abroad (New York: Doran, 1924);
The Crazy Fool (New York: Boni, 1925);
Mr. and Mrs. Haddock in Paris, France (New York & London: Harper, 1926);
Father William (New York & London: Harper, 1929);
Rebound (New York, Los Angeles & London: French, 1931);
By a Stroke of Luck! An Autobiography (London: Paddington Press; New York: Paddington Press / Two Continents, 1975).

The humorous writing of Donald Ogden Stewart treats the concerns and postures of the 1920s, when he produced most of it, in styles well suited to the period itself, parody and satire. Stewart shared with Ring Lardner, Robert Benchley, and James Thurber a concern for the "little man," and, following Lardner, he contributed his own brand of crazy humor, which relied on slapstick effects and non sequitur for its impact. The vociferous rejection of puritanism, the rebellion against authority, and the dissatisfaction with American culture in general which characterized the thinking of many young writers in the 1920s are all present in Stewart's work. At times he had a surpassing ability to compress these themes in his humor. Burton Rascoe wrote of Stewart's fifth book, *The Crazy Fool* (1925): "By writing a nonsensical narrative somewhat in the vein of Lewis Carroll, and weaving into it most of the formulas of American business organizations, Stewart has succeeded in doing in single pages what Sinclair Lewis did less effectively in thousands of words in 'Babbitt.' " Because he established his first audience on the basis of relatively light humor, however, Stewart found it difficult to pursue more serious satire, and this, plus his success as an actor and playwright, led him to give up humorous writing for Hollywood screenwriting.

Born in Columbus, Ohio, to Gilbert Holland and Clara Ogden Stewart, Donald grew up committed to the success formula he absorbed from reading Horatio Alger and *St. Nicholas* magazine. His family was, according to his later account, "in Society"; nevertheless they lived modestly, even precariously, on Gilbert's income as a lawyer and Ohio circuit court judge. Young Donald looked with great admiration on two older siblings, Gilbert

Holland, Jr., and Anne, fourteen and ten years his senior, respectively. Brother "Bert" had belonged to a high-school fraternity and lettered in football, accomplishments which Donald hoped to equal for much of his youth. His physical build and near-sightedness always kept him from athletic success, though not from athletics. His self-esteem suffered in addition from the taunts of schoolmates who called him "Duck Lip" because of his protruding upper teeth.

In 1909 Stewart was accepted at Phillips Exeter Academy, where he made a fraternity, wrote for the *Exonian*, and avoided the good grades which would have produced a social stigma. He also strung along on the second squad of the football team and, at a mere 165 pounds, threw the hammer. In 1912 his prep school career almost ended when his father informed him that he could no longer afford to pay his way, but Donald continued by getting a scholarship and working as a waiter in a dining hall.

In the summer of 1912, just before he entered Yale, Stewart endured a personal and family disaster when his father was indicted for theft of funds from the Columbus Law Library. The issue never came to trial, but this crisis, and the simultaneous discovery that his mother was an alcoholic, were the first serious jolts of disillusionment which the success-oriented Stewart suffered. The death of his brother Bert in the fall, followed shortly by that of his father, helped to complete his disillusionment. His relationship with his mother strengthened, however, after she overcame her alcoholism, and thereafter she frequently lived with or near her son, both in America and Europe.

At Yale Stewart majored in English, was tapped for Skull and Bones, an honor he coveted, and was elected assignments editor of the *Daily News*. After his graduation in 1916 a Columbus benefactor secured him a job with American Telephone and Telegraph, for which he worked in regional offices in Birmingham, Pittsburgh, and Chicago before being drafted in 1918. He enlisted in Naval Officer's Training School, managing to pass the required physical by memorizing the eye chart while the examiner was out of the room. He achieved the rank of chief quartermaster and, more important to his literary career, published his first humorous writing, a parody of Edward Streeter's *Dere Mabel* entitled "Dere Queenie," in a local Navy magazine. After World War I, having spent his time entirely on the wharf in Chicago, he returned to work for AT&T and was transferred to Minneapolis.

In 1919, across the river in St. Paul, he met F. Scott Fitzgerald and read the manuscript of *This Side of Paradise*. In the spring of 1920 he quit AT&T and took a job in a private manufacturing company. But he had begun to look seriously toward some career besides business, and before the year was out left his job and moved to Greenwich Village. In New York he again met Fitzgerald and through him gained an introduction to Frank Crowninshield of *Vanity Fair*, who politely refused him work. But he also met John Peale Bishop and Edmund Wilson, Crowninshield's assistant editors, and Wilson took the time to read a parody of Dreiser which Stewart had written. To Stewart's surprise, Wilson laughed and asked for another parody of James Branch Cabell, offering to publish both in *Vanity Fair* if they were good enough. *Vanity Fair* accepted the Cabell piece, and Stewart had found a new career.

Edmund Wilson introduced Stewart to the members of the "Round Table" group which met for lunch at the Algonquin Hotel, including Robert Benchley and Dorothy Parker, both of whom became his good friends. Stewart later said that he admired the wit and humor of the Round Table, but that he was "never really at ease in this company, partly because of the constant strain of feeling obliged to say something funny, and partly because the atmosphere seemed . . . to be basically unfriendly, too much that of dog-eat-dog." Nevertheless he found acceptance in the group, and participated in its satiric review, *No, Siree!*

Following the acceptance of his work by *Vanity Fair*, Stewart placed other pieces in George Jean Nathan and H. L. Mencken's *Smart Set*, and convinced John Farrar, editor of the *Bookman*, to publish a series of parodies of contemporary writers, including William Lyon Phelps, Sinclair Lewis, F. Scott Fitzgerald, and Ring Lardner. In November 1921 Stewart's first published short story appeared in the *Smart Set*. Entitled "The Secret of Success," it satirized the Horatio Alger office career of Richard Kennedy, who, after spending several months taking self-help courses in order to rise in the ranks, finds that real advancement comes by marrying the daughters of the company president. The eldest two having already wed, Kennedy marries the third daughter in a one-line denouement, and subsequently becomes president himself. Stewart returned to the themes of this story several times in his writing, notably in *The Crazy Fool*.

In the same month, George Doran published Stewart's first book, the collected pieces from the *Bookman* series, as *A Parody Outline of History*. Only nominally related to H. G. Wells's contemporary best-seller, it enjoyed an immediate success

Donald Ogden Stewart

any of the temptations which had turned Twain from the path of Truth. I was to be the new Mark Twain, fearless, uncorrupted." In 1922, after arranging with *Harper's Bazaar* to do a series of articles parodying the best-selling books of etiquette, and influenced like many other young writers by Harold Stearns' *Civilization in the United States*, Stewart went to Paris.

Accompanied by his mother, Clara, Stewart spent a month in Paris, where he completed the parodies of etiquette books for *Harper's Bazaar*. Some of these pieces also appeared in *Vanity Fair*. He and Clara then moved on to Vienna and Budapest, where he first read Wells's *Outline of History*. Its effect was to make him more eager to attempt a serious satire. On this first European trip Stewart also read T. S. Eliot's *The Waste Land* and met Ernest Hemingway, who later published a portion of Stewart's unpublished novel, "John Brown's Body," in the *transatlantic review*. Stewart's friendship with Hemingway continued over a number of years, and he was included in several

nonetheless. Each parody concerned some bogus episode of American history, loosely recreated around real events—Columbus at the court of Ferdinand and Isabella, the landing at Plymouth Rock, the Whisky Rebellion, Custer's "last stand," and others. Frequently the humor depended less on the reader's knowledge of the writer being parodied than on a loose familiarity with these events. But Stewart managed to juggle writing styles, historical anachronism, and items of topical interest to good effect. In "Main Street—Plymouth, Mass." he portrayed a bedtime conversation between Priscilla Kennicott and her husband, who related the decision to shut down a traveling medicine show: "This one claims to come from down south somewhere. 'Smart Set Medicine Show' it's called, run by a fellow named Mencken. Sells cheap whiskey to the Indians—makes them crazy, they say."

A Parody Outline of History enhanced Stewart's name among the members of the Algonquin Round Table and other New York literati. Encouraged, he began to take his work as a humorist more seriously: "I devoured Van Wyck Brooks' *The Ordeal of Mark Twain* and began to visualize myself as Twain's successor, but as a humorist who would not permit himself to be wooed away from devastating satire by

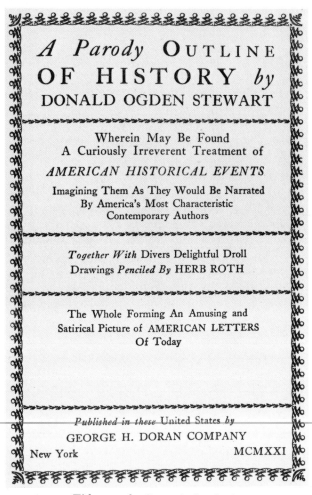

Title page for Stewart's first book

THE SMART SET MEDICINE SHOW

"'Smart Set Medicine Show, it's called, run by a fellow named Mencken. Sells cheap whiskey to the Indians—makes them crazy, they say.'"

Illustration by Herb Roth for A Parody Outline of History

visits to Pamplona to see the bullfights, but the two later split over an uncomplimentary poem about Dorothy Parker which Hemingway read aloud one evening at the home of Archibald MacLeish.

The etiquette parodies for *Harper's Bazaar* and *Vanity Fair* were collected and published by Doran in 1922 as *Perfect Behavior*, which added to Stewart's reputation as a writer of light humor. Among other things, Stewart advised his male readers about meeting young ladies: "Procure a few feet of stout manila rope or clothes-line, from any of the better-class hardware stores. Ascertain (from the Social Register, preferably) the location of the young lady's residence, and go there on some dark evening about nine o'clock. Fasten the rope across the sidewalk in front of the residence about six inches or a foot from the ground. Then, with the aid of a match and some kerosene, set fire to the young lady's house in several places and retire behind a convenient tree. After some time, if she is at home,

she will probably be forced to run out of her house to avoid being burned to death. In her excitement she will fail to notice the rope which you have stretched across the sidewalk and will fall. This is your opportunity to obtain an introduction."

The lighthearted quality of Stewart's first two books did not carry over to his third, in which he attempted to satirize middle-class American values. *Aunt Polly's Story of Mankind*, conceived while Stewart was still in Europe in 1922, completed in the MacDowell Colony in New Hampshire, and published in 1923, was Stewart's "fulfillment of [an] obligation as a humorist to be a gadfly rather than a comforter." Aunt Polly, the wife of a successful Midwestern banker, decides to "improve" her sister's fatherless children by relating the evolution of history to them, which she does in terms which justify, in the face of the children's skepticism, the values of her elite social circle. Assisted by her priggish son, David, she descends on Sam, Mary, and

Genevieve one day after school, ushers them into the family limousine, and begins her history with the cooling of the earth "sufficiently to allow life to take place so that the progress of mankind could commence." Aunt Polly's stories continue with Egypt and Mesopotamia, Greece, Rome, Europe and the American Revolution, and finally "the Glorious Present." Her moralistic lessons take an unexpectedly literal turn, however, when they prompt the children to form "Christian Scout" brigades at school, which eventually divide into factions and engage in a bloody battle at an Armistice Day pageant. Despite Stewart's high and serious hopes for the book—he proposed to Gene Saxton, his editor, that it be nominated for the Nobel Peace Prize—it was a dismal failure, and hardly attracted the attention of important critics. His friends Benchley and Parker admired it, however, and it remained his favorite, even though he abandoned heavy social satire and confined himself to humor for the sake of entertainment.

In April 1924 Stewart returned to Paris, where he began work on his first book in crazy humor style, entitled *Mr. and Mrs. Haddock Abroad*. Working rapidly, he completed it in less than a month. The protagonists, a Midwestern couple and their precocious realist of a daughter, Mildred, only manage to reach Europe by the end of the book. In an afterword written for a 1975 reprinting of the book, Stewart explained that he had gotten the idea at an Author's League dinner attended by Robert Benchley, Marc Connelly, and Ring Lardner, whose *I Gaspiri* was the model for his crazy humor, of which the chief characteristics are non sequitur and slapstick. At one point the Haddocks accompany the captain on a tour of the ship; a collision drill occurs and they are accidentally locked in a watertight compartment. Along with them is "Mrs. John ('Slugger') Gerrish—who was from Boston and very proud of her ancestry." When the captain whispers "we may have to eat one of us," the group responds by following Mrs. Gerrish's demand that they organize, and begins a raucous meeting, ostensibly governed by Robert's Rules of Order. A reading of the minutes, a marching song, debate, a prayer, voting, and a committee report by Mr. Haddock follow before the doors open and they are freed: " 'Thank God,' said Mr. Haddock.

" 'Saved,' said Mrs. Gerrish.

" 'Mildred! come back here,' said Mrs. Haddock, 'and let the older people go first. And *look* at the dirt on that dress.' "

Mr. and Mrs. Haddock Abroad returned Stewart to his readers' favor, and in the wake of its publication he returned to New York and was able to secure the contract for another book from the newly established firm of Albert and Charles Boni. He also received an offer to do a lecture tour in the United States, and helped Ernest Hemingway find an American publisher for *In Our Time* (1925). His speaking tour took him back to Columbus, Ohio, where James Thurber, then a reporter on the *Columbus Dispatch*, interviewed him. He also went for the first time to Hollywood, where he met King Vidor and remained to complete his book for the Boni firm in a small, three-story wooden hotel named "the Mark Twain." Influenced by the monetary and celebratory attractions of Hollywood, Stewart decided to write the book in a way which would please his publishers and also sell his talents to the movies. He was successful in his aims, as *The Crazy Fool* made at least one best-seller list soon after its publication, and he received assurance from King Vidor that it would make a good movie.

The Crazy Fool was Stewart's twist on a French novel, which he had heard about secondhand, concerning a young man who inherits a brothel. He substituted an insane asylum for the brothel and subordinated the problem of the inheritance to a broader plot involving the hopes of the hero, Charlie Hatch, to marry his boss's daughter. Stewart drew on his own past for the character of Charlie Hatch, and on the personalities of his friends Gerald Murphy, Robert Benchley, and Dorothy Parker for those of other characters.

Returning to Paris in 1924, Stewart visited Pamplona with Hemingway, then visited on the Riviera with his friends the Gerald Murphys, where he attempted to begin a sequel to *Mr. and Mrs. Haddock Abroad*. Unable to work, he returned to Paris, where he met his future wife, Beatrice Ames, but wrote little before he received word that Metro-Goldwyn-Mayer had bought the rights to *The Crazy Fool*. After stopping in New York for publicity photographs, he went on to Los Angeles, where he discovered that MGM had bought *The Crazy Fool* mistakenly. Thinking he was reading *The Crazy Fool*, King Vidor had actually read portions of *Perfect Behavior* to MGM production chief Irving Thalberg to secure a contract. Despite the misunderstanding, Stewart went to work for MGM writing the screenplay for an old play, *Brown of Harvard*. Unsatisfied with this work, he quit MGM and completed *Mr. and Mrs. Haddock in Paris, France* (1926), the sequel begun on the Riviera. The book had more of a message and less crazy humor than the previous Haddock volume. Mr. Haddock, in the midst of several attempts to escape his wife, who is suspicious of the French and wants to remain in the hotel, meets a longtime American resident of Paris named "The Bottin." The Bottin declares that "the soul of Europe" is sick and looking for guidance, which America can provide by realizing its own soul, "the expression of the great beautiful soul of this commercial industrial scientific age which is our own."

Stewart married Beatrice Ames on 24 July 1926, just after he had completed *Mr. and Mrs. Haddock in Paris, France*. They embarked for France, where they visited with friends at Antibes while Stewart supported them by writing weekly syndicated columns for the *Chicago Tribune*. By the end of the year they had returned to the United States, and after some time spent in Hollywood they moved to New York in 1927.

Stewart discontinued the *Chicago Tribune* pieces and attempted unsuccessfully to work on a novel, then contracted with *College Humor* for a series of stories which would become his final humorous book, *Father William* (1929). While he was writing *Father William* he also began working on short pieces for the *New Yorker*, which appeared in 1927 and 1928. The Stewart's first son, Ames Ogden, was born 21 May 1928, and shortly thereafter *Father William* was finished. The hero of *Father William* is Austin Seabury, a successful businessman and widower who sees no purpose in life but is content to enjoy himself. He finds himself compet-

ing with his son, Phillip, for the attentions of an attractive young socialite, Pussie Whitehouse. In the end Pussie sets both of the Seaburys adrift, and they are reconciled. The progress of Austin Seabury represents Stewart's view that laughter is necessary in "a purposeless but by no means gloomy world."

Stewart put his laughter into other media, however, after *Father William*. In the late summer of 1928 Philip Barry asked him to take a part in his play *Holiday*, which starred Hope Williams and had a successful run on Broadway followed by a tour. The connection with the theater encouraged Stewart to write his own play, *Rebound*, a complicated love story in which a man loses his girl friend to a wealthy suitor, marries another woman on the rebound, and loses his affection for his flirtatious first love only when his distraught wife decides to divorce him. Hope Williams starred in the play on Broadway, and it was chosen by Burns Mantle as one of the ten best plays of the year. While completing *Rebound* Stewart journeyed to Hollywood to appear in a movie, *Not So Dumb*; he also wrote the book for Joe Cook's musical comedy, *Fine and Dandy*, which opened on Broadway in the fall of 1930. After two more short trips to Europe and the birth of his and Beatrice's second son, Donald Ogden, Jr., on 5 January 1932, Stewart moved with his family to Hollywood and began a lucrative, though not always personally satisfying, career as a screenwriter. In the late 1930s and early 1940s

Stewart, Hope Williams, Ben Smith, and Barbara White in Philip Barry's Holiday

Stewart was among the most highly paid screen-writers in Hollywood, making as much as $4,600 per week.

Stewart wrote or worked on the scripts for a number of films, including *The Prisoner of Zenda* (1938), *The Philadelphia Story* (1940), for which he received an Academy Award, and *Keeper of the Flame* (1942). He also became heavily involved in political work, and served as president of the Hollywood Anti-Nazi League, president of the League of American Writers, and as a member of the board of the Screen Writer's Guild. In 1938 he and his wife divorced; he remarried, on 4 March 1939, to Ella Winter, the widow of Lincoln Steffens. In 1947 when the House Committee on Un-American Activities began its investigation of Communists in Hollywood, Stewart's career as a screenwriter was jeopardized by his political associations. By 1950 he was blacklisted, and in 1951 he and Ella moved to London. They remained there together until his death, on 2 August 1980, after an illness following a heart attack. His wife died two days later.

Although he never became the uncorrupted Mark Twain he once aspired to be, Stewart's humor remains a good indicator of the cultural trends of the 1920s. He received some censure by critics for succumbing to the temptations of Hollywood and

Stewart with his Academy Award for screenplay of The Philadelphia Story

John Howard, Cary Grant, Katharine Hepburn, and James Stewart in The Philadelphia Story, *for which Donald Ogden Stewart wrote the screenplay*

abandoning his literary efforts, a judgment for which he expresses some concurrence in his autobiography, *By a Stroke of Luck!* (1975). Nevertheless his career as humorist, screenwriter, and political activist is an intriguing document in the history of the young writers who emerged, disillusioned, after World War I.

Plays:

Los Angeles, New York, Hudson Theatre, 19 February 1927;

Rebound, New York, Plymouth Theatre, 3 March 1930;

Fine and Dandy, New York, Erlanger Theatre, 23 September 1930;

How I Wonder, New York, Hudson Theatre, 30 September 1947;

The Kidders, London, Arts Theatre, 12 November 1957;

Honour Bright, Hammersmith, U.K., Lyric Theatre, 17 June 1958.

Screenplays:

Holiday, by Stewart and Sidney Buchman, adapted from Philip Barry's play, Columbia Pictures, 1938;

Marie Antoinette, by Stewart, Claudine West, and Ernest Vajada, adapted in part from Stefan Zweig's book, MGM, 1938;

The Prisoner of Zenda, by Stewart, John Balderston, and Wells Root, adapted from Anthony Hope's novel, United Artists, 1938;

Love Affair, by Stewart, Delmer Daves, Mildred Cram, and Leo McCarey, RKO, 1939;

The Night of Nights, Independent, 1939;

Kitty Foyle, by Stewart and Dalton Trumbo, adapted from Christopher Morley's novel, RKO, 1940;

The Philadelphia Story, adapted from Philip Barry's play, MGM, 1940;

Smilin' Through, by Stewart and John Balderston, adapted from Jane Cowl and Jane Murfin's play, MGM, 1941;

That Uncertain Feeling, by Stewart and Walter Reisch, United Artists, 1941;

A Woman's Face, by Stewart and Elliott Paul, adapted from Francis de Croisset's play, *Il Etait une Fois*, MGM, 1941;

Keeper of the Flame, adapted from I. A. R. Wylie's novel, MGM, 1942;

Tales of Manhattan, by Stewart, Ben Hecht, Ferenc Molnar, and others, Fox, 1942;

Forever and a Day, by Stewart, Charles Bennett, C. S. Forrester, Lawrence Hazard, and others, RKO, 1944;

Without Love, adapted from Philip Barry's play, MGM, 1945;

Cass Timberlane, adapted from Sinclair Lewis's novel, MGM, 1947;

Life with Father, adapted from Howard Lindsay and Russel Crouse's play, Warner Brothers, 1947;

Edward, My Son, adapted from Robert Morley and Noel Langley's play, MGM, 1949.

Other:

Fighting Words, edited by Stewart (New York: Harcourt, Brace, 1940).

Periodical Publications:

"The Secret of Success," *Smart Set*, 66 (November 1921): 77-83;

"Fragment IV," *transatlantic review*, 2 (July 1924): 116-120.

References:

Matthew J. Bruccoli, Interview, *Conversations 1* (Detroit: Gale, 1977), pp. 238-250;

Burton Rascoe, "Contemporary Reminiscences," *Arts & Decoration*, 23 (July 1925): 49, 73;

Norris W. Yates, *The American Humorist* (Ames, Iowa: Iowa State University Press, 1964), pp. 15ff.

Edward Streeter
(1 August 1891-31 March 1976)

Roy Arthur Swanson
University of Wisconsin-Milwaukee

BOOKS: *Dere Mable: Love Letters of a Rookie* (New York: Stokes, 1918; London: Jarrolds, 1919);

"That's me all over, Mable" (New York: Stokes, 1919; London: Jarrolds, 1919);

Same Ole Bill, Eh, Mable (New York: Stokes, 1919; London: Jarrolds, 1919);

As You Were, Bill (New York: Stokes, 1920);

Beany, Gangleshanks and the Tub (New York & London: Putnam's, 1921);

Daily Except Sundays or, What Every Commuter Should Know (New York: Simon & Schuster, 1938);

Father of the Bride (New York: Simon & Schuster, 1949);

Skoal Scandinavia (New York: Harper, 1952; London: Hamish Hamilton, 1952);

Mr. Hobbs' Vacation (New York: Harper, 1954);

Merry Christmas, Mr. Baxter [novel] (New York: Harper, 1956);

Merry Christmas, Mr. Baxter, a comedy in two acts [play], by Streeter and William Fuson Davidson (Chicago: Dramatic Publishing Company, 1956);

Mr. Robbins Rides Again (New York: Harper, 1958);

Window on America: The Growth of a Nation as seen by New York's First Bank, 1784-1959 (New York: The Bank of New York, 1959);

Chairman of the Bored (New York: Harper & Row, 1961);

Words of Welcome; an address at the dinner for new members of the Century Association, October 5, 1961 (Stamford, Conn.: Overbrook Press, 1962);

Mr. Hobbs' Vacation, by Streeter and F. Andrew Leslie (New York: Dramatists Play Service, 1963);

Along the Ridge: From Northwestern Spain to Southern Yugoslavia (New York, Evanston & London: Harper & Row, 1964);

Ham Martin, Class of '17 (New York: Harper & Row, 1969).

Edward Streeter was one of the New England humorists, a group that includes such other Harvard men as Robert Benchley (class of '12) and Ogden Nash (a dropout). His post-*Dere Mable* humor is wry, sophisticated, and increasingly touched with wisps of sadness. The range of his humor is disclosed, appropriately, by his first few books and his last book. The *Dere Mable* books are raucously satirical and exploit near illiteracy as a comic device. Streeter's last book, *Ham Martin, Class of '17* (1969), is a somber reflection upon both his business career and his literary aspirations; its humor is heavily muted and scarcely perceptible to any but Streeter enthusiasts. Between these extremes of both time and temper lies his masterpiece, *Father of the Bride* (1949), the one work in which his particular style and his special kind of sophisticated humor are flawlessly displayed.

The gentility, restraint, charitableness, and wit of Streeter's humor reflect his Eastern WASP Establishment background, which included Eastern education at its best. Streeter was born in Chestertown, New York, to Harvey and Frances Chamberlain Streeter. He went to Pomfret School, where he edited the school paper and the class book; in 1914 he received his A.B. from Harvard, where he was editor-in-chief of the *Lampoon* and writer of the Hasty Pudding show.

During the two years following his graduation from Harvard he worked for a building-supply business in Buffalo, the city in which he grew up and in which he would be married, and he provided copy on a column-inch pay scale for the magazine section of the *Buffalo Express*. After a time, the *Express* took him on as a reporter and benefited from his availability to track leads and pursue events in his own automobile. He continued to send articles to the *Express* in 1916, when he was stationed on the Mexican border with Troop I, First Cavalry, Twenty-seventh Division (New York National Guard).

The Twenty-seventh Division's local newspaper, *The Rio Grande Rattler*, ran a column called "The Incinerator," which Streeter took over and into which he inserted the first of his "Dere Mable" letters, imitative of Ring Lardner's epistolary "You Know Me Al" series. In 1917, when the division, getting ready for its part in World War I, went on active duty at Camp Wadsworth in Spartanburg, South Carolina, the editor of the camp magazine, a Harvard college-mate of Streeter's named Richard Connell, convinced Streeter to continue "The Incinerator" and his "Dere Mable" letters. In Thomas L. Masson's *Our American Humorists* Streeter recalled how his humorous letters came to be published in book form: "In the fall of 1917 while I was serving with the 27th Division at Camp Wadsworth, South Carolina, I was assigned to the *Camp Wadsworth Gas Attack*—which I hasten to explain was a weekly paper, not a disorder. The task of editing a humorous page titled 'The Incinerator' was foisted upon me. . . .

"When the first number was assembled for press 'The Incinerator' contained two senile jokes which were originally employed by General McClellan to depress the Confederate troops across the Potomac. The remainder of the page rivalled my mind. In desperation I wrote a letter from a soldier to his 'sweetheart.'. . .

"I handed this to Dick Connell, the editor. With his usual good taste he O.K.'d the jokes as having considerable historic value. His criticism of the letter was to crumple it up and throw it under his desk. Whereupon he went to mess . . . leaving the dummy and me in the office. I quickly discovered that we had much in common. The rejected letter was smoothed out and shipped hastily to the printer with the rest of the manuscript.

"The thing didn't look so bad in print, so, the following week, I repeated. Repetition quickly grew into a habit.

"Just before the Division sailed for France I received a five-day leave. It occurred to me that, while in the North, I might stumble on some editor optimistic enough to turn my manuscript into a book. . . .

"I had a note of introduction to a publishing house which specialized in school text-books. . . . Somewhat to my indignation they turned me down after reading the title. With thirty-five minutes to catch my train for the South I looked up the publishing house nearest the station. Throwing the manuscript and my camp address on the Treasurer's desk, I ran from the office, leaving the firm somewhat doubtful as to my sanity.

"Fortunately for me the deal was finally closed. The book appeared a few days before my outfit sailed."

According to Laura Benét in *Famous American Humorists*, Streeter first submitted his manuscript to Alfred Harcourt, who was then with Henry Holt and Company. Harcourt referred Streeter to William Morrow at Frederick A. Stokes and Company, a Harvard man who would be receptive to another Harvard man's work. After considerable correspondence, Stokes agreed to publish *Dere Mable*

Edward Streeter

Front cover for Streeter's first book

(1918). Streeter sailed for France in May 1918 and was slow in learning that *Dere Mable* had become a best-seller. The book eventually sold more than 600,000 copies. The sequels *"That's me all over, Mable"* (1919) and *Same Ole Bill, Eh, Mable* (1919) sold, respectively, 275,000 and 50,000 copies. *As You Were, Bill* (1920), the fourth book in the series, sold fewer than 1,000 copies. Streeter recalled that *Dere Mable* "could not have sold better had it been suppressed by the Anti-Vice Society. Following the Descending Theory in orderly sequence my publishers disposed of only half as many copies of the second attempt. The third never achieved the dignity of four numbers, and I refrain from giving data on the fourth lest it prejudice my future."

The popularity of *Dere Mable* remained a phenomenon, whatever the fate of its sequels, and under America's imminent participation in World War II *Dere Mable* and *"That's me all over, Mable"* were reprinted in 1941 in a single volume. The original *Dere Mable* consisted of eighteen letters and a telegram sent by Pvt. Bill Smith from Camp Wadsworth to his girl friend, Mable Gimp in "Philopolis," New York; the letters were dated from 27 September 1917 to 27 February 1918 and were accompanied by thirty-five of Cpl. "Bill" Breck's illustrations. *"That's me all over, Mable"* originally comprised nineteen undated letters from Bill to Mable, a Marconigram, twenty-five Breck illustrations, and one letter to Bill from Mable. Much of the humor in these books was dependent upon misspelled words, malapropisms, and fractured French. But the best feature of the humor is Streeter's undeniable wit: for example, "They say Cleanliness is next to Godliness, Mable. I say it's next to impossible"; or the reworking of a line provided by Connell, "in the army bed and board mean the same thing"; or, "Our guns is pointed at some woods. We been shootin at em for a week and havnt hit em yet. We always seem to go over em." The 1941 edition added the "Publishers' Apology," aimed at servicemen and a war-conscious reading public, and a letter to *Dere Son*, which was signed "Dad" and offered such affectations of patriotism as the following: "Yes son, these fellos is the same as we was—all the way through. An when they get up agenst something tough whatll they do? Theyll go right on complainin. Only theyll stand up an take it just about the way we did."

Streeter attained the rank of first lieutenant in the field artillery during his service in Europe. After the war Streeter married Charlotte Lockwood Warren on 29 October 1919 (they had four children: Claire, Edward, William, and Charlotte) and finished his last *Dere Mable* book. Then he became a successful New York banker. From 1919 until 1929 he was assistant vice-president of Bankers Trust Company. In 1929-1930 he was a partner with Blake Brothers, members of the New York Stock Exchange. From 1931 until his retirement in August 1956 he was vice-president of the Fifth Avenue Bank, which in 1948 was merged with the Bank of New York.

Streeter published no books between 1921 and 1938, but he contributed short stories and articles to the *Saturday Evening Post* and *Red Book*, for which he briefly revived his Bill-to-Mable letters. He was later to contribute also to *McCall's* and *Good Housekeeping*.

Daily Except Sundays (1938) opened the second phase of Streeter's career as a humorist. Its Benchley-like humor is accented with drawings by Benchley's regular illustrator, Gluyas Williams. The setting is suburban Fairview Manor, which is also the setting for *Father of the Bride*, another Benchley-esque book illustrated by Gluyas Williams. But in *Father of the Bride*, a 1949 Book-of-the-Month Club selection, Streeter achieved his own idiom in sophistication. He was well past the derivative humor of the Mable books and well on his way to the sophisticated bittersweetness of his last two novels. Though it recalls the work of Robert Benchley and John P. Marquand, *Father of the Bride* was pure Streeter. With its concision, impeccable pace, and deft strokes of characterization, it is his most notable literary achievement. Its mixture of urbane satire and familial mellowness sets it apart from strictly Eastern humor and gives it a distinction and a universalism that Streeter nowhere else equals. *Father of the Bride* was made into a successful MGM film, starring Spencer Tracy and Elizabeth Taylor, in 1950.

Streeter's next novel, *Mr. Hobbs' Vacation* (1954) enjoyed similar success as a 1962 Twentieth Century-Fox film, starring James Stewart and Maureen O'Hara. Although *Mr. Hobbs' Vacation* became, on film, *Mr. Hobbs Takes a Vacation* and had its setting shifted from Martha's Vineyard to the Pacific Coast, it was better represented in film than *Father of the Bride*. The MGM movie was a slick and engaging comedy but it had none of the charm of its source.

Merry Christmas, Mr. Baxter (1956), with drawings by Dorothea Warren Fox, is similar in structure to *Father of the Bride*. Its sequence of Christmastime preparations and activities is parallel to the sequence of preparations and activities for a daughter's marriage; but the later novel lacks the continuity of the earlier. *Merry Christmas, Mr. Baxter*

Spencer Tracy and Elizabeth Taylor in the 1950 movie based on Streeter's novel Father of the Bride

Ham in the business world, where he knows he belongs, and alienates him from his parents, wife, and children because they take his love of business to be selfishness and fail to understand that they want him to realize their dreams and not his own. Ham's youngest son and namesake is an exception and fulfills his father's dream of a literary career; he even manages to stem Ham's jealousy of this accomplishment. Ham is fully understood and loved only by his youngest son and his devoted secretary, Miss Kelly; these two bring him to understand the creativity inherent in his financial genius. Ham dies appreciative of the fact that their love and his creativity have given his life meaning.

Streeter's contribution to travel literature with *Skoal Scandinavia* (1952) and *Along the Ridge* (1964) and to the serious novel with *Chairman of the Bored* and *Ham Martin, Class of '17* may be slight; and, as an American humorist, he may rank below Robert Benchley, James Thurber, and Ogden Nash. With the phenomenon of *Dere Mable*, however, Streeter secured himself a place in the history of American humor, and, with *Father of the Bride*, he left a solid literary achievement.

offers sentimentality instead of mellowness; and some of the humor is harsh in its effect and is not redeemed by the novel's cloying apologia for Christmas in the concluding dialogue between Mr. and Mrs. Baxter.

Chairman of the Bored (1961), marking the beginning of Streeter's last phase as a humorist, is as uneven as *Merry Christmas, Mr. Baxter*. The first two parts of the novel constitute a serious study of the trauma of retirement—and the retiring chairman, Graham Crombie, is the novel's only fully drawn and thoroughly developed character—but the last two parts are a consistently humorous account of Crombie's failure at country living and his triumphant return to the city. The tone of the serious half of this novel anticipates Streeter's last novel.

Ham Martin, Class of '17 is grim in its autobiographical portrait of a gifted young man whose plans for a literary career are permanently interrupted by his decision to make enough money to pursue that career. His genius at finance keeps

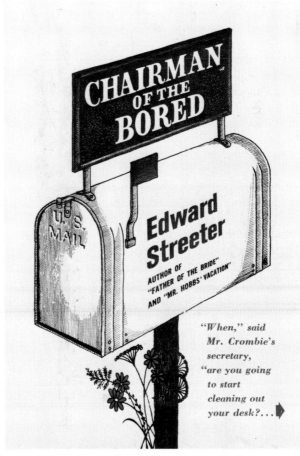

Dust jacket for Streeter's autobiographical novel

477

Frank Sullivan

(22 September 1892-19 February 1976)

Betsy Erkkila
University of Pennsylvania

BOOKS: *The Life and Times of Martha Hepplethwaite* (New York: Boni & Liveright, 1926);
The Adventures of an Oaf (New York: Macy-Masius, 1927);
Innocent Bystanding (New York: Liveright, 1928);
Broccoli and Old Lace (New York: Liveright, 1931);
In One Ear (New York: Viking, 1933);
A Pearl in Every Oyster (Boston: Little, Brown, 1938);
Sullivan at Bay (London: Dent, 1939);
A Rock in Every Snowball (Boston: Little, Brown, 1946);
The Night the Old Nostalgia Burned Down (Boston: Little, Brown, 1953);
Sullivan Bites News: Perverse News Items (Boston: Little, Brown, 1954);
A Moose in the Hoose (New York: Random House, 1959);
Frank Sullivan Through the Looking Glass (Garden City: Doubleday, 1970); republished as *Well, There's No Harm in Laughing* (Garden City: Doubleday, 1972).

The urbane smile of Frank Sullivan stretches across five decades, from the zany antics of Aunt Sarah Gallup in the 1920s to his final Christmas greeting poem for the *New Yorker* in 1974. Described by comic novelist P. G. Wodehouse as "America's finest humorist," Sullivan satirized, twitted, and otherwise entertained American readers for over fifty years with newspaper and magazine pieces, the best of which were collected in several volumes ranging from *The Life and Times of Martha Hepplethwaite* (1926) to *Well, There's No Harm in Laughing* (1972). Known in his later years as the Sage of Saratoga, Sullivan passed his youth as one of the most loved, albeit unassuming, members of the Algonquin Round Table, the group of writers and wits who gathered for luncheon conversation at the Hotel Algonquin in the 1920s. Along with such other Algonquin humorists as Franklin P. Adams, Robert Benchley, Dorothy Parker, Alexander Woollcott, and Edna Ferber, Sullivan was instrumental in creating the cosmopolitan, witty, sophisticated style of writing that came to dominate American humor in the first part of the twentieth century. He is most noted for his gentle brand of humor and his invention of several comic personae, including a no-nonsense Everyman who reflects on the absurdities of modern American life; a Knickerbocker-like historian who unearths bizarre historical facts; a travel expert who has never traveled; and his celebrated expert on cliche, Mr. Arbuthnot.

Francis John Sullivan was never quite at ease during his years as a New York City cosmopolite; he was at heart a small-town boy. He was born in Saratoga Springs, New York, where, according to Sullivan, his parents, Dennis and Shea Sullivan, "brought forth on this continent a new infant, dedicated to the proposition that all work and no play makes Frank a dull boy." Living only a few blocks from the beautiful old racetrack in Saratoga, Sullivan had an idyllic boyhood. At the age of ten he worked as a pump boy in the betting ring at the racetrack. "It was a swell job," Sullivan recalls, "easy hours, plenty to see, little to do, 10 to 15 bucks a day in tips and no income tax."

Sullivan's career as a journalist began at Saratoga Springs High School. As Sullivan tells it, in a gush of cliches: "My fate was sealed, my hash settled and my goose cooked when I was sixteen and the editor of the Saratoga Springs High School 'Recorder' accepted a story I wrote. The moment I saw those words in print I was done for." He worked as a cub reporter on *The Saratogian* until 1910, when he graduated from high school and departed for Cornell University. After graduating with a B.A. degree in 1914, Sullivan returned to *The Saratogian*, where he remained until he was drafted into the army in 1917. Summing up these early years, Sullivan said: "I am grateful I was born in 1892 and lived my first two decades in a peaceful time the world will not soon see again."

As if to signal the end of his own and the nation's youthful idyll brought about by World War I, Sullivan moved to New York City in 1919. Here he worked for the *Herald*, the *Evening Sun*, and the *World*, under such editors as William A. Willis, Keats Speed, and Herbert Bayard Swope. At the *World*, where he was hired in 1922, Sullivan became one of a galaxy of stars that included Franklin P. Adams, Walter Lippmann, Alexander Woollcott, Heywood Broun, Deems Taylor, and Laurence

Stallings. Although he was originally hired as a reporter and feature writer, Sullivan himself admits, "I was a lousy reporter but meant well. The motto at the World was, Never let Sullivan within a mile of a fact." Sullivan discovered his calling as a humorist in 1924 when he was writing a column a day on the Democratic Convention in New York. Finding himself one paragraph short, says Sullivan, "I simply added a paragraph about a fictitious old lady named Aunt Sarah Gallup, from Holcomb Landing near Ticonderoga, N.Y., who had saved her butter-and-egg money to come to the convention and root for Al Smith. To give the item piquancy I added that she was 104 years old." The next day several newspapers, along with the Associated Press, were attempting to locate Holcomb Landing and the whereabouts of the intrepid Sarah. This hoax, along with Sullivan's erroneous front-page obituary on a prominent woman, cinched his career as a humorist. It was an excellent obituary, wrote Sullivan: "There was nothing she could have taken exception to in that obit—except the statement that she was dead." Sullivan's editor, Bayard Swope, promptly transferred him from the news column to the humor column, where since the 1920s, his comic gift for turning simple facts into absurdist fantasies

Frank Sullivan

has become one of the benchmarks of Sullivan's style.

Aunt Sally Gallup, whose age was later increased to 287 years, is only one of the comic characters that Sullivan created while writing for the *World*. Others include the chandelier-swinging secretary, Miss Martha Hepplethwaite, and Joseph Twiggle, the fearless New York City street cleaner. By 1925, Sullivan was asked to fill in for Franklin P. Adams's extremely influential column, "The Conning Tower"; thereafter, he was given his own thrice-a-week column at the princely salary of $190 a week.

In January 1926, Sullivan also began contributing humorous pieces to the *New Yorker*, a magazine to which he would contribute for the rest of his life. When Harold Ross founded the *New Yorker* in 1925, he pledged himself and his columnists to standards of excellence: "It will be human. . . . It will hate bunk. . . . Its integrity will be above suspicion." These words exactly describe Sullivan's humor. His comic and unhackneyed treatment of the embattled self in a world gone mad with gadgetry and gimmickry gained him an impressive following among readers of the *World* and the *New Yorker* during the 1920s. In fact, the demand for Sullivan's humor was great enough to warrant the publication of several collections of his best pieces during the 1920s. *The Life and Times of Martha Hepplethwaite* appeared in 1926, followed by *The Adventures of an Oaf* in 1927 and *Innocent Bystanding* in 1928. With the exception of *The Adventures of an Oaf*, these volumes were published by Horace Liveright, who was a regular at the Hotel Algonquin but was never asked to join the Round Table.

The Life and Times of Martha Hepplethwaite opens with the adventures of the zany secretary and arctic explorer, who in 1918 was unearthed "a bit mildewed" from the buried family treasure by her father Colonel Hepplethwaite. The verbal and visual insanities of these pieces, which are similar to Marx Brothers slapstick, set the tone for the volume. Sullivan uses the antics of Hepplethwaite and her well-meaning boss as a vehicle for satirizing everything from high finance, industrial tycoons, war reparations, and machine technology to the new woman, Freud, and opium addiction. Some of the best pieces in the volume are in the form of personal anecdotes and letters, in which Sullivan speaks in the voice of a no-nonsense, city-dwelling Everyman who attempts to resist the depersonalization, conformity, isolation, and general discomforts of modern city life. In a comic effort to overcome loneliness, the Sullivan persona takes to answering junk mail. The most poignant of these letters sent into the void is one entitled "To Whom It May Concern." After months of searching for this elusive fellow, Sullivan discovers: "Nobody was concerned about me. People were mostly either (1) not concerned about anything or (2) they were concerned only about themselves." He concludes: "But I would—oh, how I would—like to meet you, to clasp your hand, to look into your friendly eye, to meet face to face One Who Might Be Concerned." In these pieces, where the lonely individual reaches out in protest against modern anonymity, is the darker side of Sullivan's humor—a side that would come more to the surface in the nostalgic blue mood of some of his later writings. His earliest reviewers were quick to note the more serious side of Sullivan's humor. Edwin Clark, writing for the *New York Times*, hailed Sullivan's humorous pieces as the modern equivalent of the meditative essay: Sullivan, he asserts, has "at least made us thoughtful, for humor can be a terribly serious thing, especially in large doses.... We have discovered that the essayists of today have taken refuge in the old adage that many a truth can be spoken in jest."

Innocent Bystanding contains a similar collection of humorous pieces culled from Sullivan's contributions to the *World* and the *New Yorker*. The volume opens with one of Sullivan's favorite sources of humor: a satire on literature and the conventions of literary publication. In a burlesque of literary acknowledgments, Sullivan thanks, among others, "the Acme Comma Company of Bayonne, N.J., for the commas used in the book." The remainder of the volume contains further humorous reflections on the American scene, with jabs taken at advertisers, financiers, and income tax; and another account of urban loneliness in the story of Beatrice Lillie, who receives visitors in the waiting room at Pennsylvania Station. Although one reviewer complained that Sullivan's humor was somewhat monotonous when taken in large doses, humorist Will Cuppy heaped praise upon the volume: "not to read Mr. Sullivan's books," he proclaimed, "is to argue yourself a menace to society and two-thirds Airedale."

The admiration of his readers and his fellow humorists notwithstanding, Sullivan sometimes complained of the drudgery of having to be humorous on command. In a letter to Will Cuppy in 1927, he complained: "I am so tired of dragging myself down to a newspaper office everyday to be funny on schedule, every hour on the hour, that I am thinking seriously about taking a course in bricklaying and earning an honest living.... The

last two years, since I was torn from a very comfortable, happy and cloistered sinecure as a reporter, have made a neurotic out of me." Nevertheless, Sullivan continued to brighten his readers' days with humorous accounts of American ways, and in 1931, Horace Liveright published another collection of his work, entitled *Broccoli and Old Lace*. Described by one *Saturday Review of Literature* critic as "the best slapstick satirist now writing," Sullivan continued to embroider fact with fantasy in pieces on everything from current events to the Vanderbilt family tree. Although the volume was generally well received, there is a certain strained quality in some of the pieces. One *New York Times* reviewer noted that "Mr. Sullivan belongs to the try, try again school, to the group which whips itself into a lather trying to be amusing."

If Sullivan's humor had begun to show the effects of attempting to be funny three times a week, that pressure was abruptly terminated in 1931 when the *World* closed down. Ironically, for all his complaints about the stultifying effects of the column, Sullivan ultimately came to see the close of the *World* as the close of a golden era, not only in his own life but in the life of the country. In "Thoughts Before the Undertaker Came," he nostalgically recalls: "I had eight and a half pleasant years on the *World*. I realize now what an Eden it was.... When I die I want to go wherever the *World* has gone, and work on it again." After 1931, Sullivan continued to work as a freelance writer, but he never again worked for a newspaper on a regular basis.

During the 1930s, Sullivan did most of his writing for the *New Yorker*. In December 1932, he contributed his first "Christmas Greetings, Friends!" poem to this magazine. The final couplet of his greeting for that year is indicative of the range and good-natured comedy of these greetings, which were continued until December 1974: "I greet you all *mes petits choux*, / I greet the whole goddam *Who's Who*." These Christmas greetings, in which Sullivan saluted personal friends and a cross section of American names in the news for the preceding year, became an eagerly awaited event at the *New Yorker*. Sometimes Sullivan's friends were offended if their names did not appear in his poem. At one point, Sullivan had to explain to playwright and screenwriter Nunnally Johnson that his name had not appeared in his Christmas greeting for that year because "your name doesn't rhyme with anything but Funnily."

Sullivan's continued following among American readers led to the publication in 1933 of *In One Ear*, a collection of some of the best pieces he had

Sullivan posing as Loyal Old Britches in an illustration for Corey Ford's Salt Water Taffy

written for the *New Yorker*, *Vanity Fair*, and *Harper's Bazaar*. Surprisingly, for a volume that appeared when the Depression was in full swing, there is only one piece on the depressed state of the American economy: a spoof on international finance entitled "Inflation for Ida." For the most part, Sullivan continues his wide-eyed delight in the lunacy of American life, with satirical pieces on Southerners, gangsters, Hollywood, and the opera. The volume also includes one of Sullivan's earliest spoofs on travel and travel literature by his nonvoyaging travel expert, "who has never been ten miles from land but who has seagoing friends who talk to him constantly of their voyages." Sullivan was well known for his own travel phobia; he only ventured out of New York once, on a trip to St. Louis, and on that trip he had to be accompanied by a nurse. He once confided to Marc Connelly that he was still hoping to go abroad: "Every day I'm stepping over larger puddles." His use of the nonvoyaging travel expert in several satirical pieces is a good example of the way Sullivan could turn his own personal phobias to humorous account.

In One Ear contains some of Sullivan's best work. In "Life Is a Bowl of Eugene O'Neills," Sullivan pokes fun at the mixture of sex, despair, melodrama, and amateur psychology in such currently fashionable O'Neill plays as *Mourning Becomes Electra*. In another literary burlesque, "One Year Later," Sullivan writes a mock epilogue to D. H. Lawrence's *Lady Chatterley's Lover*. And in "Yvonne," a masterful sketch on New York City street noise, Sullivan frantically plots ways to silence a little girl who stands on the corner of Beekman Place every afternoon at 3 P.M. and screams for Yvonne. So powerful was its appeal to all those who had ever suffered from street noise that the sketch inspired a response from actress Patricia Collinge entitled "Yvonnesong: an open letter to Frank Sullivan from another resident of Beckman Place, who has suffered too."

Sullivan was increasingly ill at ease with modern city life. In 1935, he returned to Saratoga Springs, where, except for occasional trips to New York City, he spent the remainder of his life in the family home at 135 Lincoln Avenue. "A small town is the place to live," he said. "I live in a small town 180 miles from New York and while I would not say it has New York beat by a mile I *would* put the distance as six furlongs."

From Saratoga in the late 1930s, Sullivan continued to contribute humorous pieces to the *New Yorker*, *Good Housekeeping*, the *Saturday Evening Post*, and *Town and Country*. Several of these pieces were collected in *A Pearl in Every Oyster*, which appeared in 1938; in 1939, a similar collection of his work, *Sullivan at Bay*, was published in London for British audiences. In these volumes, Sullivan tends to repeat himself with pieces on such old favorites as income tax, psychology, Hollywood, and the discomforts of city life. Occasionally, however, his humor hits the mark, as in "Proust and the Life Sentence," which is one of Sullivan's most memorable literary satires. Proust, Sullivan tells us, "is the inventor of the perfected Life Sentence. When the average writer starts to produce a sentence he just throws a subject and a predicate into a bag, gets aboard, and is at his destination in no time. But when Proust started out on a sentence, all the verbs kissed their families good-bye and took along their heavy underwear."

The best feature of both volumes is the inclusion of several pieces on Mr. Arbuthnot, the cliche expert whom Sullivan had invented around 1934 and who, along with Sullivan's annual Christmas poem, became an honored institution at the *New Yorker*. The name Arbuthnot probably represents a nod in the direction of eighteenth-century physician and wit Dr. Arbuthnot, who was a friend of Swift and Pope, and who was a member of another famous group of satirists, the Martin Scriblerus Club. In courtroom-style cross-examination sessions, Sullivan's cliche expert takes the stand against trite and hackneyed expression in subjects ranging from literary criticism, love, and war to baseball, gastronomy, and Roosevelt haters. One of his earliest pieces, "The Busy Cliché Expert," contains the following exchange: "Q: Mr. Arbuthnot, as an expert in the use of the cliche, you are a pretty busy man, aren't you? . . . A: Yes. At least once every day I have to beard the lion, keep the wolf from the door, let the cat out of the bag, take the bull by the horns, count my chickens before they are hatched, shoe the wild mare, and see that the horse isn't put behind the cart or stolen before I lock the barn door. You'd think I'd be rather fed up on dumb animals by this time, wouldn't you?" In this and other testimonies of Mr. Arbuthnot, Sullivan makes us aware of the way thought and expression can be trapped in cliche and the conventions of language. These cliche-expert pieces are among Sullivan's best and most enduring contributions to American humor, and, if the response of the critics is any measure of their effectiveness, they hit their mark: his reviewers sometimes find themselves tongue-tied for fear of lapsing into their usual battery of ready-made cliches.

Several of the humorous pieces that Sullivan contributed during World War II to publications such as *Atlantic Monthly*, *Good Housekeeping*, *Harper's Magazine*, the *New Yorker*, *PM*, and *Ladies' Home Journal* were collected in *A Rock in Every Snowball*, which appeared in 1946. Although Sullivan makes few direct allusions to the war itself, he does sound a new note of nostalgia. Once again, Sullivan is at his best as a satirist of contemporary manners, with the title suggesting the hard truth at the core of jest. The volume contains pieces on such subjects as "Lawyer's Lingo," "Can Ban Gluts Bean Bins," "How to Change a Typewriter Ribbon," "The Leaking Sandwich," "Jay Talking," and "The Rape of the Grape." There are several more sessions with the cliche expert, who this time takes the stand on such subjects as the atom, political jargon, yuletide, and ill health. One of the finest pieces in the volume is the delightful spoof of literary footnoting, "A Garland of Ibids for Van Wyck Brooks." In this mock review of Van Wyck Brooks's *New England's Indian Summer*, Sullivan allows his footnotes to outnumber his text by three to one; he reduces the conventions of literary documentation to inspired

insanity, and ends by yelling back at his own footnotes. *A Rock in Every Snowball* (1946) was widely and favorably reviewed by the critics, although *Saturday Review* critic James P. Wood complained of "the sentiment and avuncular impishness in some of the more serious offerings, especially those in which the author yearns toward children and childhood or reminisces nostalgically of Manhattan."

Nostalgia became the keynote of Sullivan's writings during the 1950s. Looking back over his life up to that time, he observed: "Since I reached voting age I have survived three wars (two hot, one cold, none ended) and one depression (hot) and am still here, on guard with my little wooden sword against whatever lies around the corner." Sullivan continued to brandish his wooden sword in occasional contributions to such magazines as the *New Yorker*, *Good Housekeeping*, and the *New York Times Magazine*, but he increasingly came to view himself as part of a dwindling breed of American humorists whose heyday had been in the 1920s. In an article entitled "Well, There's No Harm in Laughing," Sullivan lamented the dearth of American humorists in the 1950s: "It is not difficult to understand any reluctance a young writer might feel toward undertaking the writing of carefree humor today. In the Nineteen Twenties the atom was known intimately to only a few scientists. . . . In those days humorists about to be humorous were not in danger of being stopped dead in their tracks by coming across a photograph of Gromyko or Senator McCarthy. . . . There was plenty wrong with the Nineteen Twenties but from here they seem halcyon. The present mood, to alter a well-known definition of poetry, is one of tranquility recollected in emotion, the emotion being nostalgia." In the postwar world of the atom bomb, the cold war, McCarthyism, and widespread malaise among writers, Sullivan's brand of gentle humor, his wooden sword, seemed somehow obsolete.

His next collection of writings, entitled appropriately *The Night the Old Nostalgia Burned Down*, was published in 1953. The volume includes further adventures with such old favorites as Aunt Sally Gallup and Mr. Arbuthnot, as well as a clever spoof of the music world, "The Forgotten Bach," about a Bach who is tone deaf. But the main theme of the volume is nostalgia. There are pieces on Sullivan's days as a pump boy at the Saratoga racetrack, his affection for his hometown street, his regret over the passing of such small-town institutions as front porches and haunted houses, and his relationship with a little boy next door named Butch. The difference between these pieces and Sullivan's earlier satiric sketches is like the differences between the comedy of Buster Keaton and Charlie Chaplin: the former appeals to the head whereas the latter appeals to the heart.

The nostalgia becomes double-edged in the title piece, "The Night the Old Nostalgia Burned Down." Here Sullivan works the nostalgic vein to the point of literary parody: "Well, that was New York, the old New York, the New York of gaslit streets, and sparrows (and, of course, horses), and cobblestones. The newsboy rolled the *Youth's Companion* into a missile and threw it on your front stoop and the postmen wore uniforms of pink velvet and made a point of bringing everybody a letter every day." Once again, Sullivan is the butt of his own humor. As if Mr. Arbuthnot has caught him in the act of cliched expression, Sullivan mocks the very genre of nostalgic recollection he has been practicing throughout the volume.

Despite Sullivan's note of nostalgia and his fears about the plight of the humorist in the postwar world, the critics judged *The Night the Old Nostalgia Burned Down* to be Sullivan at his best. "One of the toughest, most tortuous jobs around these days is writing humor," observed Bernard Kalb in the *Saturday Review*. "Only a few have ever managed to locate the nation's funnybone, and of those a gent who hasn't stopped being humorous for decades is Frank Sullivan."

Unfortunately, Sullivan's humorous decades were drawing to a close. *Sullivan Bites News*, a slim volume of thirty-five "perverse news items" illustrated by Sam Berman, appeared in 1954. After that, Sullivan published only one other book, a children's story entitled *A Moose in the Hoose*, which was brought out in time for Christmas in 1959; the book is dedicated to his good friends playwright Russell Crouse, his wife, Anna, and their children. The story, which is superbly illustrated by George Price, involves a showdown between a mouse named Pomeroy and a moose named Murphy over who will play the part of the "un-stirring" mouse in the Creevy family's reading of "A Visit from St. Nicholas." Although the book received favorable notices from the critics, sales were not good.

Faced with a declining demand for his work, as well as a decline in personal health and energy, Sullivan retired completely to Saratoga Springs in the 1960s, with not even an occasional trip to New York City. Having never married, Sullivan lived his last years alone. He cultivated his garden, attended the races twice a week, frequented the local pub, and received occasional visits from his New York friends. Sullivan continued to contribute his annual

Christmas poem to the *New Yorker* and from time to time he wrote a magazine piece, but his literary output was slight during the 1960s and 1970s. Constantly hounded by his friends to produce more, Sullivan remained firm in his conviction that his days as a humorist were over. "Under separate cover, if any," he wrote to Groucho Marx in 1967, "I am not sending you a copy of the book I did not write last year or the year before, just to make you quit saying I should write more." In fact, Sullivan's

"Pomeroy stares down Murphy," illustration by George Price for A Moose in the Hoose

lengthy epistles to his friends became, in his final years, his main link with the outside world and the main vehicle for his still lively sense of humor. "In my time," said Sullivan, "I have inundated my friends with long screeds, and I guess it was because I sequestered myself up here and letters were the only way to keep in touch with the loved ones."

In 1970, George Oppenheimer edited several of Sullivan's letters and humorous pieces in a volume entitled *Frank Sullivan Through the Looking Glass* (republished in 1972 as *Well, There's No Harm in Laughing*). The collection was put together as a literary tribute to Sullivan from his appreciative friends. In the introduction, playwright Marc Connelly comments on Sullivan's prolific letter writing: "Getting a letter from Sullivan makes any morning a sunny one. This is because Sullivan is one of this

Frank Sullivan in his study

century's most engaging humorists and it's impossible for him to write a letter that doesn't have his talent and affection in it. . . . Sullivan has thousands of friends and if statistics were available, I'd bet they would show that during an average day Sullivan writes a letter every eighteen minutes." In the afterword, Oppenheimer, who was Sullivan's publisher at Viking Press, says: "This has been a labor of love—love of the material and of the man who supplied it." The labor of love began in the 1940s with Alexander Woollcott, who originally had the idea of collecting Sullivan's letters; Woollcott died before the project was completed.

Oppenheimer's collection contains Sullivan's letters to such figures as Edna Ferber, Harold Ross, Alexander Woollcott, Margaret Leech Pulitzer, Russel Crouse, Will Cuppy, Nunnally Johnson, Groucho Marx, James Thurber, and Thornton Wilder. These bright, witty, affectionate letters, signed by such aliases as Liberace, Arthur Wing Pinero, and Lionel Strongfort, reveal a Sullivan who even in his seventies has lost none of his powers as a raconteur. To author Joseph Bryan, he writes in 1963: "I must report on Sue, a four-year-old, who was visiting kinfolk next door. I presented her with

a copy of A Moose in the Hoose, a marvellous children's book I wrote but which because of the machinations of the capitalist imperialists never got the kudos nor brought in the cash I had expected. Sue said, 'Did you print this book all by yourself?' I said I did. She pondered this for a moment. Then: 'I didn't know old men could print.' "

Sullivan's last Christmas greeting appeared in the *New Yorker* in 1974. Looking back over the course his greetings had traveled, Sullivan may have suspected that this would be his last missive to the world:

These greetings started in '32,
When times were tough—but we muddled
through.
Today our frights are all redoubled,
But courage, friends, keep hearts untroubled.

Why, hardly a prophet is now alive
Who thought we'd make it to '75.
Take hope from the Star! Our course is
clear—
Full muddle ahead through the coming year!

For Sullivan, the coming year brought rapidly declining health. He was hospitalized in December 1975 for an intestinal ailment and died on 19 February 1976.

Sullivan's death marked the end of an era in American humor. He was the last of the old school of humorists, which included George Ade, Robert Benchley, Will Cuppy, Will Rogers, Ring Lardner, Booth Tarkington, and Stephen Leacock. Although Sullivan is not as well known as some of these humorists, his work spans a longer period of time, from his heyday in the 1920s and 1930s to his years in the 1960s and 1970s as the Sage of Saratoga. Saddened in his later years by the dearth of American humorists, Sullivan never gave up his belief in humor as a weapon against and a purge for the less smiling sides of life. Asked what a practicing humorist should do, Sullivan said: "Seek out the foibles of his times and hold them up to gentle ridicule. He should provoke laughter, but never forget that mirth has a serious side. . . . In its own merry way, humor tells a dreadful truth." Gentle ridicule that tells a serious truth: this is the main quality of Sullivan's humor. He occasionally lapsed into cliched sentiment, but at his best Sullivan was a champion of common sense and the triumph of the individual over the pretense and nonsense, conformity and automatism of modern life.

Other:

Jimmy Cannon, *The Sergeant Says*, edited by Sullivan (New York: Knopf, 1943);

Robert Benchley, *Chips Off the Old Benchley*, introduction by Sullivan (New York: Harper, 1949).

References:

Margaret Case Harriman, *The Vicious Circle: The Story of the Algonquin Round Table* (New York: Rinehart, 1951);

John K. Hutchens, "The Happy Essence of Frank Sullivan," *Saturday Review*, 53 (12 September 1970): 88-89;

Dale Kramer, *Ross and The New Yorker* (Garden City: Doubleday, 1951).

William Tappan Thompson
(Major Joseph Jones)
(31 August 1812-24 March 1882)

Paul R. Lilly, Jr.
State University of New York College at Oneonta

SELECTED BOOKS: *Major Jones's Courtship: Detailed, with Other Scenes, Incidents and Adventures, in a Series of Letters, by Himself* (Madison, Ga.: C. R. Hanleiter, 1843; augmented, Philadelphia: Carey & Hart, 1844; revised and augmented, New York: Appleton, 1872);

Chronicles of Pineville: Embracing Sketches of Georgia Scenes, Incidents, and Characters (Philadelphia: Carey & Hart, 1845);

John's Alive; Or, The Bride of a Ghost (Baltimore: Taylor, Wilde, 1846);

Major Jones's Sketches of Travel, Comprising the Scenes, Incidents, and Adventures in His Tour from Georgia to Canada (Philadelphia: Carey & Hart, 1848);

Major Jones's Courtship; or Adventures of a Christmas Eve: A Domestic Comedy in Two Acts (Savannah: E. J. Purse, 1850);

Rancy Cottem's Courtship. Detailed, with Other Humorous Sketches and Adventures (Philadelphia: T. B. Peterson & Brothers, 1879).

William Tappan Thompson's contribution to American humor consists of his creation of the character Major Joseph Jones, a whimsical, vernacular-speaking, upper-middle-class planter from Pineville, Georgia, who is in turn buffoon and wise man. The voice of Major Jones first appeared in 1842 in a series of letters to Thompson himself, then editing a newspaper in Macon, and the best of these letters continue through two collections, *Major Jones's Courtship* (1843), the most popular of Thompson's books, and *Major Jones's Sketches of Travel* (1848). Thompson's humor reflects his Whig-minded views of society, and Major Jones, who names his first son Henry Clay, embodies those values. In *Major Jones's Sketches of Travel*, the congenial tone of the Pineville letters darkens somewhat as Jones travels through the North confronting evidence of abolitionists.

Thompson was born in Ravenna, Ohio. Both his parents, David, a Virginian, and Catharine Kerney, were dead by the time he was fourteen, and he turned up as a teenage staff member of the *Philadelphia Daily Chronicle*. In 1830 he was named private secretary to James D. Wescott, Secretary of the Territory of Florida. Thompson traveled to Tallahassee, where he studied law in Wescott's office, and picked up stories and character sketches by keeping his eyes open in this bustling frontier town. He moved to Augusta, Georgia, in 1834 and shortly after became associated with Augustus Baldwin Longstreet, the future author of *Georgia Scenes* (1835). Thompson studied law in Judge Longstreet's office, then assisted Longstreet with the publication of the *State Rights Sentinel*, a paper Longstreet had acquired in 1834. Thompson was present at the publication of Longstreet's *Georgia Scenes* by the *Sentinel* press, and he was an enthusiastic supporter of Longstreet's writing and political views his whole life. Years later, when Thompson had established a name for himself as the author of the Major Jones books, he complimented his mentor in a sketch called "Boss Ankles": "many a scene occurred about the store door which would have afforded ample field for the graphic pen of the popular sketcher of 'Georgia Scenes and Characters.'" When Longstreet gave up the *Sentinel* in 1836 Thompson signed up with a militia unit called "The Richmond Blues" and went to Florida to campaign against the Seminole Indians. He returned to Augusta in 1837, married Caroline Amour Carrie in June of that year, and reentered the world of journalism.

In 1838 Thompson founded the semimonthly magazine, the *Augusta Mirror*, and by 1840 had his old friend, the now famous Longstreet, contributing sketches. About this time Edgar Allan Poe called Thompson's *Mirror* "a neatly printed and well-edited" journal. Thompson's own prospectus for his magazine reveals his high hopes for its role in enhancing Southern culture. The *Mirror* would be "a semi-monthly journal devoted to the development of our domestic literature; containing contributions from many of the most popular writers of the South," including "every other subject in the range of polite literature." Thompson sprinkled the issues with his own sketches, some of which described his not-so-polite soldiering days in the swamps of Florida.

In spring 1842 Thompson merged his journal with the *Family Companion and Ladies' Mirror* in Macon, owned by Benjamin Griffin and edited by his wife Sarah. Thompson and Mrs. Griffin were not compatible editors, and Thompson left in August 1842, a few weeks after the first Major Jones letters began appearing anonymously in Griffin's journal. Thompson took over as editor of the *Southern Miscellany* in August 1842, and stayed until February 1844. The rest of what became the first edition of *Major Jones's Courtship* appeared here. The book was a local success, but Thompson so underestimated its wider appeal that he agreed to have it republished in 1844 by the Philadelphia firm of Carey and Hart for the royalty of five cents a copy, which yielded him $750 for the first year. He then sold the copyright to the firm for $250. Years later (1866) he described the transaction to a friend: "Had they [Carey and Hart] asked me for the Mss., I would have freely given it them, so little confidence had I in the success of the book. . . . I have the best assurances that if I had retained the copyright it would have yielded at least $2500 at 5 cts. a copy yearly to the present time."

The second edition of *Major Jones's Courtship* was published in 1844 with twelve illustrations by F. O. C. Darley, each depicting Major Jones in top hat, cravat, waistcoat, and tails. Major Jones's getup was in fact similar to that of another Major who emerged from newspaper letters, Seba Smith's Jack Downing. Smith's bumbling but congenial Yankee was a model for the homespun wit and semiliterate, picturesque speech of Major Jones. Fifteen thousand copies of this edition of *Major Jones's Courtship* were sold that year.

Major Jones by F. O. C. Darley

Thompson's apprenticeship to the Longstreet of *Georgia Scenes* is also evident; what is different is the format. Instead of the frame tale, which provided Longstreet with a discreet distance between the refined narrator and the uncouth rustics, Jones rambles on in his colorful Georgia dialect, allowing Thompson to keep the reader's attention on the homely virtues of the Pineville community. One letter, "Major Jones Pops the Question," typifies the good-natured humor Thompson's readers found so appealing. Jones wants to ask Mary Stallins for her hand, but he is "skeered and fainty" at the prospect, and so contrives to present Mary with a

Christmas gift "to keep all your life, but it would take a two bushel bag to hold it." Mary agrees to keep whatever gift she finds, so Jones crawls inside the burlap bag Mary hangs up from the porch before going to bed. Jones fights off the cold ("thar I sot with my teeth ratlin like I had a ager") and a curious hound ("I spected every minit he'd nip me, and what made it worse, I didn't know whar bouts he'd take hold"), but when Mary finds the Major in the bag the next morning, she vows to keep her gift for life. "I tell you what," confides Jones, "it was worth hangin' in a meal bag from one Crismas to another to feel as happy as I have ever since."

The succeeding letters cover a period of two years; the Major recounts tricks played on Cousin Pete ("and the fust thing he knowd, kerslosh he went, rite into a big tub full of cold water"), his marriage to Mary, and the birth of his son, Henry Clay Jones. The parlor games, courting rites, pratfalls, and tricks Jones describes caught on so quickly with his readers that Thompson readied another collection of his sketches for publication.

In 1844 Thompson left the *Southern Miscellany* and returned to Augusta with his growing family. (Eventually the Thompsons had ten children, four of whom lived to adulthood.) The new collection, *Chronicles of Pineville* (1845), was much closer in format to Longstreet's *Georgia Scenes*. In his introduction Thompson noted that his "humble attempt" to depict in *Major Jones's Courtship* "some of the peculiar features of the Georgia backwoodsman" had been received with favor. "Influenced by these persuasions, I determined to brush up my old manuscripts, produce something new of the same sort, and thus endeavor to present to the public a few more interesting specimens of the genus 'Cracker.'" As Longstreet did, Thompson claimed he wanted to record a historical phenomenon rapidly changing because of the growth of civilization. "The vagabond and the dissolute among them [the Crackers] are only the exceptions to the rule, and in a few generations more, education will have made the mass a great people." The first sketch, "Great Attraction! or, the Doctor most oudaciously tuck in," is a satire not on the Georgia Cracker but on a pompous social climber, a Doctor who trades in his "Kentucky-jeans and thick-soled shoes" for a "shining blue cloth coat of the latest cut" and a pair of "stilt-heeled boots." The Doctor's training is superficial even by frontier standards. "He had attended one course of lectures at Augusta, and returned to his native village, rich in all the polish and refinement which a winter's residence in that Philadelphia of the south affords such ample opportunities for acquiring." The Doctor attends a circus and is outraged when a seemingly genuine Cracker, Joe Peters from Cracker's Neck, interrupts the horse show and picks a fight with a clown. The Doctor rushes to the rescue, but Joe thrusts his head between the Doctor's legs, raises him off the ground, then tosses him "pell mell on the heads of the negroes"—to the delight of the crowd. As it turns out, Joe Peters is part of the show and can ride the circus horse better than the clown. First the Doctor is fooled, then the circus audience, finally the reader. The scene looks forward to Mark Twain's treatment of Huck Finn at a circus in which a horse act is interrupted by a drunk who also turns out to be part of the show.

Thompson's satire in *Chronicles of Pineville* is corrective; the Doctor is humbled in front of his equals and deserves his comeuppance. In the sketch "Boss Ankles," Thompson describes the plight of a real Cracker. Thompson, like Longstreet before him, looks back on a Georgia that has changed; Pineville, he says, was a "very different sort of place," even less refined than the present Pineville. In the old days, Thompson continues, the country bumpkins who hung around the grocery all day sampling Mr. Harley's liquor were transformed from sleepy-eyed loafers to ring-tailed roarers. "Then, too, might be seen the torpid clay-eater, his bloated, watery countenance illuminated by the exhilaring qualities of Mr. Harley's rum, as he closed in with his antagonist, and showed by his performances that he could eat clay as well in its animate as in its inanimate form." Thompson's clay-eater is reminiscent of Longstreet's own clay-eating Ransy Sniffle. But Boss Ankles is more of a fool than the conniving Ransy. Boss is regarded by his neighbors as a "monstrous ugly varmint," and, like the Doctor, he pretends to a higher status, "basing his claim to consideration on the grounds of his being a 'school-keeper' and a professor of music." Boss, then, is fair game for the series of pranks that restore the proper social order. First Boss is treated by his friends with explosive cigars, and then he is nearly blown up by some gunpowder stored in his pocket. At the end of the sketch, the recovered Boss swears "over a sample of Mr. Harley's best" that he will not permit himself again to be "blowed up with a sky-racket." The rest of *Chronicles of Pineville* describes similar pranks played on overreachers, boasters, and blowhards. The character Major Jones appears only in the sketch "The Mystery Revealed," and contributes little to the heavy-handed plot that involves two men disguised as women. Aside from Boss Ankles, Thompson's most

interesting character is humpbacked Sammy Stonestreet, whose oversized head forms "a perfect chaos of phrenological developments—a mental Alps, with promontories and peaks, ravines and valleys, utterly defying anything like scientific exploration or systematic measurement." Sammy, like Longstreet's Ransy Sniffle, is happy only when he is at the center of chaos, and he eagerly urges the townsfolk to chase after a wagon driven by two women who, Sammy is sure, are not only men but robbers.

The tales of *Chronicles of Pineville* lack the immediacy of Major Jones's voice. The formal language sounds forced and hastily composed, and the sketches are filled with apologies about the slipshod direction of the narration. ("But our business now is not with the militia muster, or Boss's musical powers.")

The year after the publication of *Chronicles of Pineville*, Thompson moved to Baltimore to join Park Benjamin in the editorship of still another newspaper, this one called the *Western Continent*. Thompson arranged for publication in his paper of a series of letters written by his old friend, Longstreet, which attacked Massachusetts. According to Longstreet, this state was responsible for "most of the ills of an otherwise happy nation." Thompson wrote an introduction to the letters and then published them under the title *A Voice from the South* (1847). He also used the *Western Continent* to

Darley illustration for Thompson's second collection, Chronicles of Pineville

continue his Major Jones letters. Returning to the epistolary format, Thompson began a series called "Major Jones on his Travels," later collected as *Major Jones's Sketches of Travel*. Once again, Major Jones writes letters to Thompson, this time not only from Pineville but from some of the northern cities Thompson had himself recently visited—Washington, Baltimore, Philadelphia, and New York. The Philadelphia firm of Carey and Hart published the book, with eight illustrations by Darley.

The revival of Major Jones's voice gave Thompson's prose a decided advantage over *Chronicles of Pineville*. We hear in the preface not the self-conscious Thompson but Jones himself: "Reader, do you feel like gwine on a jurny to the north!" When the Major claims he wants to see the people of the North whom he has heard are "so monstrous smart and religious and refined," he sets the theme of the book—the contrast between the rapacious, abolitionist North and the simpler, more traditional South. Even before the Major leaves Pineville, the abolitionists spoil the trip: a neighbor, Mr. Mountgomery, warns Jones that the New York abolitionists will free his slave, Prissy. Upon hearing this, Prissy refuses to leave the plantation: "I aint gwine to no New York, for dem pison ole bobolitionists to cotch me." Without Prissy, Mary, Jones's wife, declines to go, so he must travel alone. The Major kisses his womenfolk good-bye, but balks at his mother-in-law: "I always did hate to kiss old wimmin what hain't got no teeth, and I was monstrous glad old Miss Stallins had her handkerchief to her face." Jones's next letter describes his journey by train and boat to Charleston, and the sea voyage to Washington. His travel commentary is a combination of shrewd observation and comic speech. He sees windmills in Wilmington, North Carolina, and guesses there are "enuff to lick all the Don Quicksots in Spain." When he reaches Washington, he is struck by the art work in the Capitol rotunda: "Over the doors ther is some sculptures representin William Penn swindlin the Ingins out of ther land, and Columbus cumin ashore in his boat, and old Danel Boon killin off the aborignees with a butcher knife, and other subjects more or less flatterin to the national character."

Like Jack Downing before him, Major Jones drops in to chat with the president, who, unfortunately, is attending a cabinet meeting. But the servant welcomes Jones, and says he knows all about him—from reading *Jones's Courtship*. Later in Philadelphia the Major is impressed by the city but leery of the Quakers—"the stiffest, starchiest,

mealy-mouthed lookin people I ever seed." Although he concedes the Quakers are "monstrous good people," they nevertheless "meddle with what don't consarn em, and keep all the time botherin the Southern people 'bout their niggers." More typical of Thompson's humor is letter 12 from "Filladelfy" in which he describes his first night at an opera. "Then the opery commenced, but for the soul of me I couldn't hardly make out hed nor tail to it, though I listened at 'em with all my ears, eyes, mouth, and nose." But the Major is not impressed. "But to sing evry thing, so that a character can't say, 'Come to supper, your excellency!' without bawlin out—'Co-ho-ho-me to-oo-oo sup-up-up-e-e-er, you-r-r ex-cel-len-cy,' with about five hundred dimmy-simmy quivers, so nobody can't tell whether he was called to supper, or whether he was told that his daddy was ded, is all nonsense." In the same letter, Thompson switches the mood of comic debunking of highbrow tastes to bitter commentary on the status of free blacks in the North. He walks through a local ghetto and is upset at seeing how the "free niggers" live: "You couldn't hardly tell the men from the wimmin for ther rags; and many of 'em was diseased and bloated up like frogs, and lay sprawlin about like so many cooters in a mud-hole, with ther red eyes peepin out of ther dark rooms and cellars like lizards in a pile of rotten logs. This, thinks I, is nigger freedom; this is the condition to which the filanthropists of the North wants to bring the happy black people of the South!" Here Thompson drops the comic mask in order to propagandize, but the piece does depict some of the grim ironies of the racial situation in America fifteen years before the Civil War.

Thompson by now saw Major Jones as something like a meal ticket. In 1848 he wrote a stage version called *Major Jones's Courtship; or Adventures of a Christmas Eve*, and the play had a successful run in Baltimore. In 1849 Thompson returned to Georgia to begin still another editorship of a newspaper, this one the *Savannah Daily Morning News*, which appeared in 1850. Thompson continued as editor—except for a short time in 1864 when he left the city to join the Confederate forces trying to hold off Sherman—until his death in 1882. After the war he made plans to continue the Major Jones saga in the *Morning News* by sending Jones to Europe. Thompson traveled to Europe in 1867, and printed a number of the Major's letters in the *Morning News*, but he never completed the project.

Thompson's skill as a humorous writer is best represented by the letters of Major Jones. The most popular were from his first collection, and his best efforts after that were attempts to exploit what he sensed was a genuine creation—the garrulous, fumbling, "yearnest" and well-meaning Major whose colloquial voice supported the values of a society Thompson knew well: close family ties, community stability, respect for women, and, increasingly in the later letters, a strident defense of white supremacy. His inspiration was his friend, Judge Longstreet, but his stylistic model was Seba Smith's Jack Downing. Still, the figure of Major Jones is unique in Southern humorous writing. Those who came after Thompson were more likely to exploit the vernacular through the mouths of rascals and subversives, such as Johnson Jones Hooper's Simon Suggs and George Washington Harris's Sut Lovingood, than to use colloquial speech to support traditional values. Thompson's popularity continued after the Civil War and was given new life with the posthumous publication of the collection *John's Alive; Or, The Bride of a Ghost, and Other Sketches* (1883), but his work was out of print by the turn of the century.

With the revival of interest in Southwestern writing in the 1930s, Thompson's achievement was reassessed. Walter Blair in *Native American Humor* (1937) praises Thompson as a "capable story-teller" writing in the tradition of the Jack Downing letters. Jay Hubbell, summing up Thompson's significance in *The South in American Literature* (1954), claims that "Thompson's women characters receive more attention and are better drawn than those in most books by Southern humorists." Kenneth Lynn in *Mark Twain and Southwestern Humor* (1959) sees Thompson's "mean-spirited attacks" on blacks symptomatic of a "society morally on the defensive." Henning Cohen, in his anthology *Humor of the Old Southwest* (1964), thinks the problem with the character of Major Jones is that he is "almost too good." Jones's respectability, Cohen argues, "makes him much less interesting than many other figures from Southwestern humor." Hamlin Hill, in *America's Humor: From Poor Richard to Doonesbury* (1978) sizes up the world of Jones—especially in contrast to the world of Sut Lovingood and Simon Suggs—this way: "There are practical jokes and good-natured high-jinks in the Major's Pineville—but not an eye-gouging in his county." Somehow Pineville seems the less for that.

Other:

A Voice from the South, edited with an introduction by Thompson (Baltimore: Western Continent Press, 1847).

References:

George R. Ellison, "William Tappan Thompson and the Southern Miscellany, 1842-1844," *Mississippi Quarterly*, 23 (Spring 1970): 155-168;

Laura Doster Holbrook, "Georgia Scenes and Life in the Works of William Tappan Thompson," M.A. thesis, University of Georgia, 1967;

Henry Prentice Miller, "The Background and Significance of *Major Jones's Courtship*," *Georgia Historical Quarterly*, 30 (December 1946): 267-296;

Miller, "The Life and Works of William Tappan Thompson," Ph.D. dissertation, University of Chicago, 1942;

Carl R. Osthaus, "From the Old South to the New South: The Editorial Career of William Tappan Thompson of the *Savannah Morning News*," *Southern Quarterly*, 14 (April 1976): 237-260.

Mortimer Thomson
(Q. K. Philander Doesticks, P.B.)
(2 September 1831-25 June 1875)

David E. E. Sloane
University of New Haven

SELECTED BOOKS: *Doesticks: What He Says* (New York: Edward Livermore, 1855);

Plu-ri-bus-tah (New York: Livermore & Rudd, 1856);

The History and Records of the Elephant Club, by Thomson (as Doesticks) and Edward F. Underhill (as Knight Russ Ockside, M.D.) (New York: Livermore & Rudd, 1856);

Nothing to Say (New York: Rudd & Carleton, 1857);

The Witches of New York (New York: Rudd & Carleton, 1858);

The Great Auction Sale of Slaves at Savannah, Georgia (New York: American Anti-Slavery Society, 1859);

The Lady of the Lake (New York: French, 1860);

The Adventures of Snoozer, A Sleepwalker (New York: J. L. Winchell, 1876).

Noting the fate of Mortimer Thomson's reputation as a humorist, Mark Twain in reviewing a volume of seventy-eight humorists in 1906 commented that Doesticks wasn't even included in the "mortuary." Yet the *New York Herald*, at the time of Thomson's death in 1875, noted that during the zenith of his fame he was the "king of American humorists." A fragment of his letter describing a visit to Niagara Falls in 1854 appears occasionally in anthologies. His major works, however, lie almost totally forgotten although they offer brilliant examples of the witty irony of pre-Civil War literary comedians. Perhaps Doesticks is a casualty of the Civil War and the loss of two talented wives, events which caused Thomson to lose optimism and idealism. After a productive ten years as a humorist, diminishing literary powers caused him to write little besides regular newspaper copy and letters for the remainder of his career from the middle 1860s until his death.

Mortimer Neal Thomson was the elder of two sons born to Edwin and Sophia Thomson at Riga, New York, a town of 3,500 west of Rochester. His father was a lawyer and his mother had modest literary pretensions, occasionally writing under the pen name Rosamund. When Mortimer was ten years old, the family moved to Ann Arbor, Michigan. Family anecdotes suggest a relaxed family atmosphere. At the age of eighteen, in the fall of 1849, Thomson enrolled in the University of Michigan in the College of Literature, Science, and the Arts. After being suspended for one prank, he was expelled for maintaining his membership in the secret society Chi Psi; he did not return for the spring 1850 semester. The *New York Times* refers to his being dismissed for too much eagerness in getting specimens for dissection, although no other evidence exists for the story; but Thomson by his own admission conducted a number of college pranks.

Little is known of the period from 1850 through 1854 when Thomson made his appearance in New York City. During part of this time he traveled with a theatrical troupe. It was also during this period that he visited Niagara Falls, providing the experience for his first Doesticks sketch, which brought him immediately to national attention. At that time, in late summer 1854, he was a clerk in the Broadway jewelry store of Sackett, Davis, and Potter. By July 1855 he was reporting for Charles A. Dana's *New York Tribune*, where he wrote comic accounts of police-court items among his reports of other city news.

The rise of the Doesticks persona to fame was meteoric, from the publication of the first letter on Niagara, "Doesticks on a Bender," in the summer of 1854 to a two-page spread of the letters in the *New York Tribune* on 23 January 1855, a sellout issue reprinted two days later in the semiweekly issue of the same paper. The first Doesticks letters seem to have been sent to Mortimer's younger brother Clifford for publication in the *Detroit Advertiser*. By the end of May 1855 twenty-nine letters had appeared in the *Advertiser* and others had appeared in the *Daily Tribune* and the *Spirit of the Times*, according to Fletcher D. Slater, Thomson's biographer.

Most of these letters, covering a variety of contemporary topics from the burlesque viewpoint of a traveling naif, were collected in Thomson's first book, *Doesticks: What He Says* (1855). The *Times* in 1875 described the initial "Niagara" sketch as a

"Doesticks on a Bender"

"funny muddle of sense and nonsense with a ludicrous refrain about taking a glass of beer." Aside from the fact that the sketch brought Q. K. Philander Doesticks, P. B.—the Q. K. for queer kritter and the P. B. for perfect brick—to national prominence, it is important in treating a highly sentimentalized natural ideal with the skeptical realism of a drunken reporter whose feet are wet. The debunking voice of the antiidealist represents a new force in American literature in the 1850s.

Other sketches in the first Doesticks volume carried the same debunking spirit into varied areas of New York City life. Railroad travel, Barnum's Museum, boardinghouses, fortune-tellers, charity balls, and the Millerites are all featured. Among the funniest of the sketches, which also carry a social point, "Running with the 'Masheen' " describes how different fire companies battle on the way to fires, while houses burn; political patronage is burlesqued in " 'Lection Day—'Paddy' versus 'Sam' " and "Police Adventures." In "A City Target Excursion," Doesticks escapes the piles of manure in the municipal streets by joining in a drunken outing with "The Lager-Bier American Volunteers, and

Native Empire City Shillelagh Guards."

Slater reports that 7,500 copies of *Doesticks: What He Says* were sold on the first day and sales continued at 1,000 per day for some time. Both the *Times* and the *Tribune* made respectful notice of Doesticks's keen powers of observation, while warning that his strain of comedy could soon grow thin. By 1857 Rudd and Carleton had 35,000 copies of the book in print. T. B. Peterson, the Philadelphia publisher, republished the book in 1859 and reprinted it as late as 1870.

Thomson's second major work, *Plu-ri-bus-tah*, was published in May 1856 and included among the bound-in advertisements at the end notice of his third book, *The History and Records of the Elephant Club*. *Plu-ri-bus-tah* is a burlesque of Longfellow's *Hiawatha*, published in November 1855. Thomson sent a respectful letter to Longfellow with a copy of the book, which he described as a lame jest rather than an attempt at ridicule, and Longfellow is supposed to have responded that Thomson's poem seemed a natural one. Using the same trochaic meter which Longfellow had borrowed from the *Kalevala*, *Plu-ri-bus-tah* was a lengthy allegorical vulgarization of American history. The book's Puritan hero, Plu-ri-bus-tah, pushes aside all obstacles in pursuing the "dirty, filthy, greasy" but "Potent and 'ALMIGHTY DOLLAR.' " The Goddess Liberty does not notice that Plu-ri-bus-tah grovels "in sanctimonious Wall-street, / On the wharves beside the seashore / In the mud beside the seashore," accepting slavery by agreeing to "Keep him on his own plantations, / And [he] called it Mah-sun-dic-sun." Ultimately, the son of Plu-ri-bus-tah and Liberty, Yunga-Merrakah, a Broadway swell, is enslaved in turn by Cuffee and crushed by a giant dollar in a heap of America's rubble.

Plu-ri-bus-tah is an outstanding representative of the genre of literary comedy. Literary and historical personages are mixed incongruously with city dandies and allegorical figures. The political ethics surrounding slavery are a central issue, but social hypocrisy and greed are the center of concern. The natural, sublime, and ideal are consistently dragged down to the vulgar, "through the alleys of the city, / Where the smell of gas escaping, / And the odors of the gutters, . . . / *Don't* remind you of the country." Political and social life is consistent with a Jersey supplication: give us this day our daily stranger. The plot climaxes in a statement about the political and social dangers facing America. Thomson's other literary burlesque, *The Lady of the Lake* (1860), a play after Sir Walter Scott's 1810 poem, featured some 120 puns and was less successful. It

Frontispiece and title page for Thomson's first book

was produced at Niblo's Garden to indifferent critical response in summer 1860.

The History and Records of the Elephant Club, although the Livermore and Rudd edition is dated 1857, appeared in November 1856. Doesticks coauthored the book with "Knight Russ Ockside, M.D.," Edward Fitch Underhill. The book is an amalgam of items which Doesticks produced as police-court sketches for the *Tribune*, loosely strung together by Underhill to make a record of the doings of green visitors to the metropolis who intend to "see the elephant" in all of its various guises. In part the work may be a satire on the Progressive Union Club, a socialist experiment organized by Stephen Pear Andrews of New York.

New York, a "mass meeting of bricks and mortar," is the locus of the sketches offered in comic reportorial format. The objective of the burlesque "elephant" club is to study metropolitan life in Manhattan, the elephant. A Turkish smoking parlor is visited, and oyster eating and a fire alarm and a fight between competing fire companies are described. A mock interview turns up a "Hard Case," in the style of Joseph C. Neal, who brings stray dogs from New Jersey to New York pounds, where he sells them for the bounty. Railroad car travels and crashes and New York hotel experiences with the new gas lights are reported to the club. The record of a Northern Negro camp meeting shows a more reportorial and less dramatic style than Southern camp meetings recorded by Thomson's Southern contemporaries Johnson Jones Hooper and George Washington Harris. When a young girl dives into the arms of pious elders, the planned vice of the city rather than the randy hypocrisy of the country seems to be illustrated. A variety of petty cheats and neighborhood pranks are described, creating a comic panorama of city life in the 1850s.

The rage of 1857 was William Allan Butler's anonymous comic poem on ladies' fashions, "Nothing to Wear," which had appeared in *Harper's Weekly* and was republished in a 20,000-copy hardcover edition by Rudd and Carleton. Capitalizing on this tremendous success, George Carleton offered Thomson $1 per line for a burlesque of the poem. Thomson's response, titled *Nothing to Say* and supposedly written in a week, was

"Charity." Riding the Astor Place Car to the Cooper Institute, transported to the North Pole, and viewing the nurses of the sick in the contagious wards of Norfolk, Virginia, Cant has "nothing to say" about these holiest works of love. Thus, Thomson defends the rich as a source of charity against the satiric charge in Butler's poem. Although brief, the poem has many of the same strengths which Thomson had shown in *Plu-ri-bus-tah*, the sharpened use of

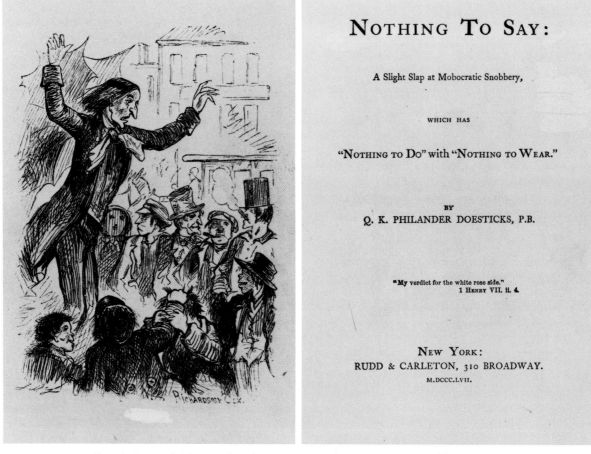

Frontispiece and title page for Thomson's satire of W. A. Butler's Nothing to Wear

305 lines long; joining a host of other burlesques, Thomson's was unusually successful, and he was paid $800. The two poems offer an interesting contrast in attitude toward wealth. Butler criticizes Miss Flora M'Flimsey for her large number of gowns and self-indulgent greed for more. Thomson's poem, however, is a social allegory in which he denies "That nowhere are found the true Christian graces, / Save closely allied to the dirtiest faces." A Miltonic devil, the "Spirit of Cant," is conducted on a tour of charities by a flashy city girl who is actually

slang and local scenery, the vulgarization of allegorical figures, and the clear statement of social meaning. *Graham's Magazine* called *Nothing to Say* a "manly and spirited defense" of the wealthy against absurd charges and implied that the poem showed an impressive new voice for Thomson. Unfortunately, it is the last significant verse that Thomson published.

In August 1857 Thomson became editor of the *New York Picayune*, a comic paper edited by T. W. Levison. The *Knickerbocker Magazine*, in reprinting his piece on garroting, had noted that he was publishing a sketch weekly in the spring of 1857, showing himself "a keen observer and clever caricaturist." He immediately expanded the *Picayune* to quarto size and attracted favorable attention, but appears to have withdrawn as editor late in the fall of 1858. The *Knickerbocker Magazine* in July 1858 favorably compared the paper with *Punch*.

In addition to his work on the *Picayune*, Thomson continued to report for the *Tribune*. In the late 1850s it was a crusading newspaper, and its reporters were noted for cavalier hats, beards and mustaches, high boots, and similar Cyrano effects. Pictures of Thomson show him in goatee and plaid beret. His own reporting included exposes of local frauds, stories on criminal types, and police-court news. In late 1858 he wrote theatrical reviews for the *Tribune* and was recognized for the high standards he set for theatrical performances. He frequented Pfaff's Cellar and was a member of the bohemian brigade which included Charles Farrar Browne, Charles G. Halpine, Frank Bellew, C. H. Webb, and Walt Whitman. He traveled to Canada with illustrator Thomas Nast of *Leslie's* to cover a major prizefight in the fall of 1858, and during this period he accepted other assignments for *Leslie's* with illustrators Nast and Sol Eytinge.

The Witches of New York was published in December 1858. It was composed of exposes of fortune-tellers which had appeared in the *Tribune* during the previous year. The investigative reporter supplies the frame for brief anecdotes and descriptions of women engaged in every imaginable crime from prostitution to infanticide. The "cash customer" pretends to seek information on a wife, a comic pretense which provides a strained continuity to the sketches. Although the whole series is a social critique, there is less generalized social irony than in other Doesticks works. The *Knickerbocker* attacked Thomson for not giving free vent to his humor and complained generally of the nonsense of Doesticks's later works, but at least found some merit in *The Witches of New York* as an expose of corruption.

Thomson's last major work was *The Great Auction Sale of Slaves at Savannah, Georgia*, written in March 1859 as a news story for the *Tribune*. On 2-3 March 436 slaves of Pierce M. Butler, a Philadelphian, were auctioned at Savannah, Georgia. Thomson, in disguise, covered the auction and wrote the story on the train north. It appeared on 9 March, causing that issue of the *Tribune* to sell out; the entire issue was reprinted two days later. Ac-

cording to Thomson's obituary in the *New York Herald*, the story rang through the North like an alarm, and its mixture of harsh irony, deadpan reportage, and sentiment was compelling. The story was reprinted, with minor deletions, in the *Times* (London) on 12 April. The whole account amounted to twenty-eight pages when reprinted as a book by the American Anti-Slavery Society. The book was respectfully reviewed by the *Atlantic Monthly*, which pointed to its clear, distinct, and eloquent style and noted the report as both a minute illustration of the phenomenon of a slave sale and an outstanding example of energetic American journalism.

"A Great Slave Auction" was presented by the *Tribune* under the heading of "American Civilization Illustrated," and its style as a social document is noteworthy. Into his detailed accounts of the auction, Thomson introduced a reportorial irony by including a number of melodramatic and sentimental vignettes about the rapacious planters and the pitiful slaves, numbered as lots, alternately acting as human beings and as merchandise. "Every shade of character capable of being implicated in the sale of human flesh and blood, was represented among the buyers," down to a red-faced Major who said that if the slave trade were reintroduced, he would have all the Negroes in America in three years and not leave enough in Africa for seed. Negroes were sold with their clothes, causing Thomson to remark, "In the North, we do not necessarily sell the harness with the horse: why, in the South, should the clothes go with the negro?" The most affecting sequences were developed around families and babies, but "The Love Story of Jeffrey and Dorcas" was overtly sentimental in its detailing of Jeffrey's attempts to interest his buyer in Dorcas, to whom he was engaged but not married, and the failure of his hopes when she came up in a family lot of four. The piece ends in a combination of sentimental nature description and outraged irony, with the refrain, "Mr. Pierce Butler gave each slave a dollar." As reportage in an ironic deadpan style of literary comedy, Thomson's "Great Slave Auction" was a literary event: the work had intrinsic literary interest and social impact. Although he lived until 1875, nothing Thomson wrote after this time shows such a combination of stylistic control and social concern.

More than any other potentially significant comedian of his era, Thomson was the victim of a series of catastrophes, both national and personal, which focused in the years from 1858 to 1864. On

23 October 1857 Thomson married sixteen-year-old Anna H. Van Cleve, the niece of a Yale professor. She died on 22 December 1858 while giving birth to a son, Marco. In May 1861 Thomson married Grace Eldridge; on 23 December 1862, two weeks after giving birth to a daughter, Ethel, Grace died of scarlet fever. These two shocking personal losses were subsumed in larger events of the Civil War, for Thomson was apparently early into the field with the troop of *Tribune* reporters. Several events of personal heroism are recorded by different sources, despite Thomson's status as a noncombatant. Perhaps even more important was an event unrecorded at the time; an almost spent shell, having already killed a Union officer, struck Thomson. Seemingly an insignificant wound, the impact of the shot cracked a rib; some time later, bone fragments were removed in a major operation conducted, inexplicably, without anesthesia. Already a heavy drinker, Thomson apparently became addicted to opium in an attempt to kill pain. He described his operation in a fugitive piece published in the December 1869 issue of *Hours at Home*, "Twenty Minutes Under the Knife."

Thomson's war reporting was most notable during the early period of the war. Throughout 1861 and 1862 Doesticks was publishing letters in the *New York Mercury*, regularly republished at the rate of about one a month in *Yankee Notions*. In the late 1850s, Thomson had developed friendships with many of the theatrical leaders of his day, and he wrote theatrical biographies for the *Tribune* toward the end of the war years. He began lecturing in 1859 and continued in 1863, reading specially prepared poems and commenting on "Pluck," "Cheek," and related qualities of personal energy. By the end of the Civil War, Thomson was connected with Street and Smith's *New York Weekly*, which prominently advertised him as a regular contributor along with Josh Billings, Max Adeler, and, less frequently, Mark Twain and John Quill, among others. The *Weekly* gave almost an entire page to humor and also offered large doses of melodrama and sentimental novels to a wide readership. Doesticks items appear from 1868 through 1876, more than a year after Thomson's death, but seemingly in his style to the end. When he corresponded with Mark Twain in 1870, he identified himself as storekeeper of a bonded warehouse for the Internal Revenue Department, evidence of a lowering of his literary fortunes.

The *New York Mercury* and *New York Weekly* columns were not reprinted as Doesticks's earlier work had been, and it might be argued that time had passed him by in 1859; however, his style changed significantly in these columns. As the columns progress, Doesticks the social critic with a quick, blunt style comes to write longer sentences dealing with less political-social topics and revolving more around problems of family life and the economic concerns of the middle class. He grapples occasionally with police kickbacks and political patronage, but the continuity of mood and the particularity of detail is weak. He becomes less a bohemian social critic and more a complainant on behalf of the established citizens. His fund of imagery and sharpness of phrase both are diminished.

Thomson spent a year in Minneapolis in 1872, joining his brother Clifford on the *Minneapolis Tribune*, but he returned, in significantly worse health, to New York City in 1873. His last two years were spent as an editor with *Leslie's Illustrated Magazine*. When he died, on 25 June 1875, he was buried from the Little Church Around the Corner, befitting his close connections to the New York theater, and was mourned by the New York press corps en masse. After Thomson's death *The Adventures of Snoozer, A Sleepwalker* (1876) was published as a comic pamphlet. Barely forty-seven pages with large illustrations, it was hardly a "culminating work" as Winchell, its publisher, claimed, although it did recapture some of Thomson's edge of social criticism in a burlesque of railroad stock manipulation by Jay Gould.

Franklin J. Meine, in the *Dictionary of American Biography*, succinctly describes Thomson as the Ring Lardner of his day: "he brought to American humor terse, vigorous, quick-moving phrases and vivid slang, and became the most popular humorist writing in the period before that of C. F. Browne." Nonetheless, a single master's thesis by Fletcher D. Slater in 1931, an article by J. L. Kuethe on Doesticks's extensive neologisms—first recorded appearances of city slang phrases—in *American Speech*, and a brief comparative essay on Doesticks and Twain's *Innocents Abroad* represent the sum of modern scholarship on Thomson.

Although contemporary literary historians accord Thomson only brief mention, a slightly different perspective on "the universal Yankee nation" could place Thomson among the most significant writers of American humor. His most important works show an unmatched ability to transform the vulgar details of city life into literary images with ironic social overtones. In an America which will have to make increasingly precise social decisions in an era of diminishing resources, many of his works offer a valuable opportunity for renewed study.

Play:

The Lady of the Lake, New York, Niblo's Garden, 21 June 1860.

References:

J. Louis Kuethe, "Q. K. Philander Doesticks, P. B., Neologist," *American Speech*, 12 (April 1937): 111-116;

Fred W. Lorch, " 'Doesticks' and *Innocents Abroad*," *American Literature*, 20 (January 1949): 446-449;

Obituary, *New York Daily Tribune*, 26 June 1875, p. 7;

Obituary, *New York Herald*, 26 June 1875, p. 10;

Obituary, *New York Times*, 26 June 1875, p. 5;

Review of *The Great Auction Sale of Slaves at Savannah, Georgia*, *Atlantic Monthly*, 4 (September 1859): 386-387;

Fletcher D. Slater, "The Life and Letters of Mortimer Thomson," M.A. thesis, Northwestern University, 1931;

George F. Williams, "When King Edward VII Visited New York," *Independent*, 54 (6 March 1902): 569-572.

Thomas Bangs Thorpe

Mark A. Keller
Middle Georgia College

See also the Thorpe entry in *DLB 3, Antebellum Writers in New York and the South*.

BIRTH: Westfield, Massachusetts, 1 March 1815, to Thomas and Rebecca Farnham Thorp.

MARRIAGE: 1838 to Anne Maria Hinckley; three children. 1857 to Jane Fosdick.

DEATH: New York, New York, 20 September 1878.

SELECTED BOOKS: *The Mysteries of the Backwoods; or Sketches of the Southwest: Including Character, Scenery, and Rural Sports* (Philadelphia: Carey & Hart, 1846);

Our Army on the Rio Grande (Philadelphia: Carey & Hart, 1846);

Our Army at Monterey (Philadelphia: Carey & Hart, 1847);

The Taylor Anecdote Book. Anecdotes and Letters of Zachary Taylor (New York: D. Appleton, 1848);

The Hive of 'The Bee-Hunter,' A Repository of Sketches, Including Peculiar American Character, Scenery, and Rural Sports (New York: D. Appleton, 1854);

The Master's House; A Tale of Southern Life, as Logan (New York: T. L. McElrath, 1854);

Reminiscences of Charles L. Elliott, Artist (New York: Evening Post, 1868).

By temperament and training an artist and an essayist, Thomas Bangs Thorpe is recognized as one of the best known of the antebellum humorists of the Old Southwest, a group of writers including, most prominently, George Washington Harris of Tennessee, Johnson Jones Hooper of Alabama, A. B. Longstreet of Georgia, and Henry Clay Lewis of Mississippi and Louisiana. Yet Thorpe's literary reputation is based mainly on two humorous sketches—"Tom Owen, the Bee-Hunter" and "The Big Bear of Arkansas." "Tom Owen, the Bee-Hunter" was perhaps the most popular single frontier humor sketch of the antebellum period, while "The Big Bear of Arkansas" is unquestionably considered to be the most famous Southwestern humor yarn produced by the aforementioned group of writers. Not only did "The Big Bear of Arkansas" provide the title for the most important anthology of native American humor published prior to the Civil War, but it also served as the basis for Bernard De Voto's creation of the term "the Big Bear School of Southern humor" to refer to the body of literature in the same tradition.

Thomas Bangs Thorpe (spelled "Thorp" before he began his publishing career) was born 1 March 1815, at Westfield, Massachusetts. He descended from the line of William Thorp, a bond servant—perhaps a political prisoner—who came from England sometime before 1639 and settled in New Haven, Connecticut, where he became a weaver. Thomas's grandfather was Elisha Thorp, a

Royalist freeman and innkeeper of St. John, New Brunswick. After Elisha's death his wife and seven children moved to Weston, Connecticut, around 1800.

Thorpe's father Thomas was born in 1792. At the age of sixteen, he converted to Methodism, and by 1814 he was a circuit-riding minister traveling in Connecticut and Massachusetts. He married Rebecca Farnham of West Springfield, Massachusetts, who had nursed him through one of his early bouts with tuberculosis, a disease that eventually took his life in January 1819. His wife was left with three children to raise—Alice, Richard Henry Sackville, and Thomas Bangs (Thomas's middle name came from Nathan Bangs, presiding Methodist elder of the church district in Westfield, Massachusetts, who may have baptized him).

In 1818 Thorpe's family had moved from Connecticut to New York, where his father had served the Allen Street Church. However, within a few months after her husband's death, Rebecca Thorp and her children moved to her family's home in Albany, New York, where her father was a whip maker by trade.

In Albany, Thorpe saw the paintings of the old Dutch masters and generally absorbed the Dutch culture offered by the city. He spent most of his boyhood summers in Connecticut with his paternal grandmother Sarah Wakeman Thorp (the widow of the Tory Elisha).

In the mid-1820s the Thorp family moved from Albany back to New York City. Thomas spent much of his time roaming the forests of Saratoga Lake and enjoying the scenery around the Hudson River. He later claimed to have known Washington Irving's *Sketch Book* and *Knickerbocker's History* by heart at this time. His experiences and interests as a youth directed him toward painting, a field that occupied his attention for much of his life.

About 1830 Thorpe began studying under John Quidor, an eccentric genius who was the only figure painter in New York City at that time. According to Thorpe's biographer Milton Rickels, Quidor influenced Thorpe's later art and writing through his appreciation of the comic and his fondness for Irving and through an artistic independence that ignored the prevailing taste of the period. At Quidor's studio, Thorpe also began a forty-year friendship with fellow art student Charles Loring Elliott.

By 1833 Thorpe had exhibited his first painting at the American Academy of Fine Arts—a genre piece, probably humorous, titled *Ichabod Crane*. During that year, Thorpe worked as a portrait painter out of the New York business location of his stepfather, Charles Albert Hinckley, a bookbinder and gilder from Maine whom Thorpe's mother had married in early 1832. After being thwarted in his desire to travel to Europe for further artistic training because of a lack of finances, nineteen-year-old Thomas enrolled in Wesleyan University in Middletown, Connecticut, in 1834.

Thorpe continued to paint while at Wesleyan, but the strict regimen of studies there no doubt limited those efforts. For example, in 1834-1835, Thorpe was enrolled in the Department of Mathematics, studying such subjects as algebra, geometry, Cambridge calculus, navigation, surveying, and astronomy; during the winter term of 1835-1836, he was enrolled in the Department of Moral Science and Belles Lettres, taking rhetoric, logic, criticism, political economy, and philosophy; in 1835-1836, he was also enrolled in the Department of Natural Science, which offered courses in chemistry, geology, mineralogy, and other subjects. Despite his time-consuming studies, however, Thorpe joined the Peithologian Society, one of three debating clubs at Wesleyan. He also made many friends, notably Newett Vick of Vicksburg, Mississippi, and John William Burruss of Woodville, Mississippi, both ministers' sons. Thorpe had

Thomas Bangs Thorpe, painting by Charles Loring Elliott

expected to graduate from Wesleyan in 1837, but bad health prevented him from receiving his degree, though he was awarded an honorary Master of Arts degree in 1847 by the school for his achievements as a writer, painter, and newspaper editor during the intervening ten years.

Thorpe left Wesleyan in the summer of 1836 and returned to his stepfather's home in New York. However, at the end of that year, at the urging of his former college classmates from Mississippi and Louisiana, Thorpe headed south to regain his health in the warmer climate. He made a rugged journey by stage to Cincinnati, arriving there by January 1837, and he apparently journeyed from there to Louisiana by way of steamboat down the Ohio and Mississippi rivers.

By September 1837 Thorpe was residing in Baton Rouge and feeling insecure over his financial status in his new home; and in 1838 he was apparently painting portraits and still lifes in New Orleans for needed money. About this time he married Anne Maria Hinckley of Maine, who was probably the daughter of his stepfather. By the summer of 1839, Thorpe was living in Jackson, Louisiana, a small town in East Feliciana parish. He lived there and in St. Francisville, Louisiana, in West Feliciana parish, for a brief time. Bennet H. Barrow, the owner of Highland Plantation, located near this latter town, hired Thorpe to paint a portrait of his daughter about this time; and Thorpe made friends with a number of other plantation owners in the area and joined them in hunting and fishing, forms of recreation that later furnished him much material on which to base sporting essays.

On 27 July 1839 Thorpe's first sketch, "Tom Owen, the Bee-Hunter," signed "By a New Yorker in Louisiana," was published in the New York *Spirit of the Times*, a sporting paper which later became an important antebellum source of American humorous literature. "Tom Owen, the Bee-Hunter" was based on an incident involving Thorpe the year before in East Feliciana parish. Thorpe had traveled with a group of friends to hear a political speech in Jackson. On the way the men met Tom Owen, an eccentric character of the community whose profession was topping trees for the Feliciana planters but whose pastime was "bee hunting"— following bees to their tree home in order to obtain their honey. Thorpe was so fascinated by this unusual backwoods character that one of the group suggested he write a sketch about Tom Owen. Thorpe wrote "Tom Owen, the Bee-Hunter" and sent it to the editor of a local Louisiana newspaper, who kept the sketch three months and returned it to

Tom Owen the Bee-Hunter, illustration by F. O. C. Darley

him unpublished. Thorpe's friend then suggested that Thorpe forward the sketch to William T. Porter, editor of the *Spirit of the Times*. Porter immediately recognized the potential appeal of the sketch to his sporting paper's audience, and he published it in the 27 July 1839 issue.

"Tom Owen, the Bee-Hunter" achieved a remarkable popularity after its publication. The sketch was quickly reprinted by newspapers and journals across America and Europe, as well as in India and other countries. It was subsequently included in two of the most famous antebellum collections of literature—Rufus Wilmot Griswold's *The Prose Writers of America* (1847) and George and Evert Duyckinck's *Cyclopaedia of American Literature* (1855).

Because Thorpe's "Tom Owen, the Bee-Hunter" is a character sketch, it lacks the exciting narrative action which typifies most of the yarns written by the humorists of the Old Southwest. The sketch is centered around only one incident—the lining of a bee to its home by Tom Owen and the subsequent felling of the tree by him. The humor of the sketch comes from the mock-heroic tone employed to describe Tom Owen and his actions, a tone established and maintained through a charming writing style reminiscent of the best of Irving's works.

To Thorpe, Tom Owen was representative of a "backwoods fraternity," "men of genius in their way," who "died unwept and unnoticed" while heroes of horse racing and hunting fame were "lauded to the skies." Thorpe compares Tom favorably with Davy Crockett and Nimrod in "hunting" ability: " 'Solitary and alone' has he tracked his game through the mazy labyrinths of the air, marked 'I hunted,' 'I found,' 'I conquered' upon the carcasses of his victims, and then marched homeward with his spoils. . . ." In the course of the sketch, when Tom follows a bee to the honey-laden tree and begins to chop it down, he turns from hunter to heroic fighter, for the bees begin to "attack" and "charge" him when they discover they are about to be "invaded." Tom triumphs, of course, at the end of the sketch, by successfully felling the tree and routing his "astonished and confused" adversaries with a thick cloud of smoke.

Thorpe's "Tom Owen, the Bee-Hunter" is important to literary history for several reasons. Its method of presenting a frontier character of the South in the essay style that prevailed at the time made it a significant transition piece between the genteel American literature represented by Irving and Cooper and the realistic, racy sketches by the humorists of the Old Southwest such as Harris and Hooper; and the sketch gained a literary audience for these later writers. Perhaps more important, Thorpe's "Tom Owen" brought the *Spirit of the Times* much-needed national attention and helped increase the *Spirit of the Times*'s popularity and circulation during a time of severe financial difficulties for the paper. Two decades later, the editor of the *Spirit of the Times* acknowledged that paper's debt to "Tom Owen, the Bee-Hunter" by noting that the sketch "inaugurated not only a new style of writing, but subsequently, through innumerable southern and western correspondents, brought together the most truly original and genuine American humor that the literature of the country can boast."

In the winter of 1839-1840, Thorpe's wife returned to New York, probably to have her first child, Anna. By the spring of 1840, Thorpe had joined his wife there, where they apparently lived with his mother and stepfather while he worked as a painter out of a studio on Bowery Street. Thorpe published his second sketch, titled "Wild Turkey Shooting," in the *Spirit of the Times* on 1 August 1840. The sketch simply described a hunting episode, but it was significant because it represented Thorpe's first attempt to reproduce realistically the frontiersman's speech. Two months later, in the 3 October 1840 issue of the *Spirit of the Times*, Thorpe's essay "Primitive Forests of the Mississippi" appeared; this essay advanced a motif that appeared frequently in Thorpe's later essays and stories—the sublimity and strength of nature. These were the first of more than sixty of Thorpe's pieces published in the *Spirit of the Times* by 1860.

In December 1840, Thorpe published an essay titled "The Mississippi" in the *Knickerbocker* Magazine, an esteemed New York literary periodical in which Thorpe published other essays in the early 1840s. Subsequently, Thorpe sold a painting of the golden age of Manahatta to Lewis Gaylord Clark, editor of the *Knickerbocker*. Clark praised Thorpe's painting and writing and generally encouraged him to continue working in both fields.

Near the end of 1840, Thorpe and his family returned to St. Francisville, Louisiana, where they remained for the next several years. During this period, he continued to write for the *Spirit of the Times*, and he made his initial contribution to an English journal, the London *New Sporting Magazine*. His writings during this time began to fall into three categories, designated by Milton Rickels as "hunting sketches, nature essays, and frontier tales of humor and character."

In this latter category is his most famous story, "The Big Bear of Arkansas," published on page one of the *Spirit of the Times* on 27 March 1841. The story is introduced by an unnamed gentleman narrator who recalls a trip he once made up the Mississippi River from New Orleans on the steamboat *The Invincible*, a trip made especially memorable because of a yarn spun by a fellow passenger named Jim Doggett. Doggett is a real ring-tailed roarer who tells a story concerning a particular bear hunt he made in Arkansas, the "creation State," where turkeys weigh forty pounds or more, mosquitoes become so large and fierce that their sting can cause a person to "swell up and bust," and corn grows so quickly in the rich soil that it can shoot up overnight and kill a sleeping hog by its "percussion." Doggett's adversary in the hunt he describes is a giant "creation bear" that takes on mythic proportions when it permits the frontiersman to kill it after earlier thwarting his attempts through a combination of extraordinary sagacity and strength. Doggett concludes that this bear "was an *unhuntable bear, and died when his time come*," and he leaves his audience of listeners on the steamboat sitting in rapt silence as he finishes the telling of his imaginative yarn.

"The Big Bear of Arkansas" is a story rich in symbolism and complex in style and structure. One

The Big Bear of Arkansas

of the themes in the story is the intrusion of civilization on the wilderness. Leo Lemay associates the killing of the bear by Doggett with the fall of man, which marked "the end of the reign of the Eden-like wilderness of the Old Southwest." John Guilds notes also that the story's "inclusion of a lengendary animal which symbolizes primitive forces and compels the hunter to pursue it incorporates a motif that recurs in American literature from Melville to Faulkner." Much of the humor of "The Big Bear of Arkansas" may be ascribed to three basic incongruities present in it: the incongruity between the polished rhetoric of the gentleman narrator and the frontier dialect of Jim Doggett; the incongruity between the time of the relating of the story and the time of the unfolding events within the tale spun by Doggett; and the incongruity between the realistic setting of the steamboat and the fantasy setting of the Arkansas locale created by Doggett. And, as Walter Blair observes, the Thorpe story even contains a subtle scatological passage, an aspect quite rare in the literature of the day.

Thorpe's years in St. Francisville were among his most productive as a writer and as an artist. In 1841 Thorpe published eight sketches in addition to "The Big Bear of Arkansas," and in 1842 seven more sketches. About this time he also sent two paintings, *A Louisiana Deer* and *Mont Du Moss*, to Porter, who included an engraving of the former work in the *American Turf Register*; and in January 1843 Thorpe displayed two portraits and two animal paintings at the second annual fair of the Louisiana Agricultural and Mechanical Association at Baton Rouge, where he won a first prize for his art.

Early in 1843, Thorpe had a minor connection with the *New Orleans Tropic*, a well-established Whig daily, to which he contributed several sketches. In the spring of that year, beginning a journalism career that would last almost twenty years, Thorpe became the editor of a short-lived sporting magazine, the *Southern Sportsman*. By June 1843 Thorpe had moved from New Orleans and joined Robert Patterson as coeditor of the *Concordia Intelligencer* at Vidalia, Louisiana. During his two-year residence there, he also served as postmaster, from May 1844 to July 1845; and he became more and more involved in Whig politics, serving as one of three secretaries at the state Whig convention at Baton Rouge in 1844. Thorpe's son Thomas was born during this time.

While serving as an editor of the *Concordia Intelligencer*, Thorpe published in that paper a noteworthy series of letters burlesquing Matthew Field's reports in the *New Orleans Picayune* of an 1843-1844 hunting expedition in the Rocky Mountains led by Sir William Drummond Stewart, baronet of Scotland and a famous world traveler. Field accompanied Stewart and his party on the expedition, but the letters he sent to the *Picayune* were full of pathos and emphasized the romantic qualities of the wilderness experience. In the summer of 1843, Thorpe began publishing his burlesque "Letters from the Far West," under the signature "P.O.F.," and the letters were reprinted by the *Spirit of the Times* and many regional papers across the country—some of which did not recognize the true purpose of them. In the letters, Thorpe satirized such romantic notions as the pleasures of outdoor life, the concept of the noble savage, and reports of fabulous wilderness animals; he also ridiculed curio collecting by travelers. The letters included several burlesques of the tall tale and parodies of some individual reports by Field. Thorpe's series of a dozen letters continued appearing in the *Concordia Intelligencer* until the spring of 1844.

In mid-May 1845 Thorpe's "The Big Bear of

Arkansas" served as the title story for the first collection of humorous stories edited by William Porter. The year before, Porter had put Thorpe in contact with his publisher, Carey and Hart of Philadelphia, to discuss a proposed volume of sketches. After Thorpe left the *Intelligencer* in June 1845—probably because of a dispute with Patterson over Thorpe's Whig politics—he journeyed to New York and Philadelphia in the summer to make final arrangements for publishing a book. Titled *The Mysteries of the Backwoods; or Sketches of the Southwest: Including Character, Scenery, and Rural Sports*, the book appeared in December 1845. The sixteen sketches in the volume were mainly romantic and sentimental in nature and intended for a genteel reading audience. Most of the selections were essays concerning Southern sporting life, such as "Piscatory Archery," "Alligator Killing," and "Grizzly Bear Hunt." However, *The Mysteries of the Backwoods* contained a revised version of "Tom Owen, the Bee-Hunter" and two of Thorpe's best stories, "A Piano in Arkansas" and "The Disgraced Scalp-Lock." The book sold poorly, and Carey and Hart thereafter advised Thorpe to write mainly humorous stories for any future books.

For the next two years, Thorpe was heavily involved in journalistic endeavors, editing or publishing at least four newspapers, three of which he established himself. From November 1845 to March 1846, Thorpe published the *New Orleans Daily Commercial Times*, a paper emphasizing financial news. In April 1846 he became a partner in the *New Orleans Daily Tropic*, a newspaper devoted to Whig interests. Four months later Thorpe severed his connection with the *Daily Tropic* after incurring heavy debts. He moved his family to Baton Rouge sometime before October 1846, purchased some printing equipment in New Orleans, and founded the *Baton Rouge Conservator* in November 1846. This business venture apparently proved unsuccessful in a very short time, for by June 1847 Thorpe had moved back to New Orleans to establish another newspaper, the *Daily National*, through which he supported Zachary Taylor for President. As editor of the paper, Thorpe advocated the cause of public schools, opposed dueling and lynching, and wrote editorials in support of sanitary regulations for New Orleans, especially during the September 1847 yellow fever epidemic there. Thorpe left the *Daily National* in December 1847, an action that marked the end of his journalistic career in the South.

During this period of his activities as a publisher and editor, Thorpe served in the Mexican War and continued his literary pursuits. In the spring of 1846, he traveled from New Orleans by ship to join the American forces on the Rio Grande. Thorpe arrived in Matamoros in late May or early June, where he probably served as a bearer of dispatches for Gen. Zachary Taylor. During his brief term of service, he sent reports of the war back to the *New Orleans Daily Tropic*. By mid-June, he had returned to New Orleans and begun preparations to publish a book through Carey and Hart based on his Mexican War experiences. The volume appeared in October 1846, under the title *Our Army on the Rio Grande*. The 196-page book purported to be "A Short Account of the Important Events Transpiring From the Time of the Removal of the 'Army of Occupation' from Corpus Christi, To the Surrender of Matamoros. . . ." Thorpe used eyewitness accounts of key battles, official military documents, and reports of camp newspapers, but the writing in the book was hasty and emotional; as a result, the volume sold poorly, as had *The Mysteries of the Backwoods*.

In December 1846 Thorpe's story "Bob Herring, the Arkansas Bear Hunter" was included in Porter's second collection of humor, *A Quarter Race in Kentucky, and Other Sketches*. In the same month, Thorpe's "Woodcock Fire Hunting" was included in a revised and expanded American edition of Peter Hawker's *Instructions to Young Sportsmen*, also edited by Porter.

Early in the next year, Thorpe became involved in the cultural life of Louisiana. In January 1847 he was appointed to the Fine Arts Committee of the annual fair of the Louisiana Agricultural and Mechanical Association. In February he helped to found the Baton Rouge Lyceum, which planned a lecture series and later established a small library. In April Thorpe delivered a series of lectures in New Orleans, an activity that he would engage in off and on throughout the rest of his life.

His second book based on the Mexican War, *Our Army at Monterey*, appeared in the fall of 1847. The 204-page book included the predictable praise of Taylor and the bravery of the American soldiers, as well as twenty pages of obituaries for officers at Monterey, statistics of soldiers killed and wounded, and some official reports.

After Thorpe's departure from the *Daily National* in December 1847, he returned to Baton Rouge where he worked on other literary manuscripts and portraits of Louisiana scenes. He completed a third volume concerning the Mexican conflict, titled *Anecdotes of the War*, made up of 313 anecdotes illustrating American bravery and wit and Mexican cruelty in the war; but Carey and Hart turned the manuscript down because of the financial failures of his earlier books from their press. However, about July 1848, D. Appleton published the book under the title *The Taylor Anecdote Book* after Thorpe added a brief life of Taylor and a short appendix of the general's political letters.

For the next few years, Thorpe became more involved in politics. He was one of two secretaries elected by the Baton Rouge Whigs for Taylor in the summer of 1848. He had been in frequent contact with Taylor from 1846 to 1848 and had painted two portraits of him; thus with Taylor's election as president in November 1848, Thorpe had hoped for a political appointment offering some type of foreign service. He was eventually offered the position of Register of the New Orleans Land Office, but he declined the appointment.

By the end of the 1840s, Thorpe was engaged primarily in painting and in writing regular editorials for the *Baton Rouge Gazette*. Thereafter he also began contributing literary pieces to national publications; his "Incidents in the Life of Audubon" appeared in *Godey's Lady's Book* in May 1851. One year later, the Louisiana House of Representatives voted to purchase Thorpe's large portrait of Zachary Taylor (who had died in 1850) for $1,000.

In the fall of 1852, Thorpe actively supported the unpopular and unsuccessful Whig nominee for

Portrait of Gen. Zachary Taylor by Thomas Bangs Thorpe

president, General Winfield Scott, making speeches in his behalf across central Louisiana. At the Whig State Convention in Baton Rouge on 29 November 1852, Thorpe received the party's nomination for the office of State Superintendent of Education; but despite carrying Baton Rouge, Thorpe lost statewide to Democrat J. H. Carrigan in the election in late December.

Thorpe's third child, a daughter named Dordie Rebecca, was born in 1853. Late that year, Thorpe began writing for *Harper's New Monthly Magazine*, a magazine to which he would contribute at least thirty-two articles in the next twenty years, but with only one humorous sketch included among them—"The Case of Lady Macbeth Medically Considered: A Western Sketch" (February 1854). At the end of 1853, Thorpe purchased the plates and rights to *The Mysteries of the Backwoods* in anticipation of the publication of another collection of sketches.

D. Appleton published Thorpe's *The Hive of 'The Bee-Hunter,' A Repository of Sketches, Including Peculiar American Character, Scenery, and Rural Sports* in the spring of 1854. For this book, Thorpe corrected and extensively revised the sketches contained in *The Mysteries of the Backwoods* and added humorous sketches published previously in the *Spirit of the Times* and elsewhere. *The Hive of 'The Bee-Hunter'* is Thorpe's best work because it generally avoids the sentimentality and careless writing associated with his earlier books. The volume was dedicated to "the Lovers of Nature, Whether Residing in the Crowded City, Pleasant Village, or Native Wild" and had as its aim "to give to those personally unacquainted with the scenery of the southwest, some idea of the country, its surface, and vegetation." The book offered the best of Thorpe's humorous sketches—"The Big Bear of Arkansas," "Tom Owen, the Bee-Hunter," and "A Piano in Arkansas"—as well as essays describing exciting encounters between men and the forces of nature, such as "A Storm Scene on the Mississippi" and "The Way That Americans Go Down Hill."

Within a few months after *The Hive of 'The Bee-Hunter'* appeared, Thorpe published pseudonymously (as Logan) *The Master's House; A Tale of Southern Life*, a novel probably written in response to Harriet Beecher Stowe's *Uncle Tom's Cabin* published two years previously. The plot of Thorpe's novel is episodic, but it revolves around the character of a young North Carolinian, Graham Mildmay, who is educated in New England, moves to Louisiana, and establishes a plantation there. Mildmay ultimately suffers personal tragedy resulting from his killing his neighbor Moreton in a duel. Thorpe uses Mildmay and the Southern plantation life to show the best and worst qualities of Southerners, their social life and culture, and their institutions. Though Thorpe clearly opposes such aspects of the South as slavery, dueling, and the abuses within regional court systems in the novel, he offers many ambivalent views and few solutions to the problems he raises. Milton Rickels calls *The Master's House* "an interesting failure."

Following the publication of his last book, Thorpe moved to New York in the summer or fall of 1854 and directed his energies mainly toward writing magazine articles and painting. Between 1854 and 1856, he published fifteen articles in *Harper's*, most of which were natural history essays, such as "The Alligator," "The Rattlesnake and Its Congeners," "The Lion and His Kind," "The Dog, Described and Illustrated," and "Bears and Bear Hunting." His "Traditions of the Natchez [Indians]" appeared in *The Knickerbocker Gallery* in 1855, among contributions by Irving, Holmes, Bryant, Lowell, Longfellow, and others. In the same year, Thorpe was listed as a joint author with Frederick Saunders of the third edition of *A Voice to America*, a work concerning the American Party's (or Know-Nothing Party) tenets; however, it is unlikely that Thorpe contributed much to the volume since he moved rapidly from Whig to Republican political allegiance. The year ended in tragedy for Thorpe, for on 4 October 1855, his wife died at the age of thirty-six.

In the fall of 1857, Thorpe joined the editorial staff of *Frank Leslie's Illustrated Newspaper*, and that November he married Jane Fosdick of New York. For the next two years, Thorpe practiced law after qualifying through an examination, and he continued writing, publishing articles in George Ripley and Charles A. Dana's *New American Cyclopaedia*.

Thorpe purchased a share of the New York *Spirit of the Times* in early 1859, joining Edward E. Jones and Richard Hays as proprietors. He remained a partner in the enterprise only until March 1861, when he sold his interest in the paper to Jones. During the period of his business association with the *Spirit of the Times*, he contributed about ten articles to it concerning art, but he wrote little on other subjects.

At the National Academy of Design exhibition in the spring of 1859, Thorpe displayed one painting; a year later, he exhibited in New York a large painting of Niagara Falls, titled *Niagara As It Is*; and in 1862 Thorpe became one of the first officers of the new Brooklyn Art Association and exhibited through it four paintings with Southern subjects—

I'll Fight It Out on This Line, Palmetto Swamp—The Banks of the Mississippi, Red Snapper—The Game Fish of the Gulf of Mexico, and *Country Wood*. In the spring of that year, he exhibited two pictures for the National Academy of Design, including one titled *Washington Irving's Grave*.

Thorpe had little time for painting and writing after the start of the Civil War. With the temporary rank of colonel, he joined the Union expedition that captured New Orleans in April 1862. In June Thorpe was assigned to manage previously unemployed laborers in performing various clean-up tasks and also to distribute food to 31,000 starving families in New Orleans. Thorpe did an exceptional job of fulfilling the responsibilities of this assignment and subsequently represented one of New Orleans's city districts in the second relief commission formed by the military government. He became active in local politics in 1864 and was elected by voters of the second district of New Orleans as a Free State candidate to the state constitutional convention held in that city in April of that year. However, Thorpe was later defeated in his bid to become one of the second district's five representatives to the Louisiana General Assembly in the election approving the new state constitution in September 1864.

Thorpe left New Orleans in October 1864 and returned by ship to New York City, where he devoted much of the next two years to painting. Probably sometime during this period, he joined the Episcopal church. Following the death of his boyhood friend Charles Elliott in the fall of 1868, Thorpe wrote and published a tribute to him in the form of an eleven-page pamphlet, *Reminiscences of Charles L. Elliott, Artist*.

From 1869 until his death in 1878, Thorpe worked in various positions in the New York Customhouse, and he began writing for national publications again during the last decade of his life. In 1868 he resumed contributing material to *Harper's*. Between 1869 and 1873 he published thirty articles in *Appleton's Journal*. He wrote twenty-one columns on "Art and Drama" for *Forest and Stream* between 1873 and 1874 and seventeen articles concerning American painters and art for *Baldwin's Monthly* from 1875 to 1878.

Thorpe died in New York City on 20 September 1878, probably as a result of Bright's disease, which had caused him much suffering previously. He was buried in the family plot at Green-Wood Cemetery in Brooklyn.

Thomas Bangs Thorpe is remembered today for his story "The Big Bear of Arkansas," a sketch

William Faulkner admired. His relatively high position among the group of Southwestern humorists is a tribute to that one masterpiece, because he wrote remarkably few other frontier humor sketches during his long and productive writing career. However, his outpouring of other kinds of writings—hunting sketches, natural history essays, art criticism essays, and other types—distinguishes Thorpe as one of the most versatile of these antebellum writers.

Biography:

Milton Rickels, *Thomas Bangs Thorpe: Humorist of the Old Southwest* (Baton Rouge: Louisiana State University Press, 1962).

References:

Walter Blair, "The Technique of 'The Big Bear of Arkansas,'" *Southwest Review*, 28 (Summer 1943): 426-435;

Eugene Current-Garcia, "Thomas Bangs Thorpe and the Literature of the Ante-Bellum South-

western Frontier," *Louisiana Historical Quarterly*, 39 (April 1956): 199-222;

Barrie Hayne, "Yankee in the Patriarchy: T. B. Thorpe's Reply to *Uncle Tom's Cabin*," *American Quarterly*, 20 (Summer 1968): 180-195;

Mark A. Keller, "T. B. Thorpe's 'Tom Owen, The Bee-Hunter': Southwestern Humor's 'Origin of Species,'" *Southern Studies: An Interdisciplinary Journal of the South*, 18 (Spring 1979): 89-101;

J. A. Leo Lemay, "The Text, Tradition, and Themes of 'The Big Bear of Arkansas,'" *American Literature*, 47 (November 1975): 321-342;

Daniel F. Littlefield, Jr., "Thomas Bangs Thorpe and the Passing of the Southwestern Wilderness," *Southern Literary Journal*, 11 (Spring 1979): 56-65;

John Francis McDermott, "T. B. Thorpe's Burlesque of Far West Sporting Travel," *American Quarterly*, 10 (Summer 1958): 175-180;

Katherine G. Simoneaux, "Symbolism in Thorpe's 'The Big Bear of Arkansas,'" *Arkansas Historical Quarterly*, 25 (Fall 1966): 240-247.

James Thurber

Peter A. Scholl
Luther College

See also the Thurber entry in *DLB 4, American Writers in Paris, 1920-1939*.

BIRTH: Columbus, Ohio, 8 December 1894, to Charles Lincoln and Mary Agnes Fisher Thurber.

EDUCATION: Ohio State University, 1913-1918.

MARRIAGE: 20 May 1922 to Althea Adams, divorced; children: Rosemary. 25 June 1935 to Helen Muriel Wismer.

AWARDS: Library Association Prize for best juvenile picture book for *Many Moons*, 1943; Ohioana juvenile-book medal for *The White Deer*, 1946; Laughing Lions of Columbia University Award for Humor, 1949; Honorary Doctorate, Kenyon College, 1950; Honorary Doctorate, Williams College, 1951; Honorary Doctorate, Yale

University, 1953; Sesquicentennial Career Medal of the Martha Kinney Cooper Ohioana Library Association, 1953; American Cartoonist's Society T-Square Award, 1956; American Library Association's Library and Justice Award, 1957, for *Further Fables for Our Time*; Antoinette Perry Special Award, 1960; Certificate of Award from Ohio State University Class of 1916 for "Meritorious Service to Humanity and to Our Alma Mater," 1961.

DEATH: New York, New York, 2 November 1961.

BOOKS: *Is Sex Necessary? Or Why You Feel the Way You Do*, by Thurber and E. B. White (New York & London: Harper, 1929; London: Heinemann, 1930);

The Owl in the Attic and Other Perplexities (New York & London: Harper, 1931);

The Seal in the Bedroom & Other Predicaments (New

York & London: Harper, 1932; London: Hamilton, 1951);

My Life and Hard Times (New York & London: Harper, 1933);

The Middle-Aged Man on the Flying Trapeze (New York & London: Harper, 1935; London: Hamilton, 1935);

Let Your Mind Alone! And Other More or Less Inspirational Pieces (New York & London: Harper, 1937; London: Hamilton, 1937);

Cream of Thurber (London: Hamilton, 1939);

The Last Flower (New York & London: Harper, 1939; London: Hamilton, 1939);

The Male Animal, by Thurber and Elliott Nugent (New York: Random House, 1940; London: Hamilton, 1950);

Fables for Our Time and Famous Poems Illustrated (New York & London: Harper, 1940; London: Hamilton, 1940);

My World–and Welcome to It (New York: Harcourt, Brace, 1942; London: Hamilton, 1942);

Many Moons (New York: Harcourt, Brace, 1943; London: Hamilton, 1945);

Thurber's Men, Women, and Dogs (New York: Harcourt, Brace, 1943; London: Hamilton, 1945);

The Great Quillow (New York: Harcourt, Brace, 1944);

The Thurber Carnival (New York & London: Harper, 1945; London: Hamilton, 1945);

The White Deer (New York: Harcourt, Brace, 1945; London: Hamilton, 1946);

The Beast in Me and Other Animals (New York: Harcourt, Brace, 1948; London: Hamilton, 1949);

The 13 Clocks (New York: Simon & Schuster, 1950; London: Hamilton, 1951);

The Thurber Album (New York: Simon & Schuster, 1952; London: Hamilton, 1952);

Thurber Country (New York: Simon & Schuster, 1953; London: Hamilton, 1953);

Thurber's Dogs (New York: Simon & Schuster, 1955; London: Hamilton, 1955);

A Thurber Garland (London: Hamilton, 1955);

Further Fables for Our Time (New York: Simon & Schuster, 1956; London: Hamilton, 1956);

The Wonderful O (New York: Simon & Schuster, 1957; London: Hamilton, 1958);

Alarms and Diversions (London: Hamilton, 1957; New York: Harper, 1957);

The Years with Ross (Boston & Toronto: Atlantic Monthly/Little, Brown, 1959; London: Hamilton, 1959);

Lanterns & Lances (New York: Harper, 1961; London: Hamilton, 1961);

Credos and Curios (London: Hamilton, 1962; New York & Evanston: Harper & Row, 1962);

A Thurber Carnival (New York, Hollywood, London & Toronto: French, 1962);

Vintage Thurber, 2 volumes (London: Hamilton, 1963);

Thurber & Company (New York, Evanston & London: Harper & Row, 1966; London: Hamilton, 1967).

In a general survey of American humor, James Thurber comes after the traditional horse-sense humorists and before the black humorists of the postatomic era. His most famous and most enduring work developed after he became associated in 1927 with the two-year-old *New Yorker* magazine, a periodical that strove to be sophisticated but not stuffy, urbane but not effete. He never completed a thoroughly unified long work, though he did produce, in collaboration with Elliott Nugent, a successful three-act play, *The Male Animal* (1940). He is best known for his short pieces, especially for his almost conversational yet elegantly crafted "casuals," a word used by *New Yorker* editor Harold Ross "for fiction and humorous pieces of all kinds." Neither Thurber nor his *New Yorker* colleagues created the so-called little man character and the sort of humor with which this well-known twentieth-century type is associated. Still, Thurber's particular elaboration of the type and the near-identity of his narrative persona with the personality of the fictional little man became a Thurber trademark, and the phrase "Thurber man" (as well as "Thurber woman"— though she is a different matter altogether) has become commonplace in discussions of American humor. As early as 1919, his friend and collaborator E. B. White wrote that "These 'Thurber men' have come to be recognized as a distinct type in the world of art; they are frustrated, fugitive beings; at times they seem vaguely striving to get out of something without being seen (a room, a situation, a state of mind), at other times they are merely perplexed and too humble, or weak, to move." The characters in his work seem headed toward some final darkness, a tendency symbolized in the title of his last book published in his lifetime, *Lanterns & Lances* (1961). The lances pierce out the eyes that see the light of humor, but it is not all darkness. The lanterns often continue to shine all the way through a Thurber piece, and in his best work the lances serve as poles to raise the lanterns high. Some of the greatest moments in modern American humor are those in which his characters hold both, but use the lanterns instead of lances. For example, in "The Catbird Seat," Mr. Martin plots carefully to "rub out" the domineering Miss Ulgine Barrows, but finds, through Thurber magic in the art of telling tales, a way to comic victory without bloodshed.

James Grover Thurber was born in Columbus, Ohio, the second son of Charles and Mary Thurber. As his secretary told his biographer Burton Bernstein, "all his life, he remained an Ohio boy at heart, with a universal sense of wisdom." Whether it was mainly ambition or his "universal wisdom," he struggled hard to leave the Midwest and ultimately made his way east like many aspiring writers before and after him. Like many of his characters, Thurber became an upper-middle-class Easterner, a self-exiled Midwesterner who restlessly sought, as he put it, "the Great Good Place, which he conceives to be an old Colonial house, surrounded by elms and maples, equipped with all modern conveniences. . . ." He made it to such a place in West Cornwall, Connecticut, but he was not at rest there. He never completely divorced himself from his Ohio roots, as he admitted in 1953: "I am never very far away from Ohio in my thoughts, and . . . the clocks that strike in my dreams are often the clocks of Columbus." His Ohio memories and relatives were fundamental influences on his best work.

Thurber's father, Charles Thurber, was not born in Columbus, but was "A Gentleman from Indiana," as the nostalgic essay about him in *The Thurber Album* (1952) was titled. He dreamed of being an actor, then a lawyer, but he ended up working at various political appointments that were dependent upon his party's fortunes at the polls. Forever miscast and ill-at-ease, "He wasn't even a politician . . . but, as they say in the theatre of a part in a bad play, it was a job." He was undoubtedly one of the prototypes of the Thurber man, as "he was always mightily plagued by the mechanical. He was also plagued by the manufactured, which takes in a great deal more ground." He was nothing like his wife Mary, or Mame, as she was nicknamed, a daughter of a large, strong-willed, influential Ohio family. After reading the fictionalized description of her in *My Life and Hard Times* (1933) and the more historical portrait of her, "Lavender with a Difference," in *The Thurber Album*, no one can wonder where the original model of the Thurber woman was found. She was a natural actress, a practical joker, a believer in the occult, a strong Methodist, a great cook, and a woman with a memory that rivaled or surpassed Thurber's own much-vaunted "total recall."

If the accident of his birth into a family of loving but eccentric relatives was without parallel for its effect on his work, another accident at a

James Thurber

young age had a powerful effect on him. In the summer of 1901, Charles Thurber took his family to live in the Washington, D.C., area where he was to work for an Ohio congressman. The three Thurber boys were playing William Tell in the yard one afternoon when Jamie turned around to see what was taking his older brother William so long—"and the arrow hit Jamie smack in the eye." There was considerable delay in removing the damaged eye, a circumstance that probably led to Thurber's total blindness by 1951. In Columbus, where the Thurbers returned in 1903, the injury set him apart from most other Columbus boys, especially the mixed-race, "laboring-class," pugnacious, and sports-minded schoolboys described in "I Went to Sullivant" (1935). In *My Life and Hard Times* Thurber says that he could never pass biology at the university because he could never see anything through a microscope, and later, he reports that he was ordered to report for an army physical innumerable times, only to be told at the end of every inspection, "Why, you couldn't get into the service with sight like that!"

Glass eye and all, Thurber was still a success in his junior and senior high-school days. Among other honors, he was given the job of writing the eighth grade class prophecy. In this document, critics have found the earliest precursor of the Thurber "Walter Ego" (a punning phrase he used in *Lanterns & Lances*). The young prophet imagines his class on an incredible journey in a "Seairoplane." When the craft catches a piece of rope in its "curobator" and threatens to crash, all are surprised "to see James Thurber walking out on the beam. He reached out and extricated the rope...," in the nerveless manner which the most famous of all Thurber characters, the hero of "The Secret Life of Walter Mitty" (1939), attributes to himself in his daydreams. Thurber's early triumphs, unlike Mitty's, were not all imaginary. He graduated from high school with honor, having studied the difficult Latin curriculum, and he was elected president of his senior class. But if he was a somebody in high school, he was a nobody in his first years at Ohio State University, where he enrolled in 1913. He did not receive a bid from a fraternity that year and he did so badly in many of his classes that he stopped attending altogether during the school year of 1914-1915, without telling anyone at home. In the fall of 1916 he met Elliott Nugent, a big man on campus, who was impressed one day with a theme Thurber had written—so impressed that he managed to get him into his own fraternity and helped him become "a regular guy." Thurber and Nugent worked together on the *Ohio State Lantern* and on the *Sundial* (the university's literary and humor magazine), and following Nugent's example, Thurber joined The Strollers (the university's dramatic group) as well as other groups and clubs. Of his teachers, Thurber was most powerfully affected by English professor Joseph Taylor, from whom he learned to admire the work of Willa Cather, Joseph Conrad, and especially Henry James. But he was influenced by the comic strips of his day, by melodramas and later by movies, by "nickel novels" and the stories of O. Henry (who had served over three years in the federal prison in Columbus), and by the humor of Robert O. Ryder, editorialist for the *Ohio State Journal*. Thurber painstakingly imitated Ryder's "paragraphs"—carefully drawn, brief comments on a variety of subjects—in his writing for his high-school paper and the *Sundial*. The restrained humor of "paragraphing" was later to appear in his columns for the *Columbus Dispatch*, and the style anticipates the comments he would write for "The Talk of the Town" at the *New Yorker*.

Thurber left Ohio State in 1918 without a degree, but he had distinguished himself sufficiently to be elected to the Sphinx, the senior honorary society. He was anxious "to go with the rest of the boys," and though his eye trouble kept him out of the military, he managed to get to Paris as a code clerk for the United States Embassy, where he served from 1918 to 1920. There he reread *The Ambassadors* several times and even retraced the steps of James's passionate pilgrims, dining at the Tour d'Argent with a former Ohio State coed, reenacting a meeting between Lambert Strether and Mme de Vionnet. Clearly he saw himself as one of James's "super-subtle fry," and in the cultural center of the world, he was trying his best to be "one of those on whom nothing is lost." Yet he was still nine-tenths Ohio boy, and his loss of virginity with a dancer in the Folies Bergères could not rid him of his Midwestern conviction that there are two kinds of women, Mme de Vionnet notwithstanding. In his letters to his brother, the Jamesian sophisticate of infinite delicacy and perception gives way to what a friend described as "the hick in him." "Of all the nations on the earth," he wrote in 1919, "the Yanks easily lead in the matter of pep and enthusiasm, endurance and gogetum stuff...."

When he returned to Columbus in early 1920, his brother Robert recalls, it was evident that he had been "Over There": "He was so independent.... He was jumpy and moody, but he seemed to know what he wanted to be—a writer of some sort." He promptly took a job as a reporter on the *Columbus Dispatch*, working under tough city editor Norman Kuehner. Kuehner, like Harold Ross, was a hardboiled type who believed that "You get to be a newspaperman by being a newspaperman," and he liked to call college men like Thurber "Phi Beta Kappa." Later on, as Thurber tells this story in *The Thurber Album*, Kuehner began to call him "Author," having heard that the young man was writing librettos for Ohio State musicals. This theatrical experience, which included writing, acting, producing, and even going on the road with the Scarlet Mask Club shows, brought him much-needed cash and helped prepare the way for his much later dramatic works *The Male Animal* and *A Thurber Carnival* (a revue that opened in 1960). His renewed contact with the dramatic society also brought Althea Adams into his view. Although she has been described as "aloof, attractive, ambitious, worldly, and very social—all the things Jim wasn't...," the two were married in 1922. The family never warmed to her, especially Thurber's mother, for as Bernstein sees it, "they were too much alike for comfort—domineering,

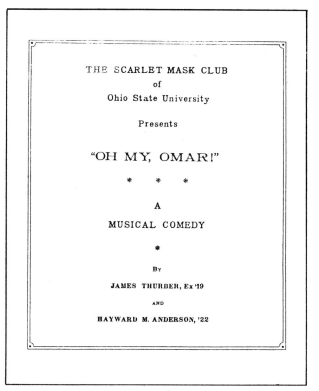

THE SCARLET MASK CLUB
of
Ohio State University

Presents

"OH MY, OMAR!"

*   *   *

A

MUSICAL COMEDY

*

BY

JAMES THURBER, Ex '19

AND

HAYWARD M. ANDERSON, '22

*Libretto for 1921 Scarlet Mask Club production, Thurber's
first published work*

aggressive, essential females. . . . An amalgam of the two of them became . . . what was later to be known to the world as the Thurber Woman."

Yet it was Althea's drive that helped Thurber leave Columbus to try his luck at free-lance writing. During the summer of 1924 they lived in a secluded cottage in the Adirondacks, where Thurber wrote and wrote. He managed to turn out "Josephine Has Her Day," the first short story for which he was paid, and had it published in the *Kansas City Star* Sunday magazine in 1926. But the experiment foundered in a tide of rejection slips, and the couple had to return to Columbus. Their ardor for escape was not cooled, however, and in 1925 they sailed for France. There they lived in a musty farmhouse in Normandy. (Their terrifying landlady is described in "Remembrance of Things Past," 1937.) Thurber was trying to write a novel, but gave it up after 5,000 words. The two fled to Paris to escape the landlady, the threat of poverty, and the agony of novel writing. Though Thurber once told interviewers that he "never wanted to write a long work," this was not the only time he started and failed to finish a novel. In a letter written in 1931 after ending work on another novel after the first chapter, he

said that he feared "all of my novels would be complete in one chapter, from force of habit in writing short pieces and also from a natural incapability of what Billy Graves would call 'larger flight.'. . ." In September 1925 Thurber secured a job as rewrite man for the Paris edition of the *Chicago Tribune*, beating out other hopeful expatriates because he was an experienced newspaperman. In December 1925 he became coeditor of the Riviera edition of the *Tribune*.

His friends in France were mainly his fellow reporters and did not include such writers as F. Scott Fitzgerald, Ernest Hemingway, or Gertrude Stein, Thurber says in "The Hiding Generation" (1936). Thurber says in "Scott in Thorns" (1951) that he only met Fitzgerald once, in New York in 1934. Thurber's imagination got good exercise, as the *Tribune* writers had to create eight to ten columns out of news cables that provided only one. It became apparent in 1926, however, that this French interlude was not furthering his career; nor was his marriage faring well, and the money was running low again. Althea stayed on behind when Thurber sailed for New York, hoping to earn money there by free-lancing.

Arriving in New York in June, he began submitting stories and manuscripts to all kinds of magazines, among them the *New Yorker*. His stories came back so fast from the *New Yorker* that he thought they must have a "rejection machine." Near despair, he took a reporting job with the *New York Evening Post*. But he kept writing and submitting humor pieces. Althea Thurber had returned, and convinced that Thurber was slaving too long over his manuscripts, she told him to time himself with an alarm clock and to send in what he had after forty-five minutes. This method worked, and he sold a piece to the *New Yorker*. "An American Romance" is a short casual about "the flagpole sitting crazes of the day." Following that initial coup in February 1927, he met E. B. White who in turn introduced him to Harold Ross, and again Thurber's newspaper experience paid off, as Ross hired him as an editor. An editor and organizer Thurber was not, but he could not convince Ross that he would be happier and more effective as a staff writer. Ross was finally convinced when Thurber returned two days late from a visit to Columbus, having overstayed his leave to look for his lost dog. Ross considered that "the act of a sis," as Thurber told the tale in *The Years with Ross* (1959). "I thought you were an editor, goddam it," Ross said, "but I guess you're a writer so write."

"I came to the *New Yorker*," Thurber was later

to say, "a writer of journalese and it was my study of White's writing, I think, that helped me to straighten out my prose so that people could see what I meant." The discipline of writing short items for "The Talk of the Town," the punctilious eye of Harold Ross, and the example of White, with whom he shared a tiny office, brought out the artless style of the Thurber casual. It is a style that refuses to call attention to itself, a "played-down" style, as Thurber was later to describe it. And it is evident in *Is Sex Necessary?* (1929), a book for which he and White wrote alternating chapters.

Thurber had long been a compulsive doodler and some of his drawings had appeared in the Ohio State *Sundial*, but he did not take himself seriously as an artist. Helen Thurber said that Thurber told her that his drawings "sometimes seem to have reached completion by some other route than the common one of intent. They have been described as pre-intentionalist, meaning that they were finished before the ideas for them had occurred to me." It was E. B. White, in the spring of 1929, who first noticed Thurber's drawings and tried to convince Ross to publish some, the first of which was a "thirteen-second sketch Thurber drew on yellow copy paper of a seal on a rock looking at two far-off specks and saying, 'Hm, explorers.'" According to Thurber, Ross asked him, "How the hell did you get the idea you could draw?" White persisted in his role as promoter, and persuaded Harper and Brothers to use Thurber's drawings to illustrate *Is Sex Necessary?* This first book introduced not only Thurber's drawings but many of the major themes that were to dominate this period of his career: the war between men and women, the trouble with marriage, the difficulties raised by easy sex stereotyping, the limitations of genteelism on the one hand and post-Freudian "liberation" on the other. White wrote that the book, published just after the Great Crash, came out of "the turbulence of the late 1920's," a time when there was a great outpouring of books on sex, marriage, and self-analysis. As Wolcott Gibbs remarked, "the heavy writers had got sex down and were breaking its arm." Thurber and White capitalized on this topic; for Thurber, this parodic vein was already quite familiar. In fact, parts of Thurber's contribution to the book are rewritten sections of "Why We Behave Like Microbe Hunters," a long parody he had tried unsuccessfully to have published in 1926. Despite the fact that *Is Sex Necessary?* was not widely advertised, it made the best-seller lists.

John Monroe, the jumpy protagonist in the first eight stories that make up *The Owl in the Attic*

and Other Perplexities (1931), a collection of some of Thurber's best *New Yorker* pieces of the period, is Thurber's typical bumbling but humane, illogical but sensitive, sympathetic character. With the publication of this book Thurber's reputation as a writer and an artist was firmly established, and the public was given more reason to associate the author with the man in Thurber's stories after reading E. B. White's introduction. There, Thurber is humorously described as a Conradian hero, a gaunt drifter White had first seen descending from a packet boat in Raritonga, "carrying a volume of Henry James and leading a honey bear by a small chain." "The Monroe stories," Thurber once said, "were transcripts, one or two of them varying less than an inch from the actual happenings." Virtually all the incidents in the battles between Monroe and his wife, between Monroe and a bat, Monroe and hot-water faucets, and so on, were based on events in the troubled married life of the Thurbers. The two other sections of this book included "The Pet Department" and "Ladies and Gentlemen's Guide to Modern English." The first of these demonstrated Thurber's ability to use his drawings in combination with brief writings that revealed his lifelong fascination with animals, real and imaginary. Some of these drawings had first been published in the *New Yorker*'s "Our Pet Department," a parody of the question-and-answer pet columns published in newspapers. In one such column Thurber's drawing of a horse with antlers tied to its head accompanies a letter from a woman who wants to know why her moose's antlers keep slipping around its head. *The Owl in the Attic* is named for another drawing that seems to show a "stuffed cockatoo" sitting on a "sort of iron dingbat." The final section reveals Thurber's early and lasting fascination with words and language as such and seems more immediately inspired by Harold Ross's fastidiousness and veneration for H. W. Fowler's *Modern English Usage* (1926), which it plays with and parodies. In these pieces he anticipates the concerns for the well-being of the language that mark his late work, but these essays are generally lighter and are not strident or precious like some of the works written after he went blind.

After the success of *Is Sex Necessary?*, Ross asked Thurber for the seal drawing he had rejected. Thurber had thrown it away. He did not get around to drawing another until December 1931 and could not recapture the original: the rock looked more like a headboard, so a headboard it became, complete with a Thurber couple in the bed and the caption "All Right, Have It Your Way—You Heard

"All Right, Have It Your Way — You Heard a Seal Bark!"

Cartoon by James Thurber

a Seal Bark!" The cartoon appeared in the *New Yorker* on 30 January 1932, and, according to Bernstein, "it became one of the most celebrated and often-reprinted cartoons of the twentieth century." This cartoon gave the title to a collection of Thurber's cartoons and drawings, *The Seal in the Bedroom & Other Predicaments* (1932). In her introduction Dorothy Parker said of the "strange people Mr. Thurber has turned loose upon us," that "They seem to fall into three classes—the playful the defeated and the ferocious. All of them have the outer semblance of unbaked cookies. . . ."

Thurber was firmly established as a *New Yorker* artist and writer by 1933, and in that year his series of casuals about growing up in Ohio was published under the title *My Life and Hard Times*. This is Thurber's best single collection of integrated stories, a series that can be read as a well-wrought and unified work of art. Here he exploits for comic effect the distance between the naive Ohio boy, just

beginning to be perplexed by the world, and the wiser but still inadequate middle-aged Easterner who is trying to appear worldly and sophisticated, chagrined by the bitter truth that "Nobody from Columbus has ever made a first rate wanderer in the Conradian tradition." Thurber, as he portrays himself in "Preface to a Life," is just a "writer of light pieces running from a thousand to two thousand words," one of those authors who, "afraid of losing themselves in the larger flight of the two-volume novel," have a genius only "for getting into minor difficulties: they walk into the wrong apartments, they drink furniture polish for stomach bitters, they drive their cars into the prize tulip beds of haughty neighbors. . . ."

Though he presents himself in the preface as a nervous person with a tenuous hold on sanity, the narrative voice in the stories themselves is remarkably calm and in clear control of the bizarre events that it relates. The manner of telling recalls the deadpan face and dry delivery of the best oral yarn spinners, who understand that the comedy is heightened by the contrast between the unexcitable delivery and the frenetic events described. The very essence of the *New Yorker*'s studied artlessness—hallmark of the casual—is evident, for example, in the opening line of "The Night the Bed Fell": "I suppose that the high-water mark of my youth in Columbus, Ohio, was the night the bed fell on my father." It is in such plain, deliberate prose as this that he introduces a parade of crazies that would indeed tax our credulity were they not reported with such apparent composure. There is, for example, cousin Briggs Beall, "who believed that he was likely to cease breathing when he was asleep," and so kept waking himself up at intervals with an alarm clock. "Then there was Aunt Sarah Shoaf, who never went to bed at night without the fear that a burglar was going to get in and blow chloroform under her door through a tube." The chaos that cuts loose in "The Night the Bed Fell" is matched in story after story, with other disasters and close calls such as those that occur "The Day the Dam Broke," "The Night the Ghost Got In," and "More Alarms at Night." The narrator is himself involved in the action of many of these tales, and is the comic protagonist of pieces such as "University Days" and "Draft Board Nights." In this last story, a fictionalized Thurber is called up for a physical examination every week, even though he was exempted from service the first time. He manages to adapt to this insanity by regarding it as comically absurd: "The ninth or tenth time I was called," he tells us, "I happened to pick up one of several stethoscopes that were lying on a table and suddenly, instead of finding myself in the line of draft men, I found myself in the line of examiners." And not surprisingly in this upside-down world, he is accepted by the other physicians as a peer—"A good pulmonary man," comments one. While Thurber feels free in this comic autobiography to stray from the facts, inventing cousins and elaborating upon familiar careers, the work displays his characteristic blending of memory and imagination, taking what Henry James called "clumsy life . . . at her stupid work," and painstakingly reshaping life into art. Here we have, as Thurber put it in an interview with Robert van Gelder, "Reality twisted to the right into humor rather than to the left into tragedy." Pathos touches the lives of these eccentrics, but the book is free from the darker shadings of absurdity that sift into his later works. On the other hand, the book is free from nostalgia, sentiment, and the concern for genealogical and historical trivia that mar his later

return to many of these scenes in *The Thurber Album*.

Most of the writings and drawings in *The Middle-Aged Man on the Flying Trapeze* (1935) were first published in the *New Yorker*, and some of them continue to use the Columbus material, particularly the essays "I Went to Sullivant," about Thurber's grammar school, and "Snapshot of a Dog," which concerns Rex. A bull terrier, Rex dragged home things like ten-foot rails and small chests of drawers and "lived and died without knowing that twelve- and sixteen-foot walls were too much for him" to jump over. This collection also includes more satiric and parodic pieces, such as "If Grant Had Been Drinking at Appomattox," "The Greatest Man in the World," and "Something to Say," the last of these a takeoff on the work of Henry James. The Thurber man is well represented here, as in "The Remarkable Case of Mr. Bruhl," in which Bruhl discovers that he bears a resemblance to a well-known mobster, high on everyone's hit lists. Badly shaken by his friends' practical jokes, "the mild little man" paradoxically takes to living the role that his friends believe to be so amusingly incongruous with his true personality. His melancholy fix is formally diagnosed by a physician as "a definite psychosis." Bruhl is assassinated, gangland style, and in his last moments, true to his psychosis, he defiantly refuses to talk to the police.

The spiritual relatives of Mr. and Mrs. John Monroe continue their marital skirmishing in this volume, and there is a notable escalation in the level of hostilities. Mr. and Mrs. Bidwell knife each other with their eyes after Bidwell persists in holding his breath for his own amusement, thus exasperating his wife. They are separating as the story ends. Things are not going so well in "Mr. Pendly and the Poindexter" either. The matrimonial warfare in this story is autobiographical, as Pendly, suffering from eye trouble, is chauffeured by his wife: "It gave him a feeling of inferiority to sit mildly beside her while she solved the considerable problems of city traffic." Prefiguring the mental adjustments of Walter Mitty and recalling the young Thurber's adventures in a Seairoplane, Pendly dreams of flying into a garden party in an "autogiro," sweeping his wife away, and zooming fearlessly into the blue. The battle is even grimmer in "The Curb in the Sky," in which Charlie Deshler makes the mistake of marrying a woman who completes sentences for people, driving him over the edge and into an asylum where she corrects and edits even his dreams.

The Thurbers' own marriage was breaking up during the time he wrote these stories (their daughter, Rosemary, was born in 1931 after the

Thurbers had briefly reconciled following an earlier separation). They were divorced in 1935. The quarrels, the fights, the infidelities, and the loneliness of these years are animated in the humorous pieces in *The Middle-Aged Man on the Flying Trapeze*; but some of the serious stories in the collection seemed so painfully autobiographical and so bleak that many of the author's friends were openly concerned about his well-being. In "Smashup," the Trinways narrowly avoid death when the nervous husband, Tommy, has to drive in city traffic and involves them in a collision. They are physically unhurt, but their marriage is irrevocably smashed. In "The Evening's at Seven," "One is a Wanderer," and "A Box to Hide In," there is very little that is funny, and the stories all chronicle the wanderings of Prufrockian souls facing forty. The anti-hero of "The Evening's at Seven" visits an old girl friend only to find that the attraction is gone; he sees it is "eighteen minutes after seven and he had the mingled thoughts that clocks always gave him." Mr. Kirk of "One Is a Wanderer," who seems in better shape, is living alone in a room where his "soiled shirts would be piled on the floors of the closet where he had been flinging them for weeks . . ." (a fitting description of Thurber's own Algonquin Hotel room, according to his biographer). Kirk cannot relax and cannot work, so he drinks one brandy after another, not caring to intrude on friends who have already seen enough of him, because "Two is company, four is a party, three is a crowd. One is a wanderer." Also disturbing is "A Box to Hide In," which concerns a man who is beyond the sort of escape that brandy can offer and is asking at grocery stores for a box that is big enough for him to hide in: "It's a form of escape . . . hiding in a box. It circumscribes your worries and the range of your anguish," he explains quite lucidly. It is precisely this melancholy light that permeates Thurber's most distinctive work.

The unique Thurber blend of the comic with the dire and the bizarre is found in "Mr. Preble Gets Rid of His Wife." In this story, as in many others in this collection, the Thurber man and woman are frankly fed up with each other. But in this instance their argument is surreal: Mrs. Preble consents to go down into the cellar, even though she knows Preble wants to kill her down there, so that he will shut up and give her a moment's peace. She is not at all unnerved at the prospect of being bludgeoned to death with a shovel, but she is disgusted with his poor choice of murder weapons, and orders him out to look for something more suitable. Dutifully, the exasperated Preble goes out to hunt up "some

piece of iron or something," as she demands, promising to hurry and to shut the door behind him, because Mrs. Preble is not about to stand in the cellar all night and freeze.

In *Let Your Mind Alone! And Other More or Less Inspirational Pieces* (1937), Thurber continued to publish stories about husbands and wives who are not getting along well together. Although no blood is spilled in "The Breaking Up of the Winships" and "A Couple of Hamburgers," these "serious" stories hardly deal with marriage optimistically. Yet the book is dedicated to Helen Wismer, the Mount Holyoke graduate and magazine editor to whom Thurber was married just one month after his first marriage officially ended in 1935. The newlyweds sought to escape the frenetic, intolerable pace and style of their New York life by escaping to a series of houses in Connecticut. There, in the relative security of a stronger marriage and a greener, more peaceful environment, Thurber developed old and new themes to create a collection that, while not as strong as his previous book, is still one of his half dozen best books.

In the first ten pieces, the "Let Your Mind Alone!" section, Thurber again parodies the writings of mental-efficiency experts, those purveyors of quick, rational, methodical fixes for what ails the human being that he had lampooned in *Is Sex Necessary?* Here he finds that humanity is in deep trouble—doomed, in fact—and he says that "scientists, statisticians, actuaries, all those men who place numbers above hunches, figures above feelings, facts above possibilities. . . ," give advice that is worse than useless in keeping the average Thurber person alive and happy. We do not need to "streamline" our minds to live more successfully; on the contrary, "The undisciplined mind . . . is far better adapted to the confused world in which we live today than the streamlined mind." Self-help writer Mrs. Dorothea Brande, "the Wake-Up-and-Live!" woman, allows daydreaming "only when it is purposeful, only when it is going to lead to realistic action and concrete achievement." This kind of advice would be of little help to the Walter Mittys of this world, and Thurber stands with this yet-to-be-created woolgatherer par excellence in "The Case for the Daydreamer," where he says, "In this insistence on reality I do not see as much profit as these Shapers of Success do." He goes on to give hilarious examples of situations in life where daydreaming presents the most masterful adaptations to the real world. The machine looms large as one of the most ominous forces that threaten human existence, as Thurber presents the case. In "Sex ex Machina,"

Thurber takes issue with the psychologists, who chalk up fears of speeding automobiles to suppressed sexual urges, to "complexes." Thurber knows a threat when he sees one, and cars are terrifying in their own right. "Every person carries in his consciousness the old scar, or the fresh wound, of some harrowing misadventure with a contraption of some sort," he says, be it with a vending machine or "an old Reo with the spark advanced."

The "Other More or Less Inspirational Pieces" prove to be less, rather than more, encouraging about the prospects for human survival. Animals, the reader is assured in "After the Steppe Cat, What?," will prevail against the combined insanities of fascism and communism and the thousand unnatural shocks of technological life; but man is doomed. Woman, however, may fare better. "Man, as he is now traveling," writes Thurber in "Women Go On Forever," "is headed for extinction. Woman is not going with him. It is, I think, high time to abandon the loose, generic term 'Man,' for it is no longer logically inclusive or scientifically exact. There is Man and there is Woman, and Woman is going her own way." In "The Case Against Women" Thurber elaborates his reasons for "hating women," which include: "they always know where things are," they never have the correct change, and "they never get anything exactly right." Thurber describes his deteriorating vision in the last essay in the volume, "The Admiral on the Wheel." Instead of having "only two-fifths vision" with its "peculiar advantages"—like seeing "bridges rise lazily into the air"—the cataract in his eye had grown, and to his ophthalmologist "it was obvious he was going blind." Helen Thurber was driving the car now in the daytime as well as at night, and soon she would have to serve as his "seeing eye wife."

Thurber put off the eye operations he would need to tour Europe with Helen Thurber, to attend the London opening of an art show including his drawings, and to generally "clear his mind." They were out of the country from May 1937 until June 1938, and a record of much of what Thurber saw and thought is in essays such as "You Know How the French Are," "An Afternoon in Paris," and "Journey to the Pyrenees," all collected in *My World–and Welcome to It* (1942). The most significant writing he produced right after returning from Europe, however, was the series gathered from the *New Yorker* and published as *Fables for Our Time and Famous Poems Illustrated* (1940). "Every writer is fascinated by the fable form," he later told Alistair Cooke; "it's short, concise and can say a great deal about life."

In Thurber's fables, there is less reassurance,

less sense of a grand consensus of common wisdom and shared values found in the fables of the ancients or even in the *Fables in Slang* (1899) of Midwestern humorist George Ade. Stylistically, Thurber's are Attic, rather than slangy or full of the wordplay and oddities in capitalization which characterize Ade's work. Written at a time when darkness was descending on the world as well as upon the artist, these fables tend toward the sardonic and register twentieth-century wariness and disenchantment. Doom lunges from every corner at unsuspecting chipmunks, humans, turkeys, and flies. Yet some of the mayhem and destruction seems preventable and is caused by ignorance and folly rather than being simply the terrible way things are. Sometimes "He who hesitates is saved." The problem is not that creatures are unredeemable and always corrupt; it is rather that they are credulous and easily swayed by Hitler-like owls and Mussolini-like foxes. The problem is that "You can fool too many of the people too much of the time." As usual, the males seem, more often than not, vulnerable to the perversity of the females. However, in "The Unicorn in the Garden," one of Thurber's best short pieces, a little man gains one of his infrequent victories. One morning, a typical Thurber husband sees the "mythical beast" in his own garden. The nagging wife, on hearing of his miraculous discovery, tells him that he is a "booby" and that she is going to have him put "in the booby hatch." When the authorities arrive, he denies ever having mentioned a unicorn, and they grab the wife for going on and on about how her husband swore he saw such a thing. She is carried away screaming and he lives "happily ever after," having sustained another victory for the imagination over the world of dull realities. The moral is "Don't count your boobies until they are hatched." Yet in 1938-1939, for Thurber's barnyard animals in "The Hen and the Heavens," "the heavens actually were falling down." And in the moral he commented, "It wouldn't surprise me a bit if they did."

The year 1939 was probably the most rewarding year in Thurber's creative life. Not only did he produce some of his best writing, he achieved great satisfaction in the summer of 1939 from collaborating with his college friend Elliott Nugent on a play. It was Thurber's idea to write *The Male Animal*, but both men participated fully in the work of writing, revising, and rewriting again during trial performances in San Diego, Santa Barbara, Los Angeles, Princeton, and Baltimore. The play was a financial and critical success and had a run of 243 performances at the Cort Theatre in New York where it opened 9 January 1940 with Howard

Shumlin as producer and Nugent playing the lead of Tommy Turner, an English professor at Midwestern University. Warner Brothers made a film version of the play in 1942, starring Henry Fonda and Olivia de Havilland. The film's March 1942 world premiere in Columbus, the Thurber family in attendance, made it clear to everyone that James Thurber had become one of the city's most celebrated offspring.

Thurber had been interested in the theater for a long time, as his participation in dramatics at Ohio State and his work on musicals for the Scarlet Mask Club between 1921 and 1925 had shown. A Broadway play was a great challenge to this writer of short pieces, who had difficulty writing tightly organized, long, and "serious" works. *The Male Animal*, though it is essentially a romantic comedy, has its serious dimensions. Nevertheless, it portrays the battle between Tommy Turner, a classical liberal and defender of good writing, individualism, and principles in the abstract, fighting against blind conformity, brute force, and the voice of money, power, and vested interests—represented partially by former football hero Joe Ferguson and chiefly by the villain of the play, university trustee Ed Keller. Tommy Turner, the professorial defender of principle, is married to an atypical Thurber woman, Ellen. Ellen is lovely and rather passive, and functions primarily as the prize to be fought over by the rival men. Tommy, on the one side, represents reason and the old-fashioned liberal ideal of the integrity of the individual; Joe Ferguson, on the other side, represents the values and virtues of animal vigor, football, and dead-level conformity on all matters considered controversial. The trustee, Ed Keller, is an antiintellectual Red-hunting Babbitt who seeks to have Tommy fired after he learns that Tommy plans to read the last statement of anarchist Bartolomeo Vanzetti. Joe Ferguson, recently divorced, becomes a rival for Ellen's affections, and Tommy appears to play the fool, the defeated Thurber man, as he fantasizes that the "male animal" within him can conquer Ferguson by dint of force. Ferguson knocks him senseless, of course, but he ultimately profits from playing the part of comic victim and butt. For he is a man of principle and of intellect, and can use his experience to gain insight and to adapt. Unlike Walter Mitty, who retreats into fantasy when the world threatens his security, Tommy Turner gains an ironic understanding of himself as a comic figure; at the same time, he can retain a realistic belief in his principles and the virtues of his role as an embattled individualist. In the end, Joe testifies that Tommy is a real "scrap-

per," and Ellen is convinced that Tommy is "wonderful." The play ends not with a divorce, but with a reaffirmation of the Turners' marriage, as "They are kissing each other very, very hard" when the curtain falls. It is not a very political play, as Thurber was not a very political man. Yet the political dimension was thrown into high relief when the play was revived on Broadway in 1952 as the country labored under the shadow of McCarthyism; it did even better at the box office then than it had originally and subsequently went on a national tour.

The Last Flower (1939) is "a parable in pictures" with a spare written text, yet it can hardly be called a cartoon. Written in the fall of 1939, after Germany had invaded Poland, the book opens with World War XII. Although armies ravage the cities, destroy civilization, and devastate the forests, one last flower remains. The few humans left alive find the flower, and nurture it. The cycle begins again and World War XIII destroys all but one man, one woman, and one flower for them to nurture. *The Last Flower* is said to have been Thurber's favorite of his own books in his later years, and E. B. White, writing in the *New Yorker*'s memorial tribute to Thurber, said that he too liked it best of all Thurber's works. "In it," he contended, "you will find his faith in the renewal of life, his feeling for the beauty and fragility of life on earth." The book was dedicated to Thurber's daughter, Rosemary, "in the wistful hope that her world will be better than mine."

"The Secret Life of Walter Mitty" presents the classic version of the Thurber man. This story is unquestionably Thurber's most famous; published first in March of 1939 in the *New Yorker* and later collected in *My World–and Welcome to It*, the story has been frequently reprinted. The name Walter Mitty, like that of George Babbitt or Don Quixote, can be found in the dictionary, defined as "a commonplace unadventurous person who seeks escape from reality through daydreaming and typically imagines himself leading a glamorous life and becoming famous." Tommy Turner indulges in fantasies of himself as a powerful "male animal," but also sees this indulgence as comical. Such ironic detachment from himself as daydreamer gives him a kind of self-awareness and insight that Mitty does not have. Walter Mitty is a compulsive daydreamer and in the story he repeatedly retreats from everyday problems by imagining himself as a pulp-fiction hero—the kind of man neither he nor anyone could ever be. "The more he depends on the escape they afford," writes Stephen Black, "the less possibility there is of his confronting his real problems...."

Yet Mitty's escapist tactics for surviving in a hostile world of domineering wives, traffic cops, automobiles, and all that goes "ta-pocketa-pocketa," seem more effective than those of even jumpier Thurber men, as other stories in *My World–and Welcome to It* reveal.

If 1939 and 1940 had been years of triumph, 1941 began a period of severe trial. Thurber's eye operation could no longer be postponed, and in fact he underwent five operations that year for cataract, glaucoma, and iritis, problems which were related to his childhood accident and the sympathetic ophthalmia induced by the loss of his left eye in 1901. Other family problems, including the death of Helen Thurber's father and the diagnosis that Mary Thurber had cancer, combined to push Thurber through "the corridors of hell," as he put it in a letter. His operations could not reverse the deterioration of his vision, and faced with the prospect of blindness, this intensely visual artist suffered a severe nervous breakdown.

The anxiety, the terror, and the anger of these months were expressed and partially exorcised in some of the darker stories collected in *My World–and Welcome to It*. One of these, possibly the darkest and least amusing little man story Thurber was ever to write, is "The Whip-Poor-Will," first published in 1941 in the *New Yorker*, just after he had begun to climb out of the mental collapse. Like Thurber, Mr. Kinstrey is an upper-middle-class former Ohioan, and the setting appears to be quite like one of the Thurber retreats in Massachusetts or Connecticut. Kinstrey's mental torment mirrors Thurber's concerns: he is plagued by insomnia and provoked by a "brazen-breasted," persistent, sleep-murdering whippoorwill, that neither his servants nor his wife will admit to having heard. His wife tells him to ignore it, to use his "will power." The pun enters his dreams and blends with the unnerving, rhythmic, intolerable birdcalls. Thurber's concern for his loss of sight, possibly manifest in the dominance of aural effects in the story, is more explicit when Kinstrey objects to his wife's use of the word *spectacle* to describe his furious yelling and cursing at the whippoorwill in the middle of the night. "I never heard such a spectacle," she says the next morning. "You can't hear spectacles," says Kinstrey. "You see them." The image returns on the night he goes completely to pieces, imagining that he can hear his wife chant, "Here are your spectacles, here are your spectacles." There is no magic to save this Thurber man, as there is in "The Unicorn in the Garden" or "The Catbird Seat," and there is no comic resolu-

tion: Kinstrey takes out a carving knife and kills his wife, two servants, and himself.

There is a similar dark ending in "A Friend to Alexander," also-collected in *My World–and Welcome to It*. Harry Andrews, the troubled husband, shares with Thurber a fascination with Aaron Burr and the song "Bye, Bye, Blackbird." He, too, is in poor physical health, worries about weight loss, and fortifies himself with all kinds of vitamins. He has terrible dreams and suffers a mental breakdown. In his recurrent dreams, Harry is threatened by Aaron Burr, and he takes to practicing, as if for a duel, with a pistol. After he dies mysteriously in his sleep, the doctor comments that his heart "Just stopped as if he had been shot." Mrs. Andrews, like the wife in "The Unicorn in the Garden," blurts out the impossible truth, that "Aaron Burr killed him the way he killed Hamilton." But when she is pronounced "stark, raving crazy" and is taken away, there is no triumphant humor. There is only grim irony.

There are signs of Thurber's return to mental stability in *My World–and Welcome to It*, however, in several lighter pieces. "You Could Look It Up" is a dialect narrative about a baseball manager who puts in a midget pinch hitter with an infinitesimal strike zone. "A Good Man," expanded and republished as "Adam's Anvil" in *The Thurber Album*, anticipates the nostalgic tone and subject matter of that later volume. Thurber's abiding and deepening interest in the sounds, shapes, and nuances of words is displayed in two other notable pieces, "What Do You Mean It Was Brillig?" and "The Gentleman in 916." Both pieces take off from linguistic anomalies uttered by a "remarkable collection of colored maids," and both reveal his increasingly evident preoccupation with his increasing blindness and the brevity of life. In the first piece, for example, Della perplexes him one day by announcing, "They are here with the reeves." Thurber has a lot of fun with this pronunciation, finally discovering that the "reeves" in question are Yuletide window decorations. In the second, Maisie writes him that she tried to see him in December, "but the timekeeper said you were in Florida." Her reference to "the timekeeper" disturbs him: "Since I have, for the time being, about one-fiftieth vision, I can't actually see him; but I can hear him. It is no illusion that the blind become equipped with the eardrums of an elk hound." Both stories make use of the traditional encounter between the shrewd but uneducated *eiron* with the *alazon*, the word-crazy author who presumes to be smarter than he is. The uneducated Della, for example, says of her employer, "His mind works so fast his body can't keep up with it. . . ," a line which gives Thurber pause. He begins to worry that soon "They will come for me with a reeve and this time it won't be a red-and-green one for the window, it will be a black one for the door."

Many of the themes in Thurber's writing are also found in his drawings. In White's note on the drawings that illustrate *Is Sex Necessary?*, White notes such subjects as "the melancholy of sex," "the implausibility of animals," and the persistent theme of warfare between the sexes. "The War Between Men and Women" is, in fact, the title to a seventeen-part series of drawings, running from the first "Overt Act" (when a man in dinner dress throws a glass of dark liquid in a woman's face) through "The Fight in the Grocery" and "Mrs. Pritchard's Leap," to the ultimate (and baffling) "Surrender" of the women to the men. The series was first collected in *Thurber's Men, Women, and Dogs* (1943), which contains many of Thurber's best and most famous cartoons. Among these is the surrealistic "House and Woman," a drawing that depicts a badly frightened and tiny Thurber man recoiling in astonishment before a three-storied house which somehow has coalesced into an enormous Thurber woman, who glares fiercely at the cowering little man below. Thurber's drawings and cartoons do more than merely illustrate most of his works (they continued to appear in his books even after he had to stop drawing new ones in 1951); they amplify, extend, and open different dimensions of his artistry.

Published in early 1945, after Thurber's five-year struggle with nervous and physical breakdowns including not only the eye operations but a nearly fatal case of appendicitis complicated by pneumonia, *The Thurber Carnival* signaled his recovery and was proof that Thurber had arrived as an important figure in American letters. In a review for the *New Republic*, Malcolm Cowley approached the book "exactly as if it were the work of any other skillful and serious American writer." The book contains six pieces not previously collected (among them one of his best stories, "The Catbird Seat," and one of his best "dark" tales, "The Cane in the Corridor," a work that clearly alludes to his recent suffering and affliction), a selection of pieces from *My World–and Welcome to It*, *Let Your Mind Alone!*, *The Middle-Aged Man on the Flying Trapeze*, *Fables for Our Time and Famous Poems Illustrated*, *The Owl in the Attic*, *The Seal in the Bedroom* (1932), *Thurber's Men, Women, and Dogs*, and the entire contents of *My Life and Hard Times*. The critical reception was extravagant and wide, and for the first time a Thurber book found a truly mass audience, as the book sold 50,000 copies in the Harper's first edition and 375,000 more with the Book-of-the-Month Club. Cowley found that eight of the pieces "are quite serious in effect and intention, and several of the others balance on the edge between farce and disaster. . . ." Many of them deal with murder, death, or "dreams of killing or being killed, and two with the hero of one and the villainess of the other reduced to raving madness." This latter category includes "The Unicorn in the Garden" and "The Catbird Seat," which repeats the pattern of "The Unicorn in the Garden" as the put-upon little man, Edwin Martin, manages to have the browbeating Mrs. Barrow fired by behaving outrageously out of character in her presence and then denying his actions after she reports him to the boss. But almost half the selections in the work, Cowley notes, are "largely based on nightmares, hallucinations or elaborate and cruel practical jokes. Entering Thurber's middle-class world is like wandering into a psychiatric ward and not being quite sure whether you are a visitor or an inmate."

Thurber found relief from some of his mental and physical troubles in writing works like the nostalgic *The Thurber Album* and in a series of romances for children and adults that included *Many Moons* (1943), *The Great Quillow* (1944), *The White Deer* (1945), *The 13 Clocks* (1950), and *The Wonderful O* (1957). These stories depart from the plain style of the typical Thurber casuals and are characterized by a more poetic density of figures and allusions, and, at times, meter and rhyme. White called *The White Deer* "Exhibit A in the strange case of a writer's switch from eye work to ear work." Thurber had always written about people who live by virtue of their power to dream, surviving in hostile circumstances with the help of their inner visions. Now this element of fantasy predominates, and these works can be called proper romances, tales of wizards and kings and enchanted forests, of spells and potions and captive princesses. As in the myth of the Fisher King, there is a blight upon the land at the beginning of each of these tales. Thurber's questing heroes manage to break the withering forces of evil and restore order, meaning, and purpose to the world. The heroes are toymakers, sensitive third sons, wandering minstrels, and jesters; in *The Wonderful O* the hero is a poet. They are all men of imagination, shapers who order the meaningless jumble of things and make sense out of them. These fantasists succeed where more practical men—represented by mathematicians, physicians,

Cartoon by James Thurber

lawyers, and experts of every type fail. The princess marries the minstrel-prince in *The 13 Clocks*, and sails away from the land of the cruel, cold duke, who lives in a land that is so cold that all the clocks have stopped, frozen. They cannot be started again until the princess holds her hand at a certain magical distance from them—at which time they thaw and begin to strike the hours. The minutes of clocks, Thurber seems to be hinting, like the words of stories, create and order the world—they humanize it, they lend it the meaning that it otherwise lacks. It is the inner vision of the artist that creates the bright shapes by which people must live. The poet as the hero of *The Wonderful O* restores the letter Os to the land from which they have been banished, and thereby returns to the inhabitants words like hope, love, valor, and freedom.

In the foreword to *The Beast in Me and Other Animals* (1948), Thurber apologized for coming out with "another collection of short pieces and small drawings," when a writer "verging on his middle fifties" "should be engaged on some work dignified by length and of a solemnity suitable to our darkening age. . . ." The darkening was first and most

immediately his nearly complete blindness, and the perceptible decline in the quality of this volume compared with earlier collections is apparent. Since 1946, he had been forced to dictate his stories to a secretary and had found this process difficult and complicated further by the need to find a secretary with whom he could be comfortable. It was a troubled time, even though he and Helen Thurber had found a large colonial house that they liked in quiet West Cornwall, Connecticut.

The Beast in Me and Other Animals included "A Sheaf of Drawings," featuring some of his last cartoons and whimsical sketches of Thurber men and women, and also three sets of drawings-with-text under the heading "Less Alarming Creatures" (less alarming than humans, that is). These were some of the last drawings Thurber was able to produce, and all of them were executed with the assistance of technical aids, such as the Zeiss loop—a magnifying helmet used during the war for precision work in defense plants. Some of the creatures are Thurber's versions of real beasts, such as Bosmon's Potto (a species of primate), but other creatures are Thurber's inventions. There are Trochees encountering Spondees, Serenades, and Victuals, for example. Ross was delighted with these pictured puns and asked the artist to continue, but the only addition Thurber could think of would be "a man being generous to a fault—that is, handing a small rodent a nut."

During the mid-1940s and early 1950s, Thurber produced relatively few casuals and stories for the *New Yorker*. His "heart wasn't in it" to write amusingly during this period he said, and Bernstein reveals that in his private life he was often behaving as a tyrannical, temperamental, and sometimes drunken and vengeful "King of Cornwall," given to dyspeptic rages and pronouncements. The pieces he collected in *The Beast in Me and Other Animals* sometimes show "the beast" in him—an opinionated and cantankerous misogynist or an old stick critical of the new, as in "Thix," where he compares the popular-culture radio serials such as "Captain Midnight" with the less harrowing adventures he followed in his own youth through the plays and nickel novels back in Columbus. Such a subject also betrays his dependence on radio for entertainment, as becomes even more evident in his long, five-part investigation "Soapland," which originally ran in the *New Yorker* as a reportorial piece in which "the humor . . . is coincidental." This investigation of radio soap opera and the sex roles and cultural values displayed therein was a popular success in the magazine and demonstrated Thurber's ability as a serious analyst of American culture. *The Beast in Me*—even in its title—also demonstrates Thurber's continued reverence for the work of Henry James, whose "The Beast in the Jungle" he elaborately imitates, more in homage than in parody, in "The Beast in the Dingle." Ross rejected the piece as too labored and literary, saying that he "understood fifteen percent of the allusions," leaving Thurber to wonder just which fifteen percent those could have been. Ross did print "A Call on Mrs. Forrester," however, Thurber's tribute to Willa Cather and Henry James, told by a sort of Lambert Strether making an imaginary call on Cather's "lost lady" and comparing her to Mme de Vionnet. "It's about a man and two women," Ross said, "and it comes over."

Thurber's love of puns, word games, and puzzles of all sorts had been evident in his work from the beginning and had been further developed in his employment as a code clerk, which led him to read books on cryptography. In this volume, as in the "fairy tales" for adults and children he had been writing, his fascination with the sounds and structures of words is expressed not only in the curious names of whimsical creatures and the loving imitations of Henry James, but with anagrammatic experimentation and wordplay in "Here Come the Tigers." Two friends demonstrate, for example, how they have "discovered a new dimension of meaning," finding "the lips in pistol / And mists in times, / Cats in crystal, / And mice in chimes." Such logomania abounds in Thurber's later work, often amounts to a preponderance of wit over humor, and sometimes becomes excessively private in its significance.

Thurber had never been intensely interested in politics, but as the fever of McCarthysim spread, he became involved in defending the rights of the individual as opposed to the growing enthusiasm for "loyalty" and conformity. In 1946 he supported the staff of the *Sundial*, the Ohio State humor magazine he had edited in his student days, after the university administration had suspended its publication for a year because the magazine had published material they considered offensive. In 1947 he wrote a letter defending E. B. White when the *New York Herald Tribune* referred to White's opinions as potentially dangerous. (White had written a letter to the editor of that newspaper condemning required loyalty oaths as unconstitutional.) And in 1951, after the administration at Ohio State instituted a gag rule for campus speakers, he again took sides and became the first alumnus of that institution to refuse the offer of an honorary degree. In his 1951 letter of refusal, he wrote that acceptance at that time might be construed as approval of Ohio State's recent trespasses against the rights of "freedom of speech and freedom of research." This concern for the rights of the embattled artist and individual is expressed briefly in *The Thurber Album* in "Length and Shadow," the profile of Ohio State English professor and dean Joseph Villiers Denney (the model for Dean Damon in *The Male Animal*). Thurber writes that Denney "must have turned restlessly in his grave" all during the fall of 1951 when "the trustees were qualifying freedom of speech at the university. . . ." But this profile represents a departure from the basic tone and subject matter of *The Thurber Album*, which is mostly nostalgic and sentimental.

He told interviewers that *The Thurber Album* "was written at a time when in America there was a feeling of fear and suspicion. It's quite different from *My Life and Hard Times*," he said, though it treats many of the same times and characters. But the earlier book is "funnier and better. . . . The *Album* was kind of an escape—going back to the Middle West of the last century and the beginning of this, when there wasn't this fear and hysteria." Besides his sense of a general public hysteria and in addition to his personal mental and physical afflictions, during 1949 he was grieved over a serious auto accident that injured his daughter, Rosemary; by the nervous breakdown of longtime friend and collaborator Elliott Nugent; and by his wife's surgery for uterine cysts. He was also deeply saddened in 1951 by the death of Harold Ross.

In the face of all these trials, *The Thurber Album* is an impressive achievement and gave Thurber an opportunity to, as his grandfather would have put it, "show his Fisher"—to show the spirit of such ancestors as his maternal great-great-grandfather Jacob Fisher, remembered in "Adam's Anvil" (the story was previously printed as "A Good Man"). This forebear is described as a virtual ring-tailed roarer in the tradition of the humor of the Old Southwest. Jacob Fisher, born in 1808 near Columbus, fought "a thousand fights in his time," including one fight, carefully described, in which he whipped the entire canal-barge crew that had been poaching on his ducks. Fisher used to move horses in his blacksmithing shop by picking them up and carrying them—"it was easier to move 'em that way

James Thurber

than to lead 'em sometimes." Not only do these exploits match those told in an earlier age, but the manner of telling also recalls the framework narrative structure as found, for example, in "The Celebrated Jumping Frog of Calaveras County" by Mark Twain. Thurber, as first-person narrator, introduces his uncle Mahlon Taylor, whom he describes and characterizes. Taylor narrates in dialect the inner tale, the yarns about Fisher—stories that seem "mostly true, with some stretchers," as Huck Finn might say. The notable difference from the stories of the horse-sense era is in the character of the first narrator: "A far lesser breed of men," Thurber admits, "has succeeded the old gentleman on the American earth, and I tremble to think what he would have said of a great-grandson who turned out to be a writer."

In *The Thurber Album*, Thurber remembers with fondness and wit Margery Albright, the midwife who had delivered him and whom he called "Aunt Margery," though she was not related to him. Aunt Margery was a formidable personage, a homeopath, and a woman of considerable resource and unquestionable resolve; in her and even more in Thurber's portrait of his mother in "Lavender with a Difference," we see the positive side of the Thurber woman. And in "Gentleman from Indiana," about his father, Charles Thurber, we see one of the originals of the Thurber man, the kind of person who, when he tried to fix a rabbit pen, could only succeed in locking himself into the cage. The "frankly nostalgic" excursion to friends and faces in the past concludes with a "Photograph Gallery," photographs of nearly all the important figures he had written about in the book, including his eccentric relatives; his Ohio State professors Denney, Taylor, and Graves; football hero Chic Harley; city editor Norman Kuehner of the *Dispatch*; and his early model, journalist Robert O. Ryder.

Despite the strain he was under from 1948 through 1952, Thurber continued to produce casuals for the *New Yorker* and short pieces for other periodicals in addition to the work he was doing on his fairy stories and *The Thurber Album*. The best of these were collected in *Thurber Country* (1953), and while, as Charles S. Holmes points out, there are "no new departures" here, the work is of a high order. A dominant theme that runs through many of the pieces concerns the difficulty of communication and the decay of meaning: the problem of closing the gap between sender and receiver. The telephone, according to "The Case Book of James Thurber," is responsible for the kind of verbal confusion in which a woman whose name seems to be

Sherlock Holmes turns out to be Shirley Combs; the maid may think that one's spouse is coming home with a "cockeyed Spaniard," but it is only a new cocker spaniel puppy. The telephone may also tangle the user in the cord, like the one the Thurbers used on one of their trips to France. There, as Thurber says in "The Girls in the Closet," it is possible to have profounder misunderstandings trying to explain in French the problem with the overabundance of *fil* ("wire") when it is mispronounced *fille* ("girl"), indicating that "There are too many girls in the closet," and opening the door to further trouble. Writing letters does not seem to reduce the confusion appreciably, as two epistolary pieces demonstrate. "File and Forget" and "Joyeux Noel, Mr. Durning" are both presented as exchanges of letters between bureaucratic officialdom and the author. In the first, ineradicable confusion persists through a long, complicated exchange between Thurber and a publishing house; and in the second, similar confusion multiplies when a Christmas gift of liqueur sent to Thurber from France is seized by customs and he tries to have it released. Literary talk about T. S. Eliot's play *The Cocktail Party* ends in meaningless doubletalk and endless proliferation of private interpretations. One character wheezes, seemingly beside the point under discussion, but right on the more general intent of these pieces: "Discipline breaking down all over the world." The search in an author's work for what James called "the figure in the carpet" is central to the movement of "A Final Note on Chanda Bell," a story that pays homage to Thurber's old master and also shows the influence of Joyce and possibly Gertrude Stein. The title character is a noted if peculiar novelist given to wordplay that recalls either Joyce's *Finnegans Wake* or Mrs. Malaprop. She draws the narrator into a frenzied search for the secret key to all her work, telling him, "You have found the figure, Thurber . . . but have you found the carpet?" He reads her work backward, upside down, in the mirror, and in the end is trying to read it sideways, but there is reason "to fear that she had perpetrated, in . . . her novels, one of the major literary hoaxes of our time. . . ." It may be that her seemingly meaningless statements are literally meaningless.

Thurber's opinion that the language was decaying and that meaning itself was threatened led to more strident protestations against lax usage in his last works. Accompanying this theme is his fascination with word games, already evident in "Here Come the Tigers" and the verbal wit of the fairy stories. One of his best pieces on word games appears in *Thurber Country* as "Do You Want to Make Something Out of It? (Or, If You Put an 'O' on 'Understo,' You'll Ruin My 'Thunderstorm')," which explains a variation of "ghosts," a word-spelling game. Thurber was a fanatical player of this and other word games during these years, and in this witty and very funny piece he shares some of the linguistic arcana he has discovered both in hours of play and later, while tossing on his sheets, coming up with "bedwords"—words that can't be found in the dictionary (and so cannot be played) but which have the right letters in the middle. "Sgra" bedwords, for example, include such Thurber coinages as "Kissgranny, 1. A man who seeks the company of older women . . . 2. An overaffectionate old woman, a hugmoppet, a bunnytalker"; and "blessgravy. A minister or cleric; . . . *Colloq.* a breakvow, a shrugholy." In a piece that is particularly interesting to the student of American humor, Thurber presents a tale of the confrontation of himself, playing the part of citified wit and *alazon*, against Zeph Leggin, "a character in the classic mold, a lazy rustic philosopher." Thurber cannot stand to be upstaged by this shrewd cracker-barrel philosopher, but in his attempts to duel verbally with the fellow he is soundly defeated. Horse-sense sayings are not to his liking, as his twisted fables reveal; yet he acknowledges their power and makes efficient use of the tradition.

The characteristic attitudes and subjects of Thurber's later work are fully evident in *Further Fables for Our Time* (1956), in which none of the fables is as good as the best in *Fables for Our Time*. Thurber's antipathy to McCarthyism is once again evident in pieces such as "The Peaceful Mongoose," where the deviant animal who tries to use his head is told that "reason is six-sevenths treason." He is condemned to banishment finally, and the moral is: "Ashes to ashes, and clay to clay, if the enemy doesn't get you your own folks may." Thurber's conviction that the lines of communication were fraying is also a prominent theme. "We live, man and worm," says Thurber in "The Weaver and the Worm," "in a time when almost everything can mean almost anything, for this is the age of gobbledygook, doubletalk, and gudda." His pessimism over the state of the language merged with his increasing cynicism and doubts that anything could be done to remedy the world's sorry state. The tools of the humorist apparently are not much use when "the truth is not merry and bright." "The truth is dark and cold," says a squirrel in "The Turtle Who Conquered Time." The sinister truth could be "twisted" in the direction of comedy in Thurber's earlier work, the comic mask providing a mode of adaptation to the darkness, but in *Further Fables for Our Time*, he seems less able to effect the twist of humor and tends to assault the truth head-on. Yet he did not seem to find this method gratifying. "Oh, why should the shattermyth have to be a crumplehope and a dampenglee?" asks the moral of the turtle fable. As "shattermyth" it is impossible to avoid dampening glee. Thurber seemed to be recognizing the change in his work when he described a hen who had been told by her psychiatrist that she had "galloping aggression, inflamed ego, and too much gall."

Alarms and Diversions (1957) is an anthology of selected prose from as far back as 1942 and of drawings from as early as 1931. There is no fiction among the ten new pieces in the volume, none of which is particularly amusing. There are essays on a variety of topics—on child-rearing; on a 1912 gangland murder and scandal (Thurber was fascinated by murders throughout his career); on forgotten American holidays; on the relative durability of men and women (women may have more of what it takes to survive, he avers); on the relative brevity of life in Thurber's generation of American authors; on the Loch Ness monster—and so on. In "The First Time I Saw Paris" Thurber casts a wistful backward glance on his youth. The subdued tone and the poignant depiction of incidents described contrast strikingly with the exuberant, boyish letters he wrote Elliott Nugent in 1918-1919 when these events were taking place. Thurber's obsession with the decay of language is presented in "The Psychosemanticist Will See You Now, Mr. Thurber," in which he condemns the "carcinonomenclature of our times" and links the health of the body politic with that of the body semantic: "Ill fares the land, to galloping fears a prey, whose gobbledygook accumulates, and words decay." This allusive, ornate sentence expresses his thesis and also reveals his late predilection for wordplay, verbal wit, and harangue—at the expense of the humor of character and the comedy of ideas.

The last two years of Thurber's life may have been difficult in many ways, filled as they were with the night fears and drunken scenes described by Bernstein. Yet there was the bright success of his reminiscence, *The Years With Ross* (1959). Thurber had intended to write something about Harold Ross for more than a decade, at one time considering a play. What he finally created was a series of anecdotal essays, published first in the *Atlantic* beginning in 1957 and collected as *The Years With Ross*. The book was an achievement of memory, research, and discipline, and constituted a "strongly autobio-

graphical" but affectionate tribute to his editor and friend, as well as providing an insider's account of the early development of the *New Yorker* and the circle of people that were associated with this important magazine. It proved to be Thurber's longest sustained piece of writing on a single subject, but it was not warmly received by a number of other *New Yorker* "insiders"; most notably, the book was disliked by E. B. and Katharine White, longtime friends of both Thurber and Harold Ross, and people whose opinions mattered very much to the author. Even so, this anecdotal memoir is in a genre at which Thurber excelled, and the book has a lasting power to entertain and move the reader. It was a best-seller and a Book-of-the-Month Club selection and, according to Holmes, "was reviewed more widely, enthusiastically, and in more detail than any of his previous books."

On 7 January 1960 *A Thurber Carnival* premiered at the Hartman Theater in Columbus, the scene of the Scarlet Mask Club productions that Thurber had worked on in the early 1920s. This Columbus homecoming was, Bernstein says, "by far the most spectacular" of all his returns to the hometown. The show opened 26 February 1960 at the ANTA Theatre in New York. Though Thurber wrote a great deal of new material, most of the sketches that were used in this "evening of words and music" consists of tried-and-true pieces, altered and adapted for the stage. The production was the joint creation of a number of people—Haila Stoddard, Don Elliott, and Burgess Meredith—but Thurber worked energetically at all aspects of preparing the show for the stage, and even managed to stimulate the box-office receipts by taking a part, playing himself in the "File and Forget" sketch in September 1960 when the play reopened in New York following a national tour. He appeared in eighty-eight performances and won a special "Tony" award for his distinguished writing. Despite this success, he was restless, often quarrelsome, unable to sleep. His health was failing and he knew he was losing his ability to write as he had written before.

Lanterns & Lances was the last of his books that Thurber saw in print. In the foreword, he defends the "lances" that now appear in his later works, cast "at the people and ideas that have disturbed me, and I make no apology for their seriousness." Though the book has material that was "written in anger" and some pieces that may seem "lugubrious," he wishes that the reader will find in the book a "basic thread of hope." And there is hope to be found, though Thurber writes about the "decline of

At: The Stafford Hotel,
       St. James's Place,
          London, S.W.1.

2nd May 1961.

Mr. Norman A. Kurland,
Chase C-42,
Harvard Business School,
Boston 63, MASS.
U.S.A.

Dear Mr. Kurland,

I had to give up public appearances when I became a hundred and went blind nearly twenty years ago, and, besides, I am now in Europe and in the Fall expect to be in Jeopardy.

Thanks anyway, and all best wishes,

Sincerely yours,

James Thurber

JAMES THURBER.

Letter written six months before Thurber's death

humor and comedy in our time" in essays such as "The Case for Comedy" and "The Duchess and the Bugs." He also continues to rail about the decline of language in pieces such as "Conversation Piece: Connecticut," "The Tyranny of Trivia," and "The Watchers of the Night." In "The Trouble with Man Is Man" he expands upon his notion, delivered frequently in interviews during these years, that humans as a species are inferior to other creatures. He echoes the sentiments of Mark Twain's satan in *The Mysterious Stranger* when in his own "Here Come the Dolphins" he points out at length that when we humans say the beast in us has been aroused, it would be more accurate to say that the human being in us has been acting up—for animals are far less brutish than people.

Doom lowers on the narrator in this book, and only rarely can he find a way to laugh at his predicament. This is the "Atomic and the Aspirin Age," and the widespread angst he describes is most acute, it would seem, among writers, particularly those in his own generation. In "The Porcupines and the Artichokes" he says, "The literary men roughly in my age group become more articulate, and less coherent, as the years go by, but their age does not keep them away from parties." In *Lanterns & Lances* the narrator is frequently depicted as a distressed, jumpy insomniac. In "The Tyranny of Trivia," for example, he discusses his "preoccupation, compulsive perhaps, but not obsessive, with words and the alphabet. . . ." The purpose of his word games and speculations "is the sidetracking of worrisome trains of thought"; but the image of this worrier is one that seems to evoke in the reader pity and fear rather than laughter. The comic mask does not seem fully in place when he says, "My own habit, in bed at home or in the hospital, of exploring words and the alphabet acts to prevent my talking back to the wallpaper, a practice that, except in the case of the upright figure, may be more alarming than amusing." On the other hand, the narrator of "The Wings of Henry James" appears to be a sensitive and erudite literary critic; and the voice that speaks in so many of the "conversation pieces" is that of the Literatus, the supersophisticated and well-known personality, who jousts idly with half-wits, usually female half-wits, replying to their inanities in his "best Henry James garden-party manner." Only in "My Senegalese Birds and Siamese Cats" do we again hear the voice of the comic and vulnerable Thurber man. This is the only piece that makes extensive use of reminiscence—the familiar Thurber mixture of narrative fact and fiction concerning the fixes he can get into with such things as

pets and appliances. In this piece he confesses that he has suffered from "decreasing inventiveness" in his later years, and also makes a remark that crystallizes the Thurber blend of memory and art: "Historicity lies so close to legend in my world that I often walk with one foot in each arena, with side trips, or so my critics declare, into fantasy."

The comic mask had allowed the narrator of *My Life and Hard Times* to make the reader laugh in spite of the awareness of doom. But the narrator in most of the late pieces, whether he is the polished Literatus or the jumpy insomniac, seldom functions as a comedian. "Humor is," as Thurber wrote in 1936, "a kind of emotional chaos told about calmly and quietly in retrospect." More and more, he seemed to lack the inner quiet and concentrated attention necessary to twist reality into comedy. "I can't hide anymore behind the mask of comedy that I've used all my life," he told Elliott Nugent during his last year. "People are not funny; they are vicious and horrible—and so is life!"

On 3 October 1961 the Thurbers attended the opening of Noel Coward's musical *Sail Away* and a dinner party that followed at Sardi's East. Their evening went badly, and after Coward made a speech, Thurber "stood up and demanded the microphone, shouting that he had something to say." Undaunted by an appalled audience, he sang "Bye, Bye, Blackbird"—a song that held private significance for him. "Suddenly, he staggered and lurched." While many other guests thought he was drunk, the problem was more serious. Later that night, Helen Thurber found him lying in a pool of blood on the bathroom floor of their hotel room; and at the hospital the surgeons removed a large cerebral hematoma and found "evidence of arteriosclerosis and several small strokes dating back at least a year. He had a senescent brain." He died on 2 November 1961 after developing pneumonia and a blood clot in a lung. His wife reported that near the end "Thurber had once seemed to whisper, 'God bless . . . God damn.'"

Helen Thurber in the foreword to the posthumously published *Credos and Curios* (1962) explains that in collecting these pieces she is trying to carry out her husband's plans, as far as she is able to reconstruct them, for another book. Quite a few of the pieces, she notes, "express in some way his credos—his beliefs and feelings about humor and comedy, for example." The most impressive essay of this sort is "The Future, If Any, of Comedy or, Where Do We Non-Go from Here?" As the title would indicate, this piece discusses the decline and fall of humor, language, and the human species in the same vein that Thurber had been following in many late interviews and in *Lanterns & Lances*. Alongside these credal essays are the "curios"—"Prefaces and short profiles of people he knew and admired"—including a 1938 piece on E. B. White, a 1940 profile of Elliott Nugent, a 1949 piece on Robert Benchley, and "Scott in Thorns," a 1951 essay about a one-night spree with F. Scott Fitzgerald. There are also three short stories, including two of the last pieces of magazine fiction, "The Other Room" and "Brother Endicott." Both of the stories are set in Paris and both involve aging centers of consciousness who reckon up the distance they have traveled since youth. The stories seem to comment, if indirectly, on the Jamesian theme of the difference between the European and the American experience. Both stories also represent Thurber's attempt to write "serious" fiction, and Helen Thurber draws attention to this dimension in his life's work by including in the volume "Menaces in May," originally published in 1928. This impressionistic piece, she says, is "interesting because it was the first Thurber story in the *New Yorker* to depart from the 'little funny casual' he was writing in those early days." The menaces that confront the protagonist are quite similar to those that might assault a "funny little man," but here they are not treated humorously. The man wonders over the events of a disturbing day and thinks: "Chaos had threatened a perfectly directed evening. Maybe his life even. . . ."

Chaos had always threatened Thurber's characters; his anti-heroic John Monroes, Walter Mittys, Mr. Martins, and Mr. Kinstreys seem, in fact, to anticipate the spiritual drifters and death-obsessed schlemiels of later *New Yorker* writers Donald Barthelme and Woody Allen. They prefigure the characters of "black humor" more often than they recall cracker-barrel philosophers, horse-sense characters, or even the little men of early *New Yorker* writers Clarence Day and Robert Benchley. Benchley's "perfect neurotics" seem well-adjusted to the world when compared with many Thurber men, who frequently wander all the way around the bend to appear as murderous psychopaths rather than mildly maladjusted but fundamentally genial human beings. Chaos threatened Thurber personae and characters early and late, and the threat intensified as the years passed and the books accumulated. Yet even at the last, when there were more alarms than diversions, more lances than lanterns, there was that "thread of hope." In "The Case for Comedy" (originally published in 1960 and reprinted in *Lanterns & Lances*), he mentions that he had heard Walter Lippmann

say on television that he "did not believe the world is coming apart," in spite of all the apparent signs of decay and the growing nuclear stockpiles; "It is high time," Thurber commented, "that we came of age and realized that, like Emily Dickinson's hope, humor is a feathered thing that perches in the soul." Introducing the same volume, he had written that it's not just "later than you think" it is also " 'lighter than you think.' In this light, let's not look back in anger, or forward in fear, but around in awareness."

Play:

The Male Animal, by Thurber and Elliott Nugent, New York, Cort Theatre, 9 January 1940;

A Thurber Carnival, Columbus, Ohio, Hartman Theater, 7 January 1960; New York, ANTA Theatre, 26 February 1960.

Interviews:

Harvey Breit, "Mr. Thurber Observes a Serene Birthday," *New York Times Magazine*, 4 December 1949, p. 17;

Alistair Cooke, "James Thurber: In Conversation with Alistair Cooke," *Atlantic*, 198 (August 1956): 36-40;

George Plimpton and Max Steele, "James Thurber," *Writers at Work: The Paris Review Interviews*, edited by Malcolm Cowley (New York: Viking, 1959).

Bibliography:

Edwin T. Bowden, *James Thurber: A Bibliography* (Columbus: Ohio State University Press, 1968).

Biographies:

Charles S. Holmes, *The Clocks of Columbus: The Literary Career of James Thurber* (New York: Atheneum, 1972);

Burton Bernstein, *Thurber* (New York: Dodd, Mead, 1975).

References:

Stephen A. Black, *James Thurber: His Masquerades* (The Hague: Mouton, 1970);

Walter Blair and Hamlin Hill, *America's Humor: From Poor Richard to Doonesbury* (New York: Oxford, 1978);

Max Eastman, *The Enjoyment of Laughter* (New York: Simon & Schuster, 1936);

Charles S. Holmes, ed., *Thurber: A Collection of Crit-*

ical Essays (Englewood Cliffs, N.J.: Prentice-Hall, 1974);

Lost Generation Journal, special Thurber issue, 3 (Winter 1975);

Robert E. Morseberger, *James Thurber* (New York: Twayne, 1964);

Joel Sayre, "Priceless Gift of Laughter," *Time*, 58 (9 July 1951): 88-94;

[William Shawn and E. B. White], "James Thurber," *New Yorker*, 37 (11 November 1961): 247;

William L. Shirer, *20th Century Journey, A Memoir of a*

Life and the Times: The Start 1904-1930 (New York: Simon & Schuster, 1976);

Richard C. Tobias, *The Art of James Thurber* (Athens: Ohio University Press, 1969);

Norris W. Yates, *The American Humorist* (Ames: Iowa State University Press, 1964).

Papers:

Most of Thurber's papers are in the Thurber Collection at the Ohio State University Library in Columbus, Ohio.

Mark Twain
(Samuel Langhorne Clemens)

Pascal Covici, Jr.
Southern Methodist University

BIRTH: Florida, Missouri, 30 November 1835, to John Marshall and Jane Lampton Clemens.

MARRIAGE: 2 February 1870 to Olivia Langdon; children: Langdon, Olivia Susan, Clara, Jane Lampton.

AWARDS: Honorary M.A., Yale University, 1888; LL.D., University of Missouri, 1902; elected to the American Academy of Arts and Letters, 1904; Litt.D., Oxford University, 1907.

DEATH: Redding, Connecticut, 21 April 1910.

SELECTED BOOKS: *The Celebrated Jumping Frog of Calaveras County, and Other Sketches* (New York: C. H. Webb, 1867; London: Routledge, 1867);

The Innocents Abroad, or The New Pilgrims' Progress (Hartford, Conn.: American Publishing Company, 1869); republished in 2 volumes as *The Innocents Abroad* and *The New Pilgrims' Progress* (London: Hotten, 1870);

Mark Twain's (Burlesque) Autobiography and First Romance (New York: Sheldon, 1871; London: Hotten, 1871);

"Roughing It" (London: Routledge, 1872);

The Innocents at Home (London: Routledge, 1872);

Roughing It, enlarged edition (Hartford, Conn.: American Publishing Company, 1872)—

combines *"Roughing It"* and *The Innocents at Home*;

A Curious Dream; and Other Sketches (London: Routledge, 1872);

The Gilded Age: A Tale of Today, by Twain and Charles Dudley Warner (Hartford, Conn.: American Publishing Company, 1873; 3 volumes, London: Routledge, 1874);

Mark Twain's Sketches, New and Old (Hartford, Conn.: American Publishing Company, 1875);

The Adventures of Tom Sawyer (London: Chatto & Windus, 1876; Hartford, Conn.: American Publishing Company, 1876);

Old Times on the Mississippi (Toronto: Belford, 1876); republished as *The Mississippi Pilot* (London: Ward, Lock & Tyler, 1877); expanded as *Life on the Mississippi* (London: Chatto & Windus, 1883; Boston: Osgood, 1883);

An Idle Excursion (Toronto: Rose-Belford, 1878); expanded as *Punch, Brothers, Punch! and Other Sketches* (New York: Slote, Woodman, 1878);

A Tramp Abroad (London: Chatto & Windus / Hartford, Conn.: American Publishing Company, 1880);

The Prince and the Pauper (London: Chatto & Windus, 1881; Boston: Osgood, 1882);

The Stolen White Elephant (London: Chatto & Windus, 1882); republished as *The Stolen White Elephant, Etc.* (Boston: Osgood, 1882);

The Adventures of Huckleberry Finn (London:

Chatto & Windus, 1884); republished as *Adventures of Huckleberry Finn* (New York: Webster, 1885);

A Connecticut Yankee in King Arthur's Court (New York: Webster, 1889); republished as *A Yankee at the Court of King Arthur* (London: Chatto & Windus, 1889);

The American Claimant (New York: Webster, 1892; London: Chatto & Windus, 1892);

Merry Tales (New York: Webster, 1892);

The £1,000,000 Bank-Note and Other New Stories (New York: Webster, 1893; London: Chatto & Windus, 1893);

Tom Sawyer Abroad by Huck Finn (New York: Webster, 1894; London: Chatto & Windus, 1894);

Pudd'nhead Wilson, A Tale (London: Chatto & Windus, 1894); expanded as *The Tragedy of Pudd'nhead Wilson and the Comedy of Those Extraordinary Twins* (Hartford, Conn.: American Publishing Company, 1894);

Personal Recollections of Joan of Arc by the Sieur Louis de Conte (New York: Harper, 1896; London: Chatto & Windus, 1896);

Tom Sawyer Abroad, Tom Sawyer, Detective, and Other Stories (New York: Harper, 1896);

Tom Sawyer, Detective, as told by Huck Finn, and Other Stories (London: Chatto & Windus, 1896);

How to Tell a Story and Other Essays (New York: Harper, 1897);

Following the Equator (Hartford, Conn.: American Publishing Company, 1897); republished as *More Tramps Abroad* (London: Chatto & Windus, 1897);

The Man That Corrupted Hadleyburg and Other Stories and Essays (New York & London: Harper, 1900); enlarged as *The Man That Corrupted Hadleyburg and Other Stories and Sketches* (London: Chatto & Windus, 1900);

A Double Barrelled Detective Story (New York & London: Harper, 1902);

Eve's Diary Translated from the Original Ms (London & New York: Harper, 1906);

What Is Man? (New York: De Vinne Press, 1906); expanded as *What Is Man? and Other Essays* (New York & London: Harper, 1917);

The $30,000 Bequest and Other Stories (New York & London: Harper, 1906);

Christian Science with Notes Containing Corrections to Date (New York & London: Harper, 1907);

A Horse's Tale (New York & London: Harper, 1907);

Is Shakespeare Dead? (New York & London: Harper, 1909);

Extract from Captain Stormfield's Visit to Heaven (New York & London: Harper, 1909);

Mark Twain's Speeches, edited by F. A. Nast (New York & London: Harper, 1910);

The Mysterious Stranger, a Romance, edited by Albert Bigelow Paine and Frederick A. Duneka (New York & London: Harper, 1916); expanded as *The Mysterious Stranger and Other Stories*, edited by Paine (New York & London: Harper, 1922);

The Curious Republic of Gondour and Other Whimsical Sketches (New York: Boni & Liveright, 1919);

Mark Twain's Speeches, edited by Paine (New York & London: Harper, 1923);

Europe and Elsewhere, edited by Paine (New York & London: Harper, 1923);

Mark Twain's Autobiography, edited by Paine, 2 volumes (New York & London: Harper, 1924);

Sketches of the Sixties, by Twain and Bret Harte (San Francisco: Howell, 1926);

The Adventures of Thomas Jefferson Snodgrass, edited by Charles Honce (Chicago: Pascal Covici, 1928);

Mark Twain's Notebook, edited by Paine (New York & London: Harper, 1935);

Letters from the Sandwich Islands Written for the Sacramento Union, edited by G. Ezra Dane (San Francisco: Grabhorn, 1937);

The Washoe Giant in San Francisco, edited by Franklin Walker (San Francisco: Fields, 1938);

Mark Twain's Travels With Mr. Brown, edited by Walker and Dane (New York: Knopf, 1940);

Mark Twain in Eruption, edited by Bernard DeVoto (New York & London: Harper, 1940);

Mark Twain at Work, edited by DeVoto (Cambridge: Harvard University Press, 1942);

Mark Twain, Business Man, edited by Samuel Charles Webster (Boston: Little, Brown, 1946);

Mark Twain of the ENTERPRISE, edited by Henry Nash Smith (Berkeley: University of California Press, 1957);

Traveling with the Innocents Abroad: Mark Twain's Original Reports from Europe and the Holy Land, edited by Daniel Morley McKeithan (Norman: University of Oklahoma Press, 1958);

Letters from the Earth, edited by DeVoto (New York: Harper & Row, 1962);

Mark Twain's San Francisco, edited by Bernard Taper (New York: McGraw-Hill, 1963);

Mark Twain's "Which was the Dream" and Other Symbolic Writings of the Later Years, edited by John S. Tuckey (Berkeley: University of California Press, 1966);

"What Is Man?" and Other Philosophical Writings, edited by Paul Baender (Berkeley: University of California Press, 1967);

Mark Twain's Satires and Burlesques, edited by Franklin R. Rogers (Berkeley: University of California Press, 1967);

Clemens of the "Call": Mark Twain in San Francisco, edited by Edgar M. Branch (Berkeley: University of California Press, 1969);

Mark Twain's Hannibal, Huck, and Tom, edited by Walter Blair (Berkeley: University of California Press, 1969);

Mark Twain's "Mysterious Stranger" Manuscripts, edited by William M. Gibson (Berkeley: University of California Press, 1969);

Mark Twain's Fables of Man, edited by Tuckey (Berkeley: University of California Press, 1972);

Mark Twain's Notebooks and Journals, volume 1, 1855-1873, edited by Frederick Anderson, Michael B. Frank, and Kenneth M. Sanderson; volume 2, 1877-1883, edited by Anderson, Lin Salamo, and Bernard L. Stein; volume 3, edited by Robert Pack Browning, Frank, and Salamo (Berkeley: University of California Press, 1975, 1979);

The Devil's Race-Track: Mark Twain's "Great Dark" Writings, edited by Tuckey (Berkeley: University of California Press, 1979).

COLLECTIONS: *The Writings of Mark Twain*, Autograph Edition, 25 volumes (Hartford, Conn.: American Publishing Company, 1899-1907);

The Writings of Mark Twain, Hillcrest Edition, 25 volumes, edited by Paine (New York & London: Harper, 1906);

The Writings of Mark Twain, Definitive Edition, 37 volumes, edited by Paine (New York: Wells, 1922-1925).

Mark Twain's work captures the child that lives in the American psyche and also presents the confusions of the American adult. As a mature writer, Twain could recreate the small-town boyhood he had known by the Mississippi River in those halcyon years before the Civil War. His philosophical ponderings, however, kept leading him back to simple views of mankind as either deservedly damned or irresponsibly determined, and then, finally, as a figment of some celestial imagination, "wandering forlorn among the empty eternities," disillusioned with the world in which he finds himself but unable to make his way to any other. Mark Twain is best known for his evocations of pre-Civil War life along the Mississippi in *The Adventures of Tom Sawyer* (1876), *Life on the Mississippi* (1883), and

The Adventures of Huckleberry Finn (1884). Still, readers have cherished almost as much his books of wandering, whether factually based travel books, such as *The Innocents Abroad* (1869), *Roughing It* (1872), *A Tramp Abroad* (1880), and *Following the Equator* (1897) or fiction like *A Connecticut Yankee in King Arthur's Court* (1889), and his later bitter contemplations of the human heart: *Pudd'nhead Wilson* (1894), "The Man That Corrupted Hadleyburg" (1900), and *The Mysterious Stranger* (1916), unfinished at the time of his death. Clemens/Twain became, to an extent, that stranger, sickened not only by what he saw as the money-mad society around him but also by his own participation in it. At the same time, he remained, however self-contradictingly, the sensation-loving boy whom he depicted as Tom Sawyer, eager to cause a stir and ready to apologize afterwards. Get-rich-quick schemes, intense personal hatreds arising from business as well as from personal dealings, equally intense loves and loyalties—the emotional nature of the man and his final confusion when the promises of the American Dream of personal satisfaction through financial success turned increasingly into nightmare—have made Mark Twain's life the subject of intensive scholarly research equal in range and in thoroughness to the critical exploration of

Mark Twain, about 1880

his written work. We study the life because of the work, but both repay attention.

From genteel but shabby beginnings, Samuel Langhorne Clemens rose to both respectability and respect, glad to belong to the wealthy upper reaches of the society that he knew well enough to laugh at while striving, meanwhile, to please. He was born in a town so small that, as he later wrote, he "increased the population by 1 per cent." He liked to jest that he "could have done it for any place—even London, I suppose." His father and mother, John Marshall and Jane Lampton Clemens, had rented a two-room clapboard house in Florida, Missouri, about 100 feet from the store owned by their brother-in-law, John Quarles, whom Twain later immortalized both in *Life on the Mississippi* and in *Mark Twain's Autobiography* (1924). The house still stands in which Sam Clemens was born thirteen days after Halley's Comet reached its perihelion. He often said that just as he came in with the comet, so he would go out with it, and so indeed he did. The comet worked on his imagination, but the house did not. Far more important were both the Quarles farm and the town in which Sam grew up, Hannibal, where the family moved in 1839. Sam, the third of four sons, was the fifth of the six children who kept adding their weight to the slender reed that was the family fortune. (This is not to count the baby boy, Pleasants, who lived for only a month or so sometime between the births of Pamela and of Margaret in 1827 and 1830.) John Marshall Clemens, in ill health and repeated financial difficulties, had moved his family from Kentucky to Tennessee and finally to Missouri. The comfortable and warmly affectionate Quarles family—so markedly in contrast with his own, where Samuel Clemens remembered "no outward and visible demonstration of affection"—and the farm itself—its woods, fields, and story-telling slaves—impressed young Sam during his childhood years when he spent his summers back in Florida. The family's final move to Hannibal, some thirty miles off, began the most famous boyhood idyll in American literature.

The dwellings, the schoolhouse, the tannery, the slaughterhouse, Holliday's Hill (Cardiff Hill, in Twain's fiction), and, above all, the Mississippi River passed from experience into now world-famous literature. Most of Sam Clemens's boyhood has found its way through Mark Twain's writing into the nation's common heritage. Although no evidence exists that young Sam ever managed the white-washing of the family's fence in Tom Sawyer's way, Tom's practical psychology has at least as much of the truth that counts as any of the equally spectacu-

lar bits of remembered past that went to form the writer's capital. The facts themselves have less importance than what the writer made of them, both in his work and in his life.

Mark Twain grew up in a family different from most of its neighbors and in an America that, for most of its ambitious citizens, turned out to be different from what they had anticipated. A conservative Whig in politics and a freethinker in religion, John Clemens (who became justice of the peace in Hannibal in 1842) took his family into a rapidly growing river community that was also conventionally and staunchly religious. By 1847, the year of his death, more than 1,000 steamboat arrivals annually kept river and wharves crowded and busy. In a vivid passage in *Life on the Mississippi*, Twain was to contrast the sleepiness of the village before and after a steamboat's interruption with the "grandeur" and "scramble" of the ship and its activities, "and such a yelling and cursing as the mates facilitate it all with!" But ten minutes afterwards, "the town is dead again." Death as the opposite of bustle and stir, and death as the guilt-producing occasion of life's ending for brothers Benjamin (1842) and Henry (1858), for sister Margaret (1839), and for his father (1847), underlies much of the later writer's humor. The corpse on the floor of his father's office and the bones of dead monks as contributions to European architecture make the basis for deliciously macabre humor in *The Innocents Abroad*. Van Wyck Brooks's version of Mark Twain as bound to the prohibitions of gentility by guilt has by now been discredited, but that Clemens was a high-strung, nervous boy, given to sleepwalking and frequently a witness to scenes of terror and violence and death, is certainly true. These dark elements were to color a great deal of the grown man's humor; fear, guilt, and an avoidance of sexuality make up a more than fair proportion of writing in the Victorian Age in general. His first discovered published work, however—written when Clemens was not yet seventeen—reveals a simpler but, for American literature, a far more important conflict at work, that between the expectations or pretensions of his family roots and what has been called the raw democracy of the frontier.

"The Dandy Frightening the Squatter" (published in the Boston weekly *Carpet-Bag* of 1 May 1852 under the initials S.L.C.) represents a step toward the formation of Mark Twain's perspective. Having ended his formal schooling at fourteen and gone to work as a printer's apprentice on his brother Orion's *Hannibal Journal*, Sam, as a matter of course, read the squibs, anecdotes, and sketches, mostly comic, that the "exchange" columns of daily papers,

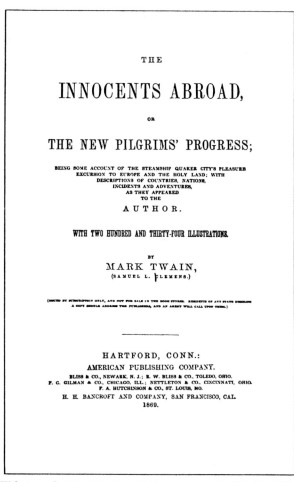

THE

INNOCENTS ABROAD,

OR

THE NEW PILGRIMS' PROGRESS;

BEING SOME ACCOUNT OF THE STEAMSHIP QUAKER CITY'S PLEASURE
EXCURSION TO EUROPE AND THE HOLY LAND; WITH
DESCRIPTIONS OF COUNTRIES, NATIONS,
INCIDENTS AND ADVENTURES,
AS THEY APPEARED
TO THE
AUTHOR.

WITH TWO HUNDRED AND THIRTY-FOUR ILLUSTRATIONS.

BY

MARK TWAIN,

(SAMUEL L. CLEMENS.)

(ISSUED BY SUBSCRIPTION ONLY, AND NOT FOR SALE IN THE BOOK STORES. RESIDENTS OF ANY STATE DESIRING
A COPY SHOULD ADDRESS THE PUBLISHERS, AND AN AGENT WILL CALL UPON THEM.)

HARTFORD, CONN.:
AMERICAN PUBLISHING COMPANY.
BLISS & CO., NEWARK, N. J.; R. W. BLISS & CO., TOLEDO, OHIO.
F. G. GILMAN & CO., CHICAGO, ILL.; NETTLETON & CO., CINCINNATI, OHIO.
F. A. HUTCHINSON & CO., ST. LOUIS, MO.
H. H. BANCROFT AND COMPANY, SAN FRANCISCO, CAL.
1869.

Title page for Twain's story of his voyage on the Quaker City

large and small, up and down the river, printed to entertain, and thus hold, their readers. As in the more memorable New York humor magazine, *Spirit of the Times*, many of the pieces printed were direct products of the frontier as experienced by literate, often educated, men of substance whose professional fortunes had taken them to the newer territories. Although these humorous tales and vignettes took a variety of tones and forms, one common and influential pattern of written telling underlined the gap between the teller and the objects of his attention. Although this gap did not always flatter the teller, it usually did more than merely present the novel facts of backcountry life. Violence and exaggeration, while part of what William Tappan Thompson refers to in his preface to *Major Jones's Chronicles of Pineville* (1845) as his effort "to catch 'manners living as they rise,'" underline the uncouthness of the local yokels, whose nonstandard language and barbaric behavior make clear to the presumably more genteel reader just how great are the blessings of true civilization. For young Sam these pieces offered a model, but they also presented a viewpoint not at all congenial to his own. "The Dandy Frightening the Squatter" echoes numerous anecdotes of Western origin in which an Eastern newcomer, certain of his superiority over any denizen of the backwoods, attempts to terrify an ignorant squatter and fails, only to end up "floundering in the turbid waters of the Mississippi," the recipient of a paralyzing punch from the fist of the doughty squatter. To clinch the point of the episode, the last sentence gives genteel sanction to the dandy's comeuppance, as the ladies, whom the dandy had sought to impress by threatening the squatter with instant annihilation, "unanimously voted the knife and pistols to the victor."

Slight though this first printed effort is, it deserves attention, as Kenneth S. Lynn has shown in his *Mark Twain and Southwestern Humor*. The narrative voice that opens the episode appears to establish the perspective of a cultivated outsider: the vernacular words "wood-yard" and "squatters" are put within quotation marks, suggesting that the writer would never use them himself. The squatter, first seen leaning against a tree, gazes at "an approaching object," apparently strange to his untutored eyes but one "which our readers would easily have discovered to be a steam boat." Unexpectedly, the representative of the educated world, to which the narrator and his readers implicitly belong, turns out to be the victim both of his own pretensions and of the backwoods boor's quick wit and quicker action. In a pattern that was to become increasingly familiar in Clemens's writing, the experienced roughneck bests the genteel newcomer.

This tale raises at least two problems that would later be important to Mark Twain: how to tell a story so that its language will not undercut or, as here, contradict its meaning, and what to do with an underlying respect for conventional, genteel society, a respect that is in conflict with a sense that that society is itself a pretentious sham. Undoubtedly, these problems, however latent in the early writing, did not emerge into Twain's consciousness until much later. With hindsight, however, one is tempted to see in Clemens's later satisfaction in mastering the craft of a Mississippi steamboat pilot (1857-1861) a great deal more than a sense of difficulty overcome and the fulfillment of what in his *Atlantic* series, "Old Times on the Mississippi" (1875), Twain calls "the one permanent ambition among my [boyhood] comrades . . . to be a steamboatman." The pilot was both respectable and alone; he was important to his world, but he stood apart from it. For a man hungry for applause but impatient with its givers, the life of a pilot must have held special delight. Much has been made, and rightly, of Twain's later insistence on the grandeur, social as well as sartorial, of piloting and on the independence and power of a pilot. Twain clearly found satisfaction also in the mastery of the difficult craft, the packing of his memory with the thousands of details necessary to recognize instantly just where on the river the boat was, day or night, with due regard for snags, bluff reefs, and all the other hazards that could "kill somebody's steamboat one of these nights." This, too, has been noted. But the position vis a vis society occupied by the pilot may be as important as any other factor in accounting for the extreme nostalgia that for the rest of his life Twain wrapped around his riverboat days that began in April 1857 and lasted for almost exactly four years. "I loved the profession far better than any I have followed since," he long afterward declared, "and I took a measureless pride in it." His first official biographer, Albert Bigelow Paine, commented that "the dreamy, easy, romantic existence suited him exactly. A sovereign and an autocrat, the pilot's word was law. . . ." *Dreamy* and *easy*, as Twain himself makes clear, seem unlikely words to apply to the demanding life of a pilot. The habit of intense and careful observation seems important, however: the river provided experience and education that the writer could seize upon. "In that brief, sharp schooling," Twain asserted, "I got personally and familiarly acquainted with about all the different types of human nature. . . . When I find a well-drawn character in fiction or biography I generally take a warm personal interest in him, for the reason that I have known him before—met him on the river." Besides pride in his work, another important analogy between the pilot and the writer lies in the position of each with respect to the rest of the social order: both depend upon society for their livelihood while at the same time both stand on the fringe. As a more recent biographer, Justin Kaplan, says of Twain, "he wanted to belong, but he also wanted to laugh from outside."

By the age of twenty-five, Sam Clemens seemed to be settling down to the life of a fully licensed pilot. Finding a possible niche had taken him quite a while; he explained his wandering years as the result of the great expectations of future wealth entertained by all the family because of land in Tennessee, 70,000 acres of it, that John Marshall Clemens had owned at his death. Twain later reflected, with considerable bitterness, on the implications for him, and equally for Orion (accent on the first syllable), of that inheritance: "It is good to begin life poor; it is good to begin life rich—these are wholesome; to begin it poor and *prospectively* rich! The man who has not experienced it cannot imagine the curse of it." Sure of eventual plenty, Twain had allowed himself to drift. He had been an itinerant printer, traveling to St. Louis, New York City, and Philadelphia in 1853, and then a printer and journalist for Orion's *Keokuk* (Iowa) *Saturday Post* until fall of 1856. Bitten once more by the wander-bug, he contributed a few comic letters to the *Post* as Thomas Jefferson Snodgrass and then set off for South America and, so he hoped, a fortune in cocoa. Instead, he met Horace Bixby, the man who "taught" him the river and made him into a pilot. Then came the Civil War, putting an end to steamboat traffic on the Mississippi. His "The Private History of a Campaign That Failed" (1885) presents one version of his brief service as a volunteer in Confederate ranks—a version that, in various after-dinner speeches, he repeatedly revised—and *Roughing It* tells of his July 1861 stagecoach journey west with his brother Orion, who had been appointed secretary to the governor of the Nevada Territory. Clemens went along, nominally to assist the secretary, in reality for the ride. Miner, prospector, and then casual contributor to the *Virginia City Territorial Enterprise* under the name "Josh," Clemens began to use the name "Mark Twain" on his work early in 1863. He had been a full-time reporter since September 1862. He became Mark Twain perhaps because he had the habit of ordering his drinks on credit and by twos, or perhaps, as used to be said, because he was resurrecting the pen name of an old river captain whom he had caused great pain by a youthful parody of the old gentleman's literary manner. In either case, the phrase, as most readers now know, comes from the river and signifies water to a depth of two fathoms, twelve feet, dangerously shallow water if one is approaching the shore in a steamboat drawing nine and a half or so feet but a welcome cry of safe water ahead if one has already come through the shoals. In Clemens's writing of river experience, the phrase, readers should note, signifies danger more frequently than safety: the pen name does not evoke Paine's "dreamy" ease. Certainly it appeared over some very unsafe columns in Virginia City and then in San Francisco, where Twain espoused the unpopular cause of the mistreated Chinese immigrants.

By 1864 it was perfectly clear that Sam Clemens was one sort of newsman and Mark Twain another. (See Henry Nash Smith's detailed com-

mentary in *Mark Twain of the "ENTERPRISE."*)
Both Clemens/Twain and the *Territorial Enterprise*,
as well as Virginia City and Carson City politicians,
"recognized two aspects of Clemens's work: routine
political reporting, a technical process without a
personal flavor, ascribed to Clemens; and personal
journalism, mostly humorous [and sometimes in-
flammatory], ascribed to Mark Twain." It may have
been—and here history gives way to legend—that
the writer's abrupt abandonment of Virginia City at
the end of May 1864 had something to do with
exceptions taken to the work of Mark Twain. Did
Twain find himself entangled in a duel? Did a helpful second, dismayed at the Missourian's inability to
hold a revolver steady, much less hit anything
smaller than the side of a barn, show him how,
blasting off the head of a small bird just as the
honored opponent was approaching the scene of
the proposed encounter? Did the duel fail to take
place because the opponent believed the remarkable marksmanship to be Twain's? Various versions
appear in various places among Twain's autobiographical writings. Twain himself, in his old age,
remarked upon the undependable ways of his
memory, including the oft-quoted lament: "I am
grown old and my memory is not as active as it used
to be. When I was younger I could remember anything, whether it had happened or not; but my
faculties are decaying now, and soon I shall be so I
cannot remember any but the things that never
happened." A good story always interested him
more than the copperplated, gilt-edged truth, or so
historical researches and his own words lead us to
believe.

In one of Twain's notebooks from early days
in California appears this entry: "Coleman with his
jumping frog—bet stranger $50—stranger had no
frog, and C. got him one:—in the mean time
stranger filled C.'s frog full of shot and he couldn't
jump. The stranger's frog won." Appearing in the
last issue of the *New York Saturday Press* (18
November 1865) as "Jim Smiley and His Frog,"
pirated by Beadle's Dime Books, and then as the
title story in *The Celebrated Jumping Frog of Calaveras
County, and Other Sketches* (1867), the tale that Twain
put together from this simple anecdotal beginning
spread his name across the country, preparing the
way for the national reputation he held for the rest
of his life. To understand an important part of what
Twain's humor is and means, one must understand
what the frog story does and is about because it is
not merely, or even mainly, about a clever stranger's
successful chicanery or about Jim Smiley's devoted
confidence in the jumping powers of his frog.

Mostly, "The Celebrated Jumping Frog of
Calaveras County" is about telling the frog's story;
that is, it is about "celebrating" the frog, about the
process by which the frog becomes a celebrity.

Always it is worth remembering that when
Ernest Hemingway observed that "all modern
American Literature comes from one book by Mark
Twain called *Huckleberry Finn*," he had in mind the
language, the quality of spoken rather than written
discourse that Twain developed into great art, beginning with simple efforts to reproduce the vernacular. In the frog story, written some thirteen
years after the dandy tried in vain to frighten the
squatter, Twain took an enormous step toward
mastery and, equally important, toward artistic
awareness of what he was doing. While the story of
the frog itself is told in the vernacular by an ill-
educated Westerner, "good-natured, garrulous old
Simon Wheeler," the story of the frog's celebration
comes to us through the first-person narrative voice
of an educated greenhorn, a newcomer to the Far
West who may even be an Easterner. "In compliance with the request of a friend of mine, who
wrote me from the East," the narrator begins his
quest for information about "*Leonidas W. Smiley—
Rev. Leonidas W.* Smiley . . . a cherished companion
of his boyhood." Those wonderful phrases, "in
compliance with" and "cherished companion,"
evoke in the first two paragraphs the genteel and
proper world of Eastern sensibility. When, at the
climax of the anecdote, Wheeler's stranger says to
Jim Smiley, owner of the now-defeated frog, "*I
don't see no p'ints about that frog that's any better'n
any other frog*," he utters a sentence that quickly
found its way into American folklore, to be quoted
in a variety of contexts over the next fifty years and
more; and he makes clear how far from the drawing
rooms of polite society literature might venture.
Twain's narrator, however, is a very foolish
greenhorn indeed. He may speak most proper English, but he lacks a sense of humor: at the start of
the story, he looks back on his encounter with
Wheeler with "a lurking suspicion" that the friend
"from the East . . . never knew such a person" as
"*Leonidas W. Smiley*" but simply wanted Simon
Wheeler to "go to work and bore me to death with
some exasperating reminiscence of . . . *Jim
Smiley* . . . as tedious as it would be useless to me."
At the end of the telling, Wheeler having presented
first Jim Smiley's penchant for betting, then a brief
summary of Smiley's fortunes with a horse, a longer
episode concerning a dog, and then the frog contest, someone calls Wheeler outside for a moment.
The genteel narrator gets up to leave, but "at the

door I met the sociable Wheeler returning, and he button-holed me and recommenced," beginning, " 'Well, thish-yer Smiley had a yaller one-eyed cow that didn't have no tail, only just a short stump like a bannanner, and—'

"However, lacking both time and inclination, I did not wait to hear about the afflicted cow, but took my leave." Here the celebration ends. Clearly, the Eastern, or at least well-spoken, narrator is a ninny. Just as clearly, Twain has created not only that fascinatingly compulsive gambler, Jim Smiley, but two other figures as well: Simon Wheeler, the hero of vernacular speech in an era when the vernacular was beyond the pale of polite literature, and that nameless narrator who embodies Eastern gentility (refinement and education) but who fails to be amused by the mildly earthy anecdote with which the unwashed Wheeler regales him.

Twain had begun in earnest to question the sufficiency of the genteel culture that the Eastern literary establishment took for granted. Ten years earlier, Walt Whitman had sounded his "barbaric yawp" over the tenements of New York City, but only a very few readers heard it, and most of them were put off. Twain, because humorists were given

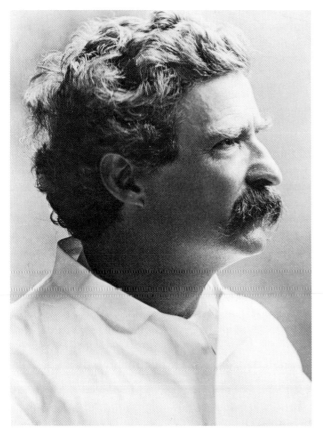

Twain in 1885

license to be at least somewhat disrespectful of propriety, not only tickled funny bones with his story but also found acceptance. He credited Bret Harte, chief among the San Francisco literati in 1864, with helping him polish his rough technique, a debt Twain always appreciated, even after he had come to despise Harte. Learning as he went, in any case, Twain grew both in skill and in understanding. When the *Sacramento Union* sent him to the Sandwich (Hawaiian) Islands in 1866, he was ready: his account of the *Hornet* maritime disaster, with interviews of the survivors, achieved national circulation in *Harper's* magazine (credited, alas, to one Mark Swain). Then his travel letters to the *San Francisco Alta California* led to lecturing engagements and, finally, to a voyage to Panama (December 1866), across the Isthmus, and then another voyage to New York City (January 1867) and the steamship *Quaker City*'s expedition to Europe and the Holy Land (June-November 1867), from which came *The Innocents Abroad, or The New Pilgrims' Progress*.

Meanwhile, however, Mark Twain was making the literary acquaintance of one of his short-lived but important creations, Mr. Brown. Indeed, the famous line at the end of the advertisements for Twain's first lecture (2 October 1866, in San Francisco) was the work of that part of the Clemens/Twain perspective that Twain in his newspaper letters referred to as "Brown." The last part of this famous ad includes such anticipations of Huck Finn's King and Duke as bold-face mention of "A SPLENDID ORCHESTRA," followed by "Is in town, but has not been engaged." Further, "A GRAND TORCHLIGHT PROCESSION may be expected; in fact, the public are privileged to expect whatever they please." And then the last line, for which Twain became widely known: "Doors open at 7 o'clock. The Trouble to begin at 8 o'clock." Irreverently "Brownist" as this was, Twain carried self-deflating irony still further seven months later when signs advertising his Hawaii lecture at the Cooper Union in New York announced: "The Wisdom will begin to flow at 8." The Brown persona became for a short while the means by which Twain could puncture genteel pretension while seeming to ally himself with it. Writing back to the *Alta California* from the steamship *America* (20 December 1866), Twain recalls his farewell to San Francisco: "Then I stood apart and soliloquized: 'Green be my memories of thee as are thy hills this bright December day, O Mistress of the Occident! May no—

" 'Oh, dang the Occident! There's lively times downstairs. The old man played his hand for all it was worth—the passengers raised him—the old man come back—they went him better—the old man passed out, and all things are lovely and the—'

" 'Say what you have got to say in plain English, Brown, and refrain from vulgar metaphor.' " Genteel passengers attitudinize—this will be innocent Twain's complaint repeatedly through *The Innocents Abroad*—affirming their respectability by striking lofty poses in loftier prose. Brown's earthy interest in the human drama below decks and his low vocabulary of the poker table undercut narrator Twain's cliches. Twain retained the services of Brown through most of his letters to the *Alta California*, but toward the end of the *Quaker City* trip, even before turning the letters into *The Innocents Abroad*, Twain began to do without Brown, taking the Brown function upon himself in some passages while echoing travel-book gentility in others. Early in the travels, Twain "did intend to write about some other wonders connected with the Cathedral [of Milan], but I have overheard Brown describing them . . . and have taken down his words in shorthand. . . . I am only sorry his language is not more refined." There follows Brown's slang-filled and irreverent description of the material grandeurs of the cathedral, ending with Brown's expression of terror and disgust when a gem-encrusted corpse shows its head: "and when I saw that, I just antied up and left." Twain then takes up the narrative "himself," in standard English with no slang, concluding with the appropriately conventional moral: "What a sermon was here upon poor human vanity!" Then, by the late letters, Twain is not only summoning up traditional associations to historic sites seen in moonlight but also providing the undercutting in his own person: "But the magic of the moonlight is a vanity and a swindle; and whoso putteth his trust in it shall fare no better than he that betteth his substance upon 'deuces *and*' when the thing the worldling calleth a flush is out against him."

The quotation marks around low phrases, such as "deuces *and*," from this point on in Twain work differently from the way they worked in "The Dandy Frightening the Squatter." Because those who indulge in such phrases as "the magic of the moonlight" have become objects of scorn, vernacular speech signals by implication a reliable perspective. By simultaneously using and undercutting the perspective that sees the world as an exhibition of preconceived ideal forms, Twain is doubling his personae, his fictional masks. His work begins to show a complicating and deepening awareness of the contradictory social pressures that Clemens/ Twain encountered and felt.

One important step was in his encountering directly the force of the East that had been primarily a matter of literary convention for the young Westerner. His brief sojourns in New York and other Eastern cities some fourteen years earlier as a young printer hardly counted. A letter of 1853 to his married sister Pamela in St. Louis underlines the social poverty of that stay: young Sam had wondered at the Crystal Palace, awed that visitors to it "average 6,000 daily—double the population of Hannibal." The Croton Aqueduct "brings in water from a distance of thirty-eight miles and, if necessary, they could easily supply every family in New York with one hundred barrels of water per day!" He spends his evenings in "a free public library containing more than 4,000 volumes" because he has "nobody at home to talk to." Above all, Pamela is to "tell Ma my promises are faithfully kept." This is the famous promise of which Van Wyck Brooks made such psychological hay, the promise that Paine records as occurring just before Clemens left Hannibal for St. Louis and points east: "I do solemnly swear that I will not throw a card or drink a drop of liquor while I am gone."

The seventeen-year-old who swore that oath and the thirty-one-year-old newspaperman, former miner, and steamboat pilot had remarkably little in common on the surface; but the "Presbyterian conscience," as Twain later and often referred to it, of the boy often forced the man to perceive what he would have been happier to ignore. The terms of the promise itself are almost beside the point; Twain as an adult could smile at his adolescent ambition to be a preacher "because it never occurred to me that a preacher could be damned. It looked like a safe job." That promise matters—and here Brooks, up to a point, is surely correct— because it implies in equal measure a human propensity for easily defined wickedness and a personal responsibility to resist the pressures of that propensity. In 1867, it was by no means clear that Twain's work was going to concern itself with questions about responsibility, but perfectly clear were the conflicting pressures of Western expansiveness and Eastern reserve, or of Western crudity and Eastern gentility. These were to be at the center of much of Twain's writing.

Two events stand out from this second New York visit. Having left the city briefly to visit friends and family and to deliver his lecture, stopping in Hannibal, Keokuk, and St. Louis, Twain came upon an announcement of the *Quaker City* excursion. Instead of going around the world (as he had planned in San Francisco to do), he suddenly decided to participate in what we would now recognize as the first cruise-ship vacation in modern times, "a novelty in the way of Excursions . . . a picnic on a grand scale," as he called it on the first page of *The Innocents Abroad*. With the *Alta California* paying his passage and twenty dollars per letter, he signed up for the voyage that led to his first book-length narrative. The facility with which he changed his plans and the enthusiasm with which he greeted this new project reveal the optimistic and mercurial sides of him as well as anything else in his active and ebullient life, just as his subsequent disgust at what he came to see as the prayer-filled hypocrisy of many of his fellow pilgrims suggests his perpetual ability to be disappointed by the vagaries of what he at times was to refer to as "the damned human race." The voyage (8 June through 19 November 1867) began and ended in New York City, and its effect on Twain's future would be hard to overestimate.

The other revealing event concerns the Cooper Union lecture of 6 May 1867, before the voyage. A newly made big fish on the West Coast, what would he be in the East? Frank Fuller, who, as acting governor of the state of Utah, had known Mark Twain in the silver country, now met him in New York and encouraged him to lecture, "but," as Paine reports, "Mark Twain was not happy." Who in the East would know or, more to the point, care to listen to him? He had little faith that even the republication of his frog story in his first book would help: " 'Fuller,' he said, 'there'll be nobody in the Cooper Union that night but you and me. . . . I would commit suicide if I had the pluck and the outfit.' " But at eight o'clock, when the wisdom began to flow, Cooper Union was "packed; there wasn't room enough left for a child. . . . I poured the Sandwich Islands out on those people, and they laughed and shouted to my entire content. For an hour and fifteen minutes I was in paradise." Fuller, on Twain's advice, had papered the house, distributing free tickets (within forty-eight hours of lecture time) to the schoolteachers of New York and Brooklyn. With their joyous acceptance of his manner and matter, and with very favorable newspaper reviews, Twain saw that he could master even an Eastern audience, and with the same satisfaction he had first known on the San Francisco stage. After the Cooper Union triumph, he could travel as a celebrity.

Aboard the *Quaker City*, Twain met Charles "Charley" Langdon, eighteen-year-old son of an Elmira, New York, coal merchant, who admired the jumping frog's celebrator. Young Langdon showed him a miniature of his older sister, Olivia. Twain's marriage to her, occurring less than fourteen months after they finally met, has elicited more commentary than any other marriage in American literary circles. After Livy Clemens had died, and shortly before his own death, Twain looked back upon his first glimpse of her person: "It is forty years ago. From that day to this she has never been out of my mind." Literally true or not, his affection

The miniature of Olivia Langdon that Twain first saw in 1867. At the end of his life he wrote, "From that day to this she has never been out of my mind."

for his wife was deep, and deeply physical, to judge from his letters to her over the years during the frequent times when lecture engagements and other business kept them apart. He relied upon her not only as a restraining force to curb his verbal attacks upon gentility, but as a focus for them as well. Her family, despite a comparative liberality in religious belief, was as safely upper middle class as could be. The values that Mrs. Fairbanks, Twain's middle-aged mentor (whom he called "Mother") on the *Quaker City*, tried to edit into or out of the travel letters that became part of *The Innocents Abroad* were indistinguishable from those dear, or repugnant, to Livy. They both took for granted a respect for property and for those who had acquired it, as signaled by conformity to the proprieties of upper-middle-class existence. They wanted regular attendance at church and respect for those who voiced approved attitudes toward protestant Christianity. Also, they appreciated the sort of ideality that had so irked "Mr. Brown." These habits and attitudes formed part of the genteel package that most of the well-meaning women in his life urged upon Twain. Paradoxically, although Livy called him "Youth" as a term of endearment and an acknowledgment of his frequent improprieties, she found herself giving up her religious faith as a result of his strident agnosticism.

Even Sam Clemens himself, however, was by no means proof against the attractions of approval by genteel society. Before encountering Livy or any member of her family, before even leaving San Francisco for good, Clemens had met, in Hawaii, Anson Burlingame, then returning to his post as American minister to China. Burlingame's son, another enthusiastic reader of "The Celebrated Jumping Frog of Calaveras County," brought the two together. Clemens valued and accepted both the encouragement and the advice that Burlingame gave him: "You have a great ability; I believe you have genius," said the authoritative Burlingame to the uneducated newspaperman, fresh from California pocket mining and Nevada silver fields and with but one nationally published piece to his credit, and that one merely vernacular fiction. Burlingame then added the revealing words of advice: "What you need now is the refinement of association. Seek companionship among men of superior intellect and character. Refine yourself and your work. Never affiliate with inferiors; always climb." Paine adds, with total approval, speaking for his era and class, "Clemens never forgot that advice. He did not always observe it, but he rarely failed to realize its gospel."

Jervis Langdon, Livy's father, would have approved of Burlingame's words, for a central concern for conventional wisdom and manners animated the life that each recommended to Twain. With the successful sales of *The Innocents Abroad*—5,170 copies of the travel book had been sold in the first month, over 31,000 by the fifth—Twain found acceptance with the Langdons. Despite the lukewarm to absolutely chilly "testimonials" that he had gathered from Twain's Western acquaintances (Twain had given names of no close friends, fearing that they would lie for him), testimonials that were supposed to justify the Langdons' entrusting of their refined and invalid daughter to this wild man

from the Pacific slopes, Jervis decided that he knew Twain better than mere Westerners could and graciously acceded to the couple's betrothal. He also burdened Twain with a house and the obligation-opportunity to buy into the *Buffalo Examiner*, a generous marriage settlement, to be sure, but one demanding a large income to keep up the house, a commitment to the newspaper rather than to any other sort of endeavor, and a geographical closeness to Elmira, all bespeaking a paterfamilial control that boded ill for artistic or any other autonomy. In 1871 the Clemenses moved to Hartford, Connecticut, and to the Nook Farm community of writers, including Charles Dudley Warner and Harriet Beecher Stowe, but the pattern was set, and set not really against the leanings of the Twain who cherished the philistine counsel of Anson Burlingame.

The forty years of Twain's life that followed marriage to Livy have become almost as public a property as the fictionalized versions of Clemens's boyhood presented in *Tom Sawyer*, *Huckleberry Finn*, numerous shorter works, many of the later manuscripts, and the *Autobiography*. The visible surface of this life was inordinately public, most spectacularly in Twain's old age when the author-as-public-figure favored white suits and dramatic entrances. The house in Hartford, elaborate both in design and in catering arrangements, signaled an increasing publicity as well as prosperity. Also, it signaled a need, always, for more and more and more money. Twain's publishing arrangements aimed from the beginning at meeting that need. The American Publishing Company, publishers of *The Innocents Abroad* and of subsequent Twain books through *A Tramp Abroad* in 1880, set the pattern of subscription sales and distribution that Twain embraced almost throughout his productive life. Sold by traveling agents for a mass market of potential readers who would not or could not frequent bookstores, books published in this way, if they succeeded, tended to bring in larger returns than were likely through ordinary bookstore sales. In return, they had to conform to patterns of length and format that demanded many words, whether aesthetically necessary or not. Profusely illustrated, at least 600 pages in length, available in a variety of bindings, a subscription book was, first of all, an imposing object and only secondarily a work of literary art. That Twain chose to have his work published in this mode reflects, as well as a need for money, his oft-expressed sense that he wanted to reach the lower strata of society and not just the cultivated and polite. In addition, it seems to confirm his uneasy sense of being an outsider in the East, a barbarian in the genteel parlors of the elite. "Poor girl," he wrote of Livy to Mrs. Fairbanks before the marriage, "anybody who could convince her that I was not a humorist would secure her eternal gratitude. She thinks a humorist is something pretty awful." Twain, despite repeated efforts to be what he at times considered "more" than a humorist, remained a humorist all his life. That is, he used language to create distance between reader and reality and thus to provoke laughter not only at what he considered the shams, pretenses, and vagaries of the polite society around him but also at the way of viewing reality that underlay that society.

When people speak of the particularly "American" quality of Twain's humor, they usually have in mind something more than the language, the use of vernacular that characterizes the spoken quality of the stories. This "something more" has been defined in different ways. Perhaps the clearest way of seeing it is in contrast with the quality that much humor of the Old Southwest shares with eighteenth-century British humor as discussed by Henry Fielding in his preface to *Joseph Andrews* in 1742. Fielding's concern was with what he called "the only source of the true Ridiculous," that is, with affectation, through which characters are made into figures of fun. Whether motivated by vanity, "which puts us on affecting false characters, in order to purchase applause," or by hypocrisy, "which sets us on an endeavor to avoid censure by concealing our vices under an appearance of their virtues," the behavior arising from affectation, when revealed by a writer, leads to a sense of "the Ridiculous—which always strikes a reader with surprise and pleasure." In haste to deny their own participation in affectation, readers side with the seemingly objective author or narrator, laughing at the affected behavior of, for example, Johnson J. Hooper's purse-proud hypocrites at a camp meeting who pretend to a sincere religious interest when their real motive for contributing to Simon Suggs's collection is a desire to appear wealthy and benevolent. No confusion, and no sympathy, exists between the reader and Simon's dupes. The narrative voice and the reader unite in recognizing the truth, which is definite, clear, knowable. One remarkable effect of Twain's humor, on the other hand, is to move a reader further and further from so simple a perspective. The world Twain created in his fictions becomes less and less knowable, less and less a world about which narrative voice and reader can confidently agree. When, in chapter 20 of *Huckleberry Finn*, the King pretends to a camp-meeting conversion and

successfully levies his collection, the imitation of Hooper's story is only superficial because the King exploits a very different sort of meeting from Suggs's of forty years earlier: his victims, not "ridiculous through affectation," neither hypocritical nor vain, are victimized because they want to believe that the King is what he says he is, an Indian Ocean pirate come up the Mississippi into Arkansas to recruit crew members. "He told them . . . he'd been robbed last night and put ashore off of a steamboat without a cent, and he was glad of it; it was the blessedest thing that ever happened to him, because he was a changed man now, and happy for the first time in his life; and, poor as he was, he was going to start right off and work his way back to the Indian Ocean" to convert the other pirates. Naturally, he will give all the credit "to them dear people in Pokeville camp-meeting . . . and that dear preacher there, the truest friend a pirate ever had!" Flattered by the apparent conversion of a scoundrel, titillated by the apparent presence of a real live pirate, victims of their own ignorance of geography, the citizens of Pokeville are badly duped, but, except for their ignorance, their victimization occurs for reasons that might apply with equal force to any reader: most of us want to think well of ourselves as influences for good, and most of us enjoy vicarious thrills. When "somebody sings out, 'Take up a collection for him, take up a collection!,' " Huck notes that "half a dozen made a jump to do it." These people, unlike Hooper's, do not pretend to a virtue that they do not have; they are not trying to purchase applause. Rather, they understand their own motives only partially, trusting their generous and pious impulsiveness but ignorant of the rest. This world, then, lacks the simple duality that underlies the humor of Twain's predecessors. Instead of a superior narrator joining with a superior reader to laugh at the pretensions of inferiors, Twain leads us to laugh at, and perhaps to acknowledge awareness of, a mutually human tendency to be mistaken about the extent to which human beings understand themselves and their surroundings. From "The Celebrated Jumping Frog of Calaveras County" on, this tendency makes itself felt in Twain's work, at first primarily through an exposure of the effects that genteel expectations have on one's capacity to perceive the truth.

The Innocents Abroad does this in almost a systematic way, "almost" because in a number of passages Twain seems to be presenting a guidebook view of foreign grandeurs with no trace of ironic distance. Dropping the character of Brown from his literary arsenal, Twain is struggling to do justice to contradictory impulses. At times the crass boor who is impressed favorably by nothing that lacks the shine and newness of what he has known in America, at times the simple innocent who marvels at whatever is old or large or famous, and at times the sophisticated traveler who is aware of what he is expected to feel and for that very reason finds himself unable to feel it, Twain-as-narrator repeatedly varies his responses to the sights, sounds, and smells of Europe and the Holy Land, and to his fellow "Pilgrims." The American boor who is bored by the old masters—"I never felt so fervently thankful, so soothed, so tranquil, so filled with a blessed peace, as I did yesterday when I learned that Michael Angelo was dead."—has become something of a cliche by now but has also been a breath of reassuring fresh air to many a traveler since Twain created him. The humor in *The Innocents Abroad*, however, frequently fights a losing battle against the weight of those genteel expectations from which the boor seeks relief. Over and over, the Pilgrim insists upon his right to his own reactions. "I set down these first thoughts because they are natural—not because they are just or because it is right to set them down. It is easy for book-makers to say, 'I thought so and so as I looked upon such and such a scene'—when the truth is, they thought all these fine things afterwards." The frequency with which narrator Twain insists upon his own "natural" response to scenes heavy with historical or aesthetic or religious associations as publicized by the "book-makers" underlines the struggle that is going on beneath the narrative surface of Twain's book. The gentle skepticism of irreverent Twain at "the tomb of Adam! How touching it was, here in a land of strangers, far away from home, and friends, and all who cared for me, thus to discover the grave of a blood relation" becomes angry irony when he summarizes his sense of the scene of the Crucifixion: "History is full of this Old Church of the Holy Sepulchre—full of blood that was shed because of the respect and the veneration in which men held the last resting-place of the meek and lowly, the mild and gentle, Prince of Peace!" But skepticism and anger yield in turn to sheer fatigue before a plethora of sights, along with an effort to manifest the proper bookmaker's assurance: "To us, Jerusalem and today's experiences will be an enchanted memory a year hence—a memory which money could not buy from us." Now, however, they are a weariness to the spirit and a reminder of inadequacy.

The humor in *The Innocents Abroad* is no less interesting, though slightly more uneven, than that in *Roughing It*. In the three-year interval between

Twain in late 1890s

the two publications, Twain had not only married Livy and moved to Hartford, he had achieved in some detail a firsthand knowledge of the pressures that genteel expectation laid upon the head of a family. As writer, he was already familiar with the gap between what was "natural" and what was expected of a "bookmaker." Both Mrs. Fairbanks and Livy had, in their ways, insisted upon proper reverence in Twain's treatment of holy matters in *The Innocents Abroad*. That so much skepticism remains in the published volume along with so much conventional respect and piety testifies to the strength of both impulses in Twain himself. During their engagement, when Twain was in Washington or on the lecture circuit, Livy sent him copies of Henry Ward Beecher's sermons, and he tried, it would seem, to develop a piety of sorts. (That Livy herself eventually gave up her religion became one more matter with which Twain reproached himself when she lay dying without the comfort of a firm belief in immortality.) In 1870, with *The Innocents Abroad* a success, Twain was pouring his energies into the *Buffalo Express* and also into the *Galaxy*, a New York City magazine that had agreed to pay him $2,400 a year for a "humorous department." His "Memoranda" column for the *Galaxy* included a recapitulation of the cruel treatment of Chinese immigrants in San Francisco, as well as amusing pieces, such as

"How I Edited an Agricultural Paper" and his own favorite, "Burlesque Map of Paris," but it also attacked Washington corruption ("The Great Beef Contract") and the hypocritical pseudosanctity of exclusively middle-class Christianity as represented by the Reverend T. DeWitt Talmage "who had delivered from the pulpit an argument against workingmen occupying pews in fashionable churches." The social anger, often vivid and hot, gives these pieces some vitality, although their main interest today lies simply in their being the work of Twain. Too often—and he quickly came to see that this was the case—his anger at injustice or sham or hypocrisy was too great for him to be able to write effective satire.

Most of his concern at this time, however, lay with meeting his financial obligations. The same hunger for cash that he was to castigate in his fellow Americans took hold of Mark Twain himself. At the same time, he remained an artist who was trying to come to grips with the aesthetic implications of his own impulses. The man in need of money invented the Mark Twain scrapbook. Sold in stores throughout the East, its special tabs and other features made it a popular item, the only one among the many inventions that excited him on which he managed to turn even a small profit. That the development of a set of empty gummed pages should occupy the time and energy of a writer is a sad irony. Sadder still, to support his house and his servants in the style to which he felt that he ought to become accustomed, Twain found himself by October 1871 separated from Livy and their sickly baby, Langdon, and out on the lecture circuit organized by James Redpath. Although he loved to dominate an audience, he was at best ambivalent about the life. Here, the artist in him drew what sustenance it could. "Notify all hands," he wrote Redpath in December 1871, "that from this time on I shall talk nothing but selections from my forthcoming book, *Roughing It*. Tried it twice last night; suits me tip top." The previous month he had written Livy, just after lecturing on humorist Artemus Ward in Bennington, Vermont, to explore with her a problem of structure and technique: "Good house, but they laughed too much.—A great fault with this lecture is that I have no way of turning it into a serious & instructive vein at will. *Any* lecture of mine ought to be a running narrative-plank, with square holes in it, six inches apart, all of the length of it, & then in my mental shop I ought to have plugs (half marked "serious" & the other marked "humorous") to select from & jam into these holes according to the temper of the audience." This had been precisely the method of *The Innocents Abroad*, with reverence and irreverence (as Henry Nash Smith says, "the ambivalence of the tourist") alternating, but with no way of expressing both feelings "simultaneously." To present attitudes as a series thus became a consciously formulated tactic; after developing it on the lecture platform, Twain eventually discovered—in *Huckleberry Finn*—how to go beyond it. Usually, however, the scramble for money remained foremost in the lecturer's mind. He wrote to Redpath, "Have paid up $4,000 indebtedness. You are the last on my list. Shall begin to pay you in a few days, and then I shall be a free man again." By the end of February 1872 he thought he was indeed free, with but one more platform appearance. He telegraphed Redpath: "How in the name of God does a man find his way from here to Amherst, and when must he start? Give me full particulars, and send a man with me. If I had another engagement I would rot before I would fill it. S. L. Clemens."

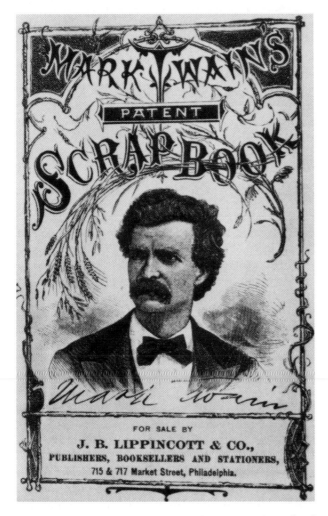

Cover of advertisement for Mark Twain's Patent Scrapbook

Out of debt and anticipating great sales from *Roughing It*, and with Livy Clemens expecting a second child, Twain had cause for rejoicing. But the birth of Susy (Olivia Susan) in March 1872 was followed in June by the death of Langdon. With or without cause—and most commentators agree that little or no cause existed, except in Twain's mind—Twain blamed himself. In Elmira for the birth of Susy, Twain had carelessly allowed the blankets around his sickly son to come loose during a drive. More than a month later, a fatal diphtheria set in, giving the conscience of the former Presbyterian more material with which to work. Huck Finn would later say, "If I had a yaller dog that didn't know no more than a person's conscience does I would pison him. It takes up more room than the rest of a person's insides, and yet ain't no good, nohow. Tom Sawyer, he says the same." Twain's revenge on his conscience was to be purely literary; so far as biographers can tell, conscience always won out in real life.

A different sort of disappointment, slow to come, came with the sales of *Roughing It*. After 40,000 copies in the first three months encouraged Twain's extravagant self-assurance that it would sell 100,000 in the first year, ten years passed before the book reached that mark, attained by *The Innocents Abroad* in three. What the modern reader finds in *Roughing It* may help explain its curious sales pattern. The stance of the narrator shifts in a way that seems first to encourage and then to condemn a rejection of Eastern gentility. The Westward thrust of the book begins as if Twain were simply retaining the tourist mask of *The Innocents Abroad*, with the difference that he presents himself as the archetypal tenderfoot who gradually becomes the initiated, experienced Westerner. Henry Nash Smith notes Twain's equation of Western slovenliness with Western freedom. In describing for Eastern readers the unprepossessing coyote of the Western plains, "a long, slim, sick and sorry-looking skeleton" of a creature, Twain paradoxically illuminates what his first-person voice calls "the gladness and the wild sense of freedom that used to make the blood dance in my veins on those fine overland mornings." Thundering across the prairie on a stage coach, narrator Twain discovers that the coyote, for all his sorry appearance, has powers not at first apparent to the self-satisfied Easterner. He imagines a "town-dog" that sets out to catch a coyote, "a dog that has a good opinion of himself, and has been brought up to think he knows something about speed. . . . he begins to get aggravated, and it makes him madder and madder to see how

gently the coyote glides along and never pants or sweats or ceases to smile; and he grows still more and more incensed to see how shamefully he has been taken in by an entire stranger. . . ." And after the coyote has grown bored with the game and turned on his real speed, "behold that dog is solitary and alone in the midst of a vast solitude! . . . And for as much as a year after that, whenever there is a great hue and cry after a coyote, that dog will merely glance in that direction without emotion, and apparently observe to himself, 'I believe I do not wish any of the pie.' " Here in one episode is the deflation of Eastern self-assurance by the facts of Western experience. For the first part of the book, this is the pattern followed by the narrator. At first a helpless, hopeless duffer, the tenderfoot gives up his Eastern style of dress for "a damaged slouch hat, blue woolen shirt, and pants crammed into boot-tops, and gloried in the absence of coat, vest, and braces." Later he goes a significant step further and gives up the cliches of Eastern gentility that pertain to the propriety and significance of deathbed repentance. Lost in a snowstorm, convinced that he is at death's door, the narrator, along with his two companions, vows permanent reformation. "I threw away my pipe, and in doing it felt that at last I was free of a hated vice . . . the thought of the good I might have done in the world, and the still greater good I might *now* do [by his example], with these new incentives and higher and better aims to guide me if I could only be spared a few years longer, overcame me and the tears came again." Huddled together for warmth, the three nod off to sleep. "Oblivion came. The battle of life was done." So ends chapter 32. Chapter 33 opens with the confused narrator awakening to what he thinks is death and then hearing a voice say, "with bitterness: 'Will some gentleman be so good as to kick me behind?' " Not only have they survived, but "there in the gray dawn, not fifteen steps from us, were the frame buildings of a stage-station. . . . We actually went into camp in a snowdrift in a desert, at midnight in a storm, forlorn and hopeless, within fifteen steps of a comfortable inn." Within an hour of a very comfortable breakfast, the three have recovered their pipes, bottles, and cards, shaken hands, "and agreed to say no more about 'reform' and 'examples to the rising generation.' "

The narrator has finally taken on the perspective and experience of the Westerner. He becomes part of the community of substantively lawless and certainly impolite miners and prospectors. The problem with *Roughing It* may well be that because Twain the author is basing the book on his own experience his narrator must now become a reporter for the *Virginia City Territorial Enterprise*. That is, the narrator becomes the sort of person who wrote the stories that Twain now draws upon for fleshing out his book. Not only does his dress change back to "the boiled shirt and black broadcloth that would not have seemed out of place in Boston or New York," his point of view becomes increasingly that of a member of an upper class, a cultivated class that speaks standard English and either scorns or smiles condescendingly at the uncouth language of "the boys" with whom he had seemed, at last, so comfortable. An example offers itself in Scotty Briggs, a Virginia City rough, as he engages in a hilariously slang-filled dialogue with a "pale theological student" for the purpose of arranging "Buck Fanshaw's Funeral," an episode part of which is often anthologized for its delightful juxtaposition of genteel and vernacular speech. During the exchange, each confuses the other with vocabulary, idiom, and grammar, as if in a war of words. If the reader sees it as indeed a war, then Scotty holds his own in the battle at hand. The anthologies usually omit the conclusion, however, in which it turns out that Scotty has lost the war. "Scotty Briggs, in after days, achieved the distinction of becoming the only convert to religion that was ever gathered from the Virginia roughs." Further, narrator Twain has learned, he became an extremely successful Sunday-school teacher because "He talked to his pioneer small-fry in a language they understood!" The exclamation point anticipates the condescension of the next paragraph: "It was my large privilege" to hear Scotty "tell the beautiful story of Joseph and his brethren . . . riddled with slang" but spoken by "that grave, earnest teacher" to "his little learners" so reverently "that they were as unconscious as he was that any violence was being done to the sacred proprieties!" "Large privilege" and "sacred proprieties!" show where the narrator's values now lie. This triumph of Eastern gentility, disappointing to readers, becomes especially striking in light of Mark Twain's omission of his own burlesque version of "the beautiful story of Joseph" from *The Innocents Abroad*: he and Mrs. Fairbanks had agreed that it was simply too irreverent.

The problem for the narrator, the problem for author Twain, a continuing problem for all writers of serious fiction about the early West, here surfaces. In the early parts of *Roughing It*, the constrained greenhorn, equipped with the sensibilities, the vocabulary, and the preconceptions of a reasonably cultivated Easterner, discovers and then comes to understand and finally to participate in a way of life that liberates him from the confines of the society he has known. Looked at from the perspective of cliches concerning the natural goodness of humanity, the repressive badness of social order, Scotty Briggs and his ilk become immensely attractive. But when the narrator looks through the spectacles of a detached observer, of a responsible reporter, he sees a different set of values reflected in the mores that accompany vernacular speech. The "boys" who rally 'round to give Buck Fanshaw a rip-roaring funeral make up precisely the same violent and amoral element that Twain-as-reporter castigates for mistreatment of the Chinese immigrants.

Twain's imagination continued to work on the contradictory assumptions latent in the presentation of characters whose vernacular speech stands at the opposite pole from genteel drawing rooms. Not until his acknowledged masterpiece, *Huckleberry Finn*, did he achieve a satisfactory solution. Meanwhile, he continued to search for ways of converting experience into literature. In the writing of *The Innocents Abroad* and *Roughing It*, he had relied heavily upon his newspaper pieces. Having exhausted these, he visited England in 1872-1873, looking into publishing rights for his books, and lecturing, but mainly trying to collect material for another travel book. Instead, however, on his return to Hartford, he and neighbor Charles Dudley Warner collaborated on the first extended work of fiction to carry Twain's name, *The Gilded Age* (1873), a title taken over by historians for the corrupt last third of the nineteenth century in America. The claims of vernacular and of experience by and large got shunted aside during this endeavor, Warner and Twain developing most of their plot from "threadbare devices borrowed from popular fiction." Still, some readers continue to find pleasure in *The Gilded Age*, primarily in the wonderful Colonel Sellers, always poor and always hopeful, whose joyful cry of "There's millions in it! Millions!" repeatedly heralds an impractical scheme doomed to failure at its inception. The irrepressible Sellers, somewhat like the speculative side of Twain himself, was drawn almost literally from James Lampton, Twain's mother's cousin, whose perpetual optimism and good-hearted bungling entertained the family when not breaking their hearts. Most of the book, however, concerns conventional love entanglements or personal and corporate corruption in Washington, D.C., as Colonel Sellers's pet project concerning railroads and a large tract of land encounters legislative bottlenecks. The story itself becomes tedious, but, as has often been said, and by Twain himself, Twain at least this once put to good use that incubus of 70,000 Tennessee acres

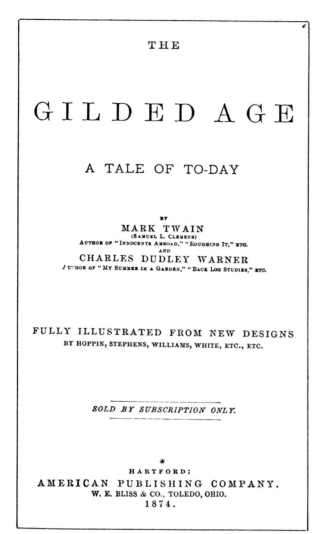

THE

GILDED AGE

A TALE OF TO-DAY

BY

MARK TWAIN
(SAMUEL L. CLEMENS)
AUTHOR OF "INNOCENTS ABROAD," "ROUGHING IT," ETC.

AND

CHARLES DUDLEY WARNER
AUTHOR OF "MY SUMMER IN A GARDEN," "BACK LOG STUDIES," ETC.

FULLY ILLUSTRATED FROM NEW DESIGNS
BY HOPPIN, STEPHENS, WILLIAMS, WHITE, ETC., ETC.

SOLD BY SUBSCRIPTION ONLY.

HARTFORD:
AMERICAN PUBLISHING COMPANY.
W. E. BLISS & CO., TOLEDO, OHIO.
1874.

Title page for Twain and Charles Dudley Warner's novel of personal and corporate corruption

lighted response to a reaction by a valued member of it, the Reverend Joseph Twichell, a good friend who had performed his marriage service and who frequently accompanied Twain on long tramps.

To understand the role of Twichell, however, one must first know about Twain's friendship with William Dean Howells, Ohio born printer, Lincoln's consul in Venice, New York journalist, and then editor-in-chief of the *Atlantic Monthly*, Boston's prestigious literary journal. Howells had first visited Boston in 1860 as a young man of twenty-three, "a pilgrim from the midwest worshiping at the feet of New England's literary great." With the rise of his own reputation as novelist, critic, editor, and finally, as people liked to say, "Dean" of American literary realism, of American literature generally, Howells retained, on the one hand, a respect for standards and values of upper-class Boston but, on the other hand, a high regard for talent, even when it was unconventional. His review of *The Innocents Abroad* in 1869 had praised "Mr. Clements' " work for the "amount of pure human nature" in it "that rarely gets into literature." With Twain living in Hartford

Mark Twain with John T. Raymond, who played Col. Mullberry Sellers in the 1874 dramatization of The Gilded Age

that his father had bequeathed to the family. Twain's insistence to Orion Clemens, a year or so before the writing of *The Gilded Age*, that he did not "want to be consulted at all about Tennessee. I don't want it even mentioned to me. . . . I beseech you never to ask my advice, opinion, or consent about that hated property" may have helped bring to mind the aggravation of owning potential but always unconvertible wealth, if help was needed; and from the conflicting emotions of hope and disappointment Twain did indeed, through the writing and sale of the book, derive a kind of return from the hated property. But *The Gilded Age* did little toward Twain's development as a writer, except as it involved him more deeply in the Nook Farm community. The next step in that development came in part as a reaction to that community and in de-

and with a friendship beginning between the two men that would last until death, Howells in 1874 urged Twain to contribute to the *Atlantic Monthly*. But Twain, having laid aside plans for "a Mississippi book" until he could get back to the river and take notes, remained persuaded that he needed a factual basis for his "narrative plank" with the spaces for serious and humorous plugs.

On 24 October 1874 Twain wrote to Howells: "I take back the remark that I can't write for the Jan. number. For Twichell & I have had a long walk in the woods & I got to telling him about old Mississippi days of steamboating glory & grandeur as I saw them (during 5 years) from *the pilot house*. He said, 'What a virgin subject to hurl into a magazine!' I hadn't thought of that before. Would you like a series of papers to run through 3 months or 6 or 9?—or about 4 months, say?" *Old Times on the Mississippi* (seven installments in the 1875 *Atlantic*) came out in Canada and England as a book, one of the most compelling recreations of a time and place and vision of life that Twain was to write. His own experience as a "cub" learning the river, his convenient memory, and his doubleness of perspective—as both neophyte and old timer—all contributed to this evocation of a world totally foreign to, but welcomed by, most *Atlantic* readers. In 1883 Twain used these seven installments, with minor revisions, to form about one third of *Life on the Mississippi*, most of which deals with a subsequent return to the river by the then famous author.

Meanwhile, Twain was passing through the first in a series of attacks of stage fever. He had begun work in 1870 on "A Boy's Manuscript," a burlesque of adult romance in an account of preadolescent puppy love concerning one Tom Sawyer. In 1872, he briefly returned to some of the same characters, but this time in dramatic form. Again he broke off, recommencing in the summer of 1874 at Quarry Farm (Livy Clemens's sister's house near Elmira, where the Clemenses usually summered and Twain wrote in a small study, "a little room of windows, somewhat suggestive of a pilot-house," that his sister-in-law had built for him). With the success of *The Gilded Age*, an unauthorized adaptation of Colonel Sellers's escapades had appeared on the San Francisco stage by May 1874. Notified of the theft by his friend Joe Goodman, owner of the *Enterprise*, Twain, as so often before and afterwards, launched into instant litigation. Finally, he paid $400 to Gilbert S. Densmore, the larcenous dramatist, worked over the script himself, appropriated Densmore's chief actor, and made a considerable financial success. In this case,

as in his future and unsuccessful attempts to capture theater audiences, Twain showed little if any talent as a dramatist. Unfortunately, John T. Raymond's masterful enactment of the title role made *Colonel Sellers* a success at the box office and encouraged Twain to pursue what was for him an artistic dead end.

Even in 1874, his best instincts must have recognized this, for when he returned to Tom Sawyer in the summer, he developed the novel, not the play. At the same time he was working on a number of other projects, some literary, some financially speculative, and of the former not all were humorous. "A True Story" and "The Curious Republic of Gondour" both ended up in the *Atlantic Monthly* (November 1874 and October 1875), the latter anonymously because he feared that no one would take it seriously if Mark Twain were known to be the author. "A True Story" presents with earned emotion the suffering and joy of an old slave woman as she tells of her separation from her favorite child at a slave auction and of their reunion twenty-two years later during the Civil War. The brutalities of slavery, understated and presented concretely through the ex-slave's memory, and the use of first-person dialect make the story especially interesting as a precursor of *Huckleberry Finn*. Here, too, are the effects of that emphasis on class and rank, of the false aristocracy that Twain saw as characterizing the antebellum South. (In *Life on the Mississippi* he was to call Sir Walter Scott's medieval romances in large measure responsible for Southern aristocratic pretension and thus for the Civil War itself.) In "The Curious Republic of Gondour," however, Twain returned to the abuses of present day American democracy latent in *Roughing It* and overt in *The Gilded Age*. His impatience with these abuses grew so rabid that by the summer of 1877 he could say, in a letter to young Mollie Fairbanks, "I hate all shades & forms of republican government, now." Only a revision of that tyrannical universal suffrage ("this wicked, ungodly suffrage, where the vote of a man who knew nothing was as good as the vote of a man of education and industry") could solve the problems of American democracy and save the country. In "The Curious Republic of Gondour," Twain's proposed solution is to expand the vote (to deny it would be unconstitutional) so that the more education or the more property, the greater number of votes an individual may cast. The Republic of Gondour is a utopia where this scheme has led to enlightenment, industry, and general good government. Twain has departed from the egalitarian memories of his boyhood in Hannibal.

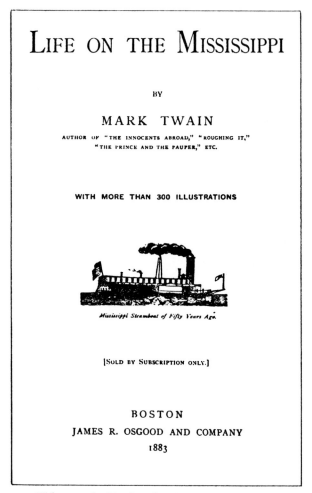

LIFE ON THE MISSISSIPPI

BY

MARK TWAIN

AUTHOR OF "THE INNOCENTS ABROAD," "ROUGHING IT,"
"THE PRINCE AND THE PAUPER," ETC.

WITH MORE THAN 300 ILLUSTRATIONS

Mississippi Steamboat of Fifty Years Ago.

[SOLD BY SUBSCRIPTION ONLY.]

BOSTON
JAMES R. OSGOOD AND COMPANY
1883

Title page for Twain's description of riverboat life

But he was, of course, to come full circle, and more than once.

One cannot know to what extent Twain's disillusionment with contemporary, corrupt, adult society stimulated his imagination to explore and to recapture the past of his boyhood. He could not, in any case, write effective extended fiction about his present world. His first book-length fictional evocation of the past, *The Adventures of Tom Sawyer*, "simply a hymn, put into prose form to give it a worldly air," has become the American boyhood idyll.

It opens as Tom, apparently nine or ten years old, flees from his Aunt Polly's wrath, climbing the back fence in his haste to escape the prohibitions and censure of adult society. Tom's punishment for playing hooky—he has to spend Saturday whitewashing a board fence thirty yards long and nine feet high—leads to his accumulation of friends' treasures as he turns drudgery into a status-bestowing object of envy. His encounters with Becky Thatcher, the new girl in town, and with Huck Finn, independent pariah about Tom's age or slightly older, help to organize the episodes of a story that is primarily an evocation of what it felt like for Sam Clemens to be young long ago in Hannibal, Missouri. Still, there is something of a plot, the two main strands of which concern Tom's relationship with Becky and the aftermath of Injun Joe's murder of a townsman, the only witnesses of the deed being Tom and Huck. These two interests finally come together as Tom and Becky, lost in the labyrinth of McDougal's Cave, survive because of Tom's bravery and sense of responsibility. In the process, Tom happens upon Injun Joe's hiding place for stolen gold. The book ends as Tom, now perhaps fourteen or fifteen years of age even though only one spring and one summer have elapsed since the episode of the fence, shares the gold with Huck and establishes himself as a member-in-good-standing of the very society whose constrictions he had found so onerous at the book's start. Injun Joe, less lucky and resourceful than Tom, has starved to death in the cave; Becky fervently admires Tom; Aunt Polly has forgiven him his various mischiefs because of his "goodheartedness."

Worth noting, however, is the somber undertone of this book that, above all other American stories—including Booth Tarkington's sentimental Penrod confections—calls to readers' minds childhood's careless raptures. Graveyard murder, tormented conscience, sudden violence, haunted dreams, grief at loss, and the final drawn-out terror of the cave episode play as large a role in the book's loose plot as boyish pranks and puppy love. The tone of the whole, however, assures the reader that, at least for Tom and those who love him, all will be well, eternally, in what has been rightly called the longest and most glorious summer in the annals of literature. In addition, *Tom Sawyer* offers a first glimpse of Huckleberry Finn, the wild huckleberries of Twain's adopted New England joining with the derelict Jimmy Finn, town drunkard of Hannibal in the 1840s, to give a name to Twain's most significant creation.

It appears that as Twain approached the ending to Tom's book late in 1875, he began to feel some awareness of a problem with his, at first, sympathetically portrayed central figure. Tom, although he dares to consort with Huck the outcast, responsibly testifies in court against the murderous Injun Joe and gallantly saves Becky and himself from the cave. Perhaps, then, it should be no surprise that he becomes spokesman for genteel re-

THE ADVENTURES

OF

TOM SAWYER

BY

MARK TWAIN.

THE AMERICAN PUBLISHING COMPANY,
HARTFORD, CONN.: CHICAGO, ILL.: CINCINNATI, OHIO.
A. ROMAN & CO., SAN FRANCISCO, CAL.
1876.

Frontispiece by True Williams and title page for first American edition

spectability, his escapes from society's trammels having been only temporary, designed as the means of purchasing society's applause. Still, there is a difference between Tom's boyishly conventional flouting of conventions during the body of the story and his final insistence that if Huck is to join Tom Sawyer's gang, he must return to the constricting care of the Widow Douglas, because "Huck, we can't let you into the gang if you ain't respectable, you know." Crestfallen, Huck agrees to "stick to the widder till I rot, Tom; and if I git to be a reg'lar ripper of a robber, and everybody talking 'bout it, I reckon she'll be proud she snaked me in out of the wet." Here the story ends, with Huck's amusing last words taking away some of the sting from Tom's betrayal of what might have seemed to be an espousal of real freedom but that is, instead, just a slight kicking up of the heels before settling into a conventional role. Twain says as much in his two-paragraph conclusion: "Most of the characters that perform in this book still live, and are prosperous and happy. Some day" he may take up their adult lives "and see what sort of men and women they turned out to be." In 1902 he learned that the par-

tial model for Huck Finn, Tom Blankenship, had become a much respected justice of the peace in Montana; but this was merely fact and had nothing to do with Twain's literary imagination. In 1891, when he jotted some notes toward a continuation of Huck's story, one of his thoughts was that "Huck comes back . . . crazy" and that "both [Tom and Huck] are desolate, life has been a failure. . . ." By the end of *The Adventures of Huckleberry Finn*, this change of heart seems already signaled. When Tom reveals that Jim is "as free as any cretur that walks this earth," Twain has anticipated through the book's action his own comment in his notebook twenty years later: "The skin of every human being contains a slave."

The greatest work so far of the American comic imagination, Huck's story begins where Tom's ends, and was begun in the summer of 1876, while Twain was still preparing the latter for publication. "You don't know about me without you have read a book by the name of *The Adventures of Tom Sawyer*," begins Huck, and then adds Twain's indictment of himself: "That book was made by Mr. Mark Twain, and he told the truth, mainly. There was things which he stretched, but mainly he told the truth." As Twain well knew, Huck is being charitable. Huck's own book is itself full of evasions, including a Victorian ignoring of the sexual nature of young adolescents, as John Seelye's recent *The True Adventures of Huckleberry Finn* (1970) so ingeniously demonstrates. It is not, however, guilty of the great lie that Tom's book revels in, and from which it draws its air of peaceful delight: the lie that evil is external to society, encapsulated in, and therefore easily exorcized by the death of, Injun Joe. In Huck's story evil exists not simply in the institution of slavery or in the exploitations engineered by the King and the Duke, but in the very fabric of genteel civilization that makes possible, in addition to these, the use of people as means to ends, even by that most innocent-seeming representative of the established order, Tom Sawyer himself.

This account makes Twain's result and intention appear to be far more congruent than they probably were. Clearly, the shaping of Huck's story—an involved, complex, uncertain process, documented in Walter Blair's *Mark Twain and HUCK FINN* (1960)—came intuitively rather than by plan. Seven years of irregular effort, punctuated by numerous excursions in other directions, lie behind the finished work. Twain at first wrote pretty steadily. Then, with chapter 16, where a steamboat crushes the raft on which Huck and the runaway slave, Jim, are drifting south, Twain abruptly put aside the manuscript. Why, exactly, Huck's story came so hard to him furnishes material for some of the most interesting biographical, historical, social, and literary speculation in which readers indulge. Twain himself saw the process simply as his own intuitive, or perhaps "hydraulic," way of working, a process that he first discusses in reference to the hiatus in the making of *Tom Sawyer*: "When the manuscript had lain in a pigeon-hole two years I took it out one day and read the last chapter that I had written. It was then that I made the great discovery that when the tank runs dry you've only got to leave it alone and it will fill up again in time while you are asleep—also while you are at work on other things and are quite unaware that this unconscious and profitable cerebration is going on." The revivification of memories of the past, he said, especially helped to stimulate the flow. Thus, in early 1880, when young Wattie Bowser, a schoolboy in Dallas, Texas, wrote as a student in Laura Wright Dake's sixth-grade class to ask some conventional questions of the rich and famous author, Twain's memory of the young Laura Wright he had known,

and apparently felt great affection for, while he was apprentice to Horace Bixby, released a flood of river reminiscence into a twelve-page letter. That is, even before Twain returned to the river in 1882 to take notes for the expansion of *Old Times on the Mississippi* into a volume of subscription-book length, his thoughts went in that direction and he wrote the Grangerford-Sheperdson chapters of *Huckleberry Finn*. Reminiscence and imagination together drew him back to his tale of life on and along the river. But why the earlier abandonment of the story? A look at some of the "other things" that Twain worked on instead suggests that part of the answer has to do with considerable conflict involving the life of the adult Samuel Clemens, his roots, and the art of Mark Twain.

The Clemens mansion in Hartford in its magnificence underlined the economic distance Twain had come from his beginnings and implied the high gentility to which he made repeated efforts to adapt himself. His election to the Hartford Monday Evening Club, to whose literary and intellectual discussions he became a regular contributor, his participation in home theatricals, and his enthusiastic readings aloud from Browning's poetry all reflect the style of life represented by that house. The house was three stories high, with three towers and seven bathrooms, a billiard room, a library, and more balconies and other rooms than are immediately apparent (twenty-eight rooms in all), and its initial cost of $122,000 (over $500,000 in today's dollars, if such a risky comparison has any meaning) was repeatedly increased by remodeling, along with continuous outlays for six servants and lavish entertaining. Here was the dream of success translated into tangible assets. One may imagine the satisfaction Twain could take in contemplating the contrast between hard times in Hannibal and contentment in Connecticut. Huck Finn, even worse off than young Sam had been, at least until the sharing of buried treasure with Tom (but this is never translated into fictional reality), might seem simply to emphasize that contrast. Two recurring motifs in Twain's work at this time, however, suggest that this is too simple an account of Twain's condition: concerns about conscience and concerns about genteel propriety recur again and again. Writing to Howells in January 1876, Twain apologetically brings up a matter of language at the end of the manuscript of *Tom Sawyer* that Howells had read and marked for revision. Twain is grateful for Howells's assumption of the chore—"This was splendid, & swept away all labor"—but "there was one expression which perhaps you overlooked." Twain had read the pas-

Recto and verso for Twain's dummy title page; frontispiece by E. W. Kemble and title page for first American edition

Twain's nineteen-room house in Hartford, Connecticut, which, with land and furnishings, cost $122,000

sage to Livy Clemens, and, on another occasion, "to her aunt & her mother (both sensitive and loyal subjects of the kingdom of heaven, so to speak,) & *they* let it pass." Still, when Huck Finn complains to Tom about "all manner of compulsory decencies" at the Widow Douglas's, "he winds up by saying, 'and they comb me all to hell.' (No exclamation point.)" Twain wonders about this word, and Howells agrees that, although it's exactly what a boy in Huck's position would say, now that the book is intended "for the children," it will not do. As a reader will notice, Huck is now combed "all to thunder." The rough language of Twain's and Howells's boyhoods must not sully young Eastern ears. Huck's freedom and independence represent a threat to Twain's own way of life, and Twain himself is more sensitive to the issue than is his Eastern wife.

Conscience (and it has often been said that *Huckleberry Finn* is a book about the workings of conscience), often an issue in Twain's earlier work, explicitly appears at the center of Twain's thought at about this same time. On 24 January 1876 he read

to the Monday Evening Club "The Facts Concerning the Recent Carnival of Crime in Connecticut," published in the *Atlantic Monthly* in June, the month before he started to write Huck's story. The carnival of crime results from the narrator's ingenious success in killing his conscience so that he can now do anything at all and feel no pang. At the story's start, the narrator, expansively generous-hearted, "thoroughly happy and contented," muses: "If my most pitiless enemy could appear before me at this moment, I would freely right any wrong I may have done him." The enemy promptly enters, a deformed creature, "nauseating" in appearance yet inescapably resembling "myself." Echoing W. E. H. Lecky's *History of European Morals from Augustus to Charlemagne* (1869), the narrator's conscience—for that is who this "conspicuous deformity," this most "pitiless enemy," turns out to be—admits that he, like all consciences, actively enjoys tormenting his victim. "The *purpose* of it is to improve the man, but *we* are merely disinterested agents. We are appointed by authority. . . . We obey orders. . . . But I am willing to admit this much: we *do* crowd the orders a trifle when we get a chance which is most of the time. We enjoy it." Here, a reader of Freud would say, is the punitive superego, producing pain for the sake of producing pain. Certainly this is the equivalent of Twain's formulation, one that reflected his subjective experience and that he had found worked out in detail in Lecky's massive two volumes on European morals, which Twain had read and discussed with brother-in-law Theodore Crane since the summer of 1874 and regularly referred to for the rest of his life. Lecky tried to distinguish between two kinds of moral theory, the intuitive, innate sort and "the inductive, the utilitarian, or the selfish." His marginal notes suggest that Twain had trouble with the logic of Lecky's distinction. Nevertheless, Lecky put clearly ideas that Twain kept coming back to, ideas whose importance to him underline his problems with his own conscience. From that time on, the question of why we value what we value was never far from the surface of Twain's fiction. Huck Finn himself finally decides to "go to hell" by committing the major crime of helping a slave escape to freedom. His "sound heart," as Twain characterized it in 1895 notes for a lecture tour, triumphs over his "deformed conscience," but only the author and the reader can see that "the conscience . . . can be trained to approve any wild thing you *want* it to approve if you begin its education early and stick to it."

All of this points to 17 December 1877 as a focus for Twain's guilt-stricken ambivalence toward genteel culture. Invited to speak at the *Atlantic*'s twentieth-anniversary dinner honoring John Greenleaf Whittier on his seventieth birthday, Twain delivered a humorous story. Howells's introduction cast him in the role of kindly humorist, "whose fun is never at the cost of anything high or good." What amounted to Howells's prayer was answered by Twain's acquiescence in the role of funny man, presenting a rough Westerner encountering Eastern literary culture. Twain's own reaction to his performance provides insight: abject apology and guilt for having besmirched the "gracious singers" of New England alternate with his strong sense that the speech was hilariously funny, most appropriate to the occasion, and perhaps, at its deepest levels of meaning, even true. Longfellow, Emerson, and Holmes, all present at the dinner, are envisioned as having cavorted in a California miner's cabin where Mark Twain, newly emboldended by his "nom de plume," "callow and conceited," has sought refuge. The miner, insulted,

imposed upon, and robbed by his previous guests, is soured on all literary figures and wants even Twain to move on. When the latter observes that "*these* [cardsharps, drunkards, and misappropriators of famous verse] were not the gracious singers to whom we and the world pay loving reverence and homage: these were imposters," the miner—the vernacular character, the irreverent Westerner—extrapolates tellingly, "Ah, imposters, were they? are *you*?" Through 1906 Twain kept on thinking about, and changing his mind about, the speech. The extent to which his unconscious evaluation of genteel literary culture spilled over into his consciousness tantalizes readers. That his aggression against that culture was in this case unconscious seems most likely, considering the reversals of feelings he later recorded. That he saw himself, for all his success, as still something of an "imposter" in the East also seems likely. As one of his characters might have put it, contemporary America was "too many" for him. The Missouri boyhood of the conventional Tom Sawyer and then of the subversive Huck Finn, the pre-Elizabethan setting of *The Prince and the Pauper* (1881), the European jaunt served up in *A Tramp Abroad*, and the heavy disillusion that informs the return-to-the-river chapters of *Life on the Mississippi* all point to an increasing unease with his American present. His humor, hilarious in places, was to become increasingly ironic and eventually sardonic.

Clearly, no single cause for Twain's perspective can be identified; neither can all the causes be known. Reading Lecky seems not to have altered his views so much as clarified them. We cannot say that only someone outside the dominant genteel culture can have a "sound heart" like Huck's, for Mary Jane Wilks, whose sincere concern for the feelings of the family slaves touches Huck as well as the reader, has more than her share of the innate decencies, despite her conventional propriety. Buy why? How? Twain never does resolve this perplexing question. He suffered increasingly violent rages at those he thought had cheated him—publishers, business agents, and, above all, James W. Paige, into whose fantastic typesetter Twain threw a total of over $200,000 during a fourteen-year period beginning in 1880. If people are simply the result of what training or environment makes of the original raw material, as Twain's fictions and characters come more and more to suggest and assert, then no basis for moral outrage exists. The mechanistic determinism preached in *What Is Man?* (1906) and presented in some of the manuscripts that were to go into *The Mysterious Stranger* represents Twain's felt perception, but so does the accompanying fury that informs so much of his unpublished, and also published, work. This combination, as much as any other single element, gives energy and bite to his mature work. Even parts of the saccharine *The Prince and the Pauper* and *Personal Recollections of Joan of Arc* (1896) transcend their author's genteel intentions in their booming excoriations of exploitation and injustice.

The second half of Twain's life, punctuated by frequent publications as well as by frequent difficulties, both financial and personal, included triumphs, honors, and joys in fair measure. His children at first gave him immense pleasure, and numerous letters and reminiscences attest to the zest for life that many visitors sensed in the Clemens household. The trip to Europe that immediately followed the Whittier birthday speech and that led to *A Tramp Abroad* was by no means an embarrassed retreat, having been planned since considerably before that occasion. Twain's numerous travels testify primarily to financial exigency as well as to itching feet. Unwise speculations, the increasing expenses of the Hartford house, and, after 1880, his disastrous expansion of his publishing house, Charles L. Webster and Company, to do full justice to the *Memoirs* of Ulysses S. Grant (Twain was extremely proud of thereby salvaging the Grant family's for-

tunes) all joined with Paige's omnivorous appetite for perfection and for expensive tinkering with his machine to lead Twain ever closer to the bankruptcy that finally came in April 1894. Exhausting lecture tours took him away from the family, but still he managed to write. His eventual decision to pay 100 cents on the dollar when, both by law and by the common business ethics of the time, he had no obligation to do so made him, finally, a popular hero.

The emotional strain seems to have been great, just as his newfound business adviser and close friend, H. H. Rogers, exacted, all unknowingly, a toll on Twain's sense of moral independence. Ironically, Rogers, one of the three men in charge of the twenty companies that made up the Standard Oil Trust, managed with equal proportions of skill and tact to bring order to the financial affairs of the author, many of whose books soundly lambasted the exploitation of the masses by large monied interests. Twain found his own views changing. By 1900, he was remembering, in "Corn-Pone Opinions," the words of a slave heard fifty years earlier: "You tell me whar a man gits his corn-pone, en I'll tell you what his 'pinions is." By "corn-pone," Twain explains, he means both the satisfaction of material self-interest and the satisfaction of the desire to be thought well of by others,

The Paige typesetting machine on which Twain lost some $300,000

"perhaps by an ass, but still an ass . . . whose approval . . . confers glory and honor and happiness and membership in the herd." Six years later, recalling a running battle of some twenty-two years' duration with Joe Twichell, Twain discovers that he has "never found any real fault with him for voting his infernal Republican ticket, for the reason that, situated as he was, with a large family to support, his first duty was not to his political conscience, but to his family conscience. . . . He sacrificed his political independence, and saved his family by it." Is Twain perhaps protesting too much? In any case, his conscience was troubling him more and more. The death of Susy, the daughter who seemed to him most like himself, had struck him as a punishment in 1896: had he and Livy Clemens been home rather than circling the globe to pay off his debts, perhaps. . . . His wife's death in 1904 left him not only bereaved but, once again, guilty. "Almost the only crime of my life which causes me bitterness now," he wrote Clara Clemens the following May, was his having deprived Livy of the "spiritual shelter and refuge that her religion had once offered." He recalled having said shortly after Susy's death, "Livy, if it comforts you to lean on the Christian faith, do so," and she had replied, "I can't, Youth. I haven't any."

Twain's writing following *Huckleberry Finn* takes numerous directions. The humor becomes more and more bitter, but its source still lies in the upsetting of cliches and popular complacencies (for example: "It is by the goodness of God that in our country we have those three unspeakably precious things: freedom of speech, freedom of conscience, and the prudence never to practice either of them"; and, "Nothing so needs reforming as other people's habits.") and in the exposure of the huge and unnoticed gap between what people intend by their actions, what they think they are, and what their actions suggest that they are indeed. Hank Morgan, nineteenth-century Connecticut Yankee at the court of King Arthur, fights for the triumph of "the magic of science" over "the magic of fol-de-rol," secure in his belief that principle is what he cares for. But the image of Sir Boss, as Hank is called, "snaking" armored knights out of their saddles with a lariat out of the American West and then, when "things" begin to look "squally," mystifying as well as killing them with two revolvers, gets much of its comic point from Hank's delight in the sheer Tom Sawyer glory of being "the focal point of forty thousand adoring eyes." Like the very knights he defeats, Hank lives for applause, perhaps even more than for principle. "Across my mind flitted

the dear image of a certain hello girl [telephone operator] of West Hartford, and I wished she could see me now." Such complexities in *A Connecticut Yankee in King Arthur's Court* help to make it one of Twain's more coherent books. Hank tries to bring democracy and industrial progress to the backward sixth century. By the time he is done trying, the evils of a machine culture have been exposed no less than the tyrannies of title and church and wealth. At the same time, readers have always enjoyed the sheer exuberance of Hank's various juxtapositions of the modern and the archaic: billboards advertising soap and toothpaste and stove polish cover the armor of "the bravest knights I could get." Not even the techniques of modern advertising, however, can reeducate Arthur's people; Hank fails disastrously, leaving 25,000 dead in a devastated society.

The principal issue beneath the action of the book has most to do with quesitons raised by Twain's old guide Lecky: do people have the power to educate themselves upward, ever upward, or are they—are we—simply victims of heredity and environment? Where, that is, does Huck Finn's "sound heart" come from? How potent a force is it? Hank, witnessing a particularly gratuitous killing, wonders how Morgan Le Fay can justify her crime. "How thou talkest!" she replies. "Crime, forsooth! Man, I am going to pay for him!" Hank speculates that what we call human "nature . . . is merely heredity and training. We have no thoughts of our own, no opinions of our own; they are transmitted to us, trained into us." Then he adds, "All that is original in us, and therefore fairly creditable or discreditable to us" is "that one microscopic atom in me that is truly me. . . ." In his rage, Hank sounds much like Twain; in his efforts to persuade himself that "blame" in human affairs is irrelevant, he also sounds like Twain. "My book is written—let it go," Twain wrote to Howells. "But if it were only to write over again there wouldn't be so many things left out. They burn in me; & they keep multiplying & multiplying, but now they can't ever be said. And besides, they would require a library—& a pen warmed up in hell." Despite even H. H. Rogers's friendship and, beginning in the midst of the Great Panic of 1893, general management of funds, business affairs, and copyrights, Twain remained a seething volcano for the rest of his life. Sentimental effusions—"A Dog's Tale" (1903), "A Horse's Tale" (1906), and others—did preserve his tie to the respectable genteel culture. Most of Twain's late output, however, he wrote as if "from the grave. By these terms only can a man be approximately frank. He cannot be straitly, & unqualifiedly frank either in the grave or out of it." Ordinarily sophisticated readers in Twain's day found, and almost all readers now find, nothing in the posthumously published works to justify this reticence. Even Twain himself on occasion changed his mind and published what he had first intended to withhold until after death; parts of his *Autobiography* (begun in 1877 and his major interest from 1906 on), *What Is Man?*, and "Captain Stormfield's Visit to Heaven" are among such instances. "The War Prayer," written in 1905 and pointing out the paradoxical fact that any Christian who prays for victory in time of war is thereby praying for the death and mutilation of fellow human beings, he would not allow to be published in his lifetime. "He did not care to invite the public verdict that he was a lunatic," explains Paine, but subsequent readers have concluded that both Twain and Paine were evaluating public opinion on the basis of the orthodoxies of Twain's childhood.

Pudd'nhead Wilson, "The Man That Corrupted Hadleyburg," and "The $30,000 Bequest" are the works published late in Twain's life that best repay today's readers. *Tom Sawyer Abroad* (1894), delightful for children, strikes most adults as a labored exploitation of Tom, Huck, and Jim, although many find merit in the semi-Platonic dialogues carried on by the three comrades in the balloon that takes them from Missouri to Africa. In the other works, and in the great masses of collected papers that have been appearing in published form over the last forty years (and especially in the last fifteen), guilt, responsibility, and dream are the primary motifs. "The Man That Corrupted Hadleyburg" emphasizes guilt. Once again, people mistake their own natures. The citizens of Hadleyburg, smugly proud of their honesty, discover how greedily crooked they are when a stranger leaves a bag purported to contain $40,000 in gold, the contents to go to the unknown person who, some years before, supposedly befriended and advised him. The test of identity is to be the words of that advice. The leading citizens all succumb to the temptation to enter as their own the words that the stranger has mailed to each of them. This is as grimly powerful a story as any that Twain ever wrote.

Pudd'nhead Wilson (1894), for all the ironic humor of the "Pudd'nhead Wilson's Calendar" quips that begin each chapter, as if with an almanac entry for a specific date, and the great fun Twain had in Wilson's use of fingerprints to solve a murder (1892 was the date of the first such success in real life), focuses on problems of responsibility, and also on miscegenation, on Southern pretensions to honor, and on the murder of a not-quite-father by a

not-quite-son. Once again, Twain takes readers back to a small riverside town in the pre-Civil War South. A black baby, identical in appearance to his mother's master's white son, grows up "white" because Roxy, the barely Mulatto mother, has switched the two babies as infants. Why is "Tom" so vicious? Does his "black blood" dominate? Does his upbringing as the spoiled darling of a widowed father and a guilty "black" nursemaid who is really his mother account for his ways? His mother blames the "blood," but Twain appears to put more weight on the question of upbringing, especially in the contrast with "Chambers," the real white scion who lives as a slave. In a complex plot that includes Tom's selling his mother down the river into the unbearable hell of a Louisiana sugar plantation, Twain ends the book in a dramatic trial and conviction of Tom for murdering his "uncle" in whose house he has lived since his "father's" death. More dramatically still, David Wilson, who is the "Pudd'nhead" of the title because the simple villagers cannot appreciate his mind, reveals through his history in fingerprints not only that Tom is indeed the murderer but also that Tom, between the ages of seven and eight months, was moved from the cradle of a slave to that of a young white master. Tom, therefore, is neither hanged nor imprisoned but, instead, because he is "a valuable slave," the governor of the state "pardoned Tom at once, and the creditors sold him down the river." Twain is still attacking slavery in this story, but primarily the slavery of the spirit. Roxy, his most satisfactorily drawn female character, undergoes a transformation when her guilt becomes public: though she has been resilient and independent despite the indignities of her status, "the spirit in her eye was [now] quenched." Similarly, the "real" white master who has grown up as a slave can "neither read nor write. . . . His gait, his attitudes" allow him to feel "at home and at peace nowhere but in the kitchen." Although he finds "himself rich and free," he is, like so many of Twain's characters, in a figurative sense, a slave for life. This bitter irony fairly represents the tone of the book, most notably in the epigraphs that begin each chapter, the excerpts from "Pudd'nhead Wilson's Calendar." "October 2, the discovery," for example, sums up the legal "discoveries" of the previous chapter in a much wider reference: "It was wonderful to find America, but it would have been more wonderful to miss it."

The central preoccupation of the last writings, however, appears to have been with the confusion of dream with reality. To an extent, this follows from Twain's continuing interest in psychic phenomena in general and especially in what he called "mind-cure," beginning with reports of Livy Clemens's recovery from various debilitating disorders just before he met her and extending to his book-length commentary on Christian Science and an active following of the work of Charcot and others at the end of the century and beyond. Perhaps more significant still is the nature of the reality from which many of Twain's late characters flee into dream. Driven by loss or guilt or some other misery, they find themselves at last in a condition that renders them incapable of distinguishing one realm from the other. Some of these narratives are black and bleak indeed. "The $30,000 Bequest," however, has its humorous side as well. Saladin and Electra Foster (Sally and Aleck), expecting any week to inherit their bequest from a rich uncle, spend hours manipulating in imagination the investments they will make once the money is theirs. Or, rather, Aleck takes care of the finances while Sally sinks into degrading debaucheries. Lost in fantasy, his face reveals to Aleck how far gone in sin—totally imaginary, of course—he has become. Finally, both of them see "all things dimly, as through a veil." Twain's comment on the story applies to many of his later pieces: "How soon and how easily our dream life and our material life become so intermingled and so fused together that we can't quite tell which is which, any more."

For a while, it was a common criticism of Twain to say that a loss of artistic vision, of aesthetic control, marred his later output, that he was so overcome by rage and grief that he could shape none of his work meaningfully and satisfyingly. More recently, as more and more material has emerged from the archives of the Mark Twain papers, one careful reader has gone on record as proclaiming "the total effect [to be] one of mature mastery and control." *Extract from Captain Stormfield's Visit to Heaven* (1909) transforms the

Twain in 1904, photographed by his biographer Albert Bigelow Paine

blasphemous Ned Wakeman, captain of Twain's ship from San Francisco to Panama back in 1866, to the delightful Stormfield whose heavenly voyage shocked only gently the evangelical proprieties and whose fictional name Twain in great good humor attached to his last residence, the house he built at Redding, Connecticut, and lived in for most of his last two years. It remains true, however, that America's greatest humorist, as seen by the biographer who knew him best, Albert Bigelow Paine, "dreaded loneliness," especially in his later years—many a night he played billiards until three or four in the morning—and presented as his image of ultimate reality an individual whose whole universe is merely "a dream" because "Nothing exists save empty space—and you!"

Unamusing though this be, the "Mysterious Stranger" manuscripts repay a reader's attention, now that they are available, for they include some of Twain's liveliest, most vivid writing. It is now perfectly clear that the posthumously published volume entitled *The Mysterious Stranger*, edited by Twain's official biographer and literary executor, Paine, and Frederick A. Duneka of Harper and Brothers, was in essence "an editorial fraud perpetrated by" the two of them. Both the 1916 version and that of 1922—the latter including what Paine said was the last chapter, finally discovered—represent Paine's combining and linking of several manuscripts. What Twain really wrote should be read by anyone desiring a clear sense of how Twain's imagination used experience, reading, and reflection to shape significant fiction. Set in various pasts, depending on which manuscript one reads, and developing fictional possibilities of the double as well as of the dream and of determinism, these writings have both intrinsic appeal and also the interest that comes from the light they throw on literary creativity.

Mark Twain has always struck his readers as an author they would have liked to know. His passion for billiards, his fascination with gadgets (he was one of the first writers to try to use a typewriter, one of the first citizens of Hartford to have a telephone), his curiosity about and his confidence in a variety of psychic phenomena—together with his healthy skepticism—his endless optimism about financial speculations, his self-education and rise to fame and fortune, his dependence on popular opinion—together with his outspoken courage—his delight in public recognition (he cherished his Oxford honorary degree), above all, his sense of humor: these make him for many an archetypal American. When he spoke of "the calm confidence of a Christian with four aces," he spoke the thought of millions in language that made blasphemy seem simple common sense. He helped shape the American idiom and, to an extent, the American mind. For Americans, he made humor not only reputable but openly necessary, publicly a part of the American repertoire of expected, and effective, behavior.

Periodical Publications:
FICTION:
"The Dandy Frightening the Squatter," *Carpet-Bag*, 1 May 1852;

"Jim Smiley and His Frog," *New York Saturday Press*, 18 November 1865;

"The Curious Republic of Gondour," anonymous, *Atlantic Monthly* (October 1875);

"The Facts Concerning the Recent Carnival of Crime in Connecticut," *Atlantic Monthly* (June 1876);

"The Great Revolution in Pitcairn," *Atlantic Monthly* (March 1879);

"A Dog's Tale," *Harper's* (December 1903);

"A Horse's Tale," *Harper's* (August-September 1906).

NONFICTION:
"Forty-Three Days in an Open Boat," as Mark Swain, *Harper's* (December 1866);

"A True Story," *Atlantic Monthly* (November 1874);

"Old Times on the Mississippi," *Atlantic Monthly* (January-July 1875);

"The Private History of a Campaign That Failed," *Century Magazine* (December 1885);

"In Defense of Harriet Shelley," *North American Review* (July 1894);

"Fenimore Cooper's Literary Offenses," *North American Review* (July 1895);

"Concerning the Jews," *Harper's* (September 1899);

"To the Person Sitting in Darkness," *North American Review* (February 1901);

"The Death of Jean," *Harper's* (December 1910).

Letters:
Mark Twain's Letters, 2 volumes, edited by Albert Bigelow Paine (New York & London: Harper, 1917);

Mark Twain's Letters to Will Bowen, edited by Theodore Hornberger (Austin: University of Texas Press, 1941);

Mark Twain to Mrs. Fairbanks, edited by Dixon Wecter (San Marino, Cal.: Huntington Library, 1949);

The Love Letters of Mark Twain, edited by Wecter (New York: Harper, 1949);

Mark Twain-Howells Letters, edited by Henry Nash Smith and William M. Gibson (Cambridge: Belknap Press/Harvard University Press, 1960);

Mark Twain's Letters to His Publishers, edited by Hamlin Hill (Berkeley: University of California Press, 1967);

Mark Twain's Correspondence with Henry Huttleson Rogers, edited by Lewis Leary (Berkeley: University of California Press, 1969).

Bibliographies:

Merle D. Johnson, *A Bibliography of the Works of Mark Twain* (New York & London: Harper, 1935);

Thomas Asa Tenney, *Mark Twain: A Reference Guide* (Boston: G. K. Hall, 1977);

Alan Gribben, "Removing Mark Twain's Mask: A Decade of Criticism and Scholarship," *ESQ: Journal of the American Renaissance*, 26 (1980): 100-108, 149-171.

Biographies:

Albert Bigelow Paine, *Mark Twain: A Biography*, 3 volumes (New York & London: Harper, 1912);

Clara Clemens, *My Father: Mark Twain* (New York & London: Harper, 1931);

Dixon Wecter, *Sam Clemens of Hannibal* (Boston: Houghton Mifflin, 1952);

Justin Kaplan, *Mr. Clemens and Mark Twain: A Biography* (New York: Simon & Schuster, 1966);

Milton Meltzer, *Mark Twain Himself: A Pictorial Biography* (New York: Bonanza Books, 1966);

Hamlin Hill, *Mark Twain: God's Fool* (New York: Harper & Row, 1973);

William R. Macnaughton, *Mark Twain's Last Years as a Writer* (Columbia: University of Missouri Press, 1979).

References:

Kenneth R. Andrews, *Nook Farm: Mark Twain's Hartford Circle* (Cambridge: Harvard University Press, 1950);

Howard G. Baetzhold, *Mark Twain and John Bull: The British Connection* (Bloomington: Indiana University Press, 1970);

Walter Blair, *Mark Twain and HUCK FINN* (Berkeley: University of California Press, 1960);

Edgar M. Branch, *The Literary Apprenticeship of Mark Twain* (Urbana: University of Illinois Press, 1950);

Van Wyck Brooks, *The Ordeal of Mark Twain* (New York: Dutton, 1920; revised, 1933);

Louis J. Budd, *Mark Twain: Social Philosopher* (Bloomington: Indiana University Press, 1962);

George C. Carrington, Jr., *The Dramatic Unity of "Huckleberry Finn"* (Columbus: Ohio State University Press, 1976);

Pascal Covici, Jr., *Mark Twain's Humor: The Image of a World* (Dallas: Southern Methodist University Press, 1962);

James M. Cox, *Mark Twain: The Fate of Humor* (Princeton, N.J.: Princeton University Press, 1966);

Bernard DeVoto, *Mark Twain's America* (Boston: Little, Brown, 1932);

Allison Ensor, *Mark Twain and the Bible* (Lexington: University of Kentucky Press, 1965);

William M. Gibson, *The Art of Mark Twain* (New York: Oxford University Press, 1976);

Alan Gribben, *Mark Twain's Library: A Reconstruction*, 2 volumes (Boston: G. K. Hall, 1980);

Sholom J. Kahn, *Mark Twain's Mysterious Stranger: A Study of the Manuscript Texts* (Columbia & London: University of Missouri Press, 1978);

S. J. Krause, *Mark Twain as Critic* (Baltimore: Johns Hopkins University Press, 1961);

Kenneth S. Lynn, *Mark Twain and Southwestern Humor* (Boston: Little, Brown, 1959);

Franklin R. Rogers, *Mark Twain's Burlesque Patterns* (Dallas: Southern Methodist University Press, 1960);

John Seelye, *The True Adventures of Huckleberry Finn* (Evanston, Ill.: Northwestern University Press, 1970);

Henry Nash Smith, ed., *Mark Twain: A Collection of Critical Essays* (Englewood Cliffs, N.J.: Prentice-Hall, 1963);

Smith, *Mark Twain's Fable of Progress: Political and Economic Ideas in "A Connecticut Yankee"* (New Brunswick, N.J.: Rutgers University Press, 1964);

Smith, *Mark Twain: The Development of a Writer* (Cambridge: Harvard University Press, 1962);

John S. Tuckey, *Mark Twain and Little Satan: The Writing of "The Mysterious Stranger"* (West Lafayette, Ind.: Purdue University Press, 1963).

Papers:

Most of Mark Twain's papers are in the Bancroft Library of the University of California, Berkeley.

Carolyn Wells

(18 June 1862-26 March 1942)

Zita Zatkin Dresner
Washington, D.C.

SELECTED BOOKS: *At the Sign of the Sphinx* (New York: Kimball & Stone, 1896);

Idle Idylls (New York: Dodd, Mead, 1900);

A Phenomenal Fauna (New York: Russell, 1902);

Folly for the Wise (Indianapolis: Bobbs-Merrill, 1904);

The Rubaiyat of a Motor Car (New York: Dodd, Mead, 1906; London: Harper, 1906);

The Carolyn Wells Year Book of Old Favorites and New Fancies for 1909 (New York: Holt, 1908);

The Rubaiyat of Bridge (New York & London: Harper, 1909);

Christmas Carollin' (New York: Bigelow, 1913);

The Re-Echo Club (New York: Bigelow, 1913);

The Eternal Feminine (New York: Bigelow, 1913);

Girls and Gayety (New York: Bigelow, 1913);

Baubles (New York: Dodd, Mead, 1917);

The Rest of My Life (Philadelphia & New York: Lippincott, 1926).

One of America's favorite parodists at the turn of the century, Carolyn Wells produced light verse and humorous articles that appeared in many little magazines as well as the popular magazines and comic papers of the late 1890s and the early twentieth century. Wells was considered the chief woman humorist of the first two decades of the 1900s and collections of her rhymes were bestsellers, as were her distinctive anthologies of humorous verse. An admirer of Lewis Carroll and Edward Lear, she was directly inspired by Gelett Burgess and Oliver Herford, and in the course of her career, she became acquainted with most of the popular humorists of the period, both in America and England. Her output and reputation were so prodigious that, as one reviewer stated, "to begin a sentence sharply with 'Carolyn Wells says' is to attract the attention of a whole tableful and silence any spasmodic, needless chatter that may be going on elsewhere around the board."

Born in Rahway, New Jersey, to parents of English ancestry and comfortable middle-class status, Wells described herself in her autobiography, *The Rest of My Life* (1926), as a precocious child who knew the alphabet at eighteen months,

read fluently and began writing verse at three years, and wrote and bound a complete book at the age of six. However, an attack of scarlet fever at age six left Wells with an ever-increasing deafness from which she suffered both physically and emotionally. Although she graduated valedictorian from high school, she declined to attend college, considering it a waste of time and preferring to study topics of her own choosing with knowledgeable friends and teachers. One of these teachers, the noted literary scholar William J. Rolfe, not only taught her Shakespeare for three seasons at the Amherst Sauveur Summer School of Languages, but also introduced her to the charade books of William Bellamy, which were in vogue in the early 1890s. Intrigued by these literary puzzles, she tried her own hand at them and, encouraged by Rolfe, produced enough for a collection entitled *At the Sign of the Sphinx*, her first book, published in 1896.

Prior to this publication, however, Wells had been contributing verses to the humorous weeklies of the 1890s, her first four-liner being accepted by *Puck* in 1892. "If the magazines I have written for in the course of my writing career could be hung on a rack," she declared in her autobiography, "they would rival any corner newsstand of today." She did not exaggerate. Among the little magazines which accepted her work were the *Chap Book*, the *Lark*, the *Philistine*, *Bibelot*, *Yellow Book*, and the *Tatler*, a short-lived daily humorous publication which she also helped to edit. Among the popular magazines to which she contributed during her career were *Bookman*, *Scribner's*, *Outlook*, *Century*, *Harper's Bazar*, *Harper's Monthly*, *St. Nicholas*, *Ladies' Home Journal*, *Life*, *Delineator*, *Woman's Home Companion*, *Putnam's*, *Good Housekeeping*, *Saturday Evening Post*, and *Collier's*.

Of the little magazines in which Wells's verse appeared, the *Lark* was most significant because of the voluminous correspondence she maintained with its founder, editor, and major contributor, Gelett Burgess. Wells began sending material to the *Lark* immediately after reading the first issue, dated May 1895, and despite repeated rejections, continued to submit material because of the education

Carolyn Wells

she acquired in the writing of nonsense verse through Burgess's critical comments on her work. "Writing nonsense came naturally to me," she said in an interview with Thomas L. Masson for his *Our American Humorists*, "but, like most other things in their natural state, my faculty was quite worthless until I began training it." One of the first lessons she learned from Burgess, she explained, was "the ability to distinguish silliness and nonsense," the latter being "organic, well-ordered, and . . . almost mathematical in its precision, and in its certainty to hit the reader or listener straight between the eyes, as it were." Wells's persistence paid off when Burgess finally accepted a piece of hers for publication fourteen months after her initial submission.

Wells claimed as her second "master" Oliver Herford, whose whimsical imagination she particularly admired. An artist as well as a writer, Herford had illustrated a number of jingles that Wells had contributed to *St. Nicholas* in the mid-1890s. Subsequently, he, she, and Burgess collaborated on one issue, dated April 1898, of what was projected to be a weekly humor journal, entitled *Enfant Terrible*. Despite the failure of the project, Wells's friendship with the two men continued, and Herford illustrated a number of her later books, including a book of jingles for children, published in 1899, and her fourth volume, *Idle Idylls*, a book of humorous verse for adults.

Idle Idylls (1900) was representative in both subject matter and style of much of the verse that Wells wrote prior to and following the publication of this book. Like Burgess, she used traditional English and, especially, French verse forms as models for her nonsense verse. Her talent for parody, a popular form at the time, was also evident in this volume, which directed its humor at such popular pieces as *The Rubaiyat* of Omar Khayyám (also parodied by Burgess), Hamlet's soliloquy "To Be Or Not To Be," the song "Old Oaken Bucket," and the sentimental and nature poetry of the period. The lightness of touch, lively fancy, and fluent rhythms for which early reviewers praised Wells are employed in this volume to poke fun at such topics as love and courtship, women's fashions, images of ideal women (for example, the Gibson Girl, the Poster Girl, the Summer Girl), fads and faddists, feminine frailties and wiles, the Christmas spirit, romantic and avant-garde poetry, and the nostalgia for the pastoral in popular culture. A review of the volume in *Bookman* commended Wells especially for her "fastidiousness," her ability to find "the *mot juste*," her "quaint way of looking at commonplace things," her "felicity of phrase," and her talent to surprise in her choice of rhyming words.

In 1902 Wells published four volumes, including *A Phenomenal Fauna*, a collection of whimsical verse, and *A Nonsense Anthology*, her first effort as an anthologist of humorous verse. Illustrated by Herford, *A Phenomenal Fauna* offered six- and eight-line rhymes about imagined creatures like the Humbug, Feather Boa, Bookworm, Shuttlecock, Welsh Rabbit, Jail-Bird, and Golf Lynx. As a whole, the book revealed a clever wit, a delight in wordplay and puns, and the ability to capture the fanciful in concrete form for the amusement and stimulation of the reader's imagination. *A Nonsense Anthology*, perhaps her single best-known volume in the field of humor, was praised both for its uniqueness at the time and for her expertise in the selection of pieces included. Like her subsequent compilations—*A Parody Anthology* (1904), *A Satire Anthology* (1905), *A Whimsey Anthology* (1906), *A Vers de Société* (1907), *Such Nonsense!* (1918), *The Book of Humorous Verse* (1920), *An Outline of Humor* (1923), *Carolyn Wells' Book of American Limericks* (1925), and *A Book of Charades* (1927)—*A Nonsense Anthology* reflected her many years experience as librarian of the Rahway Library Association, her passion as a collector of both verse and books, and her continuing interest in and devotion to humor as a literary form.

From 1902 on, Wells's output remained steady at three or four books a year, bringing her career total to some 180 volumes, of which eighty-one were mystery and detective novels, which she began to write with great success in 1910. In addition, her publications included books of games, puzzles, and brainteasers; verses and stories for children; at least two burlesque novels—one a parody of *Main Street*; and the script to *Maids of Athens*, a light opera composed by Franz Lehar, which, to her disappointment, ran only a month in New York in 1914. In her autobiography, Wells suggested that the impressive number of books that she had "to her discredit" were the result not just of a natural facility for writing but also of a personality dominated by two major characteristics, impatience and perseverance. Priding herself on the quantity and variety, if not the quality, of her publications, Wells noted that she had never kept a publisher waiting beyond a contracted deadline for a manuscript from her.

Although her reputation as humorist persisted throughout her lifetime, the bulk of her light verse was published in book form between 1900 and 1917. *Folly for the Wise* (1904), consisting mainly of nonsense verse, was similar to *A Phenomenal Fauna* in its short verses on fanciful animals such as the Clothes Horse, Red Tapir, Wall Street Bulls and

Bears, and Bananaconda, as well as on phenomenal flora (for example, Gold Carats, Wild Oats, Widow's Weeds) and on "A Baker's Dozen of Wild Beasts," such as the Cream Puffin, Bread Panther, Little Biscuitten, Meringue-Utang, and Ginger-Snapper. The volume also contained parodies of children's verse, anti-Christmas poems, limericks, and "Mixed Morals"—brief prose pieces illustrating proverbs and maxims that contradicted each other. Wells's verbal wit and ingenuity in reconciling incongruous combinations of things are again manifest in this collection.

The Rubaiyat of a Motor Car (1906) and *The Rubaiyat of Bridge* (1909), two slim volumes of parody that poked fun not just at Khayyám's work but also at the tribulations and triumphs involved in the national obsessions with motoring and playing bridge, followed *Folly for the Wise*. In 1908 appeared *The Carolyn Wells Year Book of Old Favorites and New Fancies for 1909*, a gift book containing a calendar and verse and prose pieces by Wells to go with each month. Containing a number of poems from *Idle Idylls*, in addition to some previously uncollected

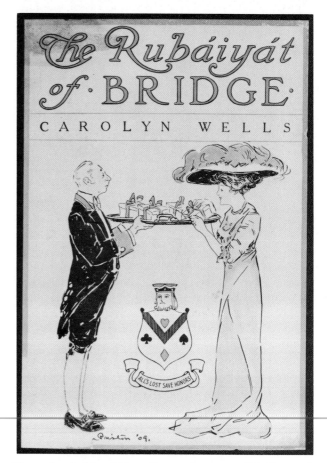

Illustration by May Wilson Preston for cover of Wells's poetic burlesque

Carolyn Wells

magazine pieces, the volume offered more of her prose parodies of maxims and morals, verse parodies of such poets as Kipling, Browning, Swinburne, Wordsworth, and Whitman, limericks, nonsense verse, and light verse dealing, as in *Idle Idylls*, with fashions, fads, conventions, and the popular culture of the time.

The financial success of Wells's books of humor resulted in the 1913 publication of a series of small, inexpensive volumes of her work, which were organized according to subject matter and included light verse and prose pieces mainly from previous publications. *Christmas Carollin'* presented those of her poems and prose pieces dealing with some of the hypocrisies, traditions, and travesties connected with the holiday season, the prevailing point of view of the pieces being perhaps best summarized in Wells's "Forgive us our Christmases as we forgive those whose Christmas against us." Another volume in the series, *The Re-Echo Club*, collected her parodies of various poets, particularly those of nineteenth- and twentieth-century England and America, whom she imagined meeting together and writing their own poems based on nursery rhymes, limericks, Burgess's "Purple Cow," and the princi-

ples of cubism. Two other volumes in the series, *The Eternal Feminine* (prose pieces) and *Girls and Gayety* (light verse), in different ways made fun of female fashions, fads, conventions, and characteristics. Presenting portraits of women who were muddleheaded, scatterbrained, self-indulgent, manipulative, as well as easily swayed, Wells targeted with her humor both the vacuous "Summer Girl" at one extreme and the strident suffragette at the other.

Wells's last volume of original verse, *Baubles*, was published in 1917. Perhaps because a majority of the poems were originally printed in *Idle Idylls*, the book was considered dated, and the newer verses—on such topics as abstract and cubist art, the popular nostalgia for a vanishing rural way of life, and the current interest in and glorification of the cowboy and the Old West—were deemed mediocre. Wells may have felt her interest in verse writing diverted by her more recent interest and, in the latter part of her career, increased activity in the field of detective novels. In any case, following her 1918 marriage to Hadwin Houghton, a member of the publishing family, and her move at that time from Rahway to New York City, her creative involvement with humor expressed itself primarily in her personal collecting of humor and in the anthologies of different types of humorous verse she continued to compile.

A private person, either by nature or perhaps in part by dint of her hearing impairment, Wells revealed little of her personal life in her autobiography but a great deal about her character. A stoic out of necessity and a realist by temperament, Wells wrote, "All my life I have looked forward, steadily forward, and never back . . . with regret for mistaken deeds, for errors of judgement, for making a fool of myself." Despite the difficulties in her life— her deafness and the excruciating operations she underwent, unsuccessfully, to cure it; the death of her husband a year after their marriage; and the diagnosis she received from doctors in 1932 that she had only two years to live (though she lived another ten)—she never indulged in self-pity. She retained her sense of humor and her capacity to take pleasure in her literary pursuits. "Crying over spilt milk," she explained, "that is not in me to do." If her humor was, to some degree, a defense against personal pain and disappointment, it was also never caustic or vindictive, but rather characterized by a warmth, wit, and lightheartedness that appealed to and was enjoyed by a wide audience of Americans. Although Carolyn Wells's name is more familiar than her work to most readers of American humor, she was important not just for her position as a woman in the field of humor but also for the great range and variety of humor she brought during the course of her lifetime to such a large portion of the reading public.

Other:
A Nonsense Anthology, edited by Wells (New York: Scribners, 1902);
A Parody Anthology, edited by Wells (New York: Scribners, 1904);
A Whimsey Anthology, edited by Wells (New York: Scribners, 1906);
A Vers de Société, edited by Wells (New York: Scribners, 1907);

Such Nonsense!, edited by Wells (New York: Doran, 1918);
The Book of Humorous Verse, edited by Wells (New York: Doran, 1920);
An Outline of Humor, edited by Wells (New York & London: Putnam's, 1923);
Carolyn Wells' Book of American Limericks, edited by Wells (New York & London: Putnam's, 1925);
A Book of Charades, edited by Wells (New York: Doran, 1927).

References:
"Carolyn Wells," *Wilson Bulletin* (April 1930): 366;
Thomas L. Masson, *Our American Humorists* (New York: Moffat, Yard, 1922), pp. 303-323.

Frances Miriam Whitcher
(1 November 1814-4 January 1852)

Clyde G. Wade
University of Missouri, Rolla

BOOKS: *The Widow Bedott Papers* (New York: J. C. Derby, 1856);
Widow Spriggins, Mary Elmer, and Other Sketches, edited with a memoir by Mrs. M. L. Ward Whitcher (New York: Carleton, 1867).

Frances Miriam Whitcher wrote some of the best Down East or Yankee humor of the nineteenth century. Historians note that she and B. P. Shillaber created the first fully developed humorous women characters in American literature and it is clear that Whitcher has stronger claims to historical priority than Shillaber. His Mrs. Partington was introduced in the *Boston Post* in 1847, while Whitcher's Widow Bedott had appeared (under the pseudonym "Frank") in the *Saturday Gazette and Lady's Literary Museum* a year earlier. Even before Widow Bedott, Whitcher had developed the Widow Spriggins; and after Bedott's triumphant appearance, she added the impressive Aunt Maguire for *Godey's Lady's Book*. Moreover, Whitcher's women characters are more numerous, more richly conceived, and more convincingly developed than Shillaber's. Her natural inclination to satirize contributes to the sense of authenticity; it gives clarity to portraits that contrast with the softer, sometimes less firmly defined characters of the always amiable Shillaber. Still

another accomplishment of Whitcher was her mastery of the "messy" humorous story that Mark Twain was to praise a generation later because of the artistic demands the form imposes upon the writer. Such stories as "Hezekiah Bedott" and "The Widow Loses Her Beau" are impressive achievements in this difficult genre and compare favorably with Twain's best efforts. Although ill health hampered her career as a writer, Whitcher's sketches and stories succeed better than the work of any other humorist in capturing the human comedy of Yankee village life in the 1840s and 1850s.

Born in Whitesboro, New York, Frances Miriam Berry was one of the thirteen children of Elizabeth Wells and Lewis Berry, who owned Berry's Tavern, an important hostelry in the region. Berry first attended the village school, then the local academy, and later studied French with excellent success in nearby Utica. She wrote both poetry and prose, preferring poetry but finally choosing prose when she was about thirty years old because she found it less demanding. A popular member of the Maeonian Circle, a social and literary society in Whitesboro, she read chapters of a humorous narrative about Widow Spriggins to the membership over a period of several meetings. The readings were so well received that she consented to Colvert

Comstock's urgings to publish the chapters in a weekly Rome, New York, newspaper. Shortly thereafter Joseph C. Neal offered to pay for contributions to his *Saturday Gazette and Lady's Literary Museum*. The wish to earn an income triumphed over her fears of the public. Thus in the summer of 1846, at the age of thirty-one, she became a professional author. The series she began for Neal, "The Widow Bedott's Table Talk" became an instant and astonishing success. The following year Louis Godey, through Neal's good offices, persuaded her to contribute a series featuring Aunt Maguire for his *Lady's Book*. Publishing concurrently in the *Gazette* and the *Lady's Book*, she became one of the best-known writers of the day.

On 6 January 1847, before contracting to write for Godey, Berry married an Episcopal minister, the Reverend B. W. Whitcher. In the spring she moved to Elmira, New York, where her husband had a parish. There the success she had suddenly realized as a writer turned bittersweet. Discovering Whitcher's identity as the author of the Widow Bedott and Aunt Maguire series, her husband's parishioners became rebellious because they wrongly perceived themselves and their loved ones in the village types that she ridiculed. One angry husband, convinced that his wife was the real-life counterpart of Mrs. Samson Savage in the Aunt Maguire stories, threatened to sue for damages. A daughter was born to the Whitchers in November of 1849. Thereafter the health of Frances Whitcher, always frail, began to deteriorate. She was able to go to her husband's new parish in Oswego but could not remain, returning to the family home in Whitesboro where she died of consumption at the age of thirty-seven. Her career as a professional writer lasted just five and a half years.

The outlines of Whitcher's concerns as a writer are perceptible in the known facts of her formative years. She always had great powers of observation and a gift for satiric humor. As she confessed somewhat ruefully to a friend years later, "I received at my birth the undesirable gift of a remarkably strong sense of the ridiculous." A frail constitution kept her from much active participation and undoubtedly contributed to the development of her role as witness to village manners. Her powers of memory were always exceptional. At the age of two she could recite Wordsworth's "We Are Seven"; and before she learned to read, she displayed the ability to commit entire poems to memory. Shy and withdrawn, she preferred a dream world to actuality, but important traits of mind and character kept her from becoming reclusive. She

was especially precocious and talented, possessing from early childhood a strong visual sense and talent for drawing and for writing verse. The need to express herself, especially in caricatures and satiric verse, was also evident at an early age. Her first sketch of "a shockingly ugly visage" was done when she was five because the owner of the face had been rude to her. She was also composing poems, dictating them to members of her family even before she learned how to write.

Sketching and versifying became means of responding to aspects of village society, church, and school that troubled her. Even family and friends grew apprehensive under her scrutiny; for a caricature or a satiric verse might result when her feelings were hurt or her sense of justice violated. "I can scarcely remember," she once observed, "the time when the neighbors were not afraid that I would make fun of them." Sometimes the satiric impulse did cause wounds where no injury was intended. At school one small boy saw a caricature she had drawn of him and did not return to the class. But there was no such lack of intent in the verses she wrote (parodying familiar verses entitled "My Mother") while smarting under the barbs of an overly critical grandfather:

> And when I let the platter fall
> Who said, as loud as he could bawl,
> "Now just came back and break them all!"
>   My Grandfather.

For all her powers of satiric humor, the young poet was a sensitive, loving girl, and her targets in later years were justly chosen.

Frances Whitcher was troubled with church and school as she grew up. Teachers and older children frightened her, and she found the sterner tenets of Calvinism oppressive. For the rest of her life she ridiculed those who put abstract theology above love and understanding. She made the sanctimonious and hypocritical her special targets, and she exposed to laughter the types of village folk who, given the power, inflicted needless injury upon the weak and defenseless. Once when she doubted the wisdom of her work, Neal, her friend, editor, and fellow satirist, responded: "An excellent critic in these matters said to me the other day that he regarded them [the Widow Bedott pieces] as the best Yankee papers yet written, and such is indeed the general sentiment." Then Neal went on to say, italicizing his words for emphasis: "It is a theory of mine that *those gifted with truly humorous genius, like yourself, are more useful as moralists, philosophers, and teachers, than whole legions of the gravest preachers. They speak more effectually to the general ear and heart even though they who hear are not aware of the fact that they are imbibing wisdom."*

The sketches and stories Whitcher wrote between the years 1846 and 1851 were gathered into two posthumous volumes. Her best and most mature work appears in *The Widow Bedott Papers* (1856). This volume enjoyed a remarkable success. It went through twenty-three editions in less than a decade and was republished to meet popular demand in 1883. According to publisher J. C. Derby, over 100,000 copies were sold. Sustained public interest in Whitcher's work brought about the second volume in 1867. That book, *Widow Spriggins, Mary Elmer, and Other Sketches*, contains earlier stories, work unfinished at her death, and other pieces not included in the first volume. The materials gathered in both volumes reveal how prominently three women characters figure in her emergence as a writer of humor. The first of these is the Widow Spriggins, the forerunner of Widow Bedott and Whitcher's most successful humorous fictional character.

Whitcher's conception of Permilla Spriggins reveals literary rather than directly experienced origins. Her plan was to create absurd scenes which demonstrated the effects of popular romantic fiction upon an impressionable young lady from Podunk, New York. Making satiric fun of sentimental literature and naive folk who regard such literature as representations of a finer reality was an old formula long before 1845. Even the novel Whitcher chose for her satire was an eighteenth-century sentimental romance by Regina Maria Roche, *The Children of the Abbey*, the first American reprint of which appeared in Philadelphia in 1798. Such fiction was still popular, and Whitcher was on target in ridiculing superficial tastes. But as the "Widow Spriggins's Recollections" progressed, it became apparent to Whitcher that her true subject was the manners of Yankee village life. The narrow literary focus of the "Recollections" could in no way do justice to the day-to-day realities of the village. So when Neal beckoned in 1846, Whitcher responded with the Widow Bedott and began to write Yankee humor that was deeply rooted in her Whitesboro experiences.

Though Whitcher first addressed her true subject with Widow Bedott, the development of Permilla Spriggins was important. "Permilly" seems at first glance merely to fit into the popular tradition of oral humor already established. She commits comic malapropisms such as "suppret" for "ex-

pressed," "devours" for "devotions," "insure" for "assure," "ridicule" for "reticule," and "manure" for "innure." Mispronunciations color the village vernacular such as "ax" (ask), "puss" (purse), "dilamby" (dilemma), "caliates" (calculates), and "alagaster" (alabaster). There are also comic figures of speech: "I was a wonderful cretur," Permilly acknowledges, "from the time I was knee-high to a hop-toad."

As a satirist burlesquing the lugubrious poetry that filled the village newspapers and journals of her day, Whitcher had no peer. A skilled, disciplined craftsman in her own voice, Whitcher was—through Widow Spriggins and, later, Hugelina and the Widow Bedott—the author of some of the best and funniest bad verse in American literature. Permilly, who can never keep swain and swine separate in her head, writes to Jabez Spriggins, the good-hearted Jonathan who will eventually marry her:

> I can't be yourn, this heart of mine
> Is plighted to another swine;
> And them besides that git besmitten,
> Must all expect to git the mitten.

Comic doggerel it may be to a sophisticated audience, but to Permilly such promptings of her poetic muse made her the "biggest genyus in Podunk."

Through Permilly, Whitcher learned to appreciate the value of a woman's perspective in exploiting the human comedy around her. Because Permilly was herself the object of Whitcher's satire, the scenes in which the woman's perspective is important tend to deal with matters of little consequence. For example, when Permilly dresses up for a party, the point of view is obviously feminine, but it serves little purpose except to create an instance of broad humor. Permilly accentuates a white dress already trimmed in blue ribbons with additional ribbons of yellow, pink, and red. With great self-assurance she converts a green shawl with spangles into a turban, sticking black ostrich feathers into it for additional effect. Around her "alagaster" neck she wears a string of glass beads "as big as bullets." The scene is enriched and probably saved from overindulgence by the conversation of Permilly and her Aunt Huldy. "Ain't ye struck with my surpassin' loveliness?" Permilly asks. "Yes, I be," replies the generous aunt, "but how do I look?" "As well as could be expected," Permilly responds, "for a woman that's past the moridion of youthful facksination." Later, with the Widow Bedott and Aunt Maguire, Whitcher is able to exploit the woman's point of view skillfully and effectively.

The "Widow Spriggins's Recollections" appear in the later 1867 volume. Almost without exception the selections that fill *The Widow Bedott Papers* surpass those in the latter volume, in large measure because both the *Gazette* and the *Lady's Book* allowed J. C. Derby to include stories of both Widow Bedott and Aunt Maguire. These characters are products of 1846 and 1847, the first significant and perhaps most vigorous years of Whitcher's brief professional career. Some of the important differences between the two women are attributable to the differences between the men for whom they were created. The Widow Bedott was certain to please Neal, a fellow humorist, and the readers of his *Gazette*. Aunt Maguire was more deliberately drawn to please the prudish tastes of Louis Godey and *Godey's Lady's Book*. For that eminently respectable middle-class journal, Whitcher created Melissa Poole Maguire (pronounced Magwire), the Widow Bedott's younger sister. Aunt Maguire, her family, and friends embody the best of small-town WASP values. Her husband, Joshua (Joshaway), a "mortal tease," is a successful shoemaker; her son Jeff, an even bigger tease, is nonetheless a serious medical student.

Whitcher's subject, the apparently inexhaustible variety that constitutes the human comedy of village life, is thus presented from the witty but good moral center of Aunt Maguire and her family. Happily, Aunt Maguire is a Poole and in possession of an authentic Yankee speech as incisive and pungent as that of her more famous sister. By her own admission, Aunt Maguire "can see as fur into a millstone as anybody." When aroused she exercises the full tartness of her tongue and thus expresses some of Whitcher's more trenchant satire. It is she who attends and then relates the incredible events of the donation party and who, as a member of the Sewin' Society of Scrabble Hill, reports the activities of the newly rich and awesomely vulgar Mrs. Samson Savage. Among the seven Aunt Maguire chapters in *The Widow Bedott Papers*, chapters 23, 24, and 25 excited the greatest amount of comment when they were published. Arguments could be made for one or more of the other chapters as superior embodiments of humor, but chapter 23, "Aunt Maguire's Description of the Donation Party," and the two following chapters on the sewing society provide imcomparable insights into village manners.

It is clear from Whitcher's savage treatment of the donation party that it no longer fulfilled its original purpose of supplementing the meager salaries of Protestant clergymen with gifts of food, clothing, and other necessities. To ridicule the donation party and laugh it out of existence, Whitcher makes Aunt Maguire attend one of them with her son Jeff, "hum" from college for a few days. With her husband's warning that public gift-giving is in bad taste, and with a six-dollar "bunnit" for the minister's wife, Aunt Maguire sets out. The parsonage is crowded with well-known village types. The well-to-do villagers who attend such things come not so much to give as to socialize and enjoy a free meal at the expense of the beleaguered minister. Deacon Peabody comes with a dozen voracious members of his family. He brings a small cheese (half a donation; half for pew rent); Cappen Smalley, a storekeeper, brings a twelve-pound box of raisins (ten pounds for pew rent) which is consumed by the overwhelming crowd who have come for dinner; Dr. Lippincott and family, including his "interesting darter Anny Marier with her six starched skirts on," bring nothing except prodigious appetites; "Widder" Grimes, well off, but "tew stingy to be decent," comes with her daughter (named with comic inappropriateness, Charity), two skeins of thread, and on her arm "an awful great workbag" into which she sneaks such amounts of food that roguish Jeff loudly seeks an invitation to the party she will give with the provisions she has stashed away. Rivaling the well-to-do in virtually unlimited appetite are some students from the village seminary where skimpy meals are such a common occurrence that out of necessity the girls must forage at village parties. For the privilege of stuffing as much as they can hold, twenty-five girls donate one rag doll to little Adeline Scrantum. After their hunger is satisfied, the girls reveal equally demanding appetites for youthful male companionship. To attract attention they proceed to outdo the other guests, including the well-to-do, in rude behavior. Theirs is no small accomplishment in this respect, for the villagers evidently regard the parsonage as community property. Guests feel entitled to open presents—including the six-dollar bonnet which is eventually ruined—and to enter the "buttry" and storeroom at will, taking such foodstuffs as appetite and whim dictate. After the seminary girls begin to amuse themselves by throwing hunks of cheese and buttered biscuits at the young men, a near riot ensues that ruins furnishings, smashes china, and damages the house itself. For all the many laughable incidents, the sketch is a cool controlled fury that expresses itself in cutting satire, the force of which may be felt today. The strength of the piece is in keeping with Whitcher's other satiric sketches touching upon aspects of church-related activity.

There are comic gossip and posturing aplenty in the chapters on the sewing society. The introduction of Mrs. Samson Savage about halfway through chapter 25 marks the beginning of Whitcher's most sensational character portrayal. Mrs. Savage's entrance is imaginatively staged. The ladies of the Stillman family refuse to consent to proposals for the expenditures of the Society's earnings on charitable causes until "there's a full meetin'": "'The fact is,' says Polly Mariar, stretchin' her great mouth from ear to ear and displayin' all her big teeth . . . , 'mar and me's of opinion that we hadent ought to vote till Miss Samson Savage is consulted.'" Miss Birsley's reply, "Miss Samson Savage ain't a member of the Society," only gives the Stillmans opportunity to emphasize the importance of Mrs. Savage to any community enterprise. At this point Mrs. Savage marches in, uninvited. She is a "great, tall, raw-boned woman, and she steps off like a trainer." Her husband is a Yankee peddler from Vermont—"wonderful fellers to make money, them Varmonters," remarks Aunt Maguire. "Husband says they come over the Green Mountains with a spellin'-book in one hand and a halter in t'other, and if they can't git a school to teach, they can steal a hoss." At the time Mrs. Savage invites herself to the sewing society, her husband is acknowledged to be the richest man in Scrabble Hill.

Mrs. Savage takes over the meeting by sheer physical presence and the loudest voice. She insults everyone present—particularly the Stillmans who fawn over her—belittles the sewing society, slanders the Reverend Mr. Tuttle and his wife, and recounts instances of tyranny she has practiced on her "waitin'-maid" Poll. "I'll forgive ye this time on account of yer ignorance," she reports of having told Poll, "but if ever you dew it agin you'll git your walkin'-ticket on short order. . . . Now start yer stumps, and fetch them things quick meeter." The voice is harshly aggressive; the language the tritest of rural figures: "green as grass," "flat as a pancake"; the Reverend Mr. Tuttle "don't know B from a broomstick, nor bran when the bag's open."

In addition to the irate husband who threatened suit, several villages in central New York State concluded that the real-life model of Mrs. Samson Savage resided in their communities. Hence there can be no doubting the authenticity of the type. Even so, the husband's public identification of his wife with Mrs. Savage is mind boggling; for Mrs. Savage, as Aunt Maguire observes, is one who "knows she ain't the ginniwine article, and so

she tries to make up for it in brass and bluster"; in the vernacular of the day, she is "*codfish gentility.*"

The vividness of Mrs. Samson Savage's characterization is one of many reminders that Widow Spriggins, Widow Bedott, and Aunt Maguire share the scenes of life with a host of memorable characters. Some are barely sketched, others fully drawn. They include Deacon Whipple, a professed votary of Godly matters who spends "the heft of his time a-pryin' into other folks' bizness"; Charity Grimes, who has been "tryin' these twenty years to get married and couldn't make it out"; Urainy Slammerkin Parsons and the Reverend Mr. Reuben Parsons who give away their eight children so they can look after the spiritual welfare of heathens in far-off lands; Sally Hugle, who writes "sunnets" for the *Scrabble Hill Luminary* and signs them "Hugelina"; Parson Jeremiah Pulsifier, another poet, whose verse sounds "like sawin' through a board of rusty nails"; Henry, who is "about as hateful a young one as ever went unflogged"; Bethiar Nobles, "an old gal that gits her livin' principally by visitin'"; the Reverend O. Shadrach Sniffles who finds the Widow Bedott irresistible after Uncle Maguire starts rumors that she has secret wealth; Jabez Clark, the unscrupulous Yankee peddler who claims to have reformed from sharp practices after he "experienced religion in Varmount"; Widder Pettibone, "a wonderful oneasy critter" who has been "a Baptist and a Presbyterian, and now she's an Episcopal" and a source of wonder over "what she'll be next"; and Deacon Hezekiah Bedott, the Widow's late husband, a schoolteacher "jawed . . . out of the world" by his wife.

In one sense Aunt Maguire represents Whitcher's finest effort. Aunt Maguire is such an admirable mixture of strength, goodness, common sense, and wit that the danger was ever present of allowing her to lapse into a stereotyped ideal of middle-class womanhood—woman as *Godey's Lady's Book* would prefer her. But Aunt Maguire is saved from that fate by a ready wit and a lively vernacular that smack of the individual, not the type. Yet for all her excellencies, Aunt Maguire does not equal the Widow Bedott as a humorous character. The source of the Widow's preeminence lies in no superiority of mind or heart. Among other things, she is a reckless, malicious gossip whose targets are mostly the widows and widowers who frustrate her desire to marry again. A woman of petty vanities, she reveals no doubts of her superiority over other folk, including her sister Aunt Maguire: "She's a very clever woman, Melissy is," the Widow remarks, "but she ain't a bit like me—hain't no genyus." The Widow can also be spiteful and cruel. She abuses a serving girl mercilessly only because the girl had been a favorite of her new husband's first wife. Thus the two sisters contrast importantly. With Aunt Maguire the comic imperfections of the village are regarded from a distance of goodness; with the Widow, they are perceived at closer range and experienced more intimately, often residing within the Widow herself.

Her shortcomings notwithstanding, Widow Bedott is worthy of admiration. She embodies the irrepressible energies of small-town life, raises two excellent, good-hearted children, and possesses resourcefulness when others come up short. It is she, for example, who found a way years before to heal wounds between Melissa and Joshua Maguire after their courtship had gone painfully awry. And the widow has spunk. She gives a thoroughly satisfying comeuppance to a Yankee peddler; and she bedevils her new husband, the Reverend Mr. Sniffles, until he prevails upon the governing body of the church to put the parsonage in suitable condition. The contrast between the experiences of the decent, honorable Scrantums who are afflicted with donation parties and Mrs. Sniffles who commands just treatment from her husband's church is instructive. Better than any other character, Widow Bedott embodies the grit and vitality of the Yankee.

Eight or nine of the twenty-one Bedott chapters are more revealing of Whitcher's concerns and techniques than others. Probably the most memorable episodes of *The Widow Bedott Papers* are those which treat the Widow Bedott's laughable endeavors to catch another husband. She comically mismanages all efforts to conceal her ambitions to marry again, including her avowal, expressed in "poitry," not to remarry out of respect for the memory of Hezekiah:

> I'll never change my single lot—
> I think 't would be a sin—
> The inconsolable Widder o'Deacon Bedott,
> Don't intent to get married again.

But she is not too disconsolate, as she versifies elsewhere: "I tell the men that's after me / To ketch me if they can."

In striving to get caught, the Widow experiences more failure than success. The most dramatic failure comes with her labors to snare the middle-aged widower Tim Crane. Oblivious to indications that Crane prefers young girls, including her own daughter, the Widow interprets Crane's faltering

overtures as the beginning of a marriage proposal to her. Never did a suitor find a rough path smoothed out more diligently. The Widow brushes aside all of Crane's feigned reluctances, especially the passage of but six months since the death of his wife. Then she is all expectant: "O, Mr. Crane . . . it's so onexpected. Jest hand me that are bottle o' camfire off the mantletry shelf—I'm ruther faint. . . ." Referring to the Widow as "the old woman," Crane asks permission to court her daughter. A splendid outburst of vituperation descends upon Crane who flees from the house. In almost no time the daughter returns with a gentleman escort to hear that her mother has spurned Crane's proposal of marriage: "for *him—Tim Crane*—to durst expire to my hand—the widder o' Deacon Bedott!" The swiftness of the comic reversal juxtaposes the Widow's anticipation and Crane's rejection more immediately than the leisurely narrative method often allows, and the result is a dramatically satisfying episode.

Another high point is the Widow's successful catching of O. Shadrach Sniffles, a Baptist minister. On this occasion, the Widow has been made irresistible by brother-in-law Joshua's spreading the rumor that Priscilla Bedott is "a rich widder." There is an even greater abundance of "poitry" in this romance since Hugelina also has an interest in the preacher. Although Hugelina often writes better bad poetry than the Widow, the day is carried by commerce—the Widow's reputed wealth—and not by art. Widow Bedott savors her triumph: " 'So I s'pose we're engaged.'

" 'Undoubtedly.'

" 'We're engaged, and my tribbilation is at an end.'

"[Her head drops on his shoulder.] 'O, Shadrach! What will Hugelina say when she hears on 't?' "

The Yankee peddler stands out among the village types. The Widow Bedott's early encounters with Jabez Clark reveal her seemingly unlimited capacity to be flattered, coaxed, and wheedled and Jabez's artful command of the legendary tricks of Yankee trading. With the advent of the daguerreotype Jabez sees even greater opportunities for making money, if only he can escape his past reputation for shady dealings. He changes his name to Augustus Montgomery and opens a gallery in Gambletown. On a visit there the Widow—now Mrs. Sniffles—recognizes Clark and gets revenge. She has with her a pin that Clark sold Mr. Sniffles some time before. A telltale green mold reveals it to be brass, not gold. She insists that the pin be accepted as payment for the "picters"; she "won't ax no boot." Clark has to accept the exchange because Mr. Sniffles and Elder Cumstock are present. The bargain made, Clark begs Mrs. Sniffles to keep his identity a secret. But she has been fleeced once too often. When she reaches the street and a large crowd of men, she looks up, shakes her "daggertypes" at Clark and cries out, "Jaby Clark, don't you feel *green?*" The exposure works, and the next morning, she recalls later, "*Mr. Montgomery was missin'.*"

As a work of art as well as of humor, Frances Whitcher's finest achievement is "Hezekiah Bedott," the first story in *The Widow Bedott Papers*. It is an outstanding example of the "messy" humorous story described by Mark Twain in "How to Tell a Story" (1895) and others including Walter Blair in *America's Humor* (1978). The humorous story was, in Twain's judgment, "strictly a work of art—high and delicate art—and only an artist can tell it." By the art of telling, Twain meant "by word of mouth, not print. . . ." An oral narrative, then, the messy humorous story is characterized by an absence of formal structure; it is rambling and apparently structureless and pointless. It consists principally or completely of a monologue. These characteristics place a heavy burden upon the writer who must, if he is to succeed, represent or recreate authentically the spoken word in print and make it suffice as a vehicle for the fiction. In this difficult genre, Whitcher is perfectly at home: one of her great achievements as a writer is the voice of Widow Bedott.

From start to finish "Hezekiah Bedott" is a comic melange of contrasts. Widow Bedott is a vigorous and assertive speaker; yet for all the energy, the narrative goes nowhere. The first two sentences are models of efficiency, purposeful and brimming with promise of immediate satisfaction. The opening sentence establishes the humorous mode perfectly: "He was a wonderful hand to moralize, husband was, 'specially after he begun to enjoy poor health." The second introduces the narrative proper. "He made an observation once when he was in one of his poor turns, that I shall never forget the longest day I live." But seldom thereafter do two consecutive sentences advance the narrative (as narrative progress is usually understood).

Four pages and some 1,200 words later, the Widow finally relates Hezekiah's comment: "*We're all poor critters.*" The emphatic italics provide an amusing contrast with the limp, anticlimactic, prosaic but, by now, hilarious conclusion. True to the tradition of the genre, Whitcher keeps the narrator innocent of anything out of the ordinary in her

manner of telling the story. Roughly halfway through, Widow Bedott gives a perfect description of the messy humorous story. Not a little of the humor in the description derives from the reader's realization that what he has guessed several passages earlier is now made explicit by the author through the Widow Bedott who alone is unaware of the joke which lies at the heart of the narrative: "—but lawful sakes! I most forgot, I was gwine to tell you what he said to me that evenin', and when a body begins to tell a thing I believe in finishin' on't some time or another. Some folks have a way of talkin' round and round and round for evermore, and never comin' to the pint." A half century later, Twain's description of the genre reveals no essential change: "The humorous story may be spun out to great length, and may wander around as much as it pleases, and arrive nowhere in particular. . . ."

The Widow's first digression is a fondly detailed account of Deacon Bedott's many ailments over the last fifteen years of his life. Memories crowd in, and a natural, unconscious surrender to free association occurs. The Widow recalls, for example, a quilting party at Squire Smith's house ten years earlier when his daughter Sal was marrying Sam Pendergrass. That recollection calls to mind Miss Jinkins, "she that was Poll Bingham" and "the tejusest individooal to tell a story that I ever see in all my born days." Reminded at that point of the name Hezekiah, the Widow goes much further back in time: "The first time I ever heard it I near killed myself laffin' " then she leaps forward in time to the naming of her son after Hezekiah. The Widow is reminded again of Hezekiah's ability to suffer illness patiently, and she recalls an occasion when the two of them were trapped in a snowbank. Finally, there is the bland, commonplace remark that concludes the narrative. The story "Hezekiah Bedott" thus arrives nowhere in particular.

Yet in another sense "Hezekiah Bedott" arrives everywhere with great particularity. Important kinds of progress have taken place within the narrative that challenge the apparent aimlessness. Briefly, Whitcher's narrative possesses an imaginative order, or logic, which helps to create the full meaning of the story. There is also an interplay between the emerging internal order and the external shapelessness that accounts for much of the distinctive quality that makes the messy humorous story a separate genre: a kind of sense emerges out of nonsense. The constant movement backward and forward in time, the teeming recollections of people, places, and events—these things thoroughly acquaint the reader with Widow Bedott and her community. For all the deceptive aimlessness, then, "Hezekiah Bedott" is a good introduction to Widow Bedott, the Yankee village, the Yankee vernacular, and the gifted humorist Frances Whitcher. It is also one of the best stories of its kind. When Walter Blair and Hamlin Hill discussed the messy humorous story in *America's Humor*, "Hezekiah Bedott" headed their list of stories and fittingly so, because "Hezekiah Bedott" is an achievement of historical importance as well as an exceptional story of its kind.

Such stories as "Hezekiah Bedott" are evidence of the artistic merit in Whitcher's popular fiction. It is difficult today to realize how popular she was; yet *The Widow Bedott Papers* continued to be republished into the 1880s. In 1879 Petroleum V. Nasby (David Ross Locke) put Widow Bedott on the stage in a four-act comedy, paying Whitcher the tribute of following the Widow's original speeches closely. It is not likely that Whitcher's fiction will approach such popularity again, in part because her works lacks sufficient technical interest for the modern audience. While her command of the vernacular is indeed a major triumph, Whitcher depends too much upon the monologue. The voices of Widow Bedott and Aunt Maguire grow wearisome; the staunchest admirer reads Whitcher today in small amounts. But the republication of *The Widow Bedott Papers* in 1969 and the inclusion of "Hezekiah Bedott" in anthologies indicates that there is still an audience.

Two considerations militate against any claim other than a minor place in American humor for Whitcher. The brevity of her career as a professional writer and the small body of work that she was able to produce do not encourage large claims on her behalf. Nevertheless, her place rests upon solid achievement that should not be overlooked. Her mastery of the Yankee vernacular and village milieu establishes an authentic sense of place; yet she escapes mere regionalism. Hers are more than local color stories and more than Down East humor. Husband-hunting widows, malicious gossips,

sanctimonious deacons, financially pressed ministers, and the vulgar newly rich transcend any one region of the nation. The vast popularity of her stories clearly indicates a larger appeal. There is more than enough evidence to confirm that Whitcher expressed universal experiences and traditional values in her fiction. In *America's Humor* Blair and Hill judiciously include Whitcher among the reputable humorists of the nineteenth century who upheld tradition, justice, and sanity. She does these things in humorous stories that faithfully express the actualities of small-town life in a style and technique that anticipates the literary realists. However, her best work presages more than nineteenth-century realism. The satiric gifts that made her neighbors fearful as well as amused are put to good use in her best work. While the kinship with Mark Twain is clearly discernible, it must not be overlooked that Whitcher also points the way to Sinclair Lewis and Flannery O'Connor.

References:

Walter Blair, *Native American Humor* (New York: American Book Company, 1937), pp. 57-107, 271-278;

Blair and Hamlin Hill, *America's Humor: From Poor Richard to Doonesbury* (New York: Oxford University Press, 1978), pp. 104, 155, 186;

J. C. Derby, *Fifty Years Among Authors, Books and Publishers* (New York: Carleton, 1884), pp. 413-419;

Max Eastman, *Enjoyment of Laughter* (New York: Simon & Schuster, 1948), pp. 163-178;

Frank Luther Mott, "Godey's Lady's Book," in his *A History of American Magazines: Volume One 1741-1850*. (Cambridge: Harvard University Press, 1930), pp. 580-594;

"Passages in the Life of the Author of Aunt Maguire's Letters, Bedott Papers, Etc, by her Sister," *Godey's Lady's Book* (July 1853): 49-55; (August 1853): 109-115.

E. B. White

(11 July 1899-   )

Edward C. Sampson
State University of New York College at Oneonta

SELECTED BOOKS: *The Lady Is Cold* (New York & London: Harper, 1929);

Is Sex Necessary?, by White and James Thurber (New York: Harper, 1929);

Every Day Is Saturday (New York & London: Harper, 1934);

Farewell to Model T, as Lee Strout White (New York: Putnam's, 1936);

The Fox of Peapack and Other Poems (New York & London: Harper, 1938);

Quo Vadimus? or The Case for the Bicycle (New York & London: Harper, 1939);

One Man's Meat (New York & London: Harper, 1942; London: Gollancz, 1943; enlarged edition, New York & London: Harper, 1944);

Stuart Little (New York & London: Harper, 1945; London: Hamilton, 1946);

The Wild Flag: Editorials from The New Yorker on Federal World Government and Other Matters (Boston: Houghton Mifflin, 1946);

Here Is New York (New York: Harper, 1949);

Charlotte's Web (New York: Harper, 1952; London: Hamilton, 1952);

The Second Tree from the Corner (New York: Harper, 1954; London: Hamilton, 1954);

The Points of My Compass (New York: Harper & Row, 1962; London: Hamilton, 1963);

An E. B. White Reader, edited by William W. Watt and Robert W. Bradford (New York: Harper & Row, 1966);

The Trumpet of the Swan (New York: Harper & Row, 1970; London: Hamilton, 1970);

Essays of E. B. White (New York: Harper & Row, 1977);

Poems and Sketches of E. B. White (New York: Harper & Row, 1981).

Generally recognized as one of the best essayists of the twentieth century, E. B. White was also a major force in the success of the *New Yorker* magazine, a writer of some of the best children's stories of our time, an inspiring advocate of world federalism, and, among other things, a spokesman for individualism and the right of privacy. He is, in E. M. Forster's sense of the word, one of the aristocracy of "the sensitive, the considerate and the plucky." Not a bohemian or an expatriate in the 1920s, nor a Marxist in the 1930s, not a joiner, and not easily classified, he is a true individualist. And at the same time, he has also been, although not exclusively so, a notable humorist.

White was born in Mount Vernon, New York; the youngest of six children of Samuel T. and Jessie Hart White, he grew up in a big Victorian house. The family was well off, White's father having risen from somewhat humble beginnings to become president of Horace Waters and Company, a New York piano firm. But as White has stated, there was nothing "fashionable" about his background: "I was a middle class public school kid whose parents were not in the swim and didn't want to be." There were pianos and other instruments in the house, and lots of music, performed with enthusiasm rather than professional dedication. White played the piano. In Mount Vernon High School, White was, as he called himself, a "writing fool." His poems, essays, and short stories were published in the Mount Vernon High School *Oracle*, and besides that, he was class artist.

In the fall of 1917, White entered the Liberal Arts College at Cornell University. The beauty of the setting at Ithaca, the intellectual activity, the cosmopolitan student body, the blend of the theoretical and the practical (engineering students surveying on the quadrangle as students went to literature classes), all had a broadening effect on White. He made the board of the *Cornell Daily Sun* his freshman year, and became editor-in-chief at the end of his junior year. He wrote most of the *Sun* editorials from 5 April 1920 to 5 April 1921, and in early May 1920 he won first prize for an editorial submitted to the Convention of Eastern College Newspapers. Arthur Brisbane, editor of the *New York Evening Journal* awarded the prize; the editorial appeared in the *Sun* later that month. White was also a member of the Manuscript Club, an organization of several faculty members and about ten students. There he got practice writing in a variety of poetic forms, particularly the sonnet. For a brief time in the fall of 1918, White was a member of the

Students' Army Training Corps. And it was at Cornell that White was first called Andy (after Andrew D. White, the first president of Cornell; it was a traditional nickname for students at Cornell named White).

After he graduated from Cornell in 1921 with a B.A., White worked as a reporter for the United Press and briefly for the American Legion News Service. Then, in the spring of 1922, restless and unsettled, he set off in his Model T Ford with Howard Cushman, a college friend, on a journey across the United States that ended six months later in Seattle, Washington, where from the fall of 1922 until June of the next year White worked as a reporter on the *Seattle Times*. After that, White went to Alaska aboard the S. S. *Buford*, starting out in first class and ending as the firemen's mess boy. The somewhat delayed literary results of White's trips west and to Alaska were two of his best pieces: the beautifully detailed essay on Model T Fords, "Farewell, My Lovely!" (1936), and "The Years of Wonder" (1961), an account of his Alaska trip.

Back in New York in the fall of 1923, White was unemployed for a while, then worked in a couple of advertising agencies as production assistant and copywriter. He had no liking for the work, but he had to earn his living. He later wrote James

Thurber that he hung on to his job in advertising because he had no confidence in his ability in the world of letters.

The *New Yorker* saved White. He started contributing small items to the magazine not long after it was founded in 1925; by 1926 he was working part-time there, and by 1927 he was working full-time, contributing a fair portion of the "Notes and Comment" department and writing tag lines for newsbreaks (a job he still does). He was beginning to find what he could do well and was doing it. For White, 1929 was the epochal year. It was not the stock market crash, however, that was important. In that year, his first two books—*The Lady Is Cold* and *Is Sex Necessary?* (with James Thurber)—were published by Harper and, on 13 November, he married Katharine S. Angell, then and for many years one of the mainstays of the *New Yorker*. Their son Joel was born on 21 December 1930.

The Lady Is Cold, White's first book, is a collection of poetry. Although most of White's poetry is light verse, his best poems are not always humorous, and his humorous ones often have an ironic twist or comment that gives them a serious tone. In most of the poems in this collection, White comments on the daily routine of city life, its minor conflicts, and its tensions. He describes late evening and early

E. B. White in his office at the New Yorker

morning rambles, the chance appearance of a pretty face, and the brief contacts with people that bring a transient sense of unity. Taking a half-whimsical look at himself, he celebrates his minor victories, and is amused by his weaknesses. He is restrained, modest, and perhaps too conscious of the danger of destroying his perceptions of life by putting them into words. As he says in "Words":

> Words but catch the moment's tint,
> Though their meaning rock you;
> Never one shall fly to print
> Will not live to mock you.

Thematically, the poems in *The Lady Is Cold* express many of White's basic ideas and views: his love of New York and his sharp awareness of the price one pays for living there, his nostalgic love of simplicity, his admiration for the stubborn endurance of natural life and beauty in an urban setting, his passion for freedom coupled with his need for love and responsibility, his sense of the transiency of life, and finally, his half-serious, ever-present fear of death. Yet there is little in these poems of permanent interest, aside from the insights they give into White's ideas and his development as a writer. Later on, White would write some better poems, but his strength was to be prose, not poetry.

Is Sex Necessary? made both White and Thurber well known. White's contributions were the foreword, chapters 2, 4, 6, and 8, and "Answers to Hard Questions." The book is a lighthearted spoof of the many books about sex that were being published in the 1920s, yet beneath its humor it makes a serious point. There was a need for the work; the subject had been overburdened with glib books that pretended to speak with authority and with better books that did speak with authority. As White said later, paraphrasing Wolcott Gibbs, "the heavy writers had got sex down and were breaking its arm." Frederick J. Hoffman has noted that in the period "there were hundreds of popular summaries, expositions, and distortions of Freud's original works, together with a growing number of works allegedly presenting the psychologies of Jung, Adler and other psychoanalysts." In short, there was room for satire. "Kiss a girl," wrote White in "Notes and Comment" (23 March 1929) "and it reminds you of a footnote."

In *Is Sex Necessary?* both authors parody the serious writers on the subject, making light of complexities, taking a mock-serious attitude toward the obvious, delighting in reducing the case-history technique to an absurdity, and making fun of those

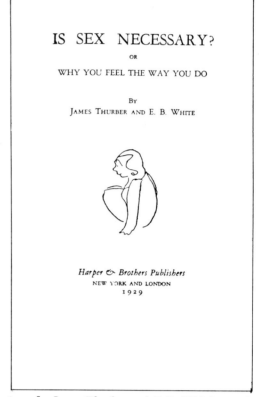

Title page for James Thurber and E. B. White's parody of sex manuals

writers who proceeded by definitions. "When I say love in this article," says White in chapter 2, "you will take it to mean *the pleasant confusion which we know exists*. When I say passion, I *mean* passion." Although some of the humorous gags of the 1920s have paled and the funny footnotes seem less funny now, the book has continued to be popular and, reprinted many times, it continues to amuse with its playful wit.

While the material in White's first two books was not written for the *New Yorker*, the majority of what he wrote from 1927 until 1938, when he left New York and went to Maine, was written for the magazine. In addition to writing the tag lines for newsbreaks (unintentionally humorous items from various newspapers and magazines) and a substantial part of "Notes and Comment," White wrote numerous sketches, articles, and short stories, most of which were published in the *New Yorker*. The best of the newsbreaks and their tag lines were collected in *Ho Hum* (1931) and *Another Ho-Hum* (1932); selections from "Notes and Comment" appear in *Every Day Is Saturday* (1934); and some of his sketches appear in *Quo Vadimus?* (1939).

Many of these items are ephemeral. The tag

lines, for example, date easily. Still, some classics remain, like the following news item: "LOST—Male fox hound, brown head, yellow legs, blue body with large black spots on left side, male. Also female, white with red head and spot on hip.—*Fayette* (Mo.) *Democrat Leader*." White's comment was, "Those aren't dogs, those are nasturtiums."

By 1932, however, a new seriousness appeared in White's writing. When Henry Ford, for example, had said something about the "normal processes of industry and business," White asked: "How do we know that two-million-men-idle isn't normal under our system of government by investigation, peace by appropriation, and happiness by aërial dissemination of dance music?" White actually wrote relatively little about the Depression; he was fortunate in not being deeply affected by it personally. Yet it certainly helped in leading him to think more deeply than he had about politics, religion, progress, the unrest in Europe, social and economic problems, and particularly about the increasing complexity of American society.

It is customary to explain White's attitude toward simplicity and complexity in terms of Thoreau, whose writing without doubt had a strong influence on him. White likely read Thoreau in college (in his senior year at Cornell he took a survey course in American literature), and he speaks of buying a copy of *Walden* in 1927. Yet even as a boy, White seemed to have been thinking of the simple life. In "Stratagem for Retirement," he says that "I find that I still hold to the same opinions that were mine when I was thirteen. I think a man should learn to swim in the pool of time, should tuck up his affairs so they fit into a canoe, and having snugged all down, should find out what bird is his eagle, and climb the tree."

In his early comments in *Every Day Is Saturday*, White remarks playfully about the complex life: when 100 clerks in an insurance office moved from one building to another, he asks incredulously, "And didn't any of the clerks escape?" In a later comment, he notes that the healthiest countries in the world are "those in which men did the most tangible tasks."

In *Quo Vadimus?* White speaks with a clearer voice about complexity. Some of the sketches here, from the late 1920s and early 1930s, represent the same playful attitude White had shown in *Every Day Is Saturday*. A later sketch, however, "The Family Which Dwelt Apart," though fanciful and humorous in part, has a seriousness that cannot be missed. (The sketch was later included in *A Subtreasury of American Humor*, 1941.) The parable, as White calls

it, begins with a description of the simple life of the Pruitts, a family of fisherfolk living on a small island: "They liked the island and lived there from choice. In winter, when there wasn't much doing, they slept the clock around, like so many bears. In summer they dug clams and set off a few pinwheels and salutes on July 4th." One winter, alas, the water freezes: the marooned family can't use a boat and the ice is too treacherous to walk on. This would have been no misfortune—the Pruitts simply stay inside and play crokinole—but the outside world begins to worry about them, and help descends upon them like a plague. The army, the state police, Pathé news, reporters—all invade the island. Through a series of man-made disasters, the whole family but one is wiped out. The survivor, having buried his kin, leaves the island of his nativity.

The source of the parable was the partly bungled rescue attempt on Tangier Island in the Chesapeake Bay, where some 1,500 inhabitants had been in real need of supplies. The matter had been reported in the *New York Times*, 2-11 February 1936.

Other themes that White takes up in *Every Day Is Saturday* and *Quo Vadimus?* involve politics, religion, progress, and, briefly, internationalism. It would have been difficult for a person writing in the 1930s not to become concerned, if not involved with politics, and White was no exception. But White, unlike many writers, belonged to no cults or groups; he was not a returning exile, nor a writer on the left. It has always been one of his qualities that he could remain an objective commentator; he was a "committed" writer, but always on his own terms. "There is a lot of the cat in me" he once wrote, "and cats are not joiners."

He writes in 1931 that "we happen to be, in a small way, on the other side of the fence from Father Coughlin on all his points." On the other hand, about a year later, he chastises the members of the John Reed Club for bad manners in their attack on Diego Rivera for "turning reactionary on them." Capitalists, White adds, are at least polite. He could never accept the philosophy of "my country, right or wrong"; "We should like," he writes, "to be a good rebel, but it has always seemed to us difficult to be a rebel in this country, where there is nothing to rebel against except one's own stupidity in electing incompetent public officers and paying taxes on a standard of living far above the simple needs of life."

White was skeptical, too, about religion. He comments with mild irony on his feelings during a rare visit to church when Dr. Fosdick was preaching on the return of people to the Christian faith to do battle against atheism and agnosticism: "It stirred us to discover . . . that we were really part of a movement against irreligion, instead of just a mousy, faintly worried man, out wandering around the town on a Sunday morning." In "Dr. Vinton," a sketch in *Quo Vadimus?*, White takes a less innocent poke at religious self-righteousness and complacency. Dr. Vinton, the sole survivor of a disaster at sea, finds in his rescue a confirmation of his own exalted sense of virtue: he is saved by Providence, in order, apparently, to preach a fatuous sermon with a sea gull as its motif. There is a *Candide* touch in the essay, and doubts as to the ultimate wisdom of Providence linger in the reader's mind, and White's.

In "The Wings of Orville," one of the most pleasant parables in *Quo Vadimus?*, White, making fun of progress, tells of Orville, a New York City sparrow with an inspired but pointless urge to tow a wren from Madison Square to 110th Street; Orville succeeds. The story is told without comment; however, in *Every Day Is Saturday* White had noted that "scientists assume that anything is progress just so long as it's never been accomplished before." "The Crack of Doom," a more explicit comment, describes how progress has gradually reduced the earth to a shambles—the elms and willows have disappeared, rainfall has increased, and tropical storms have broken out with great intensity. New man-made diseases emerge and finally the earth, thrown off its course by the effect of radio waves, collides with a fixed star and goes up in flames. White concludes: "The light was noticed on Mars, where it brought a moment of pleasure to young lovers; for on Mars it is the custom to kiss one's beloved when a star falls."

On another note, "Farewell, My Lovely!," one of White's best-known essays, was published during this period, appearing first in *The New Yorker* of 16 May 1936; it was reprinted that same year in book form as *Farewell to Model T* and has been reprinted in collections and anthologies a number of times since, including in *The Second Tree from the Corner* (1954). Suggested to White by a manuscript submitted to the *New Yorker* by Richard L. Strout, the essay was published under the pseudonym Lee Strout White. It is essentially White's, however, and belongs in the canon of his works.

The essay, a product of White's experience with his Model T, expresses as well his nostalgia for the past, for the Model T Ford was important in American history as well as in White's. "My own generation," he writes, "identifies it with Youth, with its gaudy, irretrievable excitements." With White, the identification was not so much with the gaudy excitement of youth as with his own private search for a role in life—a search that had its trials, but its vigor too: "The days were golden, the nights were dim and strange."

The main part of the essay concerns two matters: first, the gadgets and attachments one could buy for a Model T; and, second, the almost mystic lore and legends associated with the car. For the first matter, Sears and Roebuck provided much; the Model T "was born naked as a baby, and a flourishing industry grew up out of correcting its rare deficiencies and combatting its fascinating diseases." Of the lore and legends, more can be said, and White obviously delights in saying it. Of special interest is the timer, "an extravagantly odd little device, simple in construction, mysterious in function." You could hit it, blow on it, oil it; or even, as White tried once, spit on it—"You see," he writes, "the Model T driver moved in the realm of metaphysics. He believed his car could be hexed." Beyond the fun, though, is accurate and close observation; White knew his car well, as a driver had to in those days.

White's second book of poems, *The Fox of Peapack and Other Poems* (1938), was a considerable improvement over *The Lady Is Cold*. Reviews were generally favorable; David McCord noted that White had come a long way since his earlier collection. One difference between the poems in this collection and those in the earlier one is that many of these begin with a newspaper comment and develop from it. The approach may tend to produce limited and topical poems but it also suggests that White was moving closer to his material. *The Fox of Peapack* has fewer lyrical poems, fewer bits of whimsy; it has, on the other hand, stronger and more vigorous statements. Although we find, for example, references to advertising in *The Lady Is Cold*, they are light, scarcely critical; in "The Silence of the Gears" from *The Fox of Peapack* we discover a White who speaks of the "whoring Voices of the reasonable air / In fifteen-minute lozenges of pleasure."

One of White's best poems was his response to the notorious comment by Vittorio Mussolini about bombing in Ethiopia: "I remember," said Mussolini, "that one group of horsemen gave me the impression of a budding rose as the bombs fell in their midst. It was exceptionally good fun." White, seeing in the comment an attitude that violated all decent respect for life, responds with strong feeling. The poem "Flying Over Ethiopian Mountain Ranges" begins thus:

Where horsemen's blood runs sickly

To the absorbent earth,
The rose, unfolding quickly
    To give the canker birth,

Reveals a wormlike beauty
    To the new ranks of youth,
Their hands upraised in duty,
    Their heels unshod with ruth.

Equally effective, and probably better known, was "I Paint What I See," a poetic comment on the controversy over the Rivera murals in Rockefeller Center in New York City. Nelson Rockefeller had objected to some aspects of a mural that Rivera had been commissioned to paint, particularly to a portrait of Lenin that Rivera had included. Rivera offered to put in the head of Lincoln, or McCormick, though he was not willing to remove Lenin; White plays upon this nicely:

'I'll take out a couple of people drinkin'
'And put in a picture of Abraham Lincoln;
'I could even give you McCormick's reaper
'And still not make my art much cheaper
'But the head of Lenin has got to stay
'Or my friends will give me the bird today,
'The bird, the bird, forever.'

Another point Rockefeller had made, according to an account in the *New York Times*, was that Rockefeller Center was not a private house, but a public building; in the poem, his objection becomes: " 'For this, as you know, is a public hall, / 'And people want doves, or a tree in fall.' " The end of the poem may have been overly optimistic; when Rockefeller says, "And after all, / It's *my* wall," the last line has "We'll see if it is,' said Rivera." White probably wrote the poem after the first news reports, for later, of course, Rivera lost his fight. The poem is one of White's happiest combinations of wit and seriousness. His refusal to take Rivera too seriously might seem to some a lack of commitment; but, by avoiding the role of either professional liberal or conservative, White in the long run may have spoken with his most effective voice.

The best case to be made for White's poetry is in Morris Bishop's introduction to *One Man's Meat* (1942). Speaking of the poems in White's two collections, Bishop notes that many of them are "mere trifles, amusing developments of small observations." However, Bishop continues, the best of White's poems should interest the critic: "For E. B. White and a few others are creating a new mid-form between Light Verse and Heavy Verse, between the determined comic conviction of the one and the pretentious obscurity of the other." These poets, says Bishop, "aim at lucidity, at the communication of their meaning to the large number of people who are responsive to poetic form and feeling but who are rebuffed by the hermetics of our time."

In the early part of 1938, White left New York for his farm on the Maine coast, where, except for a return to New York from 1943 to 1957, he has been living ever since. He reduced considerably his contributions to the *New Yorker* and undertook to write a monthly essay for the "One Man's Meat" department of *Harper's Magazine*. White liked the country, he liked animals, and he took farming seriously—at one point (October 1941), he was sending eighty dozen eggs a week to market. In his preface to the 1944 edition of *One Man's Meat*, White describes his book and his situation: "It is a collection of essays which I wrote from a salt water farm in Maine while engaged in trivial, peaceable pursuits, knowing all the time that the world hadn't arranged any true peace or granted anyone the privilege of indulging himself for long in trivialities. Although such a record is likely to seem incongruous, I see no harm in preserving it, the more so since I have begun to receive letters from soldiers overseas assuring me that there is a positive value to them in the memory of peace and home."

After reading *Quo Vadimus?* and *Every Day Is Saturday*, one is struck by White's greater sureness of material and expression, by his clearer thinking on many topics, and above all by his more penetrating moral purpose and his deeper conviction in attitudes and feelings in *One Man's Meat*. Not surprisingly he writes a good deal about his farming and related activities in Maine: chickens, sheep, fertilizer, the weather. He also writes about many of the topics he had approached, often tentatively, in his earlier work. White at times really does seem to come closer to something solid and honest than anything he had been able to find in New York. Although there is no single theme or pattern to the essays in *One Man's Meat*, certain topics turn up more than others: a number of the essays concern war and its related problems; others are about domestic, social, and political matters. And some, like "Once More to the Lake," fit no simple category.

Certainly the coming war was on White's mind. In October 1938, in "Clear Days," he describes, among a number of other matters, roofing his barn; but like a counterpoint, Munich is on his mind: "I'm down now; the barn is tight, and the peace is preserved. It is the ugliest peace the earth has ever received for a Christmas present."

"Coon-Hunt" is another example of this counter-point effect. Before describing the coon hunt itself, White talks about civil defense, and then he notes with some sharpness how the enemy had already made his presence felt. On Halloween, some junk had been piled up in front of a Jewish merchant's store. "The enemy," says White, "slipped into town and out again, and I think there were hardly a dozen people who caught the glimpse of his coat tails. . . . There would never be a moment, in war or in peace, when I wouldn't trade all the patriots in the county for one tolerant man." These two essays, and many of the others, are made up of a variety of comments; some of his best, however, are on a single topic. Three of them are effective pieces of demolition: of the New York World's Fair ("The World of Tomorrow"), the Townsend Plan ("Camp Meeting"), and a review of Anne Morrow Lindbergh's book, *The Wave of the Future*.

The road to Tomorrow, writes White in the first of these, "leads through the chimney pots of Queens. It is a long, familiar journey, through Mulsified Shampoo and Mobilgas, through Bliss Street, Kix, Ostring-O-Sol, and the Majestic Auto Seat Covers." White epitomizes the fair with a description of a giant automaton, located outside one of the girlie shows (where, with a neat compromise between morality and eroticism, the girls were allowed to expose one breast). Several girls sat on the robot's lap and were fondled by its huge rubber hands: "Here was the Fair, all fairs, in pantomime; and here the strange mixed dream that made the Fair: the heroic man, bloodless and perfect and enormous, created in his own image, and in his hand (rubber, aseptic) the literal desire, the warm and living breast."

In August 1939, White reported on a talk given by Dr. Francis E. Townsend on the Townsend Plan (a scheme, born of the Depression, to give a pension of $200 a month to all people over sixty by a tax of 2 percent on the gross business of the country; the money was supposed to be spent within a month by the pensioner). The first part of the report is a sympathetic account of Townsend's talk—its simple appeal, the artless approach. "Maybe this Plan was it," writes White; "I never heard a milder-mannered economist, nor one more fully convinced of the right and wisdom of his proposal." The shift in the report comes when White describes the question period after the talk: "It was at this point that Dr. Francis E. Townsend (of California) began quietly to come apart, like an inexpensive toy." With a combination of calm reporting, gentle irony, and understatement, White deflates

Townsend: "It spoiled his afternoon to be asked anything. Details of Townsendism were irksome in the extreme—he wanted to keep the Plan simple and beautiful, like young love before sex has reared its head. And now he was going to have to answer a lot of nasty old questions."

Equally effective, and somewhat sharper in tone, is White's critical attack on Anne Lindbergh's book, *The Wave of the Future*. As in his treatment of Townsend, White is fair. Anne Lindbergh, he says, "wants a good world, as I do," but "she has retreated into the pure realm of thought, leaving the rest of us to rassle with the bear." Her thesis was that the "wave of the future" was the new social and economic forces being exploited in Germany, Russia, and Italy. These forces had been used badly at times, she conceded; but they are the hope for a new world. White then moves in with more vigor than he had shown against Townsend, and with good reason—for the issue was far more important, the antagonist more formidable. These forces, says White, are not new at all: they are "the backwash of the past," and have "muddied the world for centuries." Mrs. Lindbergh had argued that the new forces had emerged from the distresses of the people, and were therefore somehow good. White attacks this assumption: "The fascist ideal, however great the misery which released it and however impressive the self-denial and the burning courage which promote it, does not hold the seed of a better order but of a worse one, and it always has a foul smell and a bad effect on the soil. It stank at the time of Christ and it stinks today, wherever you find it and in whatever form, big or little—even here in America, the little fascists always at their tricks, stirring up a lynching mob or flagellating the devil or selling a sex pamphlet to tired, bewildered old men. The forces are always the same—on the people's side frustration, disaffection; on the leader's side control of hysteria, perversion of information, abandonment of principle."

Careful not to accuse Mrs. Lindbergh of being a Fascist, White is bothered not only by what she has written but also by the popularity of her ideas; for this was a time when, in certain circles in England and America, fascism had disturbingly enthusiastic partisans. Many people had spoken of the book, White notes; they would say that, though they had reservations about it, "there's something to what she says just the same." This "something" White tries to find and cannot.

In the best essay in *One Man's Meat*, "Once More to the Lake," White recounts a week's visit he made with his son to a Maine lake where he himself had vacationed as a child with his parents. During this week's visit White walked and fished with his son, and in many ways lived again the days of his childhood: there was the same excitement at arrival, the same early mornings at the lake, the same cottage with partitions that did not go up to the ceiling, the same kind of farmhouse meals, the same lake, the same kind of people visiting, the same questions, the same thunderstorms, and the same swimming in the rain afterward.

The chief values of the essay lie partly in White's skillful evocation of past and present, as details of the past recur to him, sometimes blending harmoniously with the present and sometimes clashing; and partly they lie in his moving and almost obsessive feeling of duality as he becomes both himself and his son. There is a strong awareness of the circularity of time, and of the joys of the past and of the present: the pleasures of vacation then and now. But at the end, beautifully worked out, the tone suddenly shifts. White's son, going swimming during the rain, gets his dripping trunks from the line and puts them on: "I watched him, his hard little body, skinny and bare, saw him wince slightly as he pulled up around his vitals the small, soggy, icy garment. As he buckled the swollen belt suddenly my groin felt the chill of death." Age and death are

present with frightening vividness, and time suddenly seems to reverse itself, for White is no longer young and in the past. Because the aura of death surrounds his son as well as himself, the generations are linked again, but in mortality, not in life.

Before White returned to New York, he completed another project: his editing, with the help of his wife, of *A Subtreasury of American Humor* (1941). The anthology was popular: it was a Book-of-the-Month-Club selection; in abridged form, an Armed Services edition; and later, also in abridged form, a Pocket Book edition. The Whites interpreted the term "humor" broadly: the anthology contained such selections as the first chapter of Sinclair Lewis's *Babbitt* and a *New Yorker* profile of evangelist Father Divine.

From the point of view of this study the most important part of *A Subtreasury of American Humor* was the preface by White. He explains the criteria for the selection of the items, and talks about humor. The preface has been reprinted, in a slightly changed form, in *The Second Tree from the Corner* (1954), in *The Comic in Theory and Practice* (1960), and in *An E. B. White Reader* (1966). In making the selections, says White, he and his wife rejected the goal of inclusiveness: "We asked simply that we be amused, now in 1941." Some areas of

E. B. and Katharine White at work on A Subtreasury of American Humor

humor, White notes, were not represented at all: no joke-book stuff, radio humor, or comic-strip material.

White begins his discussion of the nature of humor with some valuable and original comments on dialect and illiteracies. Petroleum Nasby's misspellings for humorous effect, for example, pose a problem to White. Nasby uses "uv" for "of," and "offis" for "office," to cite two examples. White notes that he pronounces "of" and "office" as if they were "uv" and "offis"; thus, he concludes, the humorous effect is not from the odd pronunciations but from the funny spellings themselves—as if the character involved were writing, not speaking. But then, as White says, no one who could write at all would write "uv." And in Edward Streeter's *Dere Mable*, which clearly involves characters writing, not speaking, it is unlikely that anyone would consistently leave off the "g" in "-ing" words. White concludes that "the popularity of all dialect stuff derives in part from flattery of the reader—giving him a pleasant sensation of superiority which he gets from working out the intricacies of misspelling, and the satisfaction of detecting boorishness or illiteracy in someone else."

White is perfectly well aware that this "dialect stuff" is a surface matter; the real nature of humor lies deeper and has a certain "fragility, an evasiveness," which is beyond analysis. It is not that humorists are really sad people, sad clowns; rather, "there is a deep vein of melancholy running through everyone's life and . . . a humorist, perhaps more sensible of it than some others, compensates for it actively and positively." The humorist thus comes close to the truth of human experience, but there is an irony in being a humorist—the world patronizes him: "It decorates its serious artists with laurel, and its wags with Brussels sprouts." The humorist must learn to live with a kind of injustice; he must put up with his friends who will ask the question every humorist is asked: When are you "going to write something serious?" But the real problem is the conflict between high emotion and the temptation or danger of ending with a snicker: "Here, then, is the very hub of the conflict: the careful form of art, and the careless shape of life itself. What a man does with this uninvited snicker (which may closely resemble a sob, at that) decides his destiny. If he resists it, conceals it, destroys it, he may keep his architectural scheme intact and save his building, and the world will never know. If he gives in to it, he becomes a humorist, and the sharp brim of the fool's cap leaves a mark forever on his brow." Typical of White's critical writing, the pref-

ace is neither profound nor scholarly; yet, clear, refreshing, and funny at times, it probably comes as close to the truth as most of what has been written on the subject. The comments are perceptive and perhaps defensive; for White, moreso in his earlier days than later in his career, was considered to be primarily a humorist. He was that, but never exclusively so. Often he did give in to the temptation and throw his cap in the reader's face, but just as often he did not. Still, there is no great need to classify; it is possible to combine strong emotion and a deep moral purpose with a sense of humor—as Charles Dickens and Thomas Hardy have done.

White wrote his last "One Man's Meat" piece in January 1943 and later that year returned to New York. He did not give up his Maine farm (he went there off and on, returning to full-time residence in 1957), but he wanted to be closer to the *New Yorker*, and to New York. He resumed active participation on the *New Yorker*, particularly as a writer for "Notes and Comment." Actually, he had started contributing extensively to the department in 1942—in 1941 he had written only two items; in 1942 he wrote more than fifty, and in 1943 sixty or so.

A number of those contributions were about war, peace, and the need for some sort of world government or world federalism; some were collected and published in *The Wild Flag* (1946). These, comprising some of White's most serious writing, are, except for his children's stories, his most sustained efforts on a single topic. The book had mixed reviews, including a scathing notice in the *Nation*. The modern reader might view the work as naive and idealistic—and he would probably be right. Yet even if in some ways White lacked profundity, he made a number of good observations and made them clearly. Disarmament, security leagues, treaties—all these attempts at securing peace, he said, have been and will be futile. Unless men can achieve real union, unless each nation-state can agree to relinquish some of its sovereignty, unless there can be a real basis for what we like to call international law and justice, unless, finally, men's loyalties can extend beyond those they feel for their own particular piece of territory, we have little hope. We have to have the world view; the machinery can come later. White's own retrospective comment on *The Wild Flag* is an honest and valid summation: "The book was rather dreamy and uninformed, but it was good-spirited . . . and I still think that what I said was essentially sound, although I'm not sure the timing was right."

White wrote three children's books during his career. In an October 1964 interview with the *Cor-*

nell Daily Sun, White explains why he wrote the first two of his children's books, *Stuart Little* (1945) and *Charlotte's Web* (1952) (the third, *The Trumpet of the Swan*, was not published until 1970): "I couldn't tell stories to children and they always were after me to tell them a story and I found I couldn't do it. So I had to get it down on paper." In an essay on children's books in *One Man's Meat*, White had expressed a mild distaste for the amount of geographical and linguistic information being purveyed to children that year (1938); *Stuart Little*, *Charlotte's Web*, and *The Trumpet of the Swan* are refreshingly free of studied attempts to improve young minds. What makes White's three books outstanding is that he has written them in the classical tradition of children's stories—the tradition of Lewis Carroll's *Alice in Wonderland*, Mary Molesworth's *The Cuckoo Clock*, Kenneth Grahame's *The Wind in the Willows*, and A. A. Milne's *Winnie the Pooh*. There is much to be learned from White's stories, to be sure, but it is not geography, or science, or even the habits of mice and pigs. What the child does learn—and what children learn from the other fine children's books—is a great deal about loyalty, honesty, love, sadness, and happiness.

White's first two children's books have become classics. If in *Stuart Little* there were problems of unity, *Charlotte's Web* has a near-perfect structure. White has not been given to long works, but here he found a medium that was congenial to him, and it may well be that he will be longest remembered for these stories, particularly *Charlotte's Web*. In these stories White has written clearly and simply, as he has always done. His writing is free from the bondage of current events that has dated many of his *New Yorker* pieces and independent of the pressure of literary trends and fads. Above all, White has put into these stories in unalloyed form his compassion and humanity; his delight in the physical world; his feeling for the reality and importance of the small and simple ambitions of small and simple people; and his faith in dreams and in the continuity of affection and love.

From 1944, when White published the second edition of *One Man's Meat*, until 1954, when the next collection of his pieces, *The Second Tree from the Corner* was published, White wrote—in addition to *The Wild Flag* and his first two children's stories—*Here Is New York* (1949) and the introductions to two books. He also continued writing taglines for newsbreaks, contributed to "Notes and Comment," and wrote a number of poems, stories, and sketches, mostly for the *New Yorker*; some of these were later collected in *The Second Tree from the Corner*. The two

introductions, reprinted with a few minor changes in *The Second Tree from the Corner*, were to *A Basic Chicken Guide for the Small Flock Owner* (1944) by Roy Jones, and the 1950 edition of *the lives and times of archy and mehitabel* by Don Marquis.

The introduction to *A Basic Chicken Guide* reflects the experience White had gained in raising chickens in Maine. The introduction to Don Marquis's *the lives and times of archy and mehitabel* is more serious and closer to White's heart, for he had a deep affection for Don Marquis and his humor, as well as a profound understanding of his creative problems. White sees a parallel between the cockroach hurling himself at the typewriter keys in order to hammer out his work, then falling exhausted to the floor, and the pain that creative work exacted from Marquis: "After about a lifetime of frightfully difficult literary labor keeping newspapers supplied with copy, he fell exhausted."

White makes Archy something of a symbol for literary creativity: "He cast himself with all his force upon a key, head downward. So do we all." Marquis was dogged by the question, is "the stuff literature or not?" This, admits White, is the question that "dogs us all." Behind his analysis lay a sympathy and admiration for Marquis; for White, like Marquis in one way at least, also found it hard to write sustained work—and he might have felt that he too, by a lucky accident, had found his ideal medium in the *New Yorker*. In addition, White, through his admiration for the craft of Don Marquis, shows something less than admiration for the kind of columnist that succeeded Marquis and others of his era. "Nowadays," White says, "to get a columning job a man need only have the soul of a Peep Tom or a third-rate prophet. There are plenty of loud clowns and bad poets at work on papers today, but there are not many columnists adding to belles lettres, and certainly there is no Don Marquis at work on any big daily."

White's tribute to his city, *Here Is New York*, was first published in *Holiday* (April 1949) and later that year in book form by Harper and Brothers. The book, or rather long essay—it is only forty-five pages—reveals as much about White as about New York: it helps to account for his love of New York, just as *One Man's Meat* does for his love of Maine. To the reader of White's poetry and his early *New Yorker* pieces, there are a number of familiar observations about the city in *Here Is New York*, and a few new ones. All are made with eloquence and in a kind of final form, for the book is not just an explanation of New York, but a plea for it—and a plea for peace, too; he ends the book with the observation that there is a willow tree in an interior garden near the

When the Times asked me ~~to sendxax repery~~ *for a* report
on what's being said about Watergate in my barnyard, I immediately
arranged for an interview with the goose, who is sore at me at
the moment but is always willing to talk. (between drinks) x

    ME. What is your feeling about Liddy?

    GOOSE. ~~Hxix~~ One of the greats, a man of enormous
verve, a bungler of immense premise. Liddy should be President.
He carries a gun, which is what the Oval Room needs---bungling *imagination,* and
verve, supported by gunfire.

    ME. DO You think justice was obstructed?

    GOOSE. Certainly. Justice and [justabout] everything
else. The purpose of the executive branch is to obstruct. That's
what we have these fellows there for. *Clean cut like Ehrlichman*

    ME. Sam Ervin? *How about Strachan*

    GOOSE. Don't care for ~~his~~ *the* eyebrows. You ~~don't need~~ *Nobody needs*
eyebrows—x ~~look at me.~~ I don't have ~~anyx~~ eyebrows, but I can
drink any man under the table.

    ME. SHOUld the President resign?

    GOOSE. Certainly. He should resign in favor of
Liddy, who is one of the greats.

    ME   But Liddy's in jail.

    GOOSE. ~~GstxkinxuatxvThatixxnavpraulenx~~ -I knew that,
and the jail is a better place since his arrival. *It's a going place now, with Liddy in charge.* ~~zoo~~

    ME.. What about Strachan?

    GOOSE. Gordon? An honest man. ~~Should never have~~
~~been in there.~~ (A complete misfit.)

    ~~ME. Daniel Schorr?~~

    ~~GOOSE. A fast talker but not as fast as I am. I~~

United Nations headquarters: "Whenever I look at it nowadays, and feel the cold shadow of the planes, I think: 'This must be saved, this particular thing, this very tree.' If it were to go, all would go—this city, this mischievous and marvelous monument which not to look upon would be like death."

The willow tree symbol from the end of *Here Is New York* suggests the theme of a good many of the pieces in *The Second Tree from the Corner*, especially the more recent ones: the theme, that is, that deals with the paradox of modern man, the threats to his civilization, and the hope that something, at least, can be preserved of his culture. The selections in the book are uneven. Some, in the section "Notes on the City," are largely earlier sketches that show White to be a sensitive, warm, but somehow not fully involved observer of the city. Other sketches illustrate what White calls in the foreword his "tendency to revisit." One, "Speaking of Counterweights" goes back to his days on the *Seattle Times*, and a ride he took on an odd little car around the top of the building in preparation for a feature story.

The most successful pieces in *The Second Tree from the Corner* are those dealing with the quandary, the paradox, of modern man—those that show White's skepticism about science and progress. He had written on those matters before, but some of his strongest statements and his best work are here. Of these, "The Door" (first published in the *New Yorker*, 25 March 1939) has become White's most popular story. In it, White makes extensive use of two matters recently discussed in articles in the *New York Times* (February and March 1939) and in *Life* (6 March 1939). The *Times* articles were reports about a model home exhibit in Rockefeller Center, and the one from *Life* about the effects of frustration in some experiments on rats. He also used some other briefer items from *Time* and the *New York Times*, as William R. Steinhoff has shown in a perceptive article on the story. White's use of contemporary material was characteristic, growing out of his long habit of using such material in his *New Yorker* "Notes and Comment."

"The Door," with little plot in the conventional sense, has a structure that derives from White's sources. The central character is being shown through an exhibit of a model house (everything in the house had been tested and could be laundered); and, as he is taken through, he compares himself to rats in a laboratory. That the house was being exhibited in Rockefeller Center fits the theme of the story, for such a situation is as artificial and incongruous as modern life itself. The story opens with the sterile, artificial quality of the setting made explicit: "Everything (he kept saying) is something it isn't." The names of things were "tex," "koid," "duroid"—all artificial words with no antecedents or roots.

Having established the setting of the story, and having identified man's predicament with that of the rats in a laboratory, White becomes more specific about that predicament. Doors, literal in the rat's maze, are symbolic in man's own maze. "First," says the man, "they would teach you the prayers and the Psalms, and that would be the right door . . . and the long sweet words with the holy sound, and that would be the one to jump at to get where the food was." The doors will continue being changed; and man will still jump, for "nobody can not jump." Here man and the rats differ. Another door that man learns after the prayers and the psalms, and one that works for a while, is the one "with the picture of the girl on it (only it was spring), her arms outstretched in loveliness. . . ." One would go through the door "winged and exalted (like any rat) and the food would be there . . . and you had chosen the right door for the world was young." There is one cure for man, one ironic hope of escaping the unopening door—to have the prefrontal lobe removed. But then, man will cease to be man; the work of centuries will be removed: "The higher animal becomes a little easier in his mind and more like the lower one."

But the man in the story achieves a kind of victory at the end, for he is still a man; he still keeps jumping: he goes to a door as he leaves the model house and faces the risk of a shattering bump. However, the door opens for him—he had half expected to find "one of the old doors . . . the one with the girl her arms outstretched in loveliness and beauty before him." It was not so; still, he gets out, but not quite free, not quite untouched; the symptom of his tension, the projection of his inner turmoil to the world outside, meets him as he steps off the escalator, and "the ground came up slightly, to meet his foot." But his is only a partial triumph; the story ends with the final dislocation of the ground when it moves up to meet the foot. In fact, the man has achieved not victory, not health, but the kind of uneasy truce that modern life represented for White, the kind of uneasy truce that was New York City, or any large city. We live close to the edge of collapse, and each day is survived, each jump at each door is made, with no more hope or confidence for the day to come than there was for the day just past.

The title story, "The Second Tree from the Corner" first published on 31 May 1947, has a clearer structure than "The Door," is lighter in tone, and less pessimistic. It opens with Trexler, the main character, in a psychiatrist's office. To the doctor's question, "Ever have any bizarre thoughts?" he finally answers defensively, "No." He thinks: "What kind of thoughts *except* bizarre had he had since the age of two?" Eventually Trexler's problem becomes the doctor's problem, and neither one is getting from life what he wants. At the end, Trexler sees what he wants. Symbolized by a small tree he sees—the second tree from the corner—it is a momentary glimpse of truth that gives him courage. It cannot last, but Trexler "crossed Madison, boarded a downtown bus, and rode all the way to Fifty-second Street before he had a thought that could rightly have been called bizarre." The point is basically the same as in "The Door"—no permanent cure exists for the disease of life, for the fears it engenders, for the manipulations we must endure. But there is momentary relief, the tentative victory; and, doctor or patient, the hopeful man can find it and, like Trexler, glimpse "the flashy tail feathers of the bird courage."

Not all the pieces in *The Second Tree from the Corner* deal with such serious matters. White has written an amusing parody of Hemingway's *Across the River and into the Trees*, probably Hemingway's worst novel, and one that cries out for parody. In another piece, the endearing gem "Death of a Pig," White tells how, as his pig sickens and dies, he shifts from the farmer-butcher role he started with to become, suddenly, the physician and consoler of his pig. The death of the pig takes on an unexpected dignity, unmarred by any taint of civilization: there was "no stopover in the undertaker's foul parlor." Of the twelve poems in *The Second Tree from the Corner*, "Zoo Revisited," the longest, has considerable autobiographical significance. The best of the lot, however, is "Song of the Queen Bee"—a pleasant tribute to the freedom of nature; it ends with a happy refrain:

> Oh, it's simply *rare*
> In the beautiful air,
>   And I wish to state
>   That I'll *always* mate
> With whatever drone I encounter.

The Points of My Compass (1962), the last published collection of White's hitherto uncollected pieces, includes material written from the summer of 1954 to March 1961. White has published relatively little since, and the collection contains his most personal and explicit statements on a number of matters; it also contains some of his best essays.

During the period covered by *The Points of My Compass* White continued to write for "Notes and Comment," though on an increasingly reduced scale until, by 1960, he was contributing just a few items a year. He also continued to write the tag lines for the newsbreaks department, published a number of poems and sketches that have not yet been collected, and brought out in 1959 a revised edition of William Strunk's *The Elements of Style*, to which he added an introduction and a chapter about writing.

The Points of My Compass has a curious sort of circularity about it, ending with an essay that goes back to White's days in Seattle and Washington. There is a kind of geographical circularity about it too. The book is titled as it is because White datelined his essays from the four points of the compass, depending on what direction from the *New Yorker* office in Manhattan he happened to be when he wrote them. This "geographical distortion," as he calls it, seems to broaden the dimensions of the work; but it also underlines the importance of New York City to White. It was for him a microcosm, a center, and the four corners of the world could almost be contained within its emotional if not geographical limits. Geography was to White something of an emotional matter; it is, he says, "undergoing vast shifts anyway, with populations in turmoil and the weathercock spinning wildly as the wind veers." Without trying to be pompous about it, we could say that the essays represent the culmination of White's experience, the farthest point of navigation—not quite to the heart of darkness, perhaps, but certainly to the heart of his message to his readers. Part of that message has to do with politics, national and international. A lot had happened since *The Wild Flag* to temper some of White's hope and idealism: McCarthyism, nuclear testing, the Berlin wall and Communist control over Eastern Europe in general, and, among other things, the weaknesses that kept showing up in the United Nations. To these problems White had no clear solutions; what he does, in part, is to reaffirm his view that a new international order must somehow evolve to match the new science of destruction. Some union of free nations is necessary—a union to which Communist and other totalitarian states will be admitted when they become eligible. He sums up in one of his essays—"Unity" (written 4 June 1960): what is needed, he says, "is the evolution of community, community slowly and surely invested with the robes of government by the consent of the governed. We cannot conceivably achieve a peaceful life merely by relaxing the tensions of sovereign nations; there is an unending supply of them."

In another essay from *The Points of My Compass*, "A Slight Sound at Evening" (summer 1954), White pays a centenary tribute to Thoreau. Whenever White first read Thoreau, it seems clear that his real interest in him began in 1927, when he bought a World's Classics edition of *Walden*. We should read *Walden*, White says, at an age "when the normal anxieties and enthusiasm and rebellions of youth closely resemble those of Thoreau in that that, at a certain time of life, "we are accustomed to consider every spot as the possible site of a house," he replies, "There spoke the young man, a few years out of college, who had not yet broken away from home. He hadn't married, and he had found no job that measured up to his rigid standards of employment, and like any young man, or young animal, he felt uneasy and on the defensive until he had fixed himself a den." White might have been describing

E. B. White at his farm in Maine

spring of 1845, when he borrowed an ax, went out to the woods, and began to whack down some trees for timber. Received at such a juncture, the book is like an invitation to life's dance." White himself had discovered Thoreau at such a time, and he quotes a critical sentence from *Walden*: "I learned this at least by my experiment: that if one advances confidently in the direction of his dreams, and endeavors to live the life which he has imagined, he will meet with a success unexpected in common hours." Then White adds: "The sentence has the power to resuscitate the youth drowning in his sea of doubt. I recall my exhilaration upon reading it, many years ago, in a time of hesitation and despair."

In another passage, the relevance of Thoreau to White is equally clear. To Thoreau's comment himself here. White concludes that Thoreau was at once the companion and the chider (the "hairshirt") of the "fellows who hate compromise and have compromised, fellows who love wildness and have lived tamely"; he was the man "who long ago gave corroboration to impulses they perceived were right and issued warnings against things they instinctively knew to be their enemies." This conclusion, resembling Matthew Arnold's tribute to Ralph Waldo Emerson as the friend of those who live by the spirit, is at the core of White's feeling about modern life. Man does not want to live in a culture filled with gadgets and the "multiplicity of convenience"; he wants to live simply and naturally, but not in primitiveness or barbarity—for White was never ready to surrender all progress, all conveniences.

Men should live so as to escape the charge that Thoreau once made when, in a passage White quoted, he describes a farmer fixing a hay baler: "This farmer is endeavoring to solve the problem of a livelihood by a formula more complicated than the problem itself."

Like "Once More to the Lake," the last essay in *The Points of My Compass*, "The Years of Wonder" (13 March 1961) has a circular quality, a feeling of duality about it, as White takes the reader back to his first years after college and particularly to his trip to Alaska—something White had only touched upon before. He tells us in the opening of "The Years of Wonder" that when Alaska achieved statehood, he looked into the journal he had kept while journeying to Alaska, "hoping to discover in its faded pages something instructive about the new state." As he says, a reader might not find much about Alaska in the account he wrote, but he might find something about White and about the 1920s. "The Years of Wonder" is, as White says, a "delayed account—some thirty-seven years late." In other essays White had returned to earlier times—his early dating, his unrest over what part to play in World War I, his recollections of childhood, his adolescent queries about sex. We see in these accounts White's sense of the transiency of life; we see also, from his half-belief in the cyclical quality of life, that he has faith, or something close to it, in permanency. All of his reports of the past may not be in yet, all the points of his compass not yet revealed, but one suspects that his major themes have been stated; *The Points of My Compass*, in its subject and structure, is a fitting and impressive summation. In space, it is a microcosm of his world; in time, a symbol of the unity and coherence of human experience, where youth and age, city and country, past and present, come together. The book is ultimately White's plea for a vital life where the means do not become ends, where gadgets do not create more problems than they solve, where the "advances" of science do not destroy all possibility of real advance because they have destroyed life itself.

On 15 July 1957 White wrote a sketch for the *New Yorker* entitled "Will Strunk." Beginning as a rambling account of the mosquito problems in White's New York apartment, it turns into a nostalgic tribute to Professor William Strunk, Jr., late of Cornell University, and to Strunk's book on rhetoric, *The Elements of Style*. The essay, reprinted in *The Points of My Compass*, had unexpected repercussions. Strunk's work, a short, precise guide to writing, free of jargon and written with a respect for the reader's intelligence and needs, had been used

at Cornell in White's day but had later passed out of circulation, the fate of most such books. The Macmillan Company, however, expressed an interest in reprinting the work, and asked White to revise and amplify it. The task took White a year; when the book was published in 1959, it achieved an immediate and continuing popularity.

White's *New Yorker* sketch became, with a few changes, the introduction of the book; he made some revisions to the book itself, and added a final chapter, "An Approach to Style." While giving much good advice to the student, White avoids the pitfall of considering style as something separable or isolated: "The beginner," he says, "should approach style warily, realizing that it is himself he is approaching." Many of his examples in this chapter are felicitous, and he generally manages to be precise and helpful, without being dogmatic. "Do not dress words up by adding *ly* to them, as though putting a hat on a horse," he writes, giving examples of "overly," "firstly," and "muchly."

Curiously, however, this chapter about style is not one of White's effective pieces. It is not always clear, it is sometimes inconsistent, and it is repetitious in a way rare for White. White was probably aware of some of these matters, for in the postscript to the sketch on Strunk in *The Points of My Compass*, he said that his work on *The Elements of Style* took him a lot longer than he had expected: "I discovered that for all my fine talk I was no match for the parts of speech—was, in fact, over my depth and in trouble. Not only that, I felt uneasy posing as an expert on rhetoric, when the truth is I write by ear, always with difficulty and seldom with any exact notion of what is taking place under the hood."

White has written some good short stories—"The Door," for example, and "The Second Tree from the Corner." *Charlotte's Web*, the best of White's three children's stories, is a classic in that form—it may well turn out to be the longest remembered of his works. And White has for many years been regarded as one of the best essayists in the language. Certainly his writing has long been considered almost a definition of excellence in prose style. J. W. Fuller, for example, noted that, in a survey of forty college anthologies chosen at random, there were, excluding poems, short stories, and plays, more selections by White than by any other author. Today, twenty years after Fuller's survey, an informal search shows that White is still one of the commonly selected writers, although his writings tend now to turn up in selections of essays, rather than in general college anthologies.

White was widely honored during his career,

with honorary degrees from Dartmouth, Yale, and the University of Maine in 1948; Bowdoin in 1950; and Harvard and Colby in 1954. He received the Page One Award for Literature for *The Second Tree from the Corner* in 1954; the Gold Medal Award from the National Institute of Arts and Letters in 1960; the Presidential Medal of Freedom in 1963; the Laura Ingalls Wilder Award in 1970; the National Medal for Literature in 1971; and the William Allen White Children's Book Award for *The Trumpet of the Swan* in 1973. And in 1978 White won a special Pulitzer Prize for the full body of his work.

White has been important in American letters for another reason: his connection with the *New Yorker* magazine. White contributed many stories, sketches, and essays to the *New Yorker*; and from 1927 to the late 1940s, he wrote more of the "Notes and Comment" department of the magazine than any other writer. It was that department that became the heart of the *New Yorker*, and helped set its tone. Of course, many other writers and editors have been important in the development of the *New Yorker*—Ross, Thurber, Katharine White, for example—but no such list can exclude E. B. White.

Few admirers of White, however, would be content to let his significance rest on his connection with the *New Yorker*; or on his worth as a stylist; or as a writer of essays, short stories, or children's books. He is equally important as the spokesman of our times for the right of privacy—a right threatened by the population explosion, by devices for snooping, and by repressive measures instituted through the fear of violence. It is a right that many people of the world have never known and never will know, and it is a right in danger of being forgotten by some of those who once understood it. It is a right, finally, that may turn out to be the most essential ingredient of freedom as we have known it. More fashionable today than privacy are commitment, involvement, community dialogue, confrontation. We must be a member of something, have a label—and in some measure cease to be individual. Perhaps privacy is an outmoded or irrelevant concept in today's world. If so, White's championing of it is simply another aspect of his nostalgia for the past, and it may be that we will have to give up privacy; but in so doing we must reconcile ourselves to becoming another sort of being than we have striven thus far to become.

Other:

James Thurber, *The Owl in the Attic*, introduction by

White (New York & London: Harper, 1931);

Ho-Hum: Newsbreaks from The New Yorker, edited with tag lines by White (New York: Farrar & Rinehart, 1931);

Another Ho-Hum, edited with tag lines by White (New York: Farrar & Rinehart, 1932);

A Subtreasury of American Humor, edited by White and Katharine S. White (New York: Coward-McCann, 1941);

Roy E. Jones, *A Basic Chicken Guide for the Small Flock Owner*, introduction by White (New York: Morrow, 1944);

Don Marquis, *the lives and times of archy and mehitabel*, introduction by White (New York: Doubleday, 1950);

William Strunk, Jr., *The Elements of Style*, revised, with an introduction and a new chapter, by White (New York: Macmillan, 1959; revised, 1972; revised again, 1979).

Letters:

Letters of E. B. White, edited by Dorothy Lobrano Guth (New York: Harper & Row, 1976).

References:

Warren Beck, "E. B. White," *College English*, 7 (April 1946): 367-373;

Scott Elledge, Review of *One Man's Meat*, *Carlton Miscellany*, 4 (Winter 1964): 83-87;

J. W. Fuller, "Prose Style in the Essays of E. B. White," Ph.D. dissertation, University of Washington, 1959;

Louis Hasley, "The Talk of the Town and the Country: E. B. White," *Connecticut Review*, 5 (October 1971): 37-45;

Dale Kramer, *Ross and The New Yorker* (Garden City: Doubleday, 1951);

Edward C. Sampson, *E. B. White* (New York: Twayne, 1974);

William R. Steinhoff, " 'The Door': 'The Professor,' 'My Friend the Poet (Deceased),' 'The Washable House,' and 'The Man Out in Jersey,' " *College English*, 23 (December 1961): 229-232;

James Thurber, "E. B. W.," *Saturday Review of Literature*, 18 (15 October 1938): 8-9;

Thurber, *The Years With Ross* (Boston: Little, Brown, 1959).

Papers:

Most of White's papers are in the E. B. White Collection at Cornell University.

Appendix I:
American Humor: A Historical Survey

East and Northeast
South and Southwest
Midwest
West

Artemus Ward delivering his "Great Union Speech"

East and Northeast

Stanley Trachtenberg
Texas Christian University

A couple, married for many years, had long since made the adjustments necessary to keep their warfare from destroying one another altogether. From the first the wife had been demanding, the husband long-suffering. One particular evening was more uncomfortable than most—hot, sticky. The windows were wide open, the fans did no good. Finally, after tossing and turning for many hours, the husband felt he was about to doze off when he heard his wife moaning, "Oy, am I thirsty." Shutting his eyes tightly he pretended to sleep. Again he heard, "Oy, am I thirsty." He clenched his teeth, resolved not to move. Once more, "Oy, am I thirsty." From these battles he had long come away with some dignity; but he was no fanatic. At length he got up, put on his slippers and his bathrobe, and, making his way in the dark to the bathroom, returned with a glass of water. The wife accepted it gratefully, took a long swallow, and put the glass on the night table. The husband got back into bed. Once more he shut his eyes, and again he felt sleep might soon come. At that moment he heard his wife sigh, "Oy, was I thirsty."

The sigh is more than an expression of temporary relief; it is a recognition that the denials of reality have made it difficult to accept what sweetness life has to offer without giving some thought to the pain which preceded it. It is not only a sigh; it is a historical judgment. The humor in this story, then, like that of any other, is, at least in part, at its own expense. All humor must first establish a situation of threat, a banana peel lying in wait for someone to slip on it. Then it must dispel the threat, even more, prove it groundless to begin with. We were just kidding, it says, no harm done. And the audience? We slip, dust ourselves off, and go about our business. That is why a joke can never be explained. Unless the threat is experienced, there is no satisfaction in having it shown to be harmless. In fact, there is usually a feeling of disappointment, of being let down, even of anger, when the reader is reassured and has not even been aware of any danger to begin with. That is menacing enough in itself. The explanation introduces a threat where none existed before; it is the reassurance that proves threatening. This, in fact, is the basis for that form of black humor that has come to be identified with the contemporary imagination. There is no attempt to dispel the threat, and the conventional attempts to do so are seen as sources of potential menace which must be neutralized in comedy.

But if the principle of comedy is universal, the forms which express it need to be anchored in the particularity of situation and attitude. In his introduction to an anthology of humor in America, Max Herzberg says that humor's most important literary forms include the anecdote, the pun, the limerick, the epigram, and the wisecrack, along with the humorous poem, novel, epic, satire, parody, farce, marionette, movie, variety radio program, radio comedy, comic strip, and cartoon. The list, with its now dated categories, is still comprehensive enough to serve as the model for a movie, television, or country and western awards ceremony. At the same time it mixes enough categories so that it is not certain whether Herzberg expects us to take it seriously or whether he is slipping in a category of his own—the list. In either case, Herzberg goes on to acknowledge that we can organize American comic literature according to its content, qualities, or tone as well as by its forms—according to whether it refers to professions, or subjects (such as men, women, children, animals), or even whether it refers to certain localities. He cites the humor of the South and the West and, more specifically, the humor of Texas as examples. Again it is not entirely certain whether he is kidding, though it seems a likely basis for these categories is Henny Youngman's gag file. But the implication that such regional classification is just one of a number of arbitrary ways of telling a joke misses the point that the structure of humor is itself shaped by the assumption of place.

There are, for example, the standard ethnic jokes which begin, "There was an Englishman, an Irishman and a Norwegian . . . ," a combination which in itself starts out pretty funny. But these are not regional humor so much as stereotypes, invariably the result of one culture characterizing another. We find more authentic regional humor in the conflict between the expectations historically generated within a social or political entity and the anxieties to which they give rise and from which they often evolved.

Eastern humor, for example, is associated with the urban centers, which remain its imaginative source if no longer its demographic focus. It is knowing, sophisticated, understated, self-deprecatory, ironic. It acknowledges the complexity not only of the content of experience but of its process. It accommodates the noise, the surface, the page, the frame. It is flat, and its figures, which appear to stretch toward the interior of experience, are, as in an Estes painting, brought back to the surface in reflected images. It calls attention to its own pretensions. It asserts the humor of helplessness rather than of heroism and somehow makes the helplessness the vehicle for survival.

We find these attitudes in Yiddish, a language which, in the United States at least, is associated with the urban clustering in the East and with vitality, diversity, and the process of acculturation. As Saul Bellow's fiction has shown, Yiddish has become an integral part of American spoken language. Yiddish, Bellow has pointed out, is "full of the grandest historical, mythological, and religious allusions [which] may get into the discussion of an egg, a clothesline, or a pair of pants." The acknowledgment of the immediate and material circumstances is accompanied by the refusal to accept them at their own limited assessment. It connects what exists with what one would like to see happen—without for a minute forgetting the difference between them.

In one of Grace Paley's lovely and unmistakably Eastern comic fantasies, a father urges his daughter to write a story which he can recognize as real, one with limits, "the kind De Maupassant or Chekhov used to write, one with recognizable people and what happened to them next." Try as she will, the daughter, who used to write that way, can no longer do so. "Everyone, real or invented," she tells him, "deserves the open destiny of life."

There is a thickness of detail in Grace Paley's stories that is qualified by the unlikely illumination such detail is made to yield. Ordinary facts are never allowed to get in the way of magical recognitions, and the comedy is not in what happens to people or even in what they feel or say about it but in the ability of various life-affirming voices to step around the grudging assessments of others about what they are entitled to expect of their own destinies and to counter them with some personal logic of their own.

The same kind of expectation informs the figures who animate Saul Bellow's search for an independent fate. The search is complicated on the one hand by the manipulation of social reality that isolates anyone who attempts such a search and on the other by the passive self-victimization of those who want to arrive at some informing spiritual meaning.

Bellow finds a rich source of comedy in this conflict between those who accept the contract they know they have signed with God and with other men and those who want to renegotiate its terms. The latter characteristically are vital, flamboyant figures for whom the possibilities of life are discovered chiefly in its immediate, material circumstances. They range from Mexican generals to African tribal chiefs. A typical example occurs in the novella *Seize the Day* (1956), in the person of the phony psychologist Dr. Tamkin. Restless, urgent, Tamkin is a small-time con man who swindles the hero, Tommy Wilhelm, out of his last $700. Even Tamkin's appearance betrays his character. Standing under indirect lighting, he appears to Tommy to have a "vain mustache . . . deceiver's brown eyes. His bones were peculiarly formed, as though twisted twice where the ordinary human bone was turned only once and his shoulders rose in two pagoda-like points. At mid-body he was thick. He stood pigeon-toed, a sign perhaps that he was devious or had much to hide." Even the color of Tamkin's check, made out for less than a promised amount, looks wrong to Tommy, "a false disheartening color," and his handwriting as well appears "peculiar, even monstrous . . . like a fourth grader."

From this devious character, however, comes a good deal of the book's wisdom. "Don't marry suffering," he advises the luckless hero, who earlier had learned from Tamkin that "The past is no good to us. The future is full of anxiety. Only the present is real." This wisdom in Bellow's subsequent fiction is exaggerated by more singlemindedly materialistic figures, whom Bellow characterizes as "Reality Instructors," those who want to punish the heroes with the lessons of the real. A prototype appears in the story "A Father to Be," in which Rogin, a thirty-one-year-old research chemist, dwells pessimistically on how the future will erase his individuality. In contrast to his own tenuous hold on things, Rogin encounters a delicatessen keeper whom he at once recognizes as "a New York man, toughened by every abuse of the city, trained to suspect everyone."

Against such suspecting realism is the ideal conviction of such major figures in Bellow's fiction as Herzog, Mr. Sammler, Charlie Citrine, and, most recently, Dean Albert Corde, who struggle with their separate fates but neglect the practical necessities of their environments and instead "go after reality in language." Their dreamy intellectualism serves, perhaps, as the juiciest object of Bellow's comedy, as these seekers attempt to figure things out, to understand them, to find some relationship between ideas, and, even more ambitiously, to discover a way to celebrate the particularity, the uniqueness of the individual without giving way to the inventions which attempt to disguise reality. Herzog, for example, who is credited with moments of sanity "but couldn't maintain the balance for very long," attempts to complete his dissertation showing "how life could be lived by renewing universal connections; overturning the last of the Romantic errors about the uniqueness of the Self." This ambitious project suffers a check when Herzog is abandoned by his wife, who shares with her lover, Herzog's best friend, some ideas of their own about the uniqueness of the self. Tragically sipping milk in Philadelphia (seemingly a double punishment in its own right), Herzog reassesses his situation. "Moses wanted to do what he could to improve the human condition," Bellow drily observes, "at last taking a sleeping pill, to preserve himself."

Like Herzog's effort to arrive at an "inspired condition" which would transcend the obligations of the here and now, George Grebe in "Looking for Mr. Green," a story which predates *Herzog*, attempts to match the world's energy with a complementary force of his own. In part an ideal notion like that of the welfare recipient's scheme to create a number of black millionaires, the gift of an astronomical observatory by a business tycoon, or the language courses enrolled in by Grebe's cynical boss, this attempt is also composed of the stubborn insistence that characterizes the takeover of the welfare office by Mrs. Staika, who succeeds by imposing her personality on the system. At the same time as he insists that the individual can be distinguished from the "huge hugging, despairing knot" of humanity, a knot which also appears to him as a "human wheel of heads, legs, bellies, arms," Grebe must accept the surrogate for that individual and remain content only with the possibility of finding Green rather than achieving a face-to-face confirmation of his existence. Green himself remains a symbol suggesting both the fallen world of appearances and the last things they stand for. In the real world, one set of conditions apply; in the ideal, another. Though it is not explicitly acknowledged, that necessity, too, serves as the basis for comic recognition in Bellow's fiction.

Throughout his fiction, Bellow has continued to insist on locating his comedy within a firmly rooted sense of place. "Deep down," Charlie Citrine's mistress tells him, "you're from Chicago after all," and Citrine admits that he is a city boy who has trouble telling one flower from another. Chicago is far from the East, from New York, which serves as the other pole of Bellow's imaginative landscape, just as it is equally distant from and equally close to such exotic places as Henderson's Africa. What Bellow conveys in them, however, is the exact texture of light on a given day and how the people on whom it falls are affected by it. He invests the complex windings of city streets or the atmosphere in a health club or a cafeteria with a mixture of ironic intelligence and undiminished hopefulness that provides an arena in which action is always informed by some thoughtful attempt to determine its consequences and, perhaps more importantly, its causes. It is in part the insistence on so involved and, finally, so hopeful an enterprise that marks Bellow's comic vision as unmistakably Eastern.

Paralleling the internal tension between the pragmatic and ideal elements in Eastern comedy are those characteristics which emerge in the contrasting figures of Rodney Dangerfield and Woody Allen, to take two physical extremes. Dangerfield has recently been seen in beer commercials, sweating, constantly wiping his face with a handkerchief, and surrounded by hulking athletes, none of whom seems even aware of his efforts to bring some order to their meeting. His disgusted insistence that he "don't get no respect," not his assumption that he is entitled to it, is the source of the humor. He is a big man who has been made to endure the humiliations of the little one, and the humor is also in part the result of his perplexity about what he continues to regard as a temporary if annoying situation.

Allen's humor, on the other hand, stems from what appears to be the normal order of things, a kind of hopelessness suggested by the titles of some of his collections—*Without Feathers* (1975) or *Side Effects* (1980). This hopelessness is meliorated, if at all, only by the parodic form, which allows the little man the opportunity alluded to in another title: *Getting Even* (1971). The most esoteric subjects are freighted with a recognition of a middle-class, Jewish, intellectual background which both celebrates its origins and makes fun of its pretensions. In Allen's story "The Whore of Mensa," a call girl who sells intellect rather than sex is described as coming from a Central Park West upbringing, socialist summer camps, Brandeis. Perhaps because of these credentials she is, the narrator boasts, "every dame you saw waiting in line at the Elgin or the Thalia." There are further references in the story to Alfred Kazin, *Commentary*, the Tanglewood Music Festival, Dwight Macdonald, and Hunter

College. Another story mentions Longchamps restaurant, Rutgers University, the Flat Iron Building, Saks Fifth Avenue, and the lyrics to "Rag Mop." In opposition to the chaos he sees everyplace, Allen observes that "Kant was right. The mind imposes order. It also tells you how much to tip." In still another story, a parody in the style of *The Autobiography of Alice B. Toklas*, the comic freighting of aesthetic ambition with local reference is occasioned in the narrator's boast that he went fishing with Hemingway for tuna and caught four cans.

Aware of his ineffectuality, Allen capitalizes on it to adopt an unheroic posture more resilient than, if not as glamorous as, that of more conventionally romantic figures. He owns a sword that in the event of danger turns into a cane so that he can limp away to safety. When Death comes, the manufacturer Ackerman interests him in a game of gin rummy. To Ackerman, the hooded specter is simply a businessman who bears a strong resemblance to Moe Lefkowitz. "I'm one of the most terrifying figures you could possibly imagine," Death protests, "and him I remind of Moe Lefkowitz. What is he, a furrier?" "You should be such a furrier," Ackerman assures him.

In contrast to the uncertainty the Allen character more commonly experiences, the humor of S. J. Perelman strides confidently into or out of the most exotic circumstances which turn out, after all, to be disguised versions of the same conditions so intimidating to Allen. On one occasion, Perelman finds himself "down Amboina way in the Moloccas [where] a chap buying bache-de-mer and shell in the Kai and Aru groups southeast of Ceram offers . . . a lift as far as Banda Neira in his Prahu. A filthy scow she was . . . manned by a crew of Bugi who'd slip a kris into you at the drop of a diphthong." Perelman, however, gets drunk and, when the ship sails without him, acknowledges, "It was the last ever heard of the lot of them," adding, "I probably would have heard more, except I had to rush back to New York to see about my Social Security."

Writing at a time when it was the individual, rather than the system, who was threatened, Perelman is reminded of that narrowly averted disaster only as a contrast to his more recent attempt to spend a night in his Greenwich Village apartment. Perelman described the building as a handsome old brownstone which still retained its original charm, given to it in part by "a cool, spacious stair well and a curving walnut balustrade worn smooth by the hands of many a defaulting tenant." The owner has apportioned the building among the greatest possi-

ble number of people by cutting up the premises into eight apartments. Perelman's own flat, a minute duplex in the rear of the top floor, "commanded an unbroken view of a health-food shop on Eighth Street," and was equipped with hot-water taps which supplied "a brown viscous fluid similar to cocoa." Trying to sleep, Perelman is abruptly awakened both by the frightening thought that he had forgotten to tip the janitor and by the racket made by Mrs. Purdy Woolwine, the first-floor tenant, who is attempting to anchor a galvanized rubbish can to the floor. "Her gleaming coiffure," Perelman reports, "was disordered and her face contorted like that of a wrestler in a Japanese print. At her side, a small, sallow man, whom I dimly recognized as Woolwine had driven a screwdriver under the lid with the aid of a hammer and was desperately trying to prise it off, obviously bent on disposing of a wastebasket heaped high with bottles and fruit rinds."

On another occasion, Perelman's attempts to get a night's rest are disturbed by the "annual outing of the Clan-na-Gael" beginning directly beneath his window. "Egged on by shrill cries of approval from the ladies' auxiliarity," he notes, "strapping bosthoons executed nimble jigs and reels, sang come-

S. J. Perelman

all-ye's, and vied with each other in hurling refuse cans the length of the street. The gaiety was so spontaneous and impulsive that I could not refrain from distributing several bags of water as favors. The gesture moved the crowd deeply, a few of its members even offering to come up and include me in their horseplay."

The manic humor barely concealed by a pretense of controlled urbanity that came to be identified with the *New Yorker* magazine evolved in part from the work of such writers as James Thurber and Robert Benchley, who were intimidated not by

James Thurber

the natural world but by society, not by hailstorms, drought, birth and death, but by marriage and divorce, home appliances, customs inspectors, automobiles (especially automobiles), women (especially wives), and any situation which called for a public performance. The titles of their works indicate something of the humiliations they are to endure: Benchley's *The Early Worm* (1927), *Benchley Beside Himself* (1943), *From Bed to Worse; or, Comforting Thoughts About the Bison* (1934), and *My Ten Years in a Quandary, and How They Grew* (1936), Thurber's *The Middle-Aged Man on the Flying Trapeze* (1935), *My Life and Hard Times* (1933), and *My World—and Welcome to It* (1942). Norris Yates has contrasted Benchley with the cracker-barrel school of misspellings, dialect, and general contempt for education and placed him in a tradition of university-trained humorists which found its literary anteced-

ents in the work of John K. Bangs. It was a humor of taste, of standards, and, above all, of apprehension about change and the urban forms it took. Benchley finds himself at a loss in the face of weekend visiting, looking into mirrors, any business dealing whatsoever, door keys, and any piece of machinery more complicated than a pencil sharpener. In contrast with Perelman's frenetic urbanity Benchley's whimsical acceptance of discomfort is suggested in "Do We Sleep Enough?" "Even eight hours' sleep do not do any good," Benchley decides, "if they are spent wondering what it is that is lying across the foot of the bed just over your ankles. Unfortunately I am without a dog at present, so there is no way for me to explain to myself what it is that lies across my ankles just after I get to sleep. All that I can do is hope that it is someone that I know." Known as a bad businessman "from one end of the country to just a little beyond the same end," he sees his kindergarten classmates now "dressed up in stiff shirts and . . . making marks on the back of envelopes." When he is finally invited to a business conference on the marketing of handkerchiefs, to which as a hay-fever sufferer he feels he may have something to contribute, Benchley finds most of his time spent in introductions and the rest in meaningless social small talk. With a visual imagination so limited, it "amounts practically to a squint," he finds it necessary to translate the scenes of the world's great literature into the streets of Worcester, Massachusetts, in order to picture them.

Unlike Thurber, Benchley is informal, even casual about his subjects, often seeming to arrive at them by chance, well after he has begun an essay. In "The Tortures of Week-End Visiting," he begins by discussing the labor situation, then quickly admits the irrelevance of the issue, which he introduced solely to give an element of timeliness to his essay. In "What—No Budapest?" Benchley quotes (from memory) from the 1802 Treaty of Ulm, which he cites as the authority for the decree abolishing Budapest. "The city," he writes, "has been getting altogether too large lately, and the coffee hasn't been too good, either." Later he supports his argument by quoting from Dr. Almer Doctor, Pinsk Professor of Obduracy, who in his volume *Vanished Cities of Central Europe* writes, "Since 1802 there has been so such place as Budapest. It is too bad, but let's face it!"

Where Benchley's dilemmas are, for the most part, inadvertent, Thurber's are uniformly adversarial. The difference emerges with particular clarity in their varying treatments of the same theme. In "Ladies Wild," Benchley makes the mistake of playing "Dealer's Choice" with three women sitting at the poker table. This turns out to mean "One card up, two down, the last two up. One-eyed jacks, sevens and nines wild, high low."

Robert Benchley

"I thought this was going to be poker," Benchley objects. "From then on you play it just like regular poker," the dealer reassures him. On his deal, he chooses regular draw poker, but when he wins with a full house, it is not much fun. For one thing, he has to explain what a full house is to the ladies, who suspect he is making up his own rules.

In Thurber's "Everything is Wild," Mr. Brush gets revenge for being made to endure an evening of social poker precisely by making up his own rules. First, however, he is forced to drive eighteen miles to Bronxville, where he has to ask directions from a barber with a foreign accent, who accompanies his explanation by making "swift, darting, angles in the air with his hand," at the end of which he has "turned completely around."

Brush's victory in improvising a game whose flexible rules are designed to give him the winning hand elicits from his wife an evil stare and the bitter accusation that he is a "terrible person." It is a small victory but, for Brush, a satisfying one, and it demonstrates that the "little man" can, occasionally, achieve some qualified success in overcoming the frustrations that describe the major part of his existence.

Typically these frustrations are induced by a world of machines and women; both prove not merely indifferent but actually hostile to his attempts to survive among them. Walter Mitty can intermittently retreat from his wife's insistent nagging and the insolent authority of policemen and parking-lot attendants to the triumphs of his imagination. Samuel Bruhl, who was "designed by Nature for an uneventful life [of] colorless coming and goings" and whose mild manner is reflected even in the "small stature of his dreams," finally convinces the police that he is the hardened criminal to whom he bears a superficial resemblance. And Mr. Martin in "The Catbird Seat" successfully trades on his reputation for blandness to commit the perfect crime. But for the most part, Thurber's fictional posture is that things are pretty bleak, likely to become bleaker still, and that there is not much we can do about it except, perhaps, watch out for our language.

The complexities of urban life which prompted these humorous responses to it as a means of survival were, of course, not always viewed as oppressive even when they were intimidating. Sinclair Lewis, for example, looked to cosmopolitan centers of the country and beyond them to those of Europe as a welcome escape from the deadening provinciality of the village, and even Theodore Dreiser, who saw nothing funny in it, recognized an element of wonder and vitality along with the destructive power of the city. Beyond this alternate view of the individual as a victim of isolation rather than congestion, Eastern humor began with some entirely different premises. Early examples appeared in Nathanael Ward's satire *The Simple Cobler of Aggawam in America* (1647), Ebenezer Cook's *The Sot-Weed Factor* (1708), and in Benjamin Franklin's *Poor Richard's Almanac* (1732-1757), but the dominant figure of early Eastern humor was that of the Yankee, who evolved during the first half of the nineteenth century from rustic to rascal. Though his antecedents have been traced as far back as Norse legends and the Mabinogian, the Yankee initially appeared on stage in Royall Tyler's 1787 play *The Contrast* and soon become a fixture in plays and in a growing body of newspaper verse by Tyler, William Biglow, and Thomas Green Fessenden, among others. By the turn of the century, as Jennette Tandy notes, he was fixed as a "harmless mixture of stupidity and shrewdness, intense patri-

Caricature of the Algonquin Round Table by Hirschfeld, clockwise from left: Dorothy Parker, Robert Benchley, Alexander Woollcott, Heywood Broun, Marc Connelly, Franklin P. Adams, Edna Ferber, George S. Kaufman, and Robert Sherwood; at back: Lynn Fontanne, Alfred Lunt, Frank Crowninshield, and Frank Case

otism and a talent for falling in love with the wrong girl."

In the 1830s, this low-comedy figure began to emerge as a shrewd commentator, capable of pointed social and political satire. Initially encountered in the work of Seba Smith and Charles A. Davis, he became Thomas Chandler Haliburton's Sam Slick of Slickville, Onion County, Connecticut, who often combined the image of the Yankee with the pugnacious qualities of the Kentucky ring-tailed roarer. The physical discretion, even reticence, of the Yankee peddler was thus blended with the bellicosity of his Western counterpart. Haliburton's biographer, V. L. O. Chittick, describes the conventional Yankee as "pious enough to most outward respects [but] simply not to be trusted when it came to a question of trading." Chittick continues, "Full of fun and good nature, a trait belied by his somewhat sanctimonious countenance, fond of a mirthful song or a merry jest, and adept at banter and ingratiating talk, he had, in spite of his well known

proclivities, a way of winning private confidence that usually left his customers poorer if seldom wiser. . . . He boasted inordinately about his race and his nation, and what is more, was always able to back up his most extravagant assertions with proof of fulfillment. He spoke through his nose, he drawled, and he mispronounced his words, but he was quite convinced that the New England English was better than that habitually used in the British Isles. He was as able a sailor as he was a salesman, and as competent at school-mastering as at 'fixin' a machine. . . . He was insufferably curious and inquisitive, but singularly uncommunicative when it was his turn to be interrogated. Although he was not of a combative disposition, and was even charged with cowardice, his rights were not to be infringed upon with impunity, for when hard pressed he was invariably successful, by one artful dodge or another, in bringing about his persecutor's discomfiture."

A more gentle satire about political oppor-

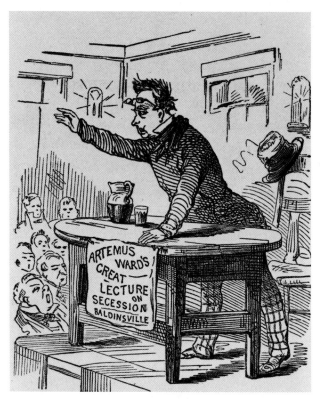

"Shall the Star Spangled Banner be cut up into dish clothes,"
Artemus Ward delivering his lecture on Secession

Thomas Chandler Haliburton

tunism was to be found in the character of Peter Brush, created by the little-known Philadelphia humorist Joseph C. Neal. Brush anticipates the small-time operator who finds himself a victim of the promises held out by more powerful social forces upon whom, he discovers, it is foolish to rely.

Although he had already become a recognizably national figure, the Yankee as an expression of political and social satire achieved what may be its definitive statement in James Russell Lowell's *The Biglow Papers* (1848) and *The Biglow Papers, Second Series* (1862). Here Lowell employs homely New England speech to comically puncture the hypocritical pieties of national sentiment which, through such doctrines as Manifest Destiny, justified a war with Mexico in which the real motives were territorial greed and the extension of slavery. The integrity of character associated with the Eastern heritage is continued in the commonsense dialect of Hosea Biglow and in the earnest if painfully pedantic moralizing of Parson Homer Wilbur. Tempted during a nostalgic reverie to trust to the renewal promised by Nature, Hosea is reminded by a Pilgrim ancestor not to depend entirely on Providence in resolving moral issues. "God hates your sneakin' creturs thet believe," Hosea is told. "He'll settle things they run away an' leave."

In contrast to Biglow's probity, Lowell opposes the picaresque opportunism of Birdofredum Sawin, who justifies his conversion to the Southern cause by pointing out the weaknesses in the democratic political system. In arriving at the character of Hosea, Lowell explained that he had "imagined to myself such an upcountry man as I had often seen at antislavery gatherings, capable of district-school English, but always instinctively falling back into the natural stronghold of his homely dialect when heated to the point of self forgetfulness." The Reverend Mr. Wilbur, he went on, "should express the more cautious element of the New England character and its pedantry, as Mr. Biglow should serve for its homely common-sense vivified and heated by conscience. The parson was to be the complement rather than the antithesis of his parishioner and I felt or fancied a certain humorous element in the real identity of the two under a seeming incongruity." Finally, Lowell found, he "needed some one as a mouthpiece of the mere drollery, for I conceive that true humor is never divorced from moral conviction. I invented Mr. Sawin for the clown of my little puppet-show. I meant to embody in him that half-conscious *un*morality which I had noticed as the recoil in gross natures from a puritanism that still strove to keep in its creed the intense savor which had long gone out of its faith and life. In the three I thought I should find room enough to express, as it was my plan to do, the popular feeling and opinion of the time."

Lowell intended to suggest the representative nature of his characters even by their names. The two sober ones were selected from memories of signboards or directories, the "impossible" Birdofredum by association with the extravagances of Manifest Destiny which signaled the "national recklessness as to right and wrong."

James Russell Lowell

Writing in 1848 to his friend C. E. Briggs, Lowell maintained he was "the first person to express the American idea," a claim which rested as much as anything else in his handling of the spoken dialect rather than the formal, written language. Offering to help Bartlett, "the Americanisms man," with a second edition of his book, he added, "I know Yankee, if I know nothing else." In addition to its topical satire, then, Lowell's humor issued from his attempt to reclaim the living language from classical authority. "It has long seemed to me," he noted, "that the great vice of American writing and speaking was a studied want of simplicity, that we were in danger of coming to look on our mother-tongue as a dead language, to be sought in the grammar and

dictionary rather than in the heart, and that our only chance of escape was by seeking it at its living source. . . ."

Lowell continued his insistence on an authentic, indigenous American literature in one of his last public addresses. Speaking at an authors' reading at New York's Chickering Hall in 1887 for the benefit of the Copyright League, Lowell acknowledged the initial American difficulty of developing a literature in the absence of historic associations but argued that the vernacular tradition pioneered by Cooper, Brockden Brown, and by William Ellery Channing, and extending as early in our history as Ward's *Simple Cobler of Aggawam*, had long since made American literature the equal of English. "We have developed [Lowell remarked], if we did not invent, a form of racy, popular humor, as original as it is possible for anything to be, which has found ideal utterance through the genius of 'Mark Twain.' I confess that I look upon this general sense of the comic among our people and the ready wit which condenses it into epigram, as one of the safeguards of our polity. If it be irreverent it is not superstitious; it has little respect for phrases; and no nonsense can long look it in the eye without flinching." Rooted in close observation of its immediate surroundings, Lowell contrasted this tradition of native humor with the work of those poets who could not free themselves from the influence of Europe. "Wut they've airly read," he wrote in *The Biglow Papers*, "Gits kind o' worked into their heart an' head / So's 't they can't seem to write but jest on sheers / With furrin countries or played-out ideers, / Nor hev a feelin', ef it doo n't smack / O' wut some critter shose to feel 'way back: / This makes 'em talk o' daisies, larks, an' things, / Ez though we'd nothin' here that blows an' sings,—" Lowell's orthography was thus an attempt to reproduce to its advantage a native dialect, not to make fun of it, and he even regretted making Hosea Biglow a poor speller. "There's no fun in bad spelling of itself," he wrote to Briggs, "but only where the misspelling suggests something else which is droll *per se*."

The regional humor which Lowell brought to its fulfillment, however, gave way to just such literary comedy in the work of such writers as Charles Farrar Browne, Henry Wheeler Shaw, and David Ross Locke. All Easterners by birth, they adopted the pose of unlettered showman and drifted across the country developing, as Walter Blair and Hamlin Hill point out, a unifying spirit of comedy. It was anchored in burlesque and in anti-intellectualism and was highlighted by mangled grammar and illiterate spelling. But while these comedians seemed to

Henry Wheeler Shaw

David Ross Locke, Samuel Clemens, and Henry Wheeler Shaw

identify themselves with the oral tradition of folk humor, it is on the recognition of its limits as perceived in literary terms that their comedy depended. Recently we have seen the reemergence of the Yankee con man, a wised up, cocky, resilient figure who, like Uncle Duke in Gary Trudeau's comic strip, believes only in his own survival. Blending the fierce personal conservatism of the National Rifle Association with the social indifference of the drug culture, Duke reveals the unlikely place at which these extremes meet. Unlike the conventional confidence man, Duke is convinced of his own competence in each of the roles he manages to adopt and is aggressive in demanding recognition of his amoral posture. As a covert government agent, for example, he is parachuted into Iran with several hundred thousand in funds designed to finance a counterinsurgency. "So I'm not Karl Malden," he tells the authorities who apprehend him, "sue me." Whether as ambassador, manager of a professional football team, or gun runner, Duke narrows the distance between the real and the ideal and thus affirms a sense of possibility that tradition-

ally has defined the American experience. It is the perspective on that experience, however, that remains Eastern. Throughout a series of panels, the scene often remains static, an ironic comment on the ballooned voices which remain foolish, suspended within it. These voices belong to a broad range of social types which include Duke's nephew Zonker, a laid-back college student whose ambition is to win the Sonny Bono Cocoa Butter Open tanning contest; Miles Potash, author of the running cult classic *Jogger Agonistes*; Lacey Davenport, a patrician congresswoman and her sometime aide, Joanie Caucus, a woman's rights activist. Yet the satire is filtered through an affectionate eagerness, in which each set of circumstances, each response is made to appear both representative and unique— and so necessary.

A complementary attitude can be seen sustaining Angel Martin of the television series *The Rockford Files*. Like Duke, Martin is similarly concerned solely with his own well-being and recognizes no scruple in formulating the many schemes he hopes will advance it. Angel's fast-talking adaptability, his single-mindedness in screening out all information other than that which will lead to some dishonest gain never deceive him about himself. He is cowardly, willing, almost at times eager to betray his friends. Above all, however, he is curious to see how far he can twist the fixed circumstances of fate to the open destiny of life. It is this quality, perhaps, more than any other that identifies Eastern humor—a going toward the world, hesitantly or confidently, to see what happens—not the discovery of self or an identification with the land. There is in Eastern humor a sense of history as meaningful, and perhaps that is what comes to us now as funny—and finally as reassuring.

South and Southwest

Sandy Cohen
Albany State College

The history of early Southern humor, like the history of all early American literature is one of slow movement from self-conscious imitation of English models to a true deep-structure humorous literature; that is, humor deeply seated in the folklore and traditions as well as the prejudices and idiosyncrasies of the area. Specifically, the models were the stylized, urbane eighteenth-century periodical essayists such as Addison and Steele. In a number of ways these models, reflecting long-established manners, customs, class, and caste that many of the new-world writers had left behind physically as well as psychologically, were inappropriate for Colonial Americans, especially in the South. Addison and Steele wrote gentle social satire that reflected their world of fashion, polished wooden ballroom floors, and gilded theater halls. The Southern colonist writer's world was one of violence, dirt streets, rough-hewn yellow pine floors, and Baptist meeting halls.

And yet the same satirical modes could be, and were, put to good effect by such early imitators as William Byrd. His *History of the Dividing Line betwixt Virginia and North Carolina*, written in 1728-1729, looks both forward and backward. Never intended for publication (it was not published until 1841), this journal which Byrd kept during his survey of the border reflects the style of the English essayists Byrd admired. But in his observations about the lazy men of North Carolina, we find elements of the sketches of frontier primitives popular around the time of the book's publication. Byrd's lazy man is a character type indigenous to the Southern humorists. The lazy man's direct descendants live in the fiction of Erskine Caldwell and William Faulkner.

With the first quarter of the nineteenth century came a new type of newspaper aimed not at large landowners alone, but at the common man as well. As Richard M. Dorson summarized it in his *American Folklore* (1959), in the 1820s "newspapers changed from four page production on good rag stock, printed in eastern seaboard cities, addressed to the educated upper class, and given over largely to foreign news. With the advent of Jacksonian democracy, a personal, chatty newspaper emerged, run by an individualistic editor in close touch with the local community he served, and conscious of his function as a dispenser of entertainment as well as news." As Walter Blair pointed out, such newspapers as the *Baltimore Observer* and the *Richmond Rainbow* published humorous sketches by local writers of local interest that aroused local readership. Much of the humor printed in these papers was of the tall-tale variety, which depended for its effect on mirthful exaggeration. Perhaps these were natural outgrowths of the very early American promotional literature of such early writers as John Smith, Thomas Morton, George Alsop, and the like, who described in all-too-glowing terms for an English audience the supposed Eden that was the New World.

Active in the early 1800s were Mason Locke Weems (1759-1825) of Mount Vernon, and James Kirke Paulding (1778-1860). Among other work, Weems wrote short, somewhat fictionalized biographies of famous Americans. His fifth edition of *The Life and Memorable Actions of George Washington* (1806), for example, first relates the story of young George and the cherry tree. Paulding's *Letters from the Old South* (1817) is both a spirited defense of the region and a small compilation of tall tales about the people and customs of the backwoods of early Virginia, which he knew from firsthand experience. These are told in the form of letters by an urbane narrator. This technique allows for comic distance and is used throughout Southern literature. Humorous almanacs were also popular in the first quarter of the nineteenth century, and the South had its share of them. Typical was *The Kentucky Farmer's Almanac of 1810*. Though for the most part this book differed little from those published in the North, it contained comic Southern tall tales.

What all of these early works have in common, what they share with the Southern humor that followed, even to the present time, is the strain of cruelty and violence they contain. They focus upon and laugh at physical deformity and moral depravity of all sorts; various forms of whippings and beatings lavished upon beast and man are humorously portrayed.

Most Southern humor of the early nineteenth century was not yet, strictly speaking, of the deep-structure type. Not only did ties still exist to the English essayists and novelists such as Maria Edgeworth, Southern humorists still very consciously wrote for an Eastern audience for two very good reasons: the publishing industry was centered in the Northeast, and most books were bought by Northerners. Southern writers did not yet feel confident enough to write their sketches and farces for any other reason than to describe their region and to preserve in writing the tall tales they heard orally. The conditions were not yet ripe for a full-blown, fully independent Southern humor.

Gradually, however, during the second quarter of the nineteenth century, Southern humor grew into an independent deep-structure form of literary expression. The first major talent of this period was Augustus Baldwin Longstreet (1790-1870). His masterwork was a collection of eighteen sketches, called *Georgia Scenes, Characters, Incidents, etc, in the First Half of the Republic*, published in 1835. Though written self-consciously for a Northern audience, and though it often reverts to the essayist style of Addison—and more often than Addison preaches about the vices it portrays—in its best passages *Georgia Scenes* retells the tall tales of the area in a vigorous, earthy style that features the dialect of the early backwoods Georgia that Longstreet knew in his youth, and which was already disappearing when he wrote. *Georgia Scenes* marks the official beginning of what is referred to as the humor of the Old Southwest. As Dorson defines it, "The 'humor of the Old Southwest,' rediscovered since 1930 by literary scholars, refers to the editions of reprinted journalistic sketches beginning with Longstreet's *Georgia Scenes* in 1835 and culminating in Harris's *Sut Lovingood's Yarns* in 1867."

In the introduction to their anthology *Humor of the Old Southwest* (1964), Hennig Cohen and William B. Dillingham describe the humorists: "The typical Southwestern humorist smiled easily but was no clown. He was a man of education and breeding who felt deeply and spoke with conviction. Usually he wanted to talk about politics. Often a devoted Whig, he was convinced that if the nation was to be saved from chaos and degradation, only the honor, reasonableness, and sense of responsibility of gentlemen—Whig gentlemen—could save it. Usually he was a lawyer and often also a judge, a state legislator, a congressman, or even a governor, but he might have been a physician, a planter, or, rarely, an actor, artist, or army officer. Frequently he was also a newspaper editor. For the South he felt a protective and defensive love, though he might have been born elsewhere. He was keenly angered by the North, which seemed to show little understanding of the South and its institutions. He defended slavery and, when the time came, secession, with passion. He was a relatively young man, but had already known frustration, and he was to know a good deal more of it before his life was over. Ambitious and hot-tempered, he endured defeat only with great personal pain."

These were hard times for the South, which was perceived by the North as a culturally primitive region that cruelly practiced slavery. The Southwest writers responded in humorous literature to this attitude with a mixture of parody and preaching. They wanted to prove that they were both humane and civilized; they also wanted to prove their vigor and masculinity. Most of their stories were told in a frame narrative that allowed them the lofty distance of the knowledgeable antiquarian on the track of gems of folklore among the back shops and markets of town and country. They wanted to be Hamlets—princes and wits who could as easily speak with a courtier as a clown. As such they used bold and even shocking imagery, hyperbole, situational comedy, slapstick, comic similes, and comic tension between urban and country folk, knowledge and ignorance. They were fond of retelling pranks, and, like the earlier Southern humorists, they laughed at deformity, misfortune, and the grave. Like much of the Southern comedy of today, the humor of the old Southwest was masculine, from lower social groups, about hunting, fishing, gambling, drinking, and fighting.

The hero of *Some Adventures of Captain Simon*

Clockwise from top: Augustus Baldwin Longstreet, Johnson Jones Hooper, William Tappan Thompson, George Washington Harris, Thomas Bangs Thorpe, Joseph Glover Baldwin; center: Charles Henry Smith

599

Suggs (1845) by Johnson Jones Hooper is an out-and-out rogue, and yet he is portrayed as the epitome of the Frontier Man. His motto is "It is good to be shifty in a new country." Like other characters created by the Old Southwestern humorists, he freely violates the Northern code of ethics. Suggs likes to take from the rich and poor, and keep it. He begins his career cheating his father at cards and ends it, appropriately, in politics. Both Mark Twain and William Faulkner acknowledged their indebtedness to this collection of picaresque tales. With Simon Suggs another conventional character in Southern humor came to full flower. That is the wise fool who plays the role of a clown to dupe his victim.

Southern humor flourished in the middle 1800s. The bear-hunting sketch is almost a separate genre in Southern humor and the single best example is Thomas Bangs Thorpe's (1815-1878) "The Big Bear of Arkansas" (1841). No other story of his ever comes close to this high point. William Tappan Thompson's (1812-1882) best work was *Major Jones's Courtship* (1843). In it he said he endeavored to "present a few more interesting specimens of the genus Cracker." The Georgia militia major, a backwoods semiliterate, is a genuine country bumpkin who wanders into and around the town in order to contrast its immoral, jaded city people with his own moral, naive country people. He mocks, sometimes bitterly, old-world manners and hypocrisy. In many respects derivative of the Northern humorists, Major Jones is something of a transitional figure between the humor of the North and the South. Henry Clay Lewis (1825-1850) wrote, under the name Madison Tensas (pronounced "tin saw"), M.D., *Odd Leaves from the Life of a Louisiana "Swamp Doctor"* (1850). This book is an account of the feverish (in both literal and figurative senses) lives of the people of the cypress bogs. Joseph Glover Baldwin's (1815-1864) *The Flush Times of Alabama and Mississippi* (1853) was a very popular and somewhat sentimental look at the earlier frontier days of his youth. Unlike the amoral Simon Suggs, Ovid Bolus, Baldwin's hero, plays pranks only on those who deserve it. Unlike the moralistic Major Jones, Ovid does not preach. The darkest and deepest of the Old Southwestern humorists was George Washington Harris (1814-1869). His master creation was *Sut Lovingood. Yarns Spun by a "Nat'ral Born Durn'd Fool"* (1867). Sut is by self-definition a man without a soul, living in a soulless world of bestiality. As Cohen and Dillingham say of him, "Sut is not merely a trickster, a Till Eulenspeigel or Pedro Urdemales. Himself the vic-

tim of a bad cosmic joke, he carefully selects his victims from a roster of prime drunkards, adulterers, lechers, sadists, bigots, and hypocrites. In the end his social role becomes clear. He has a triple function: advocate of healthy animal spirits, satirist, and scourge."

One must remember that for all their contemporary popularity, the Old Southwestern humorists faded from literary memory until they were rediscovered in the 1930s. They were not considered literarily respectable even in their own day. Most of the stories were the work not of professional writ-

F. O. C. Darley illustration for Henry Clay Lewis's Odd Leaves

ers, but of young professional men who hid behind pseudonyms in much the same way that respectable university professors of the 1940s and 1950s did when they wrote popular novels or detective fiction. Many of the Old Southwestern humorists regretted their youthful publications later in life. But the techniques, style, characters, and themes they introduced to Southern humor continued uninterrupted to succeeding generations of humorists. As Jesse Bier wrote, these Southern writers "were the first informal school to protest a growing nineteenth-century prettification of life, most absurdly idealized in the South."

The Civil War and Reconstruction years

(1861-1876) were fertile for Southern humor, the first period to produce writers of lasting international fame as well as contemporary regional celebrity. This time frame includes such minor figures as Charles Henry Smith (Bill Arp) and George Washington Cable; one major literary celebrity, Joel Chandler Harris; and one major author, Mark Twain. This new generation of writers added a bitter, satiric edge to Southern humor which often displaced their laughter, and, on occasion, made them lose their artistic perspective. Even major figures such as Twain gave in to it and paid the literary price.

Charles Henry Smith (1826-1903) is an example of a humorist who lost his perspective. He adopted the name Bill Arp and began his career in the footsteps of the Old Southwestern humorists with letters written by a semiliterate Georgia cracker who was meant to speak for the average Southerner against Northern interference in Southern affairs. But after the Civil War Smith changed the character of Arp by giving him literary pretensions. Gone were the funny misspellings and malapropisms. Arp became wise, insufferably so, and respectable.

The best and most successful guise for the Southern philosopher is the fool too naive to be corrupt. It is the naive fool, the Huck Finn, who is the most amusing, the funniest, and ultimately the

Joel Chandler Harris

most profound. To be successful comically and literarily, the Southern fool must speak more wisely than he realizes, no mean trick. This doubly ironic persona, twice removed from Joseph Addison, is the true Southern comic genius. Joel Chandler Harris (1814-1869), who wrote the Uncle Remus tales, is a case in point. Jesse Bier says in his *The Rise and Fall of American Humor* (1968) that in Harris's work "we face at once the most fetching and developed cynical inversions of the entire period and perhaps in the whole of American humor. He achieves his fame by turning traditional values inside out for a regional but dubious triumph, the true character of which he does not fully measure. The violent Uncle Remus tales are given in a duplicitous framework of gentle and charming interlocution between the boy and the old Negro retainer, and the fables themselves teach the wildest chicanery. The stories proposed a cynical ethic of success at any cost. . . . The Negro dialect is but a supreme ruse. . . . With our normal modern sensibilities, we tend to be amused and gratified at the spectacle of literal black slaves and ex-slaves seizing any psychologic means to their end. But we do not grant the ex-slave owners the same means to their renewed ends, and are scandalized when we penetrate the heavy disguise of Harris and the enormous but unconscious deception of his cynicism." But Harris's tales also play upon an assumed stereotypical view of the South and the Southerner involving a second layer of irony. In fact, survival at any cost, not success at any cost, is the ethic of Harris's tales. His laughter is not as cynical as Bier indicates; it is darker.

The War and Reconstruction period peaked and ended with the genius of Samuel Clemens/ Mark Twain (1835-1910), whose career embodies the strengths and weaknesses of the Southern Reconstructionist humorists, and, of course, went beyond it in its own original way.

In the wake of the stiff vengeance of Reconstruction there was in the South a vigorous outgrowth of a Northern school of novelists of manners. Though a minor school, these writers added a much needed lighter touch of gentle satire and social farce, though they were not primarily humorists. They included such representative figures as Ellen Glasgow (1873-1945) and James Branch Cabell (1879-1958). Ellen Glasgow, an extraordinarily prolific and popular novelist, wrote works of social history like many of the Southern novelists who followed her. The "Queensborough" of her novels was Richmond, Virginia. There were humorous elements in her work, which showed the influence of Dickens, Thackeray, and Balzac as well as her Southern literary ancestors. In turn, she exerted much influence upon the next generation of writers. She is gently satirical of the lingering vestiges of genteel Southern womanhood and of the largely sentimental view Southern writers had of a South crushed by "invasion." With Cabell and others of her school of realism, she helped remove the strains one finds in the humorists of the Old Southwest of insufferable nostalgia for a chivalric South that never existed. Twain mocked the Southern preoccupation with the pseudochivalric in his

saw it as an impediment to psychological growth, and he saw chasing after its unattainable goals as a waste of energy.

Like the mid-nineteenth-century storytellers, the early twentieth-century novelists continued the tradition of using vivid descriptions for comic effect and frame narratives for comic distance. But they discontinued the tradition of telling their stories through the eyes of a less-than-literate narrator (a technique inappropriate to a novel of manners). This last tradition was revived strongly by the next two generations of writers.

Mark Twain on lecture tour

satires set in the Middle Ages, but Glasgow satirized the chivalric attitude, the sentiment, false pride, and hypocrisy of the code of the Southern gentlemen and ladies. In this regard she certainly influenced the writers of the age of Faulkner, including Katherine Anne Porter, Eudora Welty, Thomas Wolfe, and Erskine Caldwell.

Though James Branch Cabell's satire was aimed more at the so-called New South he saw emerging out of Reconstruction, most of his career was spent in the fictional medieval town of Poictesme. He used this setting to satirize, as Twain and Glasgow did, old Southern romantic idealism. He

William Faulkner (1897-1962) was the towering figure of his age. His major tragic works, completed in the late 1920s and 1930s, contain many of the humorous elements of his later comic works. Many of those elements, including violence and physical comedy, prank playing and old-world tricksterism, farce and parody, situational comedy, comic epithets and dialogue, understatement, and hyperbole, were the progeny of Twain and the earlier Southwestern humorists, whose works he read carefully. As Walter Blair and Hamlin Hill point out in *America's Humor: From Poor Richard to Doonesbury* (1978), in his combination of slapstick and subtle

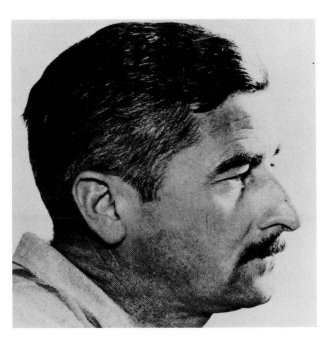

William Faulkner

humor that develops tragic themes, Faulkner anticipated the black humor that flourished after World War II.

The use of satire to challenge the underlying social structure reemerged in Southern humor between the world wars. This element was especially forceful in the 1930s. Erskine Caldwell's *God's Little*

Acre (1933), for example, uses the tall tale mixed with powerfully realistic depictions of Southern characters to portray people not so much culturally deprived as culturally bankrupt, their cultural resources having been depleted.

The next decades brought back a lighter touch to the Southern humorists, as in Jesse Stuart's *Taps for Private Tussie* (1943), about a Kentucky mountain family that defrauds the government by accepting insurance money for the "death" of their very-much-alive army son. When Mac Hyman satirized the army in *No Time for Sergeants* (1954) his intent was not social criticism, but strictly laughs.

One can see how Southern humor has come full circle in the postwar rise of the oral folk story and tall-tale tellers. The early Andy Griffith and Tennessee Ernie Ford portrayed naive backwoods babes speaking truths, seeing society from fresh new points of view, and continuing the tradition of the Old Southwest humorists. Tale-tellers such as Brother Dave Gardner and Moms Mabley reintroduced social satire to the Southern comedians' stage. And tall-tale tellers such as Jerry Clower continue the tradition of the "phunny phellows" with amusing characters to tell about and amusing stories to tell. That recordings by these comedians rarely sell well outside of the South, and that their major source of strength and income continues to be the South, attests to the fact that there is an independent Southern humor, and that it is alive and well.

Midwest

Nancy Pogel
Michigan State University

Three years ago *Chicago* magazine polled its subscribers to determine their favorite stories about the Midwest. The winner, Roger Simon's "Midwestern Friendliness," tells of a group of frontier explorers from the East who found their way to what is now Waukegan, Illinois. There they encountered their first Midwesterners, a band of Illiniwek Indians, who were known for their friendliness and their willingness to trade goods of equal value. After the explorers made a formal speech of greeting, replete with typical eastern floweriness, the strangers proceeded to trade the Midwesterners cheap beads and glass trinkets for the Indians' rich furs.

Finally, having successfully bilked the innocent natives of their riches, the Easterners prepared to leave. "We have taken your rich furs and given you our junk. You have seen our friendship, and we have seen yours. Now we go with peace." "No," said the chief, who had stood silently all this time, "You go with mustard." And the Indians fell upon the Easterners and ate them to the last man.

Although it is missing the familiar rustic narrator, the story is a throwback to nineteenth-century cracker-barrel humor: this traditional story of the triumph of wise fools over sophisticated strangers has the vestige of a frame, reminiscent of the oral tale; it includes local color to create the illusion of realism; it emphasizes the Midwesterners' fairness as well as their deflation of pomposity and sham with vernacular language. It concludes with an aphoristic moral: "Never fool with Midwesterners' friendliness" or "Never try to steal a fur coat in Waukegan." Perhaps more significantly, even though it is placed in 1621, it optimistically conveys a quality of the combined simplicity and wisdom of the common man that midwestern readers, more than 300 years after the story takes place and 100 after the tradition of this tale is supposed to have died, can recognize and respond to.

Surely the Midwest is not without its more sardonic wits and its cynics, but if there has been a dominant trend in heartland humor, it is the Midwest's persistence in recalling wisely foolish native figures, the familiar rhythms of the oral tradition, the homely common sense and the genial aphoristic style of cracker-barrel humor.

The Midwest can hardly claim that cracker-barrel humor is a heartland original, especially in the face of Jack Downing, Hosea Biglow, or Josh Billings. Nor in the light of Will Rogers's national appeal can the Midwest claim that it was the only late popularizer of cracker-barrel style in the twentieth century. What it can claim is that the Midwest contributed more to the survival of cracker-barrel characters and tales than is often believed—that its special contribution may have been the conversion of nineteenth-century humor's techniques and horse-sense perspectives from a rural to an urban environment, and that consequently nineteenth-century humor lingered in the Midwest and in our national humor long after historians mourned its passing.

Since Walter Blair wrote *Horse Sense in American Humor* in 1942, critics have conveniently divided the history of American humor into two main streams. Native American humor, variously called "horse-sense," "common-sense," or "cracker-barrel" humor, is the term generally applied to American humor from its beginnings through the nineteenth century. Modern or twentieth-century humor is usually categorized as one of several forms of so-called "dementia praecox" humor, or humor of "the little soul." Its beginnings are often associated with James Thurber, E. B. White, and

Robert Benchley, humorists for the *New Yorker* in the 1920s and 1930s.

Native American humor is traditionally the humor of the rustic yarn spinner; it is distinguished as a humor which had its foundations in solid, usually rural values; it is the humor of common sense that comes from a world that is conservative, stable, and predictable, although the humor itself may be racy and vigorous. Usually, the figures associated with native American humor range from Benjamin Franklin's Poor Richard to the local colorists and literary comedians of the late nineteenth century, and the tradition reaches its epitome in the early work of Mark Twain. This humor is a humor of "gumption and mother wit," of national self-confidence. Its heroes and spokesmen are usually ordinary men who know who they are, who exhibit some control over their predictable environment, and whose values are firmly grounded in commonsensical, everyday experience.

The humor of the little soul or dementia praecox humor, on the other hand, has often been associated with the loss of national self-confidence and the diminished lot of the ordinary individual in modern industrial times. Rather than positing a stable, predictable world of status quo values, the modern humorist finds his world bewildering and unpredictable, his values uncertain, and his ability to control the environment severely limited. His tone is anxious, neurotic, even hysterical; he sometimes escapes into his "inner space" or fantasy world of impossible dreams and horrible nightmares. He is the schlemiel, the victim in a world which often seems hopeless. This humor is often more urbane and sophisticated. According to Hamlin Hill, "It reflects the tinge of insanity and despair of contemporary society." Norris Yates has shown that the little-man character in modern American humor may be helplessly emasculated by big business, by even the simplest machines, by the mass media, by Darwinian biology, and by the rise of social science, progressive education, and Freudian psychology. Perhaps, above all, he is bedeviled by the tyranny of women.

While some observers merely lament the death of the old humor, others recognize a pattern today of relapses and reprieves; they find vestiges of the old humor in the newer form and the old humor existing alongside examples of the new. Even while he was presenting the distinction between native American humor and the dementia praecox school, Blair was reluctant to suggest that the older tradition was a cold cadaver. Later Hill and Blair found the overlap between the old and the new forms especially among stand-up comedians, on radio, and on television and concluded that, "Irreverent and irresponsible humorists, even less accommodating than other creative men and women, do not decamp when any fool can plainly see that in the interest of historical neatness they should absquatulate at once. As long as they get laughs, they don't at all mind being anachronisms."

Although scholars have long sought to define an "American" character and in so doing have tried to understand regional distinctions that make up the collective identity, they have frequently neglected the Midwest. This omission is not hard to understand, for unlike the East and the South, the Midwest does not have a clear European colonial image against which to define itself. Before the middle-western territories developed a distinctive frontier character it was preempted by the Southwest and Far West. Even though the Middle West was settled before the Far West, its population was a mobile one; its people were often only on their way somewhere else, and it was late in beginning to claim a stable regional identity for itself. By the time it did so, in the second half of the nineteenth century, its central, inland location and the diversity of its people had given rise to a national consciousness that tended sometimes to overshadow its regional character. David D. Anderson acknowledges this problem when he notes that, "So completely has twentieth century America accepted the leadership of a cultural Midwest that it fails, to see or to remember the sources of what it has made its own."

It is both the confusion of the Midwestern with the national identity and its "Johnny-come-lately" quality that best accounts for the general reluctance to come to grips with the Midwest as a distinctive region and that accounts in some part for its absence as a chapter heading in such standard histories of American humor as Jennette Tandy's *Crackerbox Philosophers in American Humor and Satire*, Constance Rourke's *American Humor*, Blair's *Horse Sense in American Humor* and *Native American Humor*, Jesse Bier's *The Rise and Fall of American Humor*, and the latest, most comprehensive Hill and Blair's *America's Humor: From Poor Richard to Doonesbury*. Therein, the traditional categories Down East, Southern, and Southwestern humor are credited with the formation of the older stream we accept as native American humor today. By the time they examine the late nineteenth century when the Midwest began to make its most significant contribution as a region, Tandy, Blair, and others have begun to

move away from considerations of regional influence to concentrate on topics such as local color and literary comedians and the gradual development of the newer, more pessimistic urban humor that they see as predominant in the twentieth century. Little time or attention, then, has been devoted specifically to the Midwest's special contribution to the history of American humor or to mainstream American humor as we know it today.

Since today's Midwest was the middle western or western frontier until around 1860, its earliest humor was the backwoods and riverman's variety that is currently anthologized under the headings of Frontier, Western, or Southwestern humor. The robust, bellowing exaggerations and tall tales of bravado ascribed to legendary heroes like riverboatman Mike Fink, the bully of Ohio; Sal Fink, the Mississippi Screamer; and frontiersman Davy Crockett traveled by word of mouth and by the rivers of the Ohio country into Illinois and Indiana just as they traveled up and down the Mississippi from New Orleans to Saint Louis. Eventually, as the population of the Midwest became less mobile, those stories were to be softened into the thrice-told, less-active tales and slower rhythms of Midwestern settlements.

Shrewd Yankee stories and cracker-barrel types imported from the eastern states were also adopted and adapted by middle western experience; early on Rourke and Tandy observed that the Yankee often came to be viewed more skeptically than positively as the newer backwoods territory began to define itself in contrast to the more commercial and settled eastern seaboard. Tandy notes that Timothy Flint was "much annoyed on his flatboat journey down the Ohio River in 1816 by the prejudice in Indiana, Ohio, and Kentucky against New England."

Emigrants and news traveled over the mountains from the East and up and down the rivers through the middle western frontier and met with additional emigration and communications from the South, and as rural Southern regional humor came to take on a distinctive character, it too, albeit in its milder, less grotesque forms, left its mark on the heartland imagination especially along the southern borders of the Midwest. All the regional branches of early American humor, then, traveled through the middle western frontier and left a residue of stories and humorous types and styles out of which the Midwest would create the amalgam that it would popularize and preserve for the twentieth century even after regional humor and the rural native tradition was reputed to have become a style of the past.

What the Midwest tended to accept and what it left behind as it was exposed to and accumulated the humor of other regions was dependent in part upon its geography and upon the people who came to live in the seven states that constitute the geographical boundaries of the Midwest—Ohio, Indiana, Illinois, Wisconsin, Michigan, Iowa, and Minnesota for the purist—and their neighbors in parts of Missouri, Kansas, Nebraska, and the Dakotas where rainfall and weather patterns are more like that of the central states than like that of the Great Plains. In *The Great Plains* Walter Prescott Webb considers the ninety-eighth meridian a convenient boundary line between areas that are either dominantly agricultural or dominantly grazing lands.

Fundamental to any sense of the midwestern imagination must be its rural agricultural character and a geography that except in the far northern, mineral-rich area, is a fertile land with adequate rain, ideal for farming. Being primarily an area of relatively isolated farms and small towns, the Midwest was receptive to the homely gossip and tales of the cracker-barrel philosophers. The Midwest was, simply speaking, an appropriate place for rural humor to flourish.

The affinity for proverbialism as well as for antiproverbialism grew not only out of the Midwest's proclivity for teaching religious lessons by means of epigrams, but also from the widespread use of *McGuffey's Reader* in the nineteenth century. The Calvinist influence from the East that made its impression in the northern Midwest of the nineteenth century may also have played a part in modifying harsher Southern and Western tales into more genial local stories.

The people who came at first for free land or in search of a more open society in the midwestern country were strongly individualistic. Their lives were influenced by those principles inherent in the Northwest Ordinance of 1787 that prepared the way for statehood—the eighteenth-century principles of rationality and order that extended into political and human affairs—and the Jeffersonian faith in the yeoman farmer. From the beginning the Midwest was abolitionist territory. In the nineteenth century those values were translated into a belief in progress and the commonsensical values espoused in the *McGuffey's Reader*. The Midwesterners were democratic in their social views and more diverse in their political affiliations than mythmakers assume. Sinclair Lewis and H. L. Mencken notwithstanding, they tended to accept human rights and tolerance of

others, in principle at least, as a rational way of life. Midwestern humor was never as overtly caste-conscious as humor in the South.

Although they respected education and encouraged it as much or more than some other regions, the Midwesterner's faith was primarily in the pragmatic and tangible, and while they sometimes emulated the established East or suffered from a sense of inferiority before it, they tended to distrust self-important demonstrations of sophistication and high culture.

In the Civil War period and well into the 1870s, a clear division is sometimes discernible in the Midwest among Eastern, Southern, and Southwestern influences. Among the earlier journalistic humorists of the period, like Joseph M. Field and John S. Robb, who both wrote in Saint Louis, the influence of the Southwest and West is most pronounced, while in the work of David Ross Locke (Petroleum V. Nasby) (1833-1888), the Southern influence prevailed.

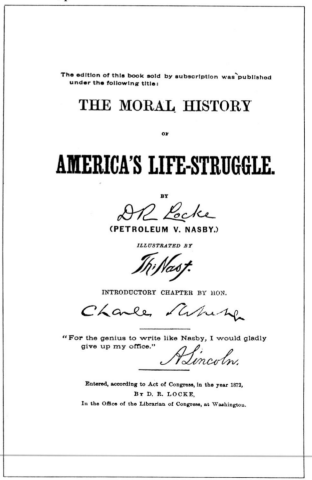

The edition of this book sold by subscription was published under the following title:

THE MORAL HISTORY

OF

AMERICA'S LIFE-STRUGGLE.

BY

D R Locke
(PETROLEUM V. NASBY.)

ILLUSTRATED BY

Th Nast.

INTRODUCTORY CHAPTER BY HON.

Charles Schurz

"For the genius to write like Nasby, I would gladly give up my office."

A Lincoln.

Entered, according to Act of Congress, in the year 1872,
By D. R. LOCKE,
In the Office of the Librarian of Congress, at Washington.

Notice about subscription edition of The Struggles (Social, Financial and Political) of Petroleum V. Nasby, *included in late printings of the trade edition*

Locke was born in New York, but he moved to Ohio, where he became writer and editor for a series of newspapers before eventually going to work for the *Toledo Blade*. Locke's greatest contribution to Midwestern humor and to the national mainstream was as a literary comedian who used verbal humor and what Walter Blair calls the humor "of phraseology rather than of character," in a manner similar to that of Artemus Ward, who also learned his trade in Ohio.

and 1950s. Modified versions of that sentimental impulse were also apparent among some of the later nostalgic local colorists such as Edward Eggleston and James Whitcomb Riley and in the journalistic humor and lectures of Robert Jones Burdette (1844-1914).

Burdette, a newspaperman from Pennsylvania, grew up in Cumminsville, Ohio, and worked on the *Peoria* (Ill.) *Review* before he went to Burlington, Iowa, to become "The Burlington Iowa

"Suffer little WHITE Children to Come unto Me," Thomas Nast drawing of Petroleum V. Nasby

While his pro-union Abolitionist point of view that so delighted Abraham Lincoln was clearly Northern, and although he often wrote about national issues using local Ohio politics as a take-off point, his Nasby letters, written in the persona of an unreconstructed Confederate sympathizer, looked stylistically more to the South than to the North or to the East. Although Nasby is more concerned with talk than with action, his humor is most reminiscent of Sut Lovingood and Simon Suggs, whose tales were frequently reprinted in his papers along with the Nasby letters.

Europe and the high culture of the urban East surely influenced the sentimental style of "sweet singer" and unconscious humorist Julia A. Moore, whose poetry was burlesqued not only by Mark Twain and others in the nineteenth century, but by writers such as Max Shulman as late as the 1940s

Hawkeye Man." He gained national fame with his "Hawketems" and soon took to the lecture circuit. His "Rise and Fall of the Mustache," a long piece that mixed a good deal of polite language and sentimentality with moments of more robust humor, was a favorite of lecture audiences.

All of these regional influences came together by the post-Civil War period in the work of the exceptional artist humorist Mark Twain of Missouri, who would go on to alter the entire course of American literary history. Although Twain surely had much to do with the survival of cracker-barrel humor, and a case could be made for Twain as a Midwestern humorist, that story requires a book, and Twain is finally a figure claimed by all regions and by the world. It is the lesser, but nonetheless important Midwestern figures that most concern us here.

The humor that emerged as Midwestern in the later nineteenth century was commonsensical, rural, cracker-barrel humor that was made up of qualities common to other rural regions with the enthusiasms of the frontier tales muted to quieter exaggerations and the grotesqueness of earlier Southern humor less prominent. While gossipy Yankee tales left their mark, Midwestern humor often retained a suspicion for the urbane and more sophisticated pretensions of the literary East.

As C. Carroll Hollis has observed in his fine article on nineteenth-century rural humor, such humor came "from a realistic country background using humorous devices of exaggeration, mala-propisms, euphemism, misquotation, mixed meta-phor, anti-climax, and understatement, and was written for an audience composed of rural, village or small town people, or if in the city, those of rural background or conviction." Often through per-sonae or through stories of regular established characters, it "surveyed the institutions and con-cerns of American people to show the disparity between what people thought some institution was supposed to perform and what actually took place, to point out folly of exaggerated concern with some part of life to the neglect of other equally important parts, to ridicule the silly sentimentality of the period."

Although earlier nineteenth-century humor created the foundations, it can be argued that the last decade of the nineteenth century and the early decades of the twentieth—when the Midwest took on a recognizable national identity and Chicago be-came the nation's second city—was the heyday of Midwestern humor. During these years Midwestern humor had its clearest definition and made its most important contributions to the mainstream. As the frontier closed and nineteenth-century cracker-barrel humor was reputed to be dying, Midwestern journalistic humorists such as Charles Bertrand Lewis, Frank McKinney Hubbard, George Ade, Finley Peter Dunne, and others like them received national recognition and showed that reports of cracker-barrel humor's death had been greatly exaggerated. While humor of the East was gradu-ally becoming more cynical and sophisticated in the face of industrialization, mass immigration, and ur-banization, rural Midwesterners in the city or in the village were reading cracker-barrel humor in the columns of newspapers, sometimes in rustic dialect and sometimes in "better" English. And graphic artists and editorial cartoonists such as John T. McCutcheon of the *Chicago Tribune*, Jay (Ding) Darling of Iowa, and even Art Young from Ohio

Caricature of Finley Peter Dunne, by Spy

drew pictures of their Midwestern small-town backgrounds for the city dailies to preserve the homespun tradition.

Unlike literary comedian Locke, whose style most closely resembles the broad Southern tales of Simon Suggs and Sut Lovingood, Charles Bertrand Lewis (M.Quad) (1842-1924), "The Detroit Free Press Man," was typical of those midwestern jour-nalists whose humor heralded the important turn-of-the-century years. His *Quad's Odds*, a collection of columns from the *Free Press*, is a curious mixture of strictly serious saccharine pieces like "little Tom," an elegy for a young boy, and items in a more humorous vein.

Included in his collection are humorous stories such as Twain incorporated into his longer works. M.Quad writes about steamboat explosions and life on rivers, railroads, funerals, mining in Nevada, courtrooms, chromo and life insurance peddlers and unrepentent reporters; he parodies or burlesques high-culture literature and its stereotypes such as elegiac poetry, the glorification of the good child, and terrifying tales of villainous Indians.

Aphoristic humor and rustic dialect, exaggeration, understatement, and comic similes pepper Lewis's columns. "Book agents," he notes, "stick to their game like a burr to a boy's head." Pretentiousness is deflated in a number of his stories. In "Up Among the Splinters," his tale of the steamboat explosion, he describes the passengers' fight to be among those who are saved. "One man got hold of a door and warned that he was a member of the legislature, and must therefore be saved, but we held a mass convention and decided that the Constitution of the United States guaranteed equal rights to all men and we crowded him along." With aphoristic good humor M.Quad wisely concludes, "It ain't good to be blown up. There are better ways of ascending and descending."

Many of Lewis's pieces are more rural than urban in their settings and subject matter, but others, like the tale of "The Self Made Men of Detroit" or "A Bribe" merge the style of the rural story

Charles B. Lewis

with the urban situation. In "A Bribe" a ragged-looking boy smoking a stub of a cigar is strolling around Detroit's Southern depot, when a philanthropist tried to give him ten cents. " 'Take it, bub, I feel sorry for you.'

" 'No yer don't,' exclaimed the boy, drawing back.

" 'Why, it's a free gift—I don't ask anything for it,' replied the man.

" 'I know you,' continued the boy, his eyes twinkling; 'You want me to promise to grow up and become President, and I ain't going to tie myself up for any man's ten cents!' "

A sidelight on this story is the commonsensical view of life that punctures false philanthropy and adult platitudes with a wise fool's aphoristic rejoinder.

In "That Smith Boy," one of M. Quad's bad-boy stories in the manner of George W. Peck, the urban setting and the boy's language that includes urban slang predate George Ade's "Artie." The narrator wakes up one morning to "loud reports of muskets," and before breakfast is over, he learns that the Smith boy has painted the lamp posts on his street red, white, and blue, barber-pole fashion. When he goes out to talk to him he finds the boy boring a hole in a shade tree in preparation for setting an explosive charge. M. Quad recalls, "I smiled kindly, and said to him: 'Good morning, bub.'

" 'Morning, old two-and six!' he replied.

" 'Are you that Smith boy?' I asked.

" 'I'll bet on't!' he answered.

" 'I'm glad to meet you,' I continued; 'I hope you'll be a good boy, go to school, and not make us any trouble. If you are good we shall all like you.'

" 'I kin take keer of myself, old Limburger!' he answered, giving my dog a kick."

In 1899 M. Quad collected his stories of the Bowsers, a tyrannical husband and a long-suffering, commonsensical wife in *Mr. and Mrs. Bowser and Their Varied Experiences*, wherein he explored the problems of an urban couple in a manner that would later become the stock and trade of radio and television domestic comedy. His book was dedicated "To the Married Women of America with the Author's fullest sympathies, but likewise his advice not to 'talk back' in case Mr. Bowser seems inclined to start a row." But in his genial fashion Lewis also acknowledged that though he wrote of Bowser's faults, "There is much good to be found in him."

Humorous personal columns such as M. Quad's that appeared in newspapers of both small towns and larger cities in the later part of the nineteenth and well into the twentieth century permitted the humorist a good deal of latitude in subject matter and approach. Norris Yates observes that humorous columns were the "most important single medium of American Humor" between 1900 and 1920. The best-known writers of such columns—Kin Hubbard, George Ade, Finley Peter Dunne, and Ring Lardner—came from and wrote in the Midwest.

Frank McKinney (Kin) Hubbard (1868-1930) from Bellefontaine, Ohio, drew Abe Martin, a thoughtful country loafer who dressed in striped pants and liked to make comments on "big wigs."

ABE MARTIN
of Brown County, Indiana

Kin Hubbard's frontispiece for Abe Martin, Hoss Sense and Nonsense

Although Hubbard wrote for the *Indianapolis News*, Martin's territory was Brown County, Indiana, from which any of Martin's neighbors, Lemmie Peters, Squire Marsh Swallow, Miss Bonnie Grimes, and Ludlow Mapes also might deliver a weekly column with a by-line. Abe Martin himself appeared in a daily cartoon beneath which appeared one or several aphoristic captions written in the cracker-barrel

style, and billboards and signs in the background to Hubbard's drawings often made a comment of their own upon the subject of the day.

As a loafer and an outsider who was, nevertheless, one of the community, Abe could comment with the special editorial freedom that has often been afforded to cracker-barrel characters. "Next t' settlin' back an' lightin' a nickel cigar at th' dinnertable, th' worst breach o' good taste is tryin' t' separate a fishbone from a mouthful o' mashed pertaters," Abe said. With cracker-barrel wisdom Abe observed that, "A feller will stop at any kind of hotel if his feet hurt," and that, "the hardest thing is writing a recommendation for someone you know." Like other Midwestern humorists of the era Hubbard was less self-righteous than he was tolerant of his neighbors' frailties when they strayed from the village ideal. Thus he reported without being judgmental that "Miss Tawney Apple has contracted neuritis from chilled cocktail shakers." And although he is concerned about the changes he sees around him, about threats to traditional institutions like the family and marriage, he is amiable in his comments. Abe thought that the 1920s flapper was "interestin' " but he hoped, too, that "She gits safly thro' an' marries an' lives as happy as could be expected." Commonsensical Abe often deflated pretentiousness as when he observed that "Tell Binkley jumped into his new $3,000 tourin' car and hurried as fast as she could to the poor farm," and when he noted, "It must be great to be rich and let th' other feller keep up appearances." He also poked fun at politics and politicians as he perceived that "The election isn't far off when a candidate can recognize you across the street" or that "Politics make strange postmasters."

In his study of Hubbard, William McCann recalls one remarkable bit of unpublished aphoristic wisdom that defies Robert Benchley's insistence that cracker-barrel humorists were only sentimental and boring. This line, that editors found in bad taste, read, "Nothing annoys a vulture like biting into a glass eye." Readers from any part of rural America who had migrated to the city, writes Norris Yates, "could feel that here was the world of horse troughs and horse sense they had left behind." Abe's syndicated cartoons and captions appeared in 300 papers and in nearly 200 cities and towns beginning in 1910. Those cartoons are still running today, reprinted on the back page of the *Indianapolis News* which only occasionally has to alter a billboard or sign in the background of the frame to bring it up-to-date.

Jesse Bier, who called Hubbard "Simply a

George Ade who stayed home," shows surprise "that the mild and rural Hubbard should be popular at all in a time of highly antithetic or ascendant urban comedy." The question implied in Bier's surprise pertains not only to Hubbard but to other popular cracker-barrel humorists such as Ade and Finley Peter Dunne in this same period. An additional question, then, is why so many of these humorists were Midwesterners.

There are, of course, a number of answers to this question. One is Bier's own, that the popularity of crackerbarrel humor in the early twentieth century is simply the "result of nostalgia in a period of accelerated urban growth" because "during transition the public values the fading types all the more as they become anachronized." C. Carroll Hollis's more positive theory credits rural humor with helping to maintain the sanity of the nation during "a time of seething social change." Seen in relationship to the rise of Chicago in a predominantly rural area, Hollis's theory goes far toward explaining the importance of Midwestern humor during this time and the special relationship of Midwestern humor to its audience.

In his sensitive study of Chicago and its humor at the turn of the century, appropriately entitled *Small Town Chicago*, James DeMuth characterizes Chicago of 1890, not as a city so much as a "frontier boomtown," whose population had increased from 368,000 to nearly 1,300,000 between 1871 and 1893. That population was made up not only of many people who had recently moved to Chicago from rural midwestern villages, towns, and farms, but a great many new foreign-born settlers who had come to Chicago predominantly from rural areas of southern and eastern Europe and Ireland. In Chicago, the newer settlers tended to gather in ghettos and neighborhoods that in some ways resembled the small European towns or midwestern villages that they had left behind. Confronted not only by the difficult experience of transplantation itself, newcomers to the city also had to face significant culture shock as they moved from slower paced cultures and traditional values into the faster, rougher life of the city. Both Chicago's population and the people who remained in the rural Midwest felt the impact of rapid social change at the beginning of the twentieth century, and both groups were disposed to accept a humor that was local and neighborly. People were reminded of their rural roots on the one hand and on the other they were provided with a perspective which helped them to adjust to a new environment. By transposing some of the values and the familiar characters and types

into the urban setting, the Midwestern cracker-barrel humorist served an important social function in providing stability and assurance and in building a bridge from rural to urban America.

While Chicago in the 1890s and early twentieth century suffered from its share of nationwide economic depressions, unemployment, painful workers' strikes, and social problems common to the rise of cities everywhere—problems that made the more perceptive question concepts of progress and the American dream—Chicago's spirit was still in great part forward looking and optimistic. Host for the Columbian Exposition of 1893, railroad and steel center, the nation's "second city," one that had rebuilt after the great fire of 1871, still retained for native Midwesterners and foreign-born settlers a promise of progressive times and conditions. It was primarily in this positive spirit that the Midwestern cracker-barrel humorists wrote in the late nineteenth and early twentieth centuries.

Chicago was also a journalistic center, boasting many great papers, most notably the *Chicago Tribune* and the *Chicago Daily News*. Enterprising young writers were given an opportunity to practice their craft as personal columnists in a town where the way had been paved by Ten Eyck White's "horse reporter" and his "Lakeside Musings" and especially by Eugene Field's local commentaries in his column, "Sharps and Flats." The tone at the Journalists' White Chapel Club was not conservative or retrogressive, but bohemian and liberal. Although they employed traditional techniques and espoused a familiar commonsense approach to life, Ade and Dunne tended to be less concerned with preserving the old than with using the rural, village style in the way native humorists always had, to allow themselves more editorial leeway and to get past the editorial censors, to comment on the habits and foibles of the population, and to poke fun on behalf of the common man—to burlesque high culture, social stuffiness, and wrongheaded politicians.

The rural cracker-barrel style that was transposed to the city in the columns and stories of humorous journalists Ade and Dunne was also evident in the editorial and social cartoons of graphic artists. John T. McCutcheon is best remembered in Chicago today for his illustrations for Ade's "Chicago Stories" and for the "Indian Summer" cartoon that is still reprinted in the *Tribune* each year. McCutcheon drew cartoons filled with rural folks, dogs, and young boys, "next-door" characters concerned about crops and near-at-hand problems. McCutcheon's own background included exchanging news and jokes around a potbellied stove in Dan Johnson's country store in Elston, Indiana, as a child. The cracker-barrel values and traditions stayed with McCutcheon through his "Bird Center" series, gathered into a book in 1903, in which he portrayed small-town life in "Bird Center," Illinois, in a mildly satirical fashion. The residents of Bird Center were regarded comically but respectfully, and McCutcheon conveyed, sometimes too sentimentally, the intrinsic innocence of the people and their lives. Although more serious students of the scene such as Sherwood Anderson, Edgar Lee Masters, and Sinclair Lewis would present a less charitable view of small-town social life, McCutcheon claimed throughout his career that his portraits were not sentimental but real and that his cartoons applied to rural as well as to city life. In his autobiography, *Drawn from Memory* (1950), he wrote: "If the series had any definite purpose, it was to show how very . . . optimistic life may be in a small town. If it seems to satirize some forms of gaiety in the smaller communities, or to poke a little good-natured fun at some of the ornate pretensions of society in the larger communities, so much the better. . . . You will find Bird Centerites in large cities as well as small ones, and it is regretted that there are not more of them . . . they are all good, generous, and genuine people." In one of the Bird Center cartoons, "Social Happenings at Bird Center, Illinois," in which "Mrs. Withersby Entertains the Bird Center Reading Circle," the motto over the door is "Live and Let Live."

McCutcheon's cartoons did not all picture rural areas; he could also concern himself with social issues in and around Chicago. Some of these, like "At Last We Are to Have Fox Hunting Near Chicago" pictures a number of little figures on horseback riding over treeless farmland. Guiding the riders are signs reading, "This way to the fox." And McCutcheon pokes fun at eastern high culture as well as Chicago politicians in a four-panel cartoon "Our Chicago Aldermen in Boston." In that drawing, when the Brahmins ask the Chicagoans, "And do you not love Holmes, the dear old Autocrat of the Breakfast Table?" the Midwesterners reply enthusiastically: "You bet! There's nobody like Sherlock for a good, rattling detective story." Although McCutcheon sometimes wielded the pen in anger or to attack corruption, as in his Bath House John cartoons or in his picture of a padlocked exit door at the Iroquois theater shortly after the famous fire there in 1904, in most instances, where McCutcheon takes a strong stand the issues are broadly humane rather than partisan or narrowly political.

McCutcheon's work from the days on the

Chicago Record through forty years with the *Chicago Tribune* was largely a testimony to the lasting appeal that Midwestern cracker-barrel humor had for his audience, even as the new humor was establishing itself in the East.

George Ade and John T. McCutcheon

Although McCutcheon's tendency to political insularity was not always the rule, the belief in the common man and his cracker-barrel style remained constant through two world wars. And that style was not unique to McCutcheon. Similar sentiments appear in the editorial cartoons of Michigan-born Jay Norwood (Ding) Darling whose canvases cluttered with local figures celebrated the common man in cracker-barrel manner for the *Des Moines Register and Tribune* and later for the *New York Herald Tribune* syndicate during the same period.

John T. McCutcheon and his Chicago roommate in the 1890s, George Ade, produced "Stories of the Streets and the Towns" for the *Chicago Record* from 1893 to 1900. These detailed pictures of the local urban scene began to do for Chicagoans what the small-town columnists had done in the villages of the Midwest during the preceding decades. From these stories Ade chose to develop several of his most popular characters. The adventures of Artie

Blanchard, a young office boy with a gift for street slang, were soon collected and published in 1896 in book form. Although Artie was clearly a city man, he always gave the impression that he was not far removed from his rustic antecedents and that his adamant insistence on a city identity and city language was a newcomer's defensive response. His sharp talk is filled with both his enthusiasm for the city and his longing to be assimilated and to be successful on the city's own terms. At the same time he struggled to hold on to his native integrity. His energetic slang is urban exaggeration reminiscent of the frontier tall tales. It implies an optimistic bravado, but it also hides his vulnerability. When Artie can't go to a charity ball, he laments his plight in slangy style but counts his savings at the same time. "Oh I could be there, I guess, if I wanted to. It's a case o' ten bucks and rentin' one o' them waiter suits. I know boys that went down there and put on a dizzy front, and next day they had to make a hot touch for a short coin so as to get the price of a couple o' sinkers and a good old 'draw one.' "

Ade's Artie must have satisfied a combination of needs in both big-city and small-town audiences. To city newcomers and to those who remained in the villages, his character and his localisms must have been a comfortable reminder of the small-town commonsense humor with which they were familiar. A wise but laughable rube who was always trying a little too hard to make it, he was also the embodiment of readers' expectations and their optimism. Readers could both identify with him and feel superior. Ade provided a significant transition from village to city as he urbanized cracker-barrel techniques and figures.

Artie encountered universal human problems while courting women and trying to make ends meet, but he also had to deal with the special difficulties of drinking, gambling, office, and city politics that were more specific to big-city life at the turn of the century.

Like Mr. Dooley's Hennessy or McKenna, Artie's Miller, a fellow employee, was there to listen and to remind him of what is decent when his best cracker common sense fades now and again before the glittery promise of big-city success and money or temptations from shrewder-than-he city types. Although city life tends to bend the rules of traditional village morality somewhat, Artie's private value system is decent, and much of his slangy, aphoristic observations are ultimately commonsensical in the old cracker-barrel style.

When Alderman Jim Landon, "a main squeeze" in his ward, seeks reelection and offers Artie a good job in a downtown office in return for his support, Artie debates whether to take on the deal. In the process Ade makes fun of the politician's false promises and of Chicago politics: "he was goin' down to city hall and change the whole works. He was goin' to clean the streets and jack up the coopers and build some schoolhouses. Jimmy says to 'em: 'Throw things my way and I'll be Johnny-on-the-spot to see that everything's on the level.' The talk was so good it went. Well, you know what happened to Jimmy when he got down there with them Indians and begin to see easy money. He hadn't been in on the whack-up six weeks till he was wearing one o' them bicycle lamps in his neck-tie and putt'n in all his time at the city hall waitin' for the easy marks to come along and throw up their hands." Although he debates with himself and with Miller over whether to join the crooked politicians, Artie commonsensically decides to play it straight. "Well, I guess I'll pass up the whole thing. Come to size it up, that ward's goin' to be floatin' in beer the next two weeks, and I'm not stuck on standin' around with them boys that smoke them hay fever torches. . . . I guess an easier way to get that roll'd be to borrow a nice kit o' tools and go round blowin' safes."

Artie's robust slang often created striking metaphors and lively commonsense aphorisms. His courtship of Mamie Blanchard led to numerous discussions of love and matrimony before Artie finally popped the question. Of Mamie, Artie would say with enthusiasm, "Talk about your peaches, why she's a whole orchard." And when Miller said, "Well, Artie, when a man's in love you can't hold him accountable," Artie replied, "That's no dream neither. Anyone that's got his head full o' girl proposition's liable to go off his trolley at the first curve."

When Artie reluctantly attends Mamie's friend's wedding, he ends up having a good time because he was "stroke oar at the doin's," and he takes sides with the common neighborhood folk, using rural images and aphoristic style to do so: "Them people up there's good enough for me. No frills, but they're on the level, and when it comes down to cases they're just as good as a lot of people that make a bigger front. They got hearts in the right place. It's like a man out at the boat club says, 'If you can't travel with the bell cows, why stick to the gang.' That's wise talk, too."

Ade's Artie was soon followed by Pink Marsh, a street-smart shoe-shine man with common sense, who predates Langston Hughes's more critical Jess Semple, and by Doc Horne, a wise old fool who told tall tales in the lobby of the Alfalfa Hotel. In "The

Fable of the New York Person Who Gave the Stage Fright to Fostoria, Ohio," and in many of his other slang fables collected in several books, Ade deflated eastern pretensions with midwestern characters, dialects, and aphorisms in the same manner.

In his introduction to *Artie and Pink Marsh* James T. Farrell noted that Ade's early hoosier years were the source of the vitality in his language, and that "He learned to make hay out of what city slickers might consider hayseed talk."

Ring Lardner, another of Ade's friends, also adapted "hayseed talk" to the urban situation. Born in Niles, Michigan, Lardner wrote during the same period as Hubbard, Ade, and Dunne, and eventually achieved a lasting national reputation as a humorist and storyteller. Although Lardner was always more ambivalent about the common man than either Ade or Dunne, in his early midwestern columns and stories before he left Chicago for the East in 1919, he wrote genially in vernacular about midwestern figures in an urban setting. In his feature columns for the *Chicago Tribune* beginning in 1913, and in his collected stories, especially *You Know Me Al* (1916), *Gullible's Travels, Etc.* (1917), and *Own Your Own Home* (1919), Lardner's characters spoke or wrote in Midwestern urban slang and exposed the follies of city life and city people in a commonsense manner.

Although he is more of a transitional figure in the development of the little-man characters of Thurber and Benchley than Ade's Artie, Lardner's Gullible of *Gullible's Travels, Etc.* shares a number of Artie's wise fool characteristics. Like Artie, he and his wife seek entrance into better social circles, and he is self-confidently aggressive rather than merely a passive victim. Gullible is usually wise later rather than earlier in his adventures, but he is finally a wise boob rather than merely a boob.

Gullible is most like Ade's and Dunne's characters as he deflates high culture pretentiousness with his vernacular perspective. Although he persistently tries to become part of the opera crowd, he maintains his integrity as a common man, and his vernacular descriptions of *Carmen* are in the Midwestern style. As he follows the opera's story line, he transposes the action to local settings and in his slangy commonsensical way makes the performance into a Midwestern folk play, peopled with ordinary characters whose world is understandable in his terms. Thus, the *Carmen* libretto as retold by Gullible is set along Chicago's Halsted Street; in Gary and Hammond, Indiana; Janesville, Wisconsin; and Des Moines, Iowa. The plot according to Gullible has to do with elevated tracks, Chinese res-

Ring Lardner

taurants, the stockyards, nickel shows, railroad trains, chewing gum, the Y.M.C.A., three-handed rummy, one-legged races, and Irish policemen.

Gullible's description of the first act of *Carmen* is typical of his several pages of vernacular commentary. "The first act opens somewheres in Spain, about the corner o' Chicago Avenue and Wells. On one side o' the stage they's a pill mill where the employees is all girls, or was girls a few years ago. On the other side they's a soldier's garage where they keep the militia in case of a strike. In the back o' the stage they's a bridge, but it ain't over no water or no railroad tracks or nothin'. It's prob'ly somethin' the cat dragged in." In Gullible's version of the opera, Carmen dies "of tobacco heart."

Gullible may sometimes be naive or banal as he goes along with his wife's attempts to improve their social status, but he hurts others only infrequently, and he exposes not only the pretensions of those "pillows o' society" above him on the social ladder, but the false posturings of lesser characters, like Bishop in "Three Kings and A Pair" and "The Water Cure," who are greater social climbers than he is. Typically, in "The Water Cure" self-interest as well as the desire to save his sentimental sister-in-law, Bessie, from a bad marriage make Gullible expose her suitor, Bishop, as a fraud and an exploiter. In aphoristic style, Gullible says, "When it comes to makin' matches I hand it to the women. When it comes to breakin' 'em leave it to the handsomer sex." And he notes in "Three Kings and A Pair," "You can't judge a mustache by seein' it oncet . . . It may be a crook at heart."

Lardner makes fun of Gullible's wife, but he is not as suspicious of women as are Thurber and the *New Yorker* writers. Gullible usually gives in to his wife's tears, and there are signs of a softer nature beneath his tough exterior when he thinks of sinking a boat because the "government checker" will not let him leave for a quick drink once he is on board. "I felt like offerin' him a lump sum to let seven or eight hundred more on the boat and be sure she went down. . . . But then I happened to think that the Missus would be among those lost; and though a man might do a whole lot better the second time, the chances are he's do a whole lot worse. So I passed up the idea. . . ."

The title story in *Gullible's Travels, Etc.* finds the Gullibles traveling to Palm Beach, Florida, to "rub elbows with the celeb's." In the course of his ill-fated trip, Gullible uses common sense to expose everything on the itinerary from high-priced hotel accommodations to sight-seeing tours. "The meals would be grand" says Gullible, "If the cook didn't keep gettin' mixed up and puttin' puddin' sauce on the meat and gravy on the pie." Gullible's remarks on the city's "oldest" architecture recalls nineteenth-century burlesque travel narratives and especially Mark Twain's *Innocents Abroad*. "First, we went to St. George Street and visited the oldest house in the United States. Then we went to Hospital Street and seen the oldest house in the United States. Then we turned the corner and went down St. Francis Street and inspected the oldest house in the United States. Then we dropped into a soda fountain and I had an egg phosphate, made from the oldest egg in the Western Hemisphere. We passed up lunch and got into a carriage drawn by the oldest horse in Florida, and we rode through the country all afternoon and the driver told us some o' the oldest jokes in the book."

While the Gullibles were foolish enough to try to keep up with the socially elite, *Gullibles Travels,*

Etc., unlike most later Lardner stories, ends with commonsense wisdom and an affirmation of common people and their values. The Gullibles breathe a sigh of relief when they arrive back in Chicago, and Mrs. Gullible exclaims, "Ain't it grand to be home!" She observes that they have learned a lesson from their experiences, and Gullible looks forward to recouping the trip's costs by playing rummy with down-home neighbors, the Hatches, who the Gullibles had decided were too common for them before they left for Palm Beach.

Lardner created vernacular characters who bend traditional ethics to meet selfish ends more often than Ade's Artie or Dunne's Mr. Dooley, but Lardner's early comic figures were eventually wise as well as foolish, and they spoke directly or indirectly for a sane, commonsense perspective not unlike Ade's or Dunne's most successful Midwestern characters. As Walton R. Patrick observes, although Jack Keefe of *You Know Me Al* and Gullible of *Gullible's Travels, Etc.* were crude ambitious characters who for much of their histories could not penetrate their false self-images, both are ultimately portrayed sympathetically. At the conclusion of their stories both Keefe and Gullible have learned or remembered the values of the small towns that arrogance, blind ambition, or social climbing had prevented them from seeing.

Once he left the Midwest for the East, Lardner's later work was more obviously shaped by his growing disillusionment, but his urban vernacular style and his lively early Chicago writings were typical of Midwestern humor in its heyday; they reflected an understanding of the common man and a commonsense outlook that were articulated even more affirmatively by Ade's other colleague, Finley Peter Dunne.

Dunne's Colonel McNeery and Martin J. Dooley (with his sidekicks Hennessy and McKenna and his parish conscience Father Kelly), like Ade's Artie, Pink Marsh, and Doc Horne, spoke for the common man in a cracker-barrel style that was translated for an urban audience. In Dunne's case the translation was into an Irish-American brogue. Archey Road, home of Mr. Dooley's tavern in Chicago's Bridgeport neighborhood was Dunne's small town within the big city, and the fads and foibles of the local population as well as the sights and sounds of windy city politics, work, and leisure-time activities became the subjects of his columns and books from December 1892 until Dunne's death in 1935. The Irish-American character was not new with Dunne, and foreign dialect had been used in Chicago in the 1870s by

Charles Harris in his creation of German-American Carl Pretzel, but Dunne was one of the most adept in combining commonsense cracker-barrel tradition with the immigrant persona in a nonpatronizing fashion.

When Dunne was forced to forego his first Chicago Irishman, Colonel McNeery, who was modeled on a friend, he sent his character McNeery back to Ireland. But while Mr. Dooley praised the Old World, he reminded the recently transplanted Irish people of Chicago that they had a new home and that they would miss good fun if they left. "So th' old boy has gone back to th' dart. Well musha, I wish him luck, an' between th' doods an th' corners an' the weight of this here stick iv timber, manny a time I've been driven to wish I was home again where I come from, with a mud wall at me back an' a roof iv rushes over th' head iv me an' a great potful iv petaties boilin' in th' turf fire. . . .

"Buy why didn't th' man stay home fr Irish Day. Sure barrin' th' shortness iv it, I'd as soon be at th' fair tomorror as I wud home. Ivrybody'll be there. Th' Lord Mayor, with th' chain around his neck, . . . an' that quare lukin' man they calls a Irish Tory he fetched over with him, an' th' ex-mimber fr'm Tipperary, an' Gawd knows who else includin' Patsy Brannegan an' Johnny Shea. . . . I'm goin' down there if I have a leg to stand on an' join in th' exercises." Dunne admires the common man and dislikes pretensions whether they are found in fancy dress or high literary culture. Talking about simple people, Mr. Dooley notes, "Whin Father Butler wr-rote a book he niver finished, he said simplicty was not wearin' all ye had on ye'er shirfront like a tin-horn gambler with his di'mon stud."

Dooley observes such local scenes as weddings, deaths, and christenings where Irish parents argue hotly over children's names. Martrimony is a common subject on Archey Road. The bachelor Dooley observes, that "A man who has his sup iv tay an' his tin cent ceegar alone be himself is th thrue philosopher, he hivens. But young min who spind their money on dhrink an' hor-rse races ought to marry. If they have to waste half their wages, they might as well be wastin' them on their wives." With the same aphoristic wisdom, Mr. Dooley also spoke up against corruption and poor judgment in a bipartisan way in everything from Chicago mayoral elections to the Spanish American War. Dooley noted with common sense that "Th' throubel with most iv us, Hennessy, is we swallow pollytical idees befure they're rep an' they don't agree with us." When the Illinois Central Railroad battled the city and the people for lakefront rights, Dunne wrote,

"They's now use teachin' th' childher what ain't thrue. What's the good iv tellin' thim that th' Lord made th' wurruld whin they'll grow up an' find it in the possission iv th' Illinye Cinthral." Although Dunne pointed out foolishness and jingoism on the local and the national scene, he also questioned the enthusiasm with which some reformers set about their work.

While his common sense and persona connected him to rural America, Dunne's Dooley was with Sandburg and with Whitman as he sang witty, slangy rhapsodies of the city: "I niver lave town meself. I take a vacation be settin' here at me front dure lookin' up at Gawd's an' the Illinye Steel Company's black-an-blue sky. Th' ilictric ca-ars go singin' by an' th' air is filled with th' melody iv goats an' curdogs. Ivry breeze that blows fr'm th' south brings th' welcome tidings that me frind Phil Armour is still stickin' to the glue business. I cannot see th' river, but I know that it's rollin grandly backward tord its sewerce laden with lumber hookers an' ol' vigitables."

Like older cracker-barrel writers, Dooley laughs at the pretensions of women's literary societies that celebrate genteel authors. He laments the day when the literary societies come to Archey Road and instead of "th' young ladies sewin' society" the ladies met for "th' Mrs. Humphrey Ward an' Pleasure Club," where "Whin anny man writes so manny pieces fr th' paper where he lives that no wan'll have annything to do with him, they send him a letter askin' him to come wou an' r-read th' pieces to thim." According to Dooley when such authors arrived, their presentations usually went something like this: " 'I doubt if anny iv ye'll undherstand anything I say,' he says, 'but I'll go ahead an r-read fr'm th' wurruk iv th' gr-reatest author that was iver foaled,' he says. 'That is,' he says, 'mesilf,' he says."

Mr. Dooley's solutions to social problems were usually genial, but he could use strong, evocative language against injustices like George Pullman's treatment of his employees during the Pullman strike, and his good-natured observations about social issues frequently carried a critical barb, especially for the better heeled citizens of Chicago. "I'd put up a social colony like Hull House downtown, ncar th' banks an' th' boord iv thrade an' th' stock exchange. I'd have ladin' citizens come in an' larn be contact with poor an' honest people th' advantage iv a life they'r on'y heard iv."

Eventually Dunne and his Mr. Dooley became so well known and respected nationally that marches, hit songs, and poems were written about them; Dunne came to earn $1,000 and more for each of his columns, and his books sold over 10,000 per month. More significantly, Dunne, like Hubbard and Ade, ensured a place for Midwestern humor in literary history. Their popularity resuscitated cracker-barrel humor and inspired followers and imitators long after they had ceased to write and long after a more cynical urban humor had become the predominant American style. Although "pure" cracker-barrel humor never again reached the heights of popularity that it had attained by 1920, it remains a part of the American humor mainstream even today.

If the Midwestern Federal Writers' Projects are any indication, cracker-barrel humor continued to interest readers throughout the regional revivalism of the 1930s, and it appears still later in comic novels of the 1940s and 1950s. In Max Shulman's midwestern novels rustic figures like Asa Hearthrug played innocents at the mercy of various citified extremists. Although Asa had some little soul qualities, he was the vehicle through which the author of *Barefoot Boy With Cheek* implied that commonsense sanity lay somewhere between the fraternity life of Alpha Cholera on one hand and the political radicalism of Yetta Samovar and the Subversive Elements League on the other. Among Shulman's more obvious rustic characters is Opie Dalrymple of *Rally Round the Flag, Boys!* who strums his guitar, delivers aphoristic wisdom, and regularly sends girls into a swoon. Opie's counsel is straight from the cracker barrel when he advises his fellow soldiers about how to get town girls: "Here me good. Put on your newest, spankin'est uniform. . . . *Look sharp.* That's half the secret. The other half is ack mis'able. Ain't nothin' attracks a gal like ackin' mis'able. . . . Tell her you're lonesome for the gal back home, so she knows she ain't scratchin' after a prize nobody wants. Then tell her you can't stay sad long around her, and begin gettin' frisky and sparklin'. If you don't get her, she ain't worth havin'. . . . *Stay loose.* . . . Remember—Man proposes, God disposes."

The nineteenth-century tradition continues to linger today among literary humorists and journalists as well, especially among journalists in the Midwest. Mike Royko, syndicated columnist for the *Chicago Sun-Times*, is a good case in point. Slats Grobnik, Royko's answer to the nineteenth-century "good boy" is a neighborhood kid, a direct heir of Ade's Artie. Using urban slang and aphoristic common sense, Slats Grobnik's observations on the world have been reprinted and gathered into several books. Slats is a neighborhood kid whose marble-shooting and knuckle-cracking abilities are

the stuff tall tales are made of. Slats, the marble champion, has thumb muscles bigger than his biceps. "The first time Slats cracked one of his knuckles," writes Royko, "dogs all over the neighborhood began barking, and a squad car came to see who had been shot." Slats is always ready with a bit of aphoristic wisdom and commentary. Joggers, according to Slats, are not to be trusted: "A guy who runs for anything except a bus can't pass a lie box test," he says. Slats is a kid whose ribs stand out, but Slats does not care. He says, "If you have muscles, someone might hire you to work." And when other kids build a tree house, Slats street-wisely quips, "If people was meant to live in trees, the squirrels would slip some nuts to the city building inspector."

Royko, speaking in his own voice, spends most of his columns poking fun at the habits of Chicago politicians. One 17 March with no additional commentary, Royko simply wished a Happy St. Patrick's Day to a list of Irish politicians and political bosses that ran the length of his whole column. He also takes delight in making fun of outsiders and of pretensions and pretentious language. "It is a strain for local newsmen," he observes, "being interviewed by visiting writers, especially the scholarly ones. They always ask if the mayor has charisma. In the mayor's neighborhood, they could get punched for talking dirty." And commonsensical Royko is not usually of the dementia praecox school of humor. "A man's identity crisis," he writes, "might hit him at about 7:45 A.M. while stuck on an expressway with the sun in his left eye. Then he might think: 'Why am I here? Why was I here yesterday? Will I be here tomorrow?' In most cases, the man manages to change lanes and feels better."

As radio comedy took the place of the newspaper column as a primary medium for humor in the 1930s and 1940s, Midwesterners such as Jack Benny and Bob Hope joked in the genial vein of the old tradition. *The Jack Benny Show* as well as *The Fred Allen Show*, *The Great Gildersleeve*, *Amos n' Andy*, *The Life of Riley*, *Fibber McGee and Molly*, and *The George Burns and Gracie Allen Show* were fashioned along lines that brought together vaudeville and music-hall comedy with native humor traditions. Built around a central humorous figure or figures, the shows all introduced a series of regular "neighbors" or "friends" who wandered in and out of places like "Allen's Alley" gossiping, delivering local wisdom, and telling jokes on themselves and others in the old-style genial way, often in native or foreign dialect. Comic strips and radio shows like *The Bumsteads* and later domestic television comedy like

I Love Lucy and Jackie Gleason's *The Honeymooners* played off the model provided by older characters like M. Quad's the Bowsers. *Duffey's Tavern* which began with the familiar, "Duffey's Tavern, Archey, the proprietor speakin' " was a direct descendant of Dunne's Martin J. Dooley and Archey Road in Bridgeport, Chicago. Jackie Gleason later adapted the character for television.

Perhaps the most constant reminder of the persistence of Midwestern "hoss sense" is the role it plays in the most popular television talk shows even today. Talk show hosts such as Dave Garroway, Steve Allen, Jack Paar, and Johnny Carson gather good talkers and put them on a couch like a "liar's bench" to tell comic anecdotes and stories. Although the talk shows include a variety of guests, according to Terry Galanoy in *Tonight!* "The house rule on 'The Tonight Show' became funny stories. If a person had ten of them, a guest appearance could be arranged, even if the guest's expertise was cancer research."

Garroway, Allen, Paar, and Carson all grew up or began their careers in the Midwest and have frequently reminded their audiences of that fact. All have adopted an easy-going, down-home, spontaneous style which Garroway has called "Old Buddy," and most have served as a commonsense center against which eccentricities can be measured. Pat Weaver, once of NBC, is reported to have hired all of them because, "They are exactly alike."

Following the model for *The Jack Benny Show* and other radio-comedy series, Steve Allen introduced a group of neighborly regulars to his programs. Tom Poston, Bill Dana, Louis Nye, and Don Knotts played these ordinary visitors with special quirks; several of the characters adopted vernacular voices and mannerisms. All of the *Tonight* show hosts have used members of the audience such as farmer John Shaefer, who became a folksy movie critic, as repeated features; they also frequently invited Midwestern cracker-barrel comedians like Herb Shriner, Charlie Weaver (Cliff Arquette), and Jonathan Winters to appear on the show. Carson's own comic personae Aunt Blabby and Floyd E. Turbo are relatives of earlier cracker-barrel figures in American humor. The best guests, according to Carson, "are the uninhibited people. . . . they know who they are, and don't try to prove they're something else." What Carson lets them do, writes Terry Galanoy is "yak, blab, chat, gab, jaw, drool, gush, yap, shoot the bull, beat their gums, and chew the rag," and as a result the *Tonight* show remains one of the most popular on nighttime television.

If black humor novels, the *New Yorker*, Firesign Theater, and *Saturday Night Live* went the Eastern way of sophisticated irony and complicated parody, then comedians such as Jack Benny and Herb Shriner, novelists such as Max Shulman, journalists such as Mike Royko, radio and television domestic comedies and television talk shows are the descendants of "hoss sense" humor. And Midwestern-style hosts such as Garroway, Allen, Paar, and Carson and their guests owe much to the nineteenth-century humorists and the persistence of their cracker-barrel manner in the heartland. If "hoss sense" humorists are stubborn anachronisms, one must wonder if perhaps the anachronisms survive because they continue to touch something basic in the American character, something that existed so vitally in America's heartland—the Midwest—that it has sustained American folk humor even into the late twentieth century.

West

David B. Kesterson
North Texas State University

The term *Western humor* almost inherently necessitates a return in our thinking to a time when the American West was raw and untamed, when the comic pens of Mark Twain, Bill Nye, Eugene Field, and the like were sporting with the West's often crude, if challenging, conditions. Indeed, what has become of Western humor? Is there much left in the later twentieth century?

Most of Western humor is gone or transformed, just as strictly Yankee humor is gone, both amalgamated by a maturing nation where urbanization, mass transit and communications, and a more mobile and more broadly educated population have diluted and modified the distinctive types of regional humor. As Max J. Herzberg has observed, "In the late 19th and 20th centuries Yankee and frontier humor were merged in an extraordinary cultural complex, in which may be found traditional elements transplanted from Europe, a persistence of cracker-barrel philosophy and of tall tales, verbal exuberance, funny business as a profession, a cult of the wisecrack and the insult, and mass production of laughter in movies, radio, television, and syndicated columns."

But Western humor was once prevalent, and, indeed, there are some surviving examples of Western humor. In roadside curio shops in the West, one can still purchase everything from "Jackalope" picture postcards to "Everything's-bigger-in-Texas" mementos, all of which still bespeak that essential trait of Western humor, exaggeration. Western climatic, geographical, and character jokes still abound, such as the one about the stranger who, while traveling through West Texas, pulls into a service station for gasoline:

> STRANGER (TO ATTENDANT AND TWELVE-YEAR-OLD SON): "Looks like it might rain today."
> WEST TEXAN (LACONICALLY): "Sure hope so. Not for my sake, but the boy's here—" (LONG PAUSE) "I've seen rain!"

The "yups" and "nopes" of the proverbial Gary Cooper stereotypical Western character still exist, but there seems to be less and less interest in such humor.

Yet in the nineteenth century, when people from the North, East, South, and Midwest were migrating to the plains and mountain boom towns, plenty of humor came with them. Especially evident were the comic oral-narrative tradition—largely from the South—and the cracker-barrel strain of homespun wisdom and humor, which emanated from the Northeast but was popular elsewhere too. The West, like the Old Southwest, soon boasted of its own raconteurs. The oral humor of the Davy Crockett and Mike Fink tales or Thomas Bangs Thorpe's "Big Bear" in the Old Southwest was matched by Mark Twain and Bill Nye in such creations as Twain's Bemis, Simon Wheeler, and Jim Blaine, or Nye's Twombley in "Twombley's Tale." Western humor, as Walter Blair and Hamlin Hill have shown in *America's Humor: From Poor Richard to Doonesbury* (1978), carried the tall tale and exaggeration out of the Old Southwest, across the Mississippi, and on out to the plains, the mountains, and all the way to the West Coast. Much of the coarse language and emphasis on dialect and local color carried over into Western humor.

Obviously, after these elements of Old Southwest and frontier humor in general reached the West, they changed to reflect the new region. They had to be assimilated into Western culture. In fact, to a major extent it is that strong sense of region (a different, distinctive region) that largely shapes the nature of what we call Western humor. Almost all the Western humorists reflect in some way this sense of region, a feel for the territory and its unique character.

Frederick Jackson Turner referred to the Western frontier as "the meeting point between savagery and civilization," and his statement identifies the matrix of Western humor. The landscape, the climate, living and working conditions, the types of people and occupations, and a definite personal and cultural image deriving from place are all key ingredients of Western humor. As Henry Nash Smith has said in *Virgin Land*, the American West was considered as a mythical realm of nature cut off from the urban East and from Europe, and the humorists writing there conveyed that feeling.

Twain's and Nye's treatments of Western landscape, climatic extremes, and living conditions are prime examples. There may be beauty in the West; in *Roughing It* (1872) Twain uses Lake Tahoe as his example, and Nye cites Rocky Mountain landscapes and sunsets as his idyllic pictures. But there was a predominance of discomfort and unpleasantness, and humor usually derives from adversity of some sort. There is the "Washoe Zephyr" of *Roughing It*, "a soaring dust drift about the size of the United States set up edgewise," a "pretty regular wind" that keeps "office hours . . . from two in the afternoon till two the next morning; and anybody venturing abroad during those twelve hours needs to allow for the wind or he will bring up a mile or two to leeward of the point he is aiming at." On the plains there are snowstorms so violent and dense that, as Twain relates in *Roughing It*, he and his party become totally lost in one, walk in circles, and give themselves up as dead before discovering the next morning that "there in the gray dawn, not fifteen steps from us, were the frame buildings of a stage station, and under a shed stood our still saddled and bridled horses!" Bill Nye cringes over futile attempts to garden in the impossible heights of Laramie, Wyoming, complaining that "winter lingers in the lap of spring till after the Fourth of July" so that "several days in midsummer . . . my cabbage plants had to . . . run up and down the garden walk to keep their feet from freezing." Communing with Western nature comfortably is impossible, Nye concludes: "Nature is all right in her place, but you don't want to get too familiar with her. The everlasting snow-capped mountains, lifting their sunlit summits to the sky, are a pretty good thing, but they look better about thirty-seven and a half miles distant than they do when they are in bed with you, because they have got such cold feet. The little dancing torrent, as it canters along to the ocean and bathes the feet of the mountain, is a pretty good thing—in a blue covered book—but when you come to grasp the reality and see that same little streamlet waddle along over the corns and chillblains on the foot of the mountain, and hear it murmur all night so that you can't sleep, the murmuring gets tiresome, and you begin to murmur yourself after a while." This passage from a man who, when he later left the West, became an ardent naturalist in the tamer country of North Carolina!

Aside from the climate, other living conditions in much of the West, until well into the twentieth century, were also relatively harsh, a state that

Advertisement for Twain's account of his adventures in the West

sometimes helped spawn violent and gruesome humor. Bill Nye's accounts of rough Western conditions carry the impact of sick humor. Frontier and Western humor such as Nye's sought to create relief from the stark reality of Western life by humorously exaggerating its dangers on the printed page. Nye's violent humorous pieces usually pertain to the treacherous Western landscape or weather, vocations such as mining or working on hazardous mountain railroads, or unruly human behavior. In "Yanked to Eternity," a work cart carrying a drunken section crew loses its brakes while speeding down a mountain. To stop the car and save the others one man is forced to leap off with a rope tied around him. The man is killed of course and shows up at the base of the mountain only "in part." Mischievous miners in "A Mining Experiment" play a trick on a youth who claims to be a mining expert by telling him to use an axe to drive a stick of dynamite into a hole. He is killed in the resulting explosion and the men are said to be trying yet to get him out of the ground "with ammonia and a tooth brush." A long tunnel on the railroad to Gunnison, Colorado, is so narrow that it is fatal for passengers to lean out the windows; "the company [has to] hire an extra man to go through the tunnel twice a day and wipe the remains of tourists off the walls." In the sketch "Desiccated Mule" a "snub" cable, drawing mules up on one side of Pike's Peak by force of a counterweight on the other side, draws too fast; the unfortunate mules "didn't touch the ground but once in three thousand feet, but they struck the canopy of heaven several times." What was left of the "desiccated mules" was "fractional." Humor associated with railroading and mining in the nineteenth century was followed in the twentieth by comic treatments of cowpunching and ranching. There is such zeal and feverish activity associated with all these enterprises, especially mining, that the humorists found ready-made targets of satire, including self-satire. As much fun as Nye and Twain had at the expense of the mining craze, they both fell victim and invested in mines—Nye in northern Colorado and Twain in Nevada, where he barely missed becoming a millionaire over a blind lead. Will Rogers's vignettes of cowboy life sprang from his own involvement in the trade.

Certain distinctive groups of people dominate Western humor of the nineteenth century especially: Indians, Mormons, Chinese, miners, bad men, women. Twain cannot ignore the bad men of the West in *Roughing It*. His humorous account of meeting desperado J. A. Slade exudes fear and uneasiness. Slade offers Twain the last cup of coffee, which Twain is reluctant to accept and "politely" declines because he fears Slade has not killed anybody that morning and "might be needing diversion." Twain's, Artemus Ward's, and Nye's accounts of the Mormons provide some of the liveliest humorous passages in their works, especially Twain's depiction in *Roughing It* of Brigham Young's endless troubles with his host of wives and offspring. Nye's views of Indians, Chinese, bad men, and Western women are a mix of scathing disapproval (of the Indians), seriocomic acceptance (of the Chinese), repulsion coupled with fascination (for the bad men), and surprising support (of courageous and right-minded Western women). Bret Harte added color to his works with humorous, often Dickensian characterizations of miners, outlaws, and other Western types, including the profane, sneaky Uncle Billy of "The Outcasts of Poker Flat," the tenacious partner of Tennessee mopping his loyal brow with the ubiquitous red bandanna,

and the sentimental "nursemaid" Kentuck of "The Luck of Roaring Camp." Harte painted a serio-comic picture of Western life that at once romanticizes it and captures its actual flavor.

Bill Nye

Not to be overlooked is a psychological factor inherent in Western humor that results partially from the cultural isolation of the West. In discussing the West as a realm of nature cut off from the urban East and from Europe, Henry Nash Smith explains that civilization in the West was considered inferior, a view that imposed on Westerners "the stigma of social, ethical, and cultural inferiority." Nye, Twain, and Will Rogers have a sharp-eyed view of the West's limitations—its provincial, crude ways of life. Yet they also defend the West and make an effort to extol certain virtues of the West over failings of East Coast culture.

Nye, for example, defended the West against Eastern effeteness, arrogance, and exploitation, openly admiring what he detected as a strong undercurrent of honesty, genuineness, and industriousness in the West. Easterners who came West with exaggerated preconceptions about its wildness, or tried to defraud the local residents in some way, or acted superior and more knowledgeable than the local folk fell prey to Nye's vindictive pen. Though he was not in favor of violence, Nye extols the Western custom of hanging as an effective deterrent to crime. The "purple and suffocated appearance of

Will Rogers

the hanged is a depressing sight," he writes in "Hung by Request," and if the murderer of President Garfield were sent West he would be hanged immediately, not set loose as Nye feared he would be in the East. If the East had vigilance committees, Nye continues, Washington, D.C.,'s census "would look as though the Asiatic cholera swept over the land." Nye felt that the West had found satisfactory solutions that the more urban, sophisticated East had not.

A similar defense of the West and attack on Eastern culture is found in the twentieth-century reactions of Will Rogers. From his attack on the learned—"All I know is just what I read in the papers"—to his counterattack on the Eastern estab-

lishment, which embraced everything from New York policemen to the absurdities of Eastern politics, Rogers carried on the tradition of Ward, Twain, and Nye. As Jesse Bier has written in *The Rise of American Humor*, "True to their mutual last stand for the provincial, countryfied type, Rogers would set himself explicitly against urban and industrial pressures and that symbol of America, the Ford car, an image for standardization."

Rogers is also the main twentieth-century Western descendant of the cracker-barrel philosopher. The titles alone of his first two books, *The Cowboy Philosopher on the Peace Conference* (1919) and *The Cowboy Philosopher on Prohibition* (1919), indicate the transformation that has been made from Eastern to Western "wise fool." Rogers embodies the same homespun humor and wisdom found in Lowell's Hosea Biglow, Franlin's Poor Richard, the sayings of Josh Billings, Bill Arp, and the writings and stage presentations of numerous others. As the supposed "natural wit," Rogers is the direct descendant of Twain, Nye, and the West's adopted son, Artemus Ward.

Thus, there is a tradition of distinctive Western humor, even if it is less identifiable and prevalent today. Western humor shares certain traits with the humor of other frontiers and has a particular kinship with humor of the Old Southwest and with cracker-barrel humor. But primarily due to the overwhelming sense of location—with all the idiosyncrasies of extreme weather and harsh living conditions, anomalous peoples and occupations—Western humor has an aura all its own, an unmistakable flavor. In chapter 20 of *Roughing It* there are four versions of Horace Greeley's harried stagecoach ride during which his coat buttons pop off and his head shoots through the roof. The incident is reported as having happened in four widely scattered locations in the West—yet the road and travel conditions are all the same. Just as those similar conditions provide a common denominator for the Greeley story, so have the distinctive characteristics of the West formed a humor indigenous to the whole region.

Appendix II:
Humorous Book Illustration

"A SNORT OF AGONY."

Fred Opper illustration for Bill Nye's Baled Hay. A Drier Book Than Walt Whitman's "Leaves o' Grass"

Humorous Book Illustration

Bill Blackbeard
San Francisco Academy of Comic Art

Comic illustration in humorous books did not enjoy a propitious position in the early development of American literature. Through much of the nineteenth century, so overwhelming was the impact on the American publishing scene of imported British comic-book and magazine illustration in terms of both quality and quantity that American talent was for the most part ill-paid and neglected. The absence of effective international copyright protection in the United States before 1890 permitted American publishers free access to current humorous illustration by such gifted English cartoonists as George Cruikshank, Hablot Knight Browne (Phiz), and John Leech. Although a few of the more responsible Yankee publishers, such as Harpers and Scribners, did negotiate abroad for formal reprint rights to much popular English and Continental illustrated work, which they often obtained at bargain rates, piracy was common. This cheaply or freely obtained mass of first-rate comic illustration from overseas not only depressed the American market for local work, it created the general public belief that all the real comic art talent was in England or Europe. (The reading public's attitude toward home-grown literary talent was often just as narrow through much of the nineteenth century, as the difficulties of such writers as Poe and Melville—who, ironically, often sold better in England than at home—attest.) Until well into the middle decades of the last century, talented Yankee cartoonists seriously interested in pursuing a creative career generally faced starvation.

When a properly humbled American comic artist did in fact find illustrating work in this period, it was frequently to do plates for pirated British or European works left unillustrated in their original publication, and he was expected to imitate closely one or another of the popular London cartoonists in style; indeed, his handiest tool in obtaining such employment was a portfolio of prints of current English fashions, city locales, and domestic interiors, which served to convince his American employers that his work would seem sufficiently authentic in even minor details that an American audience would feel comfortably certain that they were enjoying an English cartoonist's work. Other American artists worked at pirating fresh engravings of art in just-arrived copies of new English or Continental books, or at closely copying cartoons in current English humor magazines for use in Yankee comic magazines. These comic magazines did, however, print a good bit of original American cartoon humor—*their* readers, lacking the European bias of the more affluent American book-buying public, demanded comic drawings with solid Yankee satire, and a number of cartoon artists, willing to work for pennies, turned out a substantial body of work for these publications. These early comic magazines were crudely conceived and printed, and it was not until after the Civil War that talented editorship was finally established—in such once-famed weekly titles as *Puck, Judge, Life*, and *Truth*—and a sound, continuing, and well-paying market for American cartoon work was provided. Regular appearance in such magazines, and in a few other publications that displayed an enthusiastic interest in good comic art, such as *Harper's Weekly*, developed a sophisticated public awareness of, and appreciation for, the work of specific American cartoonists, notably Thomas Nast, Fred Opper, and Edward W. Kemble, among others, which led to their frequent employment as comic illustrators with by-line recognition and at a pay rate commensurate with their considerable talents.

Nevertheless, a few fortunate artists prior to the 1860s did manage book publication, often in connection with very obscure American comic texts (and possibly as a favor to the author, enabling him to appear in print with an illustrated text—a marketing advantage at the time), such as *The Adventures of Elder Triptolemus Tub* (1849), published by the author (Abel Tompkins) in Boston with amusing but uncredited cartoon illustrations. In other cases artwork was apparently well-paid-for and credited, as with John McLenan's sometimes delightful illustrations for Charles Dickens's *Great Expectations* (published unillustrated in England), published in America by T. B. Peterson and Brothers of Philadelphia in 1860—with a title-page pronouncement of publishing propriety possibly unmatched in literature: the book, we are told, was "printed from the manuscript and early proof-

625

Illustration for Abel Tompkins's The Adventures of Elder Triptolemus Tub

F. O. C. Darley illustration for Washington Irving's "The Legend of Sleepy Hollow"

sheets purchased from the author, for which Charles Dickens has been paid in cash, the sum of one thousand pounds." Earlier, McLenan had illustrated some of the prim and proper Rollo books for children with appropriately prim and proper art, but he demonstrated his comic talents fully in an 1853 American classic roguery by J. G. Baldwin called *The Flush Times of Alabama and Mississippi*. Like most other cartoon illustrators of the period (he also worked as a pork packer), McLenan was little known by the general reading public and is utterly forgotten today.

Certainly the most eminent American humorous illustrator of these middle decades was the still admired F. O. C. Darley (1822-1888), a comic draftsman of remarkable talent who—while given the usual assignments of illustrating pirated editions of Dickens, Scott, and other English writers—was also engaged to enhance new and reprinted comic works by famous American authors, including Washington Irving's *Rip Van Winkle* (1848) and *Legend of Sleepy Hollow* (1849) and Clement Moore's *A Visit from St. Nicholas* (1862). Darley's style, much more in the realistic mode than was fashionable in comic illustration of the period—which largely derived from the highly "cartoonized" style of the English pacesetters mentioned earlier, Cruikshank in particular—was nevertheless admired by the book-buying American public, and he was probably the only Yankee comic artist actually known by name and independently appreciated as an illustrator prior to the Civil War. Even so, his popular reputation did not endure even through the nineteenth century, and he has no individual entry in any edition of the various encyclopedias, including the sizable *World Encyclopedia of Cartoons* of 1980; he is mentioned in passing in the 1929 *Encyclopedia Brittanica*, but only under an entry on an engraver of his work.

The first American cartoonist to gain not only national fame in his own time but considerable European recognition and a lasting reputation as an innovative and perceptive graphic artist that is perhaps larger today than ever, was the ebullient Thomas Nast (1840-1902), whose powerful political cartoons on the front page of every issue of *Harper's Weekly* for most of the 1860s directed the feelings of a nation at war and toppled a postwar political dynasty in New York City. Nast was little interested through most of his career in illustrating anyone else's text, but he did make a notable exception for Clement Moore's classic comic poem about Santa Claus, for which his drawings of 1869 remain the definitive work (unfortunately replacing Darley's

Thomas Nast illustration for Rufus E. Shapley's Solid for Mulhooly

earlier efforts in public esteem), and for Rufus E. Shapley's raucous novel of 1889, *Solid for Mulhooly*, based on Irish-American political corruption in Baltimore. (A German immigrant himself, Nast shared the prevailing distaste of the establishment in the 1880s for the big-city political activities of the emigrants from Ireland.)

Other artists of these mid-century years were connected with humorous works of the time, although their art was not notably amusing in its own right. Perhaps the most active of these was Sol Eytinge, who illustrated the first edition of Thomas Bailey Aldrich's *Story of a Bad Boy* in 1870 and delighted Bret Harte with his extensive output for such story collections as *The Heathen Chinee* (1871) and *The Luck of Roaring Camp* (1872). Hammatt Billings illustrated *Uncle Tom's Cabin* (1852) with little display of comic concern for the novel's several humorous scenes (in which he was surpassed by George Cruikshank's work in England; Cruikshank also provided the finest illustrations for James Russell Lowell's amusing antislavery satire, *The Biglow Papers*, in the English edition of 1865). D. C. Johnson, called "the American Cruikshank" by some of his contemporaries, began work as early as 1831 with some now obscure American comic sketches (such as *The Life and Writings of Major Jack Downing of Downingville* by Seba Smith in 1833) and continued through the middle decades illustrating such pirated British comic novels as those by Frank Smedley; his work is flat and generally as derivative as his nickname suggests.

From the 1860s to the close of the nineteenth century so-called "artist factories," several of which were established in the principal centers of American publishing from Boston to Philadelphia, were extremely popular with publishers. Founded by entrepreneurs, often with little capital, and employing considerable numbers of impoverished young cartoonists and illustrators, these factories undertook, for a fee, to provide artwork for new books, magazines, and syndicated prose of all kinds. While some of the artists managed to get credit by working their initials or even signatures into their assembly-line work, they almost never received by-line recognition in the books they illustrated. (One notable exception, perhaps prompted by the authors' communal concern for comic artists, was in the 1873 first edition of *The Gilded Age* by Mark Twain and Charles Dudley Warner; the book's title page went so far as to credit, as illustrators, "Hoppins, Stephens, Williams, White, etc., etc." Later on, however, Twain joined other publishers in simply ignoring illustrators, even of his own work: his *Adventures of Tom Sawyer*, published in 1876, gives no credit to its artist, True Williams, whom Twain acquired from an artist factory maintained by an engraving firm, Fay and Cox. Williams managed to get his signature into much of the art, though.

The existence of artist factories makes it difficult to determine which illustrated comic publications with uncredited artwork from this time used free-lance illustrators and which had simply turned to the factories. Whatever the source, there were hundreds of humorous books published between the 1860s and the turn of the century, filled with often superb comic illustration—and not a line of type among them regarding the identity of the artists. A few such titles, all of popular and well-reviewed comic works, will give some small idea of

Artist factory illustrations in Mark Twain and Charles Dudley Warner's The Gilded Age

Mullen illustration for The Life and Adventures of Private
Miles O'Reilly

the range of this blackout of artist identity. *The Life
and Adventures of Private Miles O'Reilly* (1864), an
anonymously authored best-seller about the Civil
War, included highly competent comic art sometimes signed simply "Mullen"; *Sut Lovingood's Yarns*
(1867) by George W. Harris was enhanced by a
number of risible (and Rabelaisian) illustrations unsigned and uncredited; and *Human Natur'* (1885) by
W. A. Rogers, writing as "Joel Sloper," was embellished by a crude but funny comic artist who not
only illustrated the text but designed an engaging
gold-stamped design for the book's binding—all
uncredited.

The growing fame through the last decades of
the century of a number of independent comic artists, almost all known through their splendidly
showcased work in *Puck, Judge, Life,* and the other
popular humor magazines of the era, put an end to
this general exploitation of the cartoonist by the
1890s. The golden age of the comic illustrator in
America began with the turn of the century and ran
through World War II. A stunning bounty of work

was produced in this relatively short time, matching
in quality and conception the much larger lodes of
comic illustration in England and Europe from the
1700s on.

Despite the interest shown by American book
buyers in humorous books illustrated by the new
class of famous comic artists from the humor
magazines—particularly Fred Opper, E. W. Kemble, A. B. Frost, and J. M. Condé—there was a curious failure of most of the great comic writers at the
turn of the century to match their talents with those
of the leading cartoonists and create the kind of
team that characterized American humorous books
throughout the twentieth century. Thus we find
such a master of early narrative slapstick as George
W. Peck turning to a number of cartoonists to illustrate his steady stream of popular works—a very
crude artist named Gean Smith for the 1883 first
edition of his *Peck's Bad Boy and His Pa*; an unnamed
incompetent for *The Grocery Man and Peck's Bad Boy*
in 1883; and finally a better choice in D. S. Groes-
beck and R. W. Taylor for his last Peck's Bad Boy
titles, although he never again found as wholly effective an artist for his brand of comedy as True
Williams, who illustrated his 1887 magnum opus,
How Private Geo. W. Peck Put Down the Rebellion, with
graphic verve and wit.

Mark Twain was indifferently illustrated—he
seemed to have no great concern for comic graphics
per se—until he was fortunately paired almost by
accident with E. W. Kemble in *Huckleberry Finn* in
1884 (and later with Dan Beard and A. B. Frost in
other comic works about Tom and Huck). Ambrose
Bierce and Artemus Ward were either not illustrated at all, or by the factory anonyms. Robert J.
Burdette, who wrote the delightful "Hawkeyetems"
for the *Burlington Hawkeye* newspaper in the 1870s,
was saddled with a moderately effective artist
named R. W. Wallis in his major collection, *The Rise
and Fall of the Mustache* (1878). John Phoenix rather
effectively illustrated his own work of the 1850s and
later used a charming selection of old public-
domain newspaper woodcuts as illustrations in his
books, but he was not properly paired with an illustrator until John Kendrick Bangs edited a collection
of his work in 1903 with art by E. W. Kemble.

Fortunately, there were exceptions: Bill Nye
managed to be illustrated by the marvelously funny
Livingston Hopkins in his *Forty Liars and Other Lies*
(1882), a comic combination that was surpassed only
by Fred Opper's encounter with Nye in *Baled Hay. A
Drier Book Than Walt Whitman's "Leaves o' Grass"*
(1884). Unfortunately, Nye did not team up with
either of these cartoonists permanently, and some

Gean Smith illustration for first edition of George W. Peck's Peck's Bad Boy and His Pa

R. W. Wallis illustration for Robert J. Burdette's The Rise and Fall of the Mustache

later illustrations for his work by lesser artists were undistinguished. Josh Billings wisely used Livingston Hopkins's work for his series of comic almanacs in the 1870s (although in keeping with prevailing publishing practice, he did not credit him) and Hopkins had to print his own *Comic History of the United States* in 1880 to gain any public recognition for his work. Finley Peter Dunne's Mr. Dooley books and articles were often gorgeously illustrated; *Mr. Dooley's Philosophy* (1900) included art by both Opper and Kemble, and much of Dunne's later work was enhanced with the lively line drawings of John T. McCutcheon, the famed editorial cartoonist of the *Chicago Tribune*. And Edward Eggleston had great good luck in seeing his classic *Hoosier Schoolmaster* illustrated not only by the comically effective Frank Beard (in 1883), but again by Opper at the top of his form in 1892.

In some instances, the visual impact of the illustrator's work, coupled with the quantity of art involved, in effect made a book a joint project be-

E. W. Kemble illustration for Finley Peter Dunne's Mr Dooley's Philosophy

tween author and artist, a relatively commonplace occurrence in American humorous books by the 1920s. Two outstanding examples of such works at the turn of the century, both illustrated by Opper, were Eugene Field's *Complete Tribune Primer* (1901), a collection of very short sketches from Field's days on the *Denver Tribune* decorated with seventy-five drawings by Opper, who provided a sizable drawing for virtually every sketch, thus splitting the page space about equally between author and artist; and Bill Nye's comic *History of the United States* (1894), which featured a preface cosigned by Nye and Opper and an equal division of book space into closely related text and art, Nye even introducing a Whomsoever J. Opper into his story line midway through the book. Fred Opper (1857-1937) was the most active and popular cartoonist in America between 1890 and 1905, illustrating dozens of books, filling hundreds of comic magazine pages with his cartoons, pioneering in the new narrative art of the comic strip with full-color Sunday newspaper pages featuring such strips as *Happy Hooligan*, *Maud*, *Alphonse and Gaston*, and others, all the while turning out a daily political cartoon for the Hearst newspapers. His longest-lived alignment with a comic author of the time was with Bill Nye, but this was cut short by Nye's death in 1896. Opper's extensive newspaper work after the turn of the century sharply reduced his book illustration activity.

The first prolonged relationship between a major American comic author and a comic illustrator developed on the staff of the old *Chicago Record* of the 1890s between George Ade and John T. McCutcheon. McCutcheon (1870-1949) was teamed almost from the outset of his newspaper career with Ade in illustrating the latter's popular weekly series, "Stories of the Streets and of the Towns," continuing on with Ade through the famous "Fables in Slang," which followed a few years later. Book after book combining Ade's text and McCutcheon's art, largely collections of the newspaper work, were published: *Doc' Horne* (1899), *Fables in Slang* (1899), *The Girl Proposition* (1902), *People You Know* (1903), *In Babel* (1903), *Bang! Bang!* (1928), and others. Ade's growing success in writing stage musicals and plays and McCutcheon's new career on the *Chicago Tribune* had split the team up for the most part by 1905, although their collaboration continued on and off for years, mostly in magazine contributions based on the "Fables in Slang" series. In 1931, Ade wrote a book called *The Old Time Saloon*, which was illustrated by a stunning roster of many of the major cartoonists of that time: Rube Goldberg, Rea Irvin, Gluyas Williams, H. T.

John T. McCutcheon illustration for George Ade's Bang! Bang!

Kin Hubbard illustration for Abe Martin

Webster, Herb Roth, and others, but McCutcheon was oddly absent. McCutcheon himself wrote and illustrated a comic novel called *Congressman Pumphrey, The People's Friend* (1907) and illustrated a humorous collection of stories (*Anderson Crow, Detective*, 1920) by his brother, the noted novelist George Barr McCutcheon.

But the Ade-McCutcheon team was still unusual for the time. John Kendrick Bangs in the 1890s and 1900s and Irvin S. Cobb a bit later turned out a great number of comic books, managing to get a new book into the stores every Christmas for years, but most were only diffidently illustrated. McCutcheon did one or two books for Cobb, notably *Roughing It Deluxe* (1914), and Tony Sarg did some funny illustrations for *Fibble, D. D.* (1916), although his work for *A Plea For Old Cap Collier* (1921) and other Cobb titles left much to be desired. Bangs made even wider use of comic artists than Cobb, but his only really happy linkup was with Peter Newell, noted for his Lewis Carroll illustrations and comic strips, who was at his best in four Bangs titles: *A Houseboat on the Styx* (1896), *The Pursuit of the Houseboat* (1897), *The Enchanted Typewriter* (1899), and *Mr. Munchausen* (1901). The bulk of Bangs's humorous books are rarely even adequately illustrated (he was saddled more than once with the very unamusing Albert Levering), although he fared better with his sprightly children's titles, where he enjoyed the art of Clare Victor Dwiggins, Grace Weidersheim/Drayton, and Peter Newell again.

Ellis Parker Butler, author of the once famed *Pigs Is Pigs* (1905), turned out a host of small volumes in the same vein in the early years of the century, all with instantly forgettable illustrations, as did, a few years later, Charles "Chic" Sale, creator of the once-notorious book *The Specialist* (1929). But the remarkable Oliver Herford, author of over twenty volumes of comic prose and verse between the 1890s and 1930s, had no problem with art at all, since he was himself gifted with a considerable talent for drawing. Virtually all of his charming books were self-illustrated, a point he makes in the dedication to *The Bashful Earthquake* (1898), where he writes, "TO THE ILLUSTRATOR, in grateful acknowledgment of his amiable condescension in lending his exquisitely delicate art to the embellishment of these poor verses from his sincerest admirer, THE AUTHOR." Notable in terms of art were such Herford titles as *Artful Anticks* (1888), *The Rubaiyat of a Persian Kitten* (1904), *Confessions of a Caricaturist* (1917), and *Excuse It, Please* (1929). (In *Confessions of a Caricaturist*, Herford drew a caricature of George Ade accompanied by a verse which began "Somehow I always like to think, of GEORGEADE as a Summer Drink . . ." The drawing facing the verse showed a bottle of GEORGEADE being decanted into a glass.) Gelett Burgess, creator of *Goops and How To Be Them* (1900) and "The Purple Cow," drew most of the art in his numerous books from the 1890s on, as did Kin Hubbard in his several gingham-bound collections of *Abe Martin* sayings from the *Indianapolis News* between 1895 and 1915. Later cartoonist-authors, such as John Held, Jr., and Ralph Barton in the 1920s and 1930s, Bill Mauldin and Walt Kelly in the 1940s and 1950s, and Edward Gorey in the 1960s and later, produced long runs of comic titles while illustrating the works of other writers as well. The self-illustrated work of James Thurber, Ludwig Bemelmans, Clarence Day, and Milt Gross was extremely popular.

A new generation of both comic authors and

Bill Breck illustration for Edward Streeter's Dere Mable

illustrators emerged in the years following World War I. (Not surprisingly, a few writers and artists who appeared in 1917-1918 with wholly war-oriented comic work—notably Ed Streeter and Bill Breck, with their *Dere Mable* wartime rookie letter series—met with little or no success among readers in the following decade with their deliberate rejection of the war and those too intimately and exclusively connected with it.) The most famous humorous writer of this period, Ring Lardner, generally eschewed comic illustration after his first few books; an early association with the famed creator of the *Toonerville Folks* comic strip, Fontaine Fox, in two titles, *Bib Ballads* (1915) and *Own Your Own Home* (1919), offered a promising relationship that, sadly, did not develop. Other Lardner titles of this time were rather ineffectively illustrated, from the amusing drawings of *Chicago Tribune* cartoonist Gaar Williams in *The Young Immigrunts* (1920) through the stiff, gray *Saturday Evening Post* wash-style art of Wallace Morgan in *My Four Weeks in France* (1918), to the abysmal work of one Frank Crerie in *Treat 'Em Rough* (1918). His best-known and possibly funniest work, *You Know Me Al* (1916), first appeared in book form with no illustrations at all, and this became a pattern with Lardner's collections after 1924, when he switched publishers, going from Bobbs-Merrill to Scribners, although oddly the last title published in his lifetime, *Lose With a Smile* (1933), contains a number of line text drawings in a comic vein by Bill McNerney, for which the artist received no title-page or cover credit.

Don Marquis also encountered no illustrator worthy of his work until virtually the close of his career. Through some two dozen volumes of comic prose and verse published between 1912 and 1935, Marquis suffered barely adequate to poor illustrative art, and it was not until the second book in his classic three-volume series devoted to the doings of the literary cockroach, archy, and his feline buddy, mehitabel, that he was coupled with the brilliant comic-strip artist, George Herriman, whose long-running *Krazy Kat* has been termed the finest example of comic-strip art extant. So successful with the public was the marvelously comic combination of Marquis and Herriman in this book that not only did Herriman go on to illustrate the third book in the series, he was also invited to illustrate a new edition of the first, *archy and mehitabel* (1927), which originally appeared without art.

Equally as famed in its time was the long-lived book relationship between Robert Benchley and Gluyas Williams, which lasted through some sixteen volumes of Benchley sketches printed between

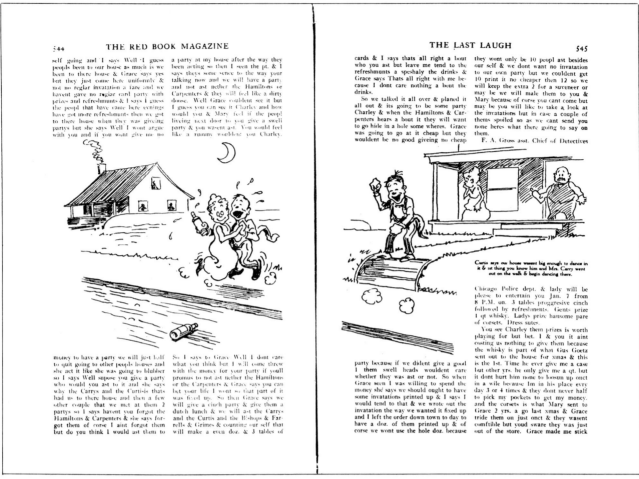

Fontaine Fox illustration for Ring Lardner's "The Last Laugh," Red Book (July 1915)

1921 and 1947, including such still risible titles as *20,000 Leagues Under the Sea; or, David Copperfield* (1928); *From Bed to Worse; or, Comforting Thoughts About the Bison* (1934); *Why Does Nobody Collect Me?* (1935); and *After 1903–What?* (1938). Gluyas Williams drew embarrassed people with a simple, telling line that made his daily comic panels a hit with newspaper readers for decades. His style exactly fitted Benchley's persona of a bumbling, well-meaning guy who was utterly confused about almost everything. Williams, with a stroke of comic genius, once drew Benchley looking at himself in a mirror and seeing E. C. Segar's classic moocher, J. Wellington Wimpy, looking back. Williams illustrated other writers' books, but never with the ideal fit between art and text that he achieved in the Benchley books.

The decade of the 1920s was notable for two curious types of illustrated comic books which ap-

peared for a short time into the 1930s and then were seen no more. One of these was initiated by the runaway best-seller by Anita Loos, *Gentleman Prefer Blondes* (1925), and extensively illustrated by Ralph Barton. Going eventually into over twenty printings, this smaller-than-normal-sized volume (5" x 7½" , 216 pages on thin, glossy paper) sparked a small host of imitations and parodies, such as *They Do Not!* (1926) by Colin Clements, *Romantic, I Call It* (1926) by Ethel Harriman, *Blondes Prefer Gentlemen* (1927) by Nora K. Strange, *Home, James* (1927) by Ethel Kelley (and illustrated by Ralph Barton), *What'll We Do Now?* (1928) by Edward Longstreth, and *Love Letters of an Interior Decorator* (1929) by Bert Green, all similarly sized and designed. Most were indifferently illustrated, except for the Barton work in *Home, James* and Bert Green's raucously funny art for his own text (featuring an exhaustive panorama of bootlegging types of the time). Loos and Barton

George Herriman illustration for archy does his part

teamed up again for a sequel to the first book in *But Gentlemen Marry Brunettes* (1928), which again went into multiple printings.

The second series of books unique to the 1920s developed from the popularity of Donald Ogden Stewart's *A Parody Outline of History* of 1921, which collected a serial of the same name which ran in the *Bookman* the year before. Illustrated by Ralph Barton, the knowing, acerbic spoofing of H. G. Wells's rather pompous best-seller, *An Outline of History* (1919-1920), caught the public fancy and stimulated the writing of a number of similar books over the next decade, all of which were packaged by various publishers in much the same format as Stewart and Barton's title: large text in a standard-format book (5½″ x 8½″), with comic illustrations roughly in the Barton manner preceding every chapter. Second in this group was another Stewart-Barton title, *Perfect Behavior* (1922), fol-

Miguel Covarrubias caricature of William Faulkner for Corey Ford's In Worst Possible Taste

Gluyas Williams illustration for Robert Benchley's The Early Worm

Ralph Barton dust jackets for Anita Loos's novels about Lorelei Lee

O. Soglow dust jacket for George S. Chappell's 1930 book

lowed by further collaborations in the same format to 1929. Notable among the imitations, all well illustrated, were *Timothy Tubby's Journal* (1922), another *Bookman* serial by George S. Chappell, illustrated by Herb Roth; *The Outline of Everything* (1923) by "Hector B. Toogood" (probably George S. Chappell), illustrated by Herb Roth; *Three Rousing Cheers For the Rollo Boys* (1925) by Corey Ford, illustrated by Gluyas Williams; *Meaning No Offense* (1928) by "John Riddell" (Corey Ford), illustrated by Miguel Covarrubias; *The Facts of Life* (1930) by H. W. Haneman, illustrated by Herb Roth; *Through the Alimentary Canal With Gun and Camera* (1930) by George S. Chappell, illustrated by O. Soglow; *The John Riddell Murder Case* (1930) by Corey Ford, illustrated by Miguel Covarrubias; *Bird Life at the Pole* (1931) by Wolcott Gibbs, illustrated by "Bruton & Bruton" (Ralph Barton); *The Gardener's Friend and Other Pests* (1931) by George S. Chappell

& Ridgely Hunt, illustrated by H. W. Haenigsen; *Evil Through the Ages: An Outline of Indecency* (1923) by George S. Chappell, illustrated by O. Soglow; and *In the Worst Possible Taste* (1932) by "John Riddell" (Corey Ford), illustrated by Miguel Covarrubias. Ancillary to these books was a series of satires on preposterous travel memoirs of a sort notorious in the 1920s, all written by either George S. Chappell or Corey Ford, and all illustrated with comic photographs involving actors and—in some cases—celebrities of the time, including Rudy Vallee, Frank Sullivan, and Heywood Broun. Typical titles were *Salt Water Taffy* (1929) and *Coconut Oil* (1931) by Ford, and *Sarah of the Sahara* (1923) and *Dr. Traprock's Memory Book* (1931) by Chappell.

The illustrator who through frequent appearance stands out in the two series of books is Ralph Barton, and there is little doubt that Barton stood second only to John Held, Jr., as the favorite cartoonist of the American literary world in the 1920s. Although Barton wrote and illustrated a few books of his own (notably *God's Country: A Short History*, 1929), he was primarily an illustrator, gifted with the rare ability to enhance almost any conceivable humorous text as if he were born to do the job. Not only was he superb with contemporary humor, he excelled with classic material, and his illustrations for Balzac's *Droll Stories* (1925) are among the best ever produced for that work. Held, on the other hand, limited his scope to the immediate subject matter of the 1920s (as well as his graphic sideline of satirizing old woodcuts to make current points) and preferred to write and illustrate either his own

Frank Sullivan as Old Britches in photographic illustrations for Corey Ford's Salt Water Taffy

Charles Addams illustration for Peter De Vries's But Who Wakes the Bugler

books or a small range of works by others dealing with flappers or speakeasy booze. Notable among Held's comic novels are *Grim Youth* (1930), *The Flesh Is Weak* (1931), and *A Bowl of Cherries* (1932), while his many illustrated books of the time are typified by *Drawn From the Wood* (1929) and *My Pious Friends and Drunken Companions* (1928), both by Frank Shay; *The Saloon in the Home* (1930) by Ridgely Hunt and George S. Chappell; *Grandfather's Follies* (1934) by James J. Geller, and *How To Behave Though a Debutante* (1928) by Emily Post. Held was so utterly one with his bathtub gin and Charleston time that he seemed unable to develop either his style or subject matter to fit the decade that followed, and despite his surviving another thirty years, he produced little after the early 1930s that was memorable or amusing.

The 1930s and 1940s were remarkable for the movement of a new generation of cartoonists who had been nurtured at the *New Yorker* into book illustration. Unfortunately, most of the books illustrated by these often gifted cartoonists were not in themselves particularly amusing or otherwise remarkable. Among the handful that were notable are Joel Sayre's 1932 comedy of gangsters in football, *Rackety Rax*, illustrated by Alan Dunn (whose wife

Syd Hoff illustration for Arthur Kober's Thunder Over the Bronx

Eyes popped like champagne corks and strong men sobbed aloud

Al Hirschfeld caricature of S. J. Perelman and himself for Perelman's Westward Ha!

and fellow *New Yorker* cartoonist, Mary Petty, produced in 1947 the best set of illustrations for Dickens's *Martin Chuzzlewit* since Hablot Browne did the originals); Arthur Kober's wry, wistful novel about a Jewish family called *Thunder Over the Bronx* (1935), illustrated perceptively by the *New Yorker*'s Syd Hoff; Peter De Vries's utterly bizarre pseudomurder mystery, *But Who Wakes the Bugler* (1940), with appropriate illustrations by Charles Addams; Geoffrey Hellman's collection of *New Yorker* comic pieces and essays, *How To Disappear For an Hour* (1947), with art by Saul Steinberg; and Robert C. Ruark's book of comic vignettes, *I Didn't Know It Was Loaded* (1948), with drawings by *New Yorker* veteran R. Taylor, who also illustrated Ruark's satire on historical novels, *Grenadine Etching* (1947). The humorous writing in these decades was often so weak that the cartoonists frequently overwhelmed the works they illustrated. Perhaps the most noteworthy example of this, because so painfully prolonged, was the endless series of comic novels about Mrs. Feeley and Mrs. Rasmussen by Mary Lasswell, which began in 1942 with *Suds In Your Eye* and was still going, nine titles later, in 1962 with *Let's Go For Broke*. All of these works were illustrated by the *New Yorker*'s inimitable George Price, whose marvelous evocation of Lasswell's dreary characters and activities (basically the old ladies drink and have escapades with oddball characters they meet) keep persuading the reader to have a go at the story. It is

Price's art, not the Lassell narratives, that makes the series noteworthy.

One very happy meeting of graphic and prose talent occurred to close out the decade of the 1940s; this was the encounter between S. J. Perelman and Albert Hirschfeld, a theatrical cartoonist since 1928 for the *New York Times*. First mated in *Westward Ha!* (1948), a collection of travel pieces Perelman and Hirschfeld had undertaken for the old *Holiday Magazine* immediately after World War II, the pair worked together again on *Listen to the Mocking Bird* (1949), an anthology of Perelman's *New Yorker* pieces and the most memorable set of illustrations any such Perelman collection had enjoyed since Perelman sprinkled a goofy potpourri of old valentines and Sears catalog cuts through his first book, *Dawn Ginsbergh's Revenge* (1929). Hirschfeld's regular regimen (and his high fees) eventually ended this collaboration, but those Perelman titles illustrated by Hirschfeld are classic comic work to rank with the best of teams of earlier years: Darley and Irving, Moore and Nest, Kemble and Twain, Opper and Nye, Ade and McCutcheon, Bangs and Newell, Lardner and Fox, Marquis and Herriman, Barton and Loos, and, of course, Benchley and Williams. If this list has something of the ring of an old-time vaudeville bill—with enough acts to last until dawn—it only underscores Jimmy Durante's enthusiastic observation that "books is the greatest show on earth!"

HOCKEY PROSPECTS FOR 1929

Cut from the Sears Roebuck catalogue illustrating S. J. Perelman's Dawn Ginsbergh's Revenge

Appendix III:
Newspaper Syndication of American Humor

Little Johnny on the Humming Bird.
Edited by Ambrose Bierce.

THE woodpecker is named that becos it wood peck a gas pipe if thare was a werm in it. It has got a red hed, and so has Missus Doppy, but she dont liv on werms, only on ole Gaffer Peters, wich is her father.

One nite Jack Brily, wich is the wicked saller, swears and chews tobacko and every thing, he was goin past Missus Doppys hous, and he stopt and hollerd, Fier, fier!

Missus Doppy she thru up a windo and stuck her red hed out and ast whare was the fier. Then Jack he sed, Never mind, mam, I ges thare isent any more danjer now that you have put out yure hed.

But it is notty for to sas.

One time Missus Doppy she was to our house and she and Uncle Ned thay et a

And the piret fled sreekin from the scen!

fillipee togather, and he was cetched. So nex day he sent her a cobm for her hair, but fore he sent it he took the box wich it was in to a printer and had it nice printed for to say, One Ferst Clas Sally Mander Cobm.

Wen eny body ses, Wot a nice cobm you hav got, Missus Doppy, she says, Yes in deed, it is a genwine Sally Mander, and is real stuck up about it.

Mister Pitchel, thats the Preecher, he says

It is wicked for to make fun of fokses unfermitys, cos thay are sent upon them for sum wise perpus, and Uncle Ned he says that is so, and Missus Doppys hed is a shining xample.

But the shinyest thing wich is in the werld is the hummy berd wich flits from flour to flour and suckx out the mlasses and makes it into hunny, for to live on during the time wen winter holes his bolstery swa!

One time there was a hummy suckin a blu bel, and thare was a buzard, and the buzard it sed, Poor little feller, you mus be mity hungry for to do that, it jes makes me sick to the stumuck of my belly to see you at it.

Go over by that tre and you wil strike a curent of deliteful fragance, and if you foller it up yule find a ded horse wich is fit for to set before a king!

Wen the butter fil gets to be old it turns in to a cattypiller, but the hummy is ferst of all a polly wog. Billy, thats my brother, he seen a wog turn in to a hummy, and he cetched it, but a saw tooth gallydoodle cum along and tride to get it for hisself, and wile Billy was a slotterin the doodle the hummy it flu away.

Billy is the bravest boy wich is in the werld, cos one time thare was a piret wich tride for to make Billy tel a lie, and sed he wude cut his hed of if he dident, but Billy wudent and the piret fled sreekin from the scen!

And now Ile tell you a piret story, wich my sisters yung man tole me.

Once there was a prizen keeper, and he was tole that the Guvener was coming for to go thru the prizen and see if evry thing was rite. The keeper he was a frade he wude ast ol sorts of questions, the Guvener wude, so he tole his depty, Jes tel him I aint in, and you sho him round yure own self.

Then the keeper he put sum stripy close on and the deputy locked him in a sel, for to conceel his identify. Blme by the Guvener and his whife and dotter thay cum to that sel, and the Guvener he ast the depty, What kind of a convick is this?

The depty spoke up and sed Piret, sir.

Then the Guvener sed, Poor feller, I dare say he is reel sory for his wicked life and wude be a good man if give a other chanc. How long has he got to stay in?

The depty sed, For his hole life if he is

spaired, unles you parden him, like you are a goin to be ast for to do, in a paper slned by ten thowsen hundred promnent sitisens. Thay say we got the rong man.

Then the Guvener he took of his spettacles and wiped them with his haukcheef, and puttum on agin, and took a other look at the keeper. After a wile he tookum of agin, and wiped um som more, and puttum on, and looked agin. Blme by he tookum of, and puttum in his pocket, and sed, I never seen this persen before, but he is the rite man in the rite place, and thare he stays.

The Guveners whife she sed, Wot a vishus face!

And the dotter she shedderd and got be-

The Guveners whife she sed, Wot a vishus face!

hine her father and sed, Wot a feend in yuman shape!

Pirets is the skerge of the seas and spairs neither age, seeks nor perdishion. And thats wy I say. Thow shal not kil.

The hummy berd livs to a considable age, but Franky, thats the baby, licks candy til his face is dobby, and then he whipes of the dob with a hanfle of dust out of the rode, and wen he is woshed he bellers lik he was catle on a thowsen hils.

Ambrose Bierce's syndicated column, 11 January 1902 (Hearst syndicate)

Newspaper Syndication of American Humor

Bill Blackbeard
San Francisco Academy of Comic Art

The distribution through the American press of humorous prose and cartoon work, a multimillion-dollar business today, came into being in the nineteenth century as the result of the sheer size of the United States and the resultant wide gaps between sizable urban-centered groups of readers. The telegraph could carry raw news over these gaps and make local newspaper publication with current news an early actuality, but the telegraph was by far too expensive a medium to carry the kind of news-paper leavening that readers enjoyed once they encountered it—popular fiction, comic stories, and humorous commentary on the news. A handful of newspapers with enormous circulations and income in a few large cities—New York, Chicago, Philadelphia—could buy and run such material from local (and often famed) writers, but papers in Indianapolis, Akron, and Richmond could not afford such work.

Thus a problem unique to the United States emerged, a problem which had never developed in England or in the generally highly centralized nations of Europe, where all that was worth printing in newspapers appeared in the dozen journals published in each capital, which were then distributed by train in a few hours to the furthest reaches of each country. The Birmingham or Edinburgh resident in England might pick up a local paper, and often did, but he also bought one or more of the freshly arrived London papers every day to keep in touch with the top writers in the capital, a situation which continues in England and Europe to the present with the result that syndicated material in newspapers there is largely limited to the same American columns and comics available here. Syndication of local copy along national lines never developed in Europe.

It was not long before a farsighted American entrepreneur realized that he could buy original copy from top writers at the same price the large metropolitan dailies were paying and distribute copies to widely separated U.S. newspapers for a much lower per-paper price which would still, due to volume sales, yield him a considerable return on his investment. This ambitious middleman was the magazine publisher S. S. McClure, who at the outset of his career in 1884 undertook the first serious attempt to buy and distribute quality fiction and entertaining prose in general to the national American press. Starting at first with short stories, McClure moved into light nonfiction, then made his first major humor acquisition with the comic essays of Bill Nye in 1885. Early newspapers to sign for the McClure packages included the *Newark Evening News*, the *St. Paul Pioneer-Press*, and the *San Francisco Call*, but in a few years the list included a daily newspaper in virtually every city in the country able to support one.

Adapting the earlier invention of "boilerplate" (eggcrate-paper mats from which pretypeset story heads and illustrations could be reproduced in hot metal for immediate duplication), McClure soon added art to his syndicated features, including a comic portrait of Bill Nye to head his pieces, and usually an illustration as well. McClure also traveled to England to sign up major British authors of the time, including Wilkie Collins, H. Rider Haggard, Robert Louis Stevenson—and even Bret Harte, who then was represented by the English literary agent A. P. Watt. Newspapers clamored for McClure's service and the money rolled in—enough to enable McClure to launch a major national magazine (appropriately named *McClure's*) in 1890.

McClure was not long alone. Several popular big-city newspapers of the 1890s loaded with comic and sensational features undertook their own syndicate operations, and a dozen independent syndicates took to the field as well. By the end of the century, it was common for reputable writers to have their works syndicated, and this included the humorists, from Mark Twain to Ambrose Bierce. Bill Nye was dead by then, but Finley Peter Dunne, like Bierce, was being distributed nationally by the Hearst newspapers, George Ade's "Fables in Slang" were sold through the *Chicago Record*, and Joel Chandler Harris was in McClure's stable of writers. Now newspaper readers in Murfreesboro, Tennessee, could open their Saturday evening paper, with its additional weekend features, and read the same columns, serials, and special articles that were being read in penthouses and on ghetto stoops in New York.

Ring Lardner's first You Know Me Al *comic strip, September 1922 (Bell syndicate)*

The major American humorists of the period, like writers in general, prospered enormously through syndication. Even those who, like Bierce, were under exclusive syndicate contract (Bierce was only allowed independent rights to sell short stories and novels and to arrange book contracts for his work) still saw their annual incomes rise regularly, since dissatisfied writers were always free to find more fertile fields when their contracts expired, and syndicate heads (in Bierce's case, William Randolph Hearst) didn't like to lose their money-makers. Some tried self-syndication at one time or another (as Mark Twain did) but often became annoyed at the bookkeeping and staff involved and turned to the professional syndicates again in relief and with no great loss in income.

English humorous writers, denied the benefits of syndication at home, soon came to agreeable terms with American firms, and writers from G. K. Chesterton to George Bernard Shaw began to appear in American papers across the country side by side with the top American comic talents. There seemed to be room for everyone, with the average sizable U.S. city then boasting between four and six daily newspapers and the smaller towns fielding at least two apiece, morning and evening, while the cost per paper for each syndicate feature used was persuasively low, being based on actual circulation units. By the early 1920s, far more of H. L. Mencken's "booboisie," whom he loved to twit to his (imagined) small audience of sophisticated and highly literate metropolitans, were reading his syndicated weekly column with relish than had ever seen the sober green issues of Mencken's *American Mercury* on a newsstand, let alone bought or read one. A new reading audience, one that actually felt its cultural interests were effectively met by local newspapers, had begun to form, and there were a great many low- to moderate-income American families between the turn of the century and World War II who—aside from a small handful of books picked up here and there—had virtually no reading matter in the house other than newspapers and the ubiquitous *Saturday Evening Post*, whose two pounds of reading matter was delivered to the door across America just like a paper for a nickel a week.

The fame of newspaper writers flourished in this situation. Ring Lardner, read through the year in the *Post* and again in the newspapers with a weekly column of comic prose and—for a time—in a daily comic strip (based on his "You Know Me Al" stories), was enormously popular; his bumbling baseball characters and his own comic persona were as familiar as Dickens's figures once were. Will Rogers received much the same reader response—and brought backward country people into town to see his films in the local movie house.

In the handling of their rosters of comic writers, there was little difference between the numerous syndicates: payment followed fame, and there was little or no attempt to direct humorists toward the development of a syndicate style or "keynote," even in the case of so tightly controlled a one-man operation as Hearst's King Features Syndicate. (There was more input from the syndicate in the case of some comic strip groups, largely because many cartoonists were hired as unknowns, to carry on a strip already made famous by someone else. In terms of total income, however, the most successful strip cartoonists made considerably more through syndication than all but a very few of the humorous writers.) Thus it matters little in considering the career of comic writer to discuss the name or function of the syndicate or syndicates that handled his work: all routinely solicited every published newspaper in the United States and Canada, and many in the English-speaking countries abroad, so that with each fresh week's array of newly announced talent, newspaper editors made their selections on the basis of the writer's advance reputation, not on the name of the syndicate or its track record in fielding successful material.

Beginning humorous writers were only offered syndication after their magazine or book writings—or newspaper columns, often in the paper that gave them their first work—had earned a certain amount of independent fame. Beginning syndication financial arrangements were based on the amount of demand the writer had generated at the time of signing, and—unless the writer (as frequently happened) promptly drank himself into creative incompetence—the rates were periodically adjusted up or down to reflect the number of subscribing newspapers. Often an author would retire from regular syndication before a decline in sales became embarrassing. A number of writers' critical reputations remained secure long after their popular appeal, as judged by newspaper editors, had all but vanished.

Syndication, however, had almost nothing to do with a comic writer's lasting critical reputation. If Ring Lardner had written nothing but the short stories included in *Round-Up*, he would be assured of a permanent and honored place in American letters, and yet few of these stories were syndicated during his lifetime; his weekly columns of casual humor in hundreds of newspapers, on the other hand, have engaged the critics' interest hardly at all, and have indeed scarcely been reprinted to any extent.

The academics and serious students of literature who make up the American critical establishment (some are even creative writers themselves) rarely take time to delve into the popular press, and in fact rather relish their calculated avoidance of its avatars, so that a writer must eventually appear notably in a periodical perused by these gentry, or in a book which reaches their hands for review or critical attention, to be given their serious attention. Thus some writers achieve their critical fame through book publication or consequential magazine appearance before syndication, while others only do so after their "obscure" local newspaper fame has earned them syndication and an eventual book collection based on their syndication success. On a very few occasions, some critics have deigned to recognize and celebrate a comic master while he is still laboring at journeyman newspaper chores, simply because he is appearing in one of the small number of newspapers they have at various times considered of sufficiently elite status to read (that is, the *New York World*, the *New York Sun*, the *St. Louis Post-Dispatch*, and so on); the classic instance of this, of course, was Don Marquis's archy and

mehitabel poems in his column in the old *New York Sun*, which gave him considerable fame in the literary community from the time of their first appearance in 1922, although Marquis was not then a wholly unknown talent, having already published a few casually received books of humor and poetry.

Not all American humorous writers entered into syndication, regardless of their fame or popularity, while some of those who did agreed only to contributions that imposed a minimal demand on their time and talent: these were usually variations on the comic-strip format, with a cartoonist adapting a character or theme of the writer's to graphic narrative and often doing the story line and dialogue as well, subject to the writer's approval. Writers prominently involved in direct syndication of their work over a good part of their lives included Will Rogers, Ring Lardner, John Kendrick Bangs, George Ade, Kin Hubbard, Finley Peter Dunne, Ambrose Bierce, Don Marquis, H. L. Mencken, Irvin S. Cobb, Damon Runyon, H. Allen Smith, Carolyn Wells, and Ed Streeter. Those with comic-strip or cartoon-panel adaptations of their work (usually rather short-lived) were Ring Lardner, Montague Glass, Will Rogers, Mark Twain, Anita Loos, George Ade, and Joel Chandler Harris, while Gelett Burgess and Milt Gross drew their own comic-strip and cartoon features for many decades, with continuing success. The writers with little or no syndication experience (notably including the major *New Yorker* writers, who were usually very well paid as permanent staff writers for that magazine) were James Thurber, S. J. Perelman, Robert Benchley, Will Cuppy, Clarence Day, Marion Hargrove, Frank Sullivan, and E. B. White.

There is no doubt that newspaper syndication brought more talent to more readers than any other development in the history of printing and supplied the purveyors of that talent with regular, assured incomes considerably beyond anything they could have expected to earn from standard magazine and book publication. On the other hand, it can well be charged, in some instances, with artificially over-farming talent and forcing the production of a great deal of second-rate material to meet arbitrary deadlines and space requirements. Luckily, the newspaper public was not hypercritical. A syndicated humorist's popularity was based on his reputation, rather than on the newspaper readers' day-to-day response to his columns. There was always the possibility that tomorrow's or next week's piece might be a knockout—which it was often enough to keep the daily readers happy.

Mr. Dooley on Discipline from the White House.

BY F. P. DUNNE.

(Copyright, 1902, by R. H. Russell.)

HERE did ye spind th' New Year's?" asked Mr. Dooley.

"I didn't go to th' White House raycip-tion," said Mr. Hennessy pleasantly.

"I see ye didn't," said Mr. Dooley. "Ye'er ar-rm is not in a sling. Man an' boy, Hinnissy, I've taken manny a chanst on me life, but I'd as lave think iv declarin' th' sintiments iv me heart in an Orange meetin' as dhroppin' in f'r a socyal call at what Hogan calls th' ixicutive mansion. That is, if I was a govermint implyee, which I aint, havin' been born wrong.

"Th' time was whin a man lost his job an' his heart to th' prisidint at th' same time. A reproof was adminis-thered to him with chloryform. He woke up an' rubbed his eyes an' says: 'Where am I?' an' th' polisman says: 'Ye'er in an ash bar'l.' He come f'rm th' White House with tears in his eyes an was tol' he was out iv wurruk. But, Hinnissy, th' prisint occypant iv th' White House is a heartier person. A reproof f'rm him is th' same thing as a compound fracture. A wurrud iv caution will lay a man up f'r a week, an' a severe riprimand will sind him through life with a wooden leg.

"There was me frind, Gin'ral Miles. No more gallant sojer iver dhrew his soord to cut out a patthern f'r a coat tain Gin'ral Miles. He's hunted th'

mas gift f'r th' hired girl who'll pizen th' soup if she gets three yards iv cal-ico, be Winnyfield Scott Schley, an' what ought to be done f'r th' Chinee, be Cap. Mahan, an' get down to what Gin'ral Miles thinks.

"'Tis always good an' full iv meaty advice. 'Is Mars inhabited?' Th' fu-ture iv th' Columbya river salmon. 'Is white lead good f'r th' complexion?' 'What wud I do if I had a millyion dollars an' it was so,' 'England's su-preemacy in Cochin China,' 'Pink gal-ters as a necissity iv warfare,' 'Is th' impire shouldhers goin' out?' 'Waist measurements iv warriors I have met,' an' so on. Gin'ral Miles is th' on'y in-an'-out up-an'-down, catch-as-catch-can, white, red or black, with or with-out journylist we have left. On anny subject, f'rm stove polish to sun wor-

Apachy, th' Sioux, th' Arypahoo, th' Commanchee, th' Congressman an' other savages iv th' plain; he's faced death an' promotion in ivry form, an' no harm come to him till he wint up th' White House stairs, or maybe 'twas till he come down.

"Annyhow, Gin'ral Miles was pur-sooin' th' thrue coorse iv a machial warryor an' enlightenin' th' wurruld on th' things he happened to think iv. 'Tis what is expicted iv him. Wan haif th' pa-apers iv th' country is edited be Schley an' th' other haif be Sampson, an' Gen'ral Miles is a con-thributor to all iv thim. If ye don't read him ye don't know what's goin' on in th' wurruld. Ivry Sundah I pick up me pa-aper an' hurry through th' articles on what's a suitable Christ-

ship. I'd take th' wurrud iv me frind Gin'ral Miles before th' man that made th' goods.

"'Twas that got him into throuble. Wan day afther inspictin' th' army, Gin'ral Miles give a chat to wan iv his fav'rite journals on what he thought about th' navy, him bein' a great authority on navy affairs before steam come in. I don't know what th' divvle he said, an' I don't care, f'r me mind was made up long ago, an' ivry-ther a Schley man or a Sampson man, an' little betther thin a thraitor or a cow'rd at that.

"But annyhow he give his opinyion, an' afther givin' it he got his bonnet out, had a goold beater in to fix up th' epylets, got th' illicthric lights goin' in th' buttons, found th' right pair iv blue an' pink pants, pulled on th' shoes with th' silver bells, harnessed to his manly hips th' soord with th' forget-me-nots on th' handle an' pranced over to th' White House. As he wint up th' hall he noticed an atmosphere iv what Hogan calls cold hatoor, f'r wan iv th' durekeepers said th' prisi-dint wasn't home, an' another lightly kicked him as he passed, but like a sojer he wint on to th' East room, where Mr. Rosenfelt, th' pa-apers tells me, shtud in front iv th' fireplace ner-vously pluckin' Sicrety Gage be th' beard.

"'I've come,' says Gin'ral Miles, 'to pay me rayspicts to th' head iv th' naytion.' 'Thank ye,' says th' prisidint; 'I'll do th' same f'r th' head iv th' army,' he says, bouncin' a coal scuttle on th' vethran's helmet. 'Gin'ral. I don't like ye'er recent conduct,' he says, sindin' th' right to th' pint iv th' jaw. 'Ye've been in th' army forty year,' he says, pushin' his head into th' grate, 'an' ye shud know that an officer who criticizes his fellow offi-cers, save in th' reg'lar way, that is to say, in a round robin, is guilty iv I dinnaw what,' he says, feedin' him with his soord. 'I am foorced to ad-minister ye a severe reproof,' he says.

"'Is that what this is?' says Gin'ral Miles. 'It is,' says th' prisidint. 'I thought it was capital punishment,' says Gin'ral Miles, as he wint out through th' window pursooed be a chan-delier. His nex' article will be entitled 'Hospital Sketches,' an' I undher-shtand he's dictatin' a few remarks to his nurse on providin' attractive suits iv steel plate f'r gin'rals in th' army.

"Well, sir, they'll be gr-reat times down there f'r a few years. A move-ment is on foot f'r to establish an

emergency hospital f'r office holders an' politicians acrost th' shtreet f'rm th' White House, where they can be threated f'r infractions iv th' Civil Sarvice law followed be pers'nal in-juries. I'll be watchin' th' pa-apers ivry mornin'. 'Rayciption at th' White House. Among th' casulties was sa-an'-so. Th' prisidint was in a happy mood. He administhered a stingin rebuke to th' chief justice iv th' su-preme coort, a left hook to eye. Sin-itor Hanna was prisint walkin' with a stick. Th' prisidint approached him gaily an' asked him about his leg.

"'Tis gettin' betther,' says th' sinitor. 'That's good,' says th' prisidint. 'Come again whin it is intirely well, an' we'll talk over that appintmint,' he says. Th' afthernoon was enlivened be th' appearance iv a Southern Con-gressman askin' f'r a fourth-class post office. Th' prisidint hardly missed him, Congressman bein' formerly wan iv Mosby's guerillas, escaped, to th' gr-reat chagrin iv Mr. Rosenfelt, who remarked on his return that life in th' White House was very confinin'. 'I will niver be able to enfoorce th' civil sarvice law till I take more exercise,' he said heartily. Th' ambulance was at th' dure promptly at five, but no important business havin' been thrans-acted, nearly all th' cabinet was able to walk to their homes.'

"Yes, sir, 'twill be grand, an' I'm goin' to injye it. F'r th' first time since I've been at it Ar-rchey road methods has been inthrajooced in nay-tional politicks. I knew th' time wud come, Hinnissy. 'Tis th' on'y way. Ye may talk about it as much as ye want, but govermint, me boy, is a case iv me makin' ye do what I want, an' if I can't do it with a song, I'll do it with a shovel. Th' ir'n hand in th' velvet glove, th' horseshoe in th' box-in' mit, th' quick right, an' th' heavy boot, that was th' way we r-run polly-ticks whin I was captain iv me pre-cinct."

"But ye niver was prisidint," said Mr. Hennessy.

"I always had too soft a spot f'r age," said Mr. Dooley, "an' 'tis th' aged that does up us young fellows. An' annyhow, I done betther."

"Yes, sir, 'twill be grand, an' I'm goin' to injye it."

"Pranced over to th' White House."

"He wint out through a window pursooed be a chandelier."

Finley Peter Dunne's syndicated column, 11 January 1902 (Hearst syndicate)

Comic-strip version of Joel Chandler Harris's Uncle Remus stories drawn by J. M. Conde, 9 August 1908 (McClure syndicate)

Comic-strip version of Mark Twain's novels, drawn by Clare Victor Dwiggins, 12 January 1919

AT THE HOUSE-BOAT ON THE STYX—In the Matter of Camouflage

Reported by Wireless to John Kendrick Bangs

Eve Doubtless Thought the Serpent was a Gentleman.

Several Miles Longer Than the Statue of Liberty.

(Copyright, 1918, McClure Newspaper Syndicate.)

"THE most interesting thing to me about this row that is going on on the other side of the river," said Michael Angelo, as he sculped the Kaiser's head out of his camembert and tossed it to Dick Whitington's cat, "is the business of camouflage and proud as I . . . . . .

pure camouflage, I mean it. They appeared to be one thing when in reality they were another. On the surface they were the most innocent looking little bits of golden sunshine that ever gloried a piece of toast. To look at 'em you'd say that as symbols of peaceful innocence they had the dove lashed to the everlasting mast—but underneath! Lago di Garda, Mike, they were seething maelstroms of destruction, and the man o . . . . German."

cob looked like a midway stunt at a World's Fair, and while I didn't want the darn thing any more than London wants Barnard's statue of Lincoln. I thought it would please the children and took it."

"And then what?" roared Wat Tyler.

"Then what?" roared Priam. "Do you mean to tell me you never heard of the Trojan horse?"

"No," said Tyler. " . . . . died mathematics."

John Kendrick Bangs's syndicated column, 24 March 1918 (McClure syndicate)

Runyon
Interviews Tad.

By Damon Runyon.

Copyright. 1920, by Star Company.

NOT long ago a friend was showing me a bunch of rare old prints.

They were drawings by Hogarth, depicting "The Rake's Progress," a famous series.

William Hogarth was an English satirical artist, who has been dead one hundred and fifty-six years.

"There's a man I wish I could have talked to," said my friend. "He must have known life, and his views must have been most interesting indeed. I wish I had lived in his time, and been acquainted with him. Aren't these pictures wonderful?"

"Well," I admitted, "I guess they're pretty good, all right, but I've got some originals of a better series up at my house. Did you ever hear of 'Indoor Sports'?"

My friend looked at me in pained surprise.

"Do you mean those things

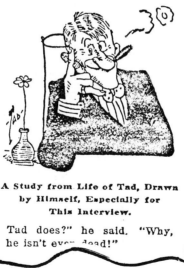

A Study from Life of Tad, Drawn by Himself, Especially for This Interview.

Tad does?" he said. "Why, he isn't even dead!"

Damon Runyon's syndicated column, 23 September 1920 (Hearst syndicate)

Comic-strip version of George Ade's "Fables in Slang," drawn by Art Helfant 1922 (Chicago Record syndicate)

Ring Learns What to "Talk About"

Finds Book That Shows How to Converse With Traffic Cops and Authors.

By RING LARDNER

To the editor:

My tension has been just drow to something that will a long felt want and something which I been wishing I had for the past 50 or 60 yrs. and I am sure others has wanted it so I make haste to tell them about it and what I refer to is a book recently published by Putnam's and wrote by a lady named Mrs. Wolcott and the title of the book is "What to Talk About."

I have read the book through and heartily recommend it either for people to get for themselfs or to give it to their friend for birthday or Labor day presents.

If a person gets a copy of this book and memorizes it from cover to cover or else always carries it in their pocket, they won't never be at a loss what to say to whoever they meet and will soon establish a reputation as brilliant talkers and have no trouble getting themselfs invited to the best homes on Long Island and other islands.

The book is got up in alphabet orders and beginning with people whose job begins with a A like artists or architects, why the author has went clear through to Z and put down just the right things to say to everybody so as to put them at their ease and at the same time make them think you are a wise cracker.

Like for inst. you are suddenly introduced to a guard on the elevated railway. Well, what would you say to a guard on the elevated railway. If you asked him if he done his own cooking he would think you was a f—l.

Well Mrs. Wolcott's book tells you what is the appropriate remarks to make and I forgot just now what she says to talk to guards but I suppose you would first ask them if they liked being guards and when they answered that would ask them if they would not rather be tackles.

In this way a conversation could be started and maintained which would be full of interest to both parties and in some cases might lead to something stronger than friendship.

Authors Hold Up Their End

Or suppose you was attracted by the appearance of a traffic policeman and wanted to get acquainted with him why the way to do would be go right up and ask him some intelligent question in regards to the duties and life of traffic policemans like you might say, "Officer would you rather whistle once or twice?" and then follow that up with "Which direction does most traffic go in, east and west or north and south?"

By this time he would be so interested that traffic would be running amuck.

When you meet a boy scout you first ask them how many knots can they tie and then whether or not they can light a fire without matches. If it is a girl scout instead of a boy scout you ask her how many scouts is in her tribe;

'You might say, 'Officer would you rather whistle once or twice?' and then follow that up with 'Which direction does most traffic go in, east and west or north and south?' "

"If you asked him if he done his own cooking he would think you was a f—l."

whether it is true that all scouts is supposed to do one good deed a day.

When you meet a person who is interested in baseball you first ask him what is the most interesting position on the diamond. Then you ask him what is the secret of the success of players like Cobb and Sisler.

When you meet a writer you ask him what kind of things does he write and whether he would rather write books or magazine articles or plays. As a gen. rule you don't half to strain your voice much keeping up a conversation with authors as the most of them insists on doing at lease their share of the talking.

When you meet the president of a bank you ask him if he clumb up from the bottom or if he got his position by a pull or else you might ask him whether more one dollar bills has odd or even numbers.

Next How to Talk to Animals

Mrs. Wolcott don't say what you ought to talk about when you meet a man that is going to the electric chair in a few days but I suppose you would ask him which he would rather have, a straight chair or a rocker and also how many volts does he think they will give him.

However all and all the book is something which they should no one be without it and personly as soon as my copy is returned I am going to have a special pocket made so as I can always carry it around with me and it is a handy size to carry without messing up your clothes and I only hope Mrs. Wolcott will follow this book up with a sequel on what to say to different kinds and _____ as I am always meeting canaries

"Ring Lardner's Weekly Letter," with cartoons by Dick Dorgan, 5 August 1923 (Bell syndicate)

Gelett Burgess's "Goops!," 20 April 1924 (Chicago Tribune syndicate)

1925 advertisement for "Ring Lardner's Weekly Letter" (Bell syndicate)

Comic-strip version of Montague Glass's "Potash and Perlmutter," drawn by Joe Irving, 1 October 1926 (Bell syndicate)

Announcement for Will Rogers's syndicated daily telegrams, 9 April 1932 (McNaught syndicate)

A Will Rogers syndicated daily telegram, 2 May 1934 (McNaught syndicate)

Appendix IV:
Selected Humorous Magazines (1802-1950)

PRICE 10 CENTS

PUBLISHED MONTHLY

AMERICAN PUNCH

JUNE

PUNCH PUB'G CO. 171 DEVONSHIRE ST. BOSTON, MASS.

TILDEN'S NEW CAMPAIGN SONG.

"Oh, I am a good little boy,
I never did any harm;
I only stole some cider
From my father's barn.

(SPOKEN)—I have that Cider Bar'l now; it is not empty.

SINGLE COPY, 10 CENTS.   SIX MONTHS, 50 CENTS. $1 PER ANNUM.

SEE GRAND LIST OF PREMIUMS.

Selected Humorous Magazines (1820-1950)

Richard Marschall
Weston, Connecticut
and
Carol J. Wilson
Columbia, South Carolina

The humor magazines in the following list represent a neglected facet of the American humor tradition. Many (certainly not all) of the humorists published in these periodicals were first-rate; yet because their work was not collected in book form, it was ephemeral. Nonetheless, these magazines were the closest contact for most readers with the currents of literary humor. They were seedbeds of trends where themes were experimented with, where conventions (such as the ethnic theme) died, where the antecedents of comics, cartoons, essays, vaudeville, movie humor, radio comedy, and every other form of American humor had origin. Moreover, because they were forced by commercial necessity to be broad-based and relevant, humor magazines are entertaining records of American opinion and accurate reflections of popular culture.

The earliest effort at a mature humor magazine (beyond the almanacs, which were sprinkled with humorous epigrams) seems to have been *Salmagundi*, which survived through twenty issues in 1807 and 1808. The editors were Washington Irving, his brother William, and William's brother-in-law, James Kirke Paulding. From then until just past the Civil War, many magazines appeared in similar format and contents, filled increasingly with woodcuts (many unsigned), short jokes (always anonymous), and essays or articles of perhaps a page in length (often pseudonymous). There was a good deal of topical humor, frequent partisan political jabs, ethnic jokes and drawings, and many burlesques of classical literature.

Publisher Frank Leslie, in the Civil War era, was responsible for many new titles. Thematically, very little was different about his magazines, but he did attract a higher quality of talent, and many of his contributors would become prominent in later years. One such contributor—an artist—was Joseph Keppler, who in 1876 founded *Puck* in New York. *Puck* became the most successful American humor magazine of that time (lasting until 1918), and it spawned many imitators. In its first decade it shed its crude image—with jokes about minorities, slapstick humor, and puns—and became a sophisticated humor magazine with longer articles and more society and suburban subjects. This was largely due to the influence of editor H. C. Bunner, one of the remarkable editors in the history of humor magazines.

Bunner died at the age of forty in 1896 and, over the next fifteen years, was succeeded as *Puck*'s editor by John Kendrick Bangs, Bert Leston Taylor ("B.L.T."), Harry Leon Wilson, and Arthur H. Folwell. In 1914 the magazine was sold by Keppler's son to the Strauss family of Macy's department store fortune; three years later they sold it to William Randolph Hearst; and in September 1918 *Puck* folded.

Puck's first major rival was *The Judge*, begun in 1881, evidently as a face-lift of *Wild Oats*. Color was added, in imitation of *Puck*, and a star cartoonist, James Albert Wales, was hired away from the rival magazine. For nearly all its existence *Judge* (as it soon was called) focused on cartoon humor; indeed, it published some of the greatest names in cartooning, while only infrequently publishing quality writers. There was always more rural and racial humor in *Judge* than in its major rivals, and laughs came via broader humor, slapstick comedy, and exaggeration.

Just after World War I *Judge* made a brief effort to be more literary. The humor became more sophisticated and, to attract a new market, college oriented. Writers included Heywood Broun, Donald Ogden Stewart, James S. Metcalfe, Benjamin deCasseres, Richard LeGallienne, Gelett Burgess, Ellis Parker Butler, George Jean Nathan, and Walter Prichard Eaton. In 1924 a new editor, Norman Anthony, set an editorial tone that once again promoted the cartoon-filled picture book look. Fortunately he discovered and nurtured some great names in American literary humor in the process of talent hunting and filling the spaces between cartoons; his most notable discoveries were S. J. Perelman and Dr. Seuss. After suspending publication in January 1939, *Judge* was resurrected later that year and struggled on until 1949.

Life, published from 1883 to 1936, set its approach toward American humor from the start and seldom deviated: it was for the cultivated reader, one involved in social causes, one familiar with society's fancies. Unlike *Puck* and *Judge* it eschewed color lithographs; it was also of a calmer political voice though its sympathies were generally Democratic (*Judge* had been staunchly Republican, even subsidized for a time by the Republican party).

Writers in its early years included its visionary founder, John Ames Mitchell, and the fecund editor, E. S. Martin—a mirror image of Bunner: humor writer, poet, essayist, and political editorialist. Tom L. Masson, *Life*'s literary editor, was among the finest hunters and managers of humorous talent of the age.

With the death of Mitchell and the end of World War I, *Life* became a straight humor magazine. If the 1920s were the golden years of American humor, then *Life* became a lightning rod for the amazing currents in the field. In its pages during that decade were contributions by Robert Benchley, Robert E. Sherwood, Dorothy Parker, Franklin P. Adams, Corey Ford, Montague Glass, Will Rogers, Ring Lardner, Marc Connelly, George S. Kaufman, Gluyas Williams, Percy Crosby, John Held, Jr., Norman Rockwell, the Leyendecker brothers, Maxfield Parrish, Charles Dana Gibson, E. W. Kemble, A. B. Frost, and T. S. Sullivant. Political spoofs, clever commentaries (editorials were still by E. S. Martin), short stories, droll essays, parodies—all of the first quality—were hallmarks of *Life* at its best.

To boost sales Norman Anthony was hired away from the raucous *Judge* in 1929, but old *Life* readers apparently disliked his college-humor approach, and *Judge* readers saw no reason to switch loyalties. That, and the Depression, pushed *Life* into a decline in the 1930s. Under the brilliant editor George T. Eggleston (now a respected revisionist historian), the last stable included S. J. Perelman, Dr. Seuss, Frank Sullivan, Paul Gallico, Baird Leonard, Kyle S. Crichton, Arthur L. Lippmann, Frank Kent, George Jean Nathan, J. P. McEvoy, and E. S. Martin, who wrote a goodbye in the last issue, in 1936, just as he had written a greeting to new readers for the first in 1883. The title was sold to the Time Corporation where it was used for a pictorial news magazine, and a wag soon referred to the "old" *Life* as the one that was *deliberately* funny.

Perhaps the most notable humor magazine of the 1920s from a historical perspective was the *New Yorker*, founded in 1925; it was soon transformed from a humor magazine into a general-interest magazine for a sophisticated metropolitan readership. Initially (and contrary to legend), established literary humorists were reluctant to join the *New Yorker* stable. Ring Lardner, for instance, wrote only one piece the first year, and George S. Kaufman was not to write until 1935 for the magazine's determined editor, Harold Ross. But eventually the *New Yorker*'s impressive list of humor writers grew to include Alexander Woollcott, Franklin P. Adams, Fairfax Downey, Arthur H. Folwell, James Thurber, S. J. Perelman, Robert Benchley, Robert E. Sherwood, Frank Sullivan, Clarence Day, Ogden Nash, Nunnally Johnson, Phyllis McGinley, Margaret Fishback, and E. B. White.

In 1931 Norman Anthony founded *Ballyhoo*, an almost nihilistic magazine of advertising spoofs, parodies, sight gags, puns, and irreverent satires. There were many imitators, and the whole spate disappeared within a few years. Hardly any piece was longer than a two-line wisecrack, and most of the work was anonymous. American humor magazine traditions have pitifully dwindled since that time to several latter-day imitations of *Ballyhoo*, including today's sophomoric (if not juvenile) *Mad* and *National Lampoon*, where scatology seems paramount to cleverness.

There are signs of new interest in humor magazines in the 1980s. The *American Bystander* and *Vanity Fair*, both national magazines that are to rely heavily on humorous material, are scheduled to debut late in 1982. Brian McConnachie, editor of the *American Bystander*, is optimistic about the chances for a revival of interest in periodicals of this type: "There is so much young talent around with no place to show their work. The readers have just gone away. They haven't died." One hopes that while they were away, the readers spawned a new generation who will extend the rich literary tradition of humor magazines in America.

Acta Columbiana, Columbia University, New York, October 1868-April 1886(?).

Ainslee's, see *Yellow Book*.

American Humorist, see *Biography; a Digest Magazine*.

American Monthly, see *Foederal American Monthly*.

American Monthly Knicker-bocker, see *Foederal American Monthly*.

American Punch, Boston, 1879-1881(?).

America's Humor, Chicago, 1927-1930.

Arkansas Thomas Cat, Hot Springs, 1890-1948.

Arkansas Traveler, Little Rock and Chicago, 1882-1916 (?).

Art Young Quarterly, see *Good Morning*.

Atlantic Monthly, see *Galaxy*.

Aw, Nerts!, ca. 1932.

Ballyhoo, New York, August 1931-August 1938.

Bee; an Illustrated Comic Weekly, New York, 16 May-2 August 1898.

Biography; a Digest Magazine, Emmaus, Pennsylvania, 1931(?)-July 1937; 1931(?)-August 1936 as *American Humorist*; October 1936-April 1937 as *New Biography*.

Boloney, ca. 1932.

Boneville Trumpet, Bridgeport, Connecticut, 1868-1869.

Boomerang, Laramie, Wyoming, 1881-(?); later *Republican-Boomerang*.

Breeze, Chicago, 1883.

Brickbat, New York, 1872.

Brown Jug, Brown University, Providence, Rhode Island, February 1920-June 1933; December 1966; September 1968.

Bubble, New York, 20 October 1849(?).

Budget, 1852-1853.

Bugle-Horn of Liberty. A Humorous Paper, Devoted to Fun, Fact and Fancy, Griffin, Georgia, August-October 1863.

Bunk, ca. 1932.

Burten's Follies, New York, 1926(?)-1929.

Bushwa, ca. 1932.

California Maverick, San Francisco, 1883-1886.

Captain Billy's Whiz-Bang, Minneapolis, 1920-1932(?).

Carl Pretzel's National Weekly, Chicago, 1874-1893.

Carl Pretzel's Pook, Chicago, 1872-1874.

Carpet-Bag, a Literary Journal; Published Weekly, for the Amusement of Its Readers, Boston, 29 March 1851-26 March 1853.

Cartoonews, New York, 13 August-December 1936; superseded by *O K*.

Cartoons, see *Wayside Tales*.

Cartoons Magazine, see *Wayside Tales*.

Chameleon, Princeton University, Princeton, New Jersey, September 1835-1836.

Champagne, an Illustrated Journal of Society, Sparkle, and Sentiment, New York, June-December 1871.

Chic, New York, 15 September 1880-31 May 1881.

Chicago Figaro. American Illustrated Society Journal, Chicago, March 1888-1893; cover and caption title of individual numbers is *Figaro*.

Chip Basket, New York, 1869-1871.

Clips: Zest of the Best; Wit of the World, New York, 21 November 1895-2 January 1897.

Cocktails, Boston, 1872.

College Humor, Chicago, 1922-December 1929; January 1930-February 1934; 1935-(?); title varies slightly.

Columbia Jester, Columbia University, New York, 1 April 1901-May 1966(?).

Comic Library, New York, 1894-1898.

Comic Monthly, New York, 1859-1881.

Comic News, New York, 1869-1872.

Comic World, New York, 1855.

Comic World, New York, January 1876-December

1879(?); cover title, *Grand Combination–Yankee Notions, The Merrymans, Comic World, Nick Nax.*

Commodore Rollingpin's Illustrated Humorous Almanac, 1875(?)-(?).

Constellation, New York, 1829-1834.

Corrector, New York, 28 March-26 April 1804.

Cozzens' Wine Press: a Vinous, Vivacious Monthly, New York, 20 June 1854-20 March 1861.

Dartmouth Jack-O'-Lantern, Dartmouth College, Hanover, New Hampshire, March 1909-current.

Diogenes, hys Lanterne, see *Lantern*.

Elephant, 1 January 1848-19 February 1848.

Epi-Lark, see *Lark*.

Every Body's Album: a Humorous Collection of Tales, Quips, Quirks, Anecdotes, and Facetiae, Philadelphia, July 1836-June 1837.

Fat Contributor's Saturday Night, Cincinnati and New York, 1872-1875.

Figaro! or, Corbyn's Chronicle of Amusements, New York, 31 August 1850-10 May 1851(?).

Film Fun, New York, August 1887-January 1922(?); 1887-January 1890 as *Judge's Serials*; February 1890-July 1912 as *Judge's Library*; August 1912-June 1915 as *Magazine of Fun*.

Flashes, ca. 1928.

Foederal American Monthly, New York, January 1833-October 1865; 1833-1862 as *Knickerbocker; or, New-York Monthly Magazine*; 1863-February 1864 as *Knickerbocker Monthly*; March-December 1864 as *American Monthly Knicker-bocker*; January-June 1865 as *American Monthly*.

Fool; by Thomas Brainless, jester to his majesty the public, Salem, Massachusetts, February-April 1807(?).

Foolish Book, New York, 1903-1904.

Frank Leslie's Budget of Fun, New York, January 1859-June 1878(?).

Frank Leslie's Budget of Humorous and Sparkling Stories, Tales of Heroism, Adventure and Satire, New York, May 1878-April 1896.

Freak, Sharon, Massachusetts, 1902-1903.

French Frolics–La Vie Parisienne, ca. 1925.

French Humor, New York, 1927(?)-1930.

Fun, New York, 1911-1917(?).

Fun Quarterly, New York and London, September-December 1903.

Funny Facts and Fiction, see *Today's Best Stories*.

Funny Side, New York, 1901-1917(?).

Funnyest of Awl, and the Funniest Sort of Phun, New York, 1865-(?).

Gag Bag, ca. 1939.

Galaxy, New York, May 1866-January 1878, merged into *Atlantic Monthly*.

Galaxy of Comicalities, Philadelphia, 2 October 1833-5 July 1834.

Gilhooley's Etchings, Pittsburgh, 1883.

Good Morning, New York, 8 May 1919-October 1921; superseded by *Art Young Quarterly*, 1922-(?).

Harvard Lampoon, Cambridge, Massachusetts, 1876-current.

Haywire, ca. 1932.

Hint, New York, 1854.

Home Magazine, Washington, Minneapolis, Indianapolis, 1888-April 1908; absorbed by *Uncle Remus's Home Magazine*.

Hooey, Louisville, Kentucky, January 1931-(?).

Hullabaloo, ca. 1932.

Humorist, New York, 1874.

Independent Balance, Philadelphia, 20 March 1817-(?).

Innocent Weekly Owl, 1860.

Jest, ca. 1933.

Jester, Boston, 14 June 1845-(?).

Jester, Philadelphia, 1889-1891; Boston, 1891-1892.

Jim Jam Jems, Bismarck, North Dakota, July 1912-October 1928.

John-Donkey, New York and Philadelphia, 1 January-21 October 1848.

Jolly Hoosier, Indianapolis, 1867.

Jolly Joker, New York, 1862-May 1878(?).

Jubilee Days. An Illustrated Daily Record of the Humorous Features of the World's Peace Jubilee, Boston, 17 June-4 July 1872.

Judge, New York, 1881-January 1939; July 1939-January 1949.

Judge's Library, see *Film Fun*.

Judge's Quarterly; a Magazine of Wit and Humor, New York, 1892-1913(?).

Judge's Serials, see *Film Fun*.

Judy, New York, 28 November 1846-20 February 1847(?).

Just Fun, That's all, New York, 1903-1904.

Kaleidoscope, New York, June 1869.

Keepapitchinin, A Semi-occasional Paper, Devoted to Cents, Scents, Sense and Nonsense, Salt Lake City, 4 July 1871-(?).

Knickerbocker Monthly, see *Foederal American Monthly*.

Knickerbocker; or New-York Monthly Magazine, see *Foederal American Monthly*.

Lantern, New York, 10 January 1852-July 1853.

Lark, San Francisco, May 1895-1 May 1897; 1 May 1897 as *Epi-Lark*.

Life, New York, 4 January 1883-November 1936.

Life's Comedy, New York, 1897-1 November 1898.

Little Joker, New York, 1863-1866.

Magazine of Fun, see *Film Fun*.

Mascot, New Orleans, 1882-1894(?).

Merry and Wise, New York, 1867.

Merry-Go-Round, ca. 1932.

Merryman's Monthly, New York, 1863-1877; 1863-February 1865 as *Mr. Merryman's Monthly*; see *Comic World*.

Merry Masker, New York, 1876.

Momus. Weekly Edition, New York, 5 May-21 July 1860.

Mr. Merryman's Monthly, see *Merryman's Monthly*.

Mrs. Grundy, New York, 1865.

Munsey's Magazine, New York, 1889-October 1929; volumes 1-5 as *Munsey's Weekly*; see *Time*.

New Biography, see *Biography; a Digest Magazine*.

New Varieties, New York, 9 January 1871-25 October 1873(?).

New Yorker, New York, 21 February 1925-current.

New York Humorist, New York, 1869.

New York Picayune, New York, January 1847-18 February 1860.

New York Time-Piece, New York, 1853.

Nick Nax, 1857-December 1875(?); see *Comic World*.

O K, New York, February 1937-December 1937/January 1938; supersedes *Cartoonews*.

Oy'Oy I'm Leffin, ca. 1930.

Phunniest of Awl, occasional title for *Funnyest of Awl, and the Funniest Sort of Phun*.

Phunniest of Phun, New York, 1865-1867.

Phunny Phellow, New York, 1859-1876.

Pick, New York, 1852-(?).

Pickings from Puck, New York, 1883-1887.

Pictorial Wag, New York, January(?) 1842-1843(?).

Princeton Tiger, Princeton University, Princeton, New Jersey, February/June 1882-current.

Puck, New York, March 1877-September 1918.

Puck on Wheels, New York, 1880-1886.

Puck's Library, New York, July 1887-1904; superseded by *Puck's Monthly Magazine and Almanac*.

Puck's Monthly Magazine and Almanac, New York, 1905-1912; 1913-1914.

Puck's Quarterly, New York, April 1896-October 1914(?).

Puck: the Pacific Pictorial, San Francisco, 7 January 1865-March 1866.

Punch and Judy, Boston, 1882.

Punchinello, New York, 2 April-24 December 1870.

Rambler. A Journal of Men, Manners and Things, Chicago, 1884-January 1887(?).

Republican-Boomerang, see *Boomerang*.

Reveille, New York, 1851-1854.

Rolling Stone, Austin, Texas, 28 April 1894-27 April 1895.

Salmagundi; or, the Whim-Whams and Opinions of Launcelot Longstaff, Esq., and Others, New York, 24 January 1807-25 January 1808; revived 30 May 1819-19 August 1820.

Satirist, Boston, 16 January-9 May 1812; numbers 11-13 as *Boston Satirist; or Weekly Museum*.

Scourge, Baltimore, 26 May-13 October 1810.

Scourge, Boston, 10 August-28 December 1811.

Sis Hopkins' Own Book and Magazine of Fun, New York, September 1899-July 1911; merged into *Judge's Library*, later *Film Fun*.

Slapstick, New York, February 1932-(?).

Smoke, a Magazine of Humor and Good-fellowship, New York, December 1906-February/March 1907(?).

Smokehouse, ca. 1933.

Snaps; a Comic Weekly of Comic Stories by Comic Authors, New York, 1899-1900.

Something, Boston, 18 November 1809-12 May 1810.

Southern Punch, Richmond, Virginia, 1863-1865.

Sunny South, Atlanta, 4 December 1805-1907; superseded by *Uncle Remus's Home Magazine*.

Texas Siftings, New York and Austin, Texas, 1881-1897.

Thistle, Princeton University, Princeton, New Jersey, September 1834-1835.

Thistle, New York, 1872.

Thistleton's Illustrated Jolly Giant, see *Thistleton's Jolly Giant, the Critic*.

Thistleton's Jolly Giant, the Critic, San Francisco, 1873-1880(?); May 1874-1877 as *Thistleton's Illustrated Jolly Giant*; superseded by *Thistleton's New Monthly Giant*, August-October 1882(?).

Thistleton's New Monthly Giant, see *Thistleton's Jolly Giant, the Critic*.

Tickle-Me-Too, ca. 1932.

Tickler. By Toby Scratch'em, Philadelphia, 16 September 1807-17 November 1813(?).

Tid-Bits, see *Time*.

Time, New York, 23 August 1884-22 February 1890; volumes 1-7 as *Tid-Bits; an Illustrated Weekly for These Times*; merged into *Munsey's Weekly*, later *Munsey's Magazine*.

Today's Best Stories, St. Paul, Minnesota, 1931-(?); 1931-March 1932 as *Funny Facts and Fiction*; April 1932-Spring 1933 as *Today's Humor*.

Today's Humor, see *Today's Best Stories*.

Truth, New York, 1886-1906(?).

Twinkles, New York, 25 October 1896-May 1897.

Uncle Remus's Home Magazine, Atlanta, May 1908-February 1913(?); supersedes *Sunny South*; absorbed *Home Magazine*, May 1908, and assumed its numbering; 1907-April 1908 as *Uncle Remus's Magazine*; May 1908-July 1909 as *Uncle Remus's, the Home Magazine*.

Uncle Remus's Magazine, see *Uncle Remus's Home Magazine*.

Uncle Sam: American Humorist, New York, October 1888(?).

Uncle Sam; the American Journal of Wit and Humor . . ., New York, 12 April-21 June 1879.

Vanity Fair, New York, 31 December 1859-4 July 1863.

Verdict, New York, 19 December 1898-12 November 1900.

Wag, Boston, 1868.

Wasp, Hudson, New York, 7 July 1802-26 January 1803.

Wayside Tales, Chicago, 1912-May 1922; 1912-May 1913 as *Cartoons*; June 1913-July 1921 as *Cartoons Magazine*; August-December 1921 as *Wayside Tales and Cartoons*.

Wayside Tales and Cartoons, see *Wayside Tales*.

Whip, St. Louis, 1885-1886.

Wild Oats. An Illustrated Weekly Journal of Fun, Satire, Burlesque and Nits at Persons and Events of the Day, New York, February 1870-1881; subtitle varies.

Williams Purple Cow, Williams College, Williamstown, Massachusetts, October 1907-January 1943.

Wit and Wisdom, New York, 20 January-15 December 1881.

Wit o' the World, New York, August 1925-August 1926.

World Humor, ca. 1925.

World's Fair Puck, Chicago, 1 May 1893-30 October 1893.

Yale Record, Yale University, New Haven, Connecticut, 1872-1969.

Yankee Doodle, New York, October 1846-October 1847.

Yankee Doodle; or, Young America, New York, February 1853-1854; (?)-1856 as *Young America*.

Yankee Humor, ca. 1928.

Yankee Notions, New York, 1852-1875(?); January-December 1852 as *Yankee Notions; or Whittlings from Jonathan's Jack-knife*; see *Comic World*.

Ye Giglampz, Cincinnati, 1874.

Yellow Book, New York, 20 March 1897-January 1898; March-July 1897 as *Yellow Kid*; superseded by *Ainslee's*, February-December 1926.

Yellow Kid, see *Yellow Book*.

Young America, see *Yankee Doodle; or, Young America*.

Young Sam, New York, 1852.

Ziffs, ca. 1925.

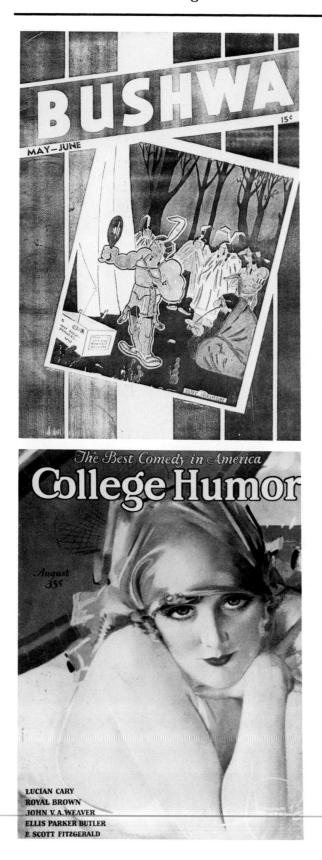

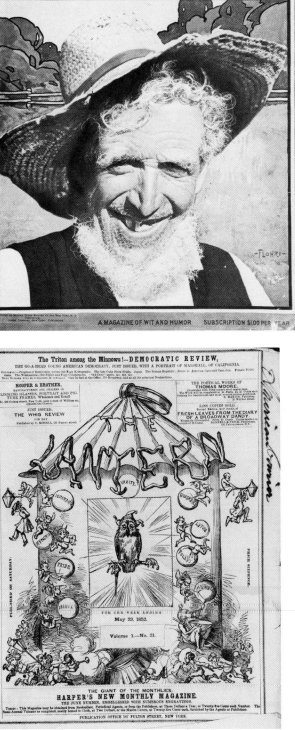

Texas, appeared on the cover of a weekly magazine that was owned and edited for a year by O. Henry while he was an Austin bank clerk. It was the profession of banking, not cartooning, that led to his imprisonment.

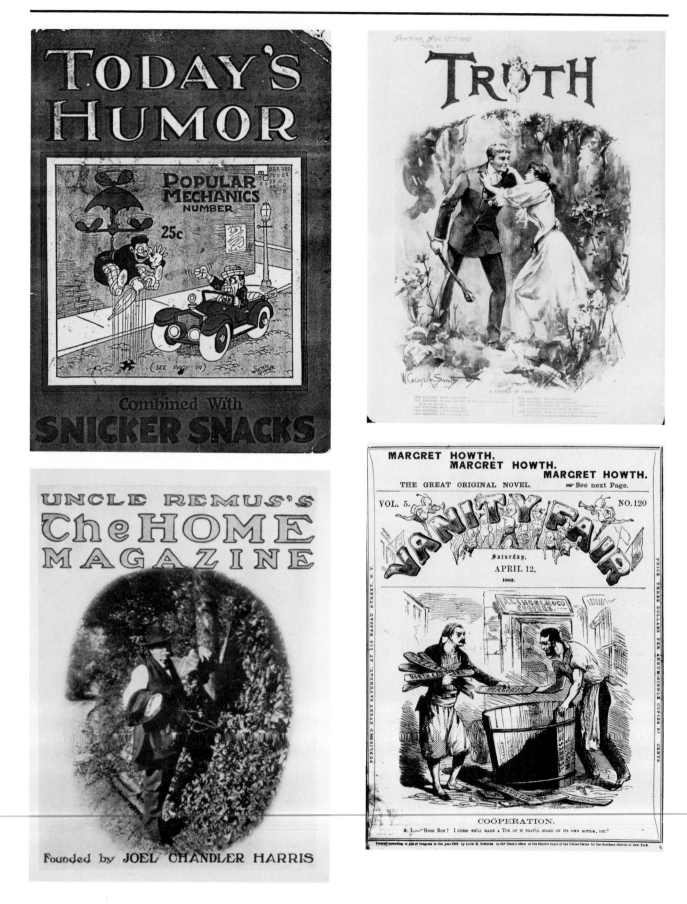

Appendix V:
Supplementary Reading List

Annotated checklists of criticism on American humor are published regularly in *American Humor: An Interdisciplinary Newsletter*.

Becker, Stephen. *Comic Art in America*. New York: Simon & Schuster, 1959.

Bier, Jesse. *The Rise and Fall of American Humor*. New York: Holt, Rinehart & Winston, 1968.

Blair, Walter. *Horse Sense in American Humor from Benjamin Franklin to Ogden Nash*. Chicago: University of Chicago Press, 1942.

Blair. *Native American Humor*. New York: American Book Company, 1937.

Blair and Hamlin Hill. *America's Humor: From Poor Richard to Doonesbury*. New York: Oxford University Press, 1978.

Boatright, Mody C. *Folk Laughter on the American Frontier*. New York: Macmillan, 1949.

Boynton, H. W. "American Humor," *Atlantic*, 90 (September 1902): 414-420.

Bradley, Sculley. "Our Native Humor," *North American Review*, 262 (Winter 1937): 351-362.

Chapman, Anthony J. and Hugh C. Foot., eds. *It's a Funny Thing, Humor*. Oxford: Pergamon Press, 1977.

Chittick, V. L. O. *Thomas Chandler Haliburton: A Study in Provincial Toryism*. New York: Columbia University Press, 1924.

Clemens, William M. *Famous Funny Fellows*. Cleveland: W. W. Williams, 1882.

Cohen, Sarah Blacher. *Comic Relief: Humor in Contemporary American Literature*. Urbana: University of Illinois Press, 1978.

Cox, Samuel S. *Why We Laugh*. New York: Harper, 1876.

DeVoto, Bernard. "Lineage of Eustace Tilley," *Saturday Review of Literature*, 16 (25 September 1937): 3-4.

DeVoto. *Mark Twain's America*. Boston: Little, Brown, 1932.

Dorson, Richard M. *Jonathan Draws the Long Bow*. Cambridge: Harvard University Press, 1946.

Eastman, Max. *Enjoyment of Laughter*. New York: Simon & Schuster, 1936.

Ferguson, J. DeLancey. "The Roots of American Humor," *American Scholar*, 4 (Winter 1935): 41-49.

Ford, James L. "A Century of American Humor," *Munsey's Magazine*, 25 (July 1901): 482-490.

Gill, Brendan. *Here at the New Yorker*. New York: Random House, 1975.

Habegger, Alfred. "Nineteenth-Century American Humor: Easygoing Males, Anxious Ladies, and Penelope Lapham," *PMLA*, 51 (1976): 884-899.

Hancock, Ernest L. "The Passing of the American Comic," *Bookman*, 22 (September 1905): 78-84.

Harriman, Margaret Case. *The Vicious Circle: The Story of the Algonquin Round Table*. New York & Toronto: Rinehart, 1951.

Hauck, Richard B. *A Cheerful Nihilism: Confidence and "The Absurd" in American Humorous Fiction*. Bloomington: Indiana University Press, 1971.

Holliday, Carl. *The Wit and Humor of Colonial Days*. New York: Ungar, 1960.

Hoole, W. Stanley. *Alias Simon Suggs: The Life and Times of Johnson Jones Hooper*. University: University of Alabama Press, 1952.

Howe, Will D. "Early Humorists," in *The Cambridge History of American Literature*. New York: Macmillan, 1948, II: 703-727.

Howells, William Dean. "Our National Humorists," *Harper's*, 134 (February 1917): 442-445.

Inge, M. Thomas, ed. *The Frontier Humorists: Critical Views*. Hamden, Conn.: Archon, 1975.

Kramer, Dale. *Ross and the New Yorker*. Garden City: Doubleday, 1951.

Lukens, Henry C. "American Literary Comedians," *Harper's*, 80 (April 1890): 783-797.

Lynn, Kenneth S. *Mark Twain and Southwestern Humor*. Boston: Little, Brown, 1959.

Masson, Thomas L., ed. *Our American Humorists*. New York: Dodd, Mead, 1922.

Matthews, Brander. "The Comic Periodical Literature of the United States," *American Bibliopolist*, 7 (August 1875): 199-201.

Meine, Franklin J., ed. *Tall Tales of the Southwest*. New York: Knopf, 1930.

Murrell, William. *A History of American Graphic Humor*, 2 volumes. New York: Whitney Museum of American Art, 1933, 1938.

Roth, Martin. *Comedy in America: The Lost World of Washington Irving*. Port Washington, N. Y.: Kennikat Press, 1976.

Rourke, Constance. *American Humor: A Study of the National Character*. New York: Harcourt, Brace, 1931.

Rubin, Louis D., ed. *Comic Imagination in American Literature*. New Brunswick: Rutgers University Press, 1973.

Tandy, Jennette. *Crackerbox Philosophers in American Humor and Satire*. New York: Columbia University Press, 1925.

Thompson, Harold W., and Henry Seidel Canby. "Humor" in *Literary History of the United States*.

New York: Macmillan, 1948, II: 728-757.

Thurber, James. *The Years with Ross*. Boston: Little, Brown, 1959.

Trent, W. P. "A Retrospect of American Humor," *Century*, 63 (November 1901): 45-64.

Turner, Arlin. "Realism and Fantasy in Southern Humor," *Georgia Review*, 12 (Winter 1958): 451-457.

Turner. "Seeds of Literary Revolt in the Humor of the Old Southwest," *Louisiana Historical Quarterly*, 39 (1957): 143-151.

Wertheim, Arthur Frank. *Radio Comedy*. New York: Oxford University Press, 1979.

Whicher, George Frisbie. "Minor Humorists," in *The Cambridge History of American Literature*. New York: Macmillan, 1933, III: 21-30.

Wilt, Napier. *Some American Humorists*. New York: Thomas Nelson, 1929.

Yates, Norris W. *The American Humorist, Conscience of the Twentieth Century*. Ames: Iowa State University Press, 1964.

Yates. *William T. Porter and the Spirit of the Times: A Study of the Big Bear School of Humor*. Baton Rouge: Louisiana State University Press, 1957.

Contributors

St. George Tucker Arnold, Jr. ....*Florida International University*
Bill Blackbeard..*San Francisco Academy of Comic Art*
Michael Butler..*University of Kansas*
Sandy Cohen..*Albany State College*
Pascal Covici, Jr...*Southern Methodist University*
Zita Zatkin Dresner ....*Washington, D.C.*
Betsy Erkkila ....*University of Pennsylvania*
Lorne Fienburg...*Iowa State University*
Steven H. Gale..*Missouri Southern State College*
Ellen Golub ....*University of Pennsylvania*
Thomas Grant ....*University of Hartford*
Terry L. Heller ....*Coe College*
Francis Hodgins...*University of Illinois*
Dan Jaffe ....*University of Missouri, Kansas City*
Mark A. Keller...*Middle Georgia College*
David B. Kesterson ....*North Texas State University*
William E. Lenz...*Chatham College*
Paul R. Lilly, Jr.............................*State University of New York College at Oneonta*
Richard Marschall ....*Weston, Connecticut*
James C. McNutt ....*University of Texas at Austin*
Elton Miles ....*Sul Ross State University*
Nancy Pogel...*Michigan State University*
Edward C. Sampson............................*State University of New York College at Oneonta*
Peter A. Scholl...*Luther College*
L. Moody Simms, Jr..*Illinois State University*
David E. E. Sloane ....*University of New Haven*
Roy Arthur Swanson ....*University of Wisconsin-Milwaukee*
Stanley Trachtenberg...*Texas Christian University*
Clyde G. Wade...*University of Missouri, Rolla*
Edward E. Waldron ....*Yankton College*
Nancy Walker ....*Stephens College*
Carol J. Wilson...*Columbia, South Carolina*

683

Cumulative Index

Dictionary of Literary Biography, Volumes 1-11
Dictionary of Literary Biography Yearbook, 1980, 1981
Dictionary of Literary Biography Documentary Series, Volume 1

Cumulative Index

Volume number only: *Dictionary of Literary Biography*, Volumes 1-11
Y before number: *Dictionary of Literary Biography Yearbook*, 1980, 1981
DS before number: *Dictionary of Literary Biography Documentary Series*, Volume 1

A

Jacob Abbott 1

Louis Adamic 9

George Ade 11

Max Adeler (see Charles Heber Clark)

Jean Louis Rodolphe Agassiz............................1

James Agee 2

Conrad Aiken 9

Edward Albee 7

Amos Bronson Alcott 1

Louisa May Alcott..1

William Andrus Alcott......................................1

Nelson Algren...9

Hervey Allen..9

Josiah Allen's Wife (see Marietta Holly)

Washington Allston 1

A. R. Ammons 5

Margaret Anderson 4

Maxwell Anderson...7

Poul Anderson 8

Robert Anderson 7

Sherwood Anderson......................4, 9, DS1

Piers Anthony 8

William Archer 10

Harriette Simpson Arnow 6

Bill Arp (see Charles Henry Smith)

Timothy Shay Arthur..3

Nathan Asch 4

John Ashbery................................5, Y81

Winifred Ashton (see Clemence Dane)

Isaac Asimov 8

Gertrude Atherton 9

Louis Auchincloss 2, Y80

W. H. Auden..10

Mary Austin 9

B

Delia Bacon...1

Wambly Bald..4

James Baldwin 2, 7

Joseph Glover Baldwin..................................3, 11

George Bancroft 1

John Kendrick Bangs 11

Amiri Baraka 5, 7

Harley Granville Barker....................................10

Coleman Barks..5

Djuna Barnes 4, 9

Margaret Ayer Barnes.......................................9

Natalie Barney 4

James M. Barrie..10

Philip Barry...7

John Barth 2

Donald Barthelme.........................2, Y80

John Bartlett..1

Cyrus Augustus Bartol 1

T. J. Bass...Y81

Thomas Joseph Bassler (see T. J. Bass)

Jonathan Baumbach.......................................Y80

Clifford Bax 10

Sylvia Beach 4

Peter S. Beagle Y80

M. F. Beal Y81

Catharine Esther Beecher 1

Henry Ward Beecher 3

S. N. Behrman 7

David Belasco 7

Ben Belitt 5

Marvin Bell 5

Saul Bellow 2

Robert Benchley 11

Michael Benedikt 5

Stephen Vincent Benet 4

Park Benjamin 3

Arnold Bennett 10

Stephen Berg 5

Thomas Berger 2, Y80

Daniel Berrigan 5

Ted Berrigan 5

Wendell Berry 5, 6

Alfred Bester 8

Ambrose Bierce 11

Lloyd Biggle, Jr. 8

Hosea Biglow (see James Russell Lowell)

Josh Billings (see Henry Wheeler Shaw)

William Bird..4

Elizabeth Bishop 5

John Peale Bishop 4, 9

Paul Blackburn..Y81

Albert Taylor Bledsoe 3

James Blish 8

Robert Bly 5

Maxwell Bodenheim 9

Charles Boer 5

Anne C. Lynch Botta.......................................3

Gordon Bottomley..10

Anthony Boucher 8

Vance Bourjaily 2

Ben Bova...Y81

Francis Bowen...1

Edgar Bowers..5

Paul Bowles...5, 6

James Boyd 9

John Boyd 8

Thomas Boyd..9

Kay Boyle 4, 9

Leigh Brackett 8

Hugh Henry Brackenridge 11

Ray Bradbury 2, 8

Marion Zimmer Bradley..................................8

William Aspenwall Bradley 4

Richard Brautigan 2, 5, Y80

James Bridie..10

Charles Frederick Briggs..................................3

Harold Brighouse 10

Albert Brisbane...3

Louis Bromfield...4, 9

Charles Timothy Brooks 1

Gwendolyn Brooks 5

Brother Antoninus (see William Everson)

John Brougham 11

James Broughton...5

Bob Brown..4

Dee Brown...Y80

Fredric Brown...8

William Wells Brown 3

Charles Farrar Browne....................................11

Orestes Augustus Brownson 1

William Cullen Bryant......................................3

Pearl S. Buck..9

William F. Buckley, Jr.....................................Y80

A. J. Budrys 8

Frederick Buechner Y80

Charles Bukowski 5

Ed Bullins..................................7

Jerry Bumpus Y81

Gelett Burgess..................................11

W. R. Burnett..................................9

Edgar Rice Burroughs..................................8

William Seward Burroughs..................2, 8, Y81

Janet Burroway..................................6

Frederick Busch..................................6

C

James Branch Cabell 9

Abraham Cahan..................................9

Erskine Caldwell 9

John C. Calhoun..................................3

Hortense Calisher..................................2

Edgar Calmer..................................4

George Henry Calvert 1

John W. Campbell, Jr...................................8

Gilbert Cannan 10

Kathleen Cannell 4

Robert Cantwell 9

Truman Capote 2, Y80

Gladys Hasty Carroll 9

Paul Vincent Carroll..................................10

Hayden Carruth..................................5

Lin Carter..................................Y81

William Alexander Caruthers 3

Michael Casey 5

R. V. Cassill 6

Willa Cather..................................9, DS1

Charles Haddon Chambers..................................10

Edward Tyrrell Channing..................................1

William Ellery Channing..................................1

William Ellery Channing II..................................1

William Henry Channing..................................1

Fred Chappell..................................6

Paddy Chayefsky..................................7, Y81

John Cheever..................................2, Y80

Ednah Dow (Littlehale) Cheney..................................1

C. J. Cherryh..................................Y80

G. K. Chesterton..................................10

Francis James Child..................................1

Lydia Maria Child..................................1

Alice Childress 7

Thomas Holley Chivers..................................3

John Ciardi 5

Charles Heber Clark..................................11

Eleanor Clark..................................6

Lewis Gaylord Clark..................................3

Walter Van Tilburg Clark..................................9

Austin Clarke..................................10

James Freeman Clarke 1

Samuel Langhorne Clemens 11

Hal Clement..................................8

Lucille Clifton 5

Robert M. Coates..................................4, 9

Irvin S. Cobb..................................11

Emily Holmes Coleman..................................4

Laurie Colwin..................................Y80

Evan S. Connell, Jr...................................2, Y81

Marc Connelly..................................7, Y80

Joseph Conrad 10

Jack Conroy..................................Y81

Pat Conroy 6

Moncure Daniel Conway..................................1

John Esten Cooke..................................3

Philip Pendleton Cooke..................................3

James Fenimore Cooper..................................3

Robert Coover..................................2, Y81

Cid Corman 5

Alfred Corn Y80

John William Corrington 6

Gregory Corso 5

Thomas B. Costain 9

Noel Coward 10

Malcolm Cowley 4, Y81

Louis Coxe 5

James Gould Cozzens 9

Christopher Pearse Cranch 1

Hart Crane 4

Geoffrey Crayon (see Washington Irving)

Robert Creeley 5

Harry Crews 6

Michael Crichton Y81

Michael Cristofer 7

David Crockett 3, 11

Caresse Crosby and Harry Crosby 4

Rachel Crothers 7

Mart Crowley 7

Homer Croy 4

Countee Cullen 4

E. E. Cummings 4

Ray Cummings 8

J. V. Cunningham 5

George Cuomo Y80

Will Cuppy 11

George William Curtis 1

D

Caroline Wells (Healey) Dall 1

T. A. Daly 11

Louis D'Alton 10

Charles A. Dana 3

Richard Henry Dana, Jr. 1

Clemence Dane 10

Avram Davidson 8

Gordon Daviot 10

Charles A. Davis 11

Clyde Brion Davis 9

H. L. Davis 9

Ossie Davis 7

Peter Davison 5

Clarence Day 11

Borden Deal 6

James D. B. De Bow 3

L. Sprague de Camp 8

Robert de Graff Y81

Samuel R. Delany 8

Nicholas Delbanco 6

Don DeLillo 6

Floyd Dell 9

Lester del Rey 8

George Horatio Derby 11

August Derleth 9

Bernard De Voto 9

Peter De Vries 6

Philip K. Dick 8

James Dickey 5

William Dickey 5

Emily Dickinson 1

Gordon R. Dickson 8

Joan Didion 2, Y81

Pietro Di Donato 9

Annie Dillard Y80

R. H. W. Dillard 5

Diogenes, Jr. (see John Brougham)

Diane DiPrima 5

Thomas M. Disch 8

Dorothea Lynde Dix 1

E. L. Doctorow 2, Y80

Q. K. Philander Doesticks, P. B. (see Mortimer Thomson)

J. P. Donleavy...6

Hilda Doolittle 4

Edward Dorn 5

John Dos Passos.......................................4, 9, DS1

Frederick Douglass 1

J. Downing, Major (See Charles A. Davis)

Major Jack Downing (see Seba Smith)

Theodore Dreiser 9, DS1

John Drinkwater 10

Alan Dugan..5

Ashley Dukes 10

Robert Duncan..5

Finley Peter Dunne..11

John Gregory Dunne Y80

Ralph Cheever Dunning 4

Edward John Moreton Drax Plunkett,
    Lord Dunsany 10

Evert A. Duyckinck...3

George L. Duyckinck..3

John Sullivan Dwight..1

E

William Eastlake..6

Walter D. Edmonds 9

George Alec Effinger 8

Larry Eigner 5

Lonne Elder III 7

T. S. Eliot...7, 10

Stanley Elkin 2, Y80

William Elliott 3

Harlan Ellison...8

Ralph Ellison...2

Ralph Waldo Emerson 1

John Erskine 9

St. John Greer Ervine.......................................10

Clayton Eshleman 5

Edward Everett...1

William Everson 5

Frederick Exley Y81

F

Philip José Farmer..8

James T. Farrell...4, 9

Howard Fast...9

William Faulkner..9, 11

Irvin Faust...2, Y80

Kenneth Fearing..9

Raymond Federman Y80

Jules Feiffer 7

Cornelius Conway Felton 1

Edna Ferber 9

Lawrence Ferlinghetti...5

Rachel Field 9

James Thomas Fields...1

Jack Finney 8

Walter Braden Finney (see Jack Finney)

Dorothy Canfield Fisher......................................9

Vardis Fisher..9

William Clyde Fitch 7

F. Scott Fitzgerald 4, 9, Y81, DS1

Robert Fitzgerald Y80

Thomas Flanagan...Y80

Janet Flanner 4

Martin Flavin 9

James Elroy Flecker..10

John Gould Fletcher......................................4

Eliza Lee (Cabot) Follen 1

Ken Follett...Y81

Shelby Foote..2

Carolyn Forché 5

Charles Henri Ford 4

Corey Ford...11

Jesse Hill Ford 6

María Irene Fornés......................................7

Michael Foster...9

John Fox, Jr...9

William Price Fox...............................2, Y81

Michael Fraenkel 4

Richard France 7

Convers Francis 1

Waldo Frank 9

Ralph Jules Frantz.....................................4

Bruce Jay Friedman 2

Krebs Friend 4

Octavius Brooks Frothingham 1

Daniel Fuchs 9

Sarah Margaret Fuller, Marchesa D'Ossoli...........1

William Henry Furness 1

G

William Gaddis..2

Ernest J. Gaines 2, Y80

Zona Gale..9

Paul Gallico 9

John Galsworthy..10

Brendan Galvin...5

John Gardner...2

George Garrett 2, 5

William Lloyd Garrison 1

William Gass..2

Virgil Geddes...4

Jack Gelber..7

Hugo Gernsback..8

David Gerrold..8

Mark S. Geston 8

William Gibson..7

A. Lincoln Gillespie, Jr...............................4

Florence Gilliam..4

Caroline H. Gilman 3

Frank D. Gilroy...7

Allen Ginsberg 5

Nikki Giovanni 5

Ellen Glasgow...9

Susan Glaspell...7, 9

Montague Glass...11

Louise Glück 5

Gail Godwin 6

Parke Godwin 3

Herbert Gold..2, Y81

Michael Gold...9

Dick Goldberg...7

Samuel Griswold Goodrich 1

Caroline Gordon...........................4, 9, Y81

Mary Gordon 6, Y81

Charles Gordone...7

William Goyen 2

Shirley Ann Grau 2

Asa Gray..1

William J. Grayson......................................3

Horace Greeley...3

Julien Green...4

Paul Green 7, 9, Y81

Asa Greene..11

Horatio Greenough 1

Walter Greenwood......................................10

Ben Greer 6

Isabella Augusta Persse, Lady Gregory 10

Zane Grey..9

Rufus Griswold 3

Milt Gross...11

Davis Grubb 6

John Guare 7

Barbara Guest 5

Arthur Guiterman 11

James E. Gunn...8

A. B. Guthrie, Jr.......................................6

Ramon Guthrie...4

Erskine Gwynne..4

H

H. D. (see Hilda Doolittle)

John Haines...5

Joe Haldeman...8

Edward Everett Hale 1

Nancy Hale...Y80

Sara Josepha (Buell) Hale 1

Thomas Chandler Haliburton 11

Donald Hall...5

Fitz-Greene Halleck 3

Albert Halper..9

Cicely Hamilton..10

Edmond Hamilton..8

Patrick Hamilton.......................................10

Earl Hamner..6

St. John Hankin..10

Barry Hannah...6

Lorraine Hansberry.....................................7

Elizabeth Hardwick.....................................6

Marion Hargrove..11

Charles L. Harness 8

George Washington Harris.............................3, 11

Joel Chandler Harris...................................11

Mark Harris 2, Y80

Harry Harrison...8

Moss Hart..7

John Hawkes...2, Y80

Nathaniel Hawthorne 1

Robert Hayden 5

Paul Hamilton Hayne...................................3

Anthony Hecht 5

Ben Hecht...7, 9

Isaac Thomas Hecker....................................1

Frederic Henry Hedge 1

Robert A. Heinlein 8

Joseph Heller 2, Y80

Lillian Hellman 7

Ernest Hemingway 4, 9, Y81, DS1

Zenna Henderson..8

Caroline Lee Hentz 3

Alan Patrick Herbert 10

Frank Herbert..8

Henry William Herbert 3

Josephine Herbst.......................................9

Joseph Hergesheimer....................................9

Robert Herrick...9

John Herrmann..4

John Hersey..6

William Heyen..5

Dorothy Heyward and DuBose Heyward 7

DuBose Heyward...9

George V. Higgins...................................2, Y81

Thomas Wentworth Higginson.............................1

Richard Hildreth 1

Chester Himes 2

Edward Hoagland.......................................6

Sandra Hochman..5

Samuel Hoffenstein 11

Charles Fenno Hoffman 3

Daniel Hoffman...5

John Hollander...5

Marietta Holley 11

Oliver Wendell Holmes...1

Edwin Honig...5

Johnson Jones Hooper.....................................3, 11

Israel Horovitz...7

Emerson Hough 9

Stanley Houghton...10

Laurence Houseman 10

Richard Howard 5

Sidney Howard 7

Julia Ward Howe 1

Andrew Hoyem 5

Kin Hubbard...11

Langston Hughes 4, 7

Richard Hugo 5

William Humphrey...6

N. C. Hunter...10

I

David Ignatow..5

Bravig Imbs...4

William Inge 7

Joseph Holt Ingraham 3

John Irving 6

Washington Irving...3, 11

J

Shirley Jackson...6

Piers Anthony Dillingham Jacob (see Piers Anthony)

William Fitzgerald Jenkins (see Murray Leinster)

Jerome K. Jerome...10

Diane Johnson..Y80

Samuel Johnson 1

Denis Johnston...10

Mary Johnston...9

Eugene Jolas 4

Henry Arthur Jones 10

James Jones...2

LeRoi Jones (see Amiri Baraka)

Major Joseph Jones (see William Tappan Thompson)

Preston Jones 7

Erica Jong...2, 5

Matthew Josephson...4

James Joyce..10

Sylvester Judd..1

K

Garson Kanin...7

Mackinlay Kantor 9

George S. Kaufman...7

Edith Summers Kelly..9

George Kelly 7

Robert Kelly 5

John Pendleton Kennedy 3

X. J. Kennedy 5

Jack Kerouac..2

Orpheus C. Kerr (see Robert Henry Newell)

Ken Kesey..2

Jed Kiley..4

Stephen King..Y80

Sidney Kingsley..7

Maxine Hong Kingston Y80

Galway Kinnell...5

Caroline Kirkland 3

Carolyn Kizer 5

Peter Klappert 5

Philip Klass (see William Tenn)

Diedrick Knickerbocker (see Washington Irving)

Damon Knight 8

Edward Knoblock 10

John Knowles 6

Arthur Kober 11

Kenneth Koch 5

Manuel Komroff 4

Arthur Kopit 7

C. M. Kornbluth 8

Jerzy Kosinski 2

Elaine Kraf Y81

Alfred Kreymborg 4

Maxine Kumin 5

Henry Kuttner 8

L

Oliver La Farge 9

R. A. Lafferty 8

Louis L'Amour Y80

Charles Lane 1

Al Laney 4

Edwin Lanham 4

Ring Lardner 11

Keith Laumer 8

D. H. Lawrence 10

Tom Lea 6

Don L. Lee (see Haki R. Madhubuti)

Harper Lee 6

Richard Le Gallienne 4

Hugh Swinton Legare 3

James M. Legare 3

Ursula K. Le Guin 8

Fritz Leiber 8

Murray Leinster 8

Charles G. Leland 11

Denise Levertov 5

Meyer Levin 9, Y81

Philip Levine 5

Benn Wolfe Levy Y81

Charles B. Lewis 11

Henry Clay Lewis 3

Sinclair Lewis 9, DS1

Ludwig Lewisohn 4, 9

A. J. Liebling 4

Paul Myron Anthony Linebarger (see Cordwainer
    Smith)

David Ross Locke 11

Ross Lockridge, Jr. Y80

Harold Loeb 4

John Logan 5

Jack London 8

Henry Wadsworth Longfellow 1

Samuel Longfellow 1

Augustus Baldwin Longstreet 3, 11

Frederick Lonsdale 10

Anita Loos 11, Y81

Phillip Lopate Y80

Sut Lovingood (see George Washington Harris)

James Russell Lowell 1, 11

Robert Lowell 5

Walter Lowenfels 4

Mina Loy 4

Alison Lurie 2

Andrew Lytle 6

M

Charles MacArthur 7

John D. MacDonald..............................8

Katherine Anne MacLean.....................8

Archibald MacLeish........................4, 7

Norman Macleod..............................4

Brinsley MacNamara.........................10

Louis MacNeice..............................10

David Madden................................6

Haki R. Madhubuti...........................5

Norman Mailer..........................2, Y80

Bernard Malamud.......................2, Y80

Barry N. Malzberg...........................8

David Mamet.................................7

Frederick Manfred...........................6

Sherry Mangan..............................4

Horace Mann................................1

D. Keith Mano..............................6

William March..............................9

Wallace Markfield...........................2

John P. Marquand...........................9

Don Marquis................................11

George Perkins Marsh........................1

James Marsh................................1

Abe Martin (see Kin Hubbard)

Edward Martyn..............................10

John Masefield..............................10

Richard Matheson............................8

Cornelius Mathews...........................3

Jack Matthews..............................6

William Matthews...........................5

Peter Matthiessen...........................6

W. Somerset Maugham.....................10

Osborne Henry Mavor (see James Bridie)

William Maxwell...........................Y80

O. B. Mayer.................................3

Robert McAlmon............................4

Anne McCaffrey.............................8

Cormac McCarthy............................6

Mary McCarthy........................2, Y81

Horace McCoy...............................9

Carson McCullers........................2, 7

Phyllis McGinley............................11

Thomas McGuane......................2, Y80

Claude McKay...............................4

Larry McMurtry........................2, Y80

Terrence McNally............................7

Mark Medoff................................7

Alexander Beaufort Meek....................3

Peter Meinke................................5

Herman Melville.............................3

H. L. Mencken..............................11

William Meredith............................5

James Merrill................................5

Thomas Merton............................Y81

W. S. Merwin...............................5

Michael Mewshaw.........................Y80

James A. Michener...........................6

Kenneth Millar..............................2

Arthur Miller................................7

Caroline Miller..............................9

Henry Miller.........................4, 9, Y80

Jason Miller.................................7

Walter M. Miller, Jr.........................8

Steven Millhauser...........................2

A. A. Milne.................................10

Donald Grant Mitchell.......................1

Langdon Mitchell............................7

Margaret Mitchell...........................9

Allan Monkhouse...........................10

Marion Montgomery.........................6

William Vaughn Moody......................7

Catherine L. Moore..........................8

George Moore...............................10

Ward Moore...8

Berry Morgan...6

Christopher Morley...................................9

Willie Morris..Y80

Wright Morris...................................2, Y81

Toni Morrison...............................6, Y81

Arthur Moss...4

Howard Moss...5

John Lothrop Motley..............................1

Gilbert Murray.......................................10

N

Vladimir Nabokov...........................2, Y80

Petroleum Vesuvius Nasby (see David Ross Locke)

Ogden Nash..11

Robert Nathan..9

Peter Neagoe...4

John Neal..1

Joseph C. Neal.......................................11

John G. Neihardt......................................9

Howard Nemerov..................................5, 6

Charles King Newcomb............................1

Robert Henry Newell 11

Frances Newman....................................Y80

Mary Sargeant (Neal) Gove Nichols 1

Josefina Niggli..Y80

John Frederick Nims................................5

Anaïs Nin..2, 4

Larry Niven...8

William F. Nolan......................................8

C. F. M. Noland.....................................11

Charles Nordhoff 9

Charles G. Norris......................................9

Alice Mary Norton (see Andre Norton)

Andre Norton..8

Andrews Norton......................................1

Charles Eliot Norton 1

Alan E. Nourse...8

Bill Nye..11

O

Joyce Carol Oates 2, 5, Y81

Tim O'Brien..Y80

Sean O'Casey...10

Flannery O'Connor.........................2, Y80

Clifford Odets...7

Frank O'Hara...5

John O'Hara...9

Chad Oliver...8

Mary Oliver...5

Tillie Olsen..Y80

Charles Olson...5

Eugene O'Neill...7

George Oppen...5

Joel Oppenheimer.....................................5

Gil Orlovitz...2, 5

Guy Owen...5

P

Robert Pack..5

Ron Padgett...5

John Gorham Palfrey.................................1

Edgar Pangborn..8

Alexei Panshin..8

Dorothy Parker..11

Theodore Parker.......................................1

Francis Parkman, Jr...................................1

Linda Pastan...5

John Patrick..7

Elliot Paul 4

James Kirke Paulding 3

Elizabeth Palmer Peabody 1

Walker Percy 2, Y80

S. J. Perelman 11

Julia Peterkin 9

David Graham Phillips 9

Jayne Anne Phillips Y80

Stephen Phillips 10

Eden Phillpotts 10

John Phoenix (see George Horatio Derby)

Josephine Pinckney 6

Arthur Wing Pinero 10

H. Beam Piper 8

Sylvia Plath 5, 6

Stanley Plumly 5

Edgar Allan Poe 3

Frederik Pohl 8

Ernest Poole 9

Eleanor H. Porter 9

Katherine Anne Porter 4, 9, Y80

William T. Porter 3

Charles Portis 6

Ezra Pound 4

William Hickling Prescott 1

Reynolds Price 2

Richard Price Y81

J. B. Priestley 10

James Purdy 2

George Palmer Putnam 3

Samuel Putnam 4

Mario Puzo 6

Thomas Pynchon 2

Q

M. Quad (see Charles B. Lewis)

R

David Rabe 7

Marjorie Kinnan Rawlings 9

David Ray 5

Ishmael Reed 2, 5

Sampson Reed 1

Mack Reynolds 8

Elmer Rice 4, 7

Adrienne Rich 5

Jack Richardson 7

Conrad Richter 9

John Riddell (see Corey Ford)

George Ripley 1

Anna Mowatt Ritchie 3

Tom Robbins Y80

Elizabeth Madox Roberts 9

Kenneth Roberts 9

Lennox Robinson 10

Theodore Roethke 5

Will Rogers 11

Anne Roiphe Y80

O. E. Rölvaag 9

Waverley Root 4

M. L. Rosenthal 5

Leonard Q. Ross (see Leo Rosten)

Judith Rossner 6

Leo Rosten 11

Philip Roth 2

Jerome Rothenberg 5

Damon Runyon 11

Joanna Russ 8

S

Fred Saberhagen 8

Howard Sackler 7

Robert Sage..4

Harold J. Salemson..4

J. D. Salinger..2

Franklin Benjamin Sanborn................................1

Mari Sandoz..9

Pamela Sargent 8

William Saroyan..................................7, 9, Y81

May Sarton Y81

Dorothy L. Sayers..10

James H. Schmitz..8

Budd Schulberg 6, Y81

James Schuyler..5

Evelyn Scott..9

William Seabrook...4

Catharine Maria Sedgwick 1

Hubert Selby, Jr...2

Mary Lee Settle..6

Anne Sexton 5

Mordaunt Shairp 10

Bernard Shaw 10

Henry Wheeler Shaw 11

Irwin Shaw..6

Robert Sheckley 8

Wilfred Sheed 6

Alice B. Sheldon (see James Tiptree, Jr.)

Edward Sheldon 7

Sam Shepard..7

Robert Cedric Sherriff 10

Robert Sherwood 7

George Shiels 10

Benjamin Penhallow Shillaber 1, 11

William L. Shirer 4

Max Shulman...11

Henry A. Shute..9

Lydia Howard (Huntley) Sigourney 1

Robert Silverberg...8

Clifford D. Simak 8

William Gilmore Simms......................................3

Neil Simon 7

Louis Simpson..5

Upton Sinclair...9

Isaac Bashevis Singer..6

Elsie Singmaster...9

L. E. Sissman...5

David Slavitt..5, 6

Sam Slick (see Thomas Chandler Haliburton)

Carol Sturm Smith Y81

Charles Henry Smith...11

Cordwainer Smith..8

Dave Smith..5

Dodie Smith...10

E. E. Smith 8

Elizabeth Oakes (Prince) Smith..........................1

George O. Smith 8

H. Allen Smith...11

Seba Smith 1, 11

William Jay Smith 5

W. D. Snodgrass..5

Gary Snyder..5

Solita Solano...4

Susan Sontag...2

Gilbert Sorrentino......................................5, Y80

Terry Southern..2

Jared Sparks..1

Elizabeth Spencer 6

Jack Spicer 5

Peter Spielberg..Y81

Norman Spinrad...8

Squibob (see George Horatio Derby)

Jean Stafford..2

William Stafford 5

Laurence Stallings 7, 9

Ann Stanford 5

David Starkweather 7

Mark Steadman.....................6

Harold E. Stearns 4

Max Steele Y80

Wallace Stegner 9

Gertrude Stein 4

Leo Stein 4

John Steinbeck 7, 9

Ann Stephens.....................3

Donald Ogden Stewart.....................4, 11

George R. Stewart.....................8

James Still.....................9

Richard Henry Stoddard.....................3

William Wetmore Story.....................1

Harriet Beecher Stowe 1

Mark Strand.....................5

Edward Streeter.....................11

T. S. Stribling.....................9

David Hunter Strother 3

Jesse Stuart.....................9

Harry Clement Stubbs (see Hal Clement)

Theodore Sturgeon 8

William Styron 2, Y80

Ruth Suckow.....................9

Simon Suggs (see Johnson Jones Hooper)

Ronald Sukenick Y81

Frank Sullivan.....................11

Hollis Summers.....................6

Alfred Sutro.....................10

Harvey Swados.....................2

May Swenson 5

John Millington Synge.....................10

T

Booth Tarkington.....................9

Allen Tate 4

James Tate 5

Bayard Taylor.....................3

Henry Taylor.....................5

Peter Taylor Y81

William Tenn.....................8

Albert Payson Terhune.....................9

Megan Terry.....................7

Paul Theroux.....................2

Richard Thoma.....................4

John Thomas 4

John R. Thompson.....................3

William Tappan Thompson.....................3, 11

Mortimer Thomson 11

Henry David Thoreau.....................1

Thomas Bangs Thorpe 3, 11

James Thurber 4, 11

George Ticknor 1

Henry Timrod 3

James Tiptree, Jr......................8

Edward William Titus 4

Alice B. Toklas.....................4

John Kennedy Toole Y81

B. Traven 9

Ben Travers 10

George Tucker.....................3

Nathaniel Beverley Tucker 3

Mark Twain (see Samuel Langhorne Clemens)

Anne Tyler.....................6

U

Boyd B. Upchurch (see John Boyd)

John Updike 2, 5, Y80

V

Laurence Vail.....................4

Jack Vance 8

John van Druten..............................10

Mona Van Duyn 5

Jean-Claude van Itallie......................7

Sutton Vane 10

Carl Van Vechten...........................4, 9

A. E. van Vogt 8

John Varley Y81

Jones Very...1

Gore Vidal...6

Peter Viereck 5

Kurt Vonnegut, Jr.................2, 8, Y80

W

David Wagoner....................................5

Diane Wakoski....................................5

Derek Walcott.................................Y81

Alice Walker.......................................6

Edward Lewis Wallant........................2

Ernest Walsh.......................................4

Joseph Wambaugh...............................6

Artemus Ward (see Charles Farrar Browne)

Douglas Turner Ward.........................7

William Ware 1

Susan B. Warner.................................3

Robert Penn Warren 2, Y80

David Atwood Wasson.........................1

Noah Webster 1

Stanley Grauman Weinbaum 8

John Weiss 1

Theodore Weiss...................................5

Carolyn Wells....................................11

Eudora Welty......................................2

Glenway Wescott.............................4, 9

Jessamyn West 6

Nathanael West................................4, 9

Edith Wharton.................................4, 9

William Wharton.............................Y80

Charles Stearns Wheeler 1

Monroe Wheeler.................................4

Colonel Pete Whetstone (see C. F. M. Noland)

Edwin Percy Whipple 1

Frances Miriam Whitcher..................11

E. B. White.......................................11

William Allen White 9

William Anthony Parker White (see Anthony Boucher)

James Whitehead Y81

Sarah Helen (Power) Whitman 1

Walt Whitman.....................................3

Reed Whittemore.................................5

John Greenleaf Whittier......................1

Richard Wilbur 5

Peter Wild 5

Oscar Wilde......................................10

Richard Henry Wilde 3

Thornton Wilder........................4, 7, 9

Kate Wilhelm 8

Nancy Willard 5

C. K. Williams 5

Emlyn Williams 10

Joan Williams 6

John A. Williams 2

John E. Williams 6

Jonathan Williams...............................5

Tennessee Williams 7

William Carlos Williams 4

Wirt Williams 6

Jack Williamson 8

Calder Willingham, Jr.........................2

Nathaniel Parker Willis 3

Harry Leon Wilson.............................9

Lanford Wilson...................................7

Margaret Wilson 9

Donald Windham 6

Owen Wister 9

Larry Woiwode 6

Gene Wolfe 8

Thomas Wolfe 9

Joseph Emerson Worcester 1

Harold Bell Wright...9

James Wright 5

Elinor Wylie 9

Philip Wylie..9

Y

Richard Yates 2, Y81

William Butler Yeats...10

Anzia Yezierska..9

Stark Young 9

Z

Israel Zangwill..10

George Zebrowski 8

Roger Zelazny 8

Paul Zimmer 5

Paul Zindel...7

Louis Zukofsky...5